1001

MEDICAL QUESTIONS & ANSWERS

Dr. Warwick Carter

MB.BS., FRACGP, FAMA

HINKLER
BOOKS

This book is intended as a reference volume only, not as a manual for self treatment. If you suspect that you have a medical problem, please seek competent medical care. The information here is designed to help you make informed choices about your health. It is not intended as a subsitute for any treatment prescribed by your doctor.

Published by
Hinkler Books Pty. Ltd.
17–23 Redwood Drive
Dingley, Victoria 3172 Australia

Cover design by Sam Grimmer

ISBN 1 865 154687

Printed in Australia

1001

MEDICAL QUESTIONS &ANSWERS

Dr Warwick Carter MB. BS. FRACGP.

Safe and practical advice for all your health queries

HB

HINKLER BOOKS

Preface

This book covers the REAL questions that REAL people REALLY ask their doctor, as they are taken from over 25 years experience as a suburban GP, and from writing medical question and answer columns for newspapers around Australia.

Some patients just can't bring themselves to ask their doctor certain confidential, embarrassing, confusing or emotional questions.

Patients want to know what is happening to them, where the diseased organs or tissue are, when they are going to get better or worse, and why it is happening to them. This book attempts to answer many of these questions.

None of the questions are invented, all are genuine. In fact, no doctor could really imagine some of the improbable questions that have been asked. At some times it is difficult to keep a straight face or believe that what is being asked is a genuine query, but amazing things worry different people, and both the questions and their answers can be fascinating.

The questions are organised under logical headings, and the topics are indexed at the back of the book, so that it may be used for reference purposes.

Dr. Warwick Carter
Brisbane

Preface

Contents

ACNE

See also SKIN; SKIN INFECTIONS

Q I have terrible zits on my face. Why do I get it more than my friends, and what can I do about it?

A Pimples, zits, spots, acne. It doesn't matter what they are called, nobody likes to have them.

Pimples are due to a blockage in the outflow of oil from the thousands of tiny oil glands in the skin. This blockage can be due to dirt, flakes of dead skin, or a thickening and excess production of the oil itself. Once the opening of the oil duct becomes blocked, the gland becomes dilated with the thick oil, then inflamed and eventually infected.

The severity of your acne will depend greatly on your choice of parents. If one or both of them had severe acne, you have a good chance of developing the same problem.

The hormonal changes associated with the transition from childhood to adult life are the major aggravating factor in acne, as the hormones cause changes to the skin and thickness of the oil, and may worsen (or occasionally improve) acne.

Acne cannot be cured, but in the majority of cases, it can be reasonably controlled by doctors. You should ensure that your skin is kept clean with a mild soap and face cloth. Then some of the many creams and lotions available from pharmacists should be tried.

If the acne is severe to start with, or the over-the-counter preparations do not help, see your general practitioner. He or she will use antibiotics and more potent skin preparations to more effectively control the problem.

Q I am 38 years old and my acne is worse than that of my teenage daughter. Why would I get it now?

A Acne in adults is unfortunately far harder to treat than in teenagers. It is due to the same causes though.

In simple terms, a change in the hormone levels causes the oil in the glands just under the skin to become thicker, and this blocks up the ducts leading from the oil glands to the surface of the skin. The glands then becomes infected and pimples develop.

Because women have more hormonal problems than men, it is far more common for women to develop adult acne. Changing the hormone levels by using a contraceptive pill (or a different strength of one) often helps solve the problem. The antibiotics and skin lotions used by teenagers are also helpful.

Q I have been taking antibiotics, including Vibra-Tabs, Minomycin and Mysteclin, for acne for many years. These keep the acne under some control, but it never completely clears up. If I stop them, the acne flares up terribly. I am worried that the antibiotics may cause my bouts of depression, and can they cause a low sperm count?

A   Acne can be controlled by antibiotics and other medications, but it cannot be cured. You are not going to have a 'peaches and cream' complexion, but there should only be a few pimples present that are not easily noticed by other people.

   If your acne is controlled by antibiotics such as those you mention, be grateful, because some victims have to use far more potent medications. The antibiotics may be combined with skin preparations if necessary.

   I am not aware of these drugs causing depression or a low sperm count, and you should be reassured on these points.

   If you are having problems with periods of depression, whether associated with your acne, other problems, or no specific problem, I urge you to discuss it further with your general practitioner, as the depression may also need to be treated to make you a far happier and more confident person.

Q   **I had a bad case of acne on my chin. I have been given Clindamycin cream to heal it. Can you tell me what this does to the pimple? Will my acne scars be permanent?**

A   Pimples are infected oil glands in the skin. Clindamycin is an antibiotic that is designed to kill the bacteria that infect the pimples, and thereby cure them. If you are finding it successful, then continue the treatment. If your pimples are still bad, you should see your doctor about using other preparations on the skin, and antibiotics or anti-acne drugs by mouth to keep the condition under control.

   Acne scars are often a deep red colour when the pimple initially subsides, but after a period of months or years, they gradually fade to a pale pink or dead white colour. These scars are unfortunately permanent, as are scars on any other part of the body. Once you have grown out of your acne, and no further skin infections are occurring, you can see a dermatologist or plastic surgeon to have one of a number of procedures performed to make the scars less obvious. Dermabrasion, in which the lumps and bumps on your face are reduced, is quite successful if the scarring is widespread.

Q   **Could you please give me information on the drug prescribed by specialists for the treatment of severe cases of acne. What are the side effects and long term effects?**

A   The drug you are referring to is Roaccutane (isotretinoin), which is a tablet that can radically improve severe acne.

   This drug is very effective, but may have serious side effects, and its prescription is limited to dermatologists only.

   The most serious complication of its use occurs if it is taken by a pregnant woman. If this does happen, the baby will almost certainly be significantly deformed. For this reason, dermatologists are very careful, when prescribing it for women, that they are well established on an effective form of contraception such as the oral contraceptive pill.

   Common non-serious side effects include a dry mouth, nose, eyes and skin; pealing of skin from palms and soles; headaches; vomiting; depression and diarrhoea. Another possible serious, but rare side effect is the development of scars in the eye.

   Roaccutane is not a drug to be used lightly, and every other form of acne treatment should be used before it is considered, but some teenagers have severe acne that could cause permanent scarring and lifelong disfigurement. Roaccutane can clear their skin and prevent this scarring, and if used under the close supervision of a dermatologist, may dramatically improve the quality of life and attitudes of an affected teenager.

Q   For how long can my son take pills for acne? He has been on Vibra-Tabs for some time now, and they control the severe pimples on his face and back. Can these pills cause any damage?

A   Vibra-Tabs are specifically designed to prevent and treat acne in teenagers. They contain a low dose of an antibiotic that is in the tetracycline class to destroy the bacteria that are responsible for this distressing problem.

If given to young children, these tablets may cause teeth discolouration and bone deformities. High doses may cause nausea and diarrhoea, and some individuals may be sensitive to the medication. These complications are uncommon, and generally in teenagers and adults they are a very safe and effective treatment for pimples.

There is no reason why your son should not take the tablets for several years if necessary. Thousands of other teenagers have done so without ill effect.

Q   I have suddenly developed pimples at 22 years of age, having not had them for seven years when I was a schoolgirl. My lifestyle has not changed. My doctor recommends antibiotics, but I am reluctant to take these. I am taking zinc tablets from the chemist, but they don't seem to be helping.

A   Pimples may develop at any age, but they are far more common in teenage years when hormone levels are increasing.

Any change to your hormone levels may trigger an attack of acne. Pregnancy is one obvious cause of hormone change, and the oral contraceptive pill may also be a cause in some women, while in others the pill may improve acne.

Treatment involves using the various pimple creams available from chemists, and taking zinc supplements, which benefit some people. If these are ineffective, then it is wise to consult a doctor who can prescribe more potent lotions and creams, along with antibiotics.

Antibiotics especially designed to combat acne are very effective, as they prevent the blocked oil ducts that cause acne from becoming infected. They are designed for long term use, and have no side effects in the majority of patients.

AIDS
(Acquired Immune Deficiency Syndrome)
See also VENEREAL DISEASES

Q   Where did AIDS come from? I believe it is a divine retribution from God against those who have sinned. What do doctors really known about the history of AIDS?

A   The story begins in Central Africa, where it is now believed a mild form of AIDS has existed for centuries. This mild form (known technically at HLTV one) has been isolated from old stored blood samples dated in the 1950s. From Africa, it spread to Haiti in the Caribbean. Haiti was ruled by a vicious dictator (Papa Doc Duvalier), and many Haitians fled to Africa to avoid persecution.

Once 'Papa Doc' and his son 'Baby Doc' were removed from power, these exiles returned, bringing AIDS with them. In the process, it mutated (to HLTV three, now known as HIV) and became more virulent, causing a faster and more severe onset of symptoms. Viruses mutate routinely (eg. different strains of influenza virus every year).

There may also have been some movement of the disease directly through Africa to Algeria and France.

American homosexuals frequented Haiti because it was very poor, and sexual favours could be bought cheaply. They returned home from their holiday with the AIDS virus, and it has spread around the world from there. The first cases were diagnosed in California in 1981.

Fortunately for most of us, it is a relatively hard disease to catch. AIDS can NOT be caught from any casual contact, or from spa baths, kissing, mosquitoes, tears, towels or clothing. Only by homosexual or heterosexual intercourse with a carrier of the disease, or by using contaminated needles or blood from a carrier can the disease be caught.

Many people who are not homosexual, promiscuous or drug addicts have been affected by this dread disease, including a number of of Australia's haemophiliacs, who depend upon blood products to stop them bleeding excessively.

Q How can you actually catch AIDS? I see all the advertisements, but I worry that it might be easier to catch than they say.

A You can catch AIDS (acquired immune deficiency syndrome) by sexual intercourse with a man or woman who is already carrying the AIDS virus (human immunodeficiency virus—HIV), by receiving blood from such a person, or by using a syringe needle previously used by a victim.

It can be transmitted by a person who is showing no signs of the disease, and may never develop the disease, but who carries the virus.

It can NOT be caught by other forms of body contact including kissing. It is not highly contagious, and is actually quite hard to catch.

Q Can you catch AIDS from a hot spa bath?

A No. Acquired immune deficiency syndrome, strange as it may seem, is a hard disease to catch. Only by sexual intercourse with a man or woman carrying the AIDS virus, by using a needle contaminated with blood from an AIDS sufferer or by receiving a blood transfusion or blood products from an AIDS carrier can you catch the disease. In these situations, there is a very high risk of the AIDS being transmitted, although it may then lie dormant for many years.

Casual contact, including kissing, cannot transmit the delicate AIDS virus.

There is some inconclusive evidence that the genital herpes virus may be transmitted by spa baths, but not the AIDS virus.

Q Can you catch AIDS by tongue kissing?

A One-line questions such as this, scribbled on a scrap of paper, indicate to me that the public education about AIDS still has a long way to go!

NO. You cannot catch AIDS from kissing—no matter how passionate. AIDS cannot be caught by any form of casual encounter. It cannot be caught by shaking hands, by a cough or sneeze, by dirty toilets or by spa baths. It is theoretically possible, although unlikely, to catch AIDS from oral sex.

Normal intercourse and anal sex, as well as any method of transfer of contaminated blood products from one person to another (eg. a shared needle) are the only methods of AIDS transmission. Injections given by doctors or dentists are given using needles that are used once only. Even ear piercing is done by the use of stud guns that cannot transmit AIDS.

AIDS is quite a difficult disease to catch, but if you are promiscuous in your sexual habits, or are involved with illegal drugs, your chances increase dramatically. Condoms offer some protection against AIDS, but not 100% protection because they can burst or come off at the wrong time.

Q   Can AIDS be cured now?

A   Unfortunately, no. Medical scientists have developed a wide range of medications that can be used to slow the progress of AIDS, particularly the transition from an inactive to an active form of the infection, and these can allow patients to lead a normal life for many years, but they do not cure this viral infection.

The drugs must be taken in quite large amounts and often while following a very strict time regime. It may be necessary to take several capsules four or five times a day. These drugs also have side effects, and some patients find these difficult to tolerate, while others have minimal problems.

It is often a decade or more from diagnosis before the infection flares up into its final stages with these medications.

The best treatment is still prevention.

Q   Is AIDS still a risk for couple who have normal male/female sex?

A   The risk in western countries of transmitting AIDS from one person to another is highest in injecting drug users and homosexuals, but it is still a problem with heterosexual sex. The saying that when you have sex with someone, you are biologically having sex with every other person that your partner has had sex with, is still true. Although less than one in ten AIDS cases occur from heterosexual sex in western countries, there is still the risk of other sexually transmitted diseases.

In Africa and Asia, the situation is vastly different, with virtually all cases of AIDS occurring with male/female sexual contacts. In some African countries, up to one in three people in the entire population have AIDS, while in southeast Asia one in 20 people in Cambodia are infected.

The incidence of AIDS has steadily dropped for several years in developed countries with better education, and safe sex techniques (eg. using condoms), but seems to have reached a plateau now, with new cases being diagnosed at about one third the rate they were at the peak of infections in the early nineties. About 600 people a year in Australia catch AIDS every year.

Q   How can AIDS be prevented? Is there a vaccine you can have?

A   Scientists from around the world have been working overtime in their laboratories for the past two decades since AIDS first appeared in order to develop a long-lasting AIDS vaccine. The scientists who succeed will not only save millions of lives, but almost certainly will win a Nobel Prize.

So far no vaccine has been developed that can be proved to work. Numerous experimental vaccines have been tried on monkeys (who can get a mild form of AIDS) and human volunteers, but without success. It is probable that one will be developed in the future, but the AIDS virus is a different type to most viruses, and no vaccine against any virus of this type has yet been developed.

AIDS can be prevented almost completely (but not totally) by using condoms when you have any sort of penetrative sex, and not sharing needles if you are an injecting drug user. The best form of protection is a long term relationship with a single sexual partner.

ALCOHOL

Q **My father consumes two casks of wine a week. Can you tell me what harm this will cause him? Are there any additives or preservatives that can cause harm?**

A There are additives and preservatives in cask wine, but their effect would be absolutely minimal in comparison to the effect of the alcohol being consumed.

Casks come in different sizes, but assuming you are referring to the standard four litre cask, your father is consuming more than 60 standard alcoholic drinks a week. A standard drink is 15 mL of spirits, 30 mL of sherry or port, 125 mL of wine or 250 mL of standard strength beer.

An alcoholic is someone who has three or more of the following habits:
- consumes more than six standard drinks a day,
- drinks alone,
- tries to hide drinking habits from others,
- disrupts work or social life because of alcohol,
- craves alcohol when none is available,
- appears to tolerate the effects of alcohol well,
- binges on alcohol,
- has abnormal liver function.

Your father is an alcoholic, and this will be causing his liver, brain, heart and other organs significant damage.

Treating an alcoholic is extraordinarily difficult, as most will not accept the diagnosis. Unless they are a danger to themselves or society, treatment cannot be forced upon them, and even if it is forced, they do not respond as well as those who accept voluntary treatment.

In his few sober moments, try to gently persuade him to seek assistance. If he has a regular general practitioner, speak to him/her, so that the next time he visits the doctor, s/he can also reinforce the message.

Q **My husband is a salesman and drinks a lot with his work. I think he uses his work as an excuse to get boozed. One of his mates has had pancreatitis. Could he get it too?**

A The pancreas is the organ that produces your digestive juices and sits in the centre of the abdomen behind the belly button. People who drink a large amount of alcohol can damage the pancreas, causing the digestive juices to leak out into the belly. These juices then try to digest your insides, which causes severe pain. The treatment is difficult and often involves long hospital stays.

Pancreatitis is not a common disease, but is a well recognised complication of alcoholism. Anyone who drinks excess amounts of alcohol, either constantly or intermittently, is placing their health at risk in many ways.

Q   I have a stupid doctor who says I must eat better and take vitamins because I drink too much. I am only a social drinker, and only get drunk every couple of weeks. He says I will get some berry disease if I don't do as he tells me. I think he's just a wowser, but I promised him I'd write you (sic) to prove him wrong.

A   I have taken the liberty of significantly shortening your three page letter, but I think readers will get the general drift of its contents from the above extract.

Beriberi is a disease caused by an acute lack of thiamine (vitamin B1). This vitamin is relatively common in the diet, and significant amounts can be found in liver, lean pork, yeast and all cereal grains. The disease occurs in those who are malnourished, and particularly in alcoholics, because alcoholics may obtain most of their calorie intake in the form of alcohol, and neglect their normal food intake.

In the early stages, the patient has a multitude of vague complaints including tiredness, loss of appetite, twitching and muscle cramps and pains. Swollen joints, shooting pains, paralysis of feet and hands, and heart abnormalities are late symptoms of a very advanced form of the disease.

Beriberi is easily treated by giving the patient thiamine (vitamin B1), and a well balanced diet. Some authorities have argued that thiamine should be added to alcoholic drinks to prevent beriberi, in the same way that iodine is added to salt to prevent goitres.

Your GP is right, you should take vitamin B and watch your diet, but better still, seriously consider your alcohol intake. Your GP can do blood tests to see if alcohol has affected your liver.

You may not want to believe it, but from your letter I would have no hesitation in diagnosing you as an alcoholic. This is not a criticism of you, but the truth, and the sooner you, and others, realise that this condition is a disease that requires specific medical treatment, the better for all concerned. Get back to that good GP of yours for further advice and help.

Q   How much can I drink and still drive?

A   The rate at which alcohol is removed from the body is constant for each person, and nothing can increase this rate, thus once alcohol is present in your blood stream, it will remain there until the appropriate period of time has passed, no matter what tricks you try to make yourself sober quickly.

The blood alcohol level depends greatly on your weight. In smaller people there is less body for the alcohol to be spread around, and so the levels for the same number of drinks tend to be higher. Fat does not help dilute alcohol very much, so a very obese person may have a much higher blood alcohol level than a person of the same weight who is all muscle and no fat.

Only a very rough guide to the amount of alcohol that is safe to drink can be given. Men may be able to consume three standard drinks in one hour to reach .05, and then one standard drink per hour thereafter to stay at that level. These figures should be reduced by $^1/_3$ for women. A standard drink is 250 mL of beer, 120 mL of wine, 60 mL of port or sherry and 30 mL of any spirit.

Q Why do alcoholics get liver damage?

A Alcohol is absorbed from the stomach into the bloodstream, and is moved to the liver, where it is broken down into its basic components. Excess amounts of alcohol are excreted through the kidneys. If the liver is regularly overloaded with alcohol, the cells in the organ are damaged (pickled) and they can no longer function properly. If enough cells are damaged, the person develops cirrhosis, which may lead to total liver failure and death.

Doctors can do a blood test to see if your liver is being damaged by alcohol. Anyone who is taking more than six drinks a day is risking permanent liver damage and is probably an alcoholic.

Q I'm not an alcoholic, but I do like a wine with dinner and an occasional beer after gardening. Can I drink alcohol with medication?

A Medication and alcohol do not mix. Alcohol may exacerbate side effects, prevent the drug from working correctly or the drug may increase the effect of the alcohol. Always ask a doctor or pharmacist about any interactions between alcohol and even common over-the-counter medicines.

ALLERGY

Q Just what is an allergy? How do they occur? I have been able to eat oysters all my life, but now I get an itchy rash if I even touch one. How can this happen?

A An allergy is an excessive reaction to a substance which in most people causes no reaction. An allergy can occur to almost any substance in our environment. It may be triggered by foods, pollens, dusts, plants, animals, feathers, furs, mould, drugs, natural or artificial chemicals, insect bites and gases. No-one is totally immune to all possible allergic substances, but some individuals are far more susceptible to a wide range of substances than other people. This tendency towards allergies tends to run through a family, but the form the allergy takes (eg. hay fever or rash) and the substances that the person reacts to (eg. oysters and bee stings) can vary from one generation to the next.

Allergy reactions may be very localised (eg. at the site of an insect bite, or in just one eye), may occur suddenly or gradually, may last for a few minutes or a few months. They may involve internal organs (eg. lungs), or be limited to the body surface (eg. skin or nose lining). Allergies that cause significant discomfort or distress to the patient occur in 10% of the population.

An allergy differs subtly from a hypersensitivity reaction, where a normal reaction, experienced by most people, is exaggerated in some individuals. Often the difference is of little consequence to the sufferer and may only be determined by measuring specific substances (called immunoglobulins) in the blood. Side effects of drugs, psychological reactions, personal dislikes and the results of over-exposure to substances, must all be differentiated from a true allergy.

When a person is exposed to a substance to which s/he is allergic, the body reacts by releasing excessive amounts of a substance called histamine from mast cells that are found in the lining of every body cavity, and in the skin. Histamine is required at times to fight invading substances, but when released in excess, it causes inflammation, redness, and swelling, and in body cavities, the excess secretion of fluid from the involved surface. Intense itching often also occurs.

It is rare for an allergy to occur on the first occasion that a person comes into contact with a substance or food (in your case, oysters), but an allergy reaction can occur on the second, third or 300th time that the substance is encountered. Developing an allergy after years of exposure is therefore, not unusual.

Q **How do you find out if you are allergic to something. Can blood tests tell you? I am already allergic to cats, but want to find out if there is something else causing my hay fever.**

A Allergies to specific substances can be detected by skin tests or blood tests. In the skin test, a minute amount of the suspected substance is scratched into a very small area of skin. The reaction of that skin area is then checked regularly over several days. In blood tests, specific antibodies (chemicals produced in the body in response to invading allergic substances) are sought and identified.

You need to have a fairly good idea what is causing your allergy before the tests are done, as the test is for a very specific substance. Several hundred things can be tested for, but each one requires a separate blood or skin test, and this can prove to be very uncomfortable and expensive, as Medicare only subsidises a limited number of these tests under very specific circumstances.

Q **How are allergies treated? Is there any permanent cure? I have to live on antihistamines for my rash that keeps flaring up for no apparent reason.**

A The treatment of an acute allergic reaction will depend on where it occurs, its severity, and its duration. Antihistamine drugs are the mainstay of treatment and may be given by tablet, mixture, injection or cream. They are best used early in the course of an allergic reaction or if an exposure to an allergy-provoking situation is expected. Unfortunately, in past years only sedating antihistamines were available, which caused drowsiness as an unacceptable side effect, but now a wide range of safe and effective non-sedating antihistamines are available.

Once the reaction is established, a severe attack may require steroid tablets or injections, adrenaline injections, or, in very severe cases, emergency resuscitation. Other drugs may be used in specific allergy situations (eg. lung-opening drugs in acute asthma).

There are a number of substances that can be used on a regular basis to prevent certain allergic reactions. These include sodium cromoglycate (Intal and Opticrom) and nedocromil sodium (Tilade—asthma spray only) which may prevent hay fever, asthma and allergic conjunctivitis if used several times a day throughout the allergy season (often spring). They are available as inhalers, nasal sprays and eye drops.

A small number of patients are so allergic to certain substances (eg. bee stings or ant bites) that they must carry an emergency supply of an injectable drug (usually adrenaline) with them at all times, and must inject themselves if they suspect that they have been exposed to the allergic substance.

Once the substances that cause an allergy in an individual have been identified, further episodes of allergic reaction may be prevented by desensitisation. This involves giving extremely small doses of the allergy-causing substance to the patient, and then slowly increasing the dose over many weeks or months until the patient can tolerate the substance at the maximum likely exposure level. The desensitisation is normally given by weekly injections.

If you can find out what is causing your allergy reaction, it may be possible to have a course of desensitisation, and be cured.

Q Every time I even see a strawberry, let alone eat one, my lips become swollen and itchy! Is this a type of allergy?

A Almost certainly you have an allergy to strawberries.

It is possible to become allergic to almost anything. Animal hair, flowers, dust, foods, drugs, materials, grasses, fish and even other people can sometimes cause allergic reactions in an individual. Protein molecules from these substances are inhaled, touched or eaten and are recognised as foreign by the defence cells of the body. They engulf and destroy the foreign protein, but in the process, a small number of cells are manufactured that remember that foreign molecule, and the next time it enters the body, the defence cells are ready for it, and can destroy it more rapidly. This memory may last life-long. Allergies occur when this reaction is inappropriate or excessive.

Most people can eat strawberries without harm, but your body has recognised one of the molecules in strawberries as harmful, and whenever it is encountered, it reacts violently. When the defence cells react excessively, a substance known as histamine is released into the tissues. This causes swelling, itchiness and secretion of mucus. Thus your lips swell up and become itchy. In other people the eyes, nose or other tissues may swell up, and your nose may water.

Treatment is by antihistamine tablets or a series of desensitising injections.

Q Could I be allergic to the limestone formations in my area? I have felt tired, moody, depressed and dizzy ever since I moved here. Can the levels of limestone be checked in the blood?

A It is possible to be allergic to almost anything, but as limestone consists mainly of calcium carbonate, which is a normal constituent of the body, it is highly unlikely that you are allergic to it.

Limestone is a very common rock formation, and I am not aware of any studies that connect exposure to limestone with any medical condition. Miners of limestone are not known to have any particular problems in the way that coal and asbestos miners do.

The level of both calcium and carbonate can be easily measured in the bloodstream by any pathology laboratory, but I would doubt that these levels would reflect in any way your environment, but they do alter with many different diseases.

ALTERNATIVE MEDICINE
See also DOCTORS

Q **Why do so many patients turn to alternative practitioners for medical care? I have found orthodox doctors marvellous, and they have saved me from a heart attack, and relieved my gout, but some of my friends insist on going to all sorts of funny 'quacks'.**

A It is rare for the practitioners of the alternative forms of medical practice to claim they can cure tonsillitis, appendicitis, urinary infections, heart attacks or gout; all of which can be successfully cured or controlled by conventional medical practice. But when it comes to emotive or difficult-to-treat conditions such as cancer, chronic fatigue syndrome, arthritis and infertility, 'quack' remedies abound

There are considerable dangers involved in the use of some of these treatments. For example, the manipulation of a sore back that is caused by bone cancer could lead to permanent paralysis, and some fad diets can lead to an imbalance in the body's potassium levels that may result in a heart attack.

Doctors are not against any new form of treatment, but it must be proved to work, and proved to be safe, before they will add it to their already comprehensive armamentarium.

Proof is usually obtained by clinical trials. In these, an experimental drug is given to volunteers who have a specific problem, and compared with another group of patients on a different medication or no medication. At all times doctors observe the patient's symptoms and signs, and the patients themselves record how they feel. Great care is taken to ensure that there is no risk to the health of the volunteers. Unfortunately, nearly all alternative medical treatments subjected to this type of trial fail. Most of them seem to work because of the placebo effect. The placebo effect is that which occurs because a patient believes he will get better on a certain drug, not because of any direct effect of that drug.

Q **My GP and specialist can't cure my problem, and I have heard of a naturopath who seems to be very good, but my doctors have both said it is a lot of rubbish. Do you think it is wise for me to seek a second opinion from a naturopath?**

A The biggest problems doctors face in dealing with naturopaths and other alternative therapists are their lack of supervised training, their exclusive dogma (everything can be cured by diet, herbs, vitamins etc.), their lack of diagnostic skill and the lack of any registration or accountability.

The reason doctors do not cooperate with these people can be described by an analogy:

When you fly in a commercial aircraft with a major airline, your life is in the hands of the pilot and his support staff. If a major airline decided to employ unqualified pilots, who had only a rudimentary knowledge of aviation, there would be a public outcry, and no-one would use that airline. If qualified pilots were asked to work with the unqualified ones, they would refuse, and resign rather than risk their passengers' lives.

When patients put their lives in the hands of unqualified therapists, there is no hue and cry, and they complain that opposing doctors are being unfair.

It is a form of double standard that the medical profession cannot accept, as they wish to put the lives of their patients first.

Q   **I have recently heard about new-age magnetic therapy which used in conjunction with a newly discovered natural treatment, can regrow hair for those suffering from baldness and hair loss. What is the validity of this claim, and is it recognised by the medical profession?**

A   In the sixteenth century, the young (and not so young) gentlemen about town used to wear cod pieces. This was a cloth sack that contained the male genitals, and was placed strategically upon the front of the tights that covered the lower abdomen and legs.

In the same way that some less developed young ladies stuff their bras with tissues today, the sixteenth century lad used to stuff his cod piece with extra material in order to make it look more impressive. The material used for this purpose was called codswallop. Thus we have the modern expression of 'a load of codswallop' to denote something that is useless rubbish.

Some less imaginative scribes believe that the term codswallop refers to the guts of codfish that are discarded during filleting.

The reason for this detailed explanation is that the magnetic therapy and natural treatments espoused for the cure of baldness are also a load of codswallop!

There is no cure for baldness, which is usually a genetically inherited trait. It can be disguised by a toupé, and plastic surgeons can use hair transplant techniques or bald patch excisions, to help improve a man's appearance.

There is no point in paying for expensive codswallop, that most certainly is not accepted by the medical profession.

Q   **I am concerned that my health may be suffering because I am not taking enough vitamins. What are the best vitamins to take?**

A   Fresh fruit and vegetables. And yes, I am serious. There is no need to take any extra vitamins in tablet or other forms unless you are suffering from specific diseases, recovering from illnesses, or have a poor diet.

Australians are brim-full of vitamins—we eat better than 95% of the people alive on this earth, and better than any population in history. All the vitamins, minerals and other nutrients required are available to use in readily obtainable foods.

Some of us eat inappropriate foods and combinations, and no-one can support a fried food and soft-drink type diet, but rather than take the necessary vitamins lacking in this type of diet in pill form, munch an apple and chew a carrot instead.

The vast majority of vitamin supplements taken by people go straight through the body in the urine and faeces, and merely enrich the sewers. There is probably quite a profit to be made by processing raw sewerage to extract all the vitamins it contains!

Vitamins in high doses can be harmful to your health, and some diseases can be caused or aggravated by them. Be sensible and save money—have a fruit and vegie day!

Q   **Is Vitamin B useful? Should I take regular capsules to supplement my diet?**

A   Vitamin B is divided into several subgroups numbered 1, 2, 6 and 12. All are water-soluble and occur in dairy products, meats and leafy vegetables. It is almost impossible to have a lack of only one in the group. If one is missing, all will be missing.

A lack of these may cause anaemia and other blood diseases. Excess is rapidly excreted from the body through the kidneys and has no harmful effects.

Vitamin B6 may be useful in mouth inflammation, morning sickness and nervous tension. Vitamin B12 is used as an injection to treat pernicious anaemia.

Unless you are suffering from one of these conditions, have an inadequate diet or are recovering from an illness there is no need to routinely take any vitamin B supplement.

Q Is excess Vitamin B harmful?

A   Vitamin B is made up from four different chemicals—thiamine (vitamin B1), riboflavin (vitamin B2), pyridoxine (vitamin B6) and cyanocobalamin (vitamin B12). These are all found in similar foods (such as dairy products, leafy vegetables and liver), and it is unusual for only one form to be missing from the diet.

All the B vitamins are water-soluble and do not accumulate in the body. If you consume more than is immediately required by the body, it is rapidly excreted through the kidneys. There is no evidence that large doses cause any serious problems.

Q Does Vitamin C really prevent or treat colds? My mother swears by it, but I'm not so sure.

A   Unfortunately, no. It would be marvellous if vitamin C (ascorbic acid), or some other compound, could prevent or treat colds. The medical profession would promote it endlessly if it worked.

Exhaustive trials have not shown vitamin C to be any more effective than placebo (sugar pills) in dealing with colds.

The placebo effect can be very strong, and if a patient sincerely believes that a particular medication will work, they may rapidly recover.

A well-balanced diet containing food from all the groups (vegetables, fruit, cereals, meat and dairy products) will give you adequate vitamins, and with a reasonable amount of exercise and adequate rest, is probably the best way to promote your own health and prevent viral infections.

Q Why do so many people use naturopathic treatments, from royal jelly to vitamins, for arthritis?

A   Arthritis is a disease that tends to come and go for no reason at all. If a sufferer is taking a medication at the time of an easing of symptoms, they will credit that medication with the result. Psychology and the placebo effect also play a large part. Up to 40% of patients who are told capsules full of sugar are the latest and greatest drug for arthritis, will get better (for a while anyway).

Q I am 65 years of age, and my problems are controlled by tablets, but I don't want to take them forever. Have you any information regarding 'chelation therapy', which I would like to use to cure my high blood pressure, high cholesterol and coronary artery disease?

A   The medical profession quite freely admits that it cannot cure all diseases, but patients often do not want to believe this, and sometimes have a far higher expectation of medical science than is reasonable.

Because of this, a few desperate people turn to the alternative forms of health care, where the words incurable and impossible are unknown.

One alternative therapy that pops up every few years is chelation.

Proponents of chelation claim that it will cure, or dramatically improve, everything from hardening of the arteries and strokes, to senility and cancer. It involves a series of 30 or more, three-hour-long intravenous injections of a chemical called EDTA.

The injections are undertaken only after a long and expensive series of high-technology investigations, that are designed more to impress the patient, than enlighten the naturopath.

The total cost of a course of chelation treatment may exceed $3000, and most of these 'clinics' demand cash in advance.

As well as the course of injections, treatment may include large doses of mineral supplements, vitamins, thyroid extract and hormones, all of which may have serious side effects.

EDTA is actually used in rare instances by doctors to treat heavy metal poisoning.

There is no scientific evidence that chelation therapy will achieve the numerous claims made for it. The claims are made by a skilful combination of accepted facts and reasonably accurate statements about theories concerning many diseases, interleaved with a subtle mixture of statements which are not supported by any scientific evidence.

Anyone contemplating undertaking a course of chelation therapy, or any other form of alternative treatment, would be well advised to discuss the matter further with their own general practitioner.

Q   **What is your opinion of the treatment of gallstones by naturopaths? I have been recommended taking a few bottles of DTM medicine, followed by five days of drinking apple juice and eating apples, then on the sixth day at 6pm taking one desertspoon full of Epsom salts in water, repeated again at 8pm. Then at 10pm take 100 mL of Olive oil mixed with 100 mL of lemon juice. Is this safe and does it work?**

A   Stones are not normally part of the human anatomy, but those that may form in the gall bladder may be just as solid and hard as those found in the average quarry.

Stones are formed by a compound being present in an excessively high concentration in a bodily fluid such as bile. The substance then precipitates out of suspension, and starts to grow with the deposition of successive layers of the substance to the original seed.

Stones in the gall bladder are smooth and rounded, and grow by addition of successive layers of substance.

A stone makes its presence felt to its owner. Pain is the main symptom, but indigestion may also occur with gall stones. Because of these symptoms, patients with a stone almost invariably require it to be removed.

The only way to remove a stone is by an operation. There is a drug available which will very slowly dissolve some types of gallstones, but this takes many months to work, is very expensive, and is reserved for those who are too frail to have an operation.

Any naturopath who claims to have a concoction that will dissolve gallstones is fooling both the patient and himself, and should be ignored. If you have a friend who has had a gall stone removed, and has saved the specimen, try soaking the stone directly in the naturopath's mixture. It will have as much effect on the gallstone as on a stone from your nearest gravel quarry!

Q   **I recently read about Coenzyme Q10 (Ubiquinone), described as an energy-producing, heart-protective anti-oxidant. I would like to know your views on this supplement.**

A   Doctors have also been inundated with information about this new product, which seems to be the 'in' thing to be taking. Every few years there is a new fad, be it chelation therapy, echinacia or megadose vitamins.

Correctly called ubidecarenone, even its chemical name has been made more catchy by the marketers who claim that it is ubiquitous (everywhere) in the body.

Many claims have been made for this preparation, but most are supported by pseudo-scientific gobbledygook, which is deliberately worded to confuse and obstruct any true scientific debate.

The gold standard for any medication, its side effects and effectiveness is the double blind cross-over trial. In these, half of a group of volunteers are given a tablet that contains the active ingredient, and the other half are given an inert placebo. After a period of time, the two groups are swapped over, but the volunteers, and their immediate supervisors, do not know which tablets are inactive and which are placebo. The reactions of the volunteers are recorded, and a report prepared, and only then are they told which tablets are which.

Not until the manufacturers of this product can demonstrate such a trial has been carried out on a good sized sample by a reputable organisation will I believe their claims.

In the meantime, you can carry out a trial yourself by taking this rather expensive supplement for a month, then stopping it to see if it makes any difference. Unfortunately, I suspect most benefit will occur because you want it to occur (the placebo effect), but on the other hand it is unlikely to cause any harm to you (except to the weight of your wallet or purse) unless you take more than three capsules a day.

Q   **I have read that one should restrict one's diet according to your blood group, so that anyone with blood group O should avoid wheat and dairy products, tomatoes, melons, olives and cauliflower. Is there much scientific evidence to support this doctrine?**

A   This is one of the weirdest health fads to come along, and a new one does come up every year or so.

The major blood groups (O, A, B, AB) are determined by reactions between protein particles on the surface of red blood cells, and are important when giving blood transfusions to prevent interactions between red blood cells in the donor and patient blood, but have no relationship to any disease or infection.

When treating patients with any medical condition, with any form of medication (tablet or injection), doctors pay absolutely no attention to the patient's blood group unless there is a possibility that a blood transfusion may be required.

If there is no interaction between any of the thousands of different medications in use (even when directly injected into the blood) and the blood group, there is no logic in the argument that foods, which are broken down into their basic constituents in the stomach before being absorbed into the body, can react in different ways in people with different blood groups.

Probably the most significant blood factor is the rhesus factor which can be negative or positive for each of the ABO major blood groups. There are also numerous minor blood group divisions, including the Kell, Duff, Lewis and Kidd factors, and groups M, N, S and U. All of these can be responsible for reactions during transfusions and may need to be specifically cross-matched. What do the proponents of these diets say about these sub-groups? I doubt that they even know about them.

There is absolutely no scientific evidence to support this diet.

Q If taken in the correct dosage, is creatine harmful or beneficial to the body?

A Creatine is a naturally occurring amino acid. These are the building blocks from which proteins are made, and are found in a variety of foods, with the richest source being lean red meat. One kilogram of steak contains about 5 grams of creatine. Creatine also increases the amount of water held in muscles, thus increasing their bulk, and making creatine attractive to muscle builders.

Muscles require energy to move, which comes from a molecule called adenosine triphosphate, (ATP). During exercise, muscles break down ATP into ADP (adenosine diphosphate). When ATP is broken down, creatine phosphate comes in and releases its phosphate to change ADP back to ATP. As creatine phosphate levels drop during exercise, performance deteriorates as skeletal muscle only stores enough creatine phosphate and ATP for about 10 seconds of high-intensity activity.

Those who use creatine phosphate supplements may increase the level of creatine in muscles, which increases the amount of phosphate available to convert ADP back to ATP, therefore increasing muscle performance and decreasing recovery time.

Dosages are usually high for the first five days with 10 to 20 grams of creatine phosphate taken every day, after that 2 to 5 grams a day is all that is necessary. There is considerable variability in creatine absorption between individuals, and those with a low initial creatine concentration will show a greater benefit. Trained athletes often have higher natural stores of creatine than non-athletes, so they will not benefit as much from supplements.

Creatine supplementation does improve performance with intermittent short exercises lasting no longer than 20 seconds (eg. body building, sprinting, throwing, jumping). It does not improve long-term aerobic exercise (medium- or long-distance running, swimming, cycling).

The most common side effects from creatine in normal doses are a rash, shortness of breath, vomiting, diarrhoea, nervousness, anxiety, fatigue and migraines. Uncommon serious side effects include muscle inflammation, seizures and irregular heartbeat. Excessive doses can cause kidney damage. There are no adverse effects from long-term use at low dosages.

Q **Ménière's disease is extremely difficult to cure, and doctors try many different medications. I have found a cure for the condition in myself, and for years I have not had any attacks of dizziness or noises in the ears. My cure is regular doses of all the B group vitamins. I would appreciate it if you could pass this on to your readers who may suffer from this distressing condition.**

A Ménière's disease causes dizziness, deafness and persistent noises in the ears. It is caused by diseases of the inner ear, and most commonly by a deterioration in the blood supply to the inner ear with age and hardening of the arteries.

As you rightly point out, it is a very difficult condition to control, and almost impossible to cure. Doctors use a wide range of medications, and rarely surgery, in attempts to assist the patient. More than half of all victims are assisted by these regimes, but the rest are left to suffer the annoying consequences of the condition.

I am delighted that you have found vitamin B has helped you, and as this group of vitamins is generally safe in all but extremely high doses, there is no reason why other sufferers should not experiment with this form of treatment. Unfortunately, very often, the treatment that helps one person does not always help others.

Anyone with Ménière's disease should consult a doctor to ensure that there is no serious cause for the disease, and to try some of the more commonly used treatments. If these fail, vitamin B could also be tried, but if unsuccessful, they should return to their doctor to continue trials of other potentially beneficial medications.

ANAESTHETICS

Q **I have to have an operation, but I'm scared about the anaesthetic. Can you please tell me what will happen to me?**

A About an hour before the operation, you are usually given an injection to relax you in preparation for the anaesthetic, and to dry up your saliva, so that it does not cause trouble while you are asleep.

You are then taken on a trolley or in a wheelchair to the theatre suite where you meet the anaesthetist, but your memory of the meeting will be brief, as s/he will be busy putting you to sleep as soon as possible.

You will breathe oxygen through a mask, while the anaesthetist places a needle in a vein in your arm or hand. Once all is ready, medication will be injected through the needle to make you drop off to sleep, and relax your muscles. This is not at all frightening, and is just like going to sleep naturally.

You are very carefully watched all the time you are asleep, as the anaesthetist is regularly checking your pulse, blood pressure, breathing and heart.

Your first memory after the operation will be of the recovery room. This is where you stay under the care of specially trained nurses, and the anaesthetist, until you are fully awake. You are then wheeled back to your ward.

Anaesthetists are highly trained doctors, who undergo many years of intensive training, and must pass difficult exams, before starting their practice. Modern anaesthetics are very effective, and complications are extremely rare.

Q **I am going to have an anaesthetic injection into my back for my operation, as I have been told I am too old to have a normal one. I am worried that I will be awake during the operation and know what is happening, and this is frightening to me. What do you suggest I do? Can you explain what will happen?**

A There is nothing to be frightened about, as you will also be given a sedative that will make you relax, and probably sleep during the operation. Although you will not be under a full anaesthetic, you will feel nothing, and see nothing because a vertical drape will be placed across your chest to block your line of vision. The anaesthetist will ensure that you will not be upset in any way.

There are two types of anaesthetic that can be given by injections into the back, a spinal and an epidural. Both can only be used when operations below the waist are being performed.

In a spinal anaesthetic, the anaesthetist places a needle into the lower back. The needle is inserted between the vertebrae so that the tip enters the spinal canal, that contains the cerebrospinal fluid that surrounds the spinal cord. The spinal cord carries all the nerve messages to and from the brain, and runs through the centre of the 24 vertebrae that form the backbone. A small amount of anaesthetic is injected into the spinal canal, so that the nerves below the level of injection no longer work and pain from the operation cannot be felt. The patient is often tilted slightly to prevent the anaesthetic from flowing further up the spine and affecting nerves above the level required for adequate anaesthesia.

The side effects of a spinal anaesthetic include low blood pressure, a headache for several days, and a slow heart rate. Nausea and vomiting are less common complications.

An epidural anaesthetic is very similar to a spinal anaesthetic, but the injection into the back does not penetrate as deeply and does not enter the cerebrospinal fluid. The spinal cord is wrapped in three layers of fibrous material (the dura), and this anaesthetic is given into the very small space between the outer two layers. The procedure is technically more difficult, but the side effects are less severe. Epidural anaesthetics are used most commonly to relieve the pain of childbirth.

Q **How do local anaesthetics work? My GP says he is going to fix my ingrown toenail with a nerve block into the base of the toe, but I am sure this will hurt. When he cut out a mole, the injection was into the mole, and it really stung a lot.**

A Local anaesthetics are used in three different ways.

A local area may be injected with anaesthetic solution to numb that area, for example while a mole is being cut out or a cut sutured. This method is commonly used by general practitioners, plastic surgeons, skin specialists and others for small procedures. The injection does sting for a few seconds, but this sensation subsides rapidly as the anaesthetic takes effect, and rarely lasts more than 30 seconds.

A local anaesthetic can also be injected around a nerve to stop that nerve from receiving pain impulses from beyond the point of injection. The injection may take several minutes to work after being given. These nerve blocks are commonly used in fingers and toes and in dental procedures, but almost any nerve in the body may be injected.

Sometimes, if a more major procedure is to be done on an arm or leg, a tourniquet can be placed around the thigh or upper arm and a large amount of anaesthetic injected into the dilated veins below the tourniquet to give a regional block. This effectively numbs the entire area below the tourniquet. This type of anaesthesia is commonly used to set minor fractures.

Your GP will ensure that you are feeling no pain before the operation commences, so do not be concerned about the procedure, and look forward to having a toe that is no longer giving you trouble.

Q **What is the drug used in local anaesthetics, is it dangerous, are there side effects, will I feel anything, and how long does it last? I need to know the answers to these questions before I let my GP cut out a mole he has found on my back, and all he says is, 'Don't worry, it will be fine.'**

A Your GP is right, you will be fine, and won't feel any pain, but it would have been sensible of him to answer your specific concerns in more detail.

The most commonly used local anaesthetic is lignocaine (also known as Xylocaine). This drug is so good that 99% of all local anaesthetics are given using this one medication. It has an anaesthetic effect that lasts for one to two hours, depending upon the site of injection, the amount injected, and the concentration of anaesthetic used. Adrenaline may be added to the anaesthetic to reduce bleeding and prolong its effectiveness for up to four hours, but adrenaline cannot be used in toes, fingers and some other areas.

Lignocaine is very safe, very rarely are there any side effects (it is actually given as an injection into a vein to regulate abnormal heart rhythms), and the only thing you will feel is a stinging sensation for a few seconds while the injection is being given. After the anaesthetic takes effect, which is in less than ten seconds, you will feel no pain in the anaesthetised area, but may feel tugging and pulling sensations as the doctor undertakes the mole removal and suturing.

ANAL PROBLEMS
See also GUT

Q **I have a haemorrhoid that came and was uncomfortable, then after a few days it went away. Is this normal? I thought that once they were present, they were there for ever.**

A Haemorrhoids are swollen veins around the anus that usually start after an episode of passing hard motions when constipated, straining or heavy lifting. Once formed, there will always be a weakness at that point unless the pile is surgically removed. Most piles settle slowly with no treatment, others settle with the help of various creams, ointments and other medications, and some need to be drained or injected, but only a very small number actually need full surgery.

Be grateful that your haemorrhoid has settled quickly and simply, but don't be surprised if it recurs at the same point next time you become constipated.

Q Why do haemorrhoids cause itching? Chemist preparations don't help much.

A Haemorrhoids (or piles—they are one and the same thing), are basically damaged veins around the anus, that balloon out, become painful and bleed. They itch because the skin over the pile is irritated by clothing, heat, sweat, scratching and hard motions.

Piles are best prevented by keeping regular at the toilet, and avoiding constipation.

Q I would be grateful if you could explain the causes and symptoms of internal piles. Can they become cancerous, and do drinks of beer exacerbate the problem?

A Piles (or haemorrhoids—which is another name for the same condition) can occur on the outside or inside of the muscle ring that forms the anus. In both situations they are caused by a dilated vein. The blood inside this vein may clot to cause a thrombosed pile. The pressure of the dilated vein or the clotted blood it contains on adjacent nerves causes pain. Twisting of the pile can also cause severe pain. The other main symptom apart from pain is bleeding, which occurs if the pile bursts.

Piles are caused in the first place by excessive stress on the anus. This stress can be in the form of constipation, prolonged diarrhoea, or heavy lifting. Weight-lifters are notorious sufferers of piles. There is no evidence that they become cancerous, and I cannot see why alcohol in any form would cause them to develop. There is certainly a tendency for piles to develop within a family due to a congenital weakness in the area.

Treatment involves creams or suppositories which contain medication to soothe the pile, anaesthetics and anti-inflammatory substances. Further treatment involves injecting, banding or excising the pile.

Q In what way can piles be treated? I suffer terribly from this embarrassing condition.

A Initial treatment involves creams or suppositories that soothe and shrink the piles. There are many types of creams available, some from chemists and others on prescription.

If these are not successful, the next step may be a simple incision of a thrombosed pile, injecting a glue like liquid into the pile or clamping a rubber band around the pile under local anaesthetic.

If these measures lead to recurrences, a formal operation to remove the segment of the anus involved may be required. These operations are uncomfortable, but not as painful as gossip and the imagination would have us believe. The most important treatment is prevention—do not get constipated!

Viewed in vertical section

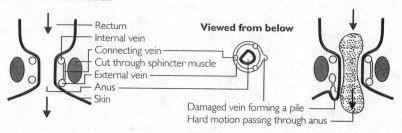

Rectum
Internal vein
Connecting vein
Cut through sphincter muscle
External vein
Anus
Skin

Viewed from below

Damaged vein forming a pile
Hard motion passing through anus

Diagrammatic representation of anal canal and the formation of a pile.

Q I am bleeding from the back passage after passing a motion. Is this serious?

A Bleeding of this nature is most commonly caused by piles. These are dilated veins that are caused by constipation and straining. When hard motions are passed, the small veins around the anus become damaged and become thin-walled and swollen. Further motions can easily rupture the veins, and this leads to bleeding after going to the toilet. Sometimes the blood in the pile becomes clotted, and they may become very tender.

There are other causes for anal bleeding that include diseases as diverse as cancer and a simple tear, so it is always wise to have this problem checked and properly diagnosed by a doctor.

Q I have two small lumps near my anus, which sometimes discharge blood and yellowish fluid, and then disappear for a while. They feel uncomfortable and I would like them to go away. Please advise.

A You could be suffering from one of a number of conditions including piles, fistulae or cysts. There are also a number of rarer possibilities. It will be necessary for a doctor to closely examine one of the less attractive parts of your anatomy in order to make the appropriate diagnosis.

Almost certainly you will need some form of surgery to remove the cause of your discomfort.

If piles are present, injecting into the piles, or placing a small rubber band around the base of them may cure the problem, but in some cases, surgical excision is the only option.

A fistula is a microscopic tube that connects the inside of the gut just inside the anus, to the skin beside the anus. These tubes become infected and painful periodically, and then discharge pus and blood. The only treatment is surgical.

A cyst can occur on any part of the skin, and may occur on your back as readily as your anus. There are many different types of cysts, including those that can be caused by blocked sweat or oil glands, ingrown hair, or infected hair follicles. Although these can burst and drain, they usually return unless they are cut out completely.

Don't continue to suffer discomfort for months, suffer embarrassment for a few minutes instead, and see a doctor soon.

Q What do you think is the cause of anus itching? I have tried several remedies, but no luck so far. I am 70 years old and 100% fit.

A The most common cause of this distressing condition is called pruritus ani. This is really just means 'itchy anus' in Latin.

Pruritus ani is caused by excessive drying out of the skin around the anus, and its continued irritation by sweat, clothing and scratching. Once the cycle is established it may continue for many years.

Treatment involves:
— never scratch the area, no matter how itchy it becomes
— avoid using soap (which dries skin) around the anus, merely rinse the area by parting the cheeks under the shower
— do not scratch the area
— patting and not rubbing the area dry when wet
— do not scratch the area
— use soft toilet paper very gently, using a dabbing rather than wiping movement
— do not scratch the area (are you getting the message?)
— applying a mild steroid cream prescribed by your doctor to help ease the itch.

Only be avoiding any irritation to the area for several weeks or months can you hope for a cure.

There are also a number of more serious diseases that may cause anal itching, and these should be excluded by a doctor, as they may be treated effectively. Common examples include piles, fungal infections, diabetes, worm infestations of the gut and psoriasis.

Q **I have a very dark red, sometimes purplish colour ring around the opening of my anus. I'm too scared to go to the doctor in case it might be cancer. I'm extremely worried I'm going to die!**

A There are many possible explanations for the discolouration around your anus, that vary from dermatitis, to fungal infections and piles; but the most likely explanation is that you are seeing a prominent vein that normally runs around the anus.

Trying to diagnose your condition without seeing the relevant part of your anatomy, is rather like trying to play chess without being able to see the board— very difficult and liable to be wrong!

You are foolish not to consult your GP if this is worrying you so much. It is extremely unlikely to be anything serious, and your doctor can therefore give you a large dose of reassurance, and if necessary, the appropriate medication to cure the problem.

In the unlikely event that it is a significant problem, seeing your doctor sooner rather than later will make the problem far easier to cure. Embarrassment is no excuse, as both male and female doctors are readily available, and both are very used to examining the most intimate parts of your anatomy without blushing, making sexist remarks or rude jokes.

Q **I had a solitary ulcer in my rectum some years ago that was diagnosed by a specialist after I was bleeding from the back passage. I have now started bleeding again. Is it worth going back to the doctor to have the ulcer reassessed?**

A Yes!! Any abnormal bleeding from the anus (back passage) must be assessed by a doctor as soon as possible.

The bleeding may just be a recurrence of your ulcer, piles or some other benign disease, but it could also be something more serious, and the sooner treatment is started, the better the chances of a cure.

Even if nothing nasty is present, treatment may remove something that is troublesome, and reassure you that all is well.

Please see your general practitioner as soon as possible for a thorough check up.

Q **I suffer from irritation and inflammation around the anus, accompanied by a wetness in the area. My personal hygiene is carefully attended to, and I can't feel any lumps like piles. I am an otherwise healthy thirty year old woman. Is there any treatment available which will eradicate it?**

A The possible explanations for your anal discomfort include excessive perspiration (more likely if you are overweight) and a constant discharge of mucus from the anus.

Excess mucus is produced by the gut if it is inflamed, and this mucus can slowly leak out through the anus. A condition called proctitis can cause this inflammation, and can be detected by a doctor inserting a small instrument (a proctoscope) into the anus to inspect the lining of the gut. If this is excessively red and moist, you will have proctitis.

The condition can be treated by using steroid suppositories (tablets inserted through the anus) to settle down the inflammation (and therefore the mucus production), but your doctor will probably also perform further tests to exclude any cause for the proctitis developing.

Q **My mother is demented in a nursing home and is now incontinent of faeces and the smell around her is appalling. Is there anything that can be done for her?**

A Incontinence is the inability to control the discharge of body waste products. Incontinence of faeces takes two forms. There are those patients who are aware of passing a small amount of faeces through the anus but are physically incapable of stopping it, and there are those who are not aware of passing the faeces but could have stopped it if they had been aware.

The first group includes patients with severe diarrhoea (eg. gastroenteritis), women after childbirth when the anal canal may be torn, and patients who have had operations on the anus (eg. dilation for an anal tear). In these cases, the condition causing the incontinence is usually of short duration and may be treatable. It is a considerable inconvenience when the incontinence occurs, but it is rarely a long-term problem.

The sadder and more difficult situation occurs with those who are not sufficiently aware of their own body to know that they are soiling themselves. This includes patients who are in a coma or unconscious (because of injury or disease), cases of paralysis of the lower half of the body (paraplegics and quadriplegics), mentally deranged people, the confused elderly (eg. advanced Alzheimer's disease), and those with subnormal mentality. Unfortunately, this is the situation with your mother, and most of these cases cannot be cured. The wearing of nappies and use of protective sheeting in beds must become routine.

Careful attention by attendants to hygiene and cleanliness is essential to avoid rashes and sores developing on the buttocks and around the anus. This will also help any odour problems.

ANTIBIOTICS

See also MEDICINES

Q   Just what are antibiotics? Doctors seem to prescribe them all the time.

A   Antibiotics are a group of very different chemicals that have the ability to destroy bacteria, but they have no effect upon viral infections. Most of the infections seen by a general practitioner are caused by viruses, and there is no need for antibiotics in these cases.

Doctors will use antibiotics if the infection appears to be bacterial, or if a person has reduced immunity, is elderly, frail, liable to recurrent infections or due for an operation, an antibiotic may be used to prevent a bacterial infection.

Major problems can occur with the overuse of antibiotics. Cost is the first one, and as the government pays part of the cost of everyone's antibiotics, this is a problem affecting every taxpayer. Side effects are another problem. These can include rashes, diarrhoea (which can stop the oral contraceptive pill from working), nausea, fever and some rarer and more serious complications. The most important problem is the development of resistance, which can enable bacteria to change in a way which makes them able to resist the actions of an antibiotic that was previously very effective.

Q   I keep hearing that there are more and more bugs becoming resistant to antibiotics. Just how many different antibiotics are there?

A   There are over 70 distinct and separate antibiotics listed in the medication guide (MIMS) that doctors use to guide them through the maze of medications available in this country.

Many of these antibiotics fit into a particular class such as penicillins or sulphas, and so it is likely that if a bacteria is resistant to one drug in this class, it will also be resistant to all the others.

Penicillins include drugs such as amoxycillin (also known as Amoxil), procaine penicillin (which is given by injection) and phenoxymethyl penicillin (also known as PVK).

The most common sulpha is sulfamethoxazole, which is used in urinary infections and marketed as Alprim. In combined with trimethoprim this medication is known as Bactrim or Septrim.

Combinations of antibiotics are becoming common to reduce the incidence of resistance, so amoxycillin is now often combined with clavulanic acid and marketed as Augmentin.

Another commonly used group of drugs is the cephalosporins, which include cephalexin (marketed as Keflex and Ibilex), and cefaclor (Ceclor and Vercef).

It is very much a matter of 'horses for courses', as specific antibiotics work better against specific bacteria, in particular places (eg. the bladder or lungs), or in certain forms (eg. as injections or creams).

A doctor must judge which antibiotic is best in each situation.

Q   Why won't a doctor give antibiotics for the flu?

A   Influenza is due to a virus particle, which is far smaller than, and totally different to, the bacteria that antibiotics will destroy. In most cases there is no cure except time and rest, for influenza, but new medications (Relenza, Tamiflu) were released in 1999 and 2001 respectively, appear to shorten the course of an attack of influenza if started within 36 hours of the first symptoms developing. Unfortunately they are quite expensive, and not subsidised by the Pharmaceutical Benefits Scheme.

There are other medications available from chemists and on prescription that will help relieve your symptoms, but giving antibiotics for flu is a waste of money and time. It may give you the side effects of the antibiotics without any benefit, and could lead to the formation of resistant forms of bacteria.

Q I am allergic to penicillin. What other antibiotics can I use?

A If you have a severe reaction to penicillin, you should wear a bracelet or pendant warning doctors of this fact. You should be able to use tetracyclines and sulpha drugs without problems, but you should be careful with erythromycin and cephalosporins as they can have a cross-sensitivity with penicillin. There are many other less common antibiotics that can be used on you when necessary, so do not fear that treatment will not be available when needed. Just make sure any doctors you consult are made aware of your allergy.

Q I have been prescribed an antibiotic called Keflex for my cystitis, but it gave me diarrhoea and I stopped it. I am also 6 months pregnant. Is this the right antibiotic to use?

A Keflex is an excellent broad spectrum antibiotic, and a member of the cephalosporin group. These are a group of relatively strong antibiotics that are divided by doctors into first, second and third generation cephalosporins. In general terms, they increase in strength and the number of types of bacteria they are active against decreases as you go from first to third generation drugs.

First generation cephalosporins such as cephalexin (also known as Keflex and Ibilex) and cefaclor (Ceclor, Keflor) are commonly used by general practitioners. They are active against a very wide range of bacteria, and are particularly useful in chest, urinary, skin and joint infections. They can interact with some other antibiotics, and must be used with care in patients with kidney failure. Side effects are uncommon with the first generation of this group, but more likely with the third generation cephalosporins which are given by injection. The most common side effect, is unfortunately the one you suffered, diarrhoea. On the other hand, it is quite safe to use in pregnancy.

You need to have your cystitis treated properly, so should return to your GP so that another antibiotic, that will hopefully not cause diarrhoea, can be prescribed.

Q I have been told that I am allergic to sulpha antibiotics, as I had a bad rash after taking Bactrim. With so many different antibiotic names, can you tell me which ones contain sulpha? Are they all yellow like normal sulpha?

A Sulpha antibiotics do not contain raw sulphur in any form, but are built around a sulphur-containing molecule. They can be any colour, but usually white, as sulphur's yellow colour only appears when it is in its pure form, uncombined with any other substance.

Sulphas were actually the very first antibiotics developed, but the ones available in the late 1930s had severe side effects and were not very effective. Sulphas today are not as widely used as many other groups of antibiotics but still play a part in the treatment of some types of infections. The most commonly prescribed sulpha preparation is co-trimoxazole (also known as Bactrim, Septrin or Resprim), which has a sulpha antibiotic combined with a second type of antibiotic.

Another commonly used sulpha drug is trimethoprim (Alprim, Trib or Triprim).

Your best option is to always tell both doctors and pharmacists who are prescribing any medication for you that you are allergic to sulphas. Virtually all are available only on prescription, but some more old-fashioned ones are available from chemists without a prescription in skin preparations.

Sulphas should be avoided in patients with liver disease and used with caution in the elderly. They are available in tablet, mixture and injection forms.

Q Can you please tell me about the antibiotics called tetracyclines? I have often had these for my bronchitis, but my GP said they were too dangerous to use on my six year old son when he got bronchitis.

A Tetracyclines are a group of antibiotics that act by preventing the multiplication of bacteria. Other antibiotics act by directly killing the bacteria. As a result, tetracyclines are sometimes slower to act than penicillins or sulphas.

Your GP was wise not to prescribe a tetracycline for your son. Although they are not actually dangerous for children, prolonged use can cause yellow discolouration of teeth and nails, but this effect occurs only under 12 years of age. They can also retard the development of the skeleton in a foetus if taken during pregnancy.

When used correctly they are very effective in the treatment of many infections, particularly in the chest and sinuses. They are frequently used long term for the treatment of pimples in teenagers, and interestingly they also inhibit the development of the malaria parasite so can be used as a form of protection against this tropical disease.

The tetracycline group include drugs such as doxycycline (Doryx, Vibramycin), minocycline (Minomycin), and tetracycline (Mysteclin).

Side effects are uncommon, but may include poor appetite, nausea, sore mouth, diarrhoea, and sun sensitivity.

ARMS

See also ARTHRITIS

Q Why does it hurt so much when you hit your funny bone?

A Because your funny bone is not a bone but a nerve. On the inside of the point of your elbow is a groove. Through this groove runs a tendon to move the elbow, and a nerve that goes from the neck to the hand. If you hit this part of your elbow, the pain that ensues is due to the nerve being compressed against the bone, and the result is not really very funny at all!

Q I have a tennis elbow. How can this be treated?

A Tennis elbow is inflammation on the inside of the elbow from excessive strain to the muscles inserted into the arm bone at that point. The most important type of treatment is rest, and this should be started as early as possible, and continued until the elbow has completely recovered. If rest is inadequate, the condition may persist for many months.

Anti-inflammatory tablets may also prove useful, and in severe cases injections of steroids are used. Physiotherapists have skills that may be of benefit to some sufferers.

There are also specially designed straps with a pressure pad attached to them, that can be worn on the affected elbow. These can prevent, as well as treat, tennis elbow.

Eventually the condition will settle, but often not until the patient has been forced to give up sport for far longer than wished.

Q For over two years I have had an obsession to scratch the outer part of my upper arm. I have changed my diet, toiletries, sheets, clothes etc., but doctors are at a loss, and nothing helps. Scratching makes it worse. Can you help?

A I suspect that you are suffering from a relatively mild, but still annoying, obsessive compulsive neurosis.

This is a condition in which the patient has a totally irrational desire to undertake a repetitive action. The desire to perform this action is constantly intruding into the patient's thoughts, and even after completing the task, the patient feels that s/he must do it again and again. At other times the activity may be subconscious.

The victim may feel that by performing the rituals, s/he will regain control of a personality and emotions that are felt to be out of control. S/he is well aware that the habit is abnormal, but is powerless to stop it.

Obsessive compulsive neurosis is more common in women than in men, and is occasionally related to previous brain injury or infection (eg. encephalitis).

Treatment involves psychotherapy, behavioural therapy and medication. Some medications are particularly successful in treating this disorder, and a number of different ones may be tried.

You should ask your GP to refer you to a psychiatrist, who will be able to advise you further.

Q My twelve year old daughter has unusually hairy arms. On her request, I trim the hairs. Will this cause stronger or darker growth of hairs?

A Repeatedly cutting the hairs will not cause them to become darker or stronger, but the short hairs will stand up on end as they regrow, making her skin feel bristly and prickly, thus resulting in a request for more shaving.

All humans, both male and female, have hair on their bodies. In some men this is very obvious, but even the most attractive of women have a fine down on them.

At a woman's puberty, the hairs may become more prominent, but as the hormones settle down, the hairs usually become finer and softer. Most body hairs are usually blonde, and do not show up markedly on the skin.

I would advise you not to trim your daughter's body hair, but allow it to grow to its full length, when it will lie down on the skin, and not feel abnormal. If the hairs are noticeable, they can be bleached.

A small number of women do have an excessive amount of body and facial hair that is embarrassing. In these situations, a tablet called spironolactone can be prescribed by your general practitioner to remove this hair.

Q **I've got elbows similar to that of an elephant's skin—greyish and wrinkly —but I'm only 18, not 81! Occasionally they become raw and painful, not to mention unsightly. Can I do anything about it?**

A There is obviously something wrong when a young woman has such unsightly elbow skin.

A number of skin diseases, varying from psoriasis and lupus to fungal infections and even birth skin defects may be responsible.

Trying to diagnose a skin condition without being able to see the affected skin, even if the condition is described very carefully, is rather like trying to play chess without being able to see the board—very difficult (if not impossible) to get the correct result.

I suggest that you see your general practitioner about the problem, and if s/he is unable to help you, seek a referral to a skin specialist (dermatologist). Do this as soon as possible, because with some conditions, delay can lead to permanent skin damage.

Q **My arm has swollen horribly after an operation for cancer of the breast. Can this be treated?**

A When the breast is removed for cancer, it is necessary to remove a lot of tissue around it in order to catch any cancer cells that may have spread. The most common place for these malignant cells to go is to the glands in the armpit. It is therefore necessary to remove these glands if the cancer is a large one.

The waste products produced by the muscles in moving your hand and arm are returned to the body through a network of fine vein-like tubes called the lymphatic system. Along these lymph channels, the lymph glands act as filters to remove any infection or abnormal cells. These are the glands situated in your armpit. If these are removed, the lymphatic channels are disrupted, and the lymphatic fluid is unable to return to the body in its normal manner. Much of it will enter the bloodstream and return via the veins, but what remains behind causes the arm to become swollen, tense and sore (lymphoedema).

It is a very difficult problem to treat. There are several techniques that can be tried, and sometimes a combination of them gives relief. Wearing a firm, correctly shaped elasticised stocking over the arm at night often gives relief. It is a matter that you will have to discuss in more detail with your own doctor.

Q **I wake up with pins and needles in my left arm most mornings. It settles after 15-20 minutes, but is most annoying. What can I do to stop this?**

A You are probably sleeping on your left side, and the pressure on the left arm along with little or no movement in the arm is affecting its blood supply. If nerves are deprived of blood for even a short time, they stop working properly and the affected area becomes numb, develops pins and needles, loses all sensation and rarely may become temporarily paralysed.

The solution to your problem is obviously to not sleep on your left side. This is easier said than done, because some people find it difficult to go to sleep in a different position, or roll onto that side during sleep. One simple solution is to sleep on two pillows rather than one. This will alter the angle of your neck, and take some of the weight off the shoulder when lying on your side.

Q **I've had a frozen shoulder for months and tried everything suggested by my doctor. What do I do now?**

A This is a very difficult problem, and the most important factor in successful treatment is time. Patients with a frozen shoulder are unable to move the joint freely, and sometimes even the slightest movement causes severe pain. They cannot brush their own hair or even clean their teeth in severe cases.

The recognised therapies for this distressing condition are exercises, heat, physiotherapy, anti-inflammatory drugs, steroid injections into the shoulder, manipulation (sometimes under anaesthetic) and occasionally cortisone tablets.

If you are not improving after some months of treatment, you should be seeing an orthopaedic specialist for his opinion.

Q **I have pain in my left arm between the elbow and shoulder. It is not only stiff, but agonising, particularly at night. The doctor calls it supraspinatus tendonitis, and has prescribed Feldene, but these are not helping. What else can be done?**

A Supraspinatus tendonitis is the inflammation of the tendon that runs across the top of your shoulder to help move your arm away from your body.

If this tendon becomes strained, stretched or damaged, it swells and does not work effectively. Sometimes tiny flecks of bone form in the tendon if it has been inflamed for a long time, and these can be seen on X-ray.

Inflammation occurs when tissue is damaged. If you hit your thumb with a hammer, it becomes swollen and painful. This in inflammation, and any attempt to use the thumb worsens the pain. In your situation, any attempt to move the arm causes pressure on the tendon, and intense pain.

The treatment includes anti-inflammatory medications such as Feldene, rest (most important), physiotherapy, and injections of cortisone around the tendon.

Q **After falling off a horse, my daughter dislocated her shoulder, but it popped back again quickly. The doctor said it was probably a subluxation and did not require any further treatment. What is the difference between a dislocation and subluxation?**

A A dislocation occurs when a the joint surfaces of the two bones forming a joint are completely separated from each other. A subluxation occurs when there is only partial separation.

Shoulder dislocation is the disruption of the joint between the scapula (shoulder blade) and humerus (upper arm bone). The shoulder is a ball and socket joint, but the socket is very shallow to allow maximum movement. A cuff of muscles and ligaments surrounds the joint to keep it in position. This joint can move through a greater range than any other, but as a result is relatively unstable, and it is the most commonly dislocated major joint. If excessive force is applied to the shoulder joint, it may dislocate forwards, or less commonly, backwards.

Patients experience severe pain, do not like the shoulder joint to be moved, and often hold the elbow of the affected arm at right angles and against their side with the other hand. The diagnosis can be confirmed by X-rays.

The dislocated shoulder can be put back into place by one of a number of different techniques, often with little or no anaesthetic if treated immediately, or after giving pain-killing injections or a brief general anaesthetic if there is any delay. After treatment the arm is kept in a sling for a month.

Any shoulder dislocation is associated with tearing and damage to the surrounding muscles and ligaments of the rotator cuff and joint capsule, and a dislocation may be associated with a fracture. After a couple of dislocations, recurrent shoulder dislocations may occur by merely picking up a heavy object or raising the arm and these patients require an operation (the Putti-Platt procedure) to repair the damaged tissues and prevent further dislocations.

Dislocation Types

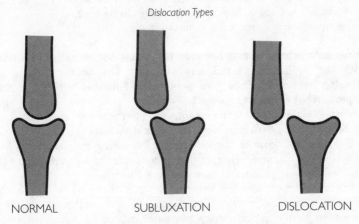

NORMAL   SUBLUXATION   DISLOCATION

Diagram demonstrating the difference between subluxation and dislocation of a joint.

ARTERIES and VEINS

See also BLOOD; HEART

Q **What is the difference between an artery and a vein? I am confused about why different blood vessels have different names.**

A When the heart contracts, it pumps blood out into arteries under considerable pressure. The blood travels along these arteries, which divide into smaller and smaller ones (arterioles), until they finally branch into microscopically thin vessels called capillaries.

Every cell in the body is in direct contact with a capillary, and can obtain oxygen and nutrients from the blood, while giving back waste products.

The blood moves out of capillaries into very small blood vessels called venules, which join up to form veins. The blood travels slowly at low pressure back to the heart through steadily larger veins. Once in the heart, the blood is pumped through the lungs to be enriched with oxygen, then returns to the heart again to be pumped out into the body through the arteries again, completing the cycle.

Because the blood in arteries is moving quickly under high pressure, arteries have thick walls containing muscle fibres. Veins are far thinner and softer, as blood in them is not under any significant pressure, but because they are weaker, those that do have an increase in pressure, for example in the legs, can dilate and form varicose veins.

Q   My doctor says I have an aneurysm in my stomach. What is this?

A   The main artery carrying blood from your heart to the rest of the body is called the aorta. This may be 2 to 3 cm in diameter, and travels down the back of your chest and abdomen just inside the backbone.

If this large artery develops a weak spot from atherosclerosis (hardening of the artery), an aneurysm can develop. The wall of the artery is made of three layers. If the weak spot allows blood to seep into the area between two of these layers, it will gradually separate them and cause a balloon-like swelling on the side of the artery.

There are several types of aneurysm. Some are like the traditional round balloon, and sit like small pimples on the side of an artery. Others are long and thin, and appear as a thickening of the artery. Both types are quite serious, as they may burst if they swell to far or you receive a blow to the vital area. As a result, doctors usually operate to correct the condition once it is found.

Q   A recent ultrasound has shown a medium-sized aneurysm of my abdominal aorta that the doctors intend to watch with repeated ultrasound examinations. Can you tell me how serious this condition is, and what can happen to me?

A   An aneurysm is the ballooning out of one part of an artery at a weak point. There are several different types of aneurysm, some of which are very dangerous, while others are quite innocuous. The aorta is the main artery of the body that runs from the heart down the back of the chest and belly.

On an X-ray or ultrasound, the size, shape and type of aneurysm can be determined. This may vary from a tiny narrow-necked balloon on the side of the artery, to a generalised swelling on one side and along the length of an artery.

If your doctor was at all concerned about the aneurysm, surgery would have been recommended. Many aneurysms develop very slowly, and can be checked by regularly repeated X-rays or ultrasound examinations. If the aneurysm does not change from one year to the next, major surgery can be avoided. If the aneurysm is shown to be enlarging, surgery can be arranged electively.

The greatest danger from an aneurysm is that it may rupture. If this occurs, the patient will be severely ill, and require emergency surgery. Certain types of aneurysm are more likely to rupture than others.

Q **What causes varicose veins? My legs look terrible, and I wear slacks all the time as I feel I look terrible in a skirt.**

A Blood is pumped from your heart out to the hands and feet and every other part of your body. The blood returns to the heart through the veins, but this process does not occur due to the action of the heart. Many people believe that blood is 'sucked' back from the feet to the heart, but this is not so.

In your legs there are veins superficially just under the skin, and veins deep within the muscles near the bones. When you walk or stand, the deep veins are compressed by the muscular action. This squeezes the blood out of them. These veins are also fitted with one-way valves, so that once the blood is pumped up the vein in your leg, it cannot run back down again. It is the muscular action of the leg muscles on the leg veins that moves blood back to the heart.

The valves also only allow the blood from the superficial veins to go to the deep veins (where the muscular action is more effective) and not the other way around.

If the pressure of blood in the veins builds up excessively due to a restriction of the flow of the venous blood back to the heart, the valves may be damaged and allow blood to pool in the leg veins. Conditions that can restrict venous blood return include pregnancy, obesity and prolonged standing. There is also a significant hereditary tendency.

The dilated veins that result from damaged valves are varicose veins.

Q **I have varicose veins that I think cause me to black out when I stand around for a long time waiting to be served in supermarkets or banks. What can be done about them?**

A When you stand still for any length of time, blood pools in your legs, as the only way that blood can move from the legs back up to the heart is by the action of the leg muscles pressing on the veins, and acting as a pump. The heart is unable to pump the blood up and out of the legs.

When soldiers stand at attention for a long period of time, they are taught to contract and relax their calf, foot and thigh muscles, so that they do not collect excess blood in the legs.

If excess blood does collect in the legs, insufficient blood is available for the heart to pump to the brain, and a faint results. The person falls to the ground, the gravitational effect on the blood in the legs is removed, and the blood can flow to the brain, and revive the patient.

Those who have varicose veins, effectively have large blood reservoirs in their legs. If you stand still for a short time, these veins swell up, and by the mechanism described above, starve the brain of blood, and cause a faint far more rapidly than in a person without varicose veins.

The simple solutions are to wear supportive stockings, and keep moving up and down on your toes instead of standing still. More definitive treatment will involve an operation to remove or destroy the varicose veins.

Q **I have broken capillaries all over my nose and face, although I am only 32. This is most distressing to me. Can they be treated by sclerosant injections? Is there any other treatment?**

A   Sclerosant injections are suitable for moderate-sized varicose veins in the legs, but are not suitable for the spider-like superficial blood vessels on the face or other parts of the body.

These disfiguring, surface veins are best dealt with by electrocautery or laser treatment. This will usually involve a referral to a plastic surgeon or dermatologist, but a small number of GPs also do this work.

The procedure is simple, and after a local anaesthetic injection (or sometimes without, particularly with the laser treatment), a fine needle is placed into the offending capillary, and an electric current is passed through it for a few seconds to destroy the blood vessel. The laser burns the vessel through the skin, without an injection. Both methods leave a small white spot scar at the point of burning.

Q   **I have been told that I am suffering from thromboses in my leg that are very painful, and are not being helped by an ointment or tubular bandage. What can I do to stop these? Do you suggest having the veins stripped?**

A   There are two types of thrombosis (clot) that can occur in the veins of the leg—those that develop in the deep veins inside the muscle, and those that develop in the superficial varicose veins.

The deep blood clots are very serious and require long-term medication to prevent sometimes fatal complications. The superficial thromboses are rarely serious, but are often a significant nuisance.

Varicose veins that develop a thrombosis can be treated by liniments, strapping and anti-inflammatory drugs (eg. Indocid and others) that reduce the inflammation. Most of these clots can also be prevented by taking half an aspirin a day every day for years. This simple measure may solve the problem for you. Low doses of stronger anti-clotting drugs may be used if the aspirin is unsuccessful. Wearing support stockings, not standing still for long periods, and exercising the legs regularly can all help to prevent superficial thromboses.

Stripping the veins will certainly stop clots in those veins, but not all varicose veins can be removed, and the problem may recur in the small number that remain.

Q   **My doctor says I have hardening of the arteries. What is this?**

A   If excess levels of cholesterol occur in the bloodstream due to a poor diet or hereditary reasons, it may form deposits on the inside of the arteries. This occurs particularly at points of turbulence where an artery divides or bends.

If a surgeon feels these arteries, they are thicker and firmer than normal, and thus the term 'hardening of the arteries'. Once it has occurred, medications can be used in mild cases to very slowly remove some of the cholesterol plaques, but in severe cases the only treatment is surgery to remove the deposits of cholesterol or bypass any blockage that may be caused by the deposits.

It can be a quite serious disease if arteries supplying vital organs such as the heart and brain become narrowed or blocked.

Q   **A specialist has told me he is going to fix my blocked arteries with a small balloon, but he hasn't explained just how. Can you help me?**

A   When an artery becomes narrowed by fatty deposits, insufficient blood may reach the part of the body beyond the narrowing, particularly during exercise, when more of the oxygen carried by the blood, is required as fuel by the muscles. When this happens, pain occurs in the affected muscle.

The area affected can be anywhere in the body, but the most commonly involved are the heart, head and legs.

In past years, the only way to overcome this blockage was an operation to bypass the damaged area of artery, or to clean out the fatty deposits from inside the artery.

In the last few years, heart surgeons have devised the technique of balloon angioplasty.

In this procedure, a fine tube is threaded into an artery, and moved along it until the blocked area is reached. The tube has a small balloon on the end of it. The hard tip of the tube is pushed through the obstructing fatty deposits, and then the balloon is gently blown up. This pushes aside the fat inside the artery, compresses it, and when the balloon is deflated, a clear channel is left for the blood to pass.

This delicate procedure saves the time, trauma and expense of a major operation, and is being used more and more where the blockage is not extensive. Large blockages will still need surgery, as sometimes the fat is too hard to be pushed away by the balloon.

Q How can I help poor circulation in my hands? They go blue and become painful whenever it gets cold.

A There is a disease known as Raynaud's phenomenon which is due to spasm of the tiny arteries in your hands in cold weather. The first sign is redness of the fingers and hands which then go white, then blue and become intensely painful. It is obviously more of a problem in cold climates, but many people go skiing and experience the problem for the first time.

The hands should be kept warm by mittens or gloves, and if the problem occurs, they can be immersed in warm water. This is often not convenient, so doctors use a number of different drugs that can be taken by mouth to dilate the arteries. Nicotinic acid is the one used traditionally, but more potent medications are available on script in severe cases.

A new and very successful treatment is the use of a very small amount of ointment on the involved area. This ointment is normally used on the chest to open the heart arteries in angina patients, but works just as well on the hands.

Q I had a drip in my arm after an operation recently. Now there is a long, hard lump running 10 cm up my arm. Is this serious?

A This is a very common complication of an intravenous drip. The presence of a small plastic tube in a vein causes irritation of the vein wall. This in turn triggers the clotting mechanism in the blood, so that after several days the vein becomes blocked by a clot. This is why a new drip must be inserted into a different vein every few days, or special drugs must be used in the drip to stop it from blocking with a clot.

Once the drip tube is removed, the area of irritation is still present, and again a clot can form. This can be felt as a hard, tender lump at the drip site, and may extend for several centimetres along the vein. If it is annoying, anti-inflammatory medications and creams can be used to relieve the discomfort. It is not a serious problem, as the veins used are superficial and any clot is most unlikely to break off and reach the lungs.

ARTHRITIS

See also ARMS; BACK; FEET; HANDS; LEGS

Q **What can a pensioner use for chronic pain from arthritis? The government only gives pensioners simple things like Panamax and Aspirin on the free list, and they are not good enough.**

A Both paracetamol (Panamax) and aspirin are very effective and very safe pain-killers. Often the reason they do not work is that not a large enough dose is taken. You should pursue this course initially. Up to eight paracetamol or aspirin tablets can be taken every day if necessary.

Unfortunately, some patients with chronic pain conditions do require stronger medications, and these people may well find themselves disadvantaged, as the government does not subsidise the cost of all of the moderate strength analgesics. There are a number of drugs in this intermediate strength range (eg. Digesic, Prodeine), but some of them are quite expensive.

The next step up the pain-killer ladder is a medication called Tramal, which helps moderate to severe pain. Beyond this comes Panadeine Forte, but this may cause drowsiness, constipation and addiction. Both of these medications are subsidised for pensioners.

The government also subsidises the very powerful narcotic pain killers, but as these may have significant side effects, they are only used in special circumstances. Several other large groups of medications are missing from the subsidised pharmaceuticals list including antihistamines (for allergies), antibiotic creams and cough mixtures.

Q **What is the cause of stiff and sore finger joints in the morning?**

A The two most likely explanations are overuse of the fingers the night before in tasks such as typing or playing the piano, or one of the many different types of arthritis that can attack the finger joints—the most common being nodal arthritis and rheumatoid arthritis. In older people, rheumatoid arthritis is more likely, but unfortunately this condition cannot be cured or prevented.

Rheumatoid arthritis can be very effectively controlled, and it is very important for sufferers to receive appropriate medical care as soon as possible to ensure that adequate control is achieved.

Q **I have been told that my kneecap is arthritic. I do not want to be an invalid in old age. What treatments are available?**

A The kneecap is designed to allow the tendons from the large muscles on the front of the thigh to slide smoothly over the front of the knee and insert into the top of the lower leg (tibia). Every time you bend your knee, the kneecap glides over the end of the thigh bone (femur). If the under surface of the kneecap (patella) is roughened by arthritis, the smooth movement does not occur, friction builds up and pain results. This is arthritis of the kneecap, and can be caused by injury, stress, chronic overuse, infection and an inbuilt tendency to arthritis.

Treatment involves physiotherapy to mobilise the knee as much as possible, anti-inflammatory tablets prescribed by your doctor, steroid injections into the joint, and surgery. The injections are very successful, but cannot be repeated too often. Surgery can be used to remove the kneecap completely or to replace the smooth surface of the kneecap with an artificial one. The treatment used will be determined by the degree of discomfort you suffer. There should be no reason why this will cause any permanent disability.

Q I have terrible arthritis in my knees, and the tablets I have been prescribed for the pain don't work. Is knee replacement surgery successful?

A Yes, very. Knees have been replaced for over 20 years, and a great deal of knowledge about the procedure is now available. If the knee is severely arthritic and causing enough pain and limitation of movement to adversely affect the patient's lifestyle, they should seriously consider this procedure.

A discussion with your general practitioner and then one or two orthopaedic surgeons is necessary. In the operation, the old knee joint is cut out, and a new steel and plastic one is inserted. You will be able to walk quite well within a few weeks, and after two or three months should not be aware of the artificial joint.

There is always a small percentage of people who do not do well with any operation. The complications of this one include infection, bleeding, instability of the joint and cracking of the long bones of the lower leg.

Q I visited the Sunshine Coast four years ago and was bitten by mosquitoes that gave me Ross River fever. This caused months of joint aches and weakness. If I get bitten again by mosquitoes that carry the virus, can I catch the disease again?

A Normally the answer is no. Once you have had this disease (or any other viral infection) you cannot catch it again, but there are always those few people who are the exception to the rule.

As with chickenpox and other childhood viruses, once you have had a viral infection you develop antibodies to that virus that remain in your system for the rest of your life.

In Australia, Ross River fever is named after the river that runs through Townsville in north Queensland, but it is a world-wide disease that is known generally as epidemic polyarthralgia. It causes severe muscle and joint swelling and pain, fever and tiredness that may last for several months. There is no cure or vaccine, but medication can be prescribed by doctors to relieve the worst symptoms.

This infection is most common in the tropics, but can occur Australia-wide (Tasmania being the one exception). It tends to flare in epidemics every few years.

You can enjoy another Sunshine Coast holiday with the expectation that it is very unlikely that you will catch the infection again.

Q I've had arthritis in my hip for years that has been giving me more and more pain. My doctor has suggested referring me to have an artificial hip put in. Can you explain what is an artificial hip?

A   Many older people with severe arthritis of the hip, and some younger ones who are born with dislocated hips, require an artificial hip to enable them to walk with ease.

In an operation lasting about an hour, the top of the thigh bone is cut off, and a metal ball is attached to the top of the bone. This fits neatly into a tough plastic cup that is inserted into the old hip socket on the pelvic bone. The operation is very successful, and most patients are up and walking within a few days.

Q   How good are artificial hips?

A   Very good. It would be quite easy to leave my answer as just those two words, because the modern artificial hip really is very good.

If one goes back in history, hip replacement is not a new operation. Ivory hip replacements, carved from elephant tusks, were first used one hundred years ago. Today, the head of the femur (the ball part at the top of the thigh bone) is made of stainless steel, titanium or other rare metals. The cup part in the pelvis is made of a Teflon type plastic that is smooth, but extremely hard.

The operation is performed on those people who have arthritis (or other disease) in their hip, that is bad enough to significantly affect their lifestyle. The operation itself takes about 60 minutes, and the patient is often up and walking a few days later with the aid of a physiotherapist.

The majority of patients find a new lease of life after the procedure, but there are always a very small number in whom the operation is not a success. It is extremely rare for anyone to be worse off after the operation than before.

Q   After a very bad motorbike accident in which my son broke his hip, my son has been doing heavy farm work, but recently he has a lot of pain and stiffness in the joint in the morning. His doctor says he will need a hip replacement as there is arthritis showing on X-rays of the joint. He is only 28. Can exercise or diet stop him from having the operation?

A   After breaking his neck of femur (hip bone) your son's leg may have reset at a slightly different angle to before. This, combined with the heavy work he is doing, may have placed abnormal stresses on the hip joint, and resulted in premature arthritis of the joint.

With rest, the joint stiffens as microscopic adhesions form in the joint. With movement in the morning, these are broken down, causing pain for a while until the joint starts moving freely again.

Unfortunately, this problem will slowly worsen with time and the only effective long-term treatment is a hip replacement operation. Anti-inflammatory medications and physiotherapy exercises may help in the short term, but there is no diet that will be of any benefit.

The operation is very successful, and young people who need such an operation usually recover rapidly. There is no reason why the steel hip replacement should not be successful in carrying your son around and allowing him to do heavy work and play sport.

The timing of the operation depends on your son. When the discomfort of the hip worries him enough to want an operation, then he should see an orthopaedic specialist to have it arranged.

Q **I have very severe rheumatoid arthritis which is controlled by taking Prednisone all the time. I am told that it has side effects. Are these serious?**

A Prednisone is an invaluable drug for controlling a vast range of diseases from asthma and psoriasis to rheumatoid arthritis. Doctors usually try to use it for short periods of time, or on alternate days, but if used long term it may have significant side effects, and it may be a matter of what is worse, the disease or the treatment. The main problems are bruising easily, poor healing, increased susceptibility to infection, weakening of bones, stomach ulcers, muscle pains and a host of other more minor problems.

Doctors do not use this drug lightly, and provided you are on the absolute minimum dose needed to control your arthritis, and your doctor is monitoring your condition regularly, you shouldn't get into too much trouble. Any patient using prednisone who experiences unusual symptoms should report them to a doctor immediately.

Q **I am 62 years old, and several of my friends have rheumatoid arthritis, and I do not want to catch it. How do you catch rheumatoid arthritis?**

A This is not a disease that you catch, but one that develops for an unknown reason, although recent theories suggest a virus that acts in susceptible people may be the culprit. There is certainly an hereditary tendency, so if your parents or grandparents suffered from rheumatoid arthritis, you have an increased chance of developing the disease.

It may develop at almost any age from childhood on, but is more common in women after the menopause.

The tissue lining the small joints of the hands and feet are particularly severely affected, and this causes the swelling and pain associated with the disease.

There is no evidence that diet or environment play any part in the development of the disease, and unfortunately vitamins and diet do not help the symptoms.

Doctors can use medications to control (but not cure) most cases.

Q **I believe that rheumatoid arthritis is not just a disease of old people, but can occur at all ages, including childhood. What do you think?**

A Rheumatoid arthritis can occur at any age, including a rare childhood form (when the disease is called Still's disease), but as the disease usually lasts life-long, the number of older people with the disease is greater than the number of young or middle-aged people.

There are some patients in whom the disease appears to 'burn out' in old age, and although they may not have the severe pain they had in earlier years, the deformed joints (particularly of the hand) with their reduced function, will remain for the rest of their lives. The most common age for the disease to actually start is between 30 and 40, and it is far more common in females than males (by a ratio of 3 to 1).

Rheumatoid arthritis cannot be cured, but there are many drugs available to control the worst of the symptoms. In some patients, it is now possible to replace the small joints in the fingers (which are particularly severely attacked by this disease) to improve both the appearance and usefulness of the hands.

Q Can you recommend some exercises for an elderly woman with osteoarthritis?

A It is most important for patients of all ages to keep their arthritic joints as mobile as possible, and exercises specifically designed for the individual are therefore a vital part of any treatment program.

Exercises for arthritis should be performed regularly, every day. You may experience some pain as you put your joints through their paces, but if this pain lasts for more than 30 minutes after the exercise, you are probably doing too much and should ease off. Doing your exercises after heating the affected joints in a bowl of warm water or after a hot bath can often ease the discomfort and give a better range of movement.

The aim of any exercises in arthritis is to move the joint through its full range of movement (eg. bending a knee as much as possible and then straightening it as much as possible) several times. Once this is readily achieved it may be possible to add some light weights to make it harder to use the joint. This will strengthen the muscles around it. Always start with an easy exercise and slowly build up to harder ones.

Booklets containing exercise programs are also available from the Arthritis Foundation (listed in your capital city phone book). The best person to teach you the appropriate exercises is a physiotherapist. Physios can also give heat, interferential and other treatments to arthritic patients to help their arthritis further.

Q I have been told I have chondromalacia of a joint in my foot. I stand a lot in my job and I'm not overweight. What can be done to relieve the pain?

A Chondromalacia is an abnormal softness of the cartilage which covers the ends of the bones in a joint. In patients with chondromalacia, this cartilage becomes pitted, uneven and damaged, and the bones grate across each other instead of gliding.

The cause of chondromalacia is often difficult to determine, but it can certainly be caused by recurrent injury to the joint, from walking long distances, carrying excess weight or jumping.

Patients complain of a pain deep in the joint, and worse pain on moving the joint. When the joint is moved, a fine grating may be felt by the patient, and by a doctor when s/he places her/his hand over the joint.

You can significantly help yourself by taking the weight off your feet, by reducing your total body weight, and by wearing shock absorbent insoles (eg. Sorbothane).

Further treatment involves firm bandaging and rest. With this the majority of cases settle. Sometimes splinting or a plaster cast may be required to totally rest the joint for a few weeks. After many months, if pain persists, surgery to modify or remove the cartilage may be necessary.

Q I am 92, live alone, and have arthritis in my hands, back and ankles. I am taking Naprosyn, but is there a better medication to ease pain when sleeping?

A There are a large number of anti-inflammatory medications that can be used to control arthritis, and it is often a matter of trial and error to find the one that suits you best.

Some medications last for longer than others, but they may not be as effective in easing the pain.

Anti-inflammatories such as Celebrex, Vioxx, Orudis and Feldene only need to be taken once a day, and they should control pain through the night. Other medications are taken twice, three times, or rarely four times a day as they have a shorter active life.

You should discuss your problem with your general practitioner so that various combinations and permutations of medications can be tried until your pain is relieved.

ASTHMA
See also LUNGS

Q Can a three year old get asthma?

A YES! Asthma is one of the most under-diagnosed conditions in medicine, and is very often overlooked in young children because their symptoms vary from those traditionally associated with asthma. There may be minimal wheezing and shortness of breath in infants, and they tend to have a chronic cough, be small for their age and suffer from repeated respiratory infections.

There is no specific diagnostic test, but if they can cooperate, abnormalities may be seen when the child breathes into a machine that tests lung function, and minor changes may be seen on an X-ray of the chest. The main diagnosis depends on the clinical acumen of the doctor. If the correct treatment is given, the child will rapidly loose the cough, and become more active and generally healthier.

Prevention is more important than treatment in asthma, and the long-term management should be designed to prevent its recurrence. Liquid medications are easy to use, but are not as effective as inhaled drugs. As soon as possible, an asthmatic child should learn to use a puffer, usually with the assistance of a spacing device which can be recommended by your doctor. The larger spacers (such as the 'Nebuhaler') are easy for children to use and are as effective as the more expensive nebulising machines, which must be used in more severe and difficult cases.

If your child has a chronic cough, it could be asthma.

Q I took my son to the doctor with a cough, and she said that he had asthma. I can't believe that this is true. Why would my son develop asthma at the age of 12?

A Asthma can develop at any age, but the most common times are at about 2 years, 5 to 7 years of age and at puberty (12 to 14 years).

Asthma may be triggered by infections (eg. common colds), allergies, exercise, temperature changes, emotional changes or hormonal changes (different times of the month in women). One of the most common presenting symptoms in children is a persistent dry cough.

Once asthma is diagnosed, attacks may occur regularly, seasonally, or very rarely. If regular attacks occur, medication will be given to prevent them. If attacks are infrequent, medication can be used when required.

It is very important to receive adequate treatment for asthma, to seek further help if the cough or wheeze continues, and to follow your doctor's instructions carefully. Poorly treated asthma can lead to growth retardation and other long-term problems.

Q My asthma cannot be controlled. My life is one continual struggle to breathe. What more can be done?

A It is unusual for patients to find that their asthma cannot be controlled—provided they are taking adequate medication, and taking it correctly. I will assume that you have seen your general practitioner regularly about this problem—if not, you should be ashamed—see her/him today.

The next step is to see a specialist respiratory physician. S/he will assess the situation thoroughly and start you on a combination of medications to both prevent and treat the asthma. These will be sprays and/or tablets.

The sprays may well be given by means of a spacer or nebuliser, which are far more effective than the hand held sprays. Nebulisers are electric or gas powered machines that break the drug down into microscopic particles that are readily inhaled and can penetrate deep into your lungs. Many different types of medications are available for use in nebulisers, and two or more may be used in combination.

Inhaled steroids will probably be used, and in quite high doses. Only as a last resort are oral steroids used. Medications to thin out and liquefy your phlegm can also be prescribed, and physiotherapy to help you drain the chest can be useful. A lot can be done to help you—go and get that help now!

Q I have heard several times said that Ventolin sprays are dangerous, and people should use different things. I have used a Ventolin spray for my asthma for many years without trouble, but now I am worried. Should I stop my Ventolin?

A Ventolin, and other similar sprays, were introduced more than 30 years ago. Over that time they have helped millions of people around the world, and saved the lives of countless asthmatics.

Today, these medications remain the principal form of treatment for acute asthma. The side effects are minimal and rare, and they are so safe that they can be purchased from a pharmacy without a prescription, but all asthmatics should have their asthma regularly monitored by a doctor to ensure they are receiving adequate treatment.

Prevention is always better than cure, and those who have regular asthma attacks should be using other medications all the time in a dose that is sufficient to prevent their asthma.

You should not stop your Ventolin, and provided your GP checks your lungs regularly, and you follow his/her advice on further treatment, you have nothing to fear.

Q Different doctors and naturopaths have told me different ways to deal with my asthma. What is the best treatment for asthma?

A The best treatment is that which completely prevents the disease. It is far better to prevent asthma than to deal with acute attacks. If the asthma only occurs every month or two, intermittent treatment may be appropriate. Most patients are being under-medicated, rather than taking too much. This applies particularly to patients who obtain their medication over the counter from chemists rather than seeing a doctor. This habit could prove expensive to your health!

Prevention involves two classes of drugs:
— Intal or Tilade
— Steroids (eg. Becotide, Becloforte, Flixotide, Pulmicort, Aldecin etc.).

Both groups are designed to be used regularly on a long term basis to prevent asthma attacks.

If an attack does occur, treatment is usually by one of a number of sprays (eg. Ventolin, Respolin, Bricanyl, Serevent). These can also be given by a nebuliser (when they are even more effective) or in a tablet or mixture (when they are less effective than a spray).

Combination inhalers are now available (eg. Seretide) that have both preventive and treatment medication in the one dose.

Tablets or mixtures of a group of drugs called theophyllines can also be given to treat an attack of asthma. These include medications such as Austyn and Theo-Dur.

If these medications do not work adequately, there are a number of add-on sprays and tablets that can be used including Atrovent and Prednisone.

I must emphasise how important it is to be under the continued care of a doctor when using any of these medications. Asthma can be well controlled with the cooperation of the patient.

Q   **I am 63 years old and a severe asthmatic. I need oxygen several times a day, but it is costing me a lot of money to have the cylinders filled. Is there something else I can do?**

A   It is initially necessary to ensure that your asthma is as well controlled as possible. With severe asthma, you should be under the regular care of both your general practitioner and a respiratory physician. Hopefully, you may be weaned off the oxygen, as it is both inconvenient and expensive.

If you must continue using oxygen regularly, it may be worthwhile buying, hiring or leasing an oxygen concentrator. These are machines that take oxygen from the air and concentrate it so that you do not have to buy your oxygen in cylinders. If you are finding that you have continuing financial problems, or if you want more information about these machines, you should contact the Asthma Foundation which will be listed in the phone book for the capital city of your state.

Q   **Is there any connection between eczema and asthma? Half of my family seems to have one disease, while the other half have the other.**

A   It seems strange that a skin and lung disease can be connected, but this is the case. In fact, there is a third disease—hay fever—that is also connected to eczema and asthma. All three are 'atopic' diseases—that is there is a specific type of reaction by the tissue in the lung, skin and nose, often to outside substances such as temperature changes, dust or pollen, but sometimes to internal triggers such as stress or hormone changes.

Patients with these conditions will know that the disease flares and settles without treatment, and usually for no apparent cause. Others will recognise that before a menstrual period, at times of anxiety, in certain seasons or with a particular type of weather, their condition will worsen.

People with one of these three diseases, also have an above average risk of developing one of the others.

It is possible for allergists to desensitise you to any allergies that may be the cause, but this procedure will not work against the other factors. Fortunately there are creams, sprays and medications that can control these diseases, but there is no cure.

AUTOIMMUNE DISEASES

Q **Would you please explain what an autoimmune disease is? I have been told this is the cause of my arthritis.**

A Autoimmune diseases can be explained as the body rejecting part of its normal tissue, that for an unexplained reason, it suddenly considers to be foreign tissue.

If you have a kidney transplant, and receive someone else's kidney, your body tries to reject this foreign organ, and you must be given medications to prevent the rejection. The same thing happens in autoimmune diseases, except that the body is triggered (for unknown reasons) to reject part of itself that has always been present.

Examples of autoimmune diseases include the nephrotic syndrome, poly-myalgia rheumatica, pemphigus, pyoderma gangrenosum, rheumatoid arthritis, scleroderma, Sjögren syndrome, systemic lupus erythematosus and temporal arteritis.

Q **I have been told by my doctor that I may have scleroderma, and he has ordered tests. Could you please explain what kind of sickness is sclero-derma, what are the symptoms, and how is it treated?**

A Scleroderma is one of the many auto-immune diseases that can beset mankind. In these diseases, the body attempts to reject part of itself as though it is foreign material, resulting in the attacked tissue becoming inflamed and damaged. Rheumatoid arthritis is the most common auto-immune disease, and the tissue being attacked is the cartilage inside the joints.

Scleroderma is a relatively uncommon condition which is caused by the widespread rejection of most body tissues. This results in thickening of the skin, arthritis, and replacement of normal tissue in other organs with fibrous scar tissue.

Raynaud's phenomenon, in which the hands and feet become cold, white (or blue), swollen and painful is a very common symptom. This is caused by a poor blood supply to the hands, and in due course the fingers and toes may develop ulcers.

Elsewhere the skin becomes blotchy, and feels leathery and thick. The same happens to the gut, causing difficulty in swallowing, bowel irregularities and difficulty in absorbing food.

Every organ in the body may be affected, including the heart, lungs and kidneys.

There is no cure for scleroderma, but quite effective controls are available to slow the spread of the condition and relieve its symptoms. Very careful tests will be performed to prove the diagnosis before any treatments are started.

Q My daughter has had SLE for twenty years. She is now getting ulcers and pains in her legs. She takes prednisone and aspirin, but no doctor can explain her problem to me.

A Systemic lupus erythematosus (SLE) is a relatively common, but seldom written about, autoimmune disorder.

In this condition, the autoimmune reaction attacks the joints, skin, liver, and kidney most commonly, but almost any tissue in the body can be affected.

85% of SLE occurs in women, and usually young women. It can have a very variable course, from a mild arthritic complaint that causes only slight intermittent discomfort, to a rapidly progressive disease that leads to death within a few months. Fortunately, most patients are towards the milder end of the scale.

The common characteristics of SLE are a red rash across both cheeks and the bridge of the nose ('butterfly rash'), rashes on other areas that are exposed to sunlight, mouth ulcers, arthritis of several joints, poorly functioning kidneys and anaemia. In addition, patients may complain of a fever, loss of appetite, tiredness, weight loss, damaged nails, loss of hair and painfully cold fingers.

The symptoms vary dramatically from one patient to another, and none will have all these problems. Arthritis is the most common link between them, but because of the varied symptoms and progress of the disease, it is often difficult for doctors to diagnose SLE.

Once suspected, specific blood tests can diagnose the condition. Anaemia and reduced kidney and liver function may also be detected on blood tests.

Treatment will depend upon the severity of the disease. Many patients, with relatively mild symptoms, will require no treatment, or occasional treatment for arthritis.

Sun exposure should be avoided, and because some drugs are known to precipitate the condition, all non-essential medications should be ceased.

In more severe cases, a wide range of drugs including steroids, cytotoxics, immunosuppressives and antimalarials (used for their anti-arthritis properties), may all be used in various combinations and dosages.

There is no cure available for SLE, but nearly 90% of patients are still alive more than ten years after the diagnosis is made. Many patients are free of symptoms for months on end before a further relapse requires another course of treatment.

Q My father keeps developing large watery blisters on various parts of his body, but particularly his thighs, hips and upper arms. His doctors say it is a condition called pemphigus, but none of their treatments are working. What do you suggest?

A Pemphigus is within a class of diseases known as autoimmune conditions, in which the body attacks part of itself in an attempt to reject it. In your father's case, the body is rejecting the skin.

It usually starts in the fifties or sixties with red patches on the skin that then become large, soft, fluid filled blisters. The problem can occur on any part of the body, and may affect only a small area, or in extreme cases, the whole body may be affected, including the inside of the mouth.

The diagnosis can be confirmed by cutting out a piece of affected skin and examining it under a microscope. There is also a specific blood test for the disease.

Treatment is very complex and involves the use of medications to suppress the reaction including steroids and other more sophisticated drugs. It is often very difficult to control, but most patients go into remission after a few months. Recurrent attacks are unfortunately common. There is no specific cure available, but some patients go into prolonged remission.

Q My horrible aches and pains have been diagnosed as polymyalgia rheumatica, and although medication seems to help, the pains keep coming back. How long will I suffer?

A Polymyalgia rheumatica (PMR) is a random inflammation of the muscles anywhere in the body. Women are affected five times more often than men. It is one of a number of post-viral syndromes that triggers an autoimmune response. In some people, for no known reason, a viral infection such as influenza is followed by a chronic inflammation of many muscles.

Symptoms include severe aches and pains in a group of muscles for a few days before the pain subsides, then another muscle group is attacked. The muscles are also weak and the patient is irritable, tired, unable to concentrate, and depressed. Other symptoms may include nausea, headache, arthritis and loss of appetite.

No investigation can confirm the diagnosis but blood tests indicate a generalised inflammation of the body.

Treatment involves heat, pain-killers and anti-inflammatory medications. If these are not successful, steroids can be used.

The condition may last for weeks or months, then recur after a long absence, but eventually complete recovery occurs in most patients.

BABIES
See also CHILDREN

Q I do not have enough breast milk and my baby is not gaining weight. I have been told that it is bad to stop breast feeding, but I feel that I should. Others have suggested supplementary feeds. What does that mean and how do I give supplementary feeds?

A There is no need for you to stop breast feeding. The production of breast milk can be encouraged by the more frequent feeding of the baby and ensuring that the breasts are completely emptied after each feed. If essential, there are also medications available that can help build up breast milk production.

If your child is not gaining sufficient weight despite these measures, supplementary feeding is essential. This can take the form of formula milk, cow's milk or solids, depending on the child's age. Your doctor or clinic sister can guide you here.

At each feed, the breasts should be given first, and emptied as much as possible. After this, the supplementation can be given, and then the breasts again, if desired, to ensure that they are empty and give comfort to both mother and child. Weighing should be done weekly until an adequate rate of weight gain is achieved.

Q Why do babies vomit so much?

A It is important to differentiate between vomiting, positing and reflux. Vomiting is not very common, and may be due to some disease process (eg. infection, food allergy). The vomitus is usually altered food and may be green in colour, indicating the presence of bile. It may occur several hours after a feed.

Positing occurs in most infants, and is the regurgitation of milk and food from the mouth, gullet and upper part of the stomach during or immediately after a feed. It is caused by over feeding, rapid feeding or burping, and it does not require any treatment.

Reflux is the regurgitation of the stomach contents immediately after a meal, and for some time afterwards. It is distressing to the child, as stomach acid is bought up, and this burns the gullet. This can be helped by posture feeding, slow feeding and mixtures (such as Infant Gaviscon) that may be given after a meal.

If you are unsure about the problem, have your child assessed by your GP.

Q My baby is always vomiting, but when I took her to the doctor, he said it was a reflux problem and not vomiting. In what way does reflux differ from vomiting in babies?

A Some babies are unlucky enough to have a defect in the muscle ring at the bottom of the oesophagus (gullet). This muscle ring is normally contracted shut, and only opens when food is swallowed. This prevents the acid and food in the stomach from running up into the oesophagus when lying down or bending over.

If the muscle is weak or defective, the acid in the stomach can burn the oesophagus, which causes considerable pain to the infant. This is known as reflux oesophagitis.

Most children will grow out of the problem, but medication must be given in the meantime to prevent the burning and pain. This is usually in the form of a mixture which is given after every feed. More sophisticated treatments are available for intractable cases.

Q   My newborn son has an umbilical hernia. The doctor told me not to worry about it, but I think it looks horrible. Can it be serious?

A   No. This is a common problem, and the vast majority correct themselves by 5 years of age. If they persist beyond this age, a small operation can be done to correct it. Most infants can have the lump in the centre of their belly button pushed back into the abdomen.

If the lump cannot be reduced, or it becomes red and tender, a doctor should be consulted immediately. This is uncommon, but sometimes a small loop of gut can get caught in the hernia.

The umbilical hernias developed by older people are actually a different disease, due to a breakdown of the fibrous tissue above or below the umbilicus, and again rarely cause problems.

Q   I am a new mother, and need to know how should I deal with colic in a 3 month old? I have received all sorts of advice, but nothing seems to work.

A   The exact cause of colic is unknown, but it is a very common problem between 1 and 4 months of age. It is thought to be due to spasms of the small intestine.

Changing the feeding position, rate of feeding, frequency of feeding, and time of feeding may all help.

If these ideas do not help, numerous gut antispasmodics of varying efficacy are available over the counter from chemists.

Changing the formula is rarely beneficial, but breast fed babies are less likely to develop colic than bottle fed ones.

Anxiety in the mother can be transmitted to the baby, and this often exacerbates the problem. If mother and/or child are very distressed, doctors can treat the condition with appropriate medications.

Q   My next-door neighbour has just had a baby with Down's syndrome. It looks almost completely normal, and seems to be alright in every way. Can you explain what is Down's syndrome?

A   All medical practitioners have seen patients with this relatively common syndrome that used to be known by the rather derogatory and racist name of 'Mongolism'. Modern medical students now call it Trisomy 21 to totally confuse their older peers.

The disease is named after a London physician who lived in the middle of the nineteenth century. One in every 600 children has Down syndrome, but the actual incidence may be two or three times greater, with these pregnancies ending in miscarriage.

The main characteristics include a 'Mongol' facial appearance, mental retardation and congenital heart disease. They also have a heavily fissured tongue, low set ears and a single transverse crease on the palm.

The effect the syndrome has can vary from one victim to another. Some seem to cope, or are not as severely affected, as others. Unfortunately, as your neighbour's child grows, the problems may become more obvious.

Despite the claims of some quacks, there is no effective treatment for this distressing condition, but it can be diagnosed during pregnancy by special tests.

Q   I am expecting my fourth child soon, and from a scan I know that it will be a boy. My first son was circumcised, but I am finding it difficult to contact a doctor who will circumcise my next son. One said he would do it under a general anaesthetic at three months, the other at twelve months. I want my sons to look the same. What do you suggest?

A   'There is no medical indication for undertaking routine circumcision of new-born male infants, and the hazards of the operation at this age outweigh any possible advantage.'

This quote is from the National Health and Medical Research Council. I have not carried out a circumcision in my general practice for many years, and public hospitals in some states now ban the procedure.

Circumcision was traditionally carried out a week after birth. While the infant was held securely by an assistant, the foreskin was clamped firmly and cut away. No anaesthetic was used. I do not believe there is any reason for this barbaric practice to be continued in the twenty-first century.

There are a small number of boys and men who will need a circumcision, but this can be performed when required, and under a general anaesthetic in hospital.

The fact that an elder brother or father had been circumcised used to influence my decision in this matter, but no more. Very rarely do brothers actually compare themselves, but if they do, the uncircumcised one can be proud that he has more than his brother.

In later life, the uncircumcised male will find sex more stimulating, as the foreskin is the most sexually sensitive area of the penis.

80% of boys are now not being circumcised in Australia, and the percentage being so mutilated is dropping each year. I suggest your son joins the majority.

Q   Is it safe to heat a baby's bottle in a microwave oven, or do they destroy the goodness in the milk?

A   Microwaves do not destroy the goodness of any food any more than heating in traditional ways. It is quite safe to heat a baby's bottle (or any food or drink) in a microwave, and retain all its goodness and nutrition.

Microwaves heat up food, and particularly liquids, very rapidly. The danger that can occur in using a microwave is the overheating (over cooking) of foods and drinks. If this occurs, some goodness is lost, as vital elements of nutrition (eg. some vitamins) may be broken down by the excessive heat. This also occurs if food is over-cooked in or on a traditional stove.

Ensure that you know just how many seconds it takes to heat a certain volume of milk to just the required temperature (about 40 degrees centigrade, or roughly body temperature), and no more, and you will save yourself hours of time waiting for conventional heating methods to work. Microwaves are particularly valuable at 2 am when you have a screaming, hungry baby!

Q   My two week old daughter has been producing milk from her nipples. Is there something wrong?

A   Witches milk is the rather off-putting term used for this rather common problem. Babies can be influenced by the hormones in their mother's milk, or may be affected immediately before birth by these same hormones. It can occur in babies of either sex, and is in no way detrimental to their health.

No treatment is needed and the milk production is usually very slight and disappears in a few weeks. Interestingly, any woman or man can be made to produce breast milk if they are given the correct hormone cocktail at almost any time in their lives.

BACK PROBLEMS

See also ARTHRITIS

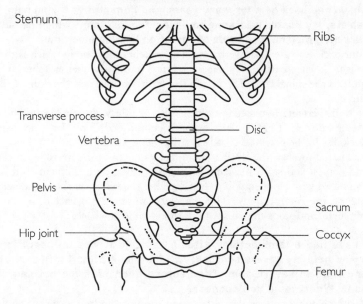

Q   I have a narrowed disc on X-rays of my back. What does this mean?

A   The discs are cushions between the bony vertebrae that form your backbone. They are like a small, thick-walled balloon, with walls made of rubbery ligaments and cartilage. The hollow centre is filled with a dense fluid, which acts as a shock absorber when you walk, run or jump.

If excessive amounts of pressure are put on a disc, it may collapse, and the space between the vertebrae on an X-ray is seen to be narrower than normal. The disc itself does not show on an X-ray, but can be seen on a special type of X-ray known as a CT scan.

Nerves leave the spinal cord between every vertebra, and if the space between them is narrowed, they may become pinched, causing pain, pins and needles and weakness in the area that the nerve supplies. Elderly people with severe arthritis of the back have narrowed discs from many years of wear and tear, but one severe injury may also cause the problem.

A slipped disc is one that has been squashed and pushed out to one side, rather like squeezing a balloon between your hands. These also appear narrowed on X-ray.

Q Would an inversion machine help my bad back?

A These machines are usually a narrow table with padded boots at one end. You strap your feet into the boots, and then tilt the table so that you are suspended head down. The idea is to stretch the back using your own body weight, and relieve the pain caused by narrowed discs in the back.

The concept does work in some people, but it can aggravate sinus conditions and has been known to cause strokes. I feel it would be wise to check with a doctor to find out if your condition can be helped by this type of back traction, and then see a physiotherapist to have traction applied professionally before purchasing this apparatus.

Q I have had back pain for many years, and I am always taking pain-killing tablets. My doctor wants me to have a laminectomy, which he says will cure my problem. What sort of operation is a laminectomy?

A Your back is made of 24 vertebrae. The vertebra has a body which is the main weight-bearing part, and there is a bony framework behind the body that protects the spinal cord. The part of this framework nearest the skin is called the lamina.

If the vertebrae are damaged by arthritis or injury, the spinal cord and/or the nerves running from it may become compressed. This leads to pain and weakness in the part of the body that the nerve supplies.

The removal of the lamina (a laminectomy) eases the pressure on the cord and nerves, and stops the pain. It causes no long-term problems and is often combined with an operation to fuse together the vertebrae above and below the site of the laminectomy. This prevents movement between two or more vertebrae, and stops the cause of arthritic pain in the back.

Q I have had a laminectomy after I was told it was an operation that would help my severe sciatica. After the operation I still cannot walk and I am in severe pain. The neurosurgeon tells me nothing can be done. What would you suggest?

A A laminectomy stiffens the vertebrae in the back and often helps people with severe back pain caused by discs in their back that have degenerated. Unfortunately no operation can ever be guaranteed, and although a laminectomy is not a major operation, it involves an area when many tissues can interact to cause nerve pain.

It would be very rare for the operation to make the situation worse. The majority are improved and a small number remain the same. It seems that you are one of the unlucky ones. If your present neurosurgeon says there is nothing more that can be done, you should obtain a second opinion from another neurosurgeon.

If it is not possible to help you further (and some unfortunate people cannot be cured or adequately helped by even the best surgeons) then you should be referred to a pain clinic at one of the major teaching hospitals. Doctors, physiotherapists and nurses can teach you how to cope with your pain and should be able to make it bearable for you.

Q Please tell me all you know about spondylitis.

A   All that I know about spondylitis may not be very much, but it would take more than the 200 words I allow for each of these answers!

Spondylitis is strictly speaking an inflammation of the spine, or a painful spine. There are many different types of spondylitis, the most common ones being rheumatoid spondylitis, ankylosing spondylitis and arthritic spondylitis.

The rheumatoid form usually affects the small joints of the hands and feet as well as causing acute pain in certain areas of the backbone. It is caused by a rejection reaction of the body to the tissue lining the small joints of the back.

Ankylosing spondylitis is a stiffening and hardening of the vertebral column so that the patient becomes steadily more bent over with a spine that cannot straighten and aches generally along much of its length.

The arthritic form also can be subdivided, but is generally a wear and tear injury to a part of the spine in heavy manual workers or those who have participated in rugged sports.

The treatments of all forms of spondylitis will involve a combination of anti-inflammatory medications, pain-killers, physiotherapy (most important), surgery and some exotic drugs (particularly for the rheumatic form).

There is no permanent cure for most forms of spondylitis, and continuing care is normally required.

Q   **My doctor has diagnosed sciatica. Is this a condition that will go away by itself, or is there anything that will alleviate the pain?**

A   Your back is made up of a number of bony vertebrae. Between each pair of vertebra, one nerve emerges from the spinal cord. In the lower part of the back, four of these nerves join up in the buttock to form the sciatic nerve. This nerve runs diagonally across the buttock, and down the back of the thigh, sending off branches to supply most of the leg. The sciatic nerve consists of individual nerve fibres that can receive sensation (eg. pain, heat), and send messages to muscles to make them contract or relax.

As they emerge from the spinal cord, and pass through narrow spaces between the vertebrae, the nerve fibres that form the roots of the sciatic nerve are easily pinched if there is any distortion or narrowing of the disc between the vertebrae, or if the ligaments joining the vertebrae together are damaged and swollen.

As a nerve is progressively pinched harder and harder, you feel pins and needles, numbness, pain and finally weakness and loss of movement in the area supplied by the nerve.

Sciatica is caused by the hard pinching of some of these nerve roots in the lower part of the back, and the pain then runs along the course of the nerve, across the buttock and down the back of the thigh.

The most effective way to relieve sciatica is to unpinch the nerve by physiotherapy manipulation, and medication to reduce inflammation and swelling in the back.

X-rays are often taken to see how badly deformed the back is, and to give the doctors and physios some idea of the appropriate treatment and the long-term outcome.

If there is significant back damage, the sciatica may come and go for years, and in severe cases, corsets may be recommended, injections given into the back and surgery performed.

Sciatica may come and go by itself, but it can usually be relieved, and sometimes cured, by the appropriate treatment.

Q **My doctor says my back X-rays show Scheuermann's disease. What is this? Is it serious?**

A This is a relatively uncommon bone condition that affects the shape of the vertebrae in rapidly growing teenagers, but may not become apparent until later in life when pain develops in the back.

The back consists of 24 vertebrae, which sit one on top of the other in precise positions to give the back its correct curvature. The vertebrae are joined together by ligaments, and their exact position and movement is controlled by muscles.

In Scheuermann's disease, the vertebrae in the middle part of the back, behind the chest, do not grow properly, and instead of being roughly square in shape, they become slightly wedge shaped. This causes the back to curve excessively giving a slightly humped appearance. The movement of the back is reduced, pain may be present due to compression of nerves, and osteoarthritis develops prematurely.

The main treatment is physiotherapy to correct the posture, anti-inflammatory medications and exercise. Rarely, surgery is recommended.

Q **I am 86 and my backbone is twisting out of shape. It is not very painful, but I look like a pretzel. What can I do to stop this?**

A Weakening of the ligaments, muscles and bones in your back lead to this disfigurement in many elderly people, particularly women. Osteoporosis, or thinning and weakening of the bones is the main cause.

The strength in bones is due to the calcium they contain. The calcium is obtained from foods, particularly dairy foods. If a person's diet has lacked calcium for many years, the bones will not be a strong as they should be.

Adding calcium later on in life cannot reverse the damage already present, but may prevent further damage developing.

In women, hormones are vital for the correct calcium balance in the bones. When hormone levels drop at the menopause, the calcium starts to leech out of the bones. As a result, doctors prescribe hormone replacement therapy for most women after the menopause. These hormones are particularly important for women who have an early menopause or a bad family history of osteoporosis.

Medications that slowly add calcium back into bones are available, but must be taken regularly for years, and will not correct any existing deformity.

Once you have developed a 'pretzel back' the only treatment is a brace to support the back, or in rare cases, surgery to strengthen it. Amazingly, grossly deformed backs in many very elderly women give remarkably few symptoms.

Q **I have three young nephews with painful back problems. Two are mechanics and one a concreter. They have seen chiropractors without success. Where should they go and what should they do?**

A They should go to their family doctor for thorough investigation and treatment of their problem. It may be simply a matter of teaching them correct posture and back care (possibly with the aid of a physiotherapist), but if more severe, anti-inflammatory medications, and regular physiotherapy will be required.

A thorough examination of the back will be performed, and an X-ray will probably be taken, but many people with very painful back strains have perfectly normal X-rays, particularly when young. As a last resort, referral to an orthopaedic surgeon may be necessary.

What they should do is modify their work practices to minimise back strain (eg. supervise work rather than perform it themselves). If the back pain persists, they may have to consider other types of work that put less stress on the back.

Q **What sort of bed should a person with a bad back sleep on? Are water beds any good?**

A Unfortunately everyone is different, but on the other hand, it makes life and medicine more interesting and challenging!

In the past, very hard beds were recommended for people with back trouble, but I believe that the ideal bed should be firm rather than hard. The simplest form of this type of bed is a 3-inch foam rubber mattress on the floor, but it is obviously better to have a supportive inner spring mattress with a foam rubber top cover or sheepskin cover. The mattress should be comfortable as well as supportive.

Water beds have often been recommended for back problems, but I have had several patients who have gone to great expense to buy one, and then found that it gives no benefit, or even makes the back worse. There are several types of water mattress with varying degrees of support due to the number of cells in them and the way in which they are constructed.

If you can arrange a try-before-you-buy deal with a water bed or any mattress retailer, that is obviously ideal, but unfortunately that may be hard to arrange. Booking a hotel room with a water bed for one night while on holiday may be worthwhile.

Q **I have a terrible back pain that the doctors can't fix. Both my parents died from bowel cancer, and I'm scared that I may have this too. Can bowel cancer cause back pain?**

A Yes, often after it has spread to the bones in your back, but sometimes because it is inflaming the nerves and muscles that it rests on.

Bowel cancer is usually detected because of irregular bowel habits, blood on the faeces, abdominal pain or progressive loss of weight. Once back pain is present, the cancer is usually quite advanced.

Bowel cancer has a better than 50% cure rate, but the later it is detected, the worse the prognosis. Any back pain should be investigated to find a cause, as should any change in bowel habits or bleeding from the bowel.

Suggest the possible diagnosis to your doctor, and s/he will arrange for an x-ray or endoscopic examination of your bowel to put your mind at ease that there is no cancer present, or confirm your worst fears, and start treatment as soon as possible.

Q **My doctor says my daughter has scoliosis. Can you explain what this really means?**

A Scoliosis is abnormal side-to-side curvature of the spine. Minor degrees of this condition are seen in many teenagers as they go through rapid growth spurts, but only significant curvature warrants medical attention.

Spine curves are usually double. If there is a curve in one direction, there must also be a curve in the opposite direction further up or down the spine. If this were not so, the shoulders would tilt to one side.

The easiest way to detect curvature is to have the child touch their toes. When looking along their back, one side will be seen to rise higher than the other, even though the spine may appear relatively straight when erect.

If scoliosis is detected, the cause must be determined. If one leg is shorter than the other due to injury or other causes, the pelvis will be tilted, and the spine will curve to compensate. Abnormal vertebrae in the back that may have been present since birth, or damaged by a severe injury, may also lead to scoliosis. Diseases of the muscles that support the vertebral bones are another cause.

Only if your daughter's scoliosis is severe, or worsens, will any specific treatment be required.

Q The orthopaedic specialist told me my back pain was caused by a problem with the bones in the back called spondylolisthesis. He wrote the name down for me and tried to explain it, but I couldn't understand him very well. Can you please tell me what this is?

A Your backbone is made up of a series of 24 bones (vertebrae) that are stacked one on top of the other, and interlocked rather like a tower of Lego blocks. The vertebrae are not in a straight line, but are gently curved. There should be no side to side curve, but the backbone curves in at the neck, out between the shoulders, in at the waist, and out again at the back of the belly.

If one of these vertebrae becomes unlocked from the vertebra below it and slips forward, you are suffering from spondylolisthesis. This usually occurs gradually over a number of years, is usually associated with arthritis of the back and may cause considerable pain because nerves that leave the spinal cord and run out between the vertebrae become pinched. Any vertebra may slip forward, but the bottom vertebra in the back, where it joins the pelvis, is the most common one involved.

The amount of forward slip can vary from a few millimetres to (in rare and serious cases) the complete width of the vertebra. The symptoms will depend upon the amount of slippage. Most commonly pain in the back and sciatica (pain down the leg) occur.

Spondylolisthesis may be congenital (present from birth), due to injury, arthritis, degeneration of the disc between the vertebrae ('slipped disc'), tumours or other bone disease.

The condition can be easily diagnosed by an X-ray of the back, but severe slips can be felt by the examining doctor.

Treatment involves bed rest, heat, traction, physiotherapy, pain-killers, anti-inflammatory medication and in severe cases surgery.

BLOOD

See also CIRCULATION

Q I have been trying to get some information on Sickle blood cells. During my student days I saw the cells under a microscope, but there was no

information about them. What does the presence of these cells typify? Are they of any importance? Are they only found in coloured and Jewish people? I am very curious about this matter.

A   Sickle cells are malformed red blood cells that have the shape of a sickle (new moon crescent) rather than a doughnut. The condition is present mainly in black Africans, with 8% of African Americans and up to 30% of Nigerians being affected. Aborigines are not affected, and it is therefore a rare condition in Australia.

The condition can cause severe, life threatening anaemia if excessive numbers of red blood cells are affected in a patient, but if the condition is mild, it gives some protection from malaria, as the malarial parasite cannot breed in these odd-shaped red blood cells. It is easily diagnosed by examining a drop of blood under a microscope which allows the abnormal cells to be seen.

The presence of sickle cells is hereditary, and passes from one generation to the next, but the severe anaemias only develop in the children of parents who both have the disease. The treatment of the anaemia is unsatisfactory.

I am not aware of the disease being present in Jews to any significant extent. It is non-existent in European and Asian races.

Q   My nephew had a blood transfusion recently, and during the transfusion his temperature rose to 39 degrees. He was not told why and he still wants to know. I told him you would know, and that's why I'm writing.

A   Your confidence in my knowledge is most flattering, and I do have an explanation for your nephew.

Most people know that it is necessary to cross-match blood before it is given to a patient, so that the blood of the patient and the donor are compatible. There are four main blood groups—A, B, O and AB. These are further divided into those that are Rhesus negative and Rhesus positive. A person can therefore be one of eight different combinations—ie: A+ or A–, O+ or O–, B+ or B–, and AB+ or AB–.

This is complex enough, and for most purposes, this is all that is required. There are about a dozen sub-groups beyond this classification. In most cases these further sub-groups make no significant difference to the patient receiving the blood, but in some cases, a transfusion reaction can occur if there is a very slight mismatch of the blood with regard to one of these minor sub-groups.

The most common transfusion reaction is a raised temperature. Other problems that can occur are muscle pains, headaches, and shortness of breath. Very rarely does any transfusion reaction become worse than this, and most patients have no reaction at all. Your nephew was just a little bit unlucky.

Q   After a blood test the other day, my doctor said I was a bit anaemic, but not to worry about it. She gave me some iron tablets, but nothing else. What are the causes of anaemia?

A   There are hundreds!

Anaemia is a lack of haemoglobin in the red blood cells. Haemoglobin is responsible for transporting the oxygen from the lungs to the rest of the body, and is bright red, giving blood its normal colour and your cheeks their ruddy glow.

The most common, and serious cause, is chronic blood loss. This may be due to prolonged heavy periods in a woman, bleeding from an ulcer into the gut, a recurrent bleeding nose or a kidney that is damaged.

The body may be unable to produce adequate amounts of haemoglobin due to lack of iron or folic acid in the diet, particularly during pregnancy. Pernicious anaemia occurs when vitamin B12 can no longer be absorbed into the system from the food, and this is also essential for the manufacture of haemoglobin.

Certain diseases may cause red blood cells to be destroyed, and cancer can cause anaemia. Some people are born with errors in their metabolic processes which cause inadequate formation of haemoglobin. Damage to the liver, thyroid gland or kidney can also lead to anaemia. And so the list could continue for several pages!

A simple blood test ordered by your GP will quickly detect anaemia. If anaemia is found, more extensive tests may be done to determine the exact cause of the anaemia before specific treatment can start.

Q   **I have been told that I am slightly anaemic, and need to eat more foods with iron. How much iron do you need in your diet, and what foods contain large amounts of it?**

A   Between 5 and 8 mg of iron is required in a person's diet every day for good health, and because of the iron loss in their monthly period, women require twice as much as men.

Infants and rapidly growing teenagers also require more iron in their diet.

Pregnant and breast feeding women require even more iron than this, up to 35 mg per day, and as this amount may be difficult to obtain in the diet, most pregnant and breast feeding women are advised to take a daily iron tablet.

These tablets contain iron in a form that is readily absorbed into the body. Only one tablet a day is necessary for prevention of iron deficiency, but two may be prescribed for a severe deficiency.

Iron is found naturally in many foods including meat, poultry, fish, eggs, cereals and vegetables. Red meat, oysters, liver, beans, nuts and wheat contain particularly high levels of iron.

Vitamin C and folic acid, vitamins that are present in fruit and vegetables, are essential for iron to be absorbed from the gut into the bloodstream. Because of this requirement, commercially prepared iron tablets often contain folic acid, and sometimes vitamin C as well. Some foods (eg. bran) and drinks (eg. strong tea) can prevent the absorption of iron, and should be taken in moderation.

Q   **My doctor says I should take more iron because I get anaemic with heavy periods. Why does the body need a metal like iron?**

A   Iron is an essential element for the functioning of the human body.

The primary use of iron in the body is to be the core element in the manufacture of haemoglobin. This compound is found in red blood cells and transports the oxygen from the lungs to the organs. If iron levels are low, haemoglobin levels drop and the body becomes starved of oxygen. You then feel tired and weak, as oxygen is required by all cells to burn fuel for energy. Other symptoms can include pins and needles in the arms and legs, palpitations, abnormal fingernails and dizziness.

Q My father has thalassaemia. I remember him telling me that I must not marry someone with this disease. How would I know if someone had it?

A Thalassaemia is a blood disease that causes severe anaemia. It is found in people who come from southern Italy, Sicily and Malaysia (how's that for a cross-cultural and geographic mix up!). It is a genetically transmitted disease, and occurs in two forms, minor and major.

Thalassaemia minor is only an inconvenience, and is almost certainly the form of the disease suffered by your father. Blood tests can be used to determine whether a person has the disease.

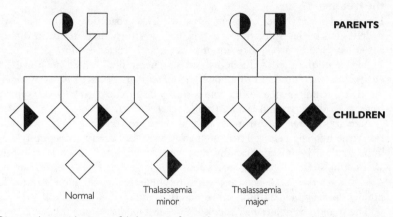

Normal	Thalassaemia minor	Thalassaemia major

Diagram showing inheritance of thalassaemia from either one or two parents with thalassaemia minor.

If someone with thalassaemia minor marries a normal person, half their children will develop thalassaemia minor. If two people with thalassaemia minor marry, one quarter of their children will have the far more serious and disabling disease of thalassaemia major. One half will have thalassaemia minor, and the other quarter will be normal.

Patients with thalassaemia major are very anaemic, weak and susceptible to other diseases. They lead a very restricted life as a result.

You should arrange through your GP to have the tests to see if you have the minor form of the disease. If you do, any likely marriage partner should also have the same test. You can then decide on your future.

Q Is excess copper in the blood dangerous?

A Copper is only required in the blood in minute quantities, and any excess is usually excreted through the liver and gut. If excess copper accumulates in the body, it affects the liver first, and can cause cirrhosis and liver failure.

It is most unusual to find a patient with excess copper unless they have been taking large quantities of the metal in tablet form. It is almost impossible to obtain too much through the diet.

There is a rare inherited disease known as Wilson's disease, in which the body is unable to cope adequately with copper, and the levels slowly increase over the years, causing more and more damage to the vital organs. There is no adequate treatment for Wilson's disease.

Q   My boyfriend has Christmas disease. Can you tell me more about it?

A   Christmas disease is an inherited disorder where one of the factors essential for the clotting of blood is lacking. As a result they bleed more easily than normal people, and may develop serious bleeding into joints that can cause arthritis. The bleeding can be controlled by regular injections of the missing factor, which is extracted from blood donations.

 If you were to marry and have children, your daughters would be carriers of the disease, but your sons would be free of it.

Q   Could you please explain what causes low blood sugar, the symptoms and the treatment?

A   Low blood sugar (hypoglycaemia) is caused by an inadequate intake of carbo-hydrate foods (ie. starvation), excess use of drugs used to treat diabetes, alcoholism and by a very rare tumour that secretes excess insulin.

 Sugars are the fuel of the body, and are chemically 'burned' to provide the energy necessary for us to function. There are many different types of sugar in our diet, including sucrose (the white stuff we sprinkle on our cereal), glucose, fructose (fruit sugar) and lactose (milk sugar).

 Starvation is rare in Australia, and so there are very few people who suffer from true hypoglycaemia. There are people who lead a very active lifestyle who burn up their body sugar rapidly, and who therefore feel much better shortly after taking sugar containing foods. Rest usually gives the same result, but more slowly, as reserves of sugars are released by the liver into the bloodstream. This problem is far more common in women than men.

 The symptoms of a transient episode of low blood sugar are tiredness, burred and double vision, headache, light headedness and personality changes.

 True, prolonged hypoglycaemia is very rare, and I have never encountered a patient with this problem in 25 years of general practice. Temporary symptoms of hypoglycaemia after exercise or stress are common, and are not a reason for concern. If you feel that you suffer from this problem regularly, suck some barley sugar before exercise or at times of stress.

Q   I keep fainting at the sight of blood. This is very embarrassing as I am a trainee nurse! What can I do?

A   Most people feel a bit uneasy when seeing blood, particularly when it is their own! You probably had an unpleasant experience early in life in which blood was involved.

 Every time you see blood now, you expect to feel unwell, and you carry out your expectations. This then makes it worse next time.

 What is required, is exposure to blood in a controlled situation. This may involve the understanding and help of theatre staff in your hospital allowing you to watch operations, or it may require the more expert help of a psychologist or psychiatrist who can help you rationalise and cope with your reaction. It is a problem that should be treated early, because every time you faint at the sight of blood makes it harder to overcome that fear.

Q   Does taking 100 mg coated aspirin a day to reduce the risk of blood clots also lead to easier bleeding, thereby increasing the risk of any stroke that may occur?

A This is actually a very good question, and one that is still a matter of some debate between doctors. Nine out of ten strokes are caused by a blood clot in the brain. The remaining 10% are caused by blood leaking out of a blood vessel (usually an artery) into the brain tissue, to cause damage. This type of stroke tends to be milder and less damaging than the sudden impact and blockage of blood flow cause by a clot.

There is no evidence that taking aspirin increases the risk of brain damage in the less common type of stroke caused by bleeding, but aspirin will significantly reduce the risk of blood clots in the brain, heart (that can cause a heart attack) and lungs (a pulmonary embolus).

On the other hand, people taking aspirin, particularly if they are elderly, will bruise more easily, and bleed for longer if cut. Overall, doctors recommend that low-dose aspirin should be taken by all people who have increased risk of blood clots, and some doctors are now saying that everyone over 50 should be taking aspirin on a regular basis, as it may also reduce the risk of bowel cancer and other diseases.

Q **I went to my doctor because I was very tired, and had no energy, and after a blood test he told me I had pernicious anaemia. Now he wants to give me a series of injections. Is that right? What causes pernicious anaemia?**

A Anaemia occurs when the body lacks haemoglobin. Haemoglobin is the red substance in blood that is essential for transporting oxygen around the body from the lungs. New haemoglobin is constantly being made and the old destroyed by the liver and spleen.

The formation of new haemoglobin requires vitamin B12. If this essential vitamin is lacking from the system, new haemoglobin cannot be made and the patient becomes anaemic.

Vitamin B12 is rarely lacking in the diet, but for it to be absorbed from the stomach into the blood stream, a special chemical is required in the stomach. Many older people fail to produce this chemical, and so are unable to absorb sufficient vitamin B12 for the synthesis of haemoglobin. Because this process occurs gradually over many years, the disease is called pernicious anaemia.

It is obviously useless to give additional vitamin B12 by mouth, and so to ensure that the anaemia is controlled, these patients are given regular injections of the vitamin every few months. This must continue for the rest of the patient's life. With these injections, the normal production of haemoglobin within the body can recommence, and the anaemia will be controlled.

BLOOD PRESSURE
See also HEART

Q **Why do doctors keep worrying about my blood pressure. Is it really that important to keep it low?**

A Any plumber will tell you that if a pipe carries water at a pressure higher than the pressure it was designed for, it will eventually rupture. If the pressure in the pipe is not only too high but varies rapidly in its level, the rupture will occur even sooner because of the excessive stresses on the pipe.

Exactly the same situation occurs in the human body when the pressure of blood in the arteries becomes too high. The arteries of a person with high blood pressure will become hardened, brittle and eventually rupture, causing a stroke, heart attack or other serious injury to vital organs.

The majority of people with high blood pressure have no symptoms of the problem for many years, and by that time it may be too late. Once diagnosed, tests will be done to see if there is any specific cause for the increased blood pressure, but the majority of people have 'essential' hypertension, for which there is no single identifiable cause. Treatment is necessary in all cases of hypertension to prevent the serious long-term problems that may occur.

There is no cure for high blood pressure, but it can be very successfully controlled in the majority of patients by taking one or two tablets a day.

Q   What is the correct figure for blood pressure? Mine is 140/90 and my doctor keeps checking it every time I see him. He says it is alright, but this constant checking worries me.

A   The actual values for blood pressure vary with many things such as exercise, anxiety, age, fitness, smoking and drinking habits, weight and medications. This is why doctors never give absolute values for what is normal and abnormal in blood pressure values.

It is a good idea to have your doctor check the pressure at regular intervals, particularly if you are over 40.

Your general practitioner is a good and careful one. It is very easy to forget that a patient might have a blood pressure problem, and not take it regularly. Your blood pressure is bordering on being too high, and that is why he is checking it every visit.

There are two figures quoted when blood pressure is measured. When the heart contracts, blood is moved around the body under high (or systolic) pressure. When the heart relaxes between beats, the blood continues to flow due to the lower (or diastolic) pressure exerted by the elasticity of the artery walls. In your case, your systolic pressure is 140, and diastolic 90.

When one, or both, of these pressures exceeds a safe level, the person is said to suffer from high blood pressure or hypertension. It is more dangerous to have the diastolic pressure high, as the systolic pressure can vary considerably due to exercise or stress. You can help prevent and treat hypertension by keeping your weight within reasonable limits, not eating excessive amounts of salt, not smoking and exercising.

Q   I am a very fit, healthy and normal weight 32 year old, but my doctor wants to start me on treatment for high blood pressure. Why?

A   Unfortunately, hypertension (high blood pressure) does not always respect youth or fitness, although these factors certainly help. 80% of people with hypertension have no specific cause for the condition, although it does tend to run in families. If a high level of blood pressure is found on several occasions, tests will be done to exclude any specific cause, and if none can be found, it is necessary to start treatment to control the pressure level of the blood.

This treatment must be continued for many years, as it does not cure the condition, but controls it only while the medication is taken. It is important to control the blood pressure adequately, despite the fact that you may have no symptoms now, because a high level for many years will greatly increase your risk of strokes and heart attacks. The only things that you can do to help the situation are keep your weight at a reasonable level, avoid salt and stop smoking.

Q **The nurse at work took my blood pressure, and said I should see a doctor. Is a blood pressure of 190/115 normal?**

A Definitely not! Normal blood pressure is difficult to define as it depends on many factors including age, sex, fitness, position, weight etc. Your doctor will take all these into account when measuring your blood pressure.

Generally speaking, a blood pressure of more than 150/90 is treated with considerable suspicion.

Blood pressure cannot be determined by only one reading. The pressure will vary during the day, may be affected by anxiety and can even rise just because a doctor is taking it. As a result, if an abnormal level is found, your doctor will take it again later in the consultation, and then at different times on different days to build up a picture of the changes your blood pressure makes.

If it is consistently high, hypertension will be diagnosed and appropriate treatment started. Smoking, obesity and salt are the greatest aggravating factors for hypertension, and correcting these may lower your blood pressure back to normal.

If you have been told that you have a blood pressure of 190/115 you need further medical attention, and should see your doctor soon.

Q **My blood pressure varies a lot. Some doctors wrap the blood pressure cuff firmly around my arm, and others do it loosely. Does it make any difference?**

A It is correct to wrap the blood pressure cuff as firmly as possible around the arm before inflating it. A loosely wrapped cuff can cause an inaccurate reading.

In larger people, a larger cuff is also necessary, as an undersize cuff will give a falsely high reading. The reverse is true for children, when a much smaller cuff is necessary, as a cuff that is too large will give a falsely low reading.

It is also necessary to ensure that the cuff is inflated to a reading at least 20 points above the highest measured pressure to ensure that the top (systolic) pressure is accurately measured.

Q **You constantly hear about high blood pressure, but what about low blood pressure. What causes this?**

A The level of blood pressure is due to a combination of the amount of blood present in the circulation, the force of contraction of the heart and the diameter of the blood vessels.

If you lose a large amount of blood your blood pressure will drop due to a lack of blood. If your heart contracts forcibly your blood pressure may rise excessively, but if it beats weakly it may fall.

If the arteries become dilated, as may happen with frights, sudden change in position or shock, the blood pressure may fall. If they are narrowed by hardening from excess cholesterol, or by spasm from chemical stimuli within the body, the blood pressure will rise.

The regulation of blood pressure is very complex, and numerous chemical and physical factors are involved. People with persistently low blood pressure need investigations to find out why it is low, but in many cases no apparent cause can be found. In the elderly, narrowing of arteries may restrict the blood supply to the brain, and even though their blood pressure is normal, they may feel light headed and dizzy when rising from a bed or chair.

BONES
See also BACK

Q **I have read how to prevent osteoporosis, but what can you do once you have got it? I have arthritis and thyroid disease, and swim every day. I am 60 years old.**

A Osteoporosis is thinning of the bones due to calcium being drained out of the bones into the bloodstream. The drop in hormone levels after the female menopause is the main cause.

An uncontrolled overactive thyroid may aggravate osteoporosis, but most older women with thyroid disease have an underactive gland. Provided your thyroid activity is being carefully controlled by a doctor, it should not cause concern.

Exercise is an excellent way to treat osteoporosis, as the mild stresses placed on the bones encourage them to become stronger. Your swimming is excellent, and should be continued.

Prevention after the menopause can be achieved by using hormone replacement therapy, in which the missing female hormones are taken on a cyclical basis as tablets.

The most effective medical treatment is the long-term use of a group of medications known as biphosphonates which include Didrocal, Fosamax and Rocaltrol. These can reverse existing osteoporosis and significantly strengthen bones. Discuss the possibility of using these with your GP.

Q **I am 55, have just been diagnosed with osteoporosis, and as I have menopausal symptoms, my doctor has suggested that I take Fosamax rather than HRT. What would you recommend, what are the side effects of Fosamax, and how long should I stay on it?**

A Osteoporosis (thinning of the bones) and the increased risk of fractures that results, is a well recognised phenomenon in menopause. There is a strong family tendency, and so if your mother or grandmother had osteoporosis, there is a good chance that you may develop the problem.

Hormone replacement therapy (HRT) is very good at preventing osteo-porosis, but once the condition is present it is necessary to use another medication to gradually build up bone strength.

Fosamax is one of a number of medications that will slowly strengthen bones over many months. It is possible to take both HRT and Fosamax together, so that you have the other benefits of HRT (eg. protecting the heart and skin from premature ageing) as well as the bone strengthening effect of Fosamax, which should be used long term.

Like all medications, Fosamax does have its side effects, but these are usually manageable. Nausea and diarrhoea, indigestion and muscle pains are the most common ones, but only occur in a very small proportion of women using the medication. It should not be used by people who have a recent history of peptic ulcers.

The dosage is also slightly complex in that the tablet must be taken at least 30 minutes before breakfast with a full glass of water, and the patient must remain upright for the next 30 minutes, so you can't half wake up and take your tablet before lying down again and waiting for breakfast. In 2001 a long-acting version was introduced that only needs to be taken once a week, overcoming a lot of these negative problems.

Overall it is far better to treat osteoporosis than to wait for the almost inevitable fracture that may be severely debilitating.

Q How can I stop myself from getting osteoporosis? My mother was severely affected.

A Before menopause—cheese, milk and yoghurt. After menopause—these foods plus hormone supplements.

Osteoporosis is due to a gradual loss of calcium from the bones in women after the change of life. The female sex hormones play a part in maintaining the concentration of calcium in bones, and as these drop after menopause, so does the calcium concentration of bone. This makes the bones soft, and with time they will bend, and with any injury will break easily.

By building up the amount of calcium in your body before menopause (and this should be done from 30 years of age onwards) you will have more to spare at an older age. Once you reach the change, your doctor can prescribe hormones that will not only control the hot flushes and irregular periods, but maintain the calcium balance of your bones.

The tendency to develop osteoporosis does run in families, and if your mother or grandmother was affected, it is wise to take these precautions. Most dairy marketers now produce a calcium-enriched milk (called 'Shape' in most markets) but all dairy products, and particularly cheese, are rich in calcium. Tablets containing calcium are also readily available.

If osteoporosis does develop, there are now sophisticated, but expensive, medications that can be given long term to prevent further deterioration, and reverse the thinning of the bones.

Q My mother has Paget's disease. How does one catch this? How does it affect the heart? What do the Calcitonin injections she is receiving do?

A Paget's disease of bone is a disorder for which there is no known cause. The bone in scattered parts of the body becomes grossly thickened and soft, causing compression of nerves, and collapse of those bones that support weight. Fractures may occur with only slight injury, and the back becomes bent and deformed. Bone pain is the earliest symptom.

The skull and thigh bone (femur) are particularly involved, giving a characteristic head appearance and bowing of the legs as they bend under the body's weight. The skull enlargement can cause pressure on nerves and a variety of unpleasant consequences, including pressure on the brain and constant headaches.

The extra blood flow to the bones can also cause circulatory and heart problems.

Paget's disease can vary from very mild to rapidly progressive, and although there are drugs available to slow its progress, there is no known cure. Tablets and/or injections (such as Calcitonin) that regulate the amount of calcium in the bone will be required regularly for the rest of the person's life to prevent softening of the bones.

Q   My father has been rather strange for some months, and now a specialist says he has acromegaly. Can you explain this disease in simple terms for me?

A   Acromegaly is a disease characterised by the excessive growth of the hands, feet, jaw, face, tongue and internal organs. Patients also suffer from headaches, sweating, weakness, and loss of vision. It is caused by excess production of growth hormone in the pituitary gland which sits underneath the brain. This hormone is required during normal growth of a child, but if it is produced inappropriately later in life, acromegaly results. The most common reason for this excess production is the development of a tumour in the pituitary gland, but occasionally, tumours elsewhere can secrete abnormal amounts of the hormone.

Laboratory tests can be used to prove the diagnosis, and X-rays and CT scans (a special type of X-ray) of the skull can detect the tumour.

Treatment will involve specialised microsurgery through the nose, and up into the base of the brain, to remove the tumour. Occasionally irradiation of the tumour may be performed. Treatment is very successful, particularly in younger adults. Sometimes, hormone supplements must be taken long term to replace the normal hormones produced by the destroyed pituitary gland. Diabetes is a common complication of the disease and its treatment.

Q   I have broken the bone in the upper part of my arm, but my doctor has not put it in plaster. Is this the correct treatment?

A   Yes. It is not normally practical to immobilise the upper part of the arm (the bone here is called the humerus) because the shoulder is such a mobile joint. It would require a plaster that encased the chest and extended down to the elbow to do this. Most fractures of the humerus set very well if left alone while hanging by the side. The wrist is normally supported by a sling, and sometimes the elbow is strapped to the body. No attempt should be made to use the arm, and it will heal in 6 to 8 weeks.

Q   I fractured my ankle a year ago, but it still causes pain. Is this normal?

A   Once a fracture has completely healed, as determined by the doctor and x-rays, there is no need for further concern about the strength of the bone, and the way in which you use it. If the fracture was a serious one, it is common for the area involved to ache and swell for months or years afterwards.

It is normally only a dull annoying ache after using the bone a lot, so I would expect that your ankle would swell and ache after a lot of walking or other exercise. This should settle overnight. Pain of this type can last for several years after a bad break, but slowly settles with time, and is normally only a nuisance rather than distressing.

If you are experiencing pain that is worse than this you should check with your doctor to see if there is some arthritis developing or some other disease or complication present.

Q Could you please explain the difference between a fracture and a break in a bone?

A The two terms mean the same thing—when a bone is broken, it is also fractured, but lay people tend to use the term fracture for a more serious break.

There are many different types of fracture (break) that can affect a bone. These include:
— Hairline fractures are the most minor of all. The bone is only just cracked, and the bone ends have not moved apart. These fractures are often quite difficult to detect on X-ray.
— Another form of minor break is the greenstick fracture that a child may sustain. Because a child's bones are still slightly flexible, they do not snap in the same way as an adult's. A fall can bend the bone, but it breaks on only one side, before returning to its correct shape and position, just like trying to break a green stick from a tree.
— The next type in order of seriousness is an avulsion fracture. In this, a small piece of bone is torn from a major bone where a ligament or tendon is embedded in it. This often occurs around the ankle when it is twisted.
— Normal or simple fractures of the long bones in the arm and leg can occur straight across the bone, in a spiral or obliquely. All these factors influence the healing time. The bone ends may be displaced sideways from each other, or may meet at an abnormal angle, or may even overlap. Manipulation of the bone ends under an anaesthetic is necessary in all these cases, as the bone ends must be in almost perfect alignment to allow for healing and satisfactory long-term appearance and function.
— Impacted fractures occur when a bone is forcibly shortened, and one fragment of bone is pushed into the other. Minor degrees of impaction can be left alone and the fracture placed in plaster.
— If a bone is broken in two places (a comminuted fracture), an operation to screw or wire the three pieces together will usually be needed.
— The most serious fractures are those where one end of the broken bone protrudes through the skin (called a compound fracture). These are likely to become infected and great care must be taken in the care of the skin wound and the bone.
— Flat bones such as the skull can have a depressed fracture, where part of the skull is pushed down into the brain.
— A joint fracture, where the line of the break enters a joint, can cause arthritis and stiffness after even the best treatment.
— A fracture and dislocation may occur simultaneously, particularly around the shoulder, and these injuries are very difficult to treat. Long-term stiffness and poor joint function are common complications.

—A pathological fracture occurs when a bone that is already weakened by disease, such as a cancer deposit in a bone, breaks with only a small amount of force. These fractures are very difficult to heal. Elderly women with osteoporosis may also fracture their bones (particularly the hip) very easily.

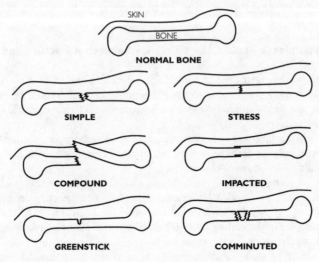

Types of bone fracture

BRAIN
See also HEADACHE

Q **I have heard from a number of people that absorption of aluminium into the human body may be a contributing factor in a person who develops Alzheimer's disease. Is this correct, and is it safe to cook in aluminium saucepans?**

A Alzheimer's disease, its treatment and prevention, is a very controversial topic. It is primarily a disease of premature senility, and it does tend to run in families, but if your parents or grandparents develop the disease, don't panic. This merely means that your chances of developing the disease are above average. It does NOT mean that you will inevitably become affected by the disease.

High levels of aluminium are found in the brains of patients who die from Alzheimer's disease, but there is no evidence that the disease is caused by aluminium. It may be that the Alzheimer's disease caused the aluminium (which is normally present in the body) to be concentrated in the brain.

The amount of aluminium eaten from cooking in aluminium pots is absolutely minimal. Far more aluminium is found in foods such as spices and baking powder, in hard water supplies, and in medications such as antacids and aspirin, than will ever be absorbed from aluminium pots and pans.

There is no necessity for anyone to alter their diet or cooking methods for fear of developing this incurable disease, as medical scientists do not know enough about it to make any rational recommendations about methods of prevention.

Q **After an MRI brain scan I have been diagnosed as having a pineal cyst. What is this?**

A The pineal gland sits between the two hemispheres at the front of the brain, behind the lower centre of your forehead. It is sometimes known as the third eye, and in some lizards is actually visible as a bump on the forehead.

In humans it acts as the clock of the body, regulating multiple biological rhythms. It is able to sense light or dark, and produces a substance known as melatonin that regulates many time-based activities in the body including the ability to awake from sleep at a desired time, menstrual periods and the onset of puberty. It is also responsible for jet lag with intercontinental travel.

A cyst of the gland may be inconsequential, may interfere with its function, or may put pressure on nearby brain tissue and nerves. Further tests, and possibly a biopsy, may need to be performed to follow the progress of the cyst and determine its cause before any specific treatment is undertaken.

Q **My 82 year old father had a stroke 20 months ago, and is now unable to talk, and has lost the use of his right hand. He worked all his life until six months before the stroke, and this happens when he should be able to lead the good life. Is there anything we can do to help him? I have considered taking him to Korea for acupuncture.**

A A stroke is devastating to both the victim and his or her family.

Strokes are caused by the blockage or rupture of an artery in the brain. The symptoms you describe fit the picture of a stroke perfectly. I would not think that there is any other likely diagnosis.

In a stroke, part of the brain is usually deprived of its blood supply. The affected part of the brain then dies and degenerates. The effects of a stroke depend upon which artery is damaged, and which part of the brain dies. Thus some people have minor effects, while others quite different major effects from a stroke.

Once part of the brain is dead, it cannot repair itself, and remains permanently non-functioning. The brain can sometimes learn new tricks to bypass the damage, but after 20 months, the residual problems will be permanent.

You and your family must accept what has happened to your father. There is no form of cure or alleviation possible. I would strongly advise against spending thousands of dollars on overseas trips in a fruitless search for the unobtainable.

Australian doctors are among the best in the world, and any form of treatment that is likely to be beneficial will be tried, but only if there is evidence of its effectiveness.

Lead your own lives, visit your father regularly to reassure and comfort him, but do not ruin your own lives by attempting to cure the incurable.

Q **My father died recently and very suddenly from a brain aneurysm. Can you explain this for me?**

A   At a point where an artery wall is weakened, the blood pressure will gradually stretch the artery to form a small balloon. This is an aneurysm.

These can occur anywhere in the body, but are most common in the brain. This weakness may have been present since birth, may be due to hardening of the arteries with age or high cholesterol levels, or may be caused by high blood pressure.

If the balloon bursts, large amounts of blood will flood into the brain, causing severe damage and possibly death. The actual effects will depend on the area of the brain involved, and a small aneurysm bursting may mimic a stroke.

If an aneurysm is discovered, the only effective treatment is an operation to remove it.

Q   **My 82 year old husband has recently developed Parkinson's disease, which is progressing quite rapidly, with shaking hands, light headedness etc. He is taking drugs and has seen several doctors, but none are able to help. Can you suggest any other treatment?**

A   Madam, I sympathise with you deeply! Parkinsonism is a dreadful disease because there is no cure, and in advanced cases, an intelligent brain can become trapped inside a body that refuses to obey even the simplest command appropriately. It is caused by a slow but steady deterioration of that part of the brain that coordinates muscle action.

Normally, if you bend a joint, the muscles on one side contract, while those on the other side relax. In Parkinson's disease, this smooth interaction of relaxation and contraction does not occur, and movements become jerky and unsteady. The brain is slow to coordinate necessary action to maintain balance, patients have a shuffling gait and falls are common. Muscles in the face are constantly in slight spasm, giving a wooden expression to the sufferer.

After all the bad news, there is some hope. There are a number of medications that will control (not cure) the condition, and slow its progression. Some are slow to act, and it can require a long period of trial and error to find the right drug combination. The medications are available only on prescription and go by many different names. No one drug is necessarily better than any other, and if your doctor feels that the response to treatment is not satisfactory, he/she will continue to experiment with different combinations and permutations to find the one best for the patient.

Physiotherapy is a very important adjunctive treatment that should be continued throughout the course of the disease.

As a last resort, in very serious cases, radical brain surgery can be undertaken.

The vast majority of patients can be given many additional useful years by these medications, and if you are not being appropriately controlled, pester your doctor to try different combinations and permutations in an attempt to ease the symptoms.

Q   **Is there anything one can do, or take, to sharpen or improve one's mind to learn and absorb things?**

A   Yes and no. There are certainly things you can do, but unless there is some disease present (such as an underactive thyroid gland), there are no tablets or capsules you can take that will help. It is always worthwhile having a check up with a doctor, just in case one of these diseases is present.

If you receive the all-clear, then it is a matter of training yourself using memory games, accurate speed reading courses, study techniques, inventing rhymes that include the topics you wish to remember and associating names or ideas with familiar objects to improve your mind skills. These training techniques can significantly improve your concentration and recall.

Q **If you take a break for a month from using aspirin to reduce the risk of a stroke from blood clotting, is one at greater risk during the break than if one had never started, or does a break not matter?**

A Aspirin only works to prevent blood clots while it is being taken. Missing an occasional dose for a day or two is unlikely to alter the risk of a blood clot significantly, but after five days, every trace of aspirin will have left the body, and the risk of blood clot, and therefore stroke, will return to that which would have been present if aspirin had never been taken.

It is therefore sensible for those who have been advised to take aspirin to prevent blood clotting complications to continue taking it regularly all the time.

Q **Recently I suffered a mild stroke which left me with a weakness in my left leg and hand and a feeling that part of my mouth and tongue are anaesthetised. Will any of these symptoms disappear with time? Is there anything I can do to help them recover? The only treatment I am having is half an aspirin a day. Is this correct?**

A A stroke is usually caused by a blood clot or blockage in one of the small arteries in the brain. The area of brain supplied by this artery can no longer obtain any blood, and so dies. The effects of a stroke depend upon the area of the brain that is affected, so that one patient may be totally paralysed down one side of the body, while another may have the relatively mild symptoms that you describe.

After a stroke, there may be recovery of some brain cells that have been damaged, but not killed, by the lack of blood. Other parts of the brain may also learn to perform some of the tasks originally undertaken by the cells killed by the stroke.

The damage caused by a stroke usually stabilises within a few hours or days. Aspirin is used as soon as possible, and lifelong after a stroke in most patients, to prevent any further blood clots from developing, and prevent the clot that is present from enlarging.

Sometimes a stroke is caused by bleeding from an artery that bursts in the brain. In this case aspirin is not used.

After a stroke, most improvement will occur in the first few weeks, some improvement after a few months, and virtually no improvement will occur after a year.

Physiotherapists, speech therapists and occupational therapists work with doctors to maximise improvements in the brain's capacity to learn new ways to perform tasks.

In your case, there is very little that can be done to improve the mouth and tongue feeling, but continued therapy for up to a year after the stroke may result in improvement of your arm and leg function. Regular exercises and physiotherapy after a year may be necessary to prevent you losing skills that you have learnt.

Q I must criticise you for saying that virtually no improvement occur one year after a stroke. My stroke occurred as the result of a haemorrhage from a blow to the head, and I had significant improvement between twelve and eighteen months after the stroke. Please do not discourage people from having further rehabilitation at this stage.

A As the saying goes, there are strokes and there are strokes.

The vast majority of strokes (technically known as cerebrovascular accidents) occur in older people and are caused by a blockage to an artery which causes part of the brain to lose its blood supply. That part of the brain then dies, and is unable to repair itself. The brain tissue around the area affected by the stroke becomes inflamed and swollen as a result of the nearby injury, but can recover over a few weeks.

A small percentage of strokes (less than 5%) are caused by a blood vessel (artery or vein) leaking blood into the brain, causing pressure and damage to part of the brain tissue, but not always tissue death. It is really a type of bad bruise to the delicate brain tissue. This type of stroke is slower to recover, but recovery progresses for a much longer period of time, as the blood that has leaked out of the vessel is slowly removed, allowing the brain to start functioning again.

Most strokes occur without a head injury, and for no apparent reason. The type of injury that you suffered is not usually referred to as a stroke as it was caused by an injury, and resulted in bleeding into the brain, but can be related to the second type of stroke above. This explains why you had a longer period of recovery than the majority of people who suffer from this most distressing, and often disabling, condition.

Q At 44 I have suffered a stroke to my optic nerve and now have blind spots and flashing lights in my vision. Can the optic nerve repair itself?

A Strokes in the optic nerve are caused by a microscopic clot in a tiny artery blocking the blood supply to part (or all) of the nerve, or a small blood vessel rupturing in the nerve and causing damage to it.

Recovery from any type of stroke occurs mostly in the first few weeks after the incident. Probably 95% of the recovery will have occurred by six months, but some further improvement can occur up to two years later.

With this type of stroke there is really nothing that doctors can do to correct the damage that has already been done, but anticoagulant medication may be prescribed to prevent any further blood clots developing.

The damaged nerve will recover if there has been only pressure damage and no death of nerve cells. Unfortunately time is the only treatment and you will just have to wait to see just how much long term disturbance you will have to your vision.

Q Why are so many people in Australia left-handed? Is this due to a malfunction of the brain?

A About one in ten people are left-handed, and there are more left-handed males than females. Traditionally left handers have been described as clumsy, but there is an impressive list of left-handed leaders, artists and sports people including Queen Victoria, Harry Truman, Gerald Ford, Michelangelo, Paul McCartney, Judy Garland, Picasso, Jimmy Connors and John McEnroe.

There is good evidence that left-handedness is more common in persons with reading disabilities, stuttering and poor coordination, but these problems may occur because until recently natural left handers were often made to use their right hand for writing, sports etc.

Hand preference does not appear to be a characteristic of animals, so is exclusive to humans. There are many theories to explain this. Some experts claim it is due to emotional contrariness in childhood, others that it is inherited, still others that it is an acquired learning process. It may well be a combination of these factors.

Some left-handers are quite hopeless using their right hand, while others are much better. There is a suggestion that this might be related to some problem with braindedness (the dominant side of the brain). Reading ability might also be tied up with this, as some left-handers have poor reading ability while others are quite normal. One side of the brain is responsible for both reading ability and speech. This may vary in left-handers leading to some confusion in the brain and clumsiness and stuttering as well as reading difficulties. A lot of research remains to be done in this area.

Parents should never try to change their child from left- to right-handed.

BREASTS, FEMALE

See also BREASTS, MALE; FEMALE PROBLEMS

Q I keep hearing how I should check my breasts regularly. Just how do I check for breast lumps?

A All women should be taught how to check their breasts for lumps by a doctor, and should perform this easy procedure every month after their period has finished.

The first step is inspecting the breasts in a mirror, with your arms at your sides and then raised above your head. Get to know the shape and size of your breasts, and note any changes that occur. Then lie down, and with one hand behind your head, examine the opposite breast with the free hand. This should be done by resting your hand flat on the chest below the breast, and then creeping the fingers up over the breast by one finger breadth at a time. You should do this twice, once over the inside half of the breast, and then over the outside half. Check under the nipple with your finger tips and finally check your arm pit for lumps. Repeat the procedure on the other breast.

It only takes two minutes a month for this simple but effective form of health care. Any lumps that are found should be shown to a doctor.

Q What is mammary dysplasia? How is it treated? Can it be cured?

A Mammary dysplasia (also called fibrocystic disease or hormonal mastitis) causes the development of tender, painful lumps in the breast. The lumps often change in their size and degree of tenderness during the month, depending on the stage of the woman's menstrual cycle. They are usually at their worst just before a period, and occur in women most commonly between 30 and 50 years, but may be found in teenagers. They are rare after the menopause.

It is obviously vital for doctors to exclude the possibility of breast cancer in these women, and a mammogram and/or ultrasound examination is often carried out before any treatment is given. If there is any lingering doubt about the nature of the disease, a biopsy (taking a sample of the lump in a minor operation) is performed so that the painful tissue can be examined under a microscope by a pathologist to confirm the diagnosis.

A number of medications can be prescribed by doctors to control the condition. It is often a matter of trial and error to find the medication that is best for each patient. The tablets must be taken on a regular basis for many months or years, as they do not give a permanent cure. Women on these treatment regimes must be followed carefully by their doctors so that no other disease can develop undetected in the breast.

Q **I am 54, and my mother and aunt both had breast cancer. My doctor is sending me for a mammogram, although I have not felt any lumps. Could you explain what is done, and is there enough radiation to harm me, or even to cause breast cancer?**

A Because of your family history of breast cancer, you are considered to be at risk of developing this disease, and you would be wise to practise regular breast examination and to have a mammogram yearly.

For the mammogram, the breast is compressed between clear plastic plates, and films are taken in two projections. If you have very little breast tissue, or very abundant breasts, the procedure may be briefly uncomfortable, but the information obtained is well worth this discomfort. There is less radiation than in a normal chest x-ray, and it will not cause breast cancer.

Q **My mother has just been diagnosed as suffering from breast cancer. Please tell me, how is breast cancer treated, and is it successful?**

A Once a breast lump is detected, a diagnosis can often be made before operation by methods such as x-rays of the breast (mammography) and needle biopsy. This is important as it allows the surgeon to discuss the diagnosis and method of treatment with the patient.

Radical mastectomy (removal of the breast and underlying muscles), and its accompanying disfigurement, is an operation of the past. It has been replaced by simple mastectomy in which only the breast is removed, leaving a cosmetically acceptable scar and scope for reconstruction of the breast by plastic surgery at a later date. Often the lymph glands under the arm will be removed at the same time, because this is the area that cancer spreads to first. Alternatively, or combined with this, a course of radiotherapy or chemotherapy (drugs) may be recommended.

In some women, equally good results in controlling the cancer can be obtained by removal of the lump alone, coupled with radiotherapy to the breast and excision of the under-arm glands. A gradually increasing proportion of women are being treated this way. Lumpectomy is only suitable for early cancers: more advanced cancers still require mastectomy. Thus delay in presentation can have a dramatic cosmetic effect as well as a prognostic one, and a return to a normal lifestyle may be only a couple of weeks away with the simpler procedure.

Two-thirds of all breast cancers may be cured. With early presentation and diagnosis, this can rise to 90%+.

Q I am 17 years old with very small breasts. The other night on the TV news there was a female model who used to be a man. This person had breasts of normal size. Why is it that an ex-male can have larger breasts than a naturally born woman? Are there hormones available to increase your breast size?

A Men who wish to change their sex do so by taking large doses of female hormones (oestrogen). Men possess breast tissue, but usually in a residual form. If this is stimulated by female hormones, the breast tissue will start enlarging in the same way as that of a teenage girl. Some teenage boys develop small breasts for a few months due to a temporary imbalance in their hormone levels.

When you start your periods and start developing breasts, it is because your ovaries start producing female hormones. Some women have breast tissue that is larger in quantity, and/or more sensitive to these hormones than other women, and they develop large breasts. The reverse can also occur. The tendency to large or small breasts is hereditary, so that if your mother and grandmother had small breasts, your chance of doing the same is quite high.

Large breasts can also be caused by obesity.

From my male doctor perspective, I feel that women with very large breasts are at a much greater disadvantage than those with small breasts, in both appearance and personal comfort.

It would be possible to increase your breast size by taking large doses of female hormone, but the side effects on the other parts of your body that respond to this hormone (the womb, ovaries and vagina) would be significant, and you would be strongly advised not to take this course.

A moderate increase in breast size can often be achieved by taking the oral contraceptive pill. During and after a pregnancy, your breast size increases significantly, and some of this increase may persist after feeding ceases. Small-breasted women can breast feed just as easily as those with large breasts.

In the long run, if you feel that your small breasts are a significant cosmetic problem, it is possible to have plastic surgery to increase their size. This is a far better option than taking hormones that may have harmful complications. Any such surgery should be delayed until you are in your early twenties, as some breast growth is possible in your late teens.

Q I am 22 years old and my breasts are too large. They are quite saggy and I get rashes under them, and they cause me great discomfort. I would like to know who I can see about getting my breasts uplifted and decreased in size, the effects of the operation and how much it would cost.

A Women with very large breasts can find them to be both uncomfortable and embarrassing. They develop fungal and heat rashes under the breast, and tired shoulder and back muscles from supporting them. They get in the way when performing some tasks, and make the woman look fatter than she is. Many women gain enormous benefit by having a breast reduction operation performed, and the sooner such a procedure is undertaken, the better.

There are a lot of plastic surgeons who perform this procedure, and you should discuss with your general practitioner who s/he recommends in your area.

There are a number of different ways of reducing the breast size, but in the most common operation, a slice of tissue and fat is removed from the underside of the breast, so that the resulting scar is in the fold under the breast, and barely noticeable.

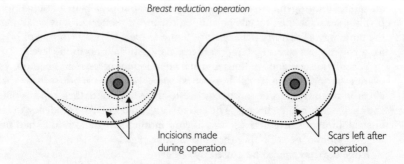

Breast reduction operation

Incisions made during operation

Scars left after operation

If nothing further was done, the nipple would be left pointing at the floor instead of straight ahead, so a further vertical cut must be made, to allow the nipple to be moved further up the smaller breast. The resultant vertical scar is below the nipple on an area of the breast that is rarely exposed to public view.

After the operation, you will feel much more comfortable, you will still be able to breast feed, and no one except your most intimate friends will ever know.

The costs involved in the operation will be partially refunded by Medicare (for the doctor's fees) and your private health fund (for the hospital charges and part of the doctor's fee). If you have no private insurance, you may have to pay $3000 to $4000. You should discuss this further at the initial consultation with the plastic surgeon, which will put you under no obligation to proceed further unless you wish to.

Q One of my breasts is markedly smaller than the other, in fact one has not developed at all. This becomes a problem when buying bras, as one side fits and the other doesn't. I am in my late teens and my breasts have always been different sizes. Am I eating the wrong foods? Is it hormonal? What is the cause, and how can I fix it without plastic surgery, or do I have to live like this for the rest of my life?

A This problem is not as uncommon as you may think. In fact, most women have slight differences in the sizes of their breasts, in the same way that most of us have one foot or hand a fraction larger than the other. In your case, the problem is extreme, and requires treatment.

All humans (male and female) have a tiny nodule of breast tissue present behind the nipple from birth. At puberty, the oestrogens in women stimulate this tissue to grow into a breast. The degree of stimulation, the size of the original nodule, and (most importantly) hereditary tendencies will determine your breast size.

In your case, you were almost certainly born with no nodule of breast tissue behind one nipple, and therefore there was nothing there for the hormones to stimulate at puberty. It has absolutely nothing to do with your diet or lifestyle.

The problem will be a permanent one, and you will not be able to breast feed a baby from the undeveloped breast, but the good breast will be able to produce adequate milk by itself (most mothers of twins successfully breast feed both babies).

There is no magical medication, cream or diet that will help, but plastic surgery will improve your self-image and appearance dramatically.

You should not instantly exclude surgery, because the operation is a very simple and safe one, that will leave a small scar under the fold of the breast that only your most intimate friends will ever discover. The surgeon will insert a bag full of soft gel behind the muscle under the nipple, so that both breasts will be exactly the same size and feel.

Ask your GP for a referral to a plastic surgeon (virtually all perform this simple procedure), and discuss the matter further with him/her. A talk commits you to nothing, and will give you a great deal more information.

Q   I have extremely itchy nipples, and I can't scratch them in public without people (especially dirty-minded men) staring at me! I don't have particularly large breasts, in fact my boyfriend teases me about my 'fried eggs' when I sunbake topless. What can I do?

A   This is a relatively common problem, particularly in summer and in women who are less well endowed. These women may go without a bra and their nipples are irritated by clothing moving across them, or have loose fitting bras that constantly move across the nipple, irritating it. Padding a bra may help this problem. Synthetic materials in the bra may also aggravate the problem—only cotton bras should be worn.

Allergies to soaps, perfumes and washing powders may cause itchy nipples. Infections such as thrush are common in breast feeding mothers, and your doctor can prescribe medication to cure this.

If no cause is apparent, lanolin and other skin moisturisers may be beneficial. As a last resort anti-itch creams can be obtained from a chemist, or your doctor can prescribe a mild steroid cream to ease the embarrassing itch.

Having plastic surgery to increase the size of your breasts may be an option if their size concerns you.

Q   I have had a mastectomy (breast removal) for cancer, and found that I avoided many complications of restricted arm movement and swelling of my arm by keeping the arm above my head on a pillow, and moving it as much as possible, starting immediately after the operation. This advice may be useful to your readers.

A   Arm movement restrictions and lymphoedema (swelling) of the arm are common complications of breast surgery when the glands in the armpit are removed to prevent the further spread of breast cancer.

Lymph is the waste products of the cells, and lymph returns from every cell through a complex network of fine tubes, rather like thin veins. These lymph ducts pass through the lymph glands that concentrate in the armpit, groin, neck and along the inside of your backbone. The glands act to remove any germs that may be attempting to penetrate deeper into the body. Eventually the lymph, having being cleaned by the glands, drains into a major vein near the heart.

The complication of lymphoedema (lymph accumulation) after breast cancer surgery varies dramatically from one patient to another, with only partial relationship to the severity of the surgery. Those who suffer severely may have an arm that is rock hard and three times its normal size. Elevation and pressure bandages are the normal treatments, but a plastic sleeve that envelopes the arm and is rhythmically inflated by a machine is the most successful treatment.

Patients requiring further help with this problem should contact the Lymphoedema Association in their state.

Q **When I was a teenager I used to squeeze my breast buds in an attempt to stimulate them to develop larger breasts, but I am now mature and my breasts are very small. Did I harm my breast buds by squeezing them?**

A Absolutely not! What you did is something many girls do as they start to develop, but there is nothing that will alter the size of the breasts during or after puberty other than manipulation of the sex hormones, a procedure that is not performed because of serious adverse effects on the other sex organs. Many women notice a small increase in breast size when taking the oral contraceptive pill, and pregnancy may result in a permanent enlargement.

Breast size is determined by your choice in parents, by the amount of oestrogen produced by your ovaries, and the individual response of your breast tissue to the oestrogen. No amount of physical stimulation is going to alter the breast size.

If you are particularly concerned by the small size of your breasts, plastic surgery techniques are available to increase your bust line. In years past, these procedures were bought into disrepute by silicon leakage from the prostheses used to increase the breast size, but better prostheses and improved operations have overcome these problems, so that the risks are now minimal.

Q **I am breast feeding, but my periods are very irregular. Is this normal?**

A Yes. While you are producing breast milk, your reproductive hormones will be suppressed by the milk producing hormones, and will not alter in level in a regular cycle to give you periods. This varies greatly from one woman to another. Some have regular periods while feeding, others have none, while most have the occasional irregular bleed.

Breast feeding is often assumed to be a form of contraception, but is most unreliable as you can ovulate and fall pregnant despite regular feeding, although the chances are reduced.

Q **I have just started breast feeding my baby, who is three weeks old. I keep hearing about the trouble some women have with breast feeding, but I am very keen to feed myself for at least six months, as I know it is better for her. What problems can occur with breast feeding and how can I avoid them?**

A Many problems can arise with breast feeding, but most are easily prevented and treated, and should not cause feeding to stop. The most common problems are engorgement and infection.

If the breasts are swollen and overfilled with milk, expressing the excess milk usually relieves the discomfort. This can be done by hand under a shower or into a container, or with the assistance of a breast pump. At other times, expressed milk may be kept and given to the baby by a sitter while the mother attends a social function. Breast feeding need not tie the mother to the home.

Mastitis is an infection of the breast that requires rapid treatment by a doctor to prevent the formation of an abscess. If one of the many lobes in the breast does not empty its milk, the milk may become infected, and the breast becomes very tender, red and sore. Fortunately, antibiotics can usually settle the problem, and it does not mean that the woman must stop feeding.

The best way to determine if the baby is receiving adequate milk is regular weighing at a child welfare clinic or doctor's surgery. Provided the weight is steadily increasing, there is no need for concern. If the weight gain is very slight, or static, then supplementation of the breast feeds may be required. It is best to offer the breasts first, and once they appear to be empty of milk, a bottle of suitable formula can be given to finish the feed.

Q I have had to stop breast feeding because of recurrent attacks of a breast infection? How can these infections be prevented and treated?

A Mastitis is an infection of the breast that requires rapid treatment to prevent the formation of an abscess. In a breastfeeding mother, if one of the many lobes in the breast does not empty its milk, the milk may become infected, and the breast becomes very tender, red and sore. It may start with a sore, cracked nipple, but often the woman wakes in the morning with breast pain as the first symptom. She may become feverish, and feel quite unwell. Women nursing for the first time are more frequently affected.

Fortunately, antibiotics can usually settle the problem, and it does not mean that the woman must stop feeding. If an abscess forms, an operation to drain away the accumulated pus is necessary.

The best form of prevention is to ensure that the breasts are empty of milk after every feed, by expressing any remaining milk or using a breast pump if necessary.

Q In a recent item you wrote on breast feeding, you neglected to mention that mastitis may be treated by ultrasound. Would you please bring this excellent form of treatment to the attention of your readers.

A Mastitis is an infection of the breast. It usually occurs in only one of the many segments of the breast in mothers who are breast feeding. The cause is a blockage in the outflow of milk from one of the segments of the breast. The milk accumulates in this area, and becomes 'sour' and infected.

As with all bacterial infections, the usual treatment is antibiotics, which are very effective.

In the early stages of the condition, when the woman first feels discomfort in the breast, ultrasound applied to the breast may break down any blockage, and allow the 'sour' milk to escape, thus curing the condition. Ultrasound is applied by a physiotherapist, and involves moving a smooth instrument over the surface of the breast. There is no pain or discomfort involved.

Both ultrasound and antibiotics may be used together.

Any woman who is breast feeding should see a doctor immediately she feels any undue pressure, pain or discomfort in the breast, so that the mastitis can be treated early, and the risk of an abscess developing is then dramatically reduced.

First-time mothers (and those who are more experienced as well) will find that the Nursing Mothers' Association (see your phone book) offers excellent support and advice to all mothers who are breast feeding their babies.

BREASTS, MALE

See also BREASTS, FEMALE

Q   I am a boy aged 16 and have very large breasts which are nearly the same as a well developed girls, and I get hassled a lot at school. I have had the breasts since I was twelve and want to get rid of them. I do not want an operation, and I'm too embarrassed to go to a doctor. Are there any non-prescription drugs I can get from a store or chemist?

A   Your problem is not unusual, but their size is unusual. Both boys and girls produce oestrogen (female hormone) and testosterone (male hormone) at puberty. Boys produce more of one hormone, and girls more of the other to change them into men and women respectively.

If the balance between these two hormones is not completely correct, or if the tissues are particularly sensitive to the hormones, boys can develop breasts, and the clitoris (penis equivalent) in a girl may become enlarged and tender. In the vast majority of cases, these problems settle in a few months or a year or two.

In a small number of cases, the problem persists, and the only solution is to have an operation to remove the offending breasts. This is not a major procedure, and will involve only a day in hospital. It is far better to have a short period of discomfort now than years more of embarrassment.

Unfortunately there are no medications available on prescription or from chemists that will help. You should not be embarrassed to see a doctor about the matter, as s/he will have seen other similar cases, and will be able to help you appropriately.

Q   I am a thirty year old MAN, and all my life I've had abnormally large breasts. I seem to gain weight only on my breasts and stomach, and my legs remain thin. I've tried doing weights, but to no avail. There is definitely something wrong with my metabolism. Can you help me with an answer?

A   There are a number of possible causes for your condition, but the one that springs most readily to mind is Cushing's syndrome. This is a condition in which the pituitary gland in the centre of the brain, or the adrenal glands that sits on top of the kidneys, become overactive and produce excessive amounts of steroid. The same condition can result from taking a large amount of steroid medications by mouth or injection for a prolonged time.

Cushing's syndrome causes fat to be deposited on the belly, chest, back and face, while the legs and arms remain thin. Other signs of the disease include mental disturbances, purple blotches on the skin and impotence.

It is possible that there are other rare causes for your problem (eg. Prader-Willi syndrome, Fröhlich's syndrome), or that you are just overweight from excessive eating.

It is important that you have your problem sorted out as soon as practical, and I would suggest that you ask your general practitioner for a referral to an endocrinologist so that you can be fully investigated and diagnosed.

Q **I am a 72 year old man. My left nipple is enlarged and hard. What could this be?**

A You should see a doctor about this immediately because it could be breast cancer. About 2% of all breast cancers occur in men, and almost invariably elderly men. Because it is an unexpected diagnosis, many men leave it too late to see a doctor, but if diagnosed early, it can be successfully treated using the same techniques that are applied to women.

As men age beyond 65 or 70 years, they go through a gradual menopause. As the male hormone levels drop, the low levels of female hormone that have always been present may take over, and fatty breasts may develop.

The other problem associated with nipples in younger men is 'joggers nipple'. In this, the nipple becomes sore, red, tender and thickened from the constant rubbing of a shirt on the nipple during jogging. A strategically placed band-aid often relieves the problem.

Q **I am now 79 years old, and very much a man, but I have started to develop breasts! Some people probably complain that I fuss around like an old woman, but this is going a bit too far. Why has this happened?**

A All of us (both men and women) have male and female hormones in our bodies. The difference between the sexes is determined by the balance between these hormones.

As men and women age, their hormone levels drop. This is the menopause. When the hormone levels are very low, there may be a slight excess of the wrong type for that sex. As a result, elderly men may develop breasts, and women may grow a scanty beard. There is no reason for any treatment unless the person finds the problem distressing.

It is possible for men to develop cancer in their breasts, so any lumps should be checked by a doctor.

CANCER
See also SKIN CANCER

Q **What are the early signs of cancer? When should I see a doctor? I don't want to be a worry-wart about a skin spot that is a wart and not a cancer!**

A The early signs of cancer are:
- a lump or thickening anywhere in the body
- sores that will not heal
- unusual bleeding or discharge
- change in bowel or bladder habits
- persistent cough or hoarseness
- change in a wart or mole
- indigestion or difficulty in swallowing
- loss of weight for no apparent reason.

If you note one of these changes in yourself, or a friend, seek immediate expert medical advice. It is far better to be reassured that there is nothing wrong now, than worry for months unnecessarily. If the condition is serious, early treatment may save your life.

Q **Several members of my family have had cancer of different sorts, and this scares me. What causes cancer? How can I avoid it?**

A Cancer, the crab of astrology, is so named because the ancients could see the cancer clawing its way into the normal tissue, destroying everything in its path. Doctors now understand a great deal about cancer, but we do not fully understand what starts the process.

Although the specific cause of cancer is unknown, sun exposure, a low-fibre diet and smoking are well-known precipitating factors.

Cancer occurs when otherwise normal cells start multiplying at an excessive rate, and the cells made by the rapid process of reproduction are abnormal in shape, size and function. Although they may have some slight resemblance to the cells around them, cancer cells cannot perform the correct work of that type of cell, and they prevent the normal cells around them from working properly, thus enabling the cancerous cells to spread.

Cancer is not just one disease process; dozens of different types of cancer occur in different parts of the body, and each type causes different problems and responds differently to treatment. Several different types of cancer can be found in the lungs for example.

Q **If I was unlucky enough to get cancer, how could this be treated?**

A Nothing can be done to help a patient with cancer until they present to a doctor, and this is one of the most frustrating aspects of medicine for general practitioners, because so many people wait for far too long before seeing a doctor with their symptoms.

At times, an otherwise intelligent human being will suspect cancer, but do nothing about it until the symptoms become so bad they are beyond help.

Over half of all cancers can be cured, and that excludes the skin cancers that rarely cause death. The cure rate is far higher in those who present early to a doctor, because the less the cancer has spread, the easier it is to treat.

Treatment may involve surgery to remove the growth, drugs that are attracted to and destroy abnormal cells, irradiation of the tumour with high-powered x-rays or combinations of these three methods.

If you are concerned about cancer, see your doctor now!

Q **Where does cancer spread to when you have a secondary cancer? I have had cancer in the breast, and I have been told that surgery has been successful and I have no secondaries, but I would like to watch out for any problems.**

A The liver, lymph nodes, and bones are the most common areas involved in the spread of cancer, but cancer can spread almost anywhere in the body from its original site.

The type of cancer will also determine where it may spread, as some types of cancer cells appear to spread more easily to one part of the body than another.

The lymph nodes are responsible for dealing with waste products and infection, and there are direct channels from them to every part of the body. Cancer cells can spread very easily along these channels, and so with most cancers, the nearest group of lymph nodes is often surgically removed, irradiated or treated with cancer-killing drugs.

The liver is responsible for processing the blood to remove abnormal and dying cells, waste products and toxins. This too can therefore be easily affected by cancer cells.

Bone marrow is responsible for producing many of the infection- and cancer-fighting cells in the body, and may itself be infiltrated by cancer cells that destroy its correct function.

Secondary cancer is certainly harder to treat than primary, but it is not an inevitable death sentence because modern anti-cancer drugs, the new radiation techniques available and delicate surgery can still remove and control many of these growths.

Q **My mother has to have yet another operation after several operations for breast cancer. This time they are going to remove her glands. Why are glands removed after operations for cancer?**

A The glands in the armpits, groin, neck and other parts of the body are really disease-fighting lymph nodes that contain millions of white cells. They can filter out abnormal cells as well as bacteria and viruses, and so they can be a site of spread for cancer.

The abnormal cells from a breast cancer can move down the lymph ducts to the nodes in the armpit. The lymph nodes in the groin can be involved in cancer of the bowel.

The lymph nodes will remove the cancerous cells from the lymph circulation, but in the process, the cancer may start in the involved nodes.

This is why it is vital for enlarged tender lymph nodes anywhere to be checked by a doctor, and it is why the nearby nodes are often removed during many forms of cancer operation.

Q My mother is on methotrexate for treatment of cancer. It is having terrible side effects. Is it worth continuing?

A This is an extremely difficult and delicate question of ethics, medical technology and common sense. The treatment of a cancer can include surgery, irradiation and drugs. The type of treatment will vary depending on the type and site of the cancer.

Methotrexate is a drug that kills cancer cells. Unfortunately it, and other cancer drugs, can have severe side effects, as they damage some normal cells while destroying the cancer. The usual problems are loss of hair and vomiting associated with constant nausea and a sense of being unwell.

Ethically, all doctors are required to do everything possible to prolong human life, and cure disease. If statistics indicate that methotrexate, or any other drug, is likely to be the best treatment, a doctor is ethically obliged to prescribe it.

Medical technology may also indicate that certain treatments are sometimes successful, and that a combination of several treatments may give a slightly higher chance of success, but with a dramatic increase in side effects.

This is where common sense is required. If a patient is likely to be cured in 50% or even 25% of cases with the use of a course of treatment that may be most unpleasant, most doctors and patients would proceed. If the success rate was only 1%, most doctors would consult with the patient and relatives and not proceed, leaving the remainder of the patient's life as calm, peaceful and free of side effects as possible.

The problem arises between these extremes. Should the patient be given a slight chance of survival after a few months of drug-induced agony, or should nature be allowed to take its course? There is no simple answer. Frank discussions between the patient, doctor and relatives is the only way for a consensus to be reached in solving the dilemma.

Q My brother has Hodgkin's disease and I am told it is serious. He lives a long way from me, and I don't like to crossexamine him on the phone about his problem. Can you please explain this condition for me?

A Hodgkin's disease is a form of cancer that attacks the lymph nodes, the spleen and liver. Its cause is not known, and it may spread widely through the body before it is detected. Surgery plays a relatively minor part in its treatment because of the insidious way it spreads through large areas of the body.

Treatment is primarily by drugs and irradiation. The drugs can often control or destroy the cancerous cells, and concentrated areas can be destroyed by high-energy X-rays. The survival rate depends on the stage at which the disease is detected. Early detection of all cancers gives a better outcome. Those with the first stages of Hodgkin's disease have an 85% chance of cure, while in advanced cases the survival rate drops below 20%.

Q Does a person who is terminally ill have to suffer excruciating pain, or can it be controlled?

A This can be a very difficult problem for doctors, patients and their families, particularly when the patient is dying from a very aggressive form of cancer.

There are undoubtedly medications available that will control the most severe pains, but the patient may be so stuporous from the side effects that they are unable to function effectively, and may end up completely unconscious.

To keep a patient alert and pain free is the challenge.

Medications, including self-administered doses of narcotics by tablet or injection, can play a part in this process, but in many cases there are other options. The use of a TENS (trans cutaneous electrical nerve stimulator) machine, which through pads on the skin stimulates nerves in a way that blocks pain, may give some patients relief.

The most radical options include injecting into the nerves that are responsible for the pain to temporarily shut them down, or permanently destroy them. Surgery to cut these nerves may also be undertaken.

The wishes of the patient must always be taken into consideration by doctors, and a discussion of the available options allows the patient to remain in control of his/her pain in the way that s/he desires.

CHEST

See also HEART; LUNGS

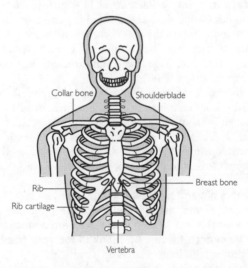

Q I keep getting pains in the centre of my chest. I am frightened it may be a heart attack. What else could it be?

A There are a score or more reasons for central chest pain, heart disease certainly being one of them.

Other causes include indigestion, hiatus hernia, muscular strains, inflammation of the chest cartilage, bronchitis, other lung diseases and tumours. Anxiety and tension can be sufficiently severe to cause muscle spasms and chest pain. Cancer of the lung, gullet and thymus (a gland in the chest) may also cause chest pain.

There is no doubt that any chest pain that does not settle rapidly should be checked by a doctor. It is far better to be reassured today that there is nothing seriously wrong, than to delay the treatment of serious lung or heart diseases. Please see your general practitioner about this as soon as possible.

Q   I wake up with a jumping sensation in my upper abdomen and lower chest. It stops when I wake completely. Is this a form of indigestion? Can I take something before going to bed?

A   Two possible causes come to mind, but there are probably more.

The first is that the problem is a spasm of the diaphragm, rather like that created by hiccoughs. There may be irritation of the gullet, as it passes through the diaphragm, while you are lying, caused by the acid in the stomach. As soon as you wake and move, the irritated tissue goes into repeated spasm until the irritation eases. You would expect this to be associated with some pain (heartburn) or burping.

The other possibility is that you are feeling an unusual, irregular heartbeat that is associated with a change in your sleep state. The heart may flutter for a few minutes with the change in position or stress.

I would suggest that you try using a reflux-preventing mixture such as Gaviscon at night, and if this fails to ease the problem, you should have your stomach and heart checked by a doctor.

Q   My GP has diagnosed my chest pain after a fall down stairs as a sprung rib, and says it is not serious. What is a sprung rib?

A   The ribs do not form a rigid cage around the chest, but are flexible so that you can expand and contract the chest when you breathe. A lot of this flexibility comes from the fact that ribs do not join directly on to the breast bone (sternum), but a strip of cartilage (the costal cartilage) runs from the end of the rib to the side of the breast bone.

Where the costal cartilages join to the bone of the rib or breast bone there is a joint (costo-chondral joint). In a fall, one or more ribs may be pushed in too far, and one or more of these joints may be damaged.

In effect, a sprung rib is a sprain of a costo-chondral joint in the rib cage.

Treatment is primarily time and rest while the damaged joint heals, but anti-inflammatory medications and pain-killers can be used to ease the discomfort.

Q   I am 47 years old and have pain in the first two left ribs where they meet the sternum. X-rays are normal, and the pain has come and gone at intervals over the last fifteen years. As I am a smoker, I am very worried this may be cancer. I would be thankful for your frank advice.

A   Tietze syndrome (also known as costochondritis).

It is often difficult from vague, rambling letters to make any guess at a diagnosis, but from your succinct description of your symptoms, I would almost bet that this relatively common syndrome is the cause of your problem.

The ribs come around the chest from the back towards the breast bone. They stop some centimetres short of the breast bone though, and a strip of cartilage (the costal cartilage) joins the end of the rib to the side of the breast bone. This strip of cartilage gives the rib cage additional spring, flexibility and resilience.

In some people, often young women, but potentially anybody, one or more of these cartilages becomes inflamed, painful, tender and slightly swollen. The cause for this reaction is unknown, but it was first described by the nineteenth-century German surgeon, Alexander Tietze—thus Tietze syndrome.

The problem may last for weeks or months before settling, and then recur at a later time. There are no serious complications of the condition, but the victim may be significantly discomforted by the pain.

Treatment involves the use of high doses of anti-inflammatory tablets, or occasionally, brief courses of steroids. These are only available on prescription, so I suggest that you discuss the possibility of this syndrome causing your pain with your GP.

Q   Can you please tell me what the thymus gland in the chest does? I am a nursing student, and I can't understand this gland at all.

A   No problem. To put it simply, the thymus in the adult is a small irregular strip of glandular tissue that lies behind the upper part of the breast bone and extends up into the front of the neck. In a child it is proportionally much larger and more important. It reaches its maximum size of about 30 grams at puberty.

It plays a major role in the development and maintenance of the immune system by producing specific types of white cells (B and T cells) that are vital in allowing the body to become immune to infection. It also secretes a hormone that maintains the competence of the cells it produces.

If the thymus fails to develop or is removed, the patient will be unable to fight off infection or cancer effectively. Excess activity of the gland can cause the disease myasthenia gravis.

CHILDREN

See also BABIES

Q   My two year old is very small, and appears to be underweight for his age. What could be the cause, as I look after him very well?

A   The first thing to do is to have your child's height and weight compared with those of other children. This can be done by a doctor using statistical tables. The height of you and your husband will also be checked to see what his genetic height is likely to be.

If a significant abnormality is found, investigations will be undertaken to determine the cause. These are extremely varied and include chronic infections, gut infestations (eg. worms), heart disease, cystic fibrosis, food allergies and intolerance and a host of other rarer conditions.

Child neglect and abuse is something that doctors have to be careful of in this situation also. If there is a problem, it can be dealt with once a cause is found.

Q   My four year old eats like a sparrow. He seems healthy enough, but I am concerned about his diet. Should I give him vitamins?

A   Children of all ages need a variety of foods to supply all the dietary essentials for their growth and energy needs. They rarely require any vitamin supplement if their diet is adequate.

Eating patterns will change between infant and teenage years. Pre-schoolers often demonstrate a decreased appetite corresponding to the slowing of their growth rate after three or four years of age. Parents are often bewildered and anxious about the finicky and capricious attitudes children of this age have towards food.

Provided foods poor in nutrition are not introduced as eating inducements, eating habits will gradually return to more normal levels in the next few years.

Q **Is aspirin safe in children? I always find it works better for my headaches than paracetamol.**

A Aspirin should not be used in children under 12 years of age unless there is no appropriate alternative, and it is given under medical supervision. This is because of the rare risk of developing Reye syndrome.

90% of the children with this syndrome have taken aspirin or similar medications for a viral infection and fever within a week or two of the onset of the syndrome's symptoms.

Children with Reye syndrome (named after the Australian doctor who first identified the condition) have vomiting, convulsions, brain inflammation, rapid breathing, mental confusion and develop liver failure.

Unfortunately there is no specific treatment for Reye syndrome, and about one third of affected children die, while another third may have permanent brain damage.

Although the syndrome is rare (affects only two to four children in Australia every year), it is still better to avoid aspirin in children when there is a good and safer alternative in the form of paracetamol.

Q **I am having no luck in toilet-training my two year old. What could the problem be?**

A Babies have no control over their bladder or bowels. They simply eliminate their waste material as the organs become full. Around the age of two, the ability to exercise control develops, and gradually, in a combination of both physical development and learning, a child acquires the ability to urinate and defecate only when appropriate. Obviously there is no point in trying to toilet-train a child who is not physically ready to control his or her bladder or bowels. To try is the equivalent of trying to teach a six month old baby to talk and will simply lead to frustration on both sides.

Parents often feel a child should be clean by the age of two, and dry at night by the age of two and a half. In fact, only about half of all children achieve these goals, and many a year or more later. Complete control is rarely reached before three in any child.

Toilet-training usually starts around 15–18 months by placing the child on the pot after meals. This is the time they are most likely to want to void, and gradually, with much praise if the pot is used, the child will learn that this is what is required. A young child, of course, has no way of knowing what is expected and patience is needed. A child with an older brother or sister who sits on a pot will usually latch on more quickly than a child without such a model to imitate.

Most toddlers react vigorously against being forced into things, and a parent who is aggressively insistent about toilet-training is likely to find the attitude counterproductive. Toilet-training can only succeed with the cooperation of the child, and if you make the process a battle ground, you are the one likely to lose out.

It is much easier for a child to learn to be clean than dry. Most children only move their bowels once or twice a day, usually at regular intervals. You are likely to be able to recognise the signs of an approaching motion and provide a pot or take them to the toilet to collect it. Generally after a few weeks, especially if you make it clear you regard it as desirable and grown-up behaviour, your child is likely to have become proud of their new skill and will seek out the pot or toilet when it is needed.

Urinating is more haphazard. Children urinate many times in a day and, since it is a less major event, they may not even notice it if they are absorbed in play. The urge to urinate is also not enough to wake them in the early days of developing control, so they remain used to urinating in their nappy while they are asleep. If a child wakes dry, make the pot available or take them to the toilet and be liberal with praise if it is used.

Gradually the child will learn that when the urge to urinate is felt they should head for the pot or toilet. It is worth remembering that all children eventually stop wetting themselves, even those who seem impossibly slow.

Q **How do you get a three year old to go to bed, and go to sleep? I am at my wits end.**

A Newborn babies sleep most of the time, but as they grow, the need for sleep diminishes until a toddler requires about ten or twelve hours of sleep a night, with a nap in the daytime.

Some children start to rebel against going to bed. After all, now that they are growing up, why should they not be able to participate in all the family activities, including those in the evening? Generally a child will be more amenable to an early bedtime if a regular routine is adhered to and there is no question that bedtime has arrived.

A child who persistently appears for a chat after being put to bed, or constantly asks for a drink of water or to go to the toilet, should have their request met once and then be put to bed firmly with no further excuses for delay allowed. Consistent routine and discipline is essential, the child must learn that there is no reward for not complying with the routine that the parents wish to establish.

Some children develop a fear of the dark at this time, and if this is the reason for a toddler's reluctance to stay in bed, a night light may solve the problem.

Once you have a problem, it is worthwhile indicating to the child that you are now going to use new rules for bedtime by moving the bed to a different position in the room, putting other pictures and furniture in new places, changing the lighting in the room and telling the child that from now on a particular routine will be applied.

CHOLESTEROL
See also DIET

Q **What is cholesterol and why should I avoid it?**

A Cholesterol is essential for the normal functioning of the human body. It is responsible for cementing cells together, is a major constituent of bile, and is the basic building block for sex hormones. Only in excess is it harmful.

If too much cholesterol is carried around in our blood stream, it may be deposited in gradually increasing amounts inside the arteries. Slowly, the affected artery narrows, until the flow of blood is sufficiently obstructed to cause the area supplied by that artery to suffer. If that area is the heart, a heart attack will result; if it is the brain, a stroke will occur.

This deposition of fat is known as arteriosclerosis, or hardening of the arteries. If you are in the high-risk group, there are several measures you can take to bring you back to normal. The first step is to stop smoking, limit your alcohol intake, take more exercise and lose weight if you are obese.

If these measures are insufficient, doctors will recommend a diet that is low in cholesterol which involves avoiding most dairy products, fatty meats, sausages, offal, fried foods, and egg yolk. Despite a strict diet, there are still some people who cannot keep their cholesterol levels under control. They will require further life-long medical management by the regular use of tablets that are designed to lower the level of fat in the blood.

Q My doctor says I have too much fat in my blood. What foods should I avoid with a low-cholesterol diet?

A Foods that are high in cholesterol include:—
— All dairy products including foods that are made with dairy products such as cream cakes and ice-cream (skim milk, cottage cheese and low-fat yoghurt are allowed).
— Eggs (egg white allowed).
— All fatty meats (eg. sausages, luncheon meat, corned beef, offal, game, goose).
— Shellfish and caviar.

It is important to keep your cholesterol levels reasonably low. If they remain too high, fat may deposit inside the arteries causing heart attacks and strokes. If diet alone does not keep the cholesterol level reasonable, medications may be required.

Q Would you please tell me in very simple terms, what foods I can and cannot eat with a high blood cholesterol level? I am very confused about all this.

A In the simplest possible terms, this is the diet you should follow to minimise your cholesterol levels:

FOODS ALLOWED
Vegetables, cereals, fruit and nuts, fish, chicken breast, lean meat, pasta, olive oil, margarine, skim milk, dark chocolate, wine and beer.

AVOID THESE FOODS
Sausages, hamburgers, pies, lamb chops, mince, offal (liver, kidneys, tripe), roasts (particularly surface fat), game meat, chicken skin and legs, pizza, cala-mari, prawns, oysters, cream cake, milk chocolate, eggs and egg products, and dairy products (cream, milk, butter, yoghurt, cheese, custard).

Q Are dairy products and sugar safe to eat? I keep hearing how cholesterol and sweets are bad for you.

A Dairy products are a staple food in the diet of nearly every civilisation around the world. The intake varies from one place to another. The Japanese have virtually none, Europeans quite a lot, and some Arab tribes live almost entirely on dairy products. They are an excellent source of carbohydrates, protein and fat, and the sugar lactose.

People can live virtually on milk alone if necessary. Some specialised dairy products, such as yoghurt and junket, are excellent aids to digestion and bowel function. Cheeses are compressed energy, and are included in survival rations.

As with all foods, too much can be harmful. Those who have a high cholesterol level in their bloodstream and the more obese members of the community should not eat whole milk products, but skim milk and fat-reduced dairy products can still be consumed. Milk with added calcium ('Shape') is now available to help prevent osteoporosis in middle-aged women.

Sugar is also an essential part of your diet, and it is found to some extent in nearly all fruit and vegetables. It acts as a natural preservative for a wide range of foods, and glucose (a form of sugar) is essential for the normal functioning of the brain. Once again, moderation is appropriate, and sugar intake should be minimised in the overweight and care should be taken not to take excess sugar in a concentrated form (sweets, soft-drinks etc.) that will cause dental caries.

Q Does fish oil help cholesterol?

A This is still a controversial subject amongst doctors. There is some evidence that the taking of large amounts of fish oil alters the balance between high-density and low-density cholesterol. It is better to have more of the high-density form.

There is no evidence that using fish oil will lower an abnormally high blood level of cholesterol without a change to the rest of the diet.

Foods high in cholesterol include milk and dairy products, fatty meats, sausages, game birds, shellfish, caviar, and egg yolk.

It is far simpler to reduce the amount of these foods in your diet to lower your cholesterol level, rather than add oils that may or may not be beneficial.

Q My doctor tells me my cholesterol is high and wants me to take tablets. Can't I just go on a diet? What do these tablets do?

A People with an excess level of cholesterol in their bloodstream are liable to an increased risk of strokes and heart attacks. For this reason it is essential for everyone to have a screening cholesterol check at the age of 40, and if this is abnormal, treatment will be necessary.

The mainstay of management is diet; and most dairy products, fatty meats, fried foods, and egg yolks are forbidden. If dietary measures are insufficient, medication is necessary to further lower the cholesterol level.

There are many medications that can be used to lower cholesterol. Further blood tests will be given a few months after the tablets are started to measure their effectiveness, and determine the long-term dose necessary to control the problem.

Q What should your cholesterol level be? My doctor tells me mine is alright at 6.3, but a friend has been told to go on a diet at a level of 5.8.

A This is a very controversial area. Cholesterol is a type of fat which is essential for the functioning of the body, but it can cause severe diseases if present in excess amounts. I have heard figures between 4.5 and 7.0 quoted as being the upper limit of normal for cholesterol, but most laboratories use a value of 5.5.

Your sex and age is important too. A higher value is accepted in older people and females than in younger males.

Doctors are more likely to treat the problem if you are overweight, have high blood pressure or diabetes, or have a family history of heart disease or stroke.

Cholesterol is divided into high-density and low-density fats. If the amount of high-density fats is high, there is less to be concerned about, as it is the low-density fats that are a factor in heart disease and hardening of the arteries.

I recommend a diet to anyone who has a level of 5.5 or more. Treatment with drugs as well as diet would certainly be given at a level of 7.0.

Q I had a cholesterol test taken in a mobile unit, and the result was 7.9. The nurse told me this was too high and I should go to a doctor and ask for medication. I am a fit woman, and eat sensibly, and I don't see why I should have high cholesterol and take tablets forever. What do you think?

A You have raised a number of very important points in your question.

Firstly, the measurement of cholesterol in the blood is technically very difficult, and there may be a 5% or greater variation in results even between major laboratories. The small machines used for screening are often poorly calibrated and maintained, and variations of up to 20% are possible. A 20% variation in your result could give a true reading between 6.3 and 9.4—quite a difference!

A cholesterol test done at random is also quite useless, as the food you had eaten in the previous few hours could significantly alter the result. The only reliable method is to take a sample after you have fasted for twelve hours (ie. overnight), and to have the test performed by a major laboratory.

Even then, if you have a high cholesterol level, there are two different types of cholesterol—high density and low density—and the ratio between them is more important than the absolute cholesterol reading. High density cholesterol is good, low density is bad.

The next point is the recommendation by the nurse. You should certainly see your doctor for further assessment, and the first thing your doctor will do after proving by further tests that your cholesterol is too high, is to assess the other risk factors in your life and family. If you smoke, have high blood pressure, are obese and have a bad family history of heart disease treatment is more necessary than in those who have none of these risk factors.

The first step in treatment is diet, and avoiding foods high in animal fats can often lower the cholesterol level significantly.

Only as a last resort is medication prescribed, and there are a number of different medications available. Your GP will determine the best medication for you, depending on your individual circumstances and characteristics.

Unfortunately the level of fitness has no effect upon cholesterol levels.

CONTRACEPTION

Q Would you please tell me about all the different forms of contraception available so that I can choose the one that will suit me best.

A Attempts to find some way of having sex without producing babies have a long history. Documents from Mesopotamia, 4000 years ago, record that a plug of dung was placed in the woman's vagina to stop conception. In Cleopatra's Egypt, small gold trinkets were inserted into the uterus of the courtesans as a form of early intrauterine contraceptive device. At the same time, camel herders pushed pebbles into the wombs of the female camels so that they would not get pregnant on long caravan treks. More recently, in the eighteenth century in France, the renowned philanderer Casanova used a thin pig's bladder as an early condom or 'French letter'. Prior to this there were similar devices made from leather or gut. Finding a safe, effective and reliable contraceptive has proved a difficult task.

Today, a very wide range of safe and effective contraceptives are available. They include:

- The contraceptive pill. Available since 1962, the pill has revolutionised modern life. It is probably the safest and most effective form of reversible contraception. There are many different dosage forms and strengths, so that most women can find one that meets their needs. The main types are the monophasic (constant dose) two-hormone pill, the biphasic (two phase), the triphasic (three phase) hormone pills in which the hormone doses vary during the month, and the one-hormone mini-pill.
- The morning-after pill. The morning-after pill is a short course of a high dose of sex hormones (often an oral contraceptive) which must be taken within 72 hours of sexual intercourse. Two doses are taken twelve hours apart and they are often given with a second medication to prevent vomiting, which is the most common side effect.
- Medroxyprogesterone injections. These are a means of contraception in which a synthetic form of the female sex hormone progesterone is injected, causing the ovaries to stop producing eggs. One injection lasts for 12 weeks or more.
- Implants. It is now possible to have an small rod shaped implant inserted into the flesh on the inside of the upper arm. This gives almost 100% protection against pregnancy for three years. In most women, their periods cease for this time, but in some, irregular bleeding leads to the implant being removed.
- Spermicides. There are creams, foams, gels and tablets which act to kill sperm on contact. A spermicide must be inserted no more than 20 minutes before intercourse and a new application must be used before each ejaculation. Generally the use of spermicides is advised with a diaphragm or condom.
- Condom. The condom is the simplest barrier method of artificial contraception. A condom is a thin rubber sheath which is placed on the penis before penetration. When the man ejaculates, the sperm are held in the rubber tip. There is also a female version of the condom, which is a thin rubber or plastic pouch that is inserted into the vagina.
- Diaphragm. The diaphragm for women works on a similar principle as the condom in that it provides a physical barrier to the sperm meeting the egg. A diaphragm is a rubber dome with a flexible spring rim. It is inserted into the vagina before intercourse, so that it covers the cervix. It is best used with a spermicidal cream or jelly to kill any sperm that manage to wriggle around the edges.
- Cervical cap. Like the diaphragm, the cervical cap is a barrier method of contraception, but it is much smaller because it fits tightly over the cervix,

rather than filling the vagina. The cap must be fitted very carefully and should be used with spermicides.

- Contraceptive sponge. This recently introduced device is a sponge impregnated with spermicide which is inserted into the vagina so that it expands to cover the cervix. Like a diaphragm it is inserted before intercourse but is disposable and thrown away after use.

- Intrauterine device. The IUD is a piece of plastic shaped like a T, that may be covered by a thin coil of copper wire. It is inserted by a doctor through the vagina and cervix to sit inside the uterus (womb). Newer IUDs contain a hormone that dramatically improves their effectiveness. The device can remain in place for two or three years before its needs to be changed.

- Natural family planning. This is a form of periodic abstinence from sex (not having sex at those times of the month when a woman is fertile). The trick is knowing just what are the safe and not so safe times. Obviously, it is essential for both sexual partners in this situation to cooperate fully in the contraceptive process. The man must be as aware of the woman's cycle as she is herself. For this reason alone, this method of contraception does not suit all couples.

- Tubal ligation. A tubal ligation (having the tubes tied or clipped) is an operation that usually renders a woman permanently unable to have children. As a contraceptive it is almost 100% effective, but as with all surgical procedures, failures may occur, and women should be aware of this when they have the procedure.

- Vasectomy. A procedure in which the vas deferens (sperm tubes) of a man are cut and tied or clipped in order to prevent him from fathering children. It is a simpler operation than the sterilisation (tubal ligation) of a woman. It should be considered to be a permanent procedure at the time it is performed, but there is always a small risk that the cut sperm tubes may spontaneously reconnect at a later time making the man fertile again.

You should discuss with your general practitioner which option suits you best.

Q How does the contraceptive pill work?

A The pill contains two hormones, an oestrogen and a progestogen, that are artificial equivalents of the two sex hormones that all women possess. These are combined in a manner which mimics the hormonal balance of pregnancy. The body is fooled into thinking that it is already pregnant, and will not allow the release of a further egg from the ovary.

The side effects of the pill are therefore the side effects of early pregnancy, but usually on a much milder scale. In addition, the pill prevents pregnancy by thickening the fluid in the neck of the womb so that there is a natural barrier to sperm, and it also alters the lining of the womb, making it more difficult for an egg to implant itself and develop.

Q What should I do if I forget a contraceptive pill?

A It is essential to take the pill properly for it to work. Forgetting even one pill could result in a very productive event nine months later!

With most types of the pill, if you forget one and then take it within eight hours, you will still be protected. With higher dose pills you have twelve hours grace, but with the single hormone mini-pills, you must take it within three hours of the same time every day for it to be effective.

If you miss a pill by more than these times, you should take the missed pill, and continue taking the rest of the pills at your usual time until the end of the pack, but take other contraceptive precautions until after you have taken at least seven of the active pills (do not count the sugar pills that you take at the end of each month).

If you miss more than one pill, stop the pill, use other contraceptive precautions (eg. condoms) until your next period starts, and then start a new pack of the pill. Do not rely on it until you have taken seven active hormone pills.

Remember, that if you have any vomiting or diarrhoea, you are effectively missing taking the pill, and must take appropriate precautions.

Q   I am worried the pill may make me sterile. Is it necessary to take a break from the contraceptive pill every year or so?

A   No! The modern pills are very low in the total dosage of hormones. You can stay on the pill for many years without a break, and when you wish to fall pregnant, the pill can be stopped and you may find yourself in the family way as soon as two weeks later. There is absolutely no evidence to implicate the pill as a cause of permanent sterility.

Some women do have a delay in the return of their periods after taking the pill, but if you are sterile after taking the pill, you would have been sterile if you had never taken it.

The greatest side effect from the regular stopping of the pill is an unwanted pregnancy. Women who are overweight or who smoke should ensure that they are on the lowest possible dose of the pill.

Q   My 14 year old daughter has a very steady 18 year old boyfriend. She insists on seeing him and I am frightened she might get pregnant. Is she too young to go on the pill?

A   There are moral, legal and medical problems in this question, and I will restrict my answer to the medical one, but be aware that the age of sexual consent in all Australian states is 16.

It would be unwise to use the oral contraceptive pill on a girl who has not finished growing, and has not had her periods for at least a year. If she does not have these or any other of the medical reasons not to use the pill, she can take it on a regular basis.

The pill is only available on prescription, and the doctor concerned will certainly discuss the matter in more personal detail with you. It may be that the barrier forms of contraception would be more appropriate in this situation.

Contraception is certainly better than pregnancy at this young age, but hopefully you and your daughter will be able to discuss the matter further with the help of your doctor or a child guidance officer at the school.

Q   I am desperately worried that I might fall pregnant. This would be a disaster as my wage is essential to pay our mortgage, and we would lose our house if I fell pregnant. I am on the oral contraceptive pill, but I really want to know how effective it is.

A The pill is the most effective form of reversible contraception known to medical science. If taken correctly, only one or two in every 1000 women will fall pregnant in a year of using the pill. By comparison, 120 women using the condom as contraceptive will fall pregnant in a year of use, 30 using the intrauterine device and between 50 and 200 using the rhythm method and its derivatives.

If no contraceptive is used, 850 out of every 1000 normally menstruating women would be pregnant after a year.

The only forms of contraceptive that are more effective are hormone implants and injections, vasectomy, tubal ligation and total sexual abstinence (the most reliable of them all!).

Most women who have fallen pregnant on the pill have missed one (that's all it takes), had diarrhoea or vomiting (it doesn't work if it doesn't stay inside you), or used antibiotics (some may affect absorption of the pill into the body). The mini-pills (Noriday, Microlut, Micronor, Microval) have a higher failure rate than the normal two-hormone contraceptive pills. These must be taken very strictly as directed.

Q **What is the difference between the mini-pill and other oral contraceptives?**

A Most oral contraceptives (known as combined pills) contain two different hormones that roughly correspond to the two types of hormone produced by your ovaries. They may be given as a steady dose of hormone throughout the month, or may have two or three different levels of hormone to correspond with the natural changes in your body. After 21 days, you stop the pill or start taking sugar pills. This drop in hormone levels allows you to have a period.

The mini-pill has only one hormone in it, and this in a very low dose. It is taken constantly, with no break for periods, and must be taken at the same time every day. Periods will still occur, but they may be irregular and are usually light. It is not as reliable as the combined form of pill, and is normally only given to older women, those who cannot tolerate the combined pill, smokers, or those who are breast feeding.

Q **I have been taking the contraceptive pill continuously, missing out the sugar pills, so that I don't have a period. How can you tell if you have fallen pregnant while on the pill if you take it this way?**

A Many women have started taking the active contraceptive pills constantly in order to stop the inconvenience of their menstrual periods, having a break only every few months to give themselves an occasional period. This can only be done with the constant-dose pills, and not those that have two or three different doses during the month.

It is quite safe to do this, and it has no effect on the future health or fertility of the woman, but you have raised a common concern, in that there is no longer that monthly reassurance that you are not pregnant. If you miss even one pill, have an episode of diarrhoea or take antibiotics that affect the function of the pill, you may fall pregnant.

The only way to be sure is to stop the pill and see if you have a period, or perform a pregnancy test on your urine. There is no other simple solution other than returning to taking the pill on a monthly cycle rather than constantly.

Q **I am taking the contraceptive pill regularly, but do not get a period until I have been taking the white sugar pills for three days. Can you get pregnant while taking the pill if you have sex on one of the days you are taking the sugar pills?**

A It is quite normal for it to take two or three days before your period starts while on the inactive sugar pills. The reason you have a menstrual period when you start these inactive pills is because there is a sudden drop in sex hormone levels in your body, and the lining of the uterus (womb) which is nurtured by these hormones becomes unstable, breaks down and is flushed away by the blood of a period.

Provided you are taking the active pills regularly, then you cannot ovulate or fall pregnant on the two or three days before your period while you are taking the inactive sugar pills.

Q **I don't like the effects I am having from the pill. Is it safe to change from one brand of the contraceptive pill to another?**

A Your doctor may consider changing the type or dosage of the pill that you are on, and his/her choice will be determined by the problems you are having with the present pill. Different hormones can suit different women, and what is very good for one, may not be as good for another.

Irregular bleeding, headaches, depression, nausea and breast discomfort are common reasons for altering the type of pill.

If you are changing from one everyday type pill to another, you should finish the pack of the pill you are on at present, and then start taking the first pill of the new pack from the day you start bleeding. If you are using 21-day packs, allow seven days between finishing the old pack and starting the new.

It is often wise to take other precautions against pregnancy for the first week on any new pill.

Q **How does the birth control pill cause thrombotic problems?**

A One of the rare side effects of taking the oral contraceptive pill is the development of a blood clot (thrombus) in a vein. This is now a very rare complication with the low dose pills that doctors have available.

If a blood clot does occur, it is usually in the veins in the calf. This causes considerable pain and tenderness of that part of the leg, and most patients would present to doctors with these symptoms for treatment.

If the clot is not treated early, it is possible for the clot to break away from the wall of the vein, and travel up the vein, through the heart and lodge in the lung. The effect this will have depends on the size of the clot, but it will block an artery in the lung, and the part of the lung affected will then die. If this is a very small area, the patient will have no serious problem, but if a major artery is blocked by a large clot, the result may rarely be fatal.

The thrombus (clot) forms because the hormones in the pill slightly alter the clotting factors in the blood, so that a minor injury to the vein (eg. repeatedly pushing back a chair with your calf as you stand) may be enough to start a clot in the blood.

Treatment involves medication to prevent the spread of the clot or further clot formation, and women who have such a problem should not use the contraceptive pill.

Q Can I take the contraceptive pill when breast feeding?

A It is possible to fall pregnant while breast feeding, and it is therefore necessary to take contraceptive precautions if you wish to avoid having a very rapidly expanding family.

The normal combined hormone contraceptive pills are probably best avoided during breast feeding, but many women can successfully use the single-hormone mini-pills. These must be taken at the same time every day, and without any break during the month. They are not quite as reliable as the combined pill, with a failure rate of 3% to 5%, and once you finish breast feeding it is wise to use the combined pill instead.

While you are feeding and on the mini-pill, you will probably have no periods, or scanty, irregular periods.

Q I have developed dense freckles on my forehead since starting the contraceptive pill. Is this a side effect?

A The side effects of the contraceptive pill are generally those of pregnancy. When you fall pregnant, the pigment cells in your skin are activated by the hormone changes, and you develop darkened nipples and often freckles and a 'pregnancy mask' of pigment on the forehead and cheeks. This is given the technical name of chloasma. The pill is probably responsible for your pigmentation, and it is for you to decide if this is an acceptable side effect or not. Your doctor may be able to prescribe different doses and types of pill in order to minimise the chloasma, but some women find it so cosmetically embarrassing that they prefer to use other methods of contraception.

Q Why do I have to go to the doctor just to get my birth control pill prescription? I have to pay for a doctor's visit as well as for the pills.

A The birth control pill is a medication which can only be obtained with a doctor's prescription. The doctor will use the consultation to make sure that you are healthy and that there are no untoward effects from taking this medication on a long-term basis.

At yearly consultations, your doctor may take your blood pressure, do a Pap smear, and internal and breast examination, enquire about your general health, and counsel you about possible problems such as obesity, smoking, alcohol, stress, family and sexual problems. In this way the doctor is practising preventive medicine, and you are getting value for your money.

Q I am allergic to the birth control pill—I get headaches and pimples, and gain weight. My doctor won't give me an IUD because he says that at 17, I am too young, and all the other birth control methods are messy and yucky. What can I do?

A Every contraceptive differs in its effectiveness, risks, side-effects and acceptability to the couple. I doubt that you are truly 'allergic' to the pill, as headaches, acne and weight gain are side effects which you may be able to avoid by changing the type of pill you are taking.

Most doctors are reluctant to use an IUD with a young patient who has never borne a child, but may wish to do so in the future.

The barrier methods (condoms and diaphragms) and spermicidal creams have few adverse side effects, and some positive benefits such as partial protection against venereal diseases, but are not as effective in preventing pregnancy. You should visit your doctor and make your choice of contraception with all the information available to you. Your partner may wish to be involved in this discussion also.

Q　**I had sex with a boy when I was drunk six weeks ago. I didn't really know what I was doing at the time, and I didn't take any precautions, and I don't think he did either. As a result, I spent three weeks desperately waiting for my period, and was scared witless until it arrived. When I told my girlfriend why I was so worried, she told me I could have had a pill to stop me getting pregnant after sex. Please tell other girls about this magic pill, so they will not get pregnant or worry the way I did.**

A　The 'morning-after pill' is by no means the ideal method of contraception, and it is far better to use a contraceptive before (eg. oral contraceptive pill) or during (eg. condom) sex, than afterwards.

Doctors can prescribe pills that can be taken up to 72 hours after sex, to prevent pregnancy. They do not always succeed in preventing pregnancy, and they work far better if taken as soon as possible after sex. In most cases, some form of irregular vaginal bleeding, or an abnormal period follows taking these pills.

Men do not get pregnant, and as a result, there is little pressure for them to use a contraceptive. Any woman who is sexually active is far better off being prepared to prevent pregnancy than desperately seeking out a doctor to prescribe a 'morning-after pill'. Women who carry condoms in their purse are not 'fast', just sensible and cautious.

Q　**I am 23, and I am absolutely decided that I never want to have children. Why can't I have my tubes tied? I feel that I should have the right to choose. If I do change my mind, can't they be joined up again?**

A　I doubt that you will find a surgeon who will agree to perform a sterilisation operation at your age. You may be very sure at 23 that you never want children, but experience has shown that you are very likely to change your mind at 30.

The operation to 'tie your tubes' is quite a simple one, but the microsurgery required to reverse this procedure is much more difficult, time-consuming and costly, and has a limited success rate. My advice would be to use another form of contraception until later in life, and then, only undertake a tubal ligation operation with the expectation that it is a permanent, irreversible procedure.

Q　**Why do so many women need a hysterectomy after a tubal ligation? I am considering having my tubes tied, but I don't want a hysterectomy, as I am only 33 years old. What should I do?**

A　Before a tubal ligation, the vast majority of women are taking the oral contraceptive. This pill regulates periods so that they are not heavy, not painful and very predictable. If the pill is stopped, the periods will return to the way they would have been if the pill had never been taken.

This sudden change can be a shock to the system because the periods may become irregular, heavy and painful. The solution to this is to start the pill again, use other hormones on a regular basis, put up with the problem or have a hysterectomy.

The high hysterectomy rate after tubal ligation is therefore not due to the operation but due to the cessation of the previous form of contraception. Hysterectomies in this situation may not be medically essential, but they can certainly improve the quality and style of life for a woman who has no intention of having further children and who may be house (or even bed) bound every few weeks by her menstrual cycle.

Q   I am scared stiff of having a vasectomy! Does it affect your masculinity? What happens to the hormones and sperm?

A   Most men are very anxious about the procedure of sterilisation, as they are not sure what happens and are concerned that it may affect their libido or masculinity. This is not so.

The male hormones which establish and maintain masculinity are produced in the testicles. These are not affected in any way by the operation as they enter the bloodstream directly from the testes and continue to function normally.

The man's ejaculation is not affected either, as the seminal (sperm nourishing) fluid from the sperm storage sac in the groin is passed as normal.

The sperm continue to be produced in the testes, but as they cannot pass down the sperm tube, these microscopic particles die and are absorbed into the body without causing any problems.

A man is not sterile immediately after the operation. Because sperm are stored in the sac above where the tube is tied, this must be emptied by about a dozen ejaculations over the next few weeks.

Q   Are there any long-term side effects from a vasectomy. Is it a safe option considering recent research?

A   A vasectomy is a very safe and effective form of permanent contraception. There are operations to reverse the operation, but success (as measured by a subsequent pregnancy in a partner) is only about 60%. Long term consequences are few and rare. A small number of men have experienced inflammation of a testicle due to a reaction against their own retained sperm, but the vast majority of men have no problems once the immediate effects of the operation have settled, and continue on with their sex life as normal.

The operation does not stop ejaculation, just removes sperm from the semen that is ejaculated. Erections, libido and hormone production are also unaffected.

Q   My wife wants me to have a vasectomy, and I think it is probably a good idea, but I would like to know a bit about what happens during this operation.

A   Sperm are produced by the testes throughout adult life at a relatively constant rate. The sperm enter a complex network of small tubules which unite to form the sperm tube (vas deferens). The sperm pass along this tube to a storage sac (the seminal vesicle) where they await the next ejaculation.

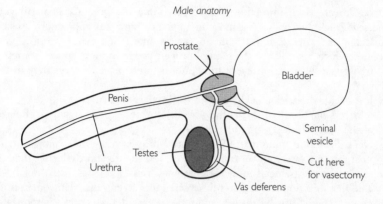

Male anatomy

The walls of the sperm storage sac secrete a fluid which nourishes the sperm, and along with an exudate from the prostate gland, forms 95% of the semen passed by the man during intercourse.

When he ejaculates, the sperm and supporting fluid (called semen when combined) pass down the sperm tube to its junction with the urethra, and then along this tube to the outside of the penis.

In the operation, a local anaesthetic numbs the side of the scrotum, and through a small incision, the doctor cuts, burns and ties the sperm tube (vas deferens) so no further sperm can pass along it from the testes. This may be done in the doctor's rooms, or as a day patient in a private hospital.

The procedure is very simple and brief, and no pain is felt. There may be some bruising and discomfort of the scrotum for a few days after the operation, but other complications are rare.

The operation should be considered to be a form of permanent sterilisation, and although reversal is sometimes possible, you should not proceed unless you are completely sure that this is what you want.

Q My GP is insisting that I have a sperm test after my vasectomy a couple of months ago. I find this very embarrassing, and do not really want to do it. Is it essential?

A The purpose of a semen test is to determine the health of a man's sperm. After a vasectomy, there should be no sperm present, and this proves that the operation was a success.

To perform the test the man must ejaculate a sperm sample into a sterile container, which is sent to a laboratory and examined to establish the number of sperm (if any) present. The semen sample must reach the laboratory as soon as possible after ejaculation.

It is essential, because it is the only way of confirming the success of the vasectomy. If one of the sperm tubes was duplicated and missed by the doctor during the operation, you may still be passing sperm to your partner during sex, and pregnancy could still occur.

Q I have heard that there is now an injection that you can have every few months instead of the pill that will stop you falling pregnant. Can you tell me about this please? Is it effective and safe?

A   Depo-Provera is an injectable contraceptive that has been used for 30 years overseas (including New Zealand and England), and was approved for use in Australia several years ago. It contains a hormone called medroxyprogesterone acetate, which is similar to the natural progesterone produced in the ovaries.

It is given by injection every three months and prevents pregnancy in two ways:
- It prevents the release of the egg from the ovary (ovulation)
- It affects the lining of the womb (uterus) and the type of mucus at the neck of the womb (cervix) to reduce fertility.

Depo-Provera is more than 99% effective in preventing pregnancy, which is comparable to a vasectomy or tubal ligation, and slightly more effective than the contraceptive pill (which can be forgotten at a vital time).

The first injection is given at a time when it is certain that the woman is not pregnant. This is usually during or immediately after a period, or soon after childbirth. The first injection will be fully effective after two weeks, and will last at least three months from the date of injection. Provided they are given regularly every three months, subsequent injections are fully effective immediately.

As with all medications there may be side effects. Many women find that their usual cycle of menstrual periods is altered by Depo-Provera, and periods often stop altogether. Other possibilities include having irregular light periods, or occasionally, constant light bleeding. Heavy bleeding rarely occurs.

Less common side effects include headaches and a prolonged delay in fertility. Rarer side effects include weight gain (usually under 2.5 kg), anxiety, acne and breast tenderness. Additional medication can be given to counteract these side effects while the injection wears off, but if any significant side effects occur, the injection is not repeated and another form of contraception must be used.

Depo-Provera may be used safely during breast feeding without affecting the baby or the mother's milk supply.

Women should be aware that the ability to fall pregnant may be delayed after using Depo-Provera by up to six months after the last injection was given. Occasionally this extends to 15 months, and very rarely up to two years.

COSMETIC and PLASTIC SURGERY

Q   **My nose looks as though it should belong on a moose rather than a human. Can it be improved by plastic surgery?**

A   You should be discussing with your general practitioner the pros and cons of plastic surgery to correct this problem. Your GP can refer you to a plastic or ear, nose and throat surgeon, and he or she will assess your face, and its problems, before explaining to you what can and cannot be done to improve your appearance.

Prominent noses with a bulb at the end, or a hump on the bridge, can be corrected by surgery that leaves no scar on the outside of your face. The entire operation is done under general anaesthetic, on the inside of the nose, with the surgeon operating through the nostrils.

Noses that are too small can also be enlarged in the same way. You will wake up with a plaster on your nose, and some bandaging around your face, but this is soon removed, and after the post-operative swelling subsides, a new-nosed you will emerge.

Q **I am very conscious of a slightly large nose and am considering plastic surgery to make it smaller. How do I go about getting in contact with a good plastic surgeon, and could you give me a rough estimate of its cost as I'm not in a private health fund?**

A Both plastic surgeons and ear, nose and throat surgeons perform operations to reduce the size, or change the shape, of noses that do not suit their owners.

The operation takes about 40 minutes, and you are in hospital for only one or two days. You feel as though a horse has kicked your nose when you wake up, and it becomes quite swollen and bruised, but after a couple of weeks, it settles down, and in a month you can proudly show your new nose in public without your best friends really knowing just why you look that little bit different.

The best person to recommend a good surgeon is your own general practitioner. S/he will be aware of the specialists in your area, and will have seen examples of their work. Using GPs to obtain referrals is an excellent way of maintaining high standards, as any specialist who does the wrong thing by a GP's patients, gets no more referrals.

Medical fees (including surgeon, assistant and anaesthetist) will vary significantly, depending on what is done, and how, but should range between $1500 and $2500. Part of these fees will be refunded under Medicare. The hospital charges will also fluctuate from one place to another, but will probably be in the $1000 to $2000 range.

Q **I am 16 years old and very embarrassed because my ears stick straight out and when I look in the mirror, they even show through my long hair that I have grown to hide them. Boys tease me about them, and call me 'Elephant' because they say I look like Dumbo. Can these be fixed?**

A Dumbo, the flying elephant, was a very gentle and kind elephant (as I recall from my childhood comics), and so you can take the jibes and jests as an indirect compliment. If you have the right attitude, a lot of the teasing will stop.

Prominent ears can cause children, teenagers and adults to be teased endlessly. If you really feel that the ears are causing you too much distress, then an operation to help pin back the bat ears can be done. Most children do not want to proceed until they are in their teen years, but then, the operation can give them new confidence that everyone is not going to stare at them and call them names.

In this procedure, a wedge of skin and tissue is excised from behind the ear, and the tissue is then sewn down again. It is a relatively simple and quick procedure for a plastic surgeon, and as recovery takes only a couple of weeks, can easily be fitted into a school holiday. The complications of these operations are uncommon, and usually involve either bruising or infection, which can be corrected by further treatment.

Anyone concerned about plastic surgery should not hesitate to discuss the matter further with a sympathetic general practitioner.

Q **Concerning cosmetic treatment for surface veins performed by a specialist—is a coagulant used, and if so, can there be any problems with blood clots following this treatment?**

A The spider webs of surface blood vessels that often appear on a woman's thighs and calves during and after childbirth, can be removed by an injection into the vein.

What is injected into the vein is not a coagulant but a sclerosant. This irritates the lining of the vein, and causes it to shrink down and its walls to stick together. The sclerosant injection is not a glue, but acts in much the same way as a small glob of glue, and completely blocks the blood vessel, thus preventing the entry of blood, and its disappearance.

After the injection, the leg is usually firmly strapped to collapse the veins, and may remain so for some weeks. There is no higher risk of blood clots from this type of operation than any other surgery of similar complexity.

These injections are only suitable for small veins, and do not work on the large, bulging varicose veins.

Q **I have a scar around the nipple after breast enlargement surgery eight years ago. Can laser surgery remove this scar in the same way as they remove tattoos?**

A When a laser is used to remove a tattoo, it acts to burn the skin. Applying a hot iron to a tattoo would have the same effect. A scar results as a result of the burn, and destroys, distorts or disguises the tattoo. Lasers must therefore be very carefully used in the treatment of tattoos or any other skin condition.

A scar around the nipple would not be appropriately dealt with by use of a laser. Plastic surgeons can almost certainly deal with the problem by re-excising the scar, and carefully repairing the wound, or by using creams on, or injections into the scar.

Discuss the matter further with your GP, and arrange for a referral to a plastic surgeon.

Q **I am curious about liposuction. Does it leave noticeable scars? After fat is removed from your thighs, does the skin sag down around your knees? Any information would be appreciated.**

A In liposuction, the plastic surgeon will inject the fatty area with a substance to partly dissolve the fat and reduce bleeding, and then through a several one-centimetre long cuts, will insert a sucker to remove some (but not all) of the excess fat.

The only scars will be those at the point where the sucker was introduced, but there may be uneven dimpling and tethering of the skin if too much fat is removed from one area.

The skin is elastic, and will shrink down to fit tightly over the tissue, but again this is provided not too much fat is removed. The older you are, the less elastic the skin, and some older people may have some skin sagging that can be corrected by further surgery.

Liposuction will not change your shape dramatically, but may reduce your thigh circumference by two to four centimetres at most.

Q **How safe is the removal of fat around the stomach by liposuction? Does the fat grow again after a while?**

A There are possible complications with any surgery, and the most common ones with liposuction are severe bruising and infection, while the most severe one is the uncommon risk of having a fat embolism which may affect the heart or brain. Generally, this commonly performed procedure is quite safe, but you should discuss the pros and cons with the plastic surgeon who will perform the procedure.

Normally, while under a general anaesthetic, a solution is injected under the skin to dissolve the fat, and then probes are inserted to suck out the slurry of solution and dissolved fat. A new technique using an ultrasound probe to break up the fat before it is sucked out from under the skin seems to increase the amount of fat removed and decrease the side effects of the operation.

Because the fat cells are removed during the operation, the fat will only grow back if you continue to eat excessively or exercise inadequately. A change of lifestyle should precede the operation.

Many patients find that they have excessive skin folds left behind after the fat is removed, and these may need to be removed during a further operation a couple of months later.

Q **After a number of prominent women have made the foray into plastic surgery, I too am thinking of having a facelift. What is involved?**

A From the outset let me state that a face lift will not make you look like your son or daughter, let alone your favourite television star, but it will significantly soften the wrinkles on your face, particularly those under the eyes, and will remove double chins and other sagging tissue.

The first step is to discuss the matter with your general practitioner. He or she will assess the situation sympathetically, and unless there is a medical reason for you not to proceed, will refer you on to a plastic surgeon. The plastic surgeon will carefully assess your face and probably take photos before explaining what can and cannot be done.

If you decide to proceed, a hospital booking will be made, and you are usually admitted the day before for assessment by the anaesthetist.

Under the general anaesthetic, the surgeon will make incisions in front of the ears, then behind the hairline above your ear, across the top of the forehead and down the other side. Through this he or she will gently lift the skin off your face and forehead, remove excess amounts of fat under the skin, tighten up the skin itself, then sew up the long incision very finely so that it cannot be seen. Separate incisions may be made under the eyes and under the chin to tighten up the tissue in those areas. The face is then firmly bandaged, and when you awake you may be blindfolded for a day or two.

The skin on the face will feel tight and sore, and when the bandages first come off it will look bruised, but after a few weeks the new you will emerge.

Q **I have heard that you can have a face lift by laser beam. Could you tell me how this is done, the cost, and the address of a surgeon who can do it?**

A Lasers are not a new miracle that allow face lifts (or hysterectomies and other operations) to be performed without an anaesthetic or leaving a scar, they are merely another useful tool in a surgeon's vast range of instruments. Almost any operation from an appendectomy up can be performed with the assistance of a laser scalpel. A fine laser beam replaces the scalpel, usually in cutting through certain types of tissue only. It has the advantage of preventing bleeding from small arteries as it heat-seals them at the same time that it cuts the tissue. The lasers themselves are very expensive, and because they only offer a slight advantage, they are only being used by a small number of surgeons, and normally for operations on areas where access is difficult and bleeding likely.

All plastic surgeons perform facelifts, and some of them will use lasers, but the main beneficiary of the laser is usually the surgeon rather than the patient, as it may make his task a little easier.

Part of the surgeon's, anaesthetist's and assistant's fees may be reimbursed by Medicare in some circumstances. Often the hospital costs will not be covered by a private health insurance fund, even if you have been a member for a number of years, as cosmetic surgery is not considered essential. The actual cost will vary between one doctor and hospital and another, so the best idea is to see the surgeon for a discussion about the procedure, and a quote. Treat it the same way as any other major purchase, and consider your options carefully.

I am not in a position to recommend any particular surgeon or doctor to anyone. The best person to approach for advice is your own general practitioner who can advise you with regard to the plastic surgeons in your area. I would strongly recommend that you use a plastic surgeon (who will have FRACS after his/her name) rather than a cosmetic surgeon.

Q At the age of 60 I have developed drooping cheeks. Can anything be done to prevent further drooping by massage or medicated creams?

A Unfortunately there are no proven rejuvenating creams or youth pills available, but there are a lot of these advertised, usually at high prices, and they often advise prolonged courses of treatment. Buyer beware.

On the other hand, there are some relatively simple surgical procedures available that will correct drooping cheeks, and droops in other parts of your anatomy.

Discuss the matter with your general practitioner, who will be able to give you an idea of the type of plastic surgery that you will need, and the costs, because a lot of these procedures are not covered by Medicare or private health insurance.

You can then be referred to a recognised plastic surgeon, who will give you greater information, show you before and after photos of other patients, and explain the risks of the surgery. If you are told there are no risks, again beware.

Consultations with plastic surgeons are rebated by Medicare, and you are under no obligation to proceed unless you wish to. Most procedures require only one or two nights in hospital, and many are done as day surgery cases.

You will never find out what can be done to help your appearance unless you ask.

Q I have a small tattoo on my wrist that I would like to have removed. Could you please tell me the methods available, and whom I should contact to have it done?

A   A small tattoo is probably best removed by cutting it out (excision). This is done in the same way as cutting out a mole, and may be performed by your general practitioner or a plastic surgeon. Tattoos up to 2 cm across can be removed this way, but the maximum size will depend where on your body the tattoo has been placed, and its shape. Obviously, a larger tattoo can be cut out from the back than the face, and a long thin tattoo is easier than a round one.

Larger tattoos may be excised in two or three stages. After each excision heals, another area can be removed.

This technique involves a local anaesthetic injection, then the tattoo is cut away without any pain, and the resulting wound is stitched. The result will be a long, thin scar, about twice as long as the tattoo is wide.

For larger, or extensive tattoos, you should be referred by your general practitioner to a plastic surgeon or dermatologist who specialises in this type of problem. There are a number of techniques that they can use, including laser burning of the tattoo, or dermabrasion (simply grinding away the tattoo). Both these techniques leave scars, but the new Q-switched lasers being used by some dermatologists seem to be very effective.

There is no way of returning your skin to its pristine natural state.

Q   **My husband would dearly love to get rid of his tattoos, that he now deeply regrets having done whilst in his teens. Surely with all this modern technology and medical advancement there must be something?**

A   Unfortunately, there are no easy solutions to removing tattoos. Lasers, acids, bleaching, deep abrasion, and surgical excision can all be tried, but all will leave some scarring. Special Q-switched lasers are the best treatment developed so far. The more experienced the doctor in these procedures, the better the result is likely to be. There are a number of plastic surgeons and dermatologists around who do this type of work, and therefore a specialist, recommended by your own GP, is your best bet. Do not expect miracles, and be prepared for a long series of procedures.

The best solution to this problem is probably tighter control of tattoo parlours. Possibly a cooling off period of two weeks after deciding to get a tattoo done, before the procedure is performed, would be one way of stopping the impetuous from disfiguring themselves for life. A large percentage of those who do get tattooed regret the decision and find that it damages their employment, promotion and social prospects.

Q   **How do plastic surgeons get rid of lines on your face with injections? I saw a show on TV about this. Can it be done in Australia?**

A   A heavily lined, wrinkled, sunken face can be considerably fleshed out and smoothed by injecting very small amounts of collagen under the skin in the appropriate places.

Initially, the face will be swollen and bruised, but after a few weeks, this will subside, and a smoother less wrinkled face should emerge.

Many plastic surgeons in Australia are now performing this procedure, but it is not suitable for all patients.

Those with sagging excess skin, or too much fat in their face, are still better helped by the traditional surgical facelift. Sometimes surgery and injections are combined to give the best result.

You should ask your GP for a referral to a plastic surgeon, and you can discuss the matter further with him or her.

DEPRESSION

Q I have depression, and it is taking years to clear up. What is this illness, what can be done for them, and what is the long term prognosis?

A There are many different types of depression. Some forms are a reaction to stresses in your life such as loss of a job or a death in the family, while others are caused by biochemical imbalances in the brain that occur for no apparent reason. Sometimes it can last for just a few weeks, while in others it may recur, or persist for years.

Psychiatrists will attempt to determine the type of depression that is affecting you before starting any treatment, but this is often very difficult, as there are no blood or other tests that can help the doctor, and s/he must depend on his/her clinical skills.

Once the diagnosis is made, the correct treatment will be started. This will usually involve the use of one or more medications, counselling, psychotherapy, and occasionally shock treatment.

There are some cases that can be cured, but others may only have their depression controlled. There are many diseases that cannot be cured, but are effectively controlled, and good examples would be diabetes and high blood pressure, where medication must be used life long.

Provided the patient is prepared to carefully follow a doctor's advice, the majority of cases of depression can be cured or controlled, so that the patient can lead a normal life with minimal side effects from the treatment. Only in cases where there is poor compliance with treatment, poor family support or other adverse factors does the patient face a life of continued depression and risk suicide.

Q Can depression be caused by an incorrect balance of the hormones I am taking for my menopause?

A Depression is a common problem in women who are passing through the menopause, and can become extremely distressing to both the woman and her family.

Hormone replacement therapy is designed to do what its name implies—replace the hormones that are lost during the menopause, and therefore prevent the complications of the menopause.

During menopause women suffer from hot flushes, irregular menstruation, breast tenderness and loss of libido as well as depression. The lack of female hormones after the menopause leads to an increase in the incidence of osteoporosis, heart attacks and strokes.

Every woman's hormonal balance is different, and sometimes it takes a considerable time, and numerous changes in both the hormone form and dosage to get just the right balance for a particular woman.

If depression is a continuing problem, it may be that the hormone replacement therapy you are taking is not quite the right balance for you, or you may require some specific anti-depressant medication. Write down exactly how you feel regarding your depression, and how the menopause is affecting you, and take the list to your general practitioner to discuss it further. Almost certainly, you will be able to receive further assistance with your problems.

Q What is the best treatment for depression? Should I keep taking drugs all the time?

A Depression may be due to an imbalance of chemicals that normally occur in the brain to control mood, and it is necessary for doctors to alter this balance, by giving medications that can control the production or activity of the depressing chemicals.

The worst problem with untreated depression is suicide, and this can be seen as a desperate plea for help in many people. The disease may not be detected or treated until a radical attempt to end life has occurred.

Medication and counselling by a general practitioner or psychiatrist will control the vast majority of cases.

The other form of treatment used is shock therapy. This has been surrounded by some controversy in the past, but is a very safe and often very effective method of giving relief to patients with severe chronic depression.

Q A week ago I saw a doctor to get some sleeping pills, and I ended up telling him off and walking out. I'm in the middle of a breakdown and can't sleep or eat. I'm tired out, stressed and fed up. I hate my housing commission flat, and feel I can't keep going any more. I need help.

A You may not be sleeping because you are depressed, and it is always better to treat the cause of the problem (the depression) rather than the effect (the lack of sleep). Your doctor may have tried to do this, but if you are unable to trust or communicate with your doctor, it is time to change to a doctor with whom you can develop a good rapport.

Treatment of your problem will involve a long discussion about the concerns that are affecting your lifestyle, and probably some medication to help you control your depression and prevent your 'breakdown' worsening. This medication will usually allow you to sleep better as well, but may take a week or two to work effectively.

Sleeping tablets only cover up the underlying problem, may be addictive, and can worsen the depression. There is no doubt that you do need assistance with your condition, and a GP who is sympathetic but firm about the correct form of treatment will be to your benefit in the long run.

Q What are the side effects of medicines used to treat depression? I am taking one called Cipramil, but I am told Efexor is better.

A Both Cipramil and Efexor are excellent medications for the treatment of depression, but they come from different classes of drugs, and so have different side effects. If you find that the medication you are taking is helping and has minimal side effects, then follow the old saying of 'When you are on a good thing, stick to it'. If you are having problems with your medication then discuss the matter with your GP, who may decide to change the dose or try a different medication.

Cipramil is in a class of antidepressants known as SSRI (selective serotonin reuptake inhibitors). The dosage can vary from 10 mg to 60 mg once a day. It should be used with caution in pregnancy, breast feeding and children, heart disease, mania and liver disease. Otherwise it is a very safe drug, but when you decide to stop the drug, you should reduce the dose slowly—do not stop suddenly.

Common side effects include nausea, diarrhoea, tiredness, dry mouth, and impotence, but these usually wear off as the medication is continued, so a trial lasting at least two weeks is the minimum. Unusual side effects include sweating, loss of appetite, tremor, agitation, watery nose, and a low libido.

Introduced in 1998 as a further advance within an excellent class of drugs that are very effective in treating depression. It is claimed to have a faster effect and fewer side effects than other SSRI antidepressants.

Efexor was introduced in 1997 for the management of more difficult cases of depression. Dosage varies from 37.5 mg to 75 mg twice a day, but the dose must be increased slowly. It must be used with caution in pregnancy, breast feeding and children, epilepsy, other psychiatric conditions, liver, high blood pressure, and kidney diseases. Once again, you should not stop the medication suddenly, but reduce the dose slowly.

Common side effects include dizziness, sleeplessness, nervousness, nausea, diarrhoea, and a dry mouth. Unusual side effects are tiredness, vomiting, excess sweating, impotence, and high blood pressure.

Please remember that all antidepressants are slow to work, and it may be two or three weeks before any improvement in mood is felt.

DIABETES

Q I have a bad family history of late onset diabetes. How can this be detected? Would a routine blood test for cholesterol find it? Are there any lifestyle changes I can make to prevent it? What are the early symptoms?

A Late onset (type 2, or maturity onset) diabetes is a totally different disease to juvenile (type 1) diabetes. The former can be controlled by diet and tablets, while the latter requires regular insulin injections. There is a family tendency to develop type 2 diabetes, but it is not inevitable that you will develop it just because close relatives have the condition.

Diabetes is diagnosed by a simple blood test for the presence of excess sugar, but a test for cholesterol will not reveal the presence of sugar and diabetes.

You can delay, or prevent the onset of this form of diabetes by reducing the amount of sugar and fat in your diet, and by keeping your weight within normal limits.

The early symptoms are excessive thirst, passing more urine than usual, tiredness, blurred vision and frequent skin infections. If you are concerned that you may develop type 2 diabetes in the near future, your general practitioner can arrange for a glucose tolerance test (GTT) to be performed by a pathology laboratory. This test takes a couple of hours to perform, and can tell more accurately if you have diabetes, and sometimes it can predict if you are likely to develop the condition in the near future.

Q What is the difference between the diabetes children get and that suffered by oldies like me?

A   There are two very distinct types of diabetes—juvenile (type one) diabetes and maturity onset (type 2) diabetes. The juvenile form may develop at any time from birth to the thirties, but the most common is between 10 and 20 years of age. Maturity type can start at any time from the thirties onwards, particularly in obese people, but is more common over 60. Juvenile diabetes is more severe and harder to control. It almost invariably requires injections of insulin once or twice a day for the rest of the patient's life, as well as a strict diet.

In the mature form, diet and weight loss alone are often sufficient to control the problem, but some sufferers require tablets to be taken regularly, and a small number need insulin injections.

Diabetes is caused by either the failure of the pancreas gland in the centre of the abdomen to produce insulin, or a reduced sensitivity of the cells in the body to insulin. The former tends to be the cause in the juvenile form, and the latter in the mature.

Insulin is essential for cells to take sugar out of the blood and into the cell, and without it, excess amounts of sugar build up in the blood and the cells are starved of a vital energy source.

Q   **What is the best blood sugar reading for someone with diabetes?**

A   Blood glucose tests are used to diagnose hyperglycaemia and hypoglycaemia (too much or too little sugar in the bloodstream), which may be associated with diabetes.

Diabetics must regularly measure their blood glucose levels, and should aim to keep them at a fasting level below 8 mmol/L and above 3.5 mmol/L. A level over 10 is considered to be dangerous, and below 3.5 there is a risk of having a 'hypo' due to excessive medication lowering the level too much.

A very sneaky test that measures the amount of a type of glucose present in red blood cells (glycated haemoglobin) can be used to give an average blood glucose level over a period of three months. This should give an average reading of between 5 and 7 to be perfect. A level over 9 is quite dangerous.

Q   **I have been suffering from type 2 diabetes, and have recently developed numb feet, and pains down the arteries of the leg. Could you explain what effect diabetes has on circulation, and what sort of specialist should I see?**

A   There are two main types of diabetes—type 1 diabetes which usually affects younger people and requires insulin injections for control, and type 2 diabetes which is far more common, usually affects the elderly, and is normally controlled by diet and tablets.

Both types of diabetes can affect the small blood vessels (capillaries) and restrict the flow of blood. The most commonly involved small blood vessels are in the feet and eyes. In patients with inadequately controlled diabetes, poor circulation to the feet may cause numbness, redness, sores that won't heal, and finally gangrene. In the eye, deteriorating vision is caused by poor circulation.

If the diabetes is well controlled, it is far less likely for these complications to occur.

Control of diabetes involves regular medication, a careful diet, checking the blood or urine levels of sugar, and checking with the general practitioner or specialist.

If a GP detects any problems that are significant, s/he will refer you to an endocrinologist (gland specialist). Some endocrinologists are super specialists, and treat only patients with diabetes.

Q   I am a diabetic and have an ulcer on my ankle that my own general practitioner can't fix.

A   Ulcers on the legs of diabetics are notoriously hard to heal, and may take months even with the best care.

The most important part of the treatment is good control of the diabetes by both diet and medication. Once this is achieved, the ulcer may heal without any further treatment.

If additional treatment is necessary, the doctor must examine the ulcer carefully to see if it is moist or dry, what type of edge it has, what sort of base it has, and what the skin around it is like. Once these factors have been assessed, an appropriate dressing can be chosen, and applied regularly for several weeks.

As a last resort, a skin graft may be necessary to heal the ulcer.

Please persist with the treatment being given by your own general practitioner.

Q   What is the best artificial sweetener for someone with type 2 maturity onset diabetes?

A   There is no best or worse in this situation, as any product that is labelled as an artificial sweetener is safe for diabetics to use. Different artificial sweeteners are added to numerous diet products (eg. Diet Coke), but you can purchase these products for your own use in cooking or adding to tea, coffee etc. Examples include Equal, Lite & Low and Nutra-Sweet and dozens of other brands.

Q   I am a 57 year old diabetic and have been told that I have autonomic neuropathy. I hate summer, as I can't bear direct sunlight, and over the past few years I have stopped sweating completely. I take Diamicron for my diabetes. Can you help me with my problem?

A   One of the complications of diabetes is the blocking of fine arteries. This may result in problems as diverse as gangrene of a toe to blindness.

If the tiny arteries supplying the nerves become blocked, that nerve does not receive the oxygen and nutrition it needs, and dies.

The autonomic nervous system performs most of the subconscious automatic tasks required by the body, including telling the sweat glands when to operate.

Neuropathy is a term that merely means nerve damage.

Your autonomic neuropathy is thus damage to the autonomic nervous system caused by diabetes, and because these nerves have died and cannot send the appropriate signals, you cannot sweat.

This will make it very difficult for your body to maintain its correct temperature, and it is vital that you do not become overheated. Cool baths or showers, and an air-conditioned room in summer, would be appropriate.

You must keep your diabetes under careful control by taking your medication (Diamicron is one of a number of excellent drugs used to control diabetes in older people), having regular blood tests, and visiting your doctor when appropriate to prevent any further damage to your body.

Q My third child was born ten days ago, and she was a whopper, weighing just over ten pounds. My obstetrician now wants me to have a special test for diabetes, because he said the baby was too big. Do women with big babies always have diabetes?

A If you have a baby that weighs more than 4.5 kg (10 lb) it is possible that you suffer from diabetes, but non-diabetics may also have big babies. After you deliver a heavy baby, doctors will routinely perform a test (the glucose tolerance test) to determine whether you have diabetes or are likely to develop the disease.

 If this test is negative, you have nothing to be worried about. If it is positive, it may only be the stress of pregnancy that has induced a temporary form of diabetes, or you may develop diabetes later in life. This form of diabetes can be very well controlled.

 Large babies also run in families, so there may be no connection with diabetes at all.

DIET
See also CHOLESTEROL; DIABETES; OBESITY

Q What is a bland diet, and when is it used?

A A bland diet consists of vegetables cooked without any sauces or spices, fish, chicken breast (no skin), most forms of cereal (eg. bread, cornflakes), and fruit taken in moderation. Fatty, fried and dairy foods should be avoided.

 This sort of diet is used to settle the bowel in many conditions, but particularly in chronic diarrhoea.

Q What foods cause gout?

A Gout is caused by the inefficient disposal of certain types of food wastes through the kidneys.

 No particular foods actually cause gout, but once you develop the disease, certain foods should be avoided to prevent excess levels of uric acid (the waste product that causes the disease) from building up. These foods include beer, liver, kidneys, sweetbreads, herring, sardines, anchovies, meat extracts, turkey, prawns and shellfish. Unfortunately, this means the end of beer and prawn nights for gout sufferers!

 Otherwise you should eat normally, but don't eat excessive amounts of fatty foods.

Q I enjoy my food, but I don't enjoy the after effects. Just because I love chili with garlic, followed by a chocolate torte smothered in cream, and washed down with a sweet bubbly wine, I don't see why I should then proceed to burp for the rest of the night. How can I help myself?

A A change in diet would obviously be the answer, and if you eat the above foods regularly, you must look like a blimp!

 An increase in fibre in the diet, and a decrease in processed foods will help the situation, but all of us over indulge, or eat inappropriate combinations of foods at different times, and suffer the consequences of stomach pain, belching, nausea and flatus (farts). The problem can be aggravated by nervous swallowing when under stress, swallowing air when eating quickly, and any fizzy drink from champagne to Coca-Cola.

A wide range of medications to relieve excess stomach gas are available. The simpler ones available without prescription from chemists contain substances such as simethicone (which breaks up the bubbles of gas), peppermint oil and charcoal. Simethicone can also be used to relieve wind in babies.

If these do not work, doctors can prescribe drugs to prevent the gut spasms, and reduce the production of gas.

Q My son eats only junk food, and is getting fat, covered in pimples and lazy. How can I stop him eating junk and start him on good foods?

A Fried chips. Licorice. Soft drinks. Tinned fruit. Popcorn. Sweets. Cream buns. Doughnuts. These are certainly fun foods, but they are not very nutritious or healthy.

A child's diet can be a constant concern to many parents, particularly if that child is a fussy eater and refuses to eat anything except hot dogs, chips and Coca-Cola.

Unfortunately, these problems are more a matter of appropriate behavioural management and discipline by the parent than a gastronomic necessity. If a child is given healthy fun foods from an early age, plus the occasional supervised dosage of 'junk' food, good eating habits can be readily established. If 'junk' foods are totally banned, they can become even more desirable than if they are special treats given occasionally. It is important to get just the right balance between 'good' and 'bad'.

Q How can I tell which dietary information is correct? If you read all the information in the paper and some magazines, it seems to be repetitive or contradictory. As a result I am very confused. Your opinion would be appreciated.

A It is easier to tell which information is incorrect, rather than which is correct. If the therapist or advisor you are consulting recommends two or more of the following points (ALL OF WHICH ARE INCORRECT)—beware!

• Most disease is due to a faulty diet.
• Most Australians are poorly nourished.
• Chemical fertilisers result in less nourishing food.
• He or she recommends you to buy something you would not otherwise purchase.
• Modern processing and storage remove all nutrition from food.
• Food additives and preservatives will poison you.
• Your need for nutrients increases with stress.
• Vitamins supplements can replace good food.
• You should take enzyme supplements.
• Everybody needs vitamin supplements.
• Natural vitamins are better than synthetic ones.
• Vitamins are never harmful.
• Sugar is poisonous.
• It is easy to lose weight with the (often expensive) plan.

- A quick, dramatic cure is guaranteed.
- Non-vitamins (eg. B15, B17) are recommended.

Q   Would you please provide information on the use of a sensible diet to control hiatus hernia?

A   A hiatus hernia occurs when part of the stomach slips up into the chest cavity. Most patients experience heartburn, indigestion, burping and a bitter taste in the mouth.

No specific foods are absolutely forbidden, as each patient will learn by experience if any particular food worsens their symptoms, and these should obviously be avoided. On the other hand, when it comes to drink, alcohol almost always worsens the symptoms of a hiatus hernia, and it should be drunk only in moderation and with a meal, if at all.

The most important part of a diet for hiatus hernia is not what you eat but how you eat it. Small frequent meals are better than large infrequent ones. You should eat slowly, chew food thoroughly, and sip a drink (non-alcoholic is of course best) after every few mouthfuls. Overfilling the stomach with rapid eating of large meals is almost guaranteed to make any hiatus hernia worse.

Q   I have dry skin. Could it be caused by my diet?

A   The dryness of your skin is determined by the amount of oil produced by the sebaceous glands in the skin. People with dry skin either have fewer oil glands than other people, or their glands produce less oil. In the vast majority of cases, the tendency towards dry skin (or oily skin) is an inherited characteristic, and there is therefore nothing that you can do about it except use moisturising creams.

In a small number of people, and if the skin dryness is a new phenomenon, there may be a skin disease present or some other internal problem (such as an underactive thyroid gland), and a doctor's opinion should be sought. Some people find that the oiliness of their skin changes at puberty, but this is a natural phenomenon.

The only connection between dry skin and diet could occur if you are lacking in vitamin A. This would be very rare in our well-fed society, as this vitamin is found in all fruit and vegetables, particularly those with an orange colour (eg. carrots, pumpkins, mangoes). On the other hand, taking excess vitamin A in the form of pills or large amounts of orange coloured food, can cause skin staining and other damage (eg. brain damage to the foetus in a pregnant woman).

I suspect that you will merely have to blame your parents for your dry skin, and use moisturising creams on a regular basis.

Q   I am elderly, and have a great deal of trouble making ends meet financially. Could I use good quality dog or cat food sometimes to stretch the budget?

A   Pet foods are not manufactured or processed to the same standards as food for human consumption, nor do they have the same nutritional balance. Many of the better pet foods cost as much or more than appropriate human foods. I cannot recommend that you use pet food, but if you are on the pension, you should be able to feed yourself properly with appropriate budgeting.

A social worker at your nearest government health centre or hospital should be able to help you with your budgeting and lifestyle. Some people tend to buy inappropriate food that is expensive because it is over packaged, convenient (eg. TV dinners, take-away foods), preprocessed (eg. frozen pizzas) or advertised frequently. Buying cheaper meats (eg. mince), fresh vegetables and less processed foods may help you to eat well but still keep within your budget.

Q **I am a school canteen convener. Can you suggest some good foods to be offered for children's lunches?**

A School tuck shops should be carefully monitored by the parent committees that run them to ensure that the healthy food available is attractively presented to offer good competition to the professionally packaged alternatives.

A few examples for canteens at school (or work) include:

— potatoes baked in their jackets, cut open and filled with cheese, tomato etc.
— hot rolls with chicken, tomato and pineapple
— attractively made salads with lean meat, cheese, fruit slices and raw vegetables on a paper plate and covered with cling-wrap
— hamburgers (no, they're not all bad) made with cheese, lettuce, tomato and lean mince cooked on a very lightly greased hotplate.

Other simple snacks could include corn cobs, fresh fruit jaffles, soup, frozen bananas, raw carrots and milk shakes. These are fun foods for children that are also nutritious.

Teenagers who have money to spend on food will make their own choices, but these will often follow eating patterns established over the past decade or so. They can be taught that fried foods, tomato sauce, cream and sweets do not have to make up the major part of their diet.

Q **I am always reading that you shouldn't eat one food or another, and should eat more of this and less of that if you want to keep to your ideal weight and stay healthy. Lots of these experts seem to contradict each other. What do you think are the best foods to eat? Are vitamins needed?**

A Put as simply as possible, human beings should eat mostly bread, cereals, vegetables and fruit; eat moderately milk, cheese, yogurt, lean meat, poultry, fish, eggs and legumes; and eat least salt, sugar, butter, margarine, oil and cream.

Food should be taken in three equal-sized meals a day, with occasional snacks between meals if not overweight. Weight should be maintained within the recommended limits for your height and build and toilet habits should be regular. Exercise is also important in maintaining a trim, taut, terrific body.

On a good diet, vitamin and fibre supplements are rarely necessary. Chomp an apple instead!

Q **All sorts of people are telling us what to eat. Some say no meat, some say no milk, some say there are too many poisons on vegetables. Eggs have cholesterol, but lots of vitamins. What should a good diet contain?**

A Humans are omnivores. They are designed to eat and utilise a wide range of foods. A well-balanced diet should contain cereals, vegetables, fruits, red and white meat, dairy products, oils and a small amount of sugar. They are listed in

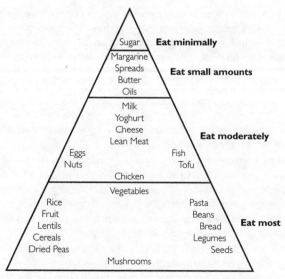

Sugar — **Eat minimally**

Margarine
Spreads — **Eat small amounts**
Butter
Oils

Milk
Yoghurt
Cheese — **Eat moderately**
Lean Meat

Eggs   Fish
Nuts   Tofu

Chicken

Vegetables

Rice   Pasta
Fruit   Beans
Lentils   Bread — **Eat most**
Cereals   Legumes
Dried Peas   Seeds

Mushrooms

Healthy Food Pyramid

order from large quantities required to small, but individual preference will determine actual amounts.

All foods break down into carbohydrates, fats and protein. Virtually all foods contain a mixture of these three basic components, but some foods contain far more of one component than the others.

Fibre is the fourth main constituent of foodstuffs, but this is not absorbed and passes out of the body in the faeces.

Vitamins and minerals are trace chemicals and elements found in varying proportions in different foodstuffs.

Numerous pamphlets and books can give details of the actual content of all foodstuffs. The best advice I can give is not to eat one type of food to the exclusion of others, but to eat sensibly a wide range of foodstuffs that you enjoy.

Q I am 59, of thin build, and still losing weight. My doctor says there is nothing wrong. Should I forget about cholesterol, and go on a diet of fattier foods?

A High cholesterol levels can occur in both fat and thin people, and the chances of developing a high cholesterol level depends as much upon your choice in parents as your choice in diet.

Cholesterol is just one factor contributing to an increased incidence of heart attacks and strokes. The other major factors are your inherited genes, smoking, obesity, and high blood pressure.

I assume that you have had your cholesterol checked by a blood test performed after fasting for 12 hours, and by a doctor (not a shopping centre entrepreneur!). At your age, I would not be concerned about your cholesterol level unless it exceeded 6.0, and unless it exceeded 7.0 I would not recommend any medication. Lower cholesterol levels are far more important in younger men.

If your cholesterol is below 6.0, then start eating dairy foods and fats again. If it is above 6.0, you should continue to avoid fatty foods, but you can build up your weight with carbohydrates (bread, pasta, vegetables, fruit, sugars).

If your weight loss continues, you should have a thorough check up to ensure that there is no other disease present.

Q My daughter is 16 and drinks 4 to 5 cups of medium strength coffee each day. Is this too much caffeine for someone her age?

A Your daughter's consumption is at the upper level of what is considered acceptable for caffeine intake in adults, and at 16 your daughter is virtually at the adult stage. Brewed coffee has higher amounts of caffeine (60 to 130 mg per 100 mL) than instant coffee (40 to 100 mg per 100 mL).

Caffeine is also found in tea and cola drinks. Tea has roughly half the amount of coffee (40 to 60 mg per 100 mL), and cola drinks less than one quarter the amount in coffee (10 mg per 100 mL). Stimulant soft drinks (eg. Red Bull) containing very large amounts of caffeine are also available.

Caffeine acts as a mild stimulant, and may cause your daughter to have difficulty in sleeping if she drinks it within an hour or two of going to bed. In higher doses (I use the word dose deliberately, because caffeine is a drug) it can cause anxiety, nervousness and an increase in the amount of urine produced. It will aggravate peptic ulcers, indigestion and heartburn.

Caffeine is also used in medications to prevent drowsiness and fatigue, ease migraines and help with motion sickness. It is forbidden in sport as it may marginally improve performance, and some athletes who have large amounts of coffee have been disqualified from international competition because of excess caffeine levels.

Provided your daughter is made aware of the problems that may occur with coffee and its caffeine content, and does not exceed her present intake, she is unlikely to come to any significant harm. Maybe she could use decaffeinated coffee sometimes.

DOCTORS

Q What should a patient do if not happy with the treatment given by their doctor?

A The first thing to do is let the doctor concerned know. It may be a little daunting to confront the doctor, but it is to the benefit of both doctor and patient if this occurs. Quite often it is a simple misunderstanding, or the patient may have expected a form of treatment that was not appropriate. If necessary, write down a list of problems to take to the consultation, or if the patient is far too anxious to see the doctor in person, write him/her a letter.

Only as a last resort, if no satisfaction is obtained on a subsequent visit, should the patient approach the Health Complaints Commissioner in their state, as the patient may be left with a completely unwarranted distrust of a doctor, or worse still, all doctors.

Q We have just moved from interstate, where we had a marvellous GP who had looked after the family for the past 23 years. What is the best way

to choose a good general practitioner to look after us in our new life here?

A   Choosing your family's general practitioner can be one of the most important decisions you make when moving in to a new area. Your life and health may depend upon him/her. The doctor who suits one person does not necessarily suit another. Doctors are human, and personality clashes can occur. The most important factor is to feel safe and confident with your GP.

When moving to a new area, friends and neighbours can be a good guide. Visit the GPs that they suggest for routine matters, and find out what they are like. Check the doctor's hours, after-hours arrangements and facilities, and observe his/her attitude to you. If you are happy with one, then tell him/her so, and arrange for your old medical records to be transferred to the new practice.

Another point you may wish to check is membership of the Australian Medical Association (most AMA members display an annual membership certificate), which will give a guide to the doctor's ethical attitudes. Doctors who have completed further study and exams in general practice will be Fellows of the Royal Australian College of General Practitioners and have the letters FRACGP after their name. Practices which have passed a very strict inspection are accredited by the government and will display a certificate of accreditation.

Q   **I have been to my doctor three times with the same pain in my side. She has tried two lots of medicine, ordered X-rays and blood tests, and still does not know what is causing my pain, which is continuing despite her useless treatments. Every time I go back she keeps charging me, but if my car doesn't go after repairs, it's fixed on warranty. Why should I have to pay if she can't make me better?**

A   Human beings are not like cars. There are only a small number of car models, they have been made by man, all are exactly the same, and spare parts are readily available. There are billions of totally different human beings, they all react in slightly different ways, and can develop slightly different forms of a disease. Even the common cold can affect people in many different ways. This makes the diagnosis of some disorders very difficult, complex and time consuming.

When repairing a car, you are able to stop the engine. Humans cannot tolerate that sort of interference, and even 'opening the bonnet' is a radical procedure in a person with a minor pain. A doctor has only their time and skill to sell, and provided that skill is being used conscientiously, carefully, and with your best interests at heart, the doctor has every right to charge for the time taken in diagnosing your complaint.

You should be pleased that your GP is prepared to undertake investigations herself, without instantly referring you to a specialist, which would result in even greater expense.

Q   **I have some very complex medical problems, but my doctor is a very busy man and I don't like to trouble him. Who do you suggest I see?**

A   No doctor should be too busy to be troubled by a patient. Some doctors have busy days or times, and if your doctor seems rushed, ask him or her if there would be a better time for you to return to discuss your problem.

If you are always being rushed out of the surgery, and you feel that your problem is not being dealt with adequately, it is time to change to another general practitioner.

Q **Is it necessary to have private hospital insurance with Medicare paying all the bills?**

A Medicare pays a percentage of all doctors bills, including specialists, x-ray and pathology, and pays the state government part of the cost of maintaining the public hospital scheme. Medicare does not cover any of the cost of a bed in a private hospital, or an intermediate bed in a public hospital which can be $600 a day for a bed, plus theatre fees ($250–$800) and dressing fees.

Unfortunately, many people have dropped private health insurance, and this means that they cannot afford to go privately. This puts an additional burden on the public hospitals, leading to long waiting lists for routine operations and procedures. The waiting time for a hernia repair may be several months, and then the operation is done at a time chosen by the hospital, by a doctor chosen by the hospital, and a medical student may be the assistant.

If you can afford private insurance it is well worthwhile as it will allow you to have an operation or medical treatment performed by your doctor in a hospital of your choice when it is convenient for you. You should obtain a brochure from a health insurance office, a chemist or your doctor's surgery so that you can consider your options.

Q **Doctors seem to love putting the full alphabet of letters after their names to impress patients, but do these letters really mean anything, or are they merely being snobs? I would appreciate it if you could let me know just what (if anything) these doctors are trying to prove.**

A The letters after a doctor's name usually show that the doctor actually has medical qualifications and where they were obtained (eg. NSW or Qld after basic medical degree), and additionally show what specialty a doctor practises. Further letters may indicate areas of special interest, or honours for service to medicine or the community.

The letters can be interpreted by patients to find out more about their doctor, but are more commonly interpreted by other doctors so that they can work out just what their colleagues have done and can do.

An explanation of the most commonly encountered qualification abbreviations follows.

BCh   Bachelor of Surgery. Part of a basic medical degree. Usually from a British University.

BMedSc   Bachelor of Medical Science. An additional degree that may be taken during or after the medical course, on a specific area in medicine (eg: Biochemistry).

BPhty   Bachelor of Physiotherapy. Basic physiotherapy degree.

BS   Bachelor of Surgery. Part of a basic medical degree.

ChB   Bachelor of Surgery. Part of a basic medical degree. Usually from a British University.

DA   Diploma in Anaesthetics. Further study undertaken in Anaesthetics, but not a specialist anaesthetist.

DCH   Diploma in Child Health. Further study undertaken in child

	health, but not a specialist paediatrician.
DFP	Diploma in Family Planning. Further study on contraceptive methods undertaken.
DObst RACOG	Diploma in Obstetrics from the Royal Australian College of Obstetricians and Gynaecologists. Further study into obstetrics undertaken, but not a specialist obstetrician.
FACRRM	Fellow Australian College of Rural and Remote Medicine.
FAMAS	Fellow Australian Medical Acupuncture Society. Doctor who has undertaken further study in acupuncture.
FRACGP	Fellow Royal Australian College of General Practitioners. Doctor who has completed further course of study, and passed exams on general practice.
FRACOG	Fellow Royal Australian College of Obstetricians and Gynaecologists. Specialist in childbirth and women's diseases.
FRACP	Fellow Royal Australian College of Physicians. Specialist physician.
FRACR	Fellow Royal Australian College of Radiologists. Specialist in X-rays etc.
FRACS	Fellow Royal Australian College of Surgeons. Specialist surgeon.
FRANZCP	Fellow Royal Australian and New Zealand College of Psychiatrists. Specialist psychiatrist.
FRCGP	Fellow Royal College of General Practitioners. English doctor who has completed further course of study, and passed exams on general practice.
FRCOG	Fellow Royal College of Obstetricians and Gynaecologists. English specialist in childbirth and women's diseases.
FRCP	Fellow Royal College of Physicians. English specialist physician.
FRCPath	Fellow Royal College of Pathologists. English specialist pathologist.
FRCPsych	Fellow Royal College of Psychiatrists. English specialist psychiatrist.
FRCS	Fellow Royal College of Surgeons. English specialist surgeon.
LRCP	Licentiate Royal College of Physicians. Old-fashioned English basic medical qualification.
MB	Bachelor of Medicine. Part of basic medical degree.
MD	Doctor of Medicine. Basic medical degree in North America and Europe. Higher qualification in Australia and Britain.
MS	Master of Surgery. Higher degree in surgery.
PhD	Doctor of Philosophy. Doctorate degree in a special area of skill, usually not involving medicine.

Q I have just arrived in Australia and I am confused by Medicare and your health system. Can you explain it simply for me? The brochures I have read seem to be very complicated.

A   Medicare is the only form of medical insurance allowed in Australia. You can take out health insurance to cover hospital fees, dental fees, medical appliances etc., but you cannot take out any other form of insurance to pay for doctors' fees.

A levy of $1.40 for every $100 of your taxable income is added to your tax bill every year to pay for Medicare. This fund pays for about 20% of the costs incurred by Medicare. The balance is paid for out of the federal government's general revenue.

When you see a private general practitioner, specialist, radiologist or pathologist, a benefit can be claimed from Medicare. It is in this area that the greatest misconceptions arise. Doctors (like all other professionals and tradesmen) are entitled to set their own fees. These fees are usually within the limits set down by the Australian Medical Association. The federal government sets the refund a patient receives from Medicare for any particular service. These refunds are set without reference to the medical profession or any court of arbitration. There is thus a gap between the doctor's fee and the Medicare refund that must be met by the patient.

A refund may be claimed by mail or in person from Medicare offices after paying the doctor; or a pay doctor cheque to pay Medicare's part of the fee may be obtained first, and forwarded with the patient's share of the fee to pay the doctor's account.

Many doctors will direct bill Medicare, or bill the patient at the lower refund level when they see pensioners or disadvantaged patients. Very few doctors will direct bill all patients.

Q **Why are doctors' fees so high? They all earn a fortune, so why do they insist on robbing sick people?**

A Doctors' fees in Australia are very reasonable by world standards. A general practitioner consultation in the United States will cost US$70 (AUS$140), in Hong Kong HK$350 (AUS$90) and a private GP in England will charge £25 (AUS$70). The AMA recommends that $45.00 is a reasonable fee for a standard general practitioner consultation, but Medicare only gives a rebate of $23.50.

Doctors in Australia earn a reasonable income, but they are not in the millionaire class by a long way! Some general practitioners are suffering considerable financial hardship.

What the public tends to forget is that it takes at least 12 years after leaving school to become a doctor in private practice. That is many years of no income or low income that has to be made up.

Doctors also take a great deal of responsibility in their job, work long hours and often have disturbed family lives. As a last straw, the expenses in running a practice take $6 out of every $10 the doctor earns, and in pathology and X-ray practice this may exceed $8.50 out of every $10 earned.

Medicare has provided a financial safety net for Australians who fall chronically ill. There should no longer be any excuse for anyone not being able to see a doctor about any medical problem for financial reasons. Patients are still expected to meet some of the cost of their medical care, but any patient who has genuine hardship with the payment of fees should discuss the matter with their doctor.

Q **I asked my GP for a referral for a second opinion, and he informed me that he had forwarded my information to the second specialist. I told him I did not like that because I wanted a proper second opinion, not**

a rehash and a biased opinion backing up the first doctor. Am I being unreasonable?

A   No. Your request for a second opinion was completely reasonable, and every patient has the right to obtain further information and options from a second (or even a third) specialist before deciding on a course of treatment.

This is not to say that every patient referred to a specialist should always obtain a second opinion. If you are happy with what you have been told by a doctor, then proceed with his/her advice. But if the proposed procedure is a major one, there are significant possible complications, or if you have a personality clash with the first specialist, by all means seek a second opinion.

Any GP refusing to refer you in person to a specialist of your choice must be able to give you good reasons why such a referral should not be given (eg. your problem does not require specialist care, the specialist does not look after your particular problem, is on holidays, is too expensive or the GP may be concerned about the quality of the specialist's work).

It is important for patients to be able to trust their GP's opinion, as well as that of any specialist.

EARS

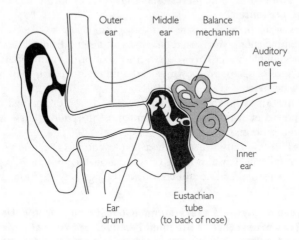

Ear anatomy

Q What are the causes of earache?

A There are hundreds of causes. The most common is infection of either the ear canal (eg. swimmer's ear), or the middle ear. These can develop very rapidly, and one of the most common causes for a 2 am call in general practice is the rapidly developing ear pain from an infection.

Infections of the sinuses may also cause ear pain, as may a blockage with phlegm of the fine tube that leads from the middle ear to the back of the nose.

If you fly or climb a mountain with this eustachian tube blocked, the air in the middle ear will be at a different pressure to that outside, the ear drum will become distorted by this difference in pressure, and pain will result. A common cold may be all that is necessary to cause this blockage.

The bones around the ear may sometimes become infected and cause earache, and the jaw joint which is just in front of the ear will cause ear pain if it becomes inflamed or injured. Impacted ear wax is another common cause of ear pain.

Dental disease can cause ear pain, and vice versa. Dentists often refer patients to a doctor for treatment of their ear or sinus condition after they have initially seen the dentist for toothache. The list goes on and on, so anyone with an earache will need assessment and treatment by a doctor (or dentist!).

Q What is the swimmer's ear that children get every summer?

A If you leave your hands in water for a couple of hours, the skin will become wrinkled and soft.

The skin inside your ears is extremely delicate, and if water is trapped in the ear after swimming or showering by a narrow ear canal or wax in the ear, the skin becomes damaged and allows infection to develop. Very rapidly the patient will develop a painful ear, that cannot be relieved by normal pain-killers.

Antibiotic and anti-inflammatory drops are the correct treatment, and the sooner treatment is started, the less pain and damage will occur.

Q How can swimmer's ear infections that my children develop every summer be prevented?

A Prevention is always better than cure, so if you or your children suffer from repeated swimmer's ear infections, you should take steps to prevent their recurrence.

Cleanliness of the water that you swim in is of primary importance, and if you have a pool or spa of your own, you should maintain it in peak condition by regular water tests.

For the majority who must use public pools, drying drops used in the ear after each period of swimming can prevent most infections. These are readily available from chemists.

Ear plugs are the only other method of prevention. The ready-made ones often leak or fall out. Custom-made ones are available and are very good, but also rather expensive. Vaseline and cotton wool plugs make a cheap alternative.

Q I seem to live at my GP's every summer because of ear infections in my children. They often start at the most inconvenient time of midnight, and cause them terrible pain for several days. I would like to prevent this problem in future and would appreciate it if you could tell me what causes ear infections in my children every summer?

A Summer is the time of year when children seem to live in swimming pools, and often seem to spend more time under the water than on the surface. The most significant medical problem associated with this phenomenon is otitis externa, or swimmer's ear.

With this disease, the outer ear canal and the outer surface of the ear drum become infected and very painful. It may occur under many circumstances, but by far the most common is retained water in the ear canal.

Bacteria normally live in the outer ear, but if the canal remains constantly wet, the type of bacteria can change from the good ones that are meant to be there, to a type that can cause tissue damage and infection. Water of any type can start this infection, but sea water is less likely to be a problem. Hot spa baths (particularly public ones) and swimming pools are the worst causes.

Private facilities are less likely to cause problems than public ones, not because the public pools and saunas are poorly cared for, but because far more people use them and introduce more bacteria. Warm water is also a greater problem than cold.

Another common cause of outer ear infections is wax. Excess wax will aid the retention of water in the ear, and itself can cause infections under hot and sweaty conditions.

Middle ear infections may also be responsible for the sudden onset of severe ear pain in children. These are more serious than outer ear infections, and often occur at the same time as a cold or runny nose due to blockage of the tube that drains from the middle ear to the back of the nose (the Eustachian tube). Medical attention is essential for these infections, because if left untreated permanent damage to the ear may occur.

momentarily forces open the walls of the eustachian tube so that the air 'pops' out of the middle ear into the back of the nose, equalising the pressure. If you are unable to equalise the pressure, the ear drum will become very distorted and painful. In the same way, swallowing pulls open the tube slightly to allow air to pass when you descend.

Your ears can hurt when you get sinusitis for the same reason. The sinus infection pushes phlegm up the eustachian tube, increasing the pressure in the middle ear to cause discomfort. The infection can also spread up the tube and into the ear.

I am concerned about my five year old daughter's hearing. Could it just be disobedience, or is a hearing problem likely?

Any parent who is concerned about their child's hearing MUST arrange for a hearing test to be performed. There is no other reliable way of determining whether the child is suffering from a defect that may cause long-term problems, or is being wilfully disobedient. The first step is to see your general practitioner who will exclude any causes such as wax or ear infection. The GP can then perform hearing tests or refer you to a specialist or audiology clinic. It is far better to be safe than sorry with this condition.

Could you tell me about the hearing problem otosclerosis which is causing me considerable confusion and embarrassment?

Otosclerosis is a relatively common ear condition that affects approximately one person in every 200 at some stage of their life.

Inside the middle ear are three tiny bones that vibrate to transmit sounds from the ear drum to the hearing mechanism in the inner ear. Otosclerosis is best described as a form of arthritis in these tiny bones and the bone that makes up the inner ear.

The bones become soft and enlarged, which reduces their ability to transmit vibration and thus sounds. It is more common in women, and usually starts in the late teens or twenties. Its onset may be triggered by pregnancy. There is a significant tendency for it to pass from one generation to the next.

The main symptoms of otosclerosis are steadily worsening deafness and a constant ringing noise in the ears. Outside noises of the right frequency may mask this ringing in the ears to make it less annoying, and enable the sufferer to hear more clearly. The noises in the head may be so severe that they are more distressing than the deafness. Dizziness occurs in some patients.

A hearing aid is the simplest form of treatment, and can be very effective, but as most patients are relatively young, a permanent operative cure in which the affected bones in the middle ear are replaced with Teflon substitutes is the treatment of choice.

Otosclerosis progresses very slowly, but never results in total deafness. The earlier in life the condition starts, the greater the final hearing loss and the worse the noises become.

I keep getting giddy all the time for no good reason. Why would this happen?

There are dozens of reasons for becoming dizzy and giddy. These sensations are

**Q I keep getting ear infections, and I'm sick of running to
I treat an ear infection myself?**

A NO! Once you have an ear infection it is important to obtain
as soon as possible. This is because untreated infections can s
the ear and cause a more serious infections in surrounding tiss

Treatment of an outer ear infection involves cleaning the
debris (don't try to do this yourself either) that may be presen
that the ear can dry out. Antibiotic drops or ointment are th
difficult cases, a wick (piece of light material) soaked in an oint
in the ear, and antibiotic tablets may be given.

Middle ear infections always require antibiotic tablets, and
supervision to ensure that the infection has cleared and no
done to the ear.

It is important that anyone with recurrent infections is tr
because each infection can injure the ear and eventually cause per

**Q My daughter has recurrent ear infections, and the spec
take out her tonsils and adenoids. I cannot see what conn
between the tonsils and the ears. Is the specialist rig
daughter have the operation?**

A Strange as it may seem, removing these lymph nodes, particula
may greatly help prevent middle ear infections.

The middle ear connects with the back of the nose with
Eustachian tube), which allows air to enter the middle ear a
leave. It is the sudden movement of air through this tube that
to pop when you go up a mountain or in an aircraft.

The adenoids are lymph nodes that surround the opening
the nose. If the adenoids are swollen, the tube is blocked, the
secretions is interrupted, and infection can develop easily in the
ear. Pressure can build up in the ear very rapidly, leading to the
associated with many ear infections.

Because the pain is due to pressure, pain-killers have little
releasing the pressure gives relief. The adenoids and tonsils ca
source of middle ear disease if they are chronically infected.

**Q Why do your ears pop when you change altitude? Why do y
with sinusitis?**

A Your ear consists of three parts. The outer ear is a dead-end
that leads from the outside to the eardrum. On the other side of
the middle ear, which is an air-filled cavity containing the three
transmit the sound vibrations from the eardrum to the inner ear
is a closed system that converts vibrations into nerve impulses.

The cavity of the middle ear is connected to the back of the
tube (the Eustachian tube). The purpose of the Eustachian tub
pressure between the middle ear and the outside air when you
(or dive underwater). This tube has a relatively soft wall and is
lapsed. When you go up a mountain or take off when flying, the
the middle ear rises above that in the air outside, and this h

controlled by semicircular canals in the inner part of the ear, so any ear disease may cause dizziness.

Common causes include colds and other virus infections that block up the ear canal with excess phlegm, ear infections, wax in the ears and sudden changes in position in older people who may have low blood pressure. Some less common reasons are Ménière's disease (an alteration of the blood supply to the inner ear), epilepsy, anaemia, heart disease, migraine, psychiatric disorders, thyroid disease, pregnancy, diabetes and some drugs. Because of this enormous diversity of causes, correct diagnosis is important before treatment starts.

Q   Why do old people like me go deaf? My television is now so loud my neighbours are complaining.

A   The gradual decrease in hearing associated with advancing age is the most common form of deafness. This is basically due to thickening of the ear drum, wear and tear on the tiny bones that conduct the vibrations of the ear drum to the hearing apparatus in the inner ear, and a loss of sensitivity in the spiral tube that senses the vibrations, and turns them into nerve impulses in the brain.

The higher frequencies of sound disappear first, and this cuts out a lot of our hearing discrimination, so that conversation in a noisy room melts into a constant blur of sound.

Medication and surgery play no part in the treatment of this condition, but hearing aids are becoming more and more sophisticated in helping these people. You can also get special hearing aids that attach to televisions and radios. This may help both you and your neighbours.

Q   I recently had a terrifying experience of extreme dizziness which required a week in hospital. A specialist pronounced that I was suffering from 'benign viral paroxysmal positional vertigo'. Can you interpret this medical jargon for me? I fear a further attack and would like to know its cause and treatment.

A   Your ear comprises three parts—the outer ear, where you accumulate wax and insert cotton buds (a bad habit); the middle ear, which is beyond the ear drum and contains three tiny bones that transmit vibrations (sound) to the inner ear; and the inner ear, which is a spiral of vibration sensitive hairs. Attached to the top of the middle ear are three semicircular fluid canals. These canals control our balance, and if they fail to work well, dizziness results.

The balance mechanism can obviously be affected by infections of the ear, but infections may occur directly in the semicircular canals themselves. These infections can be viral or bacterial. Bacterial infections can be cured with antibiotics, but viral infections must be allowed to run their course, as doctors do not have any effective broad spectrum antiviral medications.

The loose translation of your doctors diagnosis of 'benign viral paroxysmal positional vertigo' would be 'a viral infection of the balance mechanism that causes intermittent dizziness when you change position, and will get better without any serious consequences'.

Too many doctors use jargon that confuses patients. If you do not understand what your doctor is saying, ask him/her to express the idea in simpler language. It never hurts to ask, and the doctor will almost certainly oblige.

Q I have had vestibular neuronitis for 17 months, which causes dizziness that comes for a few weeks and then goes again. What causes the dizziness to come and go?

A Vestibular neuronitis is an inflammation of the balance mechanism in the inner ear. It often follows a viral infection or fever, and causes sudden, intermittent attacks of dizziness.

Unfortunately, there is no specific treatment, but a number of medications can be tried to reduce the severity of the dizziness when it occurs. Most cases settle spontaneously with time, and the younger you are, the sooner you can expect the problem to disappear. Only rarely is it permanent.

I cannot specifically explain why the attacks come and go, but the recurrence of an attack may be associated with a period when you are overtired, run down, or suffering from a minor viral illness.

Q For 30 years I have had giddy turns, which are sometimes associated with vomiting. At times I fall, and now have to use a walking stick. Attacks can last 3 to 14 days. I take Stemetil, but it's not much use. What causes it and is there any cure?

A There are many causes of giddiness that may be responsible for your attacks, but the most likely is Ménière's disease, which is an ear disorder.

The inner ear contains contains the small structures responsible for a hearing and balance. Ménière's disease is due to a poor blood supply to these structures and results in nausea, dizziness, ringing in the ears and deafness. It may occur after a head injury or ear infection, but in most patients it has no apparent cause. It is more common in men, and becomes more common with age.

There is usually a build-up in the pressure of the fluid inside the hearing and balance mechanisms of the inner ear. The increase in pressure causes the distressing symptoms of the disease. Attacks of dizziness and nausea can come and go for no apparent reason, while the deafness is usually slowly progressive and permanent. The most distressing symptom is often the constant noise (tinnitus is the technical term) in the ear.

Unfortunately, treatment is not very satisfactory, and new drugs and devices are constantly being tried to give relief. Among the drugs, one called Serc (available on prescription only) which increases the blood supply to the inner ear has been successful in some people. Other drugs tried with varying success are various antihistamines, diuretics, prochlorperazine, amitriptyline and chlorpromazine (most are on prescription). None of these have more than a 50–50 chance of success but may be tried to see if they give relief.

There are also microsurgical techniques to help the sufferers of Ménière's disease. These usually involve draining the high-pressure fluid from the affected parts of the inner ear, or as a last resort destroying the auditory nerve, leaving the patient deaf in that ear but without the distressing buzz saw noise.

Other possible causes for your symptoms are damage to the nerve to the ear, poor blood supply to the part of the brain responsible for balance, migraines (headache is not always present) and a side effect of some medications.

Q Since a short bout of the 'flu two months ago, I have had an upset stomach like travel sickness, some unsteadiness, and ringing in the ears. Will it clear up in time or will a specialist's appointment help?

A I suspect that what you are describing is vestibulitis. This is an inflammation or viral infection of the balance mechanism in one ear, and may be associated with almost any viral infection, including influenza. Excess fluid accumulates in the balance mechanism to make it malfunction.

If your balance mechanism is disturbed, you can certainly feel nauseated (in the same way that travel sickness can affect you) and of course you will be unsteady. Because the balance mechanism is beside the inner ear, a disturbance to your hearing resulting in a ringing sensation is also quite possible.

Time will heal the problem slowly, but in the meantime you can use medications such as Stemetil (prescription required) to ease the symptoms. A fluid tablet prescribed by your doctor may relieve the pressure caused by the excess fluid in the balance mechanism, and cure the problem.

Only if the problem becomes particularly prolonged should a specialist's opinion be necessary.

Q **Recently I had grommets placed in my ears. While the drainage system seems to work, I still suffer a heavy hearing loss, despite Sudafed and ear drops. Is there any solution?**

A Grommets are tiny tubes that are placed through the ear drum to allow air to pass from the outer ear to the middle ear.

The middle ear is connected by the Eustachian tube through the centre of the head to the back of the nose. This allows the air pressure in the middle ear to equalise with that in the outside air (popping of the ears) when you change altitude by going up or down a hill or in an aircraft.

If the Eustachian tube becomes blocked by phlegm from the nose, pressure can build up in the middle ear to cause discomfort, or with altitude changes, the phlegm may be forced up the Eustachian tube and into the middle ear where it settles as a thick substance known as 'glue' (thus a 'glue ear').

The glue reduces the vibrations of the eardrum and the tiny bones that transmit sounds across the middle ear to the hearing mechanism in the inner ear, causing varying degrees of deafness.

A grommet is inserted through the eardrum to allow air into the middle ear and the increased air pressure will very gradually push the glue back down the Eustachian tube to the nose, eventually clearing the ear. The grommet will be expelled naturally from the ear drum as it heals after a few months. Not until the grommet is expelled will hearing return to normal.

Sudafed reduces the amount of new phlegm being produced in the nose, while ear drops can do many tasks, depending on the type of drop, but many ear drops should be avoided while grommets are in place.

If you are continuing to have problems you should see your GP so that the amount of glue in the middle ear and the position of the grommet can be assessed, and the need for ear drops and further Sudafed determined.

Q **I have a pounding in the ears that is driving me mad! I am to scared to see a doctor in case he finds a brain tumour or something. Is there a simple cure?**

A It is most unlikely that the pounding in your ears is due to a brain tumour. The most likely explanation is high blood pressure. The increased pressure leads to movement of the ear drum in the ear with every beat, and therefore a dull pounding is heard. Other blood vessel diseases around the ear may also be responsible. Controlling the blood pressure may ease the annoying noise.

People who avoid doctors for fear of what may be found are deluding themselves. It is far better to receive any bad news now, than to wait for months or years until effective treatment may no longer be possible. The majority of people who worry themselves excessively over symptoms can be examined, investigated and then told that there is nothing seriously wrong. Please see your doctor today, rather than worry unnecessarily for a long time.

Q My ears are ringing all the time, and when I get nervous or tense they get worse. How can I help this?

A Noises in the ears are a common curse that becomes more common the older you are. Many patients are plagued with such noises to the extent that they are unable to lead a normal lifestyle.

The first step in treatment is to be thoroughly examined by your doctor to exclude any disease such as high blood pressure, wax in the ears, or an overactive thyroid gland, which may be responsible for the noise. You should also avoid possible aggravating causes such as coffee, tea and cola drinks.

After this, it is often wise to seek a referral to an ear, nose and throat specialist, or a general physician, for more detailed investigations.

Unfortunately, in all too many victims of tinnitus (the technical name for ringing in the ears), no cause can be found, and the next step is to experiment with the many different medications that may relieve your problem. This is very much a matter of trial and error, that must be carried out with the cooperation of your GP, as most of these medications require a prescription, and some may have side effects. None has a better than 30% success rate, but they should be tried in turn to see if any help.

Finally, it is possible to use a hearing-aid type device called a tinnitus masker that produces a constant tone to drown out the noises you hear, or have an operation to deafen the involved ear.

When tinnitus is combined with dizziness and deafness, the condition is called Ménière's disease.

Q After reading about tinnitus recently, I wish to know more about 'tinnitus maskers'. How are they obtained? Do you need a doctor's prescription? Can pensioners get one at a reduced rate?

A It is essential for all patients with tinnitus (a constant ringing noise in the ears) to be thoroughly assessed by a doctor to determine any specific cause for the condition. Only after thorough assessment and trials of treatments from both your GP and an ear, nose and throat specialist, should you consider a tinnitus masker.

This device produces a constant tone that 'masks' the noise in the ear. They are obtainable from hearing-aid centres in every city and major town. No doctor's prescription is required, but it may be a matter of trial and error to find the device and frequency best suited to your particular problem. Most audiologists will allow patients to take the devices on trial for a short time before they buy. Unfortunately, I am not aware of any scheme that will allow pensioners to receive them at a subsidised price.

Q **It is of very great import to me doctor that you reply, because I've been suffering from noises in my ears for twelve years. I'm also going deaf. I've been to specialists and they say there is nothing to be done. Please can you help me?**

A I believe that you are suffering from Ménière's disease. Ménière was a physician in Paris in the early part of the nineteenth century who described a syndrome that consisted of dizziness, deafness and a constant noise in the ears.

The exact cause is not known, but there is usually a build-up in the pressure of the fluid inside the hearing and balance mechanisms of the inner ear.

The most distressing symptom is the constant noise (tinnitus is the technical term) in the ear. This is usually a high-pitched ringing, but may be a dull roar in some people.

Unfortunately, treatment is not very satisfactory, and new drugs and devices are constantly being tried to give relief.

Among the drugs, Serc, Adalat and Minipress (all are available on prescription only), act to increase the blood supply to the inner ear, and have been successful in some people. Other drugs tried with varying success are various anti-histamines, diuretics, prochlorperazine, amitriptyline and chlorpromazine (most are on prescription).

None of these have more than a 50–50 chance of success, but may be tried to see if they give relief.

If medication is successful in controlling the nausea and dizziness, but not the noises, a tinnitus masker may be beneficial. This is a hearing-aid type of device that is worn in the ear and emits a constant tone that counteracts the noise already heard in the ear. It may take some experimentation to find the right one for each patient, but with persistence, many can be helped.

There are also microsurgical techniques to help the sufferers of Ménière's disease.

Those who do suffer should not despair, but keep trying the various methods of treatment that are available, in the hope that one will suit them.

Q **The Australian Tinnitus Association likes to see accurate information disseminated on this topic, and our aim is to promote research, increase community awareness, and to assist persons to cope with tinnitus.**

A Following an item I wrote in response to a reader's question about tinnitus, I received a very useful letter from this organisation, and they enclosed a 40 page book entitled *A Layman's Guide to Tinnitus and How to Live With It*. This excellent publication is a must for all sufferers of this most annoying condition.

As a medical writer, I receive more mail about tinnitus than any other subject, and as 'real' general practitioner, I see many patients whose lives are ruined because of this extraordinarily distressing complaint, for which there is no single successful form of cure or control. Many patients can be assisted by a combination of medications, psychological help, special hearing aids (a tinnitus masker) and rarely, operations.

It is also annoying to the patient that others cannot see that s/he is suffering, because there are no outward signs of tinnitus.

Tinnitus is a noise in the ears, which may be constant or intermittent. It may consist of one particular tone or varying tones. It may be very soft, so that it only becomes noticeable at night, or so loud that it drowns out normal conversation. There are many causes for the condition, including loud noise (particularly many years' work in a noisy environment), chronic middle ear infections, arthritis and other damage to the tiny bones in the middle ear (technically called otosclerosis), Ménière's disease (when tinnitus is associated with deafness and dizziness), viral infections (usually a temporary problem) and as a side effect of some drugs (eg. aspirin, alcohol, smoking) and ear operations.

EMOTIONS
See also STRESS

Q My little boy is nearly 3 and is a real 'boy', in that he likes to play with his toy cars and with his dad's tools. He is also very loving and affectionate, and climbs onto my lap for a kiss and cuddle. His father does not approve of this, and says he hates to see this trait in a boy, and I am turning him into a sissy. I would appreciate your opinion on the matter.

A. All humans, male and female, young and old, require affection and love, and if this is denied, particularly in their early life, it can adversely affect their adult attitudes.

Showing normal motherly affection and love is in no way going to turn your son into a 'sissy', in fact it will probably make him a more stable and caring person, who will be able to relate well to both sexes in his adult years.

Many studies have been undertaken by psychologists and psychiatrists into abnormal behaviour, and many of these have found that an unstable family environment, or an emotionally deprived childhood are common in these people.

Conversely, no evidence has been found, even in extreme cases where a child has been raised as though they are the opposite sex for some years, that affection has any adverse effect on the adult. Over-protection of a child from the normal consequences of life may cause later problems.

Don't use this article as a cause for confrontation with your husband, but demonstrate how other mothers treat their sons, urge him to also show some affection for your son, and gently explain that you are acting in his long-term best interests.

Q I am constantly worrying. If it's not money worries, then it's the children's schoolwork, or other silly little things. What can I do?

A It is normal to be anxious about many situations that arise in everyday life. Problems with your children at school, extra responsibility at work, financial problems, disagreements with others, illness in the family and many other circumstances will cause anxiety.

There are two main ways to deal with this type of anxiety—you can take action to remove the cause of the stress, or you can rationalise the problem.

The anxiety about financial problems will be removed if you can work overtime and earn more money, or you may be able to devise a tighter budget.

The anxiety over problems with your children may be resolved by a discussion with their teacher. Some causes of anxiety cannot be removed easily, and the rationalisation of the situation can then help.

Discussing the problem with relatives, friends, your family doctor or another sympathetic person may help you to put the problem into perspective. You may find after these discussions, that there is some action that can be taken to relieve the pressure you are suffering.

If there is nothing you can do, your friends, doctor and counsellors can offer moral support.

Q I am constantly under stress at work. My boss is very tough, and no matter how much I do, he never seems satisfied. I am constantly anxious, and this makes me slow down at work in case I make a mistake. I'm a complete mess. It is affecting my lifestyle and marriage. How can I cope with it?

A There are four basic ways to treat stress:

- The obvious, most successful, but hardest to achieve, is removing the cause of the stress.
- The next way to deal with stress is to rationalise it. This can involve a combination of several different techniques. Talking is an excellent way of relieving anxiety. Discuss the problem with your spouse, relatives, friends, doctor, work mates or anyone else who will listen. Problems often do not appear as insurmountable once bought into the open. Writing down the details of the problem is another excellent way of relieving anxiety. An insurmountable problem in your mind often appears more manageable on paper, particularly when all your possible options are diagrammatically attached to it to enable a rational view of the situation to be obtained.
- Professional assistance in discussing your problems is also very helpful. This may be given by your own general practitioner (who can often be a friend as well as counsellor), a psychiatrist (not because you may be insane, but because they have specialist skills in this area), a psychologist, or social worker. Many people are reluctant to seek this type of assistance, but it is far preferable to the fourth type of treatment for stress.
- Drugs that alter your mood, sedate or relieve anxiety are very successful in dealing with stress, but should only be used in a crisis, intermittently or for short periods of time. Some anti-depressant drugs and treatments for psychiatric conditions are designed for long term use, but most of the anxiety-relieving drugs can cause dependency if used regularly. When prescribed and taken correctly, they act as a very useful crutch to help patients through a few weeks of extreme stress, and allow them to cope until such time as the cause of the stress is removed or counselling can be started.

Q When I am nervous or worried about even little things, I get terrible pains and cramps in my gut. How can I prevent this?

A Anyone who gets nervous will notice that the muscles in their arms, neck, back etc. will tense up. These are muscles that the brain can voluntarily control, and if we consciously relax, the muscle spasms will go away.

The gut is a hollow tube made of bands of muscle that are not directly controlled by the brain. We cannot consciously direct our gut muscles to contract faster or slower. These muscles may also react to stress by going into spasm. When this occurs, you develop gut pains, much the same as those when the gut is sent into spasm by the infections or toxins of gastroenteritis.

If you relax yourself, the pains may slowly ease, but some people need to take medications that will relax the gut spasms The expression that you feel your 'stomach is tied in knots' is derived from these gut muscle spasms. The irritable bowel syndrome is a more severe manifestation of this condition, where the spasms occur for little or no reason.

Q What can I do to help a good friend of mine cope with her stress and anxiety problem?

A A sympathetic and helpful friend is the greatest aid anyone can ask for in helping with this problem. Anxiety is subtly different to stress, in that stress may cause anxiety, or it may develop for no apparent reason at all. The patient can become fearful, have feelings of unease and dread, and may develop physical symptoms such as a tremor, difficulty in swallowing or hot flushes.

Tranquillisers can play a part in controlling these symptoms on an as-required basis. When the patient feels anxious, they use a tranquilliser to control their feelings. Sometimes they may need them several times a day, at other times they may go for weeks without needing any help. The tablet is a crutch to help their fractured psyche through the day.

Anxiety affects a third of the Australian population, but nowhere near all of them will require medication to cope with this anxiety. If you feel that further help is required for your friend, convince her to see her family doctor, who can assess her, advise her, and if necessary, prescribe for her.

Q My best friend's mother has just died, and she is naturally very upset. How can I best help her?

A The way in which an individual accepts death will depend a great deal upon his/her personal philosophies and beliefs, be they religious or otherwise. Western society is sometimes very harsh on the bereaved. We expect the stiff upper lip, and tend to leave them alone, in silence, and full of heart-rending memories that can take months or years to dissipate.

Psychologists have described different stages of grief that are experienced by both the dying and those remaining behind. The five classic stages are denial, anger, bargaining, depression and acceptance. Doctors watch to ensure that there is a steady progression from one stage to the next, intervening if the individual appears to become held up unduly at one point to prevent prolonged bouts of depression.

There are steps that those close to the mourners can take to help them to recovery. It does not matter if we are referring to the person about to die, or those who are left behind. Both will grieve.

Do not isolate these people; maintain normal social contacts and activities. They do not want to be left alone most of the time, but don't go to the other extreme and start a round of frantic activity that leaves them with less time than usual for their own use. Listen and talk appropriately. A sympathetic ear, and someone who can support them emotionally is a great help to those involved. Talking always seems to make things seem easier and clearer.

Be a good friend in the true sense of the word, and be sensitive to the slight indications that are given out requesting physical help, privacy, distraction, and empathy during the natural process of grieving.

Q **I have some very important exams coming up, but I get bad exam nerves, and even though I know my work reasonably well, I feel that I might freak out in the exam and fail. Can you help me overcome this problem?**

A The best way to cope with exam nerves is to be so well prepared that the toughest questions hold no fear for you. Unfortunately, for most of us this is not possible, and relaxation techniques that can be taught by doctors or psychologists, and often involve listening to tapes that teach you how to relax, are quite successful.

Many different tablets can be used to control nerves, but most of these also sedate you slightly, which is not much use if you want to pass an exam! Propranolol is an interesting drug that is used to control everything from high blood pressure to migraines and overactive thyroid glands. It is also very useful as a 'stage-fright' pill, and in low doses it can control stress before any event that requires concentration. It must not be used in asthmatics though.

If you are having a problem, talk to your general practitioner about which of these various methods of treatment is best for you.

EPILEPSY

Q **I am terribly concerned about my two year old daughter, who has had several fever fits. Do febrile convulsions in children lead to epilepsy later in life?**

A Convulsions in children due to a high fever are not true epilepsy, and do not lead to epilepsy in later life. They are caused by a temporary short-circuit in the brain when it is overheated.

Children who develop febrile convulsions are normally given medication for a few months or years to prevent any further attacks, and any fever that develops must be treated aggressively with paracetamol, fanning and tepid baths.

Prolonged fits may cause damage, but the majority of children can be readily managed by the appropriate medication.

If a child starts fitting for any reason, he or she must be attended to by a doctor immediately, and the correct cause determined. For this reason, a child who has a febrile convulsion will be put through a complex series of tests to ensure that there is no other cause.

Q **How do you deal with someone who is having an epileptic fit?**

A Do NOT put your finger or anything else in the patient's mouth. You will only injure your finger or the mouth.

Lie the person on their side with the top arm and leg bent forward, and the bottom arm and leg straight and slightly behind the body. This is known as the coma position. To stop the person choking, place the finger tips of both hands behind the jaw on each side, pull the jaw forward and bend the neck back. Hold the patient in this position until the fit passes.

Most fits only last a minute or two. Send others for help if it lasts more than two minutes.

Q   What is epilepsy? I have been told that I have it after I had a funny turn in the street, but I don't understand it. Can you explain this condition?

A   Some people are born with epilepsy, while others acquire the disease later in life after a brain infection, tumour or injury. It can affect people in many different ways, and can vary from very mild absences, in which people just seem to loose concentration for a few seconds; to uncontrolled bizarre movements of one arm or leg; to the grand mal convulsion in which an epileptic can thrash around quite violently.

Epilepsy can be explained most easily by an analogy to a computer that develops a short-circuit. Parts of the brain are able to short-circuit after very minor and localised damage. This can stimulate another part of the brain, and then another, causing the responses that we see.

Epileptics have no knowledge of what happens during an attack. They may have a brief warning aura, but then they lose consciousness and wake up some time after the fit has finished, not knowing if they have been unconscious for a few seconds or half an hour.

After the first convulsion, several tests are performed, including an electro-encephalogram (EEG) to measure the brain waves and find out exactly where the short-circuit exists, and hopefully, what is causing it. Other investigations will include blood tests and a CT (computerised tomography) scan of the brain.

Once diagnosed, treatment can be prescribed and regular blood tests ensure that it is adequate to control the disease.

Q   What medications can be used to treat epilepsy? My teenage son has suffered from the condition for years, but keeps having fits despite taking regular medication.

A   There is a huge range a medication available, and it is often a matter of trial and error, and knowing which types of medication are more likely to treat certain types of epilepsy, in order to find the correct ones for your son. Often several different medications in low doses may be more effective than one or two in high doses. Blood levels are usually checked regularly to arrive at the correct dosage.

The drugs used to control epilepsy are known as anticonvulsants. This is a very large group of drugs. They are nearly always used as tablets, but injections and mixtures of some drugs are available.

Side effects from anticonvulsants vary widely from one person to another and between drugs. They are usually worst when treatment is first started, and wear off as time passes. Phenytoin may cause gum problems if used in the long term. All these drugs have a tendency to interact with other drugs, and the doctor must be made aware of all medications being taken and any other diseases (eg. diabetes) that may be present.

Examples of the anticonvulsant available include carbamazepine (Tegretol), clonazepam (Rivotril), ethosuximide (Zarontin), gabapentin (Neurontin), lamotrigine (Lamictal), phenytoin (Dilantin), primidone (Mysoline), sodium valproate (Epilim), sulthiame (Ospolot), tigabine (Gabitril), topiramate (Topamax) and vigabatrin (Sabril). Barbiturates (Phenobarb) and diazepam (Valium) are also used in epilepsy, but usually to treat a convulsion rather than prevent them.

Q   What are the different types of epilepsy?

A   There are several quite distinct types of epilepsy, but one patient may have fits that are combinations of the different types, or different types of fit at different times.

Grand mal is the massive fit which most people associate with epilepsy. The patient becomes rigid, falls to the ground and stops breathing. The muscles in different parts of the body become alternately rigid and slack, causing gross abnormal movements and twitching of the arms, legs and trunk. The patient may urinate, pass faeces and become blue. Epileptics who have grand mal fits have no knowledge of what happens during the attack. They may have a brief warning aura, but then they lose consciousness and wake up some time after the fit has finished, not knowing if they have been unconscious for a few seconds or an hour. After recovering from the fit, the patient is confused, drowsy, disoriented and may have a severe headache, nausea and muscle aches.

Status epilepticus is the condition where one grand mal attack follows another without the patient regaining consciousness between attacks. Urgent medical attention is required for these patients.

Petit mal (absences, drop attacks) attacks are periods of unconsciousness that may last from one or two seconds to a minute or more. There may be some unusual movements associated with them but nothing as violent as in a grand mal attack. The patient may appear totally normal during the attack, may stumble momentarily, or drop to the ground and rapidly recover. The attacks come without warning, and may appear merely as an unusual break of several seconds in a sentence while speaking. Patients are often unaware that they have had an attack. Petit mal epilepsy is far more common in children and teenagers than adults.

Partial seizures (temporal lobe epilepsy) occur when the abnormal brain wave is restricted to only one part of the brain, usually the temporal lobe of the brain on one side. The seizures can vary greatly in their severity, and in some cases the patient remains conscious while one arm and/or leg contracts and relaxes, thrashing about outside the conscious control of the patient. The fit can vary from minor twitches of the fingers or eyelid, to apparent grand mal fits, but involving only one side of the body. In other cases they may present as difficulty in talking or swallowing, as an unexplained loss of memory, or an abnormal shift of mood and emotion (eg. a sudden unexplained fear or terror, or ecstasy). At other times, partial seizures may be unnoticed by others but felt as abnormal sensations (eg. tingling, burning) by the patient. Other manifestations include flashes of light, strange smells, buzzing noises, sweats, flushes and hallucinations.

An unusual and common form of very mild epilepsy is deja vu. Deja vu is a feeling of intense familiarity when confronted with someone, something, or a place that is actually totally unfamiliar to the individual. This happens occasionally in normal people but is more commonly associated with some types of epilepsy or psychiatric disorders. *Deja vu* means 'already seen' in French.

Convulsions in children due to a high fever are not true epilepsy and do not lead to epilepsy in later life. They are caused by a temporary short-circuit in the brain when it is overheated.

EYES

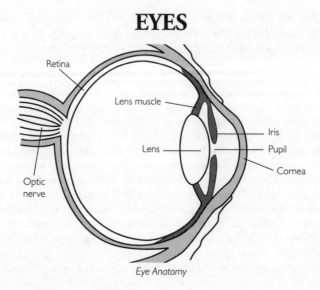

Retina

Lens muscle

Iris

Lens

Pupil

Cornea

Optic
nerve

Eye Anatomy

Q   What is colour blindness?

A   The normal form of colour blindness is an inability to differentiate between the colours red and green. In some men, other colours may be involved, but only rarely is all colour vision lost with the person seeing in black and white. Colour blindness is hereditary, and occurs nearly always in men.

Special cards covered in coloured dots, with numbers hidden amongst the dots, are used by doctors to diagnose the condition.

There is no treatment available, but most patients can live quite happily with the problem, and may have adapted so completely to the problem, that they are not aware of its existence. Those planning a to work as an electrician or commercial pilot, or in some other areas where colour differentiation is vital, may not be allowed to undertake these careers.

Q   I have just been diagnosed as having glaucoma. My mother had it too. What causes this disease?

A   Your eyeball contains a transparent liquid that has the consistency of half-set jelly. This liquid is produced by special cells that sit just behind the iris (the coloured part of the eye). There is a slow circulation of this fluid around the eyeball and out through the pupil to the area in front of the iris. Here the fluid is absorbed back into the bloodstream.

The fluid in the eyeball is under pressure to maintain the shape of the eye and prevent distortion of the light waves entering the eye. If the pressure of the fluid increases, the light-sensitive cells inside the eye will be damaged and vision will decrease—possibly to the point of blindness.

Glaucoma is the disease caused by an increase in the pressure of the fluid in the eye. The most common type of glaucoma has a slow onset over many months or years. The patient may not be aware that there is anything wrong unless a routine test by a doctor detects it.

Unfortunately, the first symptom is often deteriorating vision, and by then it may be impossible to reverse the existing damage, but any further damage can be prevented by the correct treatment.

There is an hereditary tendency to this type of glaucoma, and anyone who has parents with glaucoma should have their eyes checked every couple of years after the age of 35.

Q   How do you know if you have glaucoma? My mother is blind from it and I do not want to go the same way.

A   Unfortunately, the symptoms of glaucoma can be very mild in the early stages. Blurring of vision, headaches, watery eyes, narrowed angle of vision, eye aches and coloured halos around lights are all early signs of this condition. Glaucoma is due to an increase in the pressure of the fluid inside the eyeball. If this pressure remains high for too long it can destroy the light-sensitive cells at the back of the eye and lead to blindness.

Anyone who is suspicious that they may have this problem, or who has a bad family history of glaucoma, should have the pressure of their eyes tested regularly by a doctor. This is a simple painless procedure, and only takes a few minutes. Well worth the trouble if it saves your sight!

Once diagnosed, treatment is normally by drops that are used regularly for years on end to allow the excess fluid to drain out of the eye.

Q   My mother has been diagnosed as having mild glaucoma, but all the doctor has done is give her some eye drops. How is glaucoma treated?

A   Your sight is one of your most valued possessions. Any disease that can reduce your vision, or worse still, make you blind, is of great concern. One such disease is glaucoma.

Glaucoma is an increase in the pressure of the fluid inside the eye. If this pressure becomes too high, the eye can be permanently damaged. It is diagnosed by measuring the pressure inside the eyeball.

There are two methods of measuring the eyeball pressure. In the older method, special drops to numb the eye are used, and then an instrument is rested on the eye for a few seconds. A more sophisticated method is to use a machine that puffs air onto the eye for a fraction of a second and measures the amount of air pressure reflected from the eye. Both can give very accurate measurements of the eye pressure.

Looking at the outside of the eye at different angles, and examining the back of the eyeball with a magnifying instrument also help make the diagnosis.

There are more than 20 different types of glaucoma, with different causes and therefore different treatments. It is a complex area, that once suspected or diagnosed, is best dealt with by an ophthalmologist (specialist eye doctor).

Treatment involves the use of one or more eye drops on a regular basis, every day, usually for the rest of the patient's life. Some types of glaucoma may also require the taking of tablets. Occasionally the disease settles spontaneously in old age.

Glaucoma cannot be prevented, but it can be controlled successfully in nearly all patients, and sometimes it can be cured by surgery. The surgery increases the rate of drainage of fluid from the eye, and may involve the use of lasers to burn microscopic drain holes in the corner of the eye. With modern treatment techniques, the outcome for patients with glaucoma is normally very good, but continued follow-up by a doctor is essential.

Q Can you give me information on what causes vitreous floaters in the eye. How long do they last?

A Floaters are abnormal clumps of cells in the centre of the eyeball that cast a shadow on the light-sensitive retina at the back of the eye, and the brain perceives this shadow as an object (spot) in front of the eye.

The 'floater' can occur at any point in the field of vision, but the closer it is to the centre (ie. when looking straight ahead), the more annoying it becomes.

The cells can form in the centre of the eye because of bleeding into the eye, a detached retina, infection or no apparent cause may be found.

Diseases such as diabetes, leukaemia, high blood pressure, and a number of rarer conditions may cause bleeding into the eye. A detached retina can be repaired by laser therapy in the early stages, but if left, may result in permanent blindness.

Because there may be a serious disease causing the problem, all patients with floaters must be appropriately investigated to exclude these problems.

The condition is only treated if it is causing significant trouble, as most floaters dissipate with time.

Q I have floaters in the inside of the eye. Could you tell me if there is any treatment for this?

A Patients with floaters can 'see' one or more fine, dark spots or lines that appear to 'float' across their field of vision. Floaters are actually extremely small particles that are formed from clumps of cells, and drift in the fluid that fills the eye. This fluid has the consistency of half-set jelly.

These cell clumps break away from the inside lining of the eye, or are caused by bleeding from or damage to the lining of the eye ball. Most of them are not an indication of any serious disease, but because some floaters are caused by diseases such as diabetes, leukaemia, high blood pressure and other rarer but more serious conditions, every patient with floaters must be carefully examined by a doctor.

The only treatment necessary in the majority of cases is reassurance, but where a particular disease is found to cause the problem, this must be treated. Persistent, annoying floaters are treated by eye specialists using lasers.

Q I get flashes of black or clear spots or shapes in my eyes. My vision is still perfect. Any suggestions?

A I have several suggestions as to the cause, but they will all end the same way— you must see a doctor!

The most likely cause is that you have a floater in your eye. This is a clump of cells floating in the fluid inside the eye. They can be quite annoying, and can be destroyed by laser treatment. The problem is what has caused the floater?

The cells may have broken away for no serious reason, but it is possible that they are the first sign of significant eye problems. For this reason floaters must always be checked by an ophthalmologist (eye specialist).

Spots in your vision may also be due to migraines (and these are not always accompanied by a headache), a damaged retina (the light-sensitive layer of cells at the back of the eyeball), a cataract (cloudiness or damage to the lens in the eye), a deteriorating blood supply to the eye (for example after a stroke) or due to a tumour in or around the eye or the brain.

It is because there are so many possible nasty causes that it is essential to have an accurate diagnosis.

Q **I am sure that my son has a squint, but my GP keeps saying he hasn't. What should I do?**

A The diagnosis of squint is not as easy as one might expect. A number of normal conditions may mimic a squint, or the eye problem may not be constant and occur only when the child is very tired.

A child who has a very broad nasal bridge, may also give the false impression that the eyes are not parallel.

If you are still concerned, take him to the doctor at a time when you feel the squint is at its worst. If your GP cannot adequately explain the problem, ask for a referral to an eye specialist.

Q **The doctor is concerned about my grand-daughter's squint. What is a squint, and is it serious?**

A A squint (or strabismus, to give it its correct medical name), occurs when the two eyes do not align equally when looking at a distant object. One eye appears to be looking in one direction, while the other is looking in a different direction. This is quite normal when looking at something very close, as both eyes turn in to look at it.

If a child does have a significant squint, the brain will gradually suppress the sight in one eye, to avoid double vision. The affected eye may never learn to see again, resulting in the child becoming blind in that eye.

The correction of a squint at an early age is therefore vital. Treatment usually involves prescribing special spectacles to correct the problem. If the squint is more severe, the good eye will be covered for a period every day, as well as using the glasses. This strengthens the vision in the poor eye and prevents blindness in that eye. In marked degrees of squint, it is necessary to operate on the tiny muscles that control eye movement to shorten those that are not pulling the eye around far enough.

Q **Can glare damage your eyes?**

A Yes. Glare will cause chronic inflammation to the narrow segment of the white of the eyes that is exposed to the reflected sun's rays when squinting. Over a period of several years this can lead to the build-up of scar and fat tissue in this area. This is known as a pinguecula. They cause no harm to the eye, but are unsightly and may become inflamed and itchy.

Cataracts may also be aggravated by glare, including the glare reflected from water onto the eyes.

The problem is prevented by wearing high-quality sun glasses.

Q **What are the best sunglasses to buy?**

A There are a very wide range of sunglasses on the market, but very few manu-facturers give any information about the characteristics of the lenses, and most people buy for appearance rather than effectiveness.

A good pair of sunglasses should be large enough to prevent glare from entering the eye from around the edges. They should absorb all the ultraviolet (UV) and infra-red radiation frequencies, as these are totally unnecessary for vision, but may be harmful to the eye itself.

The total light transmission of the sunglass lenses should be reduced to below 40%, but some go as low as 15%. Polarised lenses, which reduce reflected glare markedly, are also better than non-polarised ones. The actual colour of the lens makes little difference, but the variable shaded lenses are better avoided, as they do not give adequate protection from reflected glare.

Excess sun on the eyes will aggravate cataracts, and can cause an overgrowth of tissue on the white of the eye called a pterygium. It is just as sensible to protect your eyes with good sunglasses as it is to protect your skin with a good sun screen lotion.

Q **After having gradually worsening vision for several years, I saw my GP who said I had a cataract, and he has referred me to a specialist. The GP thinks I will need an operation. Is this the best treatment for a cataract?**

A Behind the pupil in your eye is the lens. This is transparent and able to change its shape with the aid of tiny muscles attached to its edge. The change in shape enables it to focus on objects near and far.

A cataract is the clouding over of this lens. Once the vision has deteriorated sufficiently to cause significant sight impairment in both eyes, the worst eye will be operated upon, because this is the only way of treating a cataract. There are no medications or drops that will help.

The operation is technically difficult, but can be completed in half an hour and is often done under local anaesthetic. The cloudy lens is removed, and a new clear plastic lens is inserted. This new lens is not mobile, and cannot change shape, thus spectacles are normally required for close work, and sometimes distant vision as well.

Q **What is the best time to have a cataract operation? When it is only slightly annoying, or should I wait until later?**

A A cataract is the slow clouding of the lens in the eye, until it becomes like frosted glass, and impossible to see through.

There is no urgency about having a cataract operation until your sight has deteriorated to the point where glasses are unable to compensate for the clouding of the lens.

Usually one eye deteriorates faster than the other, and when reading, driving or other skills become difficult, the worst eye will be operated upon. Only very rarely are both eyes done at once.

Once the bad eye has recovered, the other eye will be treated, and most patients find a dramatic improvement in their sight. One of the most common comments by patients after a cataract operation is that they find colours far brighter and more vibrant. The slow progression of the cataract over many years has had the same effect as slowly turning down the colour control on a television to give a very washed-out effect.

Q   **My friend is to have cataract surgery to fit a new lens into one eye. Why is only one eye done? After the operation, can he read with one eye without glasses?**

A   A cataract is clouding of the lens within the eye. It has the effect of reducing the amount of light entering the eye, and blurring the vision. It is rather like trying to look through frosted glass rather than clear glass.

In the operation, the natural cloudy lens is removed and a clear artificial lens is inserted.

The most noticeable effect after the operation is the brightness of the world. Colours in particular appear far brighter than the washed out appearance they have through a cloudy lens. The ability to read and see objects clearly certainly improves after the operation, but usually not to the point where glasses can be dispensed with altogether. A few weeks after the operation your friend's eyes will be tested, and he will be fitted with new spectacles that may well have totally different strengths in each lens. He may be able to cope for short periods of time using his good eye only, but this would be awkward, and lead to a further deterioration of vision in the bad eye.

Only one eye at a time is operated upon in most patients. Surgeons like to ensure that everything has gone well with one operation before they proceed with the second eye a few months later.

Q   **I am 55 and suffer from watering eyes. It is worse when I walk or cycle, and the tears irritate the skin around the eyes, making it itchy, which annoys the eyes further.**

A   Tears are produced in the tear gland which is under the skin at the outer corner of the eye. They are produced constantly, and slowly wash across the eye to be drained into the tear duct at the inner corner of the eye. This duct leads into the back of the nose.

If you are emotionally upset, tears are produced in excessive quantities, and overflow the eyes so that you are seen to be crying. The extra tears washing down the tear duct into the nose give you the salty taste of tears at the same time. Tears are made of slightly salty water, which closely matches blood, but without the blood cells, proteins and enzymes.

In older people, the fold of skin along the lower eyelid no longer contains the tears that are normally in the eye. The lower eyelid separates from the surface of the eye, folds out just a fraction, and allows tears to overflow onto the skin. The constant exposure to salty water irritates the skin.

When wind blows into the eyes, as it does with cycling or walking, more tears are produced to protect the eyes from drying out, and in your case more tears are available to overflow from the eyes.

At your relatively young age, a minor operation can be performed by an ophthalmologist (eye specialist) to tighten the lower eyelid and correct the problem.

Q   **My eyes are constantly watering. What can be done about this?**

A   Watery eyes may be due to allergies, a blocked tear duct, contact lenses or other foreign bodies in the eye, infections, an out-turned lower eyelid in older people and numerous other reasons. As with most medical problems, correct diagnosis is essential before treatment is commenced.

The most common cause is allergy, and if you have hay fever or asthma in association with your watery eyes, the chance of the cause being an allergy is much higher. Allergic conjunctivitis is treated with simple anti-inflammatory eye drops that are available from chemists, and sometimes with antihistamine tablets. More potent medications are available on prescription if these simple remedies do not work.

Q   I keep losing the coordination of my eyes. At times I am alright, then I see double, and looking in a mirror, the eyes point different ways. What is wrong?

A   I fear that there may be reason for concern in your case. It is possible to get double vision and a squint when you are very tired, but in any other situation it is likely that there is some significant pathology present. This could be anything from thyroid diseases to a growth in the brain or multiple sclerosis. I strongly suggest that you consult a doctor as soon as possible.

Q   I would appreciate your opinion on the cause of a pterygium in the eyes. Some say it is glare, others sand or other foreign matter in the eyes. How is this condition caused, and how do you prevent it?

A   A pterygium is a fleshy overgrowth of the white part of the eye (cornea) that grows across the coloured part of the eye (iris). They develop very slowly over many years, but once they are half way across the iris, they should be removed in a simple operation to avoid growth across the pupil and blindness.

Pterygium are very common in Australia, but more so in the north than the south, as they are caused by recurrent mild sunburn to the cornea. The irritated tissue overgrows, and spreads across the eye.

Farmers, sailors, drivers, outdoor workers and sportspeople are most prone to pterygium as glare and sun exposure are the prime cause. The problem can be prevented by wearing good quality (polarised) sun glasses.

A pterygium may become irritated, red and itchy at times. Simple drops available from chemists will ease this problem.

Once present they will remain until removed surgically. There are no drops that will make them go away.

Q   My mother is having a vitrectomy. What sort of operation is this?

A   The eye contains a clear jelly-like substance called the vitreous. If this becomes discoloured, the vision in that eye will be remarkably reduced, possibly to the point of blindness.

The most common cause of discolouration of the vitreous is bleeding into the eyeball. This can occur in high blood pressure, diabetes and injury. In the last few years, a very delicate operation has been devised in which the blood-stained vitreous can be removed from the eye and a new artificial substance substituted, allowing normal vision again. It is performed under a general anaesthetic by an ophthalmologist (eye doctor) who has had specialist training in this procedure.

FEET

See also ARTHRITIS; LEGS

Q My doctor says my son has flat feet, but is ignoring the problem. Are flat feet serious?

A Flat feet have traditionally been an excuse to avoid military service, and the cause of a great deal of anxiety in parents of these children. Pes planus (medical jargon for flat feet) is no longer considered to be a serious condition, and no treatment other than well-fitting shoes is required. The commonest complications are an awkward gait and distorted shoes, but rarely any pain or discomfort. In some children in may cause knock-knees, but only gross deformities require surgery.

Q I have had a sharp pain in my foot for some years now. X-rays are normal, but the instep becomes very painful. No doctor can find anything wrong. I would be very pleased if you could give me an answer to this.

A I recently read an entire medical journal devoted to the subject of foot pain, and there are several dozen different possibilities. The one that springs most readily to mind is a condition called plantar fasciitis.

The sole of your foot is kept hard and firm by a band of fibrous tissue just under the skin. This is called the plantar fascia. If this becomes stretched, strained or inflamed, it will become very painful. If the foot is rested, the pain settles, but recurs when any prolonged walking or a small amount of running is performed. The only treatments are very prolonged rest, anti-inflammatory medications, and sometimes injections of steroids into the tender part of the foot.

Other causes of foot pain include arthritis, gout, corns, plantar warts, bunions, poor circulation, anaemia, nerve inflammation, minor cracks in the bones and scores of others. If your GP is unable to find a cause and effective treatment, request referral to an orthopaedic surgeon for further assessment.

Q I have had plantar fasciitis for nine months, and have been treated with physiotherapy, arch supports, Orudis gel, cortisone injections and osteopathy. I still have foot pain with walking. Is there anything else that I can do?

A The arch of the foot is maintained by a strong ligament along the outside of the foot and under the sole. If this ligament (the plantar fascia) becomes inflamed because of injury, the patient develops the painful condition of plantar fasciitis.

The most common place for the inflammation to occur is the point where the ligament attaches to the heel bone, and the ligament may actually tear away from the bone by a fraction of a millimetre, resulting in considerable pain that may persist for months.

You have tried all the recognised treatments for the condition with the possible exception of taking anti-inflammatory tablets, but these may upset your stomach.

Many patients suffer for months with this problem, but most eventually settle with time. My advice at this stage would be to persist with the arch supports in good shoes, walk quietly and never run or jump, ride if you can avoid walking (even riding a bike or using roller skates is better!) and try using anti-inflammatory tablets provided your stomach can tolerate them.

Q   I have plantar fasciitis that has been plaguing me with pain for years. What causes this problem? Can massage or other treatments help?

A   The problem may start after excessive exercise (eg. an unusually long run or walk), after a sudden sharp injury (eg. landing heavily after jumping), or it may start for no apparent reason.

The most important treatment is rest, and several weeks on crutches may be very beneficial. Other treatments include the anti-inflammatory tablets that you have already taken, pain-killers, physiotherapy and occasionally steroid injections into the foot. As a last resort, the foot may be put in plaster for a few weeks to ensure total rest. Massage would be more likely to irritate the problem than help.

Q   I have severe pain under my heel. It is making it very difficult to walk, and I spend a lot of time on my feet in my job. What could be the cause?

A   Pain under the heel is one of the most common problems seen by a GP. It can be caused by a spur on the bottom of the heel bone, by inflammation of the large fibrous band that maintains the arch of the foot, or from damage to the heel tissues from running on hard surfaces. Joggers are particularly susceptible to heel pain, and should ensure that they wear good running shoes, and run on grass rather than roads.

Rest is the most important part of treatment. Swimming and cycling can be substituted for exercise while the damaged tissue recovers. Anti-inflammatory medications prescribed by a doctor may ease the discomfort, but some patients require injections of steroids into the heel. These are very successful in curing what can become a chronic problem, although they may be rather painful to receive. Many doctors inject local anaesthetic with the steroid to minimise the discomfort.

Q   What are spurs in the heel, and are there any home remedies?

A   Beneath and behind your heel, large ligaments and tendons attach to the heel bone (calcaneus). The attachment of these ligaments and tendons can be stressed by prolonged over use (eg. being on your feet all day at work), or by a sudden injury. Long-distance running is a classical way in which to injure these attachments, but in older people, far milder stress can cause problems.

After injuring an attachment, the healing process will involve both the tendon or ligament, and the bone to which it attaches. During the healing process, part of the ligament or tendon may be replaced by bone, leading to a spur of bone out from the calcaneus. These spurs can be seen on an x-ray.

Spurs are subject to further injury, and may have tiny microscopic stress fractures in them, which involve the equally tiny nerves in the area to cause chronic pain. Rest will heal the spur, but further use often results in further pain.

The only home remedies are rest and thick padded insoles in shoes (eg. Sorbathane) to protect the spur. If these remedies are not successful, anti-inflammatory medication prescribed by your doctor may give some relief, but injections around the spur or surgical removal of the spur is often necessary.

Q I have a painful problem—a spur under my left heel. I have had three cortisone injections, which help for a few months, but my doctor says it is not safe to give more. What else can be done to help me?

A The treatment of heel spurs involves the use of pain-killers, heat, anti-inflammatory medications (on prescription from your doctor), physiotherapy, steroid injections, or as a last resort, an operation to remove the spur.

Steroid injections are often very effective, but if used too frequently, can actually damage the surrounding tissue.

The operation is fiddly and not particularly easy or comfortable, but is usually successful, although a very small number of patients continue to have pain or develop a recurrence of the spur.

Q What is the exact nature of a spur in the heel, and what causes this complaint?

A A thick ligament extends from the bottom of the heel bone to the base of the toes along the outside edge of the foot. This ligament holds the bones of the foot in an arch to give the foot extra spring and shock resistance.

With every step, this ligament absorbs the weight of the body, and so its attachment to the bottom of the heel bone is put under repeated stress.

In a person who does a lot of standing, walking or running, there may be minor damage to this attachment, and the resulting inflammation may result in the deposition of a small amount of bone in the ligament. This further inflames the ligament, causing more scarring and more bone formation. The end result is a spur of bone sticking out from the bottom of the heel bone into the major supporting ligament of the foot.

This spur of bone is put under pressure with every step, causing discomfort and pain.

Q I suffer severely from plantar warts, which have been unsuccessfully treated with liquid nitrogen. My GP has now prescribed Tagamet for me. Is this drug useful for warts? Is there anything that can be injected into the wart to help?

A Plantar warts are notoriously difficult and painful to treat. Liquid nitrogen can certainly be tried, particularly on smaller warts, but there is a significant failure rate. I personally prefer to use a fairly radical approach, as it seems to be the only one that works long term.

This involves injecting local anaesthetic under and around the wart (itself a painful process in the sole), then using diathermy to burn away the wart, then cutting out the burnt tissue with a scalpel or fine scissors. Any remaining wart is further burnt away, and the process continued until all identifiable wart is removed. A hole is left in the sole which is filled with Betadine ointment, but not sutured. It is covered with a bandage, and left to slowly heal over the next six weeks. It is only painful for a couple of days after the procedure. The chances of recurrence are small (but still present), and a permanent scar is left on the sole.

Tagamet is a medication that is normally used to treat stomach ulcers, but it has been serendipitously found to destroy the virus that causes warts in some patients. It is unlikely to do any harm to you, must be used for at least six months, and just might trigger the immune system to destroy your plantar wart.

I have had success in young adults who have had dozens of warts on their elbows and knees.

Another method of plantar wart treatment is to inject the anti-cancer drug bleomycin under the wart. If too much is used though, a nasty ulcer can develop, but if not enough is used, the wart will not go away.

Q The soles of my feet get very dry, scaly and itchy, particularly in summer. Sometimes there are tiny pimples present at the sides of the foot. Fungicidal creams do not help. What is it and how should it be treated?

A Dyshidrosis (also known as pompholyx) is the condition that fits your description. It is a form of eczema that is associated with excessive sweating (feet sweat in shoes), but may also be aggravated by anxiety, stress, fungal infections and chemicals that contact the area.

The small vescicles that develop are often described as small boiled rice grains under the skin.

If the cause of the problem can be removed (eg. wear sandals instead of shoes to reduce sweating) the condition will slowly resolve, but often the cause cannot be determined and it is necessary to use various medications to control the itching and irritation.

Potassium permanganate foot baths are messy but effective. Other treatments include steroid creams and steroid tablets in severe cases.

Q I suffer constantly from cold feet, mainly when in bed, and have been told it is a medical problem. I await your comments.

A Cold feet are usually due to poor circulation of blood to that area. If insufficient warm blood reaches your feet, they will feel cold, and may be white or blue, and painful.

In older people, hardening of the arteries (atherosclerosis), heart failure and diabetes are the main causes of poor circulation, while in younger people, spasm of an artery may be responsible.

Raynaud's phenomenon is a condition in which arteries go into spasm, narrow down, and fail to supply adequate blood to the hands or feet, which become cold and painful.

As you can see, a number of conditions may be responsible for your problem. You will need to be investigated to determine which problem is affecting you. Once this is known, the appropriate treatment can be given to cure or control the disease.

Q I have a painful swollen foot. What could cause this?

A Whatever the cause, you should see a doctor. There are certainly some simple explanations, such as a twist or sprain to one of the joints in the foot, but there are more sinister causes as well, including a severe deep infection, a thrombosed vein and gout. Various types of arthritis may also be responsible, as well as other diseases of muscles and ligaments.

If you are an older person, or have taken more exercise than usual recently, it is possible for a stress fracture to be present. There may be no apparent injury to cause these, but they certainly cause pain and swelling.

Q My son insists on wearing sneakers, and refuses to wear good shoes. The more worn the sneakers appear, the happier he is. Are sneakers good or bad for your feet?

A Feet need support, protection and air circulation to remain healthy. Lack of support can lead to flat feet, ankle injuries and foot pain. Lack of protection leads to injury from above, sides and below. Lack of air circulation leads to sweaty moist feet that are susceptible to fungal and bacterial infections.

By these standards, leather shoes with an arch support and air holes are the ideal footwear. Trying to keep an Australian child in such shoes, particularly during summer, is virtually impossible. Compromises are therefore necessary.

Good quality sandals and sneakers are acceptable, but those made of plastic or nylon should be avoided, as these aggravate the sweating of feet. Canvas or open weave sneakers are preferable, as are those with a good insole and support shape.

Q I have severe pain at the back of my heel that flares up whenever I start running. I am young, and trying to keep fit, and this constantly prevents my running.

A Running puts a great deal of stress on the attachment of the large Achilles tendon into the back of the heel bone. With the constant jarring and pushing on this point, the tendon may tear and separate slightly from the bone, leading to acute pain and tenderness at the site.

Treatment is by rest, and anti-inflammatory tablets. Occasionally, an injection is given into the sore point to settle the inflammation, and very rarely surgery is required. If you do not rest for long enough, or start running too hard too soon, the problem rapidly recurs.

Running is not the best form of exercise to keep fit because of the excess stress it places on feet, ankles and knees. Swimming and cycling are far more effective, and it is probably better to keep fit with these for a season until the heel has completely healed rather than run.

Q What can cause pain in the front half of the foot? I cannot recall injuring it in anyway.

A. Gout is a severe and obvious cause of foot pain, but there are several other common causes.

Metatarsalgia is a condition common in athletes. It is an inflammation of the bones that form the ball of the foot, and is due to prolonged running, jumping or walking, usually on hard surfaces. Soldiers on route marches may develop the condition. Severe pain may develop in the ball of the foot, and the treatment is primarily rest, and anti-inflammatory medications.

A 'march fracture' of the fore foot bones, due to the stress of continued walking or running on the foot may be another cause. There are minimal changes on x-ray, but excruciating pain on attempting to walk. Six weeks rest heals these fractures.

In the elderly, foot pain may be the first sign of poor circulation, diabetes, rheumatoid arthritis or neuralgia.

Because these conditions can be serious, the cause of the pain must be investigated by a doctor and the correct treatment started.

Q My daughter overseas has written to tell me that my new grand-daughter has been born with a club foot. I have heard of this condition, but do not understand what it is. Can you explain it to me?

A Club foot is a congenital (present at birth) deformity of the foot that can vary dramatically in severity and can be easily detected at birth.

It is characterised by an inturning of the foot, so that if allowed to walk, the infant would walk on the outside edge of the foot and the little toe.

Some children merely require binders and splints to correct the condition; others with a more severe condition will need corrective surgery over several years.

Q I have two bunions on each foot on the large toes. They give me pain. Would you advise operation? If so, could I have them done at the same time?

A If the big toe is constantly pushed across towards the smaller toes by high-heeled shoes, tight shoes, or a poor way of walking, the big toe may become semi-permanently deformed in this direction. The end of the long bone behind the two big toe bones in the front half of the foot (called a metatarsal) is exposed by the deflection of the toe bones, and starts pushing against the skin.

A protective, fluid-filled sac (called a bursa) forms between the bone end and the skin to protect the bone. This sac slowly enlarges to cause a lump that may become tender and painful. This is a bunion.

Bunions are becoming less common with more sensible and better-made footwear, and a wealthier society in which correctly fitted shoes can be purchased regularly for a child's growing feet. Bunions usually start in childhood, but may not cause significant discomfort until adult life.

A number of surgical procedures are available to cure a bunion, but in elderly people, it may be preferable for a protective pad to be worn inside soft or specially made shoes. When bunions are repaired, it is normal for only one side to be done at a time, but in elderly people, in whom immediate mobility is not a concern, both sides can be done at once.

Q I am experiencing hot burning feet in bed at night. Is this a medical problem?

A Any discomfort or pain in the body is a medical problem, but I assume you are concerned that it may be a symptom of some severe disease.

Hot burning feet can be due to the fact that the feet are actually hot (do they feel hot when you touch them with your hand?), or it could be that your brain perceives that the feet are hot when they are not, because of a problem with the nerves that lead from the feet to the brain.

Hot feet may be caused by an excessive blood supply to the feet, so that too much blood is pumped into them, or too little drains out. This may be due to a problem with your circulation, and sometimes is a side effect of medications that treat blood pressure by dilating arteries.

Nerve problems can be due to nerve damage from conditions such as diabetes, or pinching of the nerve somewhere in the leg, pelvis or back. Rarely nerve damage in the spine or brain could lead to inappropriate sensations of heat.

You need to see your general practitioner for a thorough check up to see if there is any significant cause for your discomfort.

Q   How do you catch athlete's foot, and what causes it?

A   Fungi are members of the plant kingdom, and are one of the types of microscopic life that can infect human beings in many diverse ways. The most common site of infection is the skin, where they cause an infection that is commonly known as tinea. The fungus that causes tinea can be found everywhere in the environment in the form of hardy spores. These are microscopic in size and may survive for decades before being picked up and starting an infection. Between the toes the fungus causes a type of tinea commonly known as athlete's foot. This is because athletes sweat and wear close-fitting shoes that lead to the ideal warm, damp environment favoured by fungi.

Q   The tendons under the arches of my feet are sore and lumpy. It feels like standing on a painful pea. Please advise me who I should see to have this problem fixed.

A   The painful pea under your foot is probably a ganglion. There are other explanations, but this is by far the most likely.

Tendons in the hands and feet are like cables that run through smooth pipes. The tendons are coated with a lubricating fluid in these pipes (called tendon sheaths) so that they run smoothly. If a tendon sheath gets a puncture, the lubricating fluid leaks out under pressure to form a fluid filled cyst. This cyst feels like a hard lump because the fluid in it is under pressure.

This type of cyst is called a ganglion. Sometimes ganglions burst and disappear, but often they re-form again over a few weeks.

They can be treated by draining out the fluid through a needle, but often they come back again, despite doctors sometimes injecting a steroid to try and reduce the inflammation and damage.

The best solution is to have a small operation to remove the ganglion permanently. This procedure is usually performed by an orthopaedic surgeon.

Q   My orthopaedic surgeon has diagnosed the lumps under my foot as Ledderhose's disease, but says there is not much that can be done for it. Can you tell me more about this condition?

A   A fibrous sheet (the plantar fascia) stretches under the skin of the sole to give it a smooth appearance, strength and firmness, and to protect and control the movement of the muscle tendons that cross under it to the toes. If damaged, the plantar fascia may become scarred, contract and thicken into hard lumps that can be felt under the skin. As the damage progresses, the contraction of the fibrous sheet pulls on the tendons that run underneath it to prevent their free movement. This is Ledderhose's disease.

Men are affected more than women, and a similar condition (Dupuytren's contracture) occurs in the hand.

The cause is unknown, but may be due to a poor blood supply to the foot (eg. diabetes), and injury to the foot from repeated blows (eg. running).

The symptoms include one or more hard, fixed nodules under the skin of the sole that gradually extend lengthwise along the sole to cause discomfort, pain with walking and loss of toe mobility. Eventually the toes cannot be fully extended, and contract into a claw-like appearance. The middle toes are usually more severely affected than the others.

Treatment involves soft shoe insoles, injection of steroids around the nodule, and in severe cases only, the nodule may be surgically excised. Unfortunately, recurrence after surgery is common, and the lumps are usually persistent.

FEMALE PROBLEMS
See also HORMONES; HYSTERECTOMY; INFERTILITY; MENOPAUSE; SEX

Q   What is the purpose of a woman's period?

A   Once a month, just after a woman releases the egg (at ovulation) from her ovary, the lining of the womb (uterus) is at its peak to allow the embedding of a fertilised egg.

If pregnancy does not occur, the lining of the womb starts to deteriorate as the hormones that sustain it in peak condition alter. After a few days, the lining breaks down completely, sloughs off the wall of the uterus, and is washed away by the blood released from the arteries that supplied it. Contractions of the uterus also help remove the debris.

After 3 to 5 days, the bleeding stops, and a new lining starts to develop ready for the next month's ovulation.

Q   I am only 55, but I am having terrible problems with urinary incontinence. Can you help me with this problem?

A   Embarrassing, unpleasant, uncomfortable, distasteful, offensive, distressing, intolerable and very annoying. Urinary incontinence is all these things, and more, but it is a topic that is never discussed with friends or family, and mentioned to doctors often only after many visits for other more socially acceptable diseases. Incontinence is usually associated with the old man lying semiconscious in a nursing home bed. But it is far more common in women, and many relatively young women in their thirties or earlier can be victims.

Incontinence is the loss of urine from the bladder at times when such loss is not desirable. It can vary from constant bed-wetting, to the occasional dribble when a woman jumps, coughs or laughs.

The most common cause of incontinence is the damage done to the genitals during childbirth, and this is the reason for women being the victims far more frequently than men. Other causes include urinary infections, strokes, confusion in the elderly, bladder injury, epilepsy and damage to the spinal cord in paraplegics and quadriplegics.

The urethra is the tube that carries urine from the bladder to the outside of the body. In women it is only 1 to 2 cm long. It leaves the bladder at an acute angle, and this angle causes the pressure of the urine inside the bladder to keep the urethra closed. It requires a voluntary muscular effort to open the urethra and allow the urine to escape. The stretching that occurs during childbirth can cause this critical angle to be lost and the urethra to become a straight tube leading from the bladder to the outside. Any pressure put on the bladder, or any significant volume of urine, can then cause incontinence. Unfortunately this straightened tube can also allow bacteria and infection to enter the bladder more easily and cause the pain and discomfort of cystitis (bladder infection).

Because the bladder is controlled by nerves, damage to the nervous system by a stroke or the cutting of the spinal cord in paraplegics may also lead to incontinence.

As with most diseases, the earlier incontinence is treated, the better the results. Prevention is even better than cure. Exercises to strengthen the muscles of the pelvic floor should be undertaken by all women immediately after childbirth. These can also be done in the early stages of incontinence to help control the bladder function as normally as possible. A patient can start by practising stopping and starting the urinary stream several times whenever they go to the toilet. Physiotherapists can teach the finer details of these exercises.

If the problem has progressed beyond control by exercises alone, the options are rather limited. In younger women, an operation to correct the abnormal bladder/urethra angle is usually successful. In older women, a specially shaped rubber ring may be worn inside the vagina to put pressure on the urethra and prevent urine from escaping. These rings must be fitted and regularly checked by a doctor.

In intractable cases it may be necessary to insert a semi-permanent catheter (tube) into a woman's bladder that drains urine into a collecting bag. A woman's concern about incontinence can become a significant mental problem and a social barrier, and should therefore be treated sooner rather than later.

Men can also have an operation, but it is not as successful as in women. In elderly and paralysed men, it is often more practical to use a collecting bag, as this can be easily attached to the penis.

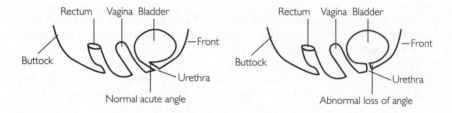

Diagrammatic cross-section through a woman's pelvis showing normal angle of urethra and bladder that prevents incontinence, and the abnormal situation after childbirth when the angle may be lost.

Q **I am a 52 year old woman. I have a dragging feeling in my groin that has been getting worse for six months. I also keep wetting myself whenever I cough or laugh. My doctor says it is a prolapse. What is a female prolapse and how can it be cured?**

A A prolapse is a protrusion of an organ into an abnormal place.

The vagina leads from the outside up to the uterus. During childbirth, it becomes very stretched and it does not always return to its original size. The muscles around the vagina may become weakened and the ligaments supporting the uterus may also become stretched and sag. After some years, this may lead to the uterus slowly moving down the vagina to a point where it completely fills it. Occasionally it may even protrude through to the outside. This is a uterine prolapse.

In some women, part of the bladder which is in front of the vagina may push back into the vagina, causing a bladder prolapse and difficulty with passing urine. The large gut, which is behind the vagina, may also push forward into the vagina as a rectal prolapse, this time causing bowel problems. Often there is a combination of these three types of prolapse.

Treatment is usually successful by means of an operation. In some older women, a ring inserted into the vagina may be used to hold everything in the correct place. Younger women can help prevent the problem by undertaking special pelvic floor exercises under the guidance of a physiotherapist both before and after the delivery of their baby.

Q   **When I attend aerobic classes I am embarrassed by an involuntary passing of urine when doing more strenuous exercises. I have children, and I believe this condition is caused by weakening of the pelvic floor muscles during childbirth. I plan to have another child, but are there any exercises that will help me, or is surgery the only answer?**

A   Surgery is the only permanent answer for this type of stress incontinence, but this should be delayed until after you have completed your family, as a further pregnancy will destroy all the surgeon's work.

Physiotherapists can benefit you in the interim by teaching pelvic floor exercises that will strengthen the muscles around the bladder. It may be possible for these exercises to completely control the problem for you, but they must be continued long term.

Q   **My doctor commented when doing a Pap smear that my womb was prolapsed. He said I shouldn't worry about it until it caused problems. What causes a prolapse of the womb?**

A   The womb (uterus) is where the baby grows during pregnancy. It therefore has the ability to expand dramatically in size, and is only loosely attached to the rest of the body. The ligaments that support it are stretched during pregnancy and may not return to their original size, allowing the uterus to move around more freely.

The more pregnancies you have, the slacker the ligaments become. With the assistance of gravity, pressure on the abdomen from lifting (eg. the result of pregnancy—children), constipation and lack of fitness it is possible for the womb to slowly slip lower and lower into the pelvis. This causes pressure on the bladder and bowel, leading to problems with these organs.

Eventually, the womb may move all the way down the vagina to expose the cervix (opening of the womb). The main symptoms are discomfort and bladder incontinence. Correction is by best performed by surgery, but elderly women may use specially shaped rings that are inserted into the vagina to keep the womb in place.

Q   **I have a terribly personal and embarrassing problem. Whenever I try to pass faeces, a lump comes out of my vagina. I can pass a little bit, but no more. As soon as I stand up, the lump goes and I need to go again. Is it cancer?**

A You probably have a rectocoele, and not cancer.

During childbirth the vaginal canal becomes very stretched. As you age, the tissues supporting the walls of the vagina becomes slack. The combination of these two factors leads to a weakness on the back wall of the vagina and the lower part of the gut (the rectum) can sag (prolapse) into the vagina.

When you attempt to pass faeces, the increased pressure in the abdomen pushes the rectum further into the vagina, even to the point where part of the back wall of the vagina is pushed outside as a lump. When this happens, the rectum takes on a very sharp S shape, and this makes it difficult for the faeces to pass down further. You can expel the small amount of faeces just inside the anus, but no further faeces can pass the S to reach the anus.

When you stand up and relax, the lump goes down, the S straightens out, faeces moves down the rectum a bit further, and you want to go to the toilet again.

The solution is to have an operation to strengthen the back wall of the vagina and suspend the rectum so that it cannot sag. In the short term, a rubber ring inserted by a doctor into the vagina may prevent the problem.

Q **I have a very embarrassing problem that I am reluctant to discuss with my doctor. It is a discharge from the vagina. What could it be?**

A Vaginal discharges fall into three major categories—excess normal secretions, infections, and bloody discharges.

The most common cause is excess production of the normal lubricating fluid that is present in the vagina. This can be due to hormonal changes at puberty, menopause and with pregnancy; the use of hormones including those in the oral contraceptive pill; sexual excitement or even stress and anxiety. Vaginal douches can sometimes irritate the vagina to cause a discharge.

Infections can include thrush (a fungus being the cause), trichomoniasis (a small organism that is transmitted sexually), various venereal diseases and a bacterial vaginitis. Doctors can usually distinguish between these by the appearance of the discharge, the smell produced or by using laboratory tests.

Bloody discharges are cause for concern. It may be just an abnormal period, but can also be a sign of significant vaginal or uterine disease.

Please do not be embarrassed, see your doctor to obtain the correct diagnosis and treatment.

Q **I have had vaginal infections before that have been treated by Flagyl, and I think I have the same infection again. Can I use the drug Flagyl if I am pregnant?**

A Flagyl is an excellent antibiotic for treating certain types of bacterial infections that occur deep inside the body. Infections of the woman's Fallopian tubes and pelvic organs are one example.

No medication should be used between the 6th and 14th week of pregnancy unless it is absolutely essential, as this is the time when the organs and limbs of the baby are developing.

Flagyl should NOT be used at this time, and it should only be used during the rest of the pregnancy and during breast feeding if there is no alternative. There is no evidence that Flagyl causes damage to the foetus, but it is known to enter the foetal circulation, so there is a potential for problems. It is better to be safe than sorry!

Q **What is the best treatment for the itch of thrush? I get this terrible infection every few months, and it drives me crazy!**

A The almost irresistible, but socially unacceptable itch is what drives most patients to the doctor.

The treatment of vaginal thrush revolves around vaginal pessaries (tablets), vaginal creams and an oral tablet. These can give rapid relief, and are given in a course that can vary from one to ten days depending on the severity of the infection and the method of treatment used.

You can prevent infections by wearing loose cotton panties, drying the genital area carefully after swimming or showering, avoiding tight clothing, wiping from front to back after going to the toilet and not using tampons when an infection is likely. Even using all these measures, it is a fortunate woman who avoids catching thrush at some time in her life.

Q **I am 19 and have had three sexual relationships with men. Over the past few months I have had a thick white discharge from my vagina, and it is itchy and sore around that area. I am getting married in two months and am worried that I might have some sort of sexually transmitted disease, and I would feel embarrassed and dirty seeing a doctor about this. What can I do?**

A What you are describing is a typical case of vaginal thrush. Tight jeans, pantihose, the contraceptive pill, nylon bathers, antibiotics and sex are the common aggravating factors involved in catching this modern woman's curse.

Thrush, also known as candidiasis or moniliasis, is a fungal infection caused by a fungus called *Candida albicans*, which lives in the gut where it causes little or no trouble. Usually when it comes out on to the skin around the anus, it dies off; but if that skin is warm, moist and irritated, it can grow and spread forward to the lips of the vagina (the vulva).

Entry of the fungus into the vagina from the skin outside is aided by the mechanical action of sex, and the alteration in the acidity of the vagina caused by the contraceptive pill.

Once established, this fungus causes an unpleasant white vaginal discharge, intense itching of the vulva and surrounding skin, and often inflammation of the urine opening so that passing urine causes discomfort.

You should see your doctor as soon as possible to confirm the diagnosis and obtain the correct treatment.

Your fiancé must also be treated with a cream, because although he may show no signs of the infection, it may be present under his foreskin, and he can give the thrush back to you after you have been successfully treated.

Q **I am 40 years old. After I had an intrauterine device (IUD) inserted my periods became much lighter. I used this method of contraception for three years, discontinuing a year ago. Now my periods are very light, regular and I have no premenstrual tension. What could cause this?**

A Light regular periods with no premenstrual tension is many women's idea of heaven. It is certainly not something to be concerned about.

Light periods in a 40 year old may be due to the early onset of menopause, or may be due to a natural change in the nature of the periods with time.

Most women find that the nature of their menstrual cycle changes gradually with over the years, and may change significantly after a pregnancy or ceasing the contraceptive pill.

The IUD is often associated with heavier and more painful periods, but your cycle is probably nothing to do with having used an IUD, just a fortunate coincidence.

The IUD is now out of favour as a contraceptive because a very small number of women had some significant side effects. On the other hand, a very large number of women found it a very convenient and effective method of controlling their fertility.

I trust that you are now using some form of contraception (even if that is abstinence) as light periods, particularly if they are regular, means that you can still become pregnant.

Q   I have not had a period for 5 months after stopping the pill. Is this normal?

A   About 10% of women who use the contraceptive pill have a delay in the return of their periods after stopping it. It is nothing to be overly concerned about, and can occur just as easily after one month on the pill as after ten years on it. Unless you are very eager to fall pregnant, doctors will wait for about six months before prescribing hormone tablets to start your cycle again. The vast majority of women will restart their periods within six months.

Some women have a tendency to miss periods for emotional, hormonal and other reasons. These women are the ones most likely to develop this problem. The pill has no effect on the long-term fertility of a couple, but is often blamed for difficulty in falling pregnancy because 15% of all couples have a delay of over a year in conceiving.

Q   I have just had an appendix operation. The doctor examined my ovaries during the operation, and he says they are very small. Is this serious?

A   Some people have small noses, others big noses. Some people have small feet, others big feet. Some people have small ovaries, others big ovaries. The actual size of the ovary has no effect upon your fertility or femininity, unless their size is due to fibrosis or disease. If this was the case, the surgeon would probably have commented about it, and referred you to a gynaecologist for a further opinion and treatment.

The ovaries are responsible for producing an egg every month that has the potential to be fertilised and implant in the womb in pregnancy. The ovaries also produce hormones that give you your appearance as a woman. The breasts, for example, develop in the first place and continue their firm shape because of the hormones produced in the ovary.

If you are concerned, you should contact the surgeon again and ask him if the small size of your ovaries was due to disease.

Q   What is a blighted ovum? My gynaecologist said it caused my miscarriage. It sounds terrible! Do I need more treatment? Can I fall pregnant again?

A   It sounds far worse than it is, and sometimes doctors are guilty of dropping these frightful medical terms into a conversation without adequately explaining them.

If you don't understand what your doctor is saying, tell him or her, so that a translation into terms more familiar to the layman can be given.

A blighted ovum is one that is not developing properly after fertilisation. It is a pregnancy that would never produce a normal baby. The ovum (or egg) may have been formed abnormally, or may not be developing properly after fertilisation by a sperm. It is probably best thought of as the placenta (or afterbirth) growing without a baby (in any way we would imagine) being present. The mother's body realises that things are not progressing properly, and stops the pregnancy by having a miscarriage.

The normal treatment would be to have the womb (uterus) cleaned out by a small operation, but after this you can get pregnant again. It will not affect any future pregnancy, and should be considered to be just bad luck. One in eight of all pregnancies ends as a miscarriage.

Q **I have been told that my painful periods are due to fibroids in my uterus. What are these, and are they cancerous?**

A The uterus (or womb) is made up of muscular tissue, fibrous tissue and glandular tissue. After childbirth, the uterus must shrink from a very large distended size, back to its usual shape and size, which resembles that of a small pear. It is thought that the stress on the uterus during pregnancy may result in some minor injury to the fibrous tissue in the uterine wall, and after the uterus contracts, this fibrous tissue repairs itself in an abnormal way. The result is the formation of one or more hard fibrous balls in the wall of the uterus, which may be the size of a golf ball or larger.

When the uterus contracts to force out the blood and wastes during a period, these fibrous balls distort the uterus, and cause the muscles to go into painful cramps.

Fibroids are not cancerous, but they can certainly cause considerable distress to a woman, and because their symptoms can mimic a cancer, they are always thoroughly investigated.

If the uterine cramps and discomfort are very distressing, the uterus can be removed in a hysterectomy operation, or if the women wishes to have more children, the individual fibroid masses can be cut out of the uterus.

Q **Is there any specific time of the month to have a Pap smear and is it normal to have an internal examination at the same time?**

A You can have a Pap smear at any time of the month, provided you are not bleeding with your monthly period. Breakthrough bleeding at other times of the month may also interfere with a Pap smear. If you have a vaginal infection with a discharge, it is sensible to have the infection treated before having the smear, as the infection will contaminate the smear and make it difficult to interpret.

A Pap smear should be performed every two years on all women who have ever been sexually active, in order to detect cancer of the cervix, vaginal infections and other abnormalities in the vagina and cervix.

An internal examination is often performed at the same time to feel the ovaries for lumps, hardness or tenderness, and to check the uterus size and shape.

Most doctors would also take the opportunity to examine your breasts and check your blood pressure as part of a thorough examination.

Q   I am 65 years old, and have never had a Pap smear. Do I have to start now?

A   There are many different opinions about this, but I would encourage you to have a Pap smear now, and another in two years. If both are normal, you may not need to continue having them.

A Pap smear could turn up a condition of the cervix that may lead to cancer in later years. This can be treated just as well at 65 as it could at 35.

Q   I am going on a school wilderness camp for a week right at the time I am due to get my period. I have heard I can take pills to delay my period. How do I do this?

A   You must visit your doctor to obtain advice about this, since you will need a prescription, and your doctor will be familiar with your medical history. There are hormone pills which will delay your period, or if you are already taking the birth control pill, your doctor will advise you how to alter the pill taking regime to avoid or delay your period. Ideally you should see your doctor at least two weeks before the period you wish to delay.

Q   My daughter is 15 but has not started her periods. Is this reason for concern?

A   In the seventeenth century, it was unusual for girls to start their periods until they were 16 or 17. Today, they may start at 12 or earlier, the change being due to the better diet, health and hygiene in the twentieth century, more rapid growth, and therefore faster maturation of the body.

The onset of periods in a girl can be estimated by the experience of her mother, sisters or cousins, but there may still be significant variations. The trend is continuing for periods to start earlier every generation.

By 15, you would expect breast buds to have developed and some early wisps of pubic hair to be present. If this is not the case your daughter should be checked by a doctor.

There are some medical conditions that can lead to a delay in the onset of periods. These include any severe illness earlier in life that may have slowed maturation, diseases of the ovaries or other glands, and some rare congenital disorders.

Q   Can you explain endometriosis for me? I have been told that this is the cause of my painful periods.

A   Your uterus (womb) is lined with special cells, which during the second half of your monthly cycle, are prepared to accept any fertilised egg and allow it to grow into a baby. If no pregnancy occurs, these cells degenerate, break away from the inside of the uterus, and with the resultant bleeding, pass out of the body in a woman's period.

From the top of the uterus, the two Fallopian tubes lead out to the two ovaries. In a very small number of unlucky women, the cells that normally go out during a period, may go in and through these Fallopian tubes. The cells are then in an abnormal position around the ovary, on the outside of the uterus or in the pelvic cavity, and they can attach to these tissues and start growing and spreading further.

They will still respond to the hormonal cycle every month, as these hormones pass through the bloodstream to every cell in the body. As a result, these cells in abnormal positions will bleed every month, releasing blood in places where it can cause pain and other symptoms. The cells may also block the Fallopian tubes causing infertility, or settle on the outside of the intestine to cause irritation and diarrhoea.

The condition can only be diagnosed by examining a woman's pelvis by means of an operation or a laparoscopy. A laparoscopy involves a small tube being put through the belly button into the abdomen, and through this a doctor can see the spots of endometriosis in its abnormal positions.

Q   **I am concerned about using tampons after reading about the toxic shock syndrome. Is this a significant risk for women, or can I still use tampons safely?**

A   The toxic shock syndrome, despite all the publicity, is actually a very rare condition, and most general practitioners have never seen a case. Only a dozen or so cases occur in Australia each year. The people who do develop the condition are extremely ill, and about 5% of them die, despite the best efforts of doctors.

Some bacteria, and particularly one called *Staphylococcus aureus* (the golden staph) which is a common cause of vaginal and other infections, may produce a toxin or poison. Most people have antibodies to protect them from this problem, but in a very small number of people, the toxin may cause severe effects.

The symptoms of toxic shock syndrome are a high fever, dizziness, severe diarrhoea, vomiting, muscle aches, fainting and sometimes a rash. An examining doctor will find the blood pressure to be low.

The syndrome can occur in anyone, but seems to be more common in women and particularly in women who are menstruating. Of the last 30 cases reported in Australia, only one was associated with tampon use.

Treatment involves antibiotics to treat the bacterial infection, and hospitalisation to replace the fluids lost with the severe diarrhoea and vomiting. There is no specific antidote to the toxin, and so the earlier the diagnosis is made, the better the chances of recovery.

There is no reason why women should not use tampons, as the risk of developing toxic shock syndrome with them is infinitesimally small. Only if the tampon becomes infected is there any chance of developing the syndrome.

To reduce the risk to a minimum, ensure your hands are clean before unwrapping and inserting the tampon; use the lowest absorbency tampon necessary for your flow; never insert more than one tampon; do not leave the tampon in for any longer than necessary; and pads may be a better alternative overnight. Make sure you don't forget to remove the last tampon of your period.

There is no evidence that any one brand or type of tampon is more likely to cause the syndrome than any other.

Relax and use the menstrual hygiene product that best suits your needs.

Q   **What causes senile vaginitis? I have had it for 9 years and I am a 75 year old pensioner.**

A   A woman's vagina is kept moist by the production of a mucus from glands in and around it. During sexual stimulation, these glands secrete more mucus, to give added lubrication. After the menopause, the female hormone oestrogen is no longer produced by the ovaries. It is this hormone that stimulates the vaginal glands to produce the mucus. Without the oestrogen, the glands do not function, and so many older women complain of a dry, sore, itchy vagina. Oestrogen also causes the formation of breast tissue and pubic hair. It is because oestrogen is lacking after the menopause that the breasts sag and the pubic hair becomes scanty.

The vaginal problem can be overcome in several ways. Simple moisturising creams can be purchased from chemists (or are available on script for pensioners) to apply when the vagina is irritated. A more effective treatment is to use creams containing oestrogen in the vagina. These creams are available under the Pharmaceutical Benefits Scheme and they usually need to be used only once or twice a week. Excess use can cause absorption of the oestrogen, which may result in nipple soreness and other symptoms of oestrogen excess.

The final method of treatment is to give oestrogen in very small doses by tablets.

Q **When I get my periods, they go on too long. Sometimes I bleed for 15 days each month. I am 25 years old. I have seen different doctors, but they don't seem to help. I'm going crazy. What do you suggest?**

A Prolonged irregular periods in a young woman require detailed investigation to exclude any cause for the obvious hormonal imbalance you are suffering. These investigations could include blood tests, a laparoscopy (looking into your pelvis with a microscope tube), and a curette (cleaning out of the uterus). If all these are negative, and the problem continues, a number of different hormones and medications can be used to regulate your cycle.

The most commonly used treatment is the oral contraceptive pill, but a relatively high dose may be necessary to totally suppress your own hormone production. After some experimentation with dosage, most women find that this will give them regular, light, pain-free periods.

Other alternatives include other types of hormones taken for the ten to fourteen days before an expected period, and hormone-blocking drugs.

You should continue to pester the doctor in whom you have the most confidence, for a successful form of control. Continued doctor shopping will only lead to confusion in your mind, and between the different doctors.

Q **I have terrible period pain, but every two weeks when I am both menstruating and ovulating! It seems to be more pronounced on the right side. What can I do?**

A You are extraordinarily unlucky to be suffering from both forms of regular gynaecological pain—uterine cramps and mittelschmerz.

When your periods come every month, the thick muscle of the uterus contracts to squeeze out the old uterine lining as blood mixed with cells. In some women, the uterus contracts too much, goes into spasm and causes severe pain, in much the same way that a leg muscle can go into cramp and cause pain.

In the middle of each month, a small cyst that contains a microscopic egg reaches the surface of a woman's ovary, ruptures, and releases the egg and a small amount of fluid. If the woman produces eggs in a large cyst instead of a small one, excessive amounts of fluid will be released at ovulation when the cyst ruptures. The fluid is irritant to the lining of the pelvis, and so pain (called mittelschmerz) results.

Often one ovary is more active than the other, and in your case the right ovary is producing more eggs than the left.

Most women experience uterine cramps with periods, or mittelschmerz with ovulation at some time of their life, but when it occurs regularly, the problem becomes distressing.

If you are not trying to fall pregnant, the simple way to treat your two problems is to take the contraceptive pill, which has the double benefit of stopping ovulation (and thus mittelschmerz), and of significantly reducing the loss at period times, thus reducing uterine cramps.

Period cramps can also be reduced by taking medication such as Ponstan or ibuprofen, but there is no other easy way to stop ovulation pain.

FIRST AID

Q **What should a good home medical chest contain?**

A A comprehensive home medical chest should contain the following items:
Paracetamol tablets
Paracetamol liquid
Charcoal tablets or solution (for overdose)
Lotion for bites and stings
Anti-itch cream
Antiseptic cream
Antiseptic liquid
Pseudoephedrine tablets and/or liquid (for nasal congestion)
Oxymetazoline nose drops
Menthol inhalant
Cough syrup
Antiseptic ear drops
Antiseptic eye drops
Sunscreen lotion or cream
Splinter forceps
Scissors
Triangular bandage (sling)
Adhesive dressing (various sizes)
Elastic bandages (wide)
Cotton gauze (NOT cotton wool)
Adhesive tape

Q **I was recently bitten by a bee, and everyone had different ideas on how to help me. What is the best first-aid treatment for a bee sting?**

A A bee is suicidal when it stings. The sting is in its tail, and is torn off after piercing the skin, which results in the disembowelment and death of the bee.

Immediately after being stung, it is necessary to remove the sting itself.

Do NOT pull it out, as this will squeeze more toxin into the victim's tissue. Brush the sting out by knocking it out of the skin sideways with the edge of a firm object (eg. back of a knife, edge of a piece of cardboard or fingernail). Then apply ice or cold water, and leave it there for 15 minutes or more. After this, anti-itch creams available from a chemist or methylated spirits applied to the bite site may ease the irritation. If severe discomfort persists, a steroid cream obtained from a doctor will give relief.

If the patient is allergic to bee stings, an antihistamine tablet should be given immediately, if available an antihistamine cream should be applied, and medical attention should be sought as soon as possible. Some allergic reactions can be severe enough to cause breathing to stop and the heart to beat irregularly. Mouth-to-mouth resuscitation should be given in this situation.

Q **I was bitten badly by ants when I trod on a nest recently. What is the best first-aid treatment for ant bites?**

A The treatment for any ant, insect or spider bite depends on several factors. The normal green or red ant bite will sting for several hours, and then itch for days. It is not likely to cause any severe reaction, but considerable discomfort can ensue.

Immediately after the bite apply ice or cold water, and leave it there for 15 minutes or more. After this, anti-itch creams available from a chemist or methylated spirits applied to the bite site may ease the irritation. If severe discomfort persists, a steroid cream obtained from a doctor will give relief. If the patient is allergic to the particular insect, an antihistamine tablet should be given immediately, if available an antihistamine cream should be applied, and medical attention should be sought as soon as possible.

Some allergic reactions can be severe enough to cause breathing to stop and the heart to beat irregularly. Mouth to mouth resuscitation should be given in this situation. If the bite is from a potentially lethal spider such as the funnel web or red-back in a child (no ants or other Australian insects come in to this category), the limb bitten should be bandaged firmly from the bite site to the groin or armpit, and then down to the foot or hand. The limb should be splinted, and the patient transported to hospital for the appropriate antivenom.

Q **I saw someone choke to death on TV after eating, and everyone in this show pretended to panic, and he died. How do you help a person who is choking?**

A Choking occurs when a foreign body gets stuck in the airway so that breathing is obstructed. It is vital to remove the object immediately. In severe cases the victim cannot breathe at all, and if left untreated will die. Adults may choke on food or broken false teeth; children may choke on bits of toys they put in their mouth or foods such as peanuts or chewing gum.

When choking occurs, the victim may have a violent fit of coughing and the face and neck will become deep red, turning to purple. They will make a superhuman effort to breathe, and if unsuccessful will claw the air and clutch at the throat before turning blue in the face and collapsing.

Often the object will be dislodged by the coughing. If not, try to remove it with your finger—but be extremely careful not to push it down further. If that is unsuccessful, two or three sharp blows between the shoulderblades may clear it. Make sure the person is in a position in which the object can fall out easily—eg. an adult should sit and lean forward. If the victim is lying down, turn them gently to one side.

If this fails, there are several ways in which you may proceed:

1. Place your arms around the victim's chest from behind, with your clenched fists over the breast bone. As suddenly and as hard as you can, push on the breast bone and squeeze the chest (Heimlich manoeuvre).

2. Lie the patient in the coma position on their side on the floor, give several sharp blows between the shoulder blades, and then if necessary, give several firm quick pushes on the side of the chest wall below the armpit.

3. Place the victim on a table so that they are hanging over the edge from the waist up, with the top of their head on the floor. Try the chest compression again so that it is aided by gravity.

Hopefully one of these methods will force the remaining air out of the lungs and up the windpipe so that the obstruction will be dislodged sufficiently for the victim to cough it up and out. If you are much bigger and stronger than the victim, try not to break too many ribs!

If all these measures fail and the victim is unconscious, lie them on their back and tilt the head backwards to maximise the airway. Sit astride the victim and place the heel of your hand on the upper abdomen just above the navel. Cover it with the heel of your other hand. Give a sharp downward and forward thrust towards the victim's head. Give up to four thrusts if necessary. If the victim does not splutter and start breathing, start mouth-to-mouth resuscitation.

As the victim starts breathing normally, place them on their side and get medical help. It is especially important to tell the doctor if chest compression has been used, so that the internal organs can be checked.

If all efforts to dislodge the object fail, you will have to blow air past it by using mouth-to-mouth resuscitation until medical help is obtained.

Q What's the best first aid for a skin burn?

A Water, water and more water. That is the immediate (and short-term) treatment for any burn, be it a burn from a flame, hot object or scald. Rope (friction) burns, sunburn, chemical burns and electrical burns are also treated this way.

The burnt part should be placed in cool water for up to half an hour, or if that is impractical, a water-soaked cloth should be held against the burnt part and kept sopping wet.

Creams, oils, butter and other treatments should NOT be used as first aid for burns, nor should a dry cloth should be applied to a burn as a dressing as it may stick.

Badly burnt patients may be given sips of water, but no other food or fluids until seen by a doctor. If shock develops, as indicated by shivering or collapse, lie the patient down and keep the body warm while the worst burns are kept moist with water.

Any burn that blisters or chars must be seen by a doctor, who will determine future treatment, dressings and pain relief depending on the severity and site of the burn. Blisters protect a burn, and should not be pricked.

Q **How should you remove a tic from your skin? I get lots of them, and I'm always worried about leaving the head behind and getting an infection.**

A A tics has a large black body from which mouth parts protrude and grasp the skin. It does not have a head as such. A tube-like mouth part-pierces the skin to suck up blood. When the tic is full of blood it drops off, and waits for its next victim. A full feed of blood may last it for a year or more.

To remove the tic, wash it and the surrounding skin with an alcohol solution such as methylated spirits. Place a pair of forceps (tweezers) flat on the skin so that the jaws are either side of the tic. Grasp the tic firmly as close to the skin as possible, twist through ninety degrees and then lift off. The tic will come away easily with minimal pain. Some tiny black marks, the mouth parts, may be left behind, but they rarely cause any trouble.

Place some antiseptic cream or lotion on the bite site and leave alone to heal over the next couple of days. If the area becomes red and angry, it may have become infected and a doctor should be consulted.

Q **I recently had a nose bleed that lasted over an hour, but stopped just before I went to hospital. How should you stop a nose bleed?**

A The patient is placed in a sitting position (NOT lying down) and the soft part of the nose just beyond the end of the nose bone is squeezed together firmly. Ideally this should be done with a cloth soaked in icy water which will cause the blood vessels in the nose to contract. If excited, the patient is calmed down, and the nostrils are held firmly for 5 minutes without letting go. When the pressure is released, the bleeding should have stopped, and the patient can go quietly on their way.

If the bleeding continues, two more five-minute periods of compression should be tried. If these fail, medical assistance should be sought, as the bleeding may be coming from further back in the nose.

The most common cause of bloody noses is drying out of the fine tissue on the nasal septum, which is covered with a network of veins designed to warm the air. If the tissue dries out too much it will split and bleeding occurs. Antiseptic and moisturising creams can be used regularly on the septum inside the nose to prevent this drying in hot weather.

Q **With three children between six and thirteen, I am always dealing with their injuries. How should you treat a bad cut, and how can you decide when a cut should be seen by a doctor or stitched?**

A There are three essentials in dealing with any cut. The first is to stop bleeding, the second to prevent infection, and the third to repair the wound.

No matter how large the wound, the best way to stop bleeding is to apply pressure directly over the injury. Tourniquets should not be used. A piece of clean cloth several layers thick (for example a clean, folded handkerchief) is the best, and usually most convenient dressing. The cloth should be applied over the bleeding area and held there firmly by a bandage. If an arm or leg is involved, that part of the body should be elevated above the level of the heart. Unless the wound is minor, the patient should lie down to avoid fainting or shock.

It is prudent to clean any dirt out of the wound with a dilute antiseptic, or clean water if no antiseptic is available. Ensure that bleeding has stopped first, and do not disturb any clots that may be present.

Minor cuts will heal without stitching, provided the edges of the wound are not gaping. If the edges do not lie comfortably together, if a joint surface is involved, if the wound continues to bleed or if the scar may be cosmetically disfiguring, then it is essential to see a doctor and have the cut correctly repaired by taping or sutures.

Q I recently came across an acquaintance who had taken an overdose. I called an ambulance, but didn't know what else to do. What should you do if someone takes an overdose of medication?

A Excessive doses of medication can be taken by accident (eg. children finding a bottle of pills, confused elderly people) or deliberately (eg. suicide attempt). The appropriate first aid by the person discovering the overdose may be life-saving.

Some medications are far more dangerous than others when taken in excess. You did the right thing in your situation, and provided an ambulance can attend within a few minutes, it is best left to the professionals to deal with the situation.

In other circumstances, for virtually all medication overdosages, the first aid treatment is to administer charcoal to neutralise the medication. Activated charcoal solutions are readily available from chemists without a prescription, and should be included in any home medicine chest.

If activated charcoal is not available, and there will be some delay in obtaining medical attention it is preferable to induce vomiting rather than allow the medication to be absorbed. Vomiting should NOT be induced if the patient is unconscious or otherwise liable to inhale any vomitus.

Activated charcoal should be given at any time after the overdose being taken. Induction of vomiting is most beneficial within 30 minutes of the overdose being taken, but even up to two hours later it may be beneficial. Many medications cause vomiting as part of their overdose effects, but by this time, the drug has already been absorbed and the vomiting is unlikely to reduce the effects of the drug significantly.

Vomiting can be induced by giving soapy water to drink, by applying pressure to the upper belly or by putting a finger down the back of the person's throat (be careful not to be bitten, particularly if the patient is likely to convulse). The patient should be lying on their side with the neck extended, or sitting up and leaning over to avoid inhaling vomitus.

Carers should seek medical advice as soon as possible, and sometimes urgent medical attention must be obtained.

Advice is available from your own general practitioner, local hospital or the Poisons Information Centre (phone 13 11 26 from any phone in Australia).

FUNGAL INFECTIONS
See also FEMALE PROBLEMS; SKIN

Q What are fungi? What sort of infections do they cause?

A Fungi are members of the plant family, and those that infect humans are effectively miniature mushrooms. Only a limited number of fungi can cause infections in humans. The vast majority of fungal infections occur on the skin to cause conditions such as tinea (ringworm and athlete's foot), but other commonly affected areas include the vagina (thrush), mouth and gut. In rare cases, fungal infections can spread to the lungs, brain and other internal organs. These infections are much more serious.

Q **What is ringworm? I keep getting this rash on my belly every summer. It settles with creams my doctor prescribes, but always comes back again.**

A Ringworm is NOT caused by a worm, but is a fungal infection of the skin (tinea). The fungus settles in one spot on the skin, and after the infection starts, a red dot may be seen but is often missed because it is quite small. This dot slowly enlarges as the fungus spreads away from its central base. After a few days, the centre of the red patch becomes pale again and similar to normal skin, because the infection is no longer active at this point. Meanwhile the infection continues to spread and forms an ever-enlarging red ring on the skin. The same phenomenon can be seen in nature with mushroom rings that form on the ground after damp weather, because mushrooms are a giant, distant relation to the microscopic fungi that are responsible for ringworm.

The spores of the fungus can settle in the base of hair follicles and sweat glands in the skin where they cannot be destroyed by creams and lotions on the skin. This enables the infection to flare up again months later when circumstances are right for the multiplication of spores.

Q **What causes athlete's foot? Is it serious?**

A Tinea pedis is the technical term for the fungal infections of the foot known commonly as athlete's foot. It is far more common in men than women, and uncommon in children. The most common site for the infection is in the skin folds under the toes, where it may cause cracking and pain. The clefts between the toes are another common site, but almost any part of the foot, including the sole, may become involved. On the sole of the foot, the fungal infection may appear as deep-seated blisters rather than a red rash. The infection is caught from infected skin fragments that may be found on damp floors (eg. communal showers, swimming pool change rooms).

It is not serious, merely annoying, and responds well to antifungal creams that are available without prescription from chemists. The treatment should be continued for several days after the rash appears to have cleared to reduce the chance of it coming back again.

Q **I have the dreaded crotch rot, and the itch drives me crazy. People look at me because I keep forgetting and scratching in public, and they think I'm a dirty old man or something. How can I fix this?**

A The very aptly named crotch rot is correctly known as tinea cruris. It is a fungal infection of the skin in the groin, and results in a red, itchy and sometimes smelly and sore rash. The infection is more common in men than women, and has a peak incidence in the 20s and 30s.

A red, scaly rash can spread out from the skin folds in the groin to cover the inside of the thighs, the lower abdomen and the buttocks. It tends to recur in summer and with exercise.

Fungi like the warm, moist area of the skin folds in the groin, so the infection is more common in people who are overweight and sweat a lot. Another concern can be diabetes, as people with this disease have a small amount of sugar in their sweat which encourages the fungus. Anyone with a recurrent fungal infection which is hard to treat should be checked for diabetes.

If simple antifungal creams from the chemist do not control your problem you should see your GP who can prescribe antifungal tablets to help kill the fungus.

Q   I have thick brown fingernails that my doctor thinks is a fungal infection. She has sent nail clippings away to be investigated. Can you tell me more about this problem?

A   Tinea unguium (also known as onychogryphosis when severe) is the notoriously difficult-to-treat fungal infection that occurs under finger and toenails. It is more common in the middle-aged and elderly.

The nails appear white or yellow and gradually thicken and infections may persist for many years, particularly in toenails, which are usually more severely affected than the fingers.

In the mid-1990s, two new treatments became available to cure this condition. Loceryl paint is an expensive lacquer which is applied to the nail weekly for many months, and gradually penetrates the nail to kill the fungus. Lamisil tablets are even more expensive, but faster at penetrating the nail through the bloodstream and curing the infection. In both cases, as the fungus is destroyed, new normal nail gradually grows out to replace the thick damaged nail.

Lamisil tablets are subsidised by the Pharmaceutical Benefits Scheme if the fungal infection can be seen in nail clippings under a microscope, or the fungus can be cultured and grown from clippings (a process which may take six weeks).

Q   Why do some women keep getting thrush? Every couple of months I am forced to suffer the indignity of using another course of vaginal cream to cure yet another of the curses of womanhood.

A   Thrush is a fungal infection of the vagina. It is caused by the fungus migrating from the back passage, or may be caught during sex from a male who is a carrier.

Heat, moisture and friction enable the fungus to migrate from the back passage. A warm climate and the aggravating factors of tight jeans, pantihose, the contraceptive pill, nylon bathers, antibiotics and sex give the area between a woman's legs the right degree of warmth, moisture and irritation to make the spread of the fungus relatively easy. Antibiotics aggravate the problem as they can kill off the bacteria that normally keep fungi under control. Entry of the fungus into the vagina is aided by the mechanical action of sex and the alteration in the acidity of the vagina caused by the contraceptive pill. Men may carry the fungus without showing any signs of infection.

Both husband and wife should therefore be treated for this condition, because the man may reinfect his wife after she has had a successful course of treatment. Women who have multiple sex partners are obviously at greater risk of catching the infection.

Tablets taken by mouth are now available to cure vaginal thrush, but they are on prescription only and more expensive than the vaginal creams.

Q   What is thrush? I have heard that babies get it in their mouths. Is it the same as the thrush that I get down below?

A   Thrush is a fungal infection that occurs in both the mouth and the vagina. The fungus *Candida albicans* is responsible for the infection in both sites.

The mouth infection (oral thrush) is quite common in infancy, particularly in bottle-fed babies, and may be triggered by a course of antibiotics that destroy the bacteria in the mouth that normally control the growth of excess fungi.

Vaginal thrush occurs for different reasons. *Candida albicans* lives in the gut, where it causes little or no trouble. When it comes out on to the skin around the anus, it dies off; but if that skin is warm, moist and irritated, it can grow and spread forward to the lips of the vagina (the vulva).

Oral thrush causes grey/white patches on the tongue, gums and inside of the cheeks that cannot be rubbed away with a fingertip or cotton bud. It may spread through the intestine and emerge to infect the skin around the anus, where it causes a bright red rash that is slightly paler towards the centre.

Vaginal thrush causes an unpleasant white vaginal discharge, intense itching of the vulva and surrounding skin, and often inflammation of the urine opening so that passing urine causes discomfort.

Q   How is thrush in a baby's mouth treated? Is it serious? Are any special tests necessary?

A   Swabs may be taken from mouth to confirm the identity of the fungus responsible for the thrush, but normally no investigations are necessary.

Treatment is simple, and involves putting antifungal drops or gels in the mouth, and if necessary antifungal creams around the anus if the infection has spread through the gut to there. Babies can sometimes reinfect themselves by touching the anus with their fingers, and then putting their fingers in their mouth, so both ends are treated, particularly in recurrent cases.

Oral thrush rarely causes serious complications and most babies respond rapidly to the correct treatment.

Q   I have white patches on my skin that spoils my otherwise excellent tan. It has been there for a couple of years now, and seems to settle a bit in winter. What could it be?

A   You are probably suffering from pityriasis versicolor. This is a mouthful of a name for a very common condition (particularly in warmer climates) but there is no simple name for this skin infection.

It is a fungal infection that affects young adults more than the elderly and children. The chest, upper arms, neck, upper back and armpits are the most commonly affected areas.

Patients develop pink/brown patches on the skin, which may have a very faint scale upon them. After a few weeks, the skin underlying the rash has less pigment, so the rash appears as white patches which are due to sunlight being unable to tan the skin underlying the fungus. Areas not exposed to sunlight (eg. armpits, breasts) may retain the pink/brown patch appearance. This effect does not occur on Aborigines, Chinese and other dark-skinned races. There are no other symptoms other than an occasional very mild itch.

No investigations are normally necessary, but diagnosis can be proved by examining skin scrapings under a microscope.

Treatment involves the regular use of antifungal lotions, rinses or creams. An antifungal tablet (ketoconazole) is used in persistent and widespread cases. The white patches will remain for some time after the fungus has been destroyed, until the sun tans the area again. Episodes of infection are quite easy to clear, but it often recurs in the next summer.

GLANDS
See also HORMONES

Q **What are glands and what do they do?**

A There are many different glands in the human, and they share one common characteristic. They all produce substances essential to life, but none of them has any ducts or tubes to take these substances away from the gland. The chemicals produced are called hormones, and each of the millions of cells in the gland that produces the hormone, discharges it directly into the microscopic blood capillary that passes beside the cell. In this way the necessary hormones enter the bloodstream and are transported to every other cell in the body.

Q **What are the glands in your neck? Mine keep coming up and getting sore every time I get a cold. Is this normal?**

A The 'glands' in the neck are really lymph nodes. They are collections of millions of infection-fighting white cells held together by a network of fibrous tissue. They are scattered throughout the body, but dense concentrations of them occur at vital areas to prevent infections from entering the main part of the body from the arms, legs and throat.

The arms and legs are more likely to be injured than the trunk, and therefore more likely to be infected, and the nose and throat are the body openings most commonly invaded by viruses and bacteria. This is why concentrations of lymph nodes in the neck, armpit and groin are so critical to our wellbeing.

All these lymph nodes, in different parts of the body, are joined together by an incredibly fine, intricate network of tiny tubes called lymph ducts. Waste products caused by the work and activity of tissue in all parts of the body, including the arms and legs, move along these lymph ducts, which slowly grow larger as they join up, and finally empty into a large vein near the heart. The wastes are transported through the bloodstream to the kidneys and liver for final disposal.

It is quite normal for lymph nodes to become swollen and painful when you have an infection, as they are doing their job of destroying the viruses and bacteria that are causing your infection. If they don't settle in a couple of days, they may need some assistance in the form of antibiotics, to finish the job.

Q **What does the thyroid gland in your neck do?**

A The thyroid gland is situated in the front of the neck. It is shaped rather like a figure 8 lying on its side, and the two lobes of the gland lie on either side of the trachea (windpipe) about halfway between the Adams apple and the top of the breast bone. There are a number of hormones produced by this gland, but they all perform a similar task, and the most common one is called thyroxine.

The task of this hormone is quite complex, but in simple terms it controls the metabolic rate of the body. This is the rate at which all the major organs of the body operate. If there is too much thyroxine the heart beats faster, you sweat more, your gut moves food along more quickly, you may feel nervous and because you burn up more energy you lose weight.

The reverse occurs if thyroxine is lacking from your system. Everything slows down and you become tired, cold and constipated. As a result, it is essential for thyroxine to be present in exactly the right concentration for you to feel in good health and perform at peak efficiency.

Q My doctor has told me that the swelling in the front of my neck is a goitre, and has sent me for blood tests. I didn't even notice that it was there. What is a goitre? Can it be serious?

A. A goitre is an enlarged thyroid gland. It may be due to an overactive gland, or lack of iodine in the diet. Iodine is essential for the formation of thyroid hormones, and if it is lacking, the gland swells up in an attempt to compensate.

At other times, swelling may be due to overactivity of the thyroid, or other diseases.

Blood tests and special scans can be done to determine the cause, and then the appropriate treatment may be given. Thyroid cysts and cancer may cause swelling of one part of the gland, but this is not strictly a goitre.

The vast majority of goitres can be completely cured, and there is no reason for concern.

Q I am 68 years old, fit as a fiddle, but get very tired at times. My GP says my thyroid gland is to blame, and I have to take tablets. Are these really necessary, and what is an underactive thyroid gland?

A The thyroid gland sits in the front of your neck, and secretes a hormone called thyroxine into your bloodstream. This hormone controls the metabolic rate of your body. This is the rate at which all cells in the body work, so that thyroxine controls the rate at which the liver, kidneys, gut and all other organs function.

If the thyroid gland becomes underactive, and secretes too little of the hormone, you feel tired, cold, constipated, have dry skin and your hair may thin out. This is a common problem in women after the menopause and is controlled by taking the correct dose of thyroxine by tablet on a regular basis.

Your GP is correct, you should take the tablets, and you may well find that you can do far more, and enjoy your life to the full again. You should have regular blood tests to ensure that the dose of thyroid hormone you are taking is adequate.

Q Fourteen years ago a specialist physician informed me that I had Hashimoto's disease. He prescribed Oroxine tablets for me to take for the rest of my life. Would you be able to explain Hashimoto's disease to me?

A Hashimoto's thyroiditis is a relatively common disease of the thyroid gland at the front of your neck.

In this disease, the thyroid gland becomes enlarged (a goitre) and ceases to function efficiently, and in due course produces less thyroxine than is required by the body. The exact cause is unknown.

The missing thyroxine is replaced by taking the same substance in tablet form. This causes the goitre to shrink, and the person can lead a perfectly normal life.

After initial stabilisation, blood tests every year or so are necessary to ensure that you are receiving the correct number and strength of thyroxine tablets. Oroxine is a trade name for one brand of thyroxine-containing tablets.

Q **I have been diagnosed as having Addison's disease. I realise it is a rare condition, and I think I understand it after my specialist has explained it to me several times, but I can't explain it properly to my family. Can you help?**

A The adrenal glands sit on top of each kidney, and produce hormones (chemical messengers) that control the levels of vital elements in the body and regulate the breakdown of food. Addison's disease occurs when the adrenal glands do not produce sufficient quantities of these vital hormones.

In most cases, the cause for the failure of the adrenal glands is unknown, but tuberculosis was a common cause in years past.

You are correct in calling it a rare disease. The common symptoms are weakness, lack of appetite, diarrhoea and vomiting, skin pigmentation, mental instability, low blood pressure, loss of body hair and absence of sweating.

The disease is diagnosed by special laboratory tests that measure the body's response to certain drugs. The complications include diabetes, thyroid disease and anaemia.

Treatment involves taking a combination of medications (different types of steroids are used) to replace the hormones missing from the body. The dosages vary greatly from one patient to another. Frequent small meals high in carbohydrate and protein should be taken, and any infections must be treated rapidly. Patients must wear a bracelet warning doctors of their condition, and carry an emergency supply of hydrocortisone with them at all times.

Treatment can give most of these patients a long and useful life, but they cannot react to stress (both physical and mental) adequately, and additional treatment (eg. hydrocortisone) must be given to cover these situations. The ultimate outcome of the disease depends greatly on the patient's ability to follow strictly all treatment regimes.

Q **My brother in England has just had an uncancerous (sic) bit taken out of his pituitary gland in his head. Where is the pituitary gland in the head, and what does it do?**

A This vital gland is situated in the very centre of your head. If you place your finger tip mid way between your eyebrows, the pituitary gland is about 9 cm inside the skull from that point.

Glands are organs that produce vital hormones that control many of the bodily functions. The testes and ovaries are glands that produce sex hormones; the thyroid gland produces a hormone that controls the body's metabolic rate; the adrenal gland produces adrenaline, which acts on the arteries, and so on.

The many glands of the body are in turn controlled by the pituitary gland, which produces chemicals that travel through the bloodstream to tell the other glands when to switch on and off their hormone production. The pituitary gland is therefore the conductor of the gland orchestra within the body, and depending on which hormones it detects in the bloodstream, it will stimulate or suppress the appropriate gland. The pituitary itself is controlled by nerves from the brain.

GUT
(Intestines)

See also ANAL PROBLEMS; LIVER and GALL BLADDER

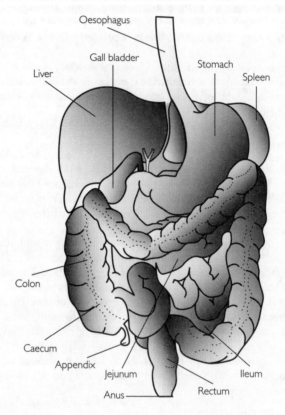

Q What are the adhesions that patients complain about after surgery?

A When you are cut, inflammation occurs to stick the edges of the wound together, and eventually heal the wound. During an operation, minor damage to all tissue in the area is inevitable, and this becomes slightly inflamed. If two areas of internal tissue in come into contact after an operation, they will heal together and form an adhesion. This is more likely when infected or damaged tissue is operated upon.

Once an adhesion forms, the bowel may become twisted around it, or it may tear and bleed, leading to pain. If at a later operation the adhesions are broken down, this damages the tissue again, and the subsequent inflammation allows the adhesions to form again. It is therefore a very difficult problem to deal with.

Q Are there any new treatments for adhesions? They plague me to the extent that my lifestyle is physically restricted.

A Adhesions are a relatively uncommon, but potentially serious and disabling complication, of any surgery within the abdomen. They form tough fibrous bands across the abdominal cavity between two points that have been inflamed or damaged during surgery. They are more common if there is an infection in the abdomen (eg. a burst appendix), but sometimes occur after a relatively minor operation. They appear to develop more readily in short, fat females, but the reason for this is unknown.

Most adhesions produce no symptoms, but can occasionally trap a loop of bowel and cause an obstruction. More commonly, they cause a persistent colic in the gut as the intestine winds tightly around these fibrous bands.

The only treatment available is further surgery to cut away the adhesions. During this further surgery, which may be done through an instrument called a laparoscope using only a 2 cm incision, extreme care is taken to prevent any bleeding into the abdomen, or any unnecessary injury to the bowel. Unfortunately, after a few months or years, the adhesions may reform and the symptoms start again. There is no permanent solution.

Q My son has worms—Ugh! Please tell me about them, in a nice way!

A The fact that your son has worms is not a reflection on his personal hygiene, but on the hygiene of someone else.

The common worms in Australia are threadworms, and these appear as short pieces (about 3 mm long) of white cotton thread on the motions. They may also be seen around the anus, particularly at night. They cause itching around the anus and slight abdominal discomfort, but rarely anything more severe. The worms lay eggs in the faeces, and if a person is not careful with their personal hygiene, the eggs may contaminate the fingers, then food, and be swallowed by another person where the eggs hatch, grow into adult worms, and start the cycle again.

Very effective treatments are available without a prescription from chemists, but if the problem recurs, a doctor's advice should be obtained.

Q I have had terrible belly pains on and off for years. My doctor now tells me it is diverticulitis, and she has given me tablets for it. These seem to help, but can you tell me what causes diverticulitis?

A Diverticulitis is the inflammation of small bubbles that develop on the large gut. They are outpocketings of the gut that form between the muscular bands that run along and around the gut. They are caused by excess pressure inside the intestine when there is inadequate bulk in the diet for the constantly contracting gut to move along towards the anus.

If you squeeze a half-inflated balloon between your fingers, it will bulge out between your fingers. This is what happens in the gut, but after a while the bulges become permanent, and these are the diverticulae.

When food waste becomes trapped in a diverticulum, it may become infected and painful and cause diarrhoea. A high-fibre diet will prevent formation of the problem.

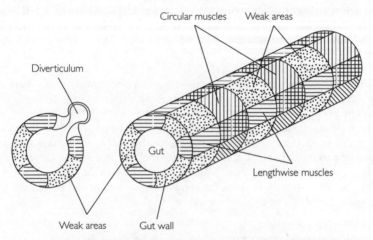

Diverticular Disease of the Colon

Circular muscles   Weak areas

Diverticulum

Gut

Lengthwise muscles

Weak areas   Gut wall

The formation of diverticulae in weak areas of the large intestinal wall.

Q Doctors have diagnosed my wife's condition as a bowel syndrome, and she has to watch her diet as eggs and meat cause diarrhoea. Her bowel X-ray shows diverticulae. Can you help us please?

A   It appears that you may be confused by two different bowel conditions, although it is possible that your wife has both of them.

The irritable bowel syndrome (IBS) causes painful spasms of the gut that result in irregular bowel activity, and is caused by anxiety, stress or depression. The treatment involves a high-fibre diet, bulking agents (eg. Normacol, Metamucil) and drugs to stop the gut spasm.

Diverticulitis is the inflammation or infection of multiple small outpocketings (diverticulae) of the large gut wall. When inflamed, these diverticulae cause diarrhoea and abdominal pain. The diverticulae are the result of a low-fibre diet over many years, and the condition is also treated with bulking agents, a high-fibre diet and antispasmodics. Antibiotics are also used sometimes to remove any infection in the diverticulae.

The symptoms of the two conditions are very similar, and only by performing an X-ray of the bowel (a barium enema) or examining the bowel with a flexible microscope tube (colonoscopy) can the diagnosis be made.

It is certainly possible for the two conditions to be present in the one patient, and one may worsen the other, but as the treatments are almost identical, the differentiation between them is not of critical importance.

Both conditions can be well controlled in most patients. The irritable bowel syndrome often comes and goes depending on stress levels, while diverticulitis will persist for the rest of the patient's life, causing occasional periods of diarrhoea and discomfort.

Q My bowels have changed. I used to be regular every day, and now I have trouble going twice a week. What could be the cause?

A   Constipation has many causes that can vary from reduced physical activity, depression and a change in diet, to pregnancy, diabetes and thyroid disease. The cause that should concern you most is the possibility of a tumour in the bowel.

Any change in your habits, be that constipation or diarrhoea, can be caused by a growth. There may be a simple explanation for your particular problem, but there is only one way to be sure, and that is to have a thorough check-up with your doctor.

Do not start using laxatives inappropriately. Once the cause of your constipation is known, the correct treatment can commence.

Q   **During the past several months I have been in agony with a bloated and cramping stomach. The pain created by these cramps is horrendous. Endoscopy, ultrasound and every other test has been normal. What could cause these pains?**

A   Unfortunately, I am less likely to make any diagnosis than the doctor who can actually lay hands on you and examine and question you in detail.

If all investigations are normal, a condition that does not show with any investigation must be considered. The irritable bowel syndrome (IBS) comes to mind.

IBS causes spasms of the gut that can be extremely painful, bloating, excess wind and episodic diarrhoea. The spasms can be triggered by diet, stress or infections, but quite often occur for no apparent reason.

There are a number of antispasmodic medications that can be used to both prevent and treat the spasms. These include Colofac, Buscopan and Merbentyl, but all require a prescription. If you are having regular attacks, it is sensible to use medications all the time to prevent the problem.

Discuss this possibility with your general practitioner.

Q   **Can you tell me about the Irritable Bowel Syndrome? This is the diagnosis my doctor has given me after doing all sorts of tests on me.**

A   People with tense personalities or continuing stress will find that their 'stomach is in knots'. This is merely the sensation that the intestine is acting more rapidly than is necessary due to the over-stimulation of the nervous system.

Over a number of years, the combination of a low-fibre diet, anxiety, stress and hereditary factors may lead to the development of the Irritable Bowel Syndrome. This syndrome is characterised by abdominal pain caused by intense spasms of the bowel muscle, alternating constipation and diarrhoea, passage of wind by mouth and anus, nausea, loss of appetite and mucus on the stools. Once established, the pattern may be very difficult to break, as the symptoms cause further anxiety in the victim, which in turn exacerbates the original symptoms.

There are no definite tests to prove the presence of the syndrome, and so all other causes of the symptoms must be excluded by exhaustive tests.

Once diagnosed, the treatment consists of a diet high in fibre and low in dairy products and processed foods. High-fibre dietary supplements are often recommended. Regular meal and toilet habits should be established, and tobacco and alcohol intake should be restricted.

The usual course is for the syndrome to occur intermittently over many years. The continued attention by a sympathetic doctor is necessary for all sufferers because the greater the confidence the patient has in the treatment and the doctor, the more likely the regime is to succeed.

Q   A recent colonoscopy has revealed bowel spasms. These are very painful and I was hoping that you could explain the cause and tell me how to prevent them.

A   Bowel spasms that have no apparent cause are called the irritable bowel syndrome.

The bowel normally contracts rhythmically to move food steadily down from the top end to the bottom. If these contractions become excessive or un-coordinated you can develop a painful colic.

The spasms may be exaggerated by stress, anxiety, certain foods, lack of food, infections, irritants, some medications and a host of other causes.

If a specific cause can be found, it obviously best to treat this, but often this is not possible.

A number of medications can be prescribed by your general practitioner to ease the gut spasms when they occur, or if the problem is constant, others may be taken on a regular basis to prevent the problem.

A high-fibre diet is often beneficial, as it gives the bowel something to work on, and directs the gut spasms in a useful way.

Q   Why do some children complain of tummy pain frequently?

A   Abdominal migraine is very common in children. It may be due to spasm of the muscles in the abdominal wall, or due to spasms of the gut. The reason for the spasm is almost invariably anxiety and stress. Thus many children only develop these pains on school days, before exams, when they have arguments with friends etc.

The best treatment is to give the child a little bit of sympathy and if necessary, a mild pain-killer. No great fuss should be made because this may cause the pains to be used as an attention-seeking device.

Children with recurrent pain must be investigated to exclude any medical cause, and if none is found, a psychologist may be able to teach the child how to cope with the problem.

Q   After many years of recurring tummy pains, my mother has been told she has Crohn's disease. Is it stress related?

A   Crohn's disease is caused by an excessive overgrowth of the tissue around one part of the small intestine. The wall of the gut at this point becomes greatly thickened and can narrow the hollow inside the gut, restricting the passage of food. This causes the severe colicky pain that sufferers experience, and can at times, completely block the gut, causing a medical emergency.

The disease can be treated by a number of medications including steroids but these usually only give temporary relief. Patients with recurrent symptoms require surgery to remove the offending section of intestine. Unfortunately, up to 60% of cases relapse after surgery, and repeated operations every few years are sometimes necessary.

A high-fibre diet is the only effective preventative measure. I am not aware of any connection between stress and the original cause of Crohn's disease (which is unknown), but it is likely that stress could precipitate an acute attack in a patient who already has the disease.

Q **I have had pain in the right lower part of my belly for three months. The pain often goes to the back, but I have no loss of weight or appetite. What could cause such a pain?**

A There are a wide range of conditions that can cause such a pain, and you will need a wide range of investigations to discover its cause.

The first step is a detailed physical examination and history by your general practitioner. This will be followed by one or more of the following tests:

— Blood tests to check liver, kidney, pancreas, to find any infection, and assess your general health.
— Urine test to check bladder and kidney.
— Ultrasound scan of ovaries, uterus and other pelvic organs.
— X-ray of back, bowel and/or kidney.
— CT scan of abdomen.
— Colonoscopy (a flexible tube passed up your back passage) to check the bowel.
— Laparoscopy (tube put through your belly button) to directly look around inside your belly.

A few of the many possible causes could include an ovarian cyst, an abscess from appendicitis, endometriosis, back arthritis, kidney stone, aneurysm (swelling) of the aorta, arterial thrombosis (clot), irritable bowel syndrome, tube infection, hernia, Crohn's disease, cancer and many more.

I can only guess at a diagnosis. Your GP and the specialists s/he may refer you to, should be able to come to a definite diagnosis that can then be treated appropriately.

Q **What is appendicitis, and how do people get this problem? My sister has just had hers removed at age 38.**

A Appendicitis is an infection of the appendix, which is a narrow dead end tube about 12 cm long that attaches to the caecum (first part of the large intestine). It is an almost unknown condition in poorer countries for dietary reasons, and the lack of fibre in Western diets is often blamed, although its incidence is steadily falling due to better dietary education. In other mammals, particularly those that eat grass, the appendix is an important structure which aids in the digestion of cellulose, but in humans it serves no useful purpose.

If the narrow tube of the appendix becomes blocked by faeces, food, mucus or some foreign body, bacteria start breeding in the closed-off area behind the blockage.

When a patient develops appendicitis, pain develops around the navel and soon moves to the lower right side of the abdomen just above the pelvic bone and steadily worsens. It is often associated with loss of appetite, slight diarrhoea and a mild fever.

There is no specific diagnostic test, but blood and urine tests are done to exclude other causes of pain. Once removed, the appendix will be sent to a pathologist to confirm the diagnosis.

The only effective treatment is surgical removal of the appendix in a simple operation (appendectomy) which takes about 20 minutes. The usual hospital stay is only two days, and patients return to work in seven to ten days. The operation is sometimes done through laparoscopes (1 cm diameter tubes). The surgeon looks through one and operates through two others, leaving only three tiny scars scattered across the belly. This speeds recovery so that sometimes only a single night is required in hospital.

If left untreated, the appendix becomes steadily more infected, full of pus, and eventually bursts to cause peritonitis. Most patients get very good results from treatment.

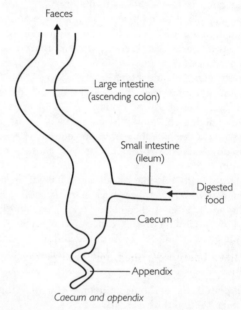

Caecum and appendix

Q **I am a 54 year old female, and for some years my bowels have caused pain. I have to use an enema to go to the toilet, but afterwards I have pain at the bottom of my stomach. Should I go to a doctor?**

A Anyone who has persistent constipation should not use laxatives or enemas regularly, but should be investigated by a doctor to find out why they are constipated. If laxatives are used regularly, the bowels become dependent upon them to work, and a long-term habit that is very difficult to break may develop.

Over-stimulation of the bowel by enemas may cause spasm and pain in the bowel. Your symptoms may be caused by the treatments you are using.

The best treatment for constipation is prevention, and that means a diet high in fibre and fluids, and passing a motion every day. The best time to do this is immediately after the main meal of the day.

You should certainly see a doctor to have your chronic bowel condition sorted out.

Q **I have unpredictable bowels! One week I'm so bound up that I can't go without taking laxatives, and the next week or so I have to go four times a day. I eat a good diet, so how can I become regular?**

A Irregular bowel habits need to be investigated thoroughly by a doctor as they may be an early sign of many different bowel diseases. It may be that something simple like stress and anxiety, hormonal changes during the month or different foods may be responsible for the problem.

Unfortunately, diverticulitis, ulcerative colitis and bowel cancer can also first show up as alternating diarrhoea and constipation. You may need to have a colonoscopy, which is a procedure in which a thin, flexible tube is passed through your anus and up into the gut. Through this a doctor can see any disease that may be present and make a definite diagnosis.

Q   What can I do to stop chronic diarrhoea?

A   The most important thing is to determine the cause of the diarrhoea. The first step is a thorough examination by a doctor, and then appropriate investigations. These would certainly include examination of your faeces in a laboratory for any infecting agents, abnormal cells or blood. Another probable investigation would be blood tests to find any diseases that may have diarrhoea as a component.

Diarrhoea has scores of different causes including infections, diseases of food absorption, allergies, cancer, gut inflammations, liver disease, tuberculosis, stress, diabetes, psychiatric diseases, kidney failure and a host of others.

Once the cause of the diarrhoea is found, the appropriate treatment can be given. Treating any chronic condition without determining its cause is foolish and dangerous.

Q   After examination and tests, doctors have diagnosed the cause of my intestinal discomfort and bloody motions as colitis. Their indication that not much can be done for the condition is not very comforting. Cortisone enemas have been prescribed, but results have not been encouraging. I would appreciate your comments.

A   Ulcerative colitis is an inflammatory condition of the last part of the bowel that causes multiple deep bleeding ulcers to form. Its cause is unknown.

Patients experience bloody diarrhoea, cramping pains in the lower belly, fevers, weight loss and sometimes anaemia.

When the diagnosis is suspected by a doctor, it is confirmed by performing a colonoscopy. In this procedure a flexible tube is passed through the anus up into the colon, and through this the examining doctor can easily see the ulcers and inflammation that are characteristic of the disease.

Unfortunately there is no cure for this condition. In acute attacks, hospitalisation may be necessary with many medications being given in high doses to bring the condition under control. Long-term treatment with steroid enemas, oral steroid tablets and special antibiotics (sulphasalazine) is then given to control the condition.

Patients with ulcerative colitis should be on a specific diet that is high in protein and low in dairy products. Each patient will learn to identify specific foods that aggravate the condition and avoid them.

As a last resort, it is sometimes necessary for the affected piece of bowel to be surgically removed.

If your condition is not adequately controlled, you should be discussing the matter further with your doctor, as good control of ulcerative colitis is essential for your long-term wellbeing.

Q **After I have anything more than a snack to eat, I have to rush to the toilet to pass a motion. It's getting embarrassing! How can I stop this?**

A In all animals there is a reflex known as the gastro-colic reflex. This acts so that when the stomach becomes distended by food, the rectum (last part of the gut) contracts to move out faeces. This reflex is easily seen in animals such as cattle and horses. In humans, the reflex is better controlled, for obvious social reasons, but it is still easier and better to go to the toilet after the main meal of the day than at other times.

Some unlucky people have an overactive gastro-colic reflex. This may be due to some disease or chronic irritation of the lower part of the gut, and it would be essential for you to see a doctor for a large bowel examination to exclude any problems in this area.

Colonoscopy involves passing a flexible tube into your back passage. Through this, the inside of your gut can be easily seen and any diseases identified. If nothing is found, exercises to improve your bowel control may be tried, dietary modification may be useful, and as a last resort medications can be prescribed to help your problem.

Q **You write a lot about hearts etc., but how about wind! My husband suffers badly from wind. Sometimes he is in agony, and nothing seems to relieve it. I would like to know what causes wind.**

A Gas can leave the bowel by burping or farting. If it is unable to leave as rapidly as it should, pressure builds up inside the gut to cause severe discomfort, loud noises and loss of appetite.

Gas can enter the bowel by swallowing air with rapid eating or nervous swallowing, or by drinking fizzy drinks such as lemonade or beer.

Gas can be formed in the bowel by fermentation of food in the gut, or by the oxygen in the blood coming out of solution, and bubbling slowly into the gut.

People who suffer from excessive wind in the gut must take measures to reduce the amount of gas entering the gut, by eating slowly and avoiding fizzy drinks. At times of anxiety, nervous swallowing can also be a significant problem, and avoiding the cause of the anxiety may help.

If excess fermentation is the problem, the wind is usually foul smelling. A course of special antibiotics can kill off the germs in the gut that are responsible for the problem.

A wide range of anti-flatulence medications are available from chemists. The simpler ones contain substances such as peppermint oil and charcoal.

If these do not work, doctors can prescribe drugs to prevent the gut spasms, and reduce the production of gas.

Q **Whenever we go away I suffer constipation and dreadful wind pains. I'm sure it's psychological as I am embarrassed about normal body functions, and don't like to use public toilets. I know I'm silly, and I should get over my fear and embarrassment, but I can't go away for more than a few days because I can't go to the toilet until I get home.**

A Your self-diagnosis of a psychological problem is obviously correct, but these problems are not silly, and can seriously affect the lives of some people.

The solution is to be taught to use public toilets and other facilities away from home. It is worth keeping in mind that even the Queen has to go to the toilet—a point many royalists who worship the Queen would never even consider!

Arrange through your general practitioner to see a good behavioural psychologist, or a psychiatrist who has an interest in behavioural problems. Over a period of several weeks you will be taught how to cope with your fear, and in due course you will be able to enjoy long holidays away from home.

Fear of almost anything can be overcome by using appropriate techniques, and your fear of strange toilets is no worse than another person's fear of heights, fear of spiders, or a fear of confined spaces.

Don't delay seeking help—a wide world away from home is waiting to be explored. A light-hearted paperback called 'London's Distinguished Dunnies' (or something similar) is available for your perusal should you venture that far afield!

Q   My father has been in hospital for weeks with pancreatitis. He seems to be suffering greatly with terrible pain that injections do not ease. Can you explain this disease?

A   The pancreas sits in the centre of your abdomen directly behind your belly button, and one of its main tasks is to produce the digestive enzymes that attack your food.

A tiny duct leads from the pancreas to the bile duct and then the small intestine to transport these enzymes to the food.

The pancreas may become infected, damaged by excess alcohol intake, or the duct leading from it may be blocked by a gallstone. In these circumstances, the digestive enzymes may leak out of the pancreas and start dissolving the pancreas itself, your intestine and other abdominal organs—this is pancreatitis.

It is an excruciatingly painful disease that leads to very rapid consultation with a medical practitioner. The treatment involves resuscitating a patient who is usually very ill and shocked, pain relief, then treating the cause of the pancreatitis. This may involve antibiotics, merely prolonged bed rest or occasionally surgery.

Q   Would you please explain a closed ileocaecal valve? What are the symptoms and is there any treatment?

A   The ten metres of gut in your belly is divided into several sections. The mouth leads to the pharynx, then the oesophagus (gullet) and the stomach. After the stomach comes about seven metres of small intestine, and the last two metres is the large intestine.

The small intestine is divided into three further sections—the short duodenum, the longer jejunum and the ileum. The large gut is also divided into three main sections—the caecum, colon and rectum.

The ileocaecal valve is a muscle ring that separates the last part of the small intestine (the ileum) from the first part of the large intestine (the caecum). Its job is to control the rate at which digested food moves from one part of the gut to the next.

It is quite rare for it to cause any trouble, but if the muscle controlling the valve goes into spasm, it causes a slow-down in the movement of food through the gut. The patient would experience severe intermittent pain in the belly (colic), become bloated and very uncomfortable.

Treatment would involve regularly using one of a number of different drugs that relax the gut muscles, or as a last resort, surgery to partly cut the valve muscle.

Q I am constantly constipated, and have had piles as a result. Can you give me some simple advice on how to control this problem?

A Common causes of constipation include:
- A low-fibre diet
- Inadequate fluid intake
- Low level of exercise
- Poor access to a toilet when nature calls
- Lack of privacy
- Weak belly and pelvic muscles after surgery or childbirth
- Some medications, particularly those containing codeine.

Actions that you can take to improve your regularity include:
- Drink five or six glasses of fluid a day
- Exercise daily
- Eat more fruit, vegetables and wholemeal cereals
- Take bulking agents (eg. Normacol, Metamucil) and fibre supplements
- Use faecal softeners (eg. Coloxyl).

If you have anal bleeding or abdominal pain, you should see your doctor.

Q Baaarrrrooooom! Grnth! Baaarrrrooooom! My tummy keeps making these terrible noises all the time, and it is most embarrassing! How can I stop it?

A Onomatopoeia is the term used to describe words that sound like what they mean. The grunts, groans and baarrrooms of your stomach are alliteratively described as borborygmi by doctors and they are due to an overactive intestine as it moves your food from one end of the gut to the other.

Some people have more active intestines than others, but everyone suffers this complaint with infections and some other disorders. A gut obstruction, gastroenteritis, the nervous swallowing of air, eating rapidly and drinking large amounts of aerated drinks can all aggravate the problem. Doctors can prescribe medications to slow down the gut activity, but avoiding the above problems is the best treatment.

Q Whenever I have a particularly good bowel movement I experience a marked feeling of tiredness and relief, not unlike an orgasm. I've been aware of this phenomenon for many years. Is it normal or common?

A There has been some delay in replying to this letter as I have been trying to find the source of a very old quote that I read many years ago about this very subject. Unfortunately I have been unable to find the original words or their author, so the following paraphrase will have to suffice (maybe some erudite reader will enlighten me).

'There are two things in life that bring organic relief to the soul. One is the discharge of semen in sexual pleasure, the other is the passing of a soft, well formed and substantial stool. I prefer the latter if given the choice, as it is free from other emotional complications.'

Q My wife and I need you to sort out a small domestic matter. My wife produces stools that sink, while I produce stools that float. My wife is convinced that her 'sinkers' are preferable to my 'floaters'. Could you settle this matter?

Some people have 'domestics' about the most extraordinary matters, but never let it be said that I refuse to answer a question, merely because it is in poor taste!

The simple answer to your query is that fat floats, fibre sinks. Faeces that contains a large proportion of fat, either due to a large fat intake, or more commonly because of a poor absorption of fat from the gut, will be a 'floater'. On the other hand, stools containing a large amount of fibre and protein are heavier than water and will be 'sinkers'.

People who are able to eat everything in sight and still remain thin tend to absorb fat poorly, and produce 'floaters', while those who gain weight at the slightest hint of an extra calorie (kilojoule) are more likely to be good absorbers of fat and produce 'sinkers'.

Bon appetite!

HAIR

Q **My father and grandfather are bald. What chance do I have?**

A Provided you are his son and not his daughter, your chances of being bald are quite good, and if there is baldness on both sides of your family tree, you will almost certainly develop some degree of baldness.

Baldness is a sex-linked genetic condition. It is very rare in women, but passes through the female line to men in later generations.

Q. **What causes baldness? I'm only 18 now, but I don't want to be like my father when I'm older.**

A By far the most common form of baldness is that caused by hereditary tendencies in men. If your father or grandfather was bald, you have a chance of developing the same problem. There is no cure for this other than wigs or hair transplants. This type of baldness does not occur in women.

There are many other causes for patchy or diffuse hair loss including ageing, skin diseases, stress, male menopause, lack of iron or zinc, an underactive thyroid gland, drugs (particularly those used to treat cancer) and a dozen or more rare diseases. Because of this, it is important for anyone with rapidly thinning hair, or patchy hair loss, that is not obviously due to an hereditary tendency, to see a doctor for thorough investigation and treatment as soon as possible.

Q **I am starting to go bald, and I don't particularly like the idea. What can I do?**

A Despite the lurid claims of magazine advertisements, there are only four ways to deal with being bald:

(1) Accept the condition.
(2) Wear a hairpiece.
(3) Use hair growth stimulating scalp lotions or tablets (eg. Propecia, Regaine).
(4) Have a hair transplant performed by a plastic surgeon.

There are no cures available, and none are likely for some time to come. The drugs available have a variable success rate and must be used consistently for many months or years. They are only available on prescription from doctors.

Q **I have read recently about some home cures for baldness and alopecia. What do you think of these remedies?**

A Alopecia (patchy hair loss) and baldness are quite separate conditions.

Male baldness is an inherited condition that passes from one generation to the next. It cannot be prevented and it cannot be cured. If the man wishes to have more hair on his head, it is possible to treat baldness in a number of ways. Wearing a hairpiece is the simplest method, and is very effective, particularly if you start wearing one when you change jobs or move to a new city. Hair transplants, and progressive scalp tightening (removing the bald area) operations can be performed by plastic surgeons. A lotion containing a drug called minoxidil and Propecia tablets (available only on prescription) are proving successful in causing hair regrowth in some men after prolonged use.

Alopecia is a sudden patchy hair loss that can occur in both sexes and all ages. It may be caused by stress, drugs (eg. for cancer), rapid weight loss, iron deficiency, an underactive thyroid gland, diabetes or a number of other diseases. Treatment of alopecia involves treating any underlying cause, using scalp irritants, and injections of powerful steroids into the scalp.

Quack practitioners are always advertising remedies for incurable conditions such as arthritis, cancer and baldness. There has never been any evidence that any of them work. If they did work, the ingredients could be patented, and sold to a major drug company for a very large sum. Buying these unproven remedies is a waste of your time and money.

Q **My hair is getting very thin at the top and front as I get older, but there is still plenty at the sides. I am a 65 year old woman. I find wigs very hot and sweaty. Do you recommend hair transplants?**

A Hair problems are very common as you age. There are fewer active hair follicles, and the hair itself becomes thinner. You would have to have very thin and sparse hair in order for hair transplantation to be warranted.

Hairdressers can perform wonders with hairstyles that can cover thinning areas, and this would be a better option than the expense and discomfort of hair transplantation. Additional hair can actually be woven into your existing hair, and this may be more comfortable than a wig or hairpiece. There are also preparations that thicken thin hairs, but they must be applied regularly.

If you are determined to have a hair transplant, you will find that most plastic surgeons undertake this procedure. There are not normally any Medicare benefits payable for cosmetic procedures, and they can be quite expensive. The best advice will be obtained from your own general practitioner, who can refer you to an appropriate plastic surgeon in your area.

Q. **I have had alopecia after my hysterectomy 10 years ago. Would you please tell me something about this disease.**

A A sudden loss of hair in a well-defined patch on the scalp, or other areas of body hair (eg. pubic area, beard, chest, eyebrows) is commonly caused by alopecia (meaning hair loss) areata (meaning a specific area).

It is different to baldness in that it can occur at any age, in either sex, and in any race. It starts suddenly, and a bare patch 2 cm or more across may be present before it is noticed. It is more common under 25 years of age and is quite common, with about 2% of patients seeing skin specialists having the condition. The hairless area may slowly extend for several weeks, before stabilising. Several spots may occur simultaneously, and may merge together as they enlarge.

If the entire scalp is affected, the disease is called alopecia totalis, but this is not a different disease, just a severe case of alopecia areata. There is a family history of the disease in up to 20% of patients but in the majority no specific cause for the disease can be found. Stress and anxiety are not considered to be a common cause. Although these may cause diffuse hair loss, they do not cause total loss of hair in an area.

Fungal infections and drugs used to treat cancer may also cause patchy hair loss, and these causes must be excluded by a doctor.

Treatment will involve using strong steroid creams, injections of steroids into the affected area, and irritant lotions. There are many other treatments undergoing trial, with varying results. In 90% of patients, regrowth of hair eventually occurs, although the new hair may be totally white. Sometimes the regrowth may take many months. The further the bare patch is from the top of the scalp, the slower and less likely regrowth of the hair becomes. It is rare for recovery from total hair loss to occur.

Q **My problem is an extremely dry scalp, the discomfort of which is making me feel very distressed. I am a 63 year old lady, and have always endeavoured to take care of my crowning glory. The irritation is almost unbearable, particularly after shampooing. I am aware ageing does not help, but would you please advise as to the best solution?**

A A dry scalp may be caused by excessive washing of the hair, particularly with medicated or perfumed shampoos and soaps. All soaps and shampoos tend to remove oil from the skin, and the first step in treatment is to recommend washing the hair no more than twice a week, and using a very mild baby shampoo. As you age, this problem often becomes more acute as the hair thins with age, and more of the soap or shampoo can penetrate to the unprotected scalp.

After washing, the gentle massaging of a small amount of baby oil into the scalp will help replace any lost oil, and thus reduce dryness and itching.

It will take several weeks for the scalp to recover, but if used consistently, most will return to normal.

In severe cases, gels or lotions containing a steroid can be prescribed by doctors to settle the scalp inflammation. These should only be used short-term until the discomfort and skin flaking have settled, and then the sensible shampooing methods outlined above should be followed.

Q **I am an eighteen year old male, and although I shave, I've hardly any hair under my armpits. Is there any need to worry?**

A Look at your father and grandfather, your uncles and older male cousins. Are they hairy chested? Do they have heavy beards? If the answer is no, then you have nothing to be concerned about.

Some men are more hairy than others, and some races are more hairy than others. The Japanese have virtually no body hair and minimal facial hair, while Greeks tend to have copious amounts of body hair and heavy beards.

Provided you are developing normally in other ways, there is no need for concern about your lack of armpit hair—it is merely your hereditary background.

Many women prefer smooth-skinned men, without hair, so there is no need to be concerned about this either.

Q **I am 18 years old, female, and suffer from an embarrassing excess of facial and body hair. It grows around my nipples, between my breasts, and leads right down to my pubic hair. I find it very hard to wear any clothes that bare my body. What would you suggest?**

A Many women suffer from excess body hair, which is often associated with severe acne, but help is readily available from your general practitioner to control this problem.

Two prescription only drugs (Aldactone and Androcur) and a type of contraceptive pill (Diane) can be prescribed long term to prevent the growth of excess body hair, reduce acne, and improve the lustre of the hair on your head. These tablets cannot be used by men.

It will be several months before they take effect, after which time the dosage can be reduced. They must normally be taken for several years to control the problem, but they do this very successfully, and with minimal side effects.

Women of all ages can benefit from these treatments, and the post-menopausal woman with a moustache will be helped as much as the young woman with nipple and body hair.

Discuss the matter further with your general practitioner to determine which treatment is the better one for you.

Q What does a trichologist do?

A By definition, a trichologist is someone who specialises in the hair. I am not aware of doctors using this term, as dermatologists (skin specialists) are the doctors who specialise in diseases of the hair.

A trichologist could be almost anyone, and you should check on what sort of training they have, particularly if you have a significant hair problem.

I suspect that you may be referring to a beautician or hairdresser, who may be trying to sell some sort of hair conditioner or other hair product.

'Caveat emptor'!

Q I am a 32 year old male with two small patches of hair on either side of my lower back. The hair causes no irritation, but is unsightly. Is there any safe way of removing these hairs?

A These patches of hair are completely normal, and are no cause for concern. If you look at other men's backs, you will see these hairs present to varying degrees on most.

Shaving the hairs will cause stubble to grow that can be more annoying than the longer hairs. Depilatory creams will work for a short time.

Hairs anywhere on the body can be permanently removed in a procedure called electrolysis. Small patches can be removed under local anaesthetic by a plastic surgeon. Ask your GP for a referral if you really wish to proceed.

Q Like many men, I am suffering from a rapidly diminishing head of hair. I can live with that, but I have found it very difficult to live (for the past 25 years!) with an excess of hair on my arms, chest and back. The problem has become so acute that I an ashamed to take my shirt off in front of others. Can medical science offer any hope?

A The same genetic factors that cause baldness also cause excessive body hair, and virtually all balding men have far more body hair than men with a dense growth of hair on their scalp.

You certainly should not be ashamed of your body hair as it is seen by some as a sign of virility and masculinity. Some men without body hair have been known to have hair transplants to give them some hair on their chests, while others love to have a tuft of chest hair showing at their collar.

Unfortunately, medical science has no more effective treatments for excessive body hair than it has for a lack of scalp hair.

The depilatory (hair removing) creams that women use for excessive hair on their legs, can be used on other parts of the body, but not extensively. Using it to remove excess hair on the neck and in the collar V on the front of the chest would be reasonable, but more extensive usage would not.

Shaving of body hair gives only temporary results and the hair grows back as a rough stubble. Waxing of the hair would be very painful and could lead to skin rashes and infections.

Electrolysis of each individual hair follicle can be performed to limited areas by plastic surgeons, but this is a very intricate and time-consuming task, as each hair must be dealt with individually.

The best solution may be changing your attitude towards your body—be proud of what you have, and don't hide it from the admiring eyes of the many women who like their men to show a bit of masculinity!

Q **What causes excessive hair growth in the ears, nose and on the back in men? I have this problem, but I am going bald on top.**

A Nature is complex, but fair. Very frequently, bald men have hairy chests, backs, legs, arms etc. This is because of many factors, but primarily your choice of parents. The genes for baldness and excess body hair passes through the generations, so you should look to your father and grandfathers to see what hair distribution is likely in your future.

The growth of ear and nose hair is also controlled by your genes. There is no practical treatment for large hairy areas, but excess nose and ear hair can be permanently removed by plastic surgeons who will destroy the hair follicle under a local anaesthetic so that no further hairs can grow.

Q **I have had hair removed from my chin by electrolysis, but it has returned. What does this mean?**

A. Electrolysis is the passage of an electric current from the tip of a needle and into the surrounding skin in a way that destroys a hair follicle. If the hair follicle is destroyed, it can no longer grow a hair.

If your chin hair has regrown after this procedure it means that the electrolysis merely destroyed the hair and damaged the hair follicle, but did not destroy the follicle. The damaged follicle can repair itself, and start producing a hair again.

Your options are to have the electrolysis procedure repeated, or to take medication such as Aldactone (available on prescription from your GP) on a regular basis to prevent hair growth.

Q **Is it safe to have electrolysis around the nipple area to remove hairs?**

A. Yes, but be careful. Hairs often grow from the areola, the dark area of slightly bumpy skin around the nipple, but rarely do hairs grow from the nipple itself.

Electrolysis is the passage of an electric current through a needle that is inserted into the hair follicle from which the hair is growing. The aim is to destroy the hair follicle so no further hair growth can occur.

If this is done on the areola, there should be no harm done, but if electrolysis is performed on the nipple itself, one or more of the 16 to 20 small ducts that transport milk from the breast tissue to the nipple itself may be damaged, which could cause problems when trying to breast feed.

Q **My hair seems to be falling out on my right side. I take Pritor and Zocor for blood pressure and cholesterol and I use a lot of hair spray. Any advice, please?**

A. If the hair on only one side of your head is affected, it is not going to be due to the use of any medication (which would affect the whole body and both sides of the head equally), and also unlikely to be due to you use of hair spray, unless this is sprayed far more on one side of the head than the other (which is a possibility, depending on your hairstyle and using one hand more than the other to apply the spray).

More likely is the possibility that the blood or nerve supply to one side of the scalp is not as good as the other. This may be due to hardening and narrowing of the arteries to the scalp with cholesterol deposits (you already know that you have this problem), or pinching of a nerve, in the neck or temple, that supplies only one side of the head.

Another possibility is a fungal infection that is attacking one side of the head more than the other.

You need to have your problem investigated properly to determine the correct cause.

HANDS

See also ARTHRITIS

Q **Would you please write something about carpal tunnel syndrome? My doctor tells me that this is the cause of my hand problems.**

A. Carpal tunnel syndrome is a form of repetitive strain injury to the wrist. It is caused by the excessive compression of the arteries, veins and nerves that supply the hand as they pass through the carpal tunnel in the wrist. This tunnel is shaped like a letter 'D' lying on its side and consists of an arch of small bones which is held in place by a band of fibrous tissue. If the ligaments become slack, the arch will flatten, and the nerves, arteries and tendons within the tunnel will become compressed. It is far more common in women and in those undertaking repetitive tasks or using vibrating tools and in pregnancy.

The symptoms include numbness, tingling, pain and weakness in the hand. The diagnosis is made by x-rays of the wrist, and studies to measure the rate of nerve conduction in the area confirm the diagnosis.

Q **I have had an aching hand for months. Finally a doctor has told me that it is caused by the carpal tunnel syndrome, and I will need surgery. Are there any other treatments for the carpal tunnel syndrome?**

A The first step is to rest the affected wrist, in a splint if necessary. Anti-inflammatory tablets may be prescribed by your doctor. Fluid tablets (to reduce swelling) and occasionally injections of steroids into the wrist are beneficial. Most people who develop the problem eventually require surgery, although the other treatments may delay this for many years.

The operation may be performed under local or general anaesthetic, takes only 15 minutes, and leaves the patient free of pain. A small cut is made across the palm side of the wrist in a 'lazy S' shape, and through this the ligaments causing the pressure are cut. It is rare for there to be any long-term problems and the operation normally gives a life-long cure.

Schematic cross-section of wrist, showing carpal tunnel

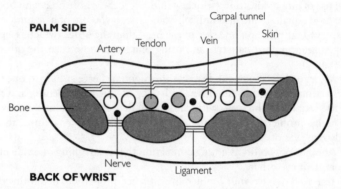

Q **What is Raynaud's phenomenon? My mother's doctor says it is the cause of her hand pain.**

A Raynaud's phenomenon is taught to medical students as the 'loyal disease' because the hands of these people go 'red, white and blue and swell up with pride'. Unfortunately it does not end there, because the colour changes and swelling of the hands is also accompanied by considerable pain.

These attacks are usually triggered by cold air, and so the condition is far commoner in the cooler states, but many find the condition so distressing that they migrate to the northern parts of Australia to escape the pain. But even in Cairns or Darwin, entering an air-conditioned building may be sufficient to trigger an attack that causes agony for many hours.

Other trigger factors may be hormonal changes, stress and anxiety, exercise and some foods. The disease usually starts in the teenage years or early twenties, and may remain life-long. Fortunately, many women find that it eases after the menopause.

One in every five women will suffer from Raynaud's phenomenon at some time in their lives. What must be detected and if possible treated in all these victims is an underlying cause for the problem. Unfortunately, frequently no specific cause can be found.

Q **My hands go numb and white in cold weather, and I have to wear gloves during winter. Is there any treatment for this?**

A Treatment of Raynaud's phenomenon is difficult as there is no cure, only control. Keeping the hands warm is the first step, but far easier said than done, and not always effective. Alcohol in low doses may be useful. A wide range of prescription drugs can be used to dilate the tiny arteries in the fingers which go into spasm to cause the blanching and pain.

As a last resort, operations to cut the nerves that cause the artery spasm can be performed.

Those who suffer from this distressing condition should be under the regular care of a doctor so that all avenues of treatment can be tried to give the best possible relief.

Q I am developing hard lumps on the palm of my right hand, and I'm finding it hard to straighten my fingers. Is this serious?

A You are probably developing Dupuytren's contractures. This is a disease of the protective membrane that covers the palm of the hand just underneath the skin. The membrane loses its elasticity and becomes fibrosed, contracted and hard.

The probable cause is an injury to the blood supply to the palm of the hand, which may occur with old age, diseases such as diabetes and hardening of the arteries, and by injury to the hand—particularly from vibrating machines (eg. jack hammers). There is an hereditary tendency in this disease, and also an increase amongst epileptics—possibly because of muscle spasms causing injury to the hand in uncontrolled epilepsy. It is much more common in men than women.

In minor cases, no treatment is necessary, but if the contractures are causing discomfort or disability, surgical treatment is available to cut away the fibrosed tissue and allow the tendons that control the fingers to move them freely again. Unfortunately, the remaining areas of fibrous tissue in the hand may contract at a later time, making repeat operations necessary.

Q I am 54 years of age and the knuckles of my fingers are very swollen and ache. Is there anything I can do to help this?

A You obviously have an arthritis of your finger joints, and the important thing to determine is what type of arthritis is present. Rheumatoid arthritis is most likely, but osteoarthritis is possible, as are a number of other rarer diseases.

Your GP can arrange X-rays and blood tests to make this diagnosis, and then the correct treatment can be given.

Treatment will depend upon the diagnosis, and can include anti-inflammatory tablets, specific anti-rheumatic drugs, heat, physiotherapy and exercise.

You are young to be developing a significant arthritis, and so it is important for the correct treatment to be started before your finger joints are permanently damaged.

Q Why do elderly people develop red palms?

A There are several dozen causes for this complaint, varying from liver disease and an overactive thyroid to blood vessel overdilation and the side effects of certain drugs.

The most likely explanation is age, because the skin is thinner in older people and this allows the blood normally circulating there to show through more easily, giving a fiery red colour to the palms.

Q I am in my 70s, and for many years have suffered with finger tips that crack and split and almost bleed. It is usually worse in winter, and very painful. Can you suggest a treatment?

A The first treatment would be the copious use of moisturising cram on the finger tips to nourish the dry skin. You cannot overuse such creams, and the cheap ones such as Sorbolene and urea cream are just as good (if not better) than the expensive perfumed ones.

If this is inadequate, a mild steroid cream can be tried as well as the moisturiser. This will require a doctor's prescription, so the doctor can check the fingers to ensure that there is not some other disease causing the problem.

Poor circulation to the finger tips, fungal infections and contact dermatitis are just a few of the many possible causes of cracked and dry finger tips.

Q **The palms of my hands and the soles of my feet have turned yellow. My husband says I eat too many paw paws. Could this be the cause?**

A Carotenaemia, also known as hypervitaminosis A, is a relatively common condition amongst health food freaks and others who overindulge in vitamin A supplements and yellow coloured foods such as pawpaw, pumpkin and carrot. The kidneys and liver are unable to remove the excess levels of carotene (the yellow pigment that gives these foods their colour) from the blood stream, and it deposits in the thick-skinned areas of the soles and palms. Eventually the whole body may become yellow, and this condition may be confused with hepatitis. The liver is also damaged in this process. The only treatment is avoidance of the offending vitamins and foods. Over several months, the body's waste removal system recovers sufficiently to remove the deposits and your colour returns to normal.

Diets should never concentrate on one type of food product, and just because a small vitamin supplement is good for you, it does not mean that large amounts of vitamins are better.

Q. **I have found it progressively more difficult to write over the past few years to the point where I now either type or write with my left hand. A doctor did electrical tests and said that my nerves weren't working and I needed an operation. Now, if I try to use my right hand, my first three fingers remain straight and cannot be bent. Should I have the operation?**

A Yes! Yes! Yes! And don't waste any more time about it or your hand may be permanently damaged.

A nerve is almost certainly being trapped and damaged, and if the damage becomes severe, the nerve may never recover.

Nerves send messages to the muscles telling them to do what the brain wishes. If the nerve is trapped or compressed, the message cannot pass, so the muscles supplied by that nerve become weak and eventually fail to work.

The probability is that the nerves supplying your fingers are being squashed as they pass through your wrist in a congested area known as the carpal tunnel.

The carpal tunnel syndrome causes tingling, numbness and then weakness of the muscles beyond the wrist. The problem can be easily and rapidly corrected by a simple operation that requires only one day (or sometimes only a few hours) in hospital. In the operation, the tissue pressing on the nerve is cut, and once free, the nerve resumes its normal function, providing it has not already been damaged too severely.

See your general practitioner immediately for a referral to an orthopaedic surgeon as soon as possible.

Q   My fingers go numb when I play the piano. What can I do about this?

A   There are many overuse syndromes in vogue at present, including RSI (repetitive strain injury).

Any form of rapid repetitive movement can cause inflammation in the arm, leg or finger involved and therefore numbness, pins and needles, pain and even weakness. It may be due to the tendons or ligaments being strained by overuse; or nerves may be damaged by rapid joint movement or the blood supply in the tiny arteries that supply the fingers may be inadequate. It is important to find out the cause of your problem, and then appropriate medications can be prescribed.

Sometimes simple remedies such as changing the position in which you play or the height of the piano stool can change the angle of your wrist to prevent constriction of nerves or arteries. If this is unsuccessful, arrange to see your doctor immediately after a long practice session so that he/she can assess the problem at first hand.

Q   I was intrigued to read that Greg Norman has a wrist injury that cannot be cured unless he stops playing golf! How does the body cope with the strain of hitting 500 golf balls a day over a period of years, and do the joints wear out, or does the body cope with no detrimental effects?

A   The problem you have raised is one that plagues virtually all world class sportspeople in almost every sport, and also significantly affects many players at far lower levels of competence.

If any piece of machinery is used excessively, it will wear out sooner than it should. If a car is repeatedly stopped using the hand brake, the hand brake will wear out and fail long before the rest of the car shows any sign of deterioration.

In a golfer, if the wrists and back are put under far greater stress than the rest of the body, these joints will develop arthritis and other problems at a far younger age than would normally be expected.

Strapping and elastic cuffs around the affected joint can protect it to some extent, as can exercises to strengthen the muscles around the joint.

Unfortunately, nothing really works adequately, and general practitioners and orthopaedic surgeons see a steady stream of middle-aged ex-athletes with significant deterioration in their joints. Footballers have bad knees, tennis players bad elbows, runners bad ankles and golfers bad wrists—almost every sport (with the possible exception of swimming) has its casualties.

HEADACHE

Q   I have a headache that won't go away for days at a time, then it comes back again after only a couple of days. What can I do?

A   The first thing you must do is determine the type of headache you have and its cause. A chronic (long-standing) headache may be due to a sinus infection, muscle spasm secondary to stress, eye strain, dental decay, medications that you may be taking for other diseases, ear diseases and several dozen other more obscure conditions. Many of these conditions can be cured or prevented.

A chronic sinus infection, for example, can be cleared up with a course of antibiotics and/or a sinus washout. Migraines may be prevented by using special medication on a regular basis for month after month. Even stress can be relieved by rationalising the problems you face with help from your general practitioner or a psychiatrist.

Please see your doctor and obtain the correct diagnosis and treatment.

Q How many different causes are there for headaches? I do not believe that doctors have really worked out what mine are due to.

A This is going to be a long answer, because a headache is probably the most common symptom to be experienced by the human race, and may be associated with problems of any of the multiple complex structures in the head, or disorders of many of the body's other organs. Fatigue, stress and anxiety may in themselves cause a headache, or may trigger muscle spasms in the temples and scalp that are responsible for the pain.

Any infection, by a bacteria (eg. tonsillitis, sinusitis, ear infection, bronchitis, urinary infection), virus (eg. influenza, common cold, glandular fever, hepatitis), fungus or parasite (eg. malaria), may cause a headache, as may a fever (see separate entry) of any cause.

Injury to any part of the head may cause a headache, but sometimes, and very seriously, the headache may occur some days after the injury due to slow bleeding from an leaking vein within the skull.

A headache is more significant when not associated with any other symptoms elsewhere in the body. The most common headaches to fit into this category are tension headaches, migraine and cluster headache.

A tension headache causes a dull, persistent pain with varying intensity that is often described as a pressure or tightening around the scalp. It occurs as a localised band around and across head, and is not aggravated by exercise or alcohol. Tension headaches are episodic, often in association with stress. Depression and anxiety are common accompanying symptoms. The pain may last for 30 minutes or a week. Muscle spasm headaches usually have a cause (eg. stress, infection, psychiatric disturbance, eye strain), and if possible this should be rectified. Simple medications are readily available to ease both the muscle spasm and pain.

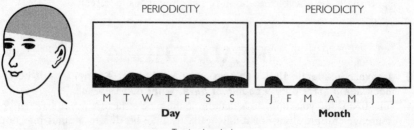

Tension headache

Migraines are often associated with visual symptoms including flashing lights, shimmering, seeing zig-zag lines and loss of part of the area of vision. They usually occur on only one side of the head, are described as throbbing, and cause intolerance of exercise, light and noise. Nausea and vomiting are common. Migraines occur periodically, and may last for a few hours to several days. The patient often looks pale and drawn. There are now effective medications available to both prevent and treat migraine.

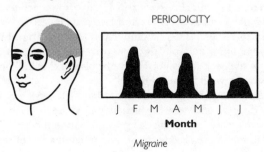

PERIODICITY

J F M A M J J
Month

Migraine

Cluster headaches are not common, but cause a very characteristic pattern of headache, usually associated with excess sweating of one or both sides of head. They occur in episodes once or twice a year to cause severe pain around or behind one eye which spreads to a temple, the jaw, teeth or chin. They often begin during sleep, and other effects may include a red, watery eye, drooping eyelid, altered pupil in the eye, stuffy nose and flushed face. Cluster headaches may be triggered by alcohol, temperature changes, wind blowing on the face or excitement. They usually last for 15 minutes to three hours, and are named because of their tendency to occur in clusters for several weeks. An unusual but effective cure is to breathe pure oxygen for 15 minutes.

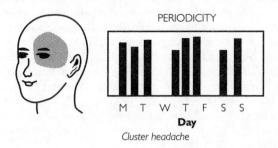

PERIODICITY

M T W T F S S
Day

Cluster headache

Many people fear that their headache may be due to a brain tumour, but this is actually very rare, most brain tumours causing other symptoms that lead to their diagnosis well before a headache develops. Cancerous and benign tumours may develop not only in the brain tissue itself, but in the other structures within the skull such as the pituitary gland, membranes around the brain (meninges), sinuses and eyes. Most brain tumours are benign and can be cured by surgery.

Anything that puts abnormal pressure on the brain may cause headaches. An abscess caused by an untreated infection in the brain or an injury that penetrates the skull are possibilities. Bleeding inside the skull caused by an injury or rupture to a blood vessel is another. An aneurysm is the ballooning out of one side of an artery. The aneurysm may put pressure on the brain to cause a headache, or rupture to cause very severe effects on the brain function.

Viral or bacterial infections of the brain (encephalitis) or surrounding membranes (meningitis) will almost invariably cause a headache.

Inflammation of nerves in the scalp and face may appear to be a headache, when really it is the tissue outside the skull that is affected. Trigeminal neuralgia is one relatively common example, as is the pain of neuralgias associated with pinched nerves in the neck that spread from the base of the skull up the back of the head and as far forward as the hairline.

Psychiatric disorders as varied as phobias (abnormal fears), depression, post-traumatic stress disorder and excessive anxiety may cause headaches.

Eye disorders that vary from increased pressure within the eye (glaucoma), to poor vision (resulting in eye muscle strain) and inflammation of the eye (iritis), may cause head pains.

Menopause, menstrual periods (premenstrual tension), contraceptive pills, pregnancy and other fluctuations in the level of the sex hormone oestrogen, may cause headaches.

Inflammation or infection of tissues around the head may be felt as a headache, but the problem may be coming from the teeth (eg. abscess or dental decay), jaw joint (eg. arthritis), neck (eg. arthritis or ligamentous strain), nose (eg. large polyp) or sinuses (eg. polyp or infection).

Cancer of any tissue in the body may cause headaches, particularly in advanced stages, due to the release of toxins into the blood. Leukaemia, a cancer of the white blood cells, is one example.

Both an underactive and overactive thyroid gland in the neck, and the subsequent variations in levels of the hormone thyroxine that it produces, can have effects on every cell in the body and result in head pain amongst other symptoms.

Diseases of any other gland (eg. adrenal glands, testes, parathyroids) in the body can affect the blood chemistry and cause headaches.

Extreme high blood pressure, or a sudden significant rise in blood pressure above normal is another cause that requires rapid medical treatment. Phaeochro-mocytoma (tumour of an adrenal gland on the kidneys) is a rare cause of extreme high blood pressure.

Anaemia (a lack of haemoglobin and/or red blood cells) reduces the amount of oxygen being supplied to cells, and as they are unable to function properly, may cause pain, particularly in the head.

A wide range of medications (eg. for control of high blood pressure, epilepsy and cancer) may cause headache as a side effect.

Poorly controlled diabetes, resulting from either high sugar levels from lack of treatment, or low blood sugar from excess medication, may result in a dull head pain.

Severe allergy reactions (anaphylaxis) may affect any part of the body, depending upon where the allergy-causing substance has entered, and what it is. A headache is almost inevitable.

Acromegaly is a thickening and enlargement of the bones in the skull and legs that results in pressure on nerves and pain.

Cushing's syndrome is caused by an overproduction of steroids such as cortisone in the body, or taking large doses of cortisone to control a wide range of diseases, including asthma and rheumatoid arthritis. Headache is a common symptom of this syndrome.

Low blood pressure from excessive medication, sudden change in position, shock or fright may cause a head pain.

Failure or inflammation of any of the body's major organs, such as the kidneys, spleen or liver, will cause a rise of waste products or abnormal cells in the blood to cause a headache.

There are many other rare causes of headache, and entire textbooks have been written on this symptom, so persistence in seeking a cause for your problem can be worthwhile.

Q **I have been getting bad migraines for two years every two to four weeks, with severe pain in the right side of my head. A CT scan was normal and Inderal did not help. Acupuncture, naturopaths and osteopath also have not helped. It is frustrating that nothing will help. Have you any suggestions?**

A A CT scan will always be normal in a migraine patient, but may be used to exclude other causes of a headache. If all other causes have been excluded, and your symptoms fit the criteria for a migraine, then further treatment can be tried.

Inderal is a very effective medication in preventing migraines in many patients, but there are always those in which it does not work. There are several other medications which can be used to prevent migraines if Inderal does not work, and here are preparations that can be used to treat any migraines that may occur.

All the preventative medications require a prescription, and you will need to discuss with your general practitioner which ones you should try. It is a matter of trial and error to see which ones work. Medications that may be used include methysergide, cyproheptadine, clonidine, pizotifen, verapamil and naproxen.

Treatment regimes vary from simple over-the-counter regimes to prescription medications. A simple regime that does not require a prescription is to take three aspirin and two Mersyndol every four hours, starting as soon as the migraine starts, but this will cause some drowsiness. The best treatment is often an Imigran tablet, inhaler or injection. Other injections and tablets are available from your doctor.

Q **I suffer terribly every few weeks—more than anyone imagines, with migraines that strike like lightening, and leave me totally disabled for hours on end. What causes migraines?**

A A migraine may occur once in a person's life, or three times a week. They may cause a relatively mild head pain, or may totally disable a victim for days on end.

Migraines are caused by an initial contraction of an artery in the brain, which may give the patient warning of an attack, followed by an overdilation of the artery within the brain.

The size of an artery is controlled by muscles in its wall, and if these muscles totally relax, excess blood passes to the part of the brain that the artery supplies. This section of the brain is then unable to function properly, and the patient feels the intense pressure, pain and other symptoms that occur with a migraine. Usually, only one artery at a time is affected.

These spasms of the arteries, may in turn be caused by many factors, including stress, illness, certain foods, allergies, hormonal changes, flashing lights, tiredness etc.

Q I am 15 years old and have been suffering from very bad migraines for three months. Is there a permanent solution for the pain?

A Migraines can be prevented and controlled, but there is no permanent cure available.

Migraines are uncommon in children, and usually start in the late teens or early twenties.

Anyone who suffers from disabling migraines more than once a month should be using preventative medication. This usually involves only one or two tablets a day, and a dosage regime free of any side effects should be possible.

Once a migraine is present, it is much harder to cure, but there are tablets and injections (called Imigran), that are very successful in stopping a migraine attack.

HEART
See also ARTERIES and VEINS

Q I need to know how the heart works for a school project.

A The heart is a hollow ball of muscle about the same size as your fist, and it acts as a very efficient pump. It is situated high in the chest behind the breast bone, and one corner extends out towards the left nipple.

The hollow heart is divided into four chambers by relatively thin walls made of muscle and fibrous tissue. The upper right chamber (right atrium) of the heart receives the blood returning through the veins from all parts of the body. With a gentle squeeze, it pushes the blood through a valve into the lower right chamber. A split second later, the lower right chamber (right ventricle) contracts quite forcibly to push the blood into the lungs. There it loses the carbon dioxide it has picked up in the body, and exchanges it for oxygen.

From the lungs, the blood flows into the upper left chamber of the heart (left atrium). This acts in the same way, and simultaneously with, the right atrium, and pushes the blood into the final chamber, the left lower one (left ventricle). This is the most powerful and important chamber of the four as it is responsible for pumping the blood out of the heart and around the body. The flow of blood to the head, all organs and down to the toes is caused by the contraction of the left ventricle.

After passing through microscopic capillaries, the blood moves back through the veins to the heart's right atrium, completing the cycle.

Q Can you tell me please how many beats does a normal heart do in one minute. I am over 70 and my heart when I wake in the morning, and am still in bed, beats only 52 times a minute. Is that too low?

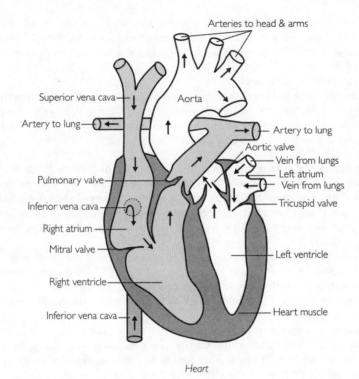

Arteries to head & arms

Superior vena cava

Aorta

Artery to lung

Artery to lung

Aortic valve

Vein from lungs

Pulmonary valve

Left atrium

Vein from lungs

Inferior vena cava

Tricuspid valve

Right atrium

Mitral valve

Left ventricle

Right ventricle

Inferior vena cava

Heart muscle

Heart

A The normal heartbeat rate, according to textbooks, is 72 beats per minute, but there are wide variations on this depending upon what you are doing, how you are doing it, your age, and how fit you are.

 If exercising vigorously, a young person's heart rate may increase to 250, while an Olympic athlete's may not go above 150.

 Younger people tend to have a higher heart rate than the elderly. At rest, a baby may have a heart rate of 85, a child 80, a young person 70, and an elderly person 60.

 If you are anxious or frightened, your heart rate will also increase. Illness, fevers and many disorders of the body (eg. overactive thyroid, heart disease) will also increase the pulse rate.

 If you are totally relaxed and comfortable, as you should be in a warm bed on waking from a good night's sleep, your pulse rate will be at its minimum, and a rate of 52 under these circumstances is nothing to be concerned about. An extremely fit athlete in the same circumstances could have a heart rate of 40.

Q **The hospital doctor said that I probably had mitral valve stenosis. Is this serious?**

A The mitral valve is situated between the upper and lower chambers of the heart. It acts to prevent the blood going in the wrong direction in the heart.

 Stenosis is the medical turn for narrowing. If the valve is narrowed, blood may be slow in passing from one chamber of the heart to the next. If the problem is mild it will cause no symptoms and require no treatment. If it is severe, the heart will start to fail, and fluid may build up in your lungs. This can be treated in the early stages by medication, but if it becomes more severe you will require surgery to replace the valve. Surgery is very successful and a relatively routine operation these days.

A doctor can detect the condition by listening to your heart, and an abnormal murmur will be heard as the blood rushes through the narrowed valve. Further investigations involving X-rays and other examinations of the heart would be necessary before surgery was contemplated.

Q **I am concerned about the occasional irregular heartbeat I get for no apparent cause. It happens about once a week for just two or three beats. I am a woman in my 20s and would like to know what it could be.**

A There is a remote possibility that you may have a conduction abnormality in your heart, and to exclude this you should have an electrocardiograph performed by your family doctor.

By far the most likely reason for your occasional irregular heart beat is a condition known as paroxysmal atrial tachycardia (PAT). This is a very common problem, but is usually more annoying than serious. It is far more common in women than in men, and tends to occur at certain times of the month—usually just before a period.

In some women the rapid heartbeats can last for an hour or two, and be quite distressing. In these cases, medication can be prescribed on a regular basis to prevent the problem. Most cases are similar to yours—a rapid pulse for just a few seconds or minutes.

Provided your medical check-up is normal, you can be reassured that there is nothing to be concerned about.

Q **My wife has been told that her 'funny turns' are due to PAT. Can you tell me who or what is PAT?**

A PAT stands for paroxysmal atrial tachycardia. Paroxysmal means occurring suddenly and irregularly for no apparent reason. Atrial refers to the atrium, which is the small upper chamber of the heart, and which regulates the rate at which the heart beats. Tachycardia means 'rapid heart' in Latin, and indicates that the heart is beating far faster than it should. Medical terminology does have some logic behind it!

PAT is relatively common in women, may be triggered by hormonal, emotional or other factors, and is not harmful. Most attacks last only a few minutes, and cause minimal discomfort to the victim. If they last for longer periods or occur very frequently, medication can be given to prevent them.

There are also a few tricks that can be used to stop the attacks once they have developed. These can be taught by a doctor and include firm massage of the eyeballs, taking a deep breath, closing your throat and trying to breathe out hard to increase the pressure in your chest, and dunking your face in icy water.

The need for treatment depends on the severity and frequency of attacks.

Q **I have been asked by my specialist doctor, who looks after my dickey heart, to go for an echo test on my heart. I've had some unpleasant**

experiences with tests on my heart before, and would like you to tell me what is involved.

A   Echocardiograms are sound waves that can show the movement of the heart valves. It is rather like a machine that can be placed on the outside of a car to visualise the movement of the pistons of an engine that is running.

    While lying down, the patient's chest is smeared with gel, and an instrument is then placed on the chest and moved slowly from one point to another over the heart. The instrument sends out high-frequency sound waves, and receives back an echo of these waves as they are reflected by the heart. The reflected waves are recorded on a moving sheet of paper to give a complex tracing.

    Any diseases of the valves can be detected, and the severity determined. The test takes 15 to 30 minutes, and there is no discomfort whatsoever.

    Expert doctors (usually cardiologists) can interpret this tracing to see if the heart valves are working properly (eg. if they are leaking or narrowed) and to check the contraction of each chamber of the heart.

    Because there is no risk, no pain and no discomfort involved with this procedure, it is often performed before progressing to more sophisticated and invasive tests on the heart. If no abnormalities show on the echocardiograph, the other tests may be unnecessary.

Q   **I am a 16 year old competitive mountain biker. Recently, after working out on a rowing machine for 2 minutes, my pulse rose to 320. My resting pulse is 45. Is this normal?**

A   It is normal for your pulse to rise when exercising, as your heart must work harder to pump the necessary amount of blood to the muscles that are working hard.

    A pulse of 45 is quite slow, but not abnormal in a very fit athlete. In a person of average fitness it could be a sign of some abnormality, from an underactive thyroid gland to drug overdose or heart damage.

    For your heart rate to increase sevenfold after only two minutes of exercise is not normal. An athlete would be expected to have a four or five-fold increase, but only after extreme exertion. A heart rate as high as 320 is of concern to any doctor, as it is unlikely that the heart could pump efficiently at that speed. I strongly recommend that you have a thorough heart check by your GP, who may well arrange an exercise cardiograph to see just what is happening in your heart.

Q   **I'm a 57 year old male, and reasonably fit as I exercise daily with a 20 minute run. After running, while I am cooling down, my pulse drops from 140 to normal in ten minutes, but during this time I notice that I miss a beat every six to eight beats. Is this acceptable, as I would feel foolish going to a doctor if it is normal?**

A   What you describe is completely normal under the circumstances. As you get older, missing the occasional beat is a common event, and many elderly people cope quite well while always missing every third or fourth beat.

    Provided you are not missing heartbeats when completely rested, and provided you are not suffering any other symptoms related to your heart, you can relax.

    All men of your age should have their blood pressure and cholesterol levels checked every couple of years to exclude any other heart risk, and you obviously should not smoke, as this can aggravate heartbeat irregularities.

Any sign of chest pain, ankle swelling or excessive breathlessness should be reported to your doctor immediately.

No-one should ever feel foolish about going to a doctor with a problem that is concerning them. Having a doctor say that there is nothing wrong can relieve long-standing anxiety, and therefore improve your quality of life. Doctors do not laugh at such people, but consider them sensible for obtaining appropriate advice.

Q I am 50 years of age and a bit overweight. When my heart races as a result of an emotional upset, or when I walk quickly, I have an uncomfortable tightness in the chest and a funny feeling in my left arm. Could this be angina?

A Yes it certainly could be, and you should see your general practitioner immediately.

Any chest pain or tightness, neck pain, arm pain or even upper belly and back pain, may be due to angina.

The only way to find out if it is a heart problem is to see your doctor, but even then, doctors sometimes find it very difficult to be sure whether the pain and tightness is due to angina, muscle pain, lung disease or indigestion.

Sophisticated tests are often necessary to exactly determine the cause, but these can only be performed if the patient presents to a doctor.

Angina occurs because one or more of the arteries supplying blood to the heart muscle becomes narrowed by excessive deposits of cholesterol. The first sign is chest discomfort or tightness when exercising, but as mentioned above, the pain may be felt elsewhere or occur at other times.

It is far better to be reassured that your pain is merely indigestion than to suddenly drop dead from a heart attack because you have been ignoring the warning signs of angina.

Q My heart keeps jumping! Every few minutes it gives a funny beat. How can I stop this?

A Everyone has extra heart beats at some time or other, and they cause no problems. If it become a frequent occurrence, it may be annoying, but is not normally serious.

The first step is to have a cardiograph (ECG) done by your GP to demonstrate the type of abnormal beat, and possibly its cause. After this you may merely be reassured, or medication can be prescribed to prevent the extra beats. Unfortunately, this medication does not cure, only control, so it may have to be taken for many years.

The heart rate is determined by a pacemaker at the top of the heart. The pacemaker usually slows the heart down, as the heart would beat much faster if the pacemaker were disconnected. If you exercise, the inhibiting effect of the pacemaker is reduced, and then the opposite effect may be applied to speed the heart rate even further if you exercise very vigorously. At times, the natural tendency of the heart to beat faster than the pacemaker wishes can break through, and an extra, premature beat occurs, which you feel as a jump in your heart.

Q **My daughter aged 42 is suffering from pericarditis which she has had for ten months. She is getting injections of cortisone. I am very worried about her, and I'm afraid for her. Can you please tell me what can be done for this disease?**

A The heart is contained in a thin sack made from fibrous tissue. This sack acts to support and protect the heart, but if it becomes inflamed or infected, the patient is suffering from pericarditis.

There are three main types of pericarditis—a bacterial infection, a viral infection, and a non-specific inflammation that may be related to heart attacks and a number of other rare diseases including tuberculosis, cancer, lupus erythematosus and kidney failure. Pericarditis may be a rapidly developing infection like tonsillitis, or a very slowly developing one that takes many months or years to cause problems. Your daughter seems to have the latter form.

The most serious complication of the disease is called constrictive pericarditis, in which the fibrous pericardial sack starts to shrink due to the infection or inflammation, and squeezes the heart so that it cannot beat effectively. This constriction can sometimes be relieved by surgery. Fluid may also accumulate between the pericardial sack and the heart to cause problems.

Cortisone injections are used to reduce the inflammation of the pericardium, and prevent the complications of the disease. The treatment and outcome depend upon the cause of the pericarditis and its severity, and from the information you have given me it is impossible to come to a more detailed conclusion.

In all cases, where a relative is concerned about a patient, it is best, with the patient's permission, to talk to the doctors looking after the case, who will be able to give more accurate information.

Q **I get very short of breath when I walk up stairs. It has only just started and I'm only 56. What can I do to help this?**

A Shortness of breath on exercising is a sign of heart or lung disease in middle-aged or elderly people.

You will need to be investigated to find the exact cause, but most patients respond very well to treatment for heart failure or chest conditions such as asthma.

When you exercise (eg. climb stairs), your body demands more oxygen, and this requires the heart to pump blood through the lungs at a faster rate. If your heart is not strong enough to do this, or the lungs are damaged by smoking or recurrent infection, you will not be able to get sufficient oxygen and you will become short of breath.

It is important to see your general practitioner as soon as possible to obtain an exact diagnosis, and to prevent any further deterioration in your condition.

Q **I am 86 years old, but do not have high blood pressure or cholesterol. My heart is good, but for a long time now I get breathless even if I walk a short distance. I have been advised to take little heart tablets, but am unwilling to do so if I can find any other way to overcome the shortness of breath. What do you suggest?**

A To work effectively, the body requires oxygen to be supplied to every cell. This is received from the lungs through the bloodstream.

If the heart is not beating and pumping as effectively as it should, not enough blood reaches the cells of the body, and as a result they do not receive enough oxygen (fuel) to work effectively. Signals are then sent to the lung to breathe faster, and the heart to beat faster, to improve the amount of oxygen entering the lungs and being pumped around the body in the blood.

Unfortunately, unless the heart beats more effectively, as well as faster, the body still does not receive sufficient oxygen, and you develop tiredness, muscle pains and shortness of breath.

This condition is called heart failure, and it is a very common problem in older people, but not normally serious. Tablets can be taken to strengthen the heart contractions and overcome the condition.

The most common medication used for mild heart failure is Lanoxin, but others are also available. This drug has been known for over 200 years (it was originally made from the Foxglove flower and drunk as a tea), is very safe, and very effective. I suggest you use the tablets prescribed by your doctor—you may find them remarkably effective, and your quality of life may improve significantly.

Q **I heard a nurse in the hospital say that I had a 'tacky cardia' just before I was discharged. I didn't get a chance to ask her if this was serious. Can you tell me?**

A Doctors—and nurses—love using long technical words, but not just to confuse patients. It is easier to say 'tachycardia' than 'a faster than normal heart rate'. And tachycardia means nothing more than that, so that when you exercise, or even climb stairs, you develop a tachycardia because your heart beats faster at these times.

Anxiety and stress can also cause a tachycardia, and the excitement of going home from hospital may have been sufficient cause in your case. There are, of course, many diseases that can cause a rapid heart rate. Anyone with a fever will have tachycardia, and other conditions as varied as pain, thyroid disease, heart attacks and cancer may be the cause.

Many drugs can also be responsible, and the most common of these is alcohol, which can significantly increase your heart rate. By itself, tachycardia is meaningless, but if taken in context it can give doctors and nurses additional information about your condition. I am sure that if your tachycardia was significant, you would not have been allowed to leave hospital.

Q **My mother-in-law had a heart attack 3 years ago, and she suffers from knee arthritis. Her doctor and physiotherapist tell her to exercise but she won't. All she does is lie on her bed or sit and watch TV all day. My husband and I are fighting as I say she should do as the doctor says, but he says she doesn't have to. What do you think?**

A Your mother-in-law's doctor and physio are quite correct in their advice. Those who exercise and control their weight after a heart attack do much better, and survive far longer than those who remain sedentary. Appropriate exercise (eg. swimming) will also help her knee arthritis.

Conversely, your mother-in-law has the right to reject their advice and do whatever she wishes. Provided she has had the risks of her inactivity explained to her, and she understands those risks, there is nothing more that you can do.

You and your husband should stop fighting, and get on with your lives, after you have explained to your mother-in-law that you are looking forward to receiving some benefit from her will in the near future, now that she has rejected all your good advice.

Q I am 63 years old and have recently been getting pains in my back at about heart height. Is this a cause for concern?

A Pain in the back of the chest can be caused by local problems in the back, such as arthritis, but it may also be a sign of heart or lung disease.

Depending upon the part of the heart affected, angina may sometimes be felt in the back. This is obviously a significant medical problem that must be dealt with by a doctor.

Lung problems as varied as pleurisy, pneumonia and an embolus (blockage of an artery) may cause back pain, and these must also be effectively treated.

Your problem may simply be a sprained muscle, but because it could be a serious problem, you should have a check-up with your general practitioner. It is far better to be reassured that nothing is wrong than miss a serious diagnosis that may have long-term consequences.

Q I suffer from heart palpitations known as paroxysmal supraventricular tachycardia. These attacks are frequent and distressing, and a wide range of medications has failed to control them. One heart specialist has suggested heart surgery to cut the nerves in the heart that are causing the problem, but another has cautioned me against this operation. What do you think I should do?

A Heart palpitations can be distressing, but are very rarely serious or life-threatening. The vast majority of patients with this condition can be controlled by medications. These include Inderal, Isoptin and Lanoxin (all only available on prescription) and similar drugs. All these drugs should be tried at various dosages for a reasonable period of time before other procedures or surgery are contemplated.

A new technique called radio frequency ablation can also be used to treat palpitations in some patients. After extensive preparatory investigations, a catheter is threaded through a vein or artery into the appropriate part of the heart and a high-frequency radio wave is used to destroy the abnormal pathway.

Surgery will cure most cases of palpitations if undertaken for the right reasons, but it is quite major surgery with risks of its own.

Surgery is the absolute last resort in this situation, and every other option should be exhausted before it is contemplated. Even then, undertaking major surgery for a problem that itself is not serious (although it may be very annoying) needs to be very carefully considered.

Q Despite having a coronary artery bypass graft after a heart attack, I continue to get pain in my left arm and chest wall. Why is this so? I have arthritis in my neck. Could this be responsible?

A Arthritis in the neck may cause narrowing of the small gaps between the vertebrae through which the nerves that supply the arm and upper chest escape from the spinal cord. If a nerve is pinched in the neck, pain will be felt in the area that is supplied by that nerve, and possibly also in the neck. It may well be the cause of your arm and chest pain, but it is also possible that you are still getting angina from an inadequate blood supply to the heart (angina) or damage to the heart from the heart attack, despite the surgery you have had to bypass blocked arteries.

It is important that you have investigations to determine the cause of your pain so that it can be properly treated. A stress test, during which you walk on a treadmill while attached to machines that measure your heart function, will be able to diagnose angina as the cause of your pain. A CT scan (special type of x-ray) may be able to detect a pinched nerve in the neck.

Once the cause is known, appropriate treatment can be given.

Q   What causes the heart to miss a beat now and then? Is it dangerous?

A   If a piece of heart muscle is taken from the body and kept alive in a nutrient solution, it will spontaneously contract at about 40 beats per minute.

There is an area near the top of the heart that is made from a complex network of nerves. This is the natural pacemaker of the heart, and it sends electrical signals to the heart muscle to contract at faster rate of approximately 70 beats a minute. This pacemaker is itself controlled by nerves running to the brain, so that anxiety and exercise can cause the heart to beat faster.

Certain chemicals in the blood stream can also act on the pacemaker, and the heart muscle itself, to alter the rate at which the heart contracts. It is therefore a very complex process.

The occasional dropped (missed) heart beat is due to a blockage of the nerve signal to the heart muscle, a lack of signal from the pacemaker, chemical disturbances in the body and many other factors. Alcohol, smoking, drugs, caffeine, high blood pressure and several diseases can all cause missed heart beats.

If the dropped beats occur only once every minute or so, there is no cause for concern, as this is a common phenomenon, particularly in older people. If you find that every third or fourth beat is being missed, you should be under regular medical care and probably on medication. Patients with problems within these extremes should discuss the matter further with their doctor. S/he will almost certainly perform an ECG (heart electrical test) and probably order blood tests to exclude any serious disease. The treatment will depend on the result of these tests.

Missed heart beats are not in themselves dangerous, unless they become very frequent.

Q   My doctor says I have an enlarged heart on X-ray. Is this dangerous?

A   Probably not. If your doctor was concerned, he or she would certainly have given you treatment or referred you to a specialist. An enlarged heart is common in older people, those who are overweight and in first class athletes. Athletes and the obese put a greater demand on the blood pump (heart) and over several years it slowly enlarges to take the additional strain. In older people the heart may become weaker and thin walled, leading to a stretching and enlarging of the heart. If there are no associated symptoms or problems shown on the X-ray, it is unlikely for treatment to be needed.

Q   My doctor says my weakness is due to cardiomyopathy. He has given

me tablets but no explanation. Can you help?

A   Most medical problems that have long fancy names can have those names dismembered into their Latin and/or Greek origins to reveal their meaning. Cardiomyopathy means heart muscle disease (cardio = heart, myo = muscle, pathy = disease). Diseases and weakness of the heart muscle are very common in older people due to the ageing process. Medications such as digoxin, ACE inhibitors and a number of others, may be prescribed to strengthen the heart muscle and make it contract more efficiently.

Almost any disease from an infection to a heart attack can cause cardio-myopathy, and so the term is often used when the exact nature of the heart disease present is unknown. I am sure that your doctor will have prescribed something to help your heart, and therefore ease your lethargy.

Q   **I am desperately worried, because my doctor says that my daughter has a heart murmur. He won't treat it and says I shouldn't worry, but I can't help it. How significant is a heart murmur in a 5 year old child?**

A   It depends on many factors! Heart murmurs can vary from the totally innocuous to the deadly serious. A general practitioner will make a decision on whether or not a murmur is serious on the appearance of the child (colour, weight, activity level etc.), the position of the sound in relation to the other heart sounds heard through the stethoscope, the loudness of the sound, the size of the heart and the position on the chest where the murmur is most easily heard. Using this information, it is often possible to tell which part of the heart is responsible for the murmur, and how serious the problem is likely to become.

Many children have heart murmurs that are quite innocent, and never cause any problem. There may even be a tiny hole in one part of the heart, but many of these close over as the child matures. If there is any doubt about the severity of the problem, your GP will refer you to a heart specialist (cardiologist) who will undertake more specialised ultrasound, X-ray, pathology and other investigations to find out the exact diagnosis.

Q   **I have an irregular pulse (1–2 seconds silence every few beats), and and I can hear the pulsation in my ears. Why would this be so? My pulse rate is 90 to 100.**

A   Your heart is showing signs of strain, and a poor conduction of nerve impulses. In most cases, dropping the occasional heart beat is of no consequence, and only reassurance is required from your general practitioner, but in other patients, particularly in those with a relatively rapid heart rate, there may be cause for concern.

Most cases can be corrected by taking one or two tablets a day that strengthen and regulate the heart rate. You should discuss this problem further with your doctor. To ensure that if treatment is necessary, it is given sooner rather than later.

Hearing the pulsing of your heart in your ears is normal, but most of us block out that noise subconsciously. Anyone who concentrates in a quiet environment, can hear their heart beating. It may be louder in those who have hardening of the arteries, and so older people tend to complain quite frequently about hearing their heart beat.

Q What is a congested heart? I am told I have one. My nose sometimes gets congested, but how can it happen to a heart?

A When your nose is congested, it becomes blocked and full of phlegm. In congestive heart failure, the heart is not pumping effectively, and as a result is cannot move the blood out of your lungs and around your body. It is therefore not your heart that is congested, but your lungs, which become blocked and overfull of blood. This leads to coughing and shortness of breath.

Medications, such as digoxin and Capoten, are used to strengthen the heart and help it pump the excess blood out of the lungs. Fluid tablets may also be used to help remove excess fluid from the body. It is a common problem in older people, but not normally a serious one, as medications can usually control it adequately if they are taken correctly.

Q My grandfather is very proud that he has a little computer in his chest that he says is a pacemaker. He claims that he is the only computerised grandfather I have! What does a heart pacemaker do?

A The heart has a collection of nerve cells near its top end that act as a natural pacemaker. This fires off signals about once a second to make the muscles of the heart contract and pump the blood around the body. If this natural pacemaker is damaged, or the nerve fibres leading away from it are damaged, it will not function properly, and the heart will beat irregularly, at the wrong rate or not at all.

There are many reasons for the heart's pacemaker malfunctioning, but the most common is a heart attack.

To correct the failure of the natural pacemaker, a small electrical device is surgically implanted in the chest with tiny wires leading to the appropriate part of the heart. This device is an artificial pacemaker, and it sends electrical signals to the heart on a regular basis to make the heart contract correctly. The pacemaker contains a battery, a timing device and the electrical stimulation mechanism. The battery has to be replaced every year or two.

The latest more sophisticated pacemakers contain a computer that actually monitors the heart, and only sends off an artificial signal when the heart's natural rhythm is disrupted. Variable-rate pacemakers, which increase the heart's rate with exercise, are also available.

These marvels of electronic miniaturisation are keeping many people alive, and giving many more a much better quality of life.

HERNIAS

Q I have a hernia and have had conflicting advice on whether to have the operation in view of my age (65 years), and also due to the fact that I have had this condition for two years, and do not experience any pain or discomfort. Your opinion would be very much appreciated.

A A hernia in the groin may remain pain free, and give no trouble for many years —but it is not going to get any smaller, and will probably steadily enlarge until it does become very uncomfortable, and much more difficult to repair.

At 65, you can reasonably look forward to another 20 years of life, most of which will be relatively active, but your general health in this time will slowly deteriorate, increasing the risks of any anaesthetic or operation.

The hernia can be uncomfortable, but the main reason to repair a hernia by an operation is to prevent the bowel inside it from becoming pinched, twisted and gangrenous. Strangely, the larger the hernia, the less chance there is of this strangulation of the gut occurring, but obviously the larger it is, the more uncomfortable it becomes.

The only people who should not have their inguinal hernia repaired are those who are too old, inactive or ill to reasonably withstand the operation.

For these reasons, I would urge you to put your fears behind you, and place your trust in a surgeon, who will repair your hernia in a relatively minor and simple operation.

Q **I have a hernia in my groin. It looks pretty ugly, but no-one ever sees it, and it causes me only slight discomfort. Why do these occur?**

A When you were a foetus in your mother's womb, the testicles were inside the abdomen. Just before birth, the testicles moved through the muscles and other tissue of the lower abdomen to sit in the scrotal sac.

Behind the testicles as they migrated to their new position, they left a canal through which the arteries, nerves, veins and sperm tube returned to the inside of the abdomen. In later years, due to heavy lifting, straining at stool, laxity of the muscles, obesity etc. this canal can open up, and allow some of the intestine inside the abdomen to slip down into the scrotal sac. This is an inguinal hernia.

Q **I have had a double inguinal hernia repair, and now the skin low down on my stomach is numb. Will this get better?**

A If the operation was performed more than two years ago, the numbness will probably remain. If the operation has been more recent, there is some chance that sensation may gradually return.

When the operation to repair an inguinal hernia is performed, it is very easy for the surgeon to cut through the fine nerves that supply the skin of the lower abdomen. If this is done, the area of skin supplied by that nerve will become numb. The nerve may grow back after the operation, but if sensation has not returned within a couple of years, recovery is unlikely. The numbness does not cause any concern in most people, and is more a curiosity than an inconvenience.

Q **My baby has an umbilical hernia. It looks funny, but does not seem to worry him. I have heard conflicting advice on treatment for this problem. What do you think should be done for this?**

A Umbilical hernias occur when there is a weakness in the wall of the abdomen where the umbilical cord goes through the muscle layers into the baby's body. Crying and straining force a piece of gut or fat through this weakened area leading to a lump under the belly button. This lump should go down when the child is lying at rest.

The vast majority of these require no treatment and close over spontaneously by the time the child is two or three years old. Only if it lasts beyond this time is corrective surgery necessary.

If the infant starts screaming, and the hernia is found to be hard, red and tender, an urgent operation will be required to reduce the trapped piece of gut. This problem is unusual.

Q My belly button gets a bulge that comes and goes. What could this be? Is it serious?

A You probably have an umbilical hernia. This occurs commonly in children, where it often disappears by five years of age, and also in elderly people who are overweight or injure themselves.

An umbilical hernia rarely causes problems in children, but in older people, a small piece of fat, or even gut can protrude into the belly button hernia and become trapped there. This causes severe pain, and is quite serious if gut is involved.

It is generally sensible to have these hernias repaired when they are small, because as they enlarge, the problem becomes harder to correct with surgery. If you are overweight, losing those excess kilos will improve your chance of successful surgery and may reduce the risk of gut entrapment.

Q What is a hiatus hernia?

A The chest cavity is separated from the abdominal cavity by a sheet of muscle (called the diaphragm) that runs across the body from front to back. Your stomach is immediately below the diaphragm, and is connected to the mouth by the gullet (oesophagus), which has to pass through a hole in the diaphragm.

Under certain circumstances, a small part of the stomach may slide through the hole in the diaphragm from the abdominal cavity into the chest cavity. This is a hiatus hernia.

The stomach may slide backwards and forwards, or may be stuck in the diaphragmatic hole.

The hernia will allow the acid in the stomach to flow up into the oesophagus, where the cells are not protected from the stomach acid. This causes heartburn, an acid taste in the mouth, burping and in severe cases, ulcers.

The factors that lead to the development of a hiatus hernia are obesity, stress, smoking, rapid eating, large meals, alcohol, heavy lifting and straining, repeated or constant bending and vomiting.

Treatment will involve avoiding these factors, antacids, medications to empty the stomach, drugs to reduce acid and spasm, and in very severe cases surgery may be tried.

Q My husband has a hiatus hernia after developing peritonitis from gall stones stuck in a duct, and is in constant discomfort, particularly after eating certain foods. His doctor has told him to put up with the pain but I don't think that's good enough. What can be done to help him?

A Peritonitis is a severe infection of the belly cavity that can leave scars, adhesions (gut sticks together instead of sliding smoothly) and other damage that may allow a hiatus hernia to develop.

The pain caused by a hiatus hernia can be treated in a number of ways. The first step is to eat small frequent meals so that the stomach is not over-filled. After eating you can take Gaviscon (available without a script) to neutralise any excess acid and prevent it from going up into the oesophagus.

The next step is to use medications that must be prescribed by a doctor to reduce acid secretion in the stomach (eg. Tazac, Zantac), and increase the rate at which the stomach empties (eg. Motilium, Prepulsid).

If these do not work (which is uncommon), more potent medications (eg. Zoton, Losec) may be prescribed, but these are normally only given after a gastroscopy is performed to confirm the diagnosis and exclude any other problems.

In a gastroscopy, a flexible tube is passed down the throat of the sedated patient so that the doctor can see what is happening in the oesophagus and gullet.

As a last resort, operations are available to relieve a hiatus hernia, but surgeons would be reluctant to perform this procedure on your husband because of his previous operations and peritonitis.

You should discuss these matters further with your general practitioner, as s/he can prescribe all these treatments if necessary.

HORMONES

See also GLANDS

Q **Would you please explain what hormones are? I do not understand how they work.**

A Most people think of hormones in terms of the sex hormones (oestrogen and testosterone), but there are actually over 100 hormones that affect the functioning of every cell in the human body.

Hormones are chemicals of various types that are released by glands such as the pituitary gland (in the brain), thyroid and parathyroid glands (in the neck), pancreas (in the centre of the belly), adrenal glands (on each kidney), ovaries, testes and other less-well-known glands. These chemicals enter the bloodstream, and in this travel to every single cell in the body.

They give instructions to the cells on an enormously wide range of matters that affect the way in which all cells work.

The system is orchestrated by a part of the brain called the hypothalamus, which in turn gives instructions to the pituitary gland which is attached to it. The pituitary releases hormones which travel to other glands through the blood, telling them what to do.

As an example, one of the hormones that the pituitary gland releases is thyroid-stimulating hormone (TSH). This stimulates the thyroid gland to produce more of the hormone thyroxine. Thyroxine controls the rate at which every cell in the body works. If there is more thyroxine, the cell works faster, if there is less thyroxine, it works slower. As the level of thyroxine rises in the blood, the pituitary gland senses this and reduces the amount of TSH produced.

This feedback mechanism regulates not only the thyroid gland and its production of thyroxine, but every other gland in the body, including the production of the sex hormones from the ovaries and testes.

Q **What do sex hormones do? How do they affect men and women? How are they used by doctors?**

A Sex hormones are produced by the ovaries in the woman and the testes in the man to give each sex its characteristic appearance. In men, they are responsible for the enlargement of the penis and scrotum at puberty, the development of facial hair and the ability to produce sperm and ejaculate. In women, the sex hormones that are produced for the first time at puberty cause breast enlargement, hair growth in the armpit and groin, ovulation, the start of menstrual periods, and later act to maintain a pregnancy.

If the sex hormones are reduced or lacking, these characteristics disappear. This happens naturally during the female menopause. During the transition from normal sex hormone production to no production in the menopause, there may be some irregular or inappropriate release of these hormones, causing the symptoms commonly associated with menopause such as irregular periods, irritability and hot flushes. After the menopause, the breasts sag, pubic and armpit hair becomes scanty, and the periods cease due to this lack of sex hormones. Men also go through a form of menopause, but more gradually, so the effects are far less obvious than in the female.

Sex hormones, and many synthesised drugs that act artificially as sex hormones, are used in medicine in two main areas—to correct natural deficiencies in sex hormone production; and to alter the balance between the two female hormones (oestrogen and progestogen) that cause ovulation, to prevent ovulation, and therefore act as a contraceptive.

Female sex hormones can also be used to control some forms of recurrent miscarriage and prolong a pregnancy until a baby is mature enough to deliver, to control a disease called endometriosis, and to treat certain types of cancer.

Uncommonly, sex hormones can be used to alter the appearance of a person who wishes to change their sex. A small dose of male testosterone can increase the libido (sex drive) in women who are lacking this normal instinct.

Q I have been given a drug called Premarin for my hot flushes, but I am worried that it might cause cancer.

A   Premarin is a form of female hormone (oestrogen) that is used in women who are having symptoms during their menopause, to prevent osteoporosis, to control abnormal menstrual bleeding, to treat some types of breast cancer and to prevent breast engorgement after a confinement. It is therefore a very valuable drug.

There are no problems with womb cancer if used for less than a year. If taken for long periods of time, there is some evidence that the incidence of cancer of the womb may increase slightly. This problem may be overcome quite easily. The Premarin may be taken cyclically (ie. for only three weeks of every month), and a second hormone (progestogen) should be added for the last ten to 14 days of the Premarin dose each month.

Some doctors use other variations of this combined dosage schedule such as a constant dose of both Premarin (or other oestrogen) and a very low dose progestogen.

All women on these regimes should have full gynaecological examination every year.

If used strictly as directed, there is no increase in risk of womb cancer, and excellent control of many quite serious or disabling conditions can be achieved. If you are concerned, discuss the matter further with your doctor.

Q **How can premenstrual syndrome be treated successfully? I (and my husband indirectly) suffer terribly every month from my depression, headaches and temper.**

A Virtually every woman suffers from this syndrome to a greater or lesser extent. It is characterised by any one or more of bloating, headaches, mood changes, irritability, depression, pelvic discomfort, breast tenderness, worsening acne, nausea, bowel habit changes, insomnia and a host of other symptoms.

The treatment should start with a medical examination to exclude any specific diseases as a cause. The next step is the use of fluid tablets to remove the excess fluid that is retained by the body prior to a period. If necessary, hormones can be added or substituted for the fluid tablets.

One of the most successful hormones is the contraceptive pill, and many women find that when they stop the pill because they have had a tubal ligation, they develop terrible premenstrual syndrome, and have to start it again. A number of other hormones can also be used, depending on the woman's symptoms.

Other treatments that may be tried are hormone blocking agents, e.g. bromocriptine and danazol, which require a doctor's prescription. Some women find low doses of vitamin B6 beneficial.

Every woman is different, and all will require different treatments. If you persist, the correct combination can be determined by your doctor to give you a more comfortable and pleasant life.

Q **When does physical growth stop for females? I am 21 years old and very short. Other women in my family are much larger. Can I use growth hormone?**

A Unfortunately, I would be very surprised if you grow any taller at your age. Most women stop growing at 18 years, and often much younger. Men can grow for a year or two longer.

Your height is determined to some extent by your parents, but it is your total genetic picture (including grand and great grandparents), plus your diet and other environmental factors that all combine to determine your final height.

Numerous medical conditions may also be responsible. For various reasons (eg. pituitary gland malfunction) you may produce less growth hormone than normal, which will result in a reduction in growth.

Growth hormone can be given to children who are very small, but this must be done very carefully, and only before growth stops in the mid-teens. You are far too old for this form of treatment.

I am afraid that at this stage there is nothing medically that can be done to increase your height. Adjust your attitude so that you enjoy being petite, know you are able to fit into small places, and be comfortable in aircraft seats that others find a torture to squeeze into.

Q **Could you explain the function of the adrenal glands and their connection to adrenalin?**

A The adrenal glands are part of the system that produces the body's hormones (called the endocrine system). They sit on top of each kidney, a bit like a beanie. The glands are tiny—less than 5 cm long and weigh only a few grams—and yet produce more than three dozen hormones. The glands are divided into two quite distinct parts—an inner, reddish brown section called the medulla and an outer, yellow-coloured section called the cortex. Each part has its own distinct function.

The hormones produced by the medulla in the adrenal gland include adrenalin, which causes the well-known 'fight or flight' response to danger. The medulla is part of the autonomic (unconscious) nervous system, and when the body becomes aware of danger through one of its senses, these hormones literally spurt out making the heart beat faster, increasing the blood sugar level, altering the blood flow and generally increasing the body's capacity to deal with the emergency. Because many of the stresses of modern life do not require such a physical response, the release of adrenalin is sometimes inappropriate and the body has no way of using it up. If it happens too often it may eventually cause health problems.

The hormones produced by the cortex are steroids, of which there are three main groups. One group controls the balance of minerals in the body. Another group regulates the use the body makes of carbohydrates, and also plays a part in our ability to handle stress (cortisone is the most important hormone of this group). The third group affects the operation of our sex glands and influences our sexual development. Steroids are made from cholesterol, so a certain amount of cholesterol is necessary in our diet, provided it isn't more than we need, which can cause heart problems.

Like other glands in the endocrine system, the adrenal cortex is controlled by the pituitary gland, which sits under the brain.

If the adrenal glands are destroyed because of disease (eg. tuberculosis or cancer) or are overactive, the functioning of our entire body can be impaired. The most common disorders are called Addison's disease and Cushing's syndrome.

Q **My father's weakness and general deterioration has been diagnosed as Addison's disease, but I can't understand what it is all about. Your help would be appreciated.**

A Addison's disease is a rare condition due to underactivity of the outer layer (cortex) of the adrenal glands, which sit on top of each kidney and produce hormones (chemical messengers) such as cortisone that control the levels of vital elements in the body and regulate the breakdown of food. In most cases, the reason for adrenal gland failure is unknown, but tuberculosis is a possible cause.

The symptoms include weakness, lack of appetite, diarrhoea and vomiting, skin pigmentation, mental instability, low blood pressure, loss of body hair and absence of sweating.

It is diagnosed by special blood tests that measure the body's response to stimulation of the adrenal gland.

Treatment involves a combination of medications (eg. steroids such as cortisone) to replace the missing hormones. Dosages vary greatly from one patient to another. Frequent small meals high in carbohydrate and protein are eaten, and infections must be treated rapidly. Patients must carry an emergency supply of injectable cortisone with them at all times.

The main complications are diabetes, thyroid disease and anaemia.

Treatment can give most patients a long and useful life, but they cannot react to stress (both physical and mental) adequately, and additional treatment must be given in these situations. The ultimate outcome depends greatly on the patient's ability to strictly follow all treatment regimes.

HYSTERECTOMY

See also FEMALE PROBLEMS; MENOPAUSE

Q **I am confused about what happens during a hysterectomy. My gynaecologist told me I had a total hysterectomy plus an ovary removed. Can you explain the different parts of me that I have lost?**

A The female reproductive organs consist of two ovaries, each of which has a Fallopian tube leading from it to the uterus (womb). The narrow opening of the uterus into the vagina is the cervix. The vagina is the part used during sexual intercourse. The lips around the outside opening of the vagina are the vulva.

In a hysterectomy (or total hysterectomy), the uterus, cervix and usually both Fallopian tubes are removed. In a sub-total hysterectomy, the cervix is left behind. This latter operation is rarely performed.

In most women who have a hysterectomy, one ovary is removed in an operation called oophorectomy. If the operation is for cancer, or other serious disease, both ovaries may be removed (a bilateral oophorectomy).

If you are confused, it is better to ask the gynaecologist performing the operation to describe in simple terms (and preferably using a diagram such as the one opposite) exactly which parts s/he intends to remove.

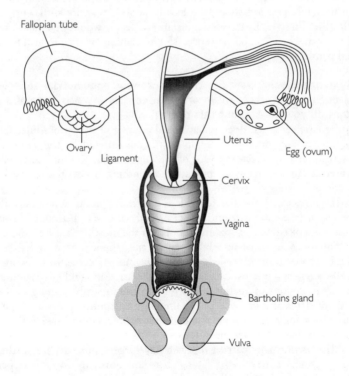

Fallopian tube

Ovary

Ligament

Uterus

Egg (ovum)

Cervix

Vagina

Bartholins gland

Vulva

Q I am 50, and my doctor has advised me to have a hysterectomy. Will I still get my periods, and will the operation make any difference to my sex life?

A A hysterectomy is removal of the uterus (womb), and since your period is the monthly shedding of the lining of the uterus, you will not have periods after the operation.

There is now some evidence that stimulation of the cervix (the opening to the uterus) during sexual intercourse causes some women to feel pleasure, so that there may be a slight difference in how you respond to love-making after the operation. For most women who have sexual difficulties following hysterectomy, the cause is psychological rather than physical.

Q My doctor has recommended a hysterectomy for my bad periods. I have tried all sorts of pills for the last two years, but is this operation really necessary?

A The last resort in controlling heavy and painful periods is a hysterectomy, but this is sometimes the only practical option. All other methods should be tried first, and this will include hormones, fluid tablets, hormone-blocking agents and pain killers. If these are not working adequately, or the woman is taking large amounts of medication, or the side effects are unacceptable, a hysterectomy may be a very reasonable option.

The woman involved should be in middle life, obviously should not want any further children, and should be having periods that are sufficiently severe to affect her lifestyle. In these circumstances I feel it would be cruel to refuse this operation, which can be very successful in enabling women to lead far more free and comfortable lives.

Q My gynaecologist wants to try a microwave endometrial ablation before he does a hysterectomy in order to control my heavy painful periods. What do you think about this operation?

A In the last few years, doctors have tried a range of new procedures to preserve the uterus and prevent the symptoms being suffered by the woman without resorting to a hysterectomy. One of the more recent, and most successful, is the procedure (it isn't really an operation as nothing is cut) known as microwave endometrial ablation (MEA).

The reason for heavy painful periods is excessive production of the lining inside the uterus (the endometrium) which is shed with every period, and comes away with some bleeding and spasms (cramps) of the muscle that forms the uterus.

The procedure involves a brief general anaesthetic for ten to fifteen minutes. A thin probe is introduced through the vagina and cervix into the uterus. The probe contains a microwave generator that is carefully calibrated to produce just the right amount of energy to destroy the endometrium (lining of the uterus) without damaging the wall of the uterus or surrounding organs. The probe is turned on for a few minutes and gently moved around inside the uterus to destroy all the endometrium.

MEA is normally carried out as a day surgery procedure, and the woman can go home a few hours later. There are normally some bad period-like uterine cramps for a few days, and a bloody discharge for two or three weeks, but after that, 90% of women have no periods at all, and can therefore avoid a hysterectomy.

The worst outcome is that the procedure fails and a hysterectomy is eventually necessary, but if it works, a simple procedure has replaced significant surgery. You should probably give it a try.

Q   Ten years ago I had a hysterectomy for fibroids, and my ovaries were removed. Do I need to have a Pap smear?

A   When a Pap smear is performed, the area examined is the cervix, and the test is primarily performed in order to find cancer of the cervix at an early stage. The cervix sits at the top of the vagina, and is the rubbery piece of tissue that forms the opening into the uterus (womb).

In a hysterectomy, the uterus and cervix are removed, but the vagina is left behind. After a hysterectomy, there is nothing left behind to perform a Pap smear on, you therefore do not require an annual trip to the doctor for this test. The one exception to this rule, is those women who have had a hysterectomy because of cancer. There is a very slight risk that the cancer can spread to the top of the vagina, and so vaginal vault smears should be performed regularly in these women.

The Pap smear test is one that should be performed on all women who have ever been sexually active. A test every two years is ideal, but if there have been abnormal tests of some sort, this may be reduced to 6 or 12 months.

Many other conditions other than cancer can be detected by a Pap smear. These include infections, abnormal discharges, erosions of the cervix and ulcers.

Q   I am due to have a hysterectomy because of fibroids. I want to keep my cervix, which is perfectly normal, but my gynaecologist is reluctant to do this. If I have a regular Pap smear, why shouldn't I have a sub-total hysterectomy and keep my cervix?

A   A sub-total hysterectomy in which the body of the uterus (the womb) is removed, but the neck of the uterus (the cervix) and the ovaries are retained, is certainly an option, but it is not one that is commonly preferred.

The advantage is that you continue to have a cervix, which some experts claim is important for the full sexual satisfaction of the woman.

The disadvantages are that the operation is technically more difficult, and more prone to complications, as the thick muscle of the neck of the womb must be cut through and secured, instead of the thin tissue at the top of the vagina. Your gynaecologist will certainly be more experienced at doing a full hysterectomy than a partial one. As you mention, you also have the continued risk of cancer of the cervix, which can be detected early by a regular Pap smear.

My advice would be to have a full removal of your uterus and cervix (retaining one or both ovaries).

Q   I have had a total hysterectomy and oophorectomy and have to take pills all the time. Why is this so?

A   A total hysterectomy and oophorectomy involves the removal of both ovaries as well as the uterus, tubes and cervix. Without ovaries, a woman produces no female hormones. These hormones are responsible for the control of body hair, breast shape and tone, sex drive, bone strength and the characteristic figure of a woman. Oestrogen is the most important sex hormone, and to prevent deterioration of the woman's figure and health, the hormone is given in pill form until the age that the menopause would normally have occurred.

To prevent these complications of the operation, female hormones are given in tablet form on a regular basis, and should be continued until the woman is well past the normal age for her menopause (change of life). It is therefore very important that you continue these pills for as long as necessary.

ILLEGAL DRUGS

Q **What is the difference between the drugs people are arrested for and those prescribed by a doctor?**

A The word 'drugs' makes most people think of the illegal drugs such as marijuana, cocaine and heroin. But drugs are also the legal medications that are prescribed by your doctor or purchased over the counter from chemists. Everything from aspirin to antibiotics, and fluid tablets to vitamin C (ascorbic acid) are drugs. Any substance that has an effect on the function of the body is a drug.

It is always important to take drugs in the correct way in order to maximise their effect. Some interact with food to reduce their effectiveness; alcohol may exacerbate the side effects of others; different drugs may interact to give more potent or less effective results. Even over-the-counter preparations may interact with each other and with prescribed drugs. Check with your pharmacist or doctor.

Q **Is marijuana harmful?**

A Marijuana is far more harmful to the human than alcohol, and is also more addictive. It is stored in the body fat, and can cause flash-backs that may disorientate and hallucinate the user at inappropriate times days or weeks later. Mothers who use the drug can cause congenital abnormalities in their babies, and regular users may suffer brain damage, behavioural changes, breast enlargement, reduction in sex hormone levels, lung damage and many more biochemical changes to the body.

It is also possible that addiction to marijuana may be the start of a very slippery slope to hard drug addiction.

Q **What are the anabolic steroids that athletes take? Are they really dangerous?**

A Anabolic steroids are drugs that build up body tissue. Oxymetholone and nandrolone (Deca-Durabolin) are examples. They are used clinically to treat severe blood diseases (eg. aplastic anaemia), some types of cancer, osteoporosis and kidney failure.

They are used illegally by athletes and body-builders in both tablet and in-jection form to increase muscle mass. There are many serious side effects and problems associated with their long-term use, including liver disease and damage, the development of male characteristics and cessation of periods in women, stunting of growth and early onset of puberty in children, swelling of tissue, water retention, infertility, personality disorders and voice changes. Their use must be actively discouraged, because the short-term benefits gained by athletes are often followed by long-term medical problems.

Q I've heard a lot recently about teenagers taking drugs like Ecstasy at parties. I have a teenager. How would I know if he had been trying Ecstasy?

A There is no easy or definite way in which to determine if someone is using Ecstasy unless a specific blood test is performed. From a parent's point of view, it is almost impossible, as the symptoms of its use could also be explained by the variable moodiness of the average teenager.

The symptoms of Ecstasy are rapid in onset and brief in duration. The rapid onset explains its popularity as the user gets a high quickly after taking the tablet. The effects are increased if used with alcohol, as this increases its rate of absorption, and this also explains the fatalities that can occur.

Serious adverse effects result in an irregular heart beat that may become so serious that a heart attack and death occurs. Most users experience a period of increased perception of sounds, sights and smells that makes the world seem a more exciting place. It can also result in sexual disinhibition, hallucinations and general euphoria.

After the high has worn off the user may be moody, drowsy, have red and sore eyes, be nauseated and vomit, and have poor coordination.

Teenagers need to be made aware of the dangers of the use of Ecstasy but parents are unlikely to be able to detect specifically if their child is using the drug unless they observe them during the hour or so that the drug is active after its use.

Q. Where does heroin come from? Does it have any medical uses?

A Heroin is refined from the milky juice of the opium poppy, which is grown legally for medical purposes in north-eastern Tasmania. Most illegal supplies reaching this country originate in Afghanistan and south-east Asia, particularly northern Thailand and Burma. Heroin is one of the most addictive substances known.

Codeine, pethidine, morphine and oxycodone are all derived from heroin and can be abused if taken regularly or excessively. These substances are collectively called narcotics. Codeine and oxycodone are found in low doses in many readily available pain-killers, diarrhoea medications and cough mixtures. Codeine in higher doses, along with pethidine and morphine, are used by doctors as tablets or injections to relieve severe pain after operations, in cancer patients, and in other similar situations.

Q Would you please tell me all about heroin? Its use seems to becoming an epidemic.

A Heroin is a drug that causes exaggerated happiness, relief of pain, a feeling of unreality, and a sensation of bodily detachment. It is normally administered by addicts to themselves as an injection directly into the veins. As sterile techniques are often not followed, the veins and skin at the injection site become infected and scarred. Heroin and other narcotics may also be inhaled or eaten, but they have a much slower effect than if injected.

Most abusers of heroin have personality disorders, antisocial behaviour, or are placed in situations of extreme stress. One quarter of heroin addicts will die within ten years of commencing the habit as a direct result of the heroin use. A rising proportion will die from complications of the intravenous injections such as AIDS, septicaemia and hepatitis B, C and D.

Heroin abuse is often combined with abuse of alcohol, smoking and synthetic drugs.

Physiological problems associated with narcotic addiction include vomiting, constipation, brain damage (personality changes, paranoia), nerve damage (persistent pins and needles or numbness), infertility, impotence, stunting of growth in children, difficulty in breathing (to the point of stopping breathing if given in high doses) and low blood pressure.

Withdrawal causes vomiting, diarrhoea, coughing, twitching, fever, crying, excessive sweating, generalised muscle pain, rapid breathing and an intense desire for the drug. These symptoms can commence within 8 to 12 hours of the last dose, and peaks at 48 to 72 hours after withdrawal. Mild symptoms may persist for up to six months.

Most people with heroin addiction who wish to withdraw from the drug are placed on methadone, a narcotic which is less addictive and less damaging than heroin. This is supplied on a daily basis (usually in liquid form) by a clinic or pharmacist, then slowly withdrawn over many months. A new drug, naltrexone, is being used experimentally to flush out heroin from the body, and relieve the addiction within a few days. This process must be undertaken under strict supervision in a specialised clinic.

Q My 20 year old daughter uses cocaine every weekend to help her party till dawn, and I can't stop her. How dangerous is this?

A Cocaine is also known as crack or coke. In medicine, derivatives of cocaine are used as local anaesthetics, but it is also a stimulant and a psychoactive drug that causes euphoria (artificial happiness), and it is for these purposes that your daughter is using the drug.

Cocaine is used in many forms and may be smoked, injected or sniffed.

Its effects may be much more serious if the person suffers from a psychiatric condition, and it may affect a person's ability to drive a car, operate machinery, swim or undertake any activity that requires concentration. Obviously it should never be used in pregnancy due to an increased risk of organ malformation and heart disease in the baby.

The common side effects of cocaine are damage to nostrils from repeated snorting, fever, headache, irregular heart rate, dilation of pupils, loss of libido (sex drive), infertility, impotence, breast enlargement and tenderness in both sexes, menstrual period irregularities, psychiatric disturbances and abnormal breast milk production, and it may lead to a desire for more frequent use or stronger drugs of addiction.

Uncommonly it may cause high blood pressure, perforation of the nasal septum, difficulty in breathing, convulsions, stroke, dementia, heart attack, and rarely death.

Cocaine also interacts with other drugs including other stimulants, antidepressants and medications acting on the brain. It also reacts with alcohol, heroin and marijuana. These reactions are all likely to make any side effects more serious.

An overdose may lead to convulsions, difficulty in breathing, irregular heart rate, coma and death. If you think someone has taken an overdose of cocaine, seek urgent medical assistance.

The more refined version of cocaine known as 'crack' is the only form that can be smoked, and is ten times more potent than cocaine base, and is therefore more dangerous and is highly addictive. When smoked, sniffed or injected, cocaine works within seconds to cause euphoria (artificial happiness) and stimulates the brain to increase all sensations. After use, many people feel worse than before, hence they want to repeat the artificial high. The more frequently it is used, the higher the dose necessary to achieve the same sensations, and the greater the risk of serious side effects.

At 20, you cannot stop your daughter from doing anything, only advise her and counsel her to the best of your ability to be aware of the risks she is taking.

INFERTILITY

Q I am trying to get pregnant, but so far haven't had any luck. Can you tell me just when is a woman fertile during the month?

A The day a woman starts bleeding with her period is day one. A woman ovulates 14 days before her next period. If she has a 28 day cycle, she will ovulate on day 14, but if the cycle is 35 days, she will ovulate on day 21, and with a 24 day cycle, ovulation is on day 10.

If the cycle is regular, it is easy to work out the day of ovulation, but if the cycle is irregular, it can be much harder.

Other clues to ovulation are are rise in the basic temperature and a change in the vaginal mucus.

A woman is fertile from two days before ovulation (the sperm can survive this long in her body after sex) to 4 days after ovulation. With a regular 28 day cycle, she is fertile from days 12 to 18. If you wish to avoid pregnancy, sex should be avoided for an additional two days either side of this fertile time.

If pregnancy is desirable, sex on the day of ovulation and for the two days afterwards is best.

Q I am trying to fall pregnant, but having no luck. How long should I wait before starting to worry if there is something wrong with me?

A After 12 months of 'normal marital endeavour' (as the textbooks so politely put it), 85% of couples should have conceived. The remaining 15% can be considered to have below-normal fertility. With the aid of medical techniques, all but 3% of couples can eventually have children.

Relax and enjoy the 'trying'. The harder you try to fall pregnant, the less likely you are to succeed. Often a good holiday relaxes both partners enough for fertilisation to occur.

Also remember, if there is a problem, it may not be your problem, but his.

Q What can cause problems in falling pregnant? My husband and I have not used contraception for almost two years, and we're starting to get worried.

A Firstly, remember that fertility is a joint property, not just a feature of the male or female. One third of infertility is due to the male partner. It takes two to tango!

In the male, the causes of infertility include premature ejaculation, undescended testes (which fail to work because of overheating), injury to the testicles, mumps infection of the testes, testicular and sperm tube venereal infections (eg. non-specific urethritis, gonorrhoea), chromosome abnormalities, and hormonal disorders.

Infertility in the female may be caused by failure of the ovaries to develop (eg. Turner syndrome), endometriosis, abnormal development of the uterus, pelvic inflammatory disease, venereal infections of the Fallopian tubes (eg. chlamydia, gonorrhoea), hormonal imbalances, and in rare cases a reaction to the husband's sperm can develop.

Strangely, infrequent sexual intercourse, due to both partners having career, life or study stresses is sometimes the cause. It may be all too easy to miss those few days a month when the woman is fertile if you are only having sex every few weeks.

Q **How do doctors investigate couples who are infertile? I have heard all sorts of horror stories and I'm very worried about what may happen.**

A Doctors start their investigations by checking the couple's sexual habits. A woman is only fertile for four to six days a month, and if sex is infrequent, it is quite easy to miss these days.

The first step in specific testing is a sperm analysis in the man. The sperm from an ejaculation is collected in a sterile container and must be examined in a laboratory within two hours. The number of sperm, their shape and their activity are all checked to ensure that they are adequate to fertilise the woman's egg. If these tests are normal, it is not usually necessary to perform any further tests on the man.

In a woman, the first step is a temperature chart. This involves marking on a graph the woman's temperature immediately upon waking every morning, the days of the period or other bleeding, and the days when intercourse has occurred. From this and a blood test, a doctor can often see problems with ovulation. There is normally a rise in temperature for the second half of the cycle after the egg has been released from the ovary.

After these simple tests, investigations become more complex. It is necessary to exclude any blockage in the tubes leading from the ovary to the womb, and to assess the woman's hormonal and biochemical function by a series of blood tests. A careful gynaecological examination is performed, and this may be followed by special X-rays or ultrasound scans that outline the uterus (womb) and tubes. The final stage of investigation is an operation called a laparoscopy, in which a small tube is poked through a cut in the lower part of the abdomen. To prevent scarring, the navel is often used for this purpose. Through this tube the doctor can directly examine the female reproductive organs to detect any problems.

Please be assured that although these investigations may not sound very nice, you should suffer no more than discomfort and some indignity, as appropriate anaesthetics are given for the more invasive procedures.

Q **How is infertility treated? I have heard about IVF, but what are GIFTs and all the other funny terms? What do they do for infertile men?**

A In the male, hormone supplements, storage and concentration of sperm (artificial insemination by husband—AIH), or fertilisation by donor sperm (artificial insemination by donor—AID) can be tried. In the woman, fertility drugs can be used to promote ovulation (eg. clomiphene), other drugs may be used to treat endometriosis, or antibiotics may be needed to treat infections. If there is an anatomical abnormality, it may be correctable by surgery.

As a last resort, a very small number of couples may be considered suitable for IVF (in-vitro fertilisation or 'test-tube babies'), or GIFT (gamete intra-Fallopian transfer). GIFT involves giving ovulation-stimulating (egg-producing) hormones to an infertile woman, then harvesting an egg directly from her ovary using a laparoscope, and transferring this unfertilised egg along with sperm from her partner, directly into her Fallopian tube. This is done by using a very fine instrument that passes through her cervix and uterus to the internal opening of a Fallopian tube. If necessary the sperm or egg may be donated by another man or woman.

Most infertility treatment is carried out in private clinics and hospitals, and Medicare benefits for these procedures are restricted. Centres in every Australian capital and many major provincial centres now perform both IVF and GIFT. Australia is one of the leading countries in the world with this technology.

The treatment of infertility has progressed by leaps and bounds over the past few years, and the techniques used are at the leading edge of medical technology. New procedures are constantly being introduced and then discarded in favour of yet another improvement, so that it is difficult for even GPs to keep up. Gynaecologists who specialise in this area are the best source of information.

Q   I am desperate to fall pregnant, but I am 18 stone and only 5ft 5in tall. The doctor says I can't fall pregnant until I lose weight, but I can't seem to stop eating. I want to lose weight very badly, and to have a baby. Please help me!

A   There are lots of expensive ways to lose weight, there are lots of different diets, every woman's magazine ever printed contains weight loss diets, and there are lots of promoters with quick loss schemes. None of these are more successful than a simple low-calorie diet, and in the long run, any weight loss depends upon the 'won't power' of the patient. My simple, cheap, and effective (if followed) diet plan is as follows:
  — EAT ONLY THREE TIMES A DAY. Never eat between, before or after your normal meals. Drink only water, black tea/coffee or diet drinks if thirsty.
  — EAT THE RIGHT FOODS. Lists of the correct low-calorie foods are readily available from doctors and chemists. Eat a well-balanced diet with foods of all types, but in small quantities.
  — EXERCISE DAILY. Exercise to the point where you are hot, sweaty and breathless at least once a day. The exercise can be anything from running up and down stairs, to using an exercise bike or swimming, but preferably should be something that is enjoyable and easily accessible.
  — IF NECESSARY, EAT LESS. If you are not losing weight at the rate of one kilogram (2 lbs) per week, you need to eat less. Weigh yourself at the same time each week, and not every day.
  — KEEP GOING until you reach your target weight, and continue dieting to maintain that weight. Any relapse in the diet can see you balloon back to your old self. A weight loss diet is for years, not months.

You will need lots of determination, but there is no other more effective way of achieving your aim.

If you cannot control your desire for food, your doctor may consider a brief course of an appetite-reducing drug. Group therapy such as weight watchers may also give encouragement to weight loss.

K KIDNEYS and BLADDER

Q Why do I keep getting bladder infections every few months? I am a 35 year old woman who is happily married.

A Sex. That one word describes the cause of 90% of bladder infections (cystitis) in women. Because the urethra (the tube leading out from the bladder) is only 1 to 2 cm long in women, it is easy for skin bacteria to be massaged up into the bladder during intercourse. Honeymoon cystitis is a very well recognised medical entity.

The simplest forms of prevention are taking plenty of fluids to keep the bladder working regularly, emptying the bladder after sex, and using urinary alkalinisers (available from chemists) to make the urine harder for bacteria to survive. Once a woman has cystitis, antibiotics should be obtained from a doctor as soon as possible because untreated the bacteria may migrate up to the kidneys and cause severe problems.

Q My doctor has given me tablets for a pain in my belly that he says is cystitis. What is this disease?

A Uncomfortable, embarrassing and common. Cystitis (a bladder infection) is all three to many women.

Cystitis is one of the most common conditions seen by general practitioners, but some women can barely get away from the toilet for long enough to visit the surgery!

The symptoms of burning pain on passing urine, pain in the pelvis, and the desire to pass urine every 10 minutes that are associated with cystitis are not limited entirely to women, but only 10% of cases occur in men because the longer length of their urethra (the tube leading from the bladder to the outside) gives them considerable protection from infection. When it does affect males, it is often more serious and requires more aggressive investigation and treatment.

Most women will have at least one bladder infection in their lives, and some have repeated attacks that require constant medication to prevent them.

Q How is a bladder infection best treated? I keep getting one every few months, and I find them most annoying and painful.

A When a patient arrives at a surgery with symptoms of a bladder infection (cystitis), a urine sample will be checked for infection. A plastic strip covered with spots that are sensitive to different constituents of the urine is used for this purpose. This can give a quite accurate picture of what is happening to cause the patient's symptoms.

The sample is then sent to a laboratory for further testing to find out which bacteria is causing the infection, and which antibiotics will kill it. These tests may take a few days to complete, so the patient is usually started on an appropriate antibiotic immediately, which can be changed at a later date if the tests results indicate that this is necessary.

Other medications (in the form of a powder that makes a fizzy drink) to alkalinise the urine and remove the unpleasant burning sensation are also prescribed. Drinking extra fluid will help wash the infection out of the kidneys and bladder.

If several infections occur, further investigations such as ultrasound scans or X-rays of the bladder and kidneys are performed, to exclude some of the rarer more serious causes of recurrent cystitis.

In most patients, cystitis is a considerable nuisance, not a serious disease, that can be easily and effectively treated provided the patient presents to a doctor at the first sign of trouble.

Q For the past twelve months I have been plagued by a bacteria causing a urinary tract infection. I feel better on antibiotics, but two or three weeks after stopping it is back again. Can you suggest a solution?

A Recurrent urinary tract infections occur because the responsible bacteria is not completely removed by the antibiotics, because there is an anatomical problem with the kidney, bladder or its control, or you have another medical condition that allows an infection to re-enter the urinary tract.

The first step would be to determine what bacteria is responsible for the infection by doing laboratory tests on the urine, and then giving a long course (a month or so) of the antibiotic that has been found to be capable of destroying this bacteria.

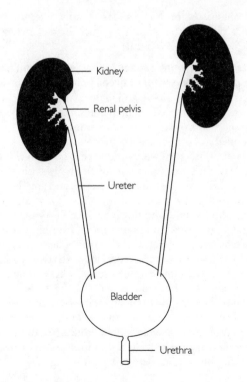

Kidney

Renal pelvis

Ureter

Bladder

Urethra

If the infection still recurs, investigations such as special ultrasound scans, X-rays or cystoscopy (looking into the bladder) need to be performed to find any anatomical abnormality. If possible, this abnormality should then be repaired, or if this is not practical, a long-term course of special antibiotics needs to be prescribed for months or years to prevent further acute attacks of infection.

Blood and other tests on kidney and general body functions may be necessary to find another condition (eg. diabetes) that may be lowering your resistance to infection.

By using the appropriate treatment, it should be possible to remedy the cause of the repeated infections, or at least prevent them from recurring.

Q I have just experienced the most excruciating pain of a kidney stone. Why do they hurt so much? Mine was only 3 mm long!

A The kidneys sit in your loins at the side of your abdomen, just below the ribs. The urine from the kidney is collected into a relatively large chamber, which has a fine tube (the ureter) leading from it down the back of the abdomen to the bladder.

Everyone forms kidney stones, but most are less than a millimetre across and pass unnoticed.

If the stone is slightly larger than the diameter of the ureter, it will be forced down the tube by the pressure of urine behind it, but will scratch the inside of this long tube causing the excruciating pain that runs across the abdomen to the scrotum and penis. When the stone is at rest, only a dull ache is felt. Once it starts moving and scratching the tube, severe pain (described as far worse than childbirth) occurs.

Once the stone passes into the bladder, it easily passes out when you urinate with no further pain. If the stone gets stuck in the ureter, surgery or other procedures are necessary to remove it.

Q My wife wants to know what causes kidney stones and how can she avoid having more, as she has suffered great pain with them in the past.

A The kidney acts to filter the blood, and removes excess water and wastes. If these wastes become too concentrated, or altered in some way, they can precipitate out and form a crystal that slowly grows into a stone.

Once the stone has formed, one of three things can happen to it.

Most stones are flushed down the tube that leads to the bladder from the kidney (the ureter) and are passed out of the body with the urine while still microscopic in size. These cause no trouble at all, and you do not know that they have been present.

A small number of stones may slowly and steadily grow in size until they are the size of a grape, or even a ping-pong ball. These big stones may completely fill the urine collection chamber of the kidney. They usually cause no trouble, but they may be the source of repeated kidney infections and pain.

The third group is the most troublesome. These stones, from one to five millimetres in length, can enter the ureter. This fine tube is very sensitive, and as the stone is pushed along the tube by the pressure of urine behind, it scrapes the tube wall causing the intense pain that sufferers experience.

There is no simple way to avoid kidney stones, but drinking plenty of fluids (mainly plain water) will help flush the kidneys out regularly and reduce the chance of anything but the smallest crystals forming.

Q I am 69 years of age, and despite being told age is only in the mind, my body's messages tell me differently. In particular, my prostate is causing trouble, and I have to dash from the tennis court to quickly find a toilet, and I have to get up through the night. What do you suggest?

A I would suggest that you are looking after yourself very well by playing tennis at 69, and that your prostate is not necessarily the cause of your problems.

Men with prostate problems usually have trouble passing urine. They have to wait for a minute or two for the stream to start, and then the urine dribbles out rather than shoots out. The desire to pass urine frequently can be a feature of prostate trouble, but usually because the bladder cannot be completely emptied, as the enlarging prostate squeezes the urine tube.

There are many other reasons for needing to rush to the toilet. One of the most common in men in their late middle age (as you say, your not in old age until your mind is), is diabetes. This is a very common condition in mature men and women, and is not nearly as serious as the juvenile form. It comes on very slowly over several months or years, and is characterised by frequent passing of urine and an increased thirst.

Other causes of urinary frequency and urgency include numerous kidney diseases, low grade infections of the urine, a number of rare diseases, and some medications that may be prescribed by doctors.

You need to see your GP to have a few investigations so that a correct diagnosis for your problem can be made, then the appropriate treatment can be given.

Q I am 30 years old, and since the birth of my third child 6 months ago, I find I urinate a little whenever I cough or sneeze, and especially when I jump in aerobic class. I am too embarrassed to mention this to my doctor. Please help me.

A This is a very common problem, so please don't be afraid to mention it to your doctor. The muscles of the pelvic floor become weaker with successive pregnancies, and the bladder may bulge into the vagina to cause 'stress incontinence'. A simple exercise to strengthen these muscles is:

— Tighten up your pelvic muscles as though you are preventing urine from escaping when you have an over-full bladder. Hold for as long as you can, and then relax. Repeat as often as possible.

When driving a car, you can do this every time you stop at a red light. Breathe normally, and hold the muscles tight until the light turns green. Physiotherapy can also be successful in treating this condition, but sometimes surgery is necessary.

Q We are very worried about our grandchildren who have kidney tract problems. The little girl has already had a crossover operation, and now the little boy is having troubles. Our daughter in law has had a lot of urinary infections in the past, and her mother had a dual kidney. Is this problem hereditary, or is it due to the infections of the mother? Should they have more children?

A Urologists are the surgical specialists who operate on kidneys and the bladder, and they can now work wonders with children who are born with serious abnormalities of the urinary tract.

Your granddaughter presumably had a blockage in the tube leading from one kidney. This tube has now been crossed over to the opposite kidney, and both kidneys now use a common tube to drain the urine to the bladder. Although this is a quite delicate operation, there should be no further problems, and she should be able to lead a normal life.

I am quite sure that the problems your grandchildren are suffering are not connected to their mother's urinary infections. On the other hand, it is possible that the kidney problems are inherited. The actual chances of inheriting further problems is extremely difficult to work out, but a geneticist at one of the large children's hospitals may be able to give you some statistics on the chances of a problem arising in future children.

As the abnormalities can usually be corrected, I can see no reason why your son and daughter in law should not have more children. Hopefully, further children may miss out on the slightly abnormal gene combination that has led to the kidney problems in the other children.

Q   My 26 year old daughter has a problem of always wanting to pass urine. She goes to the toilet every hour or two, passes urine at night several times, and always has the feeling that she needs to empty her bladder. She was a bed-wetter into her teens, and has a craving to eat sweet things like chocolate bars at all hours of the day and night. I would be grateful if you could help her with your advice.

A   After reading your letter, the disease that came immediately to mind was diabetes.

Diabetics are constantly passing copious quantities of urine, are very thirsty and often crave sweets. There are a number of other diseases that could cause her symptoms including a chronic low-grade urinary infection, kidney diseases, abnormal activity of the pituitary gland in the brain and structural abnormalities of the bladder, but no matter what the cause, she requires further assessment by a doctor as soon as possible.

All these conditions can be controlled or cured, but if treatment is delayed some permanent damage may result.

Q   I have a dull pain in both sides of the side of my back. I pass very little urine during the day, but lots at night. I have had blood and urine tests and a kidney x-ray which are all normal. What could this be?

A   Any pain in the loins at the side of your mid-back may be caused by a problem in the kidneys, but when it occurs on both sides, it is less likely, as usually only one kidney at a time is inflamed. If appropriate blood, urine and x-ray tests of the kidneys are normal, another cause for the pain must be sought.

Arthritis or other problems in the back can cause pressure on the nerves that run out from the back to surrounding tissues, and this may be the cause of pain in both loins. Other possible causes may be problems in the muscles, the gut or even the liver and spleen.

Passing excessive amounts of urine at night may be normal with aging, but may also be a symptom of other diseases such as diabetes, malfunctioning of the parathyroid glands in the neck, Addison's disease and a number of other uncommon conditions.

Ask your doctor to look further to try and find the cause of your problem.

Q **I have started urinating more than usual and have to get up at 3 am to pass water. I also have a dry mouth, but my GP tested me for diabetes, and I don't have that disease, and a bladder ultrasound was also normal. What could be the problem?**

A Normally the amount of urine produced by the kidneys varies between day and night, with the kidneys being more active during the day so that you do not normally have to empty your bladder at night.

Unfortunately, as the years go by, this variation in kidney function between day and night reduces, until in the elderly it disappears altogether. As a result, older people have to rise from their beds to empty their bladder in the early hours of the morning.

Provided diseases such as diabetes and infection, which can cause excessive urination have been excluded by your doctor, there is no cause from concern about this problem, as it is just another joy of advancing maturity!

Q **I have protein in my urine. My doctor keeps testing the urine, but does nothing. What could cause this?**

A Protein in the urine can be due to any one of several dozen reasons, some of which are not of any concern, while others are very serious. I would hope that your doctor, or another doctor, has performed detailed investigations in the past to exclude any serious disease such as infection, nephritis, high blood pressure or a tumour.

If these tests are negative, it may be that you have a mild degree of kidney failure, which is very common in older people, and he may just be checking the urine regularly to make sure it does not get any worse. If the amount of protein in the urine increased, he would then undertake further treatment.

Another possibility is that you have had protein in your urine since birth. This congenital problem is of no consequence, provided it does not worsen.

Q **I am 73 and incontinent. Every time I move I wet my panties and I wet my bed at night. It is extremely embarrassing and I need help.**

A As you age, and with the trauma of childbirth, the muscles on the floor of your pelvis become stretched and slack. It is these muscles that control the outflow of urine from the bladder.

In younger women, an operation to tighten these muscles and reconstruct the bladder opening can give enormous relief. Older women often do not want the discomfort of a moderately major operation, or may not be well enough for the procedure. They can be helped by a special device that is inserted into the vagina. These ring pessaries are fitted by a gynaecologist, and remain in place for many months. They act to stretch the vagina, and therefore tension the muscles around the bladder opening to give you control of your water works again. I suggest you discuss this matter further with your own doctor.

L
LEGS
See also ARTHRITIS

Q I have severe cramps in my legs at night. I have been told various remedies, including eating bananas at night (to increase body potassium), and taking large doses of magnesium tablets (up to six a night). What do you think of these remedies? Are they safe?

A Magnesium has been known for many years to help nocturnal cramps, and provided it is not taken in extremely high doses, is quite safe. The main side effect of excessive magnesium compound ingestion is diarrhoea, and it should not be used in the elderly who have poor kidney function. Bananas are, of course, quite safe—I cannot imagine anyone eating enough of them to cause any harm.

This is one situation where doctors have to use common sense. If the patient finds that a particular, unorthodox treatment helps, then the patient should be encouraged to continue the treatment—provided there are no long-term side effects or dangers of which the patient may not be aware. The doctor may even try the treatment on other patients, and if they also find the treatment successful, s/he may write a paper for a medical journal so that other doctors are made aware of the breakthrough.

In this way, apparently unorthodox treatments become accepted into main-stream medicine.

Keep peeling those bananas—the growers will love you!

Q Every night, I am woken between midnight and 2 am with agonising pain in my left leg. I can't cope with this any more, and nothing seems to help. What can cause my leg muscles to go into spasm?

A Night time leg cramps are a very common problem. It worsens with age and pregnancy, and most commonly they occur after heavy exercise during the day.

Some hours after ceasing the exercise, the muscles in the leg go into painful spasm, causing you to leap from your chair or bed. Stretching the affected muscles by standing on tip toe or pushing against an immovable object often eases the pain.

The spasms are caused by a combination of minor muscle injury, a build up of waste products in the muscle and dehydration—all of these problems being caused by the exercise.

Prevention is better than cure, and taking adequate amounts of fluid during and after the activity may wash away excess waste products and prevent dehydration.

If this simple measure is insufficient, medications can be prescribed to be taken after sport to prevent the cramps. Quinine and Akineton are the drugs most commonly used. The two methods of prevention can be simply prescribed if tonic water or bitter lemon is drunk after exercise. These drinks contain quinine to give them the bitter taste, and so acts to prevent dehydration and muscle spasms.

Q My daughter has a badly inturned ankle. How should this be treated?

A This depends on your daughter's age and the severity of the deformity. If detected as an infant, splinting and strapping the ankle in the correct position for a few months may be all that is necessary. In older children braces or even surgery may be required, again depending on the severity.

Some children do grow out of the problem, so no doctor will act rapidly in deciding on surgery, but measurements will be taken of the angle of inturning on several occasions over a year or more. Physiotherapy may be given during this period to encourage a natural correction.

If the deformity is significant, it will require treatment to prevent severe arthritis in the joint, and to correct the problems she will encounter in sport, and possibly even walking. Anyone who detects any form of deformity in their child should have it assessed at an early stage by a medical practitioner to ensure the best possible outcome.

Q When I do knee bends, my joints make a noise, and a friend told me to drink a lot of milk. Is this true? I am 55 years old, but very fit after years of doing Karate, Judo and Tai Chi.

A Milk is an excellent food, full of essential vitamins and minerals, as well as carbohydrates, fats and protein, but it cannot lubricate noisy knees!

Joints can grate, click or pop under pressure (such as bending), and the cause varies from one sound to another. Grating noises can be due to arthritis or cartilage damage, clicks can be caused by ligament or cartilage damage, and popping noises may be quite normal (as in popping finger joints) and caused by a sudden reduction of pressure on the lubricating fluid within the joint.

With a long history of martial art exercises, you could have some chronic knee damage, but the only way to find out is to have the knee carefully examined (and possibly x-rayed) by your doctor. Once a correct diagnosis is made, appropriate treatment may be commenced.

Q My doctor has told me that I have Milroy's disease of the leg. Could you please explain this to me?

A Milroy's disease is a rare condition in which the lymphatic system in one or both legs is faulty, and fails to remove the waste products from the leg. As a result, the leg becomes swollen, puffy and uncomfortable. The condition is hereditary (tends to pass from one generation to the next), and usually starts at puberty (12 to 14 years of age). It is far more common in women than men.

The lymphatic system is an incredibly fine network of tubes that parallel the veins throughout the body, and take some forms of waste from every cell back into the bloodstream. The lymphatic system eventually drains into a main vein near the heart.

The only treatment is elevation of the leg as much as possible, and wearing a firm elastic stocking. The main complication is infections of the swollen tissue, which must be treated with antibiotics. Some patients require constant antibiotics to prevent these infections.

Q After having a knee replacement on one of my knees, I can't bend my knee completely, and this stops me riding a bike. Is there anything I can do?

A It's delightful to hear that someone who has had a knee replacement wants to ride a bike, as most people who have this operation are well over 60.

Unfortunately, a replacement knee is never as good as the young original, but most people can eventually bend their knee to a right angle. If this is not possible within six months of the operation, it is unlikely that any significantly greater movement will be achieved.

Regular physiotherapy in the first few months after the operation is essential to gain the maximum mobility in the new knee.

Considering the fact that the old knee would have been very painful and had limited strength and movement before the operation, most patients find a replacement knee a marked improvement.

I trust that you have adjusted the bicycle seat to give the knees the least possible necessary flexion, but other than this I regret that I cannot offer any further advice for your problem.

Q **I am 76 years old and in good general health. Two years ago I had a knee replacement operation. It was not a success, and after two years of pain and not being able to walk any distance, my surgeon wants to open it up again and cement it. I am very apprehensive about this operation, and would like your opinion on how necessary it is.**

A Unfortunately, not all operations turn out the way that the surgeon (or patient) would wish. Knee replacement operations have a very high success rate, and often give dramatic relief from chronic, severe arthritis. People who have been barely able to walk find themselves to walk freely for long distances within a few months of the operation.

You have been one of the unfortunate failures. This is probably a matter of bad luck, not incompetence on the part of the surgeon, nurses or hospital. After two years, your knee is not going to improve, and it is reasonable to let the surgeon try to correct the problem that has developed. Loosening of the joint, so that the artificial joint is not firmly cemented to the bone, is one of the commonest complications, and can usually be corrected without too much trouble.

Without further surgery you will continue to suffer constant knee pain. With surgery, you have a chance of significantly improving the knee discomfort, and possibly recovering completely. At worst, the operation cannot make your knee more painful than it is now.

Q **My ankles keep swelling, and get worse as the day goes on. What can I do about it?**

A The simple (but often not practical) answer is 'sit down and put your feet up'!

There are many reasons for swollen feet that get worse as the day goes on. The most common causes are advancing age with dilated veins in the legs, prolonged standing in one position (eg. hairdresser, shop assistant), a slowly weakening heart, hormonal changes before periods and with menopause, and failure of the kidneys.

There are many other rarer (and more serious) causes too, so the first step is to exclude any of these nasties by having the appropriate tests arranged by your general practitioner.

If a specific cause is found, that will be treated, but most people with this problem have swollen feet because of their age, hormones or occupation. In these situations, a fluid tablet can be prescribed that is taken when necessary to remove the excess fluid from the legs.

If you can, keep your feet elevated when sitting and wear support stockings that exert some pressure on the slack veins in the leg.

Q **I am a 20 year old woman who has spidery varicose veins, and despite regular exercise, they have not gone away. My questions to you are:**
— **Is having varicose veins a sign of heart or artery disease?**
— **Will exercise get rid of them?**
— **What else can be done to get rid of them?**
— **Are there any negative effects upon the body other than their ugliness?**

A —Varicose veins are not a sign of heart or artery disease. They are caused by a failure of the one way valves in the veins that normally only allow blood to flow towards the heart. If these valves in the veins leak, blood pools in the veins and they dilate, further damaging the valves and worsening the problem. Prolonged standing and pregnancy are the usual causes.

—Unfortunately, exercise will not get rid of them, but appropriate leg exercises during pregnancy and in jobs such as a shop assistant or hairdresser, may prevent the problem.

—Varicose veins can be treated with support stockings, injections into the veins to destroy them, or surgical removal of the veins. The form of treatment depends on their severity and position.

—Occasionally they can ache, they will bleed copiously if cut, and in older patients they may lead to the development of skin ulcers, but otherwise their main effect is on the appearance of the legs rather than the health of their owner.

Q **On the outside of my ankle, just below the ankle bone, there is a second bone that when pressed is quite tender and swells up. I run a great deal, and this sometimes causes a burning feeling in the tender area. If it is knocked, it causes a fair amount of pain. X-rays of my ankle are normal and I have tried many treatments with little success. What more can I do?**

A There is no naturally occurring structure at the point you are describing that would normally cause this complaint, but it is possible for damage to the area to cause some hardening of the underlying tissues.

Tight shoes, high sides on shoes, and a foot that tends to turn in or roll in when walking or running, could damage the tissues in this area. Obviously, a more serious injury from a blow to the area could also cause damage. The injury to the area may cause a callous to form, which may be as hard as bone, but it would be attached to the skin and not the underlying bone. In the next layer of tissue, a hard fibrous nodule may form as a result of injury.

A tendon in the area can become partly calcified to form a bony lump that may become painful with further injury.

The bone itself may be injured and produce a fibrous overgrowth that is very hard, and although it does not show on X-rays, it is attached to the bone.

Because there are so many possibilities, it is important for you to see an orthopaedic surgeon, who can thoroughly assess your foot. Treatments could include shoe inserts to correct any deformity and prevent further injury, injecting steroids around the tender lump, or surgically removing the lump. If it is annoying you enough to write to me, you should arrange to see a specialist as soon as possible.

Q   What could cause sharp stabs of pain that run from my buttock down my leg?

A   Almost certainly you are suffering from sciatica. This is caused by the pinching of a nerve as it emerges from the spinal cord between two vertebrae low in your back. The pain is not always felt at the point of pinching, but where the nerve runs.

The sciatic nerve is made up of many spinal nerves that join together in the middle of your buttock, at a point where the pain is often first felt. The nerve then runs down the back of your thigh and calf, giving off branch nerves to supply the muscles and other structures of the leg. Some unlucky victims feel the shooting pains associated with sciatica all the way from the back to the foot.

Investigation of the problem will involve careful examination of your back by a doctor, and x-rays to determine why the nerve is being pinched. Most patients can be helped by adequate treatment in the form of medication, physiotherapy, and occasionally surgery.

Q   When I go to bed, I can't get to sleep because I feel that I have to keep moving my legs. They feel as though they want to go on a marathon run. What can I do about it?

A   Before reading the answer to this question you must promise not to laugh! Are you ready? Well your problem is almost certainly due to the restless legs syndrome—and NO, I'm not kidding—there is such a medical entity! It is also a very distressing problem for many people. Its cause is not understood, and it does not seem to be related to exercise. Getting out of bed and going for a run doesn't help either.

Treatment involves keeping the legs cooler than the body, using paracetamol, or taking a very small dose of a mild muscle relaxant such as Valium, or one of a number of similar drugs that may be prescribed by your doctor.

Q   Could you please explain what causes restless legs?

A   The restless legs syndrome is the simple name for what doctors technically call the Wittmaack-Ekbom syndrome. A patient's legs feel as though they want to exercise when body is trying to rest, and they can't get to sleep because they feel that they have to keep moving their legs.

The cause is unknown, but it is more common in women, made worse by pregnancy and heat, and sometimes is aggravated by antihistamine medications. It is not related to previous exercise.

It may be a distressing problem but is not serious, and tends to occur episodically for years. It is usually well controlled by treatment.

Q   My knee keeps aching, and I can't sleep or rest comfortably. I am at my wits end. What could cause this problem?

A   Any one of several dozen diseases and conditions can cause knee pain, so your question is impossible to answer in definite terms. The most common cause of knee pain is osteoarthritis. This can cause a deep ache that is often worse at rest, but although exercise gives temporary relief, any heavy exercise will make it worse when you do rest.

Treatment will involve anti-inflammatory medications from your doctor, pain-killers, liniments and physiotherapy. As a last resort, surgery to totally replace the knee joint can be undertaken.

Other causes of knee pain include any sort of injury (eg. falling on your knee), a strain or tear to the ligaments or cartilages in or around the knee, cysts, infections, a mal-aligned knee joint and numerous rarer diseases.

Let your doctor examine and x-ray your knee so that a proper diagnosis can be made. If osteoarthritis is present it will probably show on an X-ray.

Q   What are growing pains?

A   Many doctors do not believe that growing pains occur, and they receive scanty attention in medical textbooks. I do believe they occur and they are probably due to inflammation of the soft growing areas at the ends of the long bones in the arms and legs. Children can be extremely active and this places excessive force on the growing areas, leading to pain in the bones. Rest, heat and paracetamol or aspirin are the only necessary treatments.

Q   I am 65 and fell twice on my left hip recently. The hip is sore now when I walk, and I cannot sleep on the left side. What is it?

A   You must be examined by a doctor, who will almost certainly x-ray the hip. It may be that you have merely bruised the tissue over the hip joint, but there is always a concern that there may be a minor fracture of the top end of the thigh bone (the femur) which may have serious consequences if left untreated.

Q   What is housemaid's knee? My doctor tells me this is the cause of my swollen knee.

A   Water on the knee, or housemaid's (do such people still exist?) knee is cause by the swelling and inflammation of the bursa on the front of the kneecap.

Bursae are small sacs, rather like deflated balloons that are connected by a fine tube to the joint cavity. They secrete the essential synovial fluid which acts as an oil for the moving part of the joint. There are several of these around every joint.

One of those supplying the knee is in front of the kneecap, and if it is damaged by kneeling on it for long periods, or in any other way, it will become painful and swollen. Treatment involves rest, avoiding kneeling and occasionally draining the excess fluid from the knee.

Q   I have trouble walking distances—my legs ache, and when I stop, the pain goes. I have taken Vitamin E and lecithin every day to no avail. Can you recommend any treatment for this trouble?

A   The pain you are describing in your legs is called claudication, and is caused by narrowing of the arteries to the legs, probably as a result of atherosclerosis (hardening of the arteries). This in turn is caused by a combination of high cholesterol levels and high blood pressure over many years.

When you exercise, the muscles in your legs require more oxygen as energy. The oxygen is obtained from the blood. Because the arteries to the leg are hardened and narrowed, they cannot dilate to supply more blood, so the muscles (particularly in the calf) become starved of oxygen. The result is a painful leg that forces you to stop and rest, at which point the muscle does not need the extra oxygen of exercise, and can recover using the reduced blood supply available to it.

There are a number of drugs obtainable from doctors on prescription that are designed to open up the arteries, or allow the blood to flow more freely through them. These should be tried initially, but if they are unsuccessful, further investigations and special x-rays can be undertaken to find where the arteries are narrowed.

If only a limited blockage of the arteries is present, there are operations available to bypass the blockage and allow a better blood flow to the leg muscles.

Q I would like to ask you why my feet and legs get very hot in bed? I have to get out of bed and cool them. I will be 88 if I live until 25th December, and generally well, but take blood pressure tablets.

A You feel heat in the skin when the blood vessels just under the skin dilate. This typically happens when you have a fever or blush. Many medications to lower high blood pressure work by opening up (dilating) the blood vessels everywhere in the body to allow the blood to flow through them more freely through them and therefore lower the pressure. A sensation of warm skin is a common minor complaint of patients who are taking tablets to control high blood pressure.

It is not serious, and causes no long-term problems, but if you are finding it a nuisance, you should discuss the matter further with your general practitioner, as a different combination of tablets for your blood pressure may be possible.

Q I get a recurring itchy rash on my foreleg about 6 inches above my ankles. It settles with Sorbolene cream but recurs every few weeks. It seems to flare more after I play soccer. What do I do to get rid of it?

A The most likely explanation is a form of eczema that is flaring because of exposure to something at soccer. Your bare shins may react to the grass, chemicals or fertilisers on the playing field, the detergent used to wash your socks, the material of the socks themselves, or any one of several million other substances in the environment.

It is possible that only when you are stressed by exertion or excitement while playing soccer that you are susceptible to the particular substance.

Using a barrier cream on the shins before a match may prevent exposure to the irritant, but generally, if it settles readily with a simple cream such as Sorbolene, no further treatment should be necessary, although there are medicated steroid creams that may settle it faster.

Q Our 16 year old son has been diagnosed as having Osgood-Schlatter's disease in his left knee. He has been to an acupuncturist, physiotherapist and two doctors, none of whom could offer relief or cure. He usually plays a lot of sport and would like to continue his involvement. Is there a cure?

A   Osgood-Schlatter's disease is a relatively common condition of rapidly growing children between 12 and 16. It is a self-limiting condition that usually gets better by itself, but the condition is prolonged by sport or other activity.

Just below the knee on the front of the calf bone (the tibia) there is a small swelling or lump on the bone. This is where the large tendon that runs from the kneecap to the tibia is attached. When the large muscles on the front of the thigh contract, they pull on the knee cap, which then pulls on the tibia to straighten the knee. With running and other exercises involving the knee, enormous forces are placed on both the knee cap and the tendon attachment into the top of the tibia.

In rapidly growing children, the bones are softer than at other times. Osgood-Schlatter's disease is the result of sport on soft bone, as the lump on the front of the tibia is slightly pulled away from the rest of the soft bone, resulting in pain and tenderness.

The only treatment is prolonged rest, with no stress to the knee. In severe cases, the patient is put on crutches, or even in plaster.

If your son stops sport for a season and rests his knee it will get better. If he does not, his pain will persist.

LIVER and GALL BLADDER
See also GUT

Q   **What does the liver actually do? I can't work this out, but unlike the gall bladder, it seems to be essential to the body.**

A   The liver is the largest gland and internal organ in the body. Wedge-shaped, it lies behind the lower few ribs on the right side. It weighs about 1.5 kg and has the same reddish brown colour as the animal livers we are familiar with in the butcher shop. When food has been digested it still has to be absorbed into the body. The liver plays an integral part in this process.

The liver is a mass of complex tissue containing millions of cells and blood vessels. Among its functions, it regulates the amount of blood sugar, assists in producing the blood-clotting mechanisms, helps to nourish new blood cells, destroys old blood cells, breaks down excess acids to be eliminated as urine, stores and modifies fats so they can be more efficiently utilised by cells all over the body, stores certain vitamins and minerals, and removes poisons from harmful substances such as alcohol and drugs. The liver is also an important source of the heat which is essential to maintain the body's temperature.

The liver manufactures bile, which mixes with the digestive juices in the duodenum. Bile is a thick, yellowy-green liquid containing salts that breaks down fat into small droplets so that it can more easily be digested.

Another of the functions of the liver is to remove a yellow pigment called bilirubin, produced by the destruction of old red blood cells, from the blood. If the liver becomes diseased and cannot function properly, this yellow pigment stays in the bloodstream and gives a yellowish tinge to the skin and whites of the eyes—the jaundice that is such a striking symptom of the liver disease, hepatitis.

The chemical processing capabilities of the liver are very complex. Substances which enter as one thing frequently leave as something else, depending on the body's needs. For example, most amino acids are converted into proteins, but if

241

the body is short of glucose, the liver will combine some of the amino acids with fat to make extra sugar. Similarly, if the level of blood sugar is too high, glucose is converted into a substance that can be stored.

The liver also stores vitamins. If more vitamins are consumed than the body needs, some will be stored to be released if needed later. A person may survive as long as 12 months without taking in any vitamin A, and for up to four months without new supplies of vitamins B12 and D.

Q   What is the gall bladder? What does it do? I'm told that it is essential for digestion, but I have to have mine taken out because of stones, even though they only give occasional pains.

A   The liver, which sits behind the lower ribs on the right side of the body, produces bile at a more or less constant rate. This bile moves through a series of collecting ducts, which join up to form the common bile duct. This duct leads to the small intestine. There is a side duct to the common bile duct that leads to the gall bladder.

Bile is required to help in the digestion of food, but as we do not eat constantly, it is not needed in the gut all the time. There is a valve at the lower end of the common bile duct where it opens into the intestine. This valve opens when food passes to allow bile to be added to the food in the gut. When the valve is closed, the bile must be stored, and this is where the gall bladder fits in to the picture.

The Liver and Gall Bladder

The gall bladder is a storage area for bile not immediately required, and the bile from the liver is directed into it when the valve is closed. When extra bile is required in the gut to digest food, the gall bladder contracts to squeeze the bile out through the open valve onto the food.

If your gall bladder is removed, the bile trickles into the gut constantly, and although not an ideal situation, the bile and food will eventually mix together, and digestion will occur, with minimal consequences to you or your gut.

Q I had a laparoscopic gall bladder removal four years ago, but still have discomfort in the area, particularly after a large meal. Is this normal?

A Laparoscopic removal of the gall bladder involves cutting three or four one-centimetre long holes in the abdomen, and inserting tubes through these holes, which are used for the surgeon to see what he or she is doing and the passage of instruments to perform the operation. Recovery is usually far faster than the open operation in which a 12 to 15 cm cut is necessary.

With any operation there is some scarring, and it may be that scar tissue has formed around the site of the gall bladder which is pinching nerves or adhering to surrounding structures. This is the most common cause of post-operative pain.

It may be that the cause of your pain is due to some other disease process in the liver, stomach, intestine, pancreas or overlying muscles, and totally unrelated to your surgery.

Rarely, a gallstone may be left behind in the bile duct, and may be responsible for continuing post-operative discomfort.

In all cases you should return to your doctor so that a further examination and investigations can be performed to determine the exact cause of your problem.

Q Ten weeks ago I had my gall bladder removed by laparoscopy. I was discharged after three days, but since then I have had discomfort under the right rib cage and in the shoulder blade. Is this pain normal?

A Laparoscopic surgery is marvellous innovation that enables medium level surgery, such as removing the gall bladder, to be performed through tiny holes using long thin tubes to look into the belly and operate through.

The main advantages are far less pain from the incision, and being able to leave hospital in a very short time.

During the operation, the belly is blown up with gas in order to separate the organs from each other and enable the surgeon to see what he or she is doing. At the end of the operation, every attempt is made to remove this gas, but it is impossible to remove all of it.

As you recover, the remaining gas is slowly absorbed into the bloodstream, but this may take some weeks.

One of the places the gas tends to accumulate is above the liver, and under the diaphragm, behind the ribs on your right side. Here it can cause some irritation and discomfort. The nerves that supply the diaphragm run down from the shoulder, so it is not unusual to experience referred pain in the shoulder from the gas under the diaphragm.

All your symptoms should settle gradually in the three months after the operation, and there is no cause for concern unless the pain worsens.

Q I had my gall bladder removed recently, a cholestomy (sic) it is called, and I would like to know what parts are missing. I am frightened about what foods I can eat. Can you advise me?

A In a cholecystectomy, the only part of you removed is the gall bladder.

Bile is produced constantly in the liver, but is only required in the gut when food is present. As a result, the bile is stored in the gall bladder, and when food is eaten, the gall bladder contracts to squirt bile onto the food, and help its digestion (see diagram on page 242).

If the bile becomes too concentrated, stones may form, and cause pain and discomfort. The only way to remove these is to remove the entire gall bladder.

After the operation, you will still produce bile, but it will trickle into the gut constantly. Some patients find they get a bit bloated after a cholecystectomy, and have intermittent indigestion, but generally there are minimal symptoms.

There are no general rules on foods to avoid, but some people find that fried and fatty foods upset them. By trial and error, you will find those foods that cause problems, and learn to avoid them.

The vast majority of people who have their gall bladder removed have no problems afterwards and lead a totally normal life.

Q I've just learnt that my belly pain is caused by gallstones. How do you get gall stones?

A Gallstones form in the gall bladder which is a storage sac for bile. When food enters the gut, the gall bladder contracts and squirts bile onto the food to aid in its digestion. If the bile becomes too concentrated or infected, the bile will crystallise, and these small crystals may slowly grow into stones as big as an egg. Most stones are smaller than a pea though. Twice as many women than men will get gall stones, and they are also more common in fat people. Hereditary factors also increase your chance of developing these annoying stones.

Q My parents both had gall stones. I am worried that I might too. Who gets gall stones and how are they treated?

A Fair, fat, female, forty and flatulent. These are the people who, according to traditional medical textbooks, are more likely to suffer from gall stones. Of course the problem can occur in many people outside this group, but I find it quite surprising just how many do belong to this '5F' group.

Problems occur when the bile in the gall bladder becomes too concentrated and precipitates out as a crystal or stone. Small stones can pass out along the ducts, but larger stones block up the bile ducts, and when the gall bladder contracts, the movement of the stone in the duct causes severe pain.

The only effective treatment is surgery to remove the gall bladder and the stones it contains. If there are no acute problems, it can be carried out routinely at the patient's convenience. Some patients can have stones very low in the common bile duct removed by an instrument that is passed through the mouth and stomach into the intestine. Patients who are too old or ill for an operation may use an expensive drug that slowly dissolves some gall stones over many months.

A newer technique to disintegrate gall stones by ultrasound waves is being trialed in some hospitals, but this is not routinely available yet.

Q Following an extensive liver resection for metastatic cancer my husband developed intense itching all over but there is no sign of a rash. What could cause this?

A The liver is an extraordinarily complex organ that is responsible for the production of many of the body's essential chemicals and enzymes, and for removing waste products from the blood stream. Any surgery to the liver may interfere with these processes, and metastatic deposits of cancer may also have an effect.

If any one of the hundreds of substances produced in the liver is being manufactured in excess, or in insufficient quantities, there may be a minor imbalance in the body's metabolism. The same applies if one particular waste product is not being removed efficiently. Either problem can lead to a wide variety of symptoms, one of which could easily be an itch.

Identifying the chemical imbalance can be very difficult or impossible, as it may be an interaction between two or more different substances. If nothing obvious is found on routine investigation, it is often just a matter of time while your husband waits for the liver to repair itself (which it usually does).

In the meantime, there are medications that can be prescribed by your general practitioner to ease the itch and discomfort. You should discuss the various options further with him/her.

LUNGS
See also ASTHMA

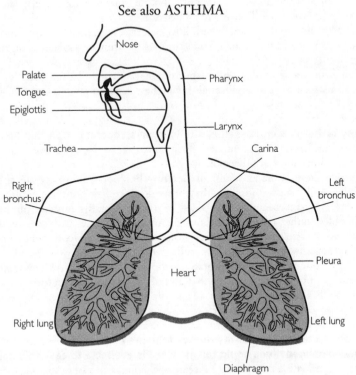

Respiratory System

Q **My son suffers from asthma, but he was recently sent in to hospital with a pneumothorax. Can you explain this?**

A Your lung is made up of millions of air bubbles that all connect together by means of fine air-filled tubes. The entire lung lies in a sack that has a smooth inner surface, allowing the lung tissue to slide over it as you breathe in and out.

If the lung develops a puncture (ie. one or more of the tiny air bubbles or tubes bursts) air will leak into the sack around the lung, and will be unable to escape. More and more air steadily accumulates in the sack, causing pressure on the lung, shortness of breath and pain. These punctures can occur for no apparent reason, or may be due to lung diseases such as asthma, which put an excessive stress on the lungs.

Once diagnosed, urgent medical attention is required. A tube is placed through the chest wall to remove the escaped air, and this allows the lung to expand and refill the sack.

Pneumothorax resembles asthma in that the the patient is short of breath, but asthmatics are not normally in pain.

Q **I am coughing a lot, and I am a smoker. How can a doctor tell if you have lung cancer?**

A It is difficult for lung cancer to be diagnosed without an X-ray or sputum test. Most lung cancers show up quite well on a normal chest X-ray, but if there is suspicion of the disease, and a normal X-ray shows no cancer, a special type of X-ray known as a CT scan will be performed.

Most people (but not all) with lung cancer have a chronic cough, and another way to make the diagnosis is to examine the sputum under a microscope for cancer cells.

If you are a smoker and suspicious that you may be a victim of this very serious form of cancer, arrange for a chest X-ray now. Nine out of ten lung cancers occur in smokers.

Q **My father has emphysema, and is always coughing. Can this be cured?**

A No. Emphysema is a permanent form of damage to the lungs caused by smoking or the inhalation of other noxious gases.

The lung is made of millions of tiny bubbles, but if they are chronically inflamed by cigarette smoke, they break down to larger and larger bubbles. The lung gradually becomes composed of a much smaller number of these large bubbles, rather than the millions of microscopic ones. These have a smaller surface area to absorb the oxygen inside them into the bloodstream. The victim thus becomes starved of oxygen and short of breath.

It is essential for these people to stop smoking to prevent any further lung damage, but they often slowly deteriorate as the lung fails to function.

Medications are available to maximise the efficiency of the lungs, but supplementary oxygen is often required as the years go by.

Q **I am 78 years old and my doctor tells me I have emphysema. I would be much obliged if you could tell me what is available to ease this condition.**

A Emphysema is a degenerative disease of the lungs caused by smoking, recurrent lung infections, or the inhalation of toxic gases. Unfortunately, there is no cure for the condition, but there are many medications (most of which require prescriptions) and techniques that can be used to control the cough and shortness of breath that occur.

The treatments available include:

- Medication to prevent any spasm of the air tubes (bronchi) in the lungs, and prevent the excess production of mucus. These are in the form of inhalers such as Flixotide, Becotide, Pulmicort and Aldecin.
- Bronchodilators that open up the airways to allow more air into the lungs. Examples include Ventolin, Respolin, Atrovent, Seretide, Oxis and Bricanyl. They can be taken using either an inhaler or a nebuliser.
- Tablets such as Theo-Dur and Nuelin that open up the airways, but often cause the heart to race as a side effect.
- A tablet or mixture called Bisolvon which liquefies the phlegm in the lungs so that it can clear away more easily.
- Antibiotics that are used to treat any infection at the earliest possible stage.
- Steroid tablets or injections which are used as a last resort to treat severe episodes, or prevent a recurrence if no other medication works.
- Physiotherapy, which is very important to assist in the clearance of excess mucus from the lungs.

By using combinations and permutations of the above treatments, most emphysema victims can lead useful and comfortable lives.

Q My wife recently died from emphysema after being a smoker most of her life. I was not present at the time of her death, and would relieve my mind greatly to have your advice on how she would have passed away. Would she have suffered much?

A Emphysema is a disease that is suffered by smokers and others who have had recurrent lung infections. It results in the slow destruction of the lung tissue.

In the advanced stages, victims are constantly short of breath, lack energy and cough repeatedly. They require a large range of medications, both inhaled and as tablets, to force the lungs to function as much as they can. Oxygen is also required constantly via prongs in the nose or a mask.

Despite all these measures, the patient eventually reaches the stage where there is not enough oxygen being absorbed into the blood from the lungs, and too much carbon dioxide builds up in the bloodstream.

Your wife would have been very tired for weeks or months before her death due to lack of oxygen. This tiredness would have progressively worsened until she fell asleep, never to wake again.

She would not have suffered at the end and her death would have been very peaceful. She was very lucky to have a husband as devoted to her welfare as you obviously were.

Q Apparently I have a collapsed left lung. I have been told there is no help for it (sic). Could you tell me if this is true?

A There are many causes for a collapsed lung that vary from tuberculosis and surgery to chronic infection and a pneumothorax (air inside the chest but outside the lung).

Without knowing the cause of your problem, I cannot comment any further, but I suspect you may have had the problem for some time without being particularly aware of it.

It is quite possible to live a normal life with only one lung.

If you do not understand your problem you should discuss the matter further with your general practitioner who will have more information about you, or will be able to obtain the necessary details from the doctors who have been treating you.

Q   I have been told by my general practitioner that my persistent cough and shortness of breath are due to a condition called bronchiectasis. Would you please explain this condition to me.

A   Bronchiectasis is unfortunately an incurable condition in which there is permanent damage to the lungs. The damage may be caused by serious diseases such as cystic fibrosis, but far more commonly by smoking, recurrent lung infections or other noxious gases. Passive smoking aggravates the condition.

It is not a particularly common condition, and most general practitioners would only have two or three cases in their practices.

Within the lungs, the disease is characterised by permanent abnormal dilation and inflammation of the small airway tubes (the bronchi). The inflamed bronchi secrete excess amounts of phlegm and are easily infected. This infection may be difficult to eradicate, and most patients must remain on antibiotics long term to prevent flare ups.

The symptoms of bronchiectasis include shortness of breath, a persistent productive cough, general malaise, weight loss, tiredness, anaemia and reduced exercise tolerance due to inability of the lungs to process oxygen efficiently.

Doctors diagnose the condition by listening to characteristic sounds at the base of the lungs, chest X-rays and in severe cases by a procedure in which a thin tube is put into the lungs through the mouth to enable a sample of lung tissue to be taken and analysed (bronchoscopy).

Treatment involves intermittent or constant use of antibiotics, chest physiotherapy and inhaled medications to open up the airways. Other medications to loosen mucus and promote effective coughing may also be used. In severe cases, surgical removal of constantly infected sections of the lung may be necessary.

Complications can include deteriorating lung function from repeated infections, the formation of an abscess in the lung and the spread of infection to a distant site in the body.

Most patients can lead a normal active life provided they remain on medication, see their doctor regularly for check-ups and do not stress their bodies excessively.

Q   My mother recently nearly died from pneumonia. I know it is a lung infection, but how do you tell if someone is getting pneumonia, what part of the lung is affected and how is it treated?

A.   Pneumonia is an infection of the tiny air bubbles that form the major part of the lung, and enable the oxygen to cross into the bloodstream. The infection is caused by bacteria, miniature microscopic animals that are inhaled with every breath. Normally these bacteria are destroyed by the body's defence mechanisms, but if the person is tired, run down, overworked, bedridden or suffering from other illnesses the bacteria may be able to get a hold, and start multiplying.

The symptoms of pneumonia may be obvious with fever, cough and chest pains, but some bacteria are far more insidious, and cause minimal symptoms for some months. The patient may just feel tired, short of breath and have intermittent sweats.

A chest X-ray is always necessary when a doctor suspects pneumonia, as the damaged section of lung can be seen, and the extent of the infection assessed. A sample of sputum is taken before treatment is started, and this is sent to a laboratory where the infecting bacteria can be identified, and the correct antibiotics to destroy it can be determined.

Treatment may be started before the laboratory results are received, but sometimes the antibiotic has to be changed to a more appropriate one at a later date. Medications to open up the airways and loosen the phlegm may also be prescribed. Regular physiotherapy is very important to drain the foul collection of pus out of the chest.

The other important factors in treatment are rest and the cessation of smoking. If you try to keep working, the body cannot gain enough energy to help the antibiotics fight off the infection. Anyone who continues to smoke while they have pneumonia is effectively frustrating every effort of the doctors and therapists to cure him or her.

Q I have recently been very ill with double pneumonia. Why is double pneumonia different to ordinary pneumonia?

A Pneumonia occurs when a bacteria enters the tiny air bubbles that fill your lung, and starts multiplying to cause an infection. Usually only one part of the lungs, often at the bottom of your chest, is affected at first, but the problem soon spreads to other parts of the lung.

If a sample of the sputum you cough up is sent to a laboratory, the specific bacteria causing your pneumonia can be identified. Once one bacteria is in residence, your resistance to further infection is lowered, and it is much easier for a second type of bacteria to infect the lungs as well. When this happens, both types of bacteria can be identified by the laboratory, and you are said to have double pneumonia. It is possible to have triple, and rarely even quadruple pneumonia if you are particularly unlucky!

The laboratory will also be able to tell which antibiotics will kill the various types of bacteria infecting your lungs. The appropriate combination of antibiotics can then be given by the doctor to cure the condition. Expectorants and chest physiotherapy are the other mainstays of treatment in any type of pneumonia.

Q I cough up pale yellow to green coloured phlegm during the day. Could this be serious? My doctor says it is Pseudomonas infection, but as I am allergic to Gentamicin, he hasn't given me any treatment.

A A Pseudomonas infection is certainly serious, and can produce yellow to green phlegm. Pseudomonas is the name of a bacteria that causes bronchitis and pneumonia. If it is left untreated, it can cause permanent lung damage, and chronic poor health. You should return to your doctor and ask for sputum cultures to be taken to determine which antibiotic is appropriate to kill the infection.

Gentamicin is commonly used to treat this type of infection, but there are others available. If necessary, your degree of reaction to Gentamicin may need to be tested again. If your own GP is unable to help you further, you should request referral to a respiratory physician. These are doctors who are specialists in lung diseases.

Q **They have recently removed lots of asbestos from inside the ceiling of our office. When and why is asbestos dangerous?**

A Asbestos is made from long, thin microscopic fibres. If this fibre is inhaled, it sticks in the tiny tubules deep inside your lung and cannot escape. In this position, it causes constant irritation which can lead to emphysema, chronic bronchitis or cancer. Usually a considerable amount of asbestos fibre must be inhaled for any significant disease to develop.

In commercial use, asbestos is normally combined with cement to make building boards or pipes. In this form it is totally safe. Only if the material is sawed or broken can the fibres escape to be inhaled. Anyone using asbestos cement should wear a face mask to prevent inhalation of any particles when sawing.

Asbestos as a dust or powder is also used as an insulating material. This is usually placed in walls or ceilings, and again it is unlikely to be inhaled in these situations, but if someone walks in the ceiling space and stirs up the asbestos dust, or if the plaster wall is broken allowing the asbestos to escape, inhalation may be dangerous.

It takes many years for any disease to develop after the asbestos is inhaled, and in many people, no disease ever develops. Asbestos is safe if used carefully and workers are adequately protected.

Q **About 6 months ago I was moving a quantity of asbestos sheets without any protection, and that night I coughed a lot and felt irritation on my chest. This has persisted ever since. I would appreciate it if you could advise me what to do.**

A Asbestos can only cause harm to humans if inhaled. Touching, or even swallowing small amounts of asbestos, is quite harmless. To be inhaled, asbestos must be in a dust or powder form, and it is sometimes used in this way as insulation in ceilings and between walls. The sawing of asbestos sheets also produces asbestos dust that can be inhaled, and particles of asbestos may be widespread in asbestos mines and factories that manufacture asbestos products.

Old asbestos sheets may deteriorate to the point where the surface breaks down and crumbles, and a small amount of asbestos dust may be produced in this way.

If small amounts of asbestos dust are inhaled infrequently, the lungs can cope adequately and expel the particles. Only long exposure to considerable amounts of asbestos dust will result in severe lung disease.

The asbestos particles are quite long and thin fibres when viewed under a microscope, which makes them difficult for the lung to remove by coughing up the mucus that accumulates around them. Over a number of years, they can irritate the lung lining to the point where the cells become cancerous. The most common form of lung cancer caused by asbestos is called mesothelioma, and this is virtually untreatable.

The casual handling of sheets of asbestos for a short period of time is not going to cause any lasting lung disease, and I suspect your cough is coincidental. x-rays would not show the presence of small quantities of asbestos dust in the lungs. Please be reassured.

Q How serious is lung cancer? Can it be cured?

A Lung cancer is extremely serious. The majority of victims have been smokers, and this is the most serious consequence from many years of inhaling toxic fumes into the lungs.

Treatment may involve combinations of surgery, radiation and medication, but even in the best cancer centres, fewer than one in ten victims will survive. The best cure is prevention—everyone who smokes is taking this terrible gamble with their lives.

Q I have a cousin who has just been diagnosed as suffering from cystic fibrosis. Can you tell me about this disease?

A Cystic fibrosis is a disease that you are born with. It is due to a lack of digestive enzymes and an inability to protect the lungs from recurrent infections, and sterility in males. The sweat of these patients is also excessively salty, and the presenting symptom to a doctor may be the mother's comment that the child tastes salty when kissed.

About one in every 2000 children has the disease.

The digestive enzymes are produced in the pancreas, an organ that sits behind the belly button in the abdomen. The enzymes are not produced and the pancreas is not properly developed in these patients, but this part of the disease can be overcome by taking capsules of the required enzymes at meal times. Some babies are born with their gut blocked up with mucus because of the lack of enzymes.

The lung condition is more serious and requires chest physiotherapy several times a day, drugs to clear mucus from the lungs and regular antibiotics to cure infections.

The disease cannot be cured yet, but long-term control is now possible and genetic engineering may produce a cure in the next decade or so.

MALE PROBLEMS
See also PROSTATE PROBLEMS; SEX

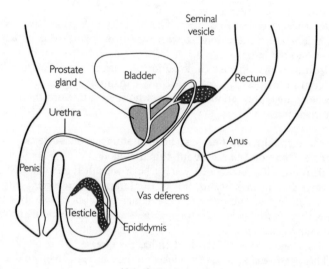

Male Genital Anatomy

Q **I am pregnant, and my husband wants any son of his to be circumcised. I am not so sure, and would like your opinion. Should it be done? Why is it done?**

A Circumcision as a religious ritual is known in many different cultures, but the idea that circumcision is 'normal' in countries of the British Commonwealth, is relatively recent. It started only at the end of the nineteenth century, and appears to stem from the hygiene problems, penile infections, and subsequent adult circumcisions suffered by soldiers in the Crimean wars, and to some extent in the First World War. Fathers at that time swore that they would not put their sons through such agony in adult life, and started the ritual of infant circumcision.

Today there is no medical reason to support the continuation of this ritual. Hygiene is not a problem in modern society, and it is possible for parents and children to adequately clean their penis, as much as their ears or any other part of the anatomy.

Removing the foreskin may adversely affect the man in later life. The foreskin is the most sexually sensitive part of the penis, and if excess is removed, it may decrease sexual pleasure.

If performed under the age of 6 weeks, circumcision is normally done without any anaesthetic, as the risk of this makes the operation even more dangerous. It is thus a traumatic experience for both the baby and the doctor.

There are also risks associated with the procedure. Although any bleeding from the penis may appear to be adequately controlled when the child leaves the surgery, catastrophic bleeding may occur unnoticed into a nappy that night. Scarring of the penis due to infection may also occur.

Some men will need to be circumcised later in life, but fewer than 1% of men will need this operation for infections, tight bands, cancer or other reasons. Some of us will also need to have our tonsils removed later in life, but this is not a valid reason for removing them at birth.

Many public hospitals in Australia are now refusing to allow this operation. This is because the vast majority of the medical profession can see the disadvantages of the procedure. It really is no more than a left-over tribal ritual.

Q My doctor says my son should not have a circumcision as it is an unnecessary operation. What men will require circumcision as an adult?

A As a general rule, very few men require circumcision. If a recurrent infection occurs under the foreskin it may need to be removed. Some children have ballooning of the foreskin when they pass urine, and this requires circumcision too. Rarely, the foreskin may retract over the head of the penis and form a tight band. This requires urgent surgery to remove the constriction.

There is no justification for routine circumcision of the newborn, as there are significant risks associated with this procedure, and it is not appropriate for the prevention of infection. Good hygiene is all that is required. Remember that a boy's foreskin may not fully retract until puberty, and it should never be forced back for cleaning.

Q I am writing about a problem of mine that has been apparent for some time. Around the base of my penis and on my scrotum there are a number of small pimple-like spots or lumps. A hair appears to grow from each lump. I am sure it is not an STD, but my girlfriend and I have agreed to have sex in the near future, and I fear she may notice these lumps. I am 15, and have had the problem for two years. Your help would be greatly appreciated.

A Relax! You do not have anything to be concerned about. Two years ago, you developed from a boy into a man, and at that time your scrotum and penis enlarged. The scrotum is normally smooth in boys, but in men, a large number of sebaceous (oil) glands and sweat glands develop in the skin of the scrotum to give it a 'plucked chicken' appearance.

You are describing a completely normal scrotum, and if you get a chance, take a sidelong look at other young men in a changing room, and you will see that they will have the same small lumps.

If you do become sexually active, ensure that you use adequate contraception (eg. a condom). I am sure you have no desire to become a father at 15!

Q. I am a 47 year old man who has never married. I am starting to see my life slip by now, and feel as though I would like to settle down with a younger woman and have a child. I have not had success in meeting the ideal partner as yet. Do you think I have left my run too late in life to settle down and have a child?

A. At 47 years of age you are still capable of fathering a child—men into their early seventies have achieved this—and from this biological point of view, you have not left your run too late.

When it comes to finding and choosing a mate for life, I am in no position to offer any constructive comment, as this is a matter of individual chemistry.

You will probably need to find a woman considerably younger than yourself. Women are incapable of child-bearing after the menopause (the change of life), and this occurs between the mid-forties and early fifties, but the risks of child-bearing increase steadily with each year over forty. I have abbreviated your letter here, but the full version gives me the feeling that you are a sincere and sensitive person, and I wish you luck in your endeavour.

Q **My son's right testicle will not retract, and doctors want to operate for this. Will this problems affect his fertility in adult life?**

A Small muscles are attached to the upper end of the testicle, and these muscles contract to draw the testicle closer to the body during cold weather, and relax during hot weather so the testes drops away from the body to keep cool. This keeps the testicles at a fairly constant temperature, which is slightly lower than normal body temperature. This is necessary for the health of the sperm, and a testicle that is too hot or too cold will not produce healthy sperm.

If the testicle will not retract, the testicle may be more prone to suffer from low temperatures, and may be more likely to suffer injury. A man is completely fertile with just one testicle, so this problem will not affect your son's fertility, but as correcting it is a relatively simple procedure, there is no reason why it should not proceed.

Q **I am 16 and one of my testicles doesn't descend at all into my scrotum. I've kept this low-key because I didn't know who to tell. I hope you can help.**

A The testicles start their life inside the lower belly, and about the time of birth, move through a canal in the groin to rest in the scrotum. Occasionally in babies, one or both testicles may retreat into this canal, but should always come down easily with rest (check them when the baby is asleep, and not when crying) or with light finger manipulation.

If the testicles do not rest easily in the scrotum by five years of age, they should be placed there surgically.

By 16, your testes should certainly be in the scrotum. If one is not, you should see your GP at once to arrange for a minor operation (performed by a surgeon) that will move the testicle into its correct position. If it is left up in the groin, it will not function properly, and in later life may become cancerous.

A man may function normally sexually, and father children, with only one testicle, but the risk of cancer is a significant one, and a man of any age with an undescended testicle should seek a surgical repair.

Q **I recently cut off the blood supply to my penis while wearing tight shorts on a car journey. I have been left with a white patch on the glans of the penis which won't go away despite treatment with hot water and massage. How can I cure the problem?**

A   Almost certainly, the white patch on your penis has nothing to do with your tight shorts. A superficial fungal infection of the skin is a far more likely diagnosis.

Hot water and massage will not help in the slightest, and may actually encourage the growth of a fungus, as they start in areas that are affected by heat, moisture and friction.

Be sensible and see your doctor so that a proper diagnosis can be made, appropriate treatment started, and your mind laid to rest.

Q   My four year old son has had a successful operation for hypospadias. Will this problem now affect him in his relationships with women in later life?

A   Hypospadias is a developmental abnormality in which the tube carrying the urine through the penis (the urethra) fails to close properly in the foetus, and the opening is on the lower side of the penis rather than the end. The opening can occur anywhere from the base of the penis to very near the end, depending on the severity of the abnormality.

Boys with hypospadias are more likely to develop urinary infections, must pass urine sitting down, and later in life when they have sex, will ejaculate through this same opening in a place that makes it difficult for the woman to fall pregnant.

The operation to correct this abnormality and place the urethral opening in the usual position at the end of the penis, requires considerable skill, but is completely successful in the vast majority of patients. Your son's future sex life should be completely normal.

Q   What is the cause of Peyronie's disease, and can anything be done to correct it by means of drugs, surgery or laser treatment?

A   Peyronie's disease was named after French surgeon Francois de la Peyronie (1678–1747) who was surgeon to Louis XIV, founded the Royal Academy of Surgeons in Paris, and who first described the condition. It is an uncommon problem that causes significant side-to-side (not vertical) curvature of the erect penis and a less firm than normal erection, as the normal tissue of the penis is replaced by fibrous tissue on one side only.

It may be caused by an injury to the penis, narrowing of the artery to one side of the penis (commonly with poorly controlled diabetes or high cholesterol), abnormal nerve supply to the penis or, most frequently, for no known cause. Its incidence increases with age.

There is usually a hard piece of tissue at the base of the penis on the affected side, and ultrasound scans can show the abnormal fibrous tissue in the penis.

Unfortunately, treatment is not very effective. Surgery, steroid injections and even radiotherapy may be tried, but none of these procedures have a good track record.

The most radical, and most successful treatment, is surgical replacement of the contents of the penis with an inflatable bladder that can be pumped up when an erection is desired. Although complications can occur, 80% success is quoted in reputable centres.

Q   I am told my son has a hydro-seal! (sic). His testicle is swollen, but it sounds more like a plumber's term than a doctor's! Can you tell me if it is serious?

A   A hydrocele has nothing to do with fur-covered aquatic animals or leaking pipes, but is a collection of fluid around a testicle.

   If you injure your knee, it often becomes swollen with 'fluid on the knee'. The same can apply to the testicle, although injury is not always apparent. The fluid causes no harm to the testicle, but can cause discomfort. If it persists the fluid can be drained away by a needle. Unfortunately it often comes back again, and sometimes an operation is required to correct the problem.

Q   I have a very embarrassing problem. In the past month one of my testes has blown up to twice its normal size. It's not painful, but I'm terribly worried and embarrassed. What could it be?

A   The most likely cause of your problem is a hydrocele.

   The testes are surrounded by a fine layer of tissue called the tunica vaginalis. Fluid may accumulate between the testes and the tunica to cause an apparent swelling of the testicle that is often painless. They may occur at almost any age, and may follow an injury or infection in the scrotum, or may occur for no apparent reason.

   A needle can be used by a doctor to drain off the fluid, but it often reaccumulates after this and an operation is usually necessary to give a permanent cure.

   There are other cysts and growths that can occur in the scrotum, including cancer, which may not be painful. For this reason, any swelling of the testes, whether painful or not, must be checked by a doctor.

   Pain in the testes, particularly in a teenager, is a medical emergency.

Q   I have pain and tenderness in my left testicle that causes nausea when the testicle is bumped. The left testicle also hangs higher in the scrotum than the right. Should I be concerned?

A   As all members of the male gender know, and cricket players in particular, testicles are very sensitive structures that cause their owner considerable distress (including pain and nausea) if they are knocked or squeezed in any way. If one testicle is more sensitive or tender than the other, medical attention is necessary as the affected testicle may be infected, inflamed or (worst of all) starting to twist.

   A twisted (or torted) testicle is a very serious condition, as it can result in the blood supply to the testicle being cut off, and the organ dying.

   An infected testicle is uncommon, but can result in sterility if left untreated.

   On the other hand, it is completely normal for one testicle to hang slightly lower than the other.

Q   What is the normal size of the erect male penis? I am concerned that I may be quite inadequately endowed.

A   A lot of rubbish is spoken of about penis size in locker rooms and other areas where men congregate, but medical texts indicate that the average male erect penis is 12.9 cm in length, and 90% of men have an erect penis that is between 9 cm and 17 cm in length, measured along the top from the groin to the tip. The other 10% of men are evenly divided between longer and shorter. The longest medically recorded erect penis was 32 cm long, but this is as much of a freak as the man who is 270 cm (nine feet) tall. There is no direct correlation between height, or any other obvious physical attribute, and penis size.

Q   **I am a young man with a sensitive problem. I believe my penis is too small. Although I know this does not directly affect the function in sexual intercourse or reproduction, it has been an issue of embarrassment and self-image while growing up. Could you please advise me as to a treatment or technique that I could use to make my penis larger?**

A   As you correctly state, a small penis has no effect upon your ability to father children, and continued reassurance on this point may help you gain confidence in your 'manhood'.

The size of the penis varies from one person to another, in the same way that some people have big noses while others are small. There are no prizes for having the largest nose on the block, nor are there for the size of any other parts of your anatomy. The only people who will ever need to be aware of your problem are yourself and your wife or other sex partners.

The size of the penis does not determine whether a man is a good lover or not. Women appreciate the foreplay and fondling as much as the sex act itself, and if you can become skilled in the former, you will keep any woman happy. Even during intercourse, the most sensitive part of a woman's sexual organs are the clitoris, which is at the outside entrance to the vagina, and the so-called 'G spot' which is just inside, and on the front wall of the vagina, at a point where even the shortest penis can give stimulation.

As a last resort, if you really do want to compete with others in size, there is a plastic surgery technique available.

Do not underestimate your prowess, you will be able to satisfy the sexual appetite of any woman if you approach her in the right way.

Q   **I am 58 and I have had a constant embarrassment because of an underdeveloped penis and testicles. As a result, I have never married or indulged in sexual intercourse. Do you know of anyone who can help me?**

A   Small testicles and penis may function just as well as large ones, and may be merely a developmental problem, in the same way that some people are tall and others are short.

At your age, hormonal treatments are not likely to be successful, but you should be examined by a general practitioner to ensure that your testicles are not developing any sort of tumour, and that the hormonal balance in your body is correct.

When seeing your GP, I would suggest that you ask for a referral to a psychiatrist. This is not because I think you are mad or crazy in any way, but a psychiatrist may be able to help improve your self-esteem, and cope with a problem that has obviously preyed on your mind for several decades.

Provided your GP's check up shows no problems, there is no reason why you should not enjoy normal sexual relations, because you are certainly not too old for that. There are many lonely, older women who would love to have a caring partner.

As a last resort, and one I would not recommend without psychiatric counselling, you could see a plastic surgeon to have penile and testicular implants inserted. This is a radical procedure, and not without its problems.

Q My foreskin is too tight to be drawn back over the head of my penis during an erection. This makes intercourse uncomfortable for me. Do I need circumcision, and if so, what does this involve?

A It may be that you do need circumcision, as your problem may be eased by a minor procedure that can be done in cases such as yours that is far less radical than circumcision. Under local anaesthetic, a few small cuts can be made into the end of the foreskin to effectively increase its circumference, thus allowing it to retract easily over the head of the penis. Your general practitioner will need to refer you to a urologist for further assessment of your problem to decide what procedure is appropriate.

If circumcision is considered necessary, you will be admitted to hospital as a day patient, or possibly overnight. The operation is usually done under general anaesthetic. The foreskin is cut away, and the cut edges stitched to promote healing and prevent bleeding.

It will be painful to have an erection for a couple of weeks, but otherwise the discomfort is not serious. Normal sexual activity can usually be resumed after a month.

Q The problem I have is a curved penis. I am almost 18 and it curves about 3 cm to the left. I'm also uncircumcised. Can my problem be helped by a device or operation? I don't want to go out with girls as I don't want them to know my problem.

A It is not unusual for the erect penis to have some curve in it, and this rarely causes any problem.

Even with the degree of curvature you describe, you would still be able to have sex successfully, and I doubt that any girlfriend would be particularly concerned about the degree of curvature of your penis at that time—presumably she would be rather preoccupied.

The fact that you are not circumcised will have nothing to do with the curvature.

My advice would be to ignore the problem for the time being, but if you find after some sexual experimentation that it causes some discomfort, and you wish to take things further, ask your general practitioner to refer you to a urologist, who will examine you and decide if an operation is appropriate.

Q I am seventeen years old, and I was wondering if it is normal to have a bent penis, and if there is any way of straightening it?

A A slight sideways curve in the penis when it is erect is not unusual, and should not in any way interfere with normal sexual activity. A slight upward curve in the erect penis is totally normal. An injury to the penis may cause scarring on one side and a significant curve. This could be corrected by plastic surgery. Unless the curve is quite severe, all you require is a large dose of reassurance.

If you are still concerned, trace the outline of your penis on a piece of paper when it is erect. You can then take this to your own doctor to demonstrate to him the extent of the problem. Your doctor will not laugh at you, and you should not be embarrassed to discuss this further because doctors are used to dealing with very personal problems in a totally sincere and confidential manner.

Q **I have this very embarrassing problem. I am 18 years old and my left testicle is much smaller than the right. This is really starting to bother me. I don't have the courage to see a doctor personally about this but would like you to tell me what to do.**

A It is not unusual for there to be a difference in size between the testicles, but this is usually no more than 25%. If one testicle is markedly larger than the other, it is possible that one is too small or the other too large.

A small testicle can be a developmental abnormality caused by a poor blood supply to one testicle, or it can be caused by an injury to the testicle at a later time.

An over-large testicle is commonly caused by an accumulation of fluid in the sac that supports the testicle. This problem can be easily corrected by a small operation. A tumour in a testicle is another possibility.

A man can function sexually and father children quite successfully with only one testicle.

You should overcome your shyness and see a doctor so that the appropriate diagnosis can be made, and any necessary treatment undertaken. Doctors are very used to examining the most private parts of your anatomy, and will not cause you to be embarrassed. Just knowing what the problem is will make you feel a lot better.

Q **I have noticed a pale oval shaped patch on the foreskin of my penis that is slowly spreading. There are no other symptoms. What could it be?**

A The most likely explanation is that you have a fungal infection present on the skin of the penis. These are easily treated with antifungal creams available from your chemist without a prescription. If this does not settle the problem, you should see a doctor.

Any skin condition can affect the penis as well as any other part of your anatomy, and patches can be due to a wide range of conditions including psoriasis, reactive dermatitis and a number of rarer conditions. Venereal diseases do not normally start in this way.

Q **My teenage son recently had one of his testes removed because of torsion. Please warn parents about this dreadful disease!**

A A man's testes and a woman's ovaries both start life together inside the abdomen of a foetus. Just before birth, the testes start migrating through the wall of the lower abdomen to settle in the scrotum, while the ovaries remain behind in the abdomen to lie beside the womb.

As they migrate through the muscles, fat and fibrous tissue of the abdominal wall, the testes trail behind them the arteries, veins, nerves and sperm tube that connect them to the body and keep it nourished and healthy. These pass through a tube called the inguinal canal back into the abdomen.

Torsion of the testes is a medical emergency, and treatment delayed for more than 12 hours can have serious consequences.

If the testis, hanging from its network of veins, arteries and nerves, twists horizontally, these vital connections to the body may have undue pressure placed upon them, and the blood supply to the testicle can be cut off. The testis then dies unless the tubes are surgically untwisted.

The victim experiences pain, and the testes become red, swollen and tender.

This problem usually occurs in teenage boys, and is almost unknown over 30 years of age. Any such symptoms should result in immediately seeing a doctor.

Q   **I am an 80 year old male, and have a distressing complaint. I urinate far too much night and day, and cannot hold my urine, but must go to the toilet at once. I am otherwise in good health and don't smoke or drink. Hoping you may have a remedy for me.**

A   Unfortunately, as you become older, it is not only the muscles of the arms, legs and back that weaken. The muscle ring (sphincter) around the base of the bladder, that controls whether you pass urine or not, also weakens.

As the bladder fills up with urine, at the rate of about one millilitre per minute (depending on how much you drink), the pressure on the muscle sphincter also increases. In a young man this causes no problems, but in an older person with a weaker sphincter, the pressure from the increasing volume of urine rapidly becomes too much, and a sudden desire to pass urine develops.

You should not avoid drinking fluids throughout the day to prevent this problem, as this may cause dehydration and damage to other parts of the body, but if you have to go out for a few hours, restricting your fluid intake during and immediately before this time may give considerable relief.

There are no simple medications or surgical operations to help men with this problem, although your doctor may try using a drug called probanthine, which helps a small number of men. In women, an operation is available to give relief.

There are two devices available that can give control and confidence, although they sound rather horrendous. The first is a soft rubber clamp which can be placed across the base of the penis to prevent the escape of urine, and which is released as required. The second is a sheath of rubber (rather like a condom) which fits over the penis, but has a tube leading from the end to a bag that is strapped to the inside of the thigh to collect the urine.

Neither of these devices should be dismissed out of hand as they can easily be concealed under clothing, the user is barely aware of their presence, and they can give freedom to move more than a few metres from a toilet.

Q   **I have a number of small hard white lumps on my scrotum. I am concerned about these and would appreciate your advice.**

A   Sebaceous glands produce the oil that keeps the skin soft and supple. Because the skin of the scrotum is very loose, these glands tend to become prominent as small lumps. Elsewhere in the body the skin is firmer and elastic, and these glands are buried. Almost certainly your small lumps are sebaceous glands that have become blocked or damaged in some way so that they harden. This is a very common phenomenon that becomes more noticeable with age. Most men have these lumps and they are nothing to be concerned about unless they become infected, in which case they will be red, tender and painful.

Q   **My testicle bag keeps contracting. There is no pain, but it will not stop contracting day or night. I have seen 12 doctors and had one operation, but nothing helps. Could you give me some advice?**

A   The scrotum in males is the sac that holds the testicles. The testicles must be kept at exactly the right temperature in order to produce sperm and hormones properly. This temperature is slightly lower than normal body temperature, and this is why the testicles are slung outside the body in the scrotum.

A muscle in the scrotum, called the detrusser, contracts to make the scrotum smaller, or relaxes to make it larger. In cold weather, the detrusser contracts, brings the testicles closer to the body, and thus keeps them warm. In hot weather, the reverse occurs, with the detrusser relaxing to allow the scrotum to sag, and the testicles to move away from the body and keep cool.

I suspect that you are having spasms of the detrusser muscle, which are causing your scrotal contractions. These may be very difficult to stop, but a low dose of a muscle relaxant such as Valium may be tried.

Q   How effective are the operations to insert an inflatable prosthesis in the penis to overcome impotence in a 64 year old man?

A   This operation is the absolute last resort in the treatment of erectile failure in a man. It is necessary to start with investigations to find any cause of his impotence. These causes can be as diverse as diabetes, psychological problems, pituitary tumours, thyroid disease and alcoholism, as well as a host of less common problems.

Once a cause of impotence has been found, that should be dealt with, or if no specific cause can be found, other forms of treatment can be tried.

Other treatments include using a simple vacuum tube that 'sucks up' the penis, and a rubber ring around the base of the penis then keeps it erect.

Medications such as Viagra, and the injection into the penis known as Caverject, can also give a very effective erection in many impotent men.

If all else fails, and the man is keen to proceed, an operation to replace the internal organs of the penis with an inflatable balloon can be used. The overall results of this operation (which is quite expensive) are good, but as with all operations, there is always a small chance of failure or complications.

It is essential that all the pros and cons of such a procedure are discussed in detail with both a doctor who is not directly involved in the procedure (eg. your general practitioner) and the surgeon.

MEDICINES

See also ANTIBIOTICS

Q   Is it compulsory for a patient in the eyes of the doctor to take all medications prescribed? I've had open heart surgery and have been given Lanoxin and Warfarin. I've stopped seeing doctors, and stopped my tablets because I find the Warfarin difficult to tolerate, although I do miss the Lanoxin. I would value your reply.

A   Unless a patient is a certified inmate of a psychiatric hospital, it is not compulsory to take any medication, or undergo any procedure recommended by a doctor. On the other hand, any patient who does not follow a doctor's advice with regard to medication and operations should be well aware of any possible consequences. In your case, I would be very concerned for your future without these vital medications. The Lanoxin is designed to strengthen the heart and keep it beating regularly. The Warfarin will stop blood clots forming in the heart and major blood vessels.

Blood clots are a common problem after heart surgery, and may be fatal. Warfarin dosages must be monitored very carefully by regular blood tests, but not taking it, or using it without the close supervision of a doctor, is taking an enormous risk. Without the Lanoxin, your heart may fail, or start to beat irregularly, which could lead to very serious complications.

If you wish to take these risks, no-one can stop you, but there are members of your family and close friends who may be distressed by your premature demise. At least consider their feelings if not your own health. See your doctor today—tomorrow may be too late!

Q **While watching a health segment on television, I saw a report on a new drug in America for the treatment of obesity. I was wondering if there is any chance that this will be available in Australia soon?**

A From the time a new drug is announced for the treatment of any condition, there is usually a five to ten-year period during which it is extensively tested before being released to the general medical community. Many new drugs that are announced with great fanfare in the press never make it to the market because somewhere along the way it fails the stringent criteria that the licensing bodies have put in place to prevent any serious consequences or side effects of the drug.

Australia is often one of the last places in the world for any new medication to come on the market, as the criteria in place in Australia are particularly strict, and as we have a small population by world standards, many pharmaceutical companies are not interested in fulfilling these requirements until the new medication is established and profitable in larger markets.

Some new medications that are for critical conditions such as cancer and AIDS may be fast-tracked through the system, but an anti-obesity drug certainly does not fit into that category.

Rather than wait for something that may be of dubious benefit, I would suggest that you use the conventional (and cheaper) ways to lose weight—eat less and exercise more.

Q **I have had a lot of funny turns lately, and all my doctor has given me is aspirin. How can this help?**

A Aspirin acts to prevent blood clots. Many types of funny turns in elderly people are due to miniature strokes in the brain. These are not serious, but cause you to feel strange and act peculiarly at times. If they are allowed to continue, they sometimes lead to a full stroke.

All patients with these attacks should be thoroughly investigated to exclude any treatable disease before being started on aspirin. Aspirin in low doses has recently been found to prevent these mini-strokes, and often prevents large strokes too. Only one tablet a day is required, but it should be continued long term.

Q **Are aspirin and Panadol safe in pregnancy?**

A Generally speaking—yes. There has never been any evidence to link these medications with any form of birth defect.

Specifically, it is probably better not to use any medication in the first three months of pregnancy unless it is essential. Aspirin should be avoided in the last month of pregnancy because it reduces the ability of the blood to clot, and if you come into labour, it is possible for you to bleed more heavily if you have been taking aspirin. You can use Paracetamol (Panadol, Dymadon, Panamax, Tylenol etc.) quite safely in that last month for your backache and headaches.

Q What are dieureticks (sic)? My doctor has said that is what I am taking.

A Diuretics are tablets that remove excess fluid from the tissues by making the kidneys work harder. They are used in heart and kidney failure, high blood pressure and to relieve premenstrual tension. There are many different brands including Dyazide, Hydrene, Moduretic, Lasix and Navidrex.

They are available only on prescription and some types may cause loss of potassium from the body. For this reason, potassium tablets or mixtures, or diets high in potassium, are often prescribed with them.

If your doctor uses a term such as 'diuretics' that you do not understand, never feel embarrassed to ask him/her what it means. The more you know and understand, the better!

Q I have a fluid build-up in my tissues, which gives me a bloated appearance. I take one Navidrex tablet each morning and Plendil twice a day for high blood pressure. I never pass much fluid. What do you suggest?

A Plendil is an excellent medication for controlling high blood pressure, but it is well known to have swelling and bloating of the arms and legs as a side effect.

Navidrex is a mild fluid tablet, that removes excess fluid from the body.

You need to talk to your doctor about your problems, and s/he may consider restabilising you on a different combination of tablets to minimise your bloating while maintaining your blood pressure.

Q I have heard that people can get addicted to some drugs like tranquillisers that can bomb you out. My doctor wanted me to take some, but I said no. Was that the right thing to do?

A Tranquillisers reduce anxiety, stress and tension. Marriage breakups, loss of job, low income, troublesome children, illness and innumerable other causes of the multiple problems of modern society may necessitate their short-term use.

Tranquillisers include drugs such as Valium, Ativan, Xanax and Serepax. In their right place these are very useful drugs, and only if they are overused or abused do they cause problems. Many patients with short-term stress, muscle spasms or sleep disorders benefit greatly from their use.

They must be used strictly as directed, and the temptation to take extra doses should be resisted. They interact with alcohol, and may cause sedation. If you are taking or are prescribed medications in this group, discuss any fears you may have with your doctor.

Q I have glaucoma, and as well as eye drops I have been prescribed Diamox tablets. I have had pins and needles in my fingers since they started. What are the side effects of Diamox?

A   Glaucoma is an increase in the pressure of the jelly-like fluid inside the eyeball. If left untreated, it will result in blindness, but most patients can be successfully treated by a combination of eye drops and tablets.

Diamox is a medication that can be used to treat an extraordinarily wide range of diseases including glaucoma, epilepsy and heart failure. It is not a new drug, and a great deal is known about its actions and effects.

Most patients have minimal side effects, but some patients do experience the pins and needles in their fingers that you describe. Other side effects may include frequent passing of urine, loss of appetite, thirst, flushing and fatigue.

Many of these side effects will wear off as treatment is continued, or are minor nuisances rather than a significant problem. If your pins and needles are worrying you, discuss alternative treatments with your doctor.

Q   Could you tell me about Roaccutane? What effect does it have on the body and how safe is it?

A   Roaccutane is the most potent medication available for very severe cases of acne that do not respond to any other medication.

The prescription of Roaccutane is restricted to dermatologists only, and cannot be prescribed by your family doctor. The main reason for this restriction is that this drug will severely damage a foetus if it is given to a pregnant woman. It is therefore essential for any woman using the drug to totally abstain from sex while on treatment, and for some time afterwards, or be well established on a very reliable contraceptive.

The most common side effects of the drug are dry eyes, lips, nose and mouth. Others include muscle pains, thinning of the hair and changes in some liver enzymes and fat levels in the blood stream.

On the other hand, Roaccutane can result in dramatic improvements to the skin, and almost complete resolution of disfiguring acne.

No dermatologist will start this medication without trying every other form of treatment first, but if started, it will be for very good reasons.

Q   I am taking Endep and Epilim for the prevention of migraine, but I have found that I have put on a lot of weight since starting these medicines. Why is this so?

A   Many medications can cause you to gain weight, and a few can have weight loss as a side effect.

Weight gain is due to one of four effects:
— retention of fluid
— increasing appetite
— reducing the body's metabolic rate
— increasing the absorption of food from the intestine.

Normally a combination of two or more of these effects is responsible for a gain in weight, and if this is a problem for you, you should discuss the matter with your doctor, as alternative medications may be available.

Retention of fluid can be overcome by giving diuretics (fluid removal medication), but this is far from the ideal situation, as using one medication to remove the side effects of another is only appropriate if the first medication is absolutely essential. The second medication may also have side effects.

Increasing appetite can be controlled by a careful diet and watching when and what you eat.

The metabolic rate is the rate at which the body's basic functions (eg. heartbeat, intestinal activity, glandular secretions) operate. People with a very high metabolic rate burn fuel (food) at a very rapid rate, and can eat everything in sight without gaining weight. The reverse is also true, and if a medication has a side effect of reducing your metabolic rate, despite eating the same amount of food, your body will require less, and the excess will add weight to your frame.

Very few medications increase the uptake of food from the intestine, but smoking is notorious for reducing food absorption, which is why many smokers gain weight when they stop this socially unacceptable and unhealthy habit.

Q   I have been put on a medicine called Phenelzine by my doctor, and I am told I have to stay on a strict diet, and mustn't stop the tablets. Can you tell me something about these please?

A   Phenelzine (also known as Nardil) is a very effective medication for the treatment of depression and phobias (abnormal fears). It is not usually the first medication to be tried, but is used in patients who do not respond to other types of treatment.

The main reason for this is the reaction it has with a wide range of foods and medicines. These include cheese, liver, raisins, sour cream, fermented foods (eg. wine and beer), pickled foods (eg. herrings, cucumbers), broad beans, game meats, yeast-containing foods (eg. Vegemite, Bonox) and many cough mixtures and cold remedies. If combined with these substances, a severe and dangerous reaction can occur in the patient.

When used correctly, it is a perfectly safe form of treatment, but it must normally be used for many years, and should not be stopped without discussing the matter with a doctor. All doctors and dentists responsible for your care must know that you are on this medication, because reactions may also occur to anaesthetics and other prescribed drugs.

Q   My doctor has started me on a drug called Digoxin. What is this used for and does it have side effects?

A   Digoxin (also known as Lanoxin) is one of the oldest drugs still in current use by doctors. It is used to strengthen the action of the heart and reduce irregular heartbeats. It is particularly useful in older patients with a mild degree of heart failure, and in children with inborn heart irregularities. It is very safe, and has very few side effects, and there is no reason why it should not be taken for many years on end.

Doctors sometimes take regular blood tests to determine how much of the drug is entering the bloodstream, and usually check patients taking the medication every few months to ensure they are receiving an adequate dosage, and that the heart condition is not deteriorating.

Q   How good is Zovirax? At $150 for a course it should be brilliant! My doctor has suggested I use them for my cold sores, as I get them badly every couple of weeks.

A Zovirax tablets and similar medications are used to prevent and control attacks of genital herpes, shingles and cold sores. There is no other form of effective treatment available, but treatment MUST be started as soon as possible after the symptoms appear, and no later than three days after the start.

Cold sores are known to most people, and only very severe forms require the use of Zovirax tablets. Zovirax cream is also available, is cheap, and available without prescription, but must be used at the first sensation that a cold sore may be developing.

A course of Zovirax tablets will certainly shorten an acute attack of any of these diseases, and if taken regularly it prevents recurrences in most people.

The use of Zovirax, and other similar antivirals, is subsidised by the government when used for shingles and genital herpes, but not for cold sores.

Unfortunately, Zovirax is not a permanent cure for cold sores or genital herpes, and repeat courses are necessary for every attack.

Q **I have been taking Aldactone three times a day for 8 months for the reversal of excessive facial hair. It has been 75% successful, but my doctor says I must keep taking it to maintain the results. I am worried about any side effects, and I would rather not take any tablets, but am dubious about what would happen if I stop them. I would appreciate your opinion.**

A Aldactone (also known as Spironolactone) is a very effective drug in significantly reducing the amount of excess facial and body hair present on some women. It is very slow to have an effect, and should be taken for at least four months before any judgment on its effectiveness is made.

Quite high doses are also required, but as it is not a new drug, doctors understand a lot about its interactions, and have found it to be very safe in high doses for long periods of time.

After six to twelve months, it is usually possible to reduce the dose of Aldactone, and retain its beneficial effects, but if it is stopped altogether, the facial and body hair usually slowly returns.

Q **What are antihistamines? I see some cold remedies boast that they don't have them, but my doctor told me to get some for a cold. What is best?**

A Antihistamines are a group of drugs that control allergic reactions, dry up phlegm, stop itching, and relieve watery eyes. All can be purchased without a prescription. Most of them cause drowsiness to some extent, but this varies greatly from one person to another. This is why some preparations label their product to be free of antihistamine.

Non-sedating antihistamines are now available, but are more expensive than the older ones.

Alcohol must be avoided, and care taken if operating machinery or driving.

Q **I have been prescribed a variety of tablets for my arthritis over many years. I believe that these are all classed as anti-inflammatory drugs. I never like taking drugs, but they do seem to help me. I would still like to know what are the side effects of anti-inflammatory pills?**

A Anti-inflammatories are used in arthritis and injuries to muscle, bones and joints to reduce the amount of inflammation. Inflammation is not infection, but is the redness, swelling and pain associated with damage to any tissue.

Drugs in this group include Indocid, Brufen, Clinoril, Naprosyn, Orudis, Feldene and Voltaren amongst many others. They should always be taken with food as they can cause stomach problems in sensitive people. Newer versions such as Celebrex and Vioxx have far fewer side effects than the older preparations, and are just as effective.

If you develop abdominal discomfort while taking these drugs, stop the course of tablets and see your doctor immediately. They may also cause sedation, and care should be used in pregnancy.

Q **What is the Inderal my doctor has prescribed for me used for? I always like to know about my medication, and several friends have told me they are on this drug, but for different reasons. Your advice would be appreciated.**

A Inderal (also known as propranolol) is one of the most interesting drugs in the pharmacopoeia as it can be used for an amazingly wide range of conditions. It has been available for more than 25 years so a great deal is known and understood about the drug.

Its uses include treatment of high blood pressure, control of irregular heartbeats, control of an overactive thyroid gland, control of fine tremors, prevention of migraines, prevention of heart attacks, control of anxiety in actors and examination candidates, prevention of angina and use in several other rare diseases and conditions. It is quite incredible that one drug can do so much.

There are some people who should not use it though. They include asthmatics and diabetics, and in some forms of heart failure it must be used with caution.

Inderal is generally a very safe drug, and can be taken in very high doses if necessary. Side effects are uncommon but may include allergies, dizziness, nightmares, tiredness and impotence.

Q **Can people who have had stomach ulcers take aspirin? Can enteric-coated aspirin be used in these people?**

A Unfortunately it does not matter how you take aspirin, be it by tablet, in solution, coated with a substance that delays absorption (enteric-coated) or even as a rectal suppository. Once it is in the body, it may affect the balance between the acid in the stomach and the thick mucus that lines the stomach. The mucus protects the stomach from the concentrated hydrochloric acid that it contains, but if the production of mucus is reduced, or the mucus is less thick, the acid will penetrate through to the stomach wall and cause inflammation, pain and eventually an ulcer.

Many of the medications used to treat arthritis, including Indocid, Voltaren, Naprosyn, Brufen, Dolobid, Orudis, Feldene etc. act the same way as aspirin, and can affect the mucus lining of the stomach. Newer anti-arthritis medications such as Vioxx and Celebrex can sometimes be taken by some people with stomach ulcers.

The vast majority of people taking aspirin and anti-arthritis drugs suffer no side effects from them, but if you have a past history of stomach ulcers, it is wise to avoid these medications if at all possible. Paracetamol can be used as a substitute for aspirin, as it has no adverse effects on the stomach.

Q **As a 77 year old, my doctor has suggested that I take 100 mg of aspirin every day to reduce my risk of having a stroke or heart attack, but I have had a stomach ulcer in the past and take Zantac every day. I was told that I should never take aspirin again because of my ulcer. What should I do?**

A Aspirin is a marvellous medication, and one of the oldest in current medical use, having being first marketed by a German chemist (Bayer) in 1899. It may be used to relieve pain, reduce inflammation (eg. in arthritic joints), decrease the risk of bowel cancer and reduce the ability of blood to clot.

This last use makes it suitable to reduce the risk of blood clots in the brain (stroke) or coronary arteries (heart attack), and as a result it is widely recommended by doctors to be taken regularly by all patients over 50.

When used to relieve pain, aspirin is taken in doses of 600 mg (two tablets), four times a day, but when used to reduce blood clotting, only a very small dose of 75 to 100 mg a day is necessary, and strangely, higher doses may be less effective in reducing the risk of clots.

Aspirin also has side effects, most commonly resulting in stomach pain, and sometimes bleeding from the stomach, but this effect is dose dependent, and the higher the dose, the greater the risk of side effects.

Low-dose aspirin is available in special formulations that reduce, but do not entirely eliminate, the risk of stomach side effects. These are marketed as Astrix, Cartia and Cardiprin, and are subsidised by the government for pensioners under the pharmaceutical benefits scheme.

It is possible that you will suffer stomach side effects from taking low dose aspirin long term, and if this occurs there is a substitute medication (Plavix), that is much more expensive than aspirin, but it does not have some of the added benefits of aspirin (eg. against bowel cancer). It is only subsidised by the government under very stringent conditions.

Q **Are sleeping pills harmful?**

A Most sleeping pills are very safe, provided they are taken in the recommended manner, but if used constantly for many weeks or months, patients may find it very difficult to stop them as they become dependent upon them. The greatest problem with the use of sleeping pills is that they are taken unnecessarily, particularly by elderly people who do not need large amounts of sleep. These pills are better taken intermittently when really needed, and they will work far more effectively.

Q **What is the difference between a decongestant and an expectorant? I find these medical terms very confusing.**

A A decongestant is designed to unplug the phlegm that is blocking the nose, sinuses and throat of someone with a cold or flu. It will contain drugs that prevent the formation of phlegm, liquefy the phlegm that is produced, and shrink down the lining of the nose and sinuses. Some also contain painkillers.

An expectorant is designed to remove the excess secretions that have accumulated in the lung. Someone with tightness in the chest and a productive cough would be helped by an expectorant, as the drugs it contains will open up the airways, liquefy the phlegm and assist effective coughing.

Many brands of both types of medication are available without prescription from chemists.

Q **Eight years ago, a blood test showed an excess of uric acid, and although I had no problems with gout or arthritis, my doctor put me on Zyloprim each day, saying failure to take the tablet could result in gout. A health shop proprietor said Zyloprim could actually cause problems if taken long term. Can you advise me?**

A High levels of uric acid in the blood stream can cause recurrent attacks of gout. Because of the severe pain associated with gout, these attacks are very obvious to the sufferer.

Uric acid has another more sinister effect on the kidneys. These can be slowly damaged, and unless kidney stones form, the presence of excessive levels of uric acid may not show up until the kidney starts to fail, and the patient presents with a totally different set of symptoms.

Zyloprim (also known as Progout and allopurinol) is a drug that lowers the amount of uric acid in the blood stream. It has been available for over 40 years, so a great deal is known about its side effects and complications. A very small number of patients do have long-term problems with its use, but the risks of using Zyloprim are far less than the risks of high uric acid levels.

Regular blood tests should be performed every year while you are taking the medication to check the level of uric acid, and the liver and kidney function. Some patients require only a low dose of Zyloprim to reduce their uric acid levels, and this can be judged by the blood test results. The drug is available in both 100 and 300 milligram sizes, so reduction of dosage in those patients who can be controlled more readily can be easily achieved.

Follow the advice of your doctor rather than a 'health' shop proprietor, whose advice may be biased by a desire to sell you his products.

Q **Can you tell me about a drug called Capoten that my doctor has prescribed for me?**

A Capoten (also known as captopril) is a quite modern drug that is widely and successfully used to treat high blood pressure and heart failure. Its only absolute contraindication is pregnancy, but it should be used with caution in patients with poor kidney function, and care must be used if the patient has a general anaesthetic.

It has few side effects, the most common ones a being a cough and light-headedness because the blood pressure has dropped too far. Anyone on treatment with blood pressure medication should be checked regularly by a doctor, and provided no problems are found, this medication can be used confidently for many years.

Q **I am a pensioner, but despite having to pay $3.30 for my medications, there are some that I will have to pay a lot more for. Why aren't all the medicines essential for a pensioner subsidised?**

A Every four months, the Commonwealth Department of Health forwards a book to all doctors and chemists in the country. This contains the list of medications that the Commonwealth Government will subsidise for pensioners. It also states how much of each medication may be given and how often it may be repeated. In many cases, the actual diseases for which the medication may be prescribed are also stated. For this reason, some medications may be provided for $3.30 to one patient, while the next has to pay a lot more for it because they have a different disease.

The list of Pharmaceutical Benefits covers the vast majority of essential medications required by the Australian community. Unfortunately, there will always be those whose condition cannot be catered for by the medications on the list. Doctors will then offer their patients medications that must be paid for.

The government is limited in the amount of money available to pay for these subsidised prescriptions, and allocates this money in the best way it can. This may sound rather like a propaganda exercise to defend the government policies, but I do have some sympathy for the dilemma faced by the bureaucrats because the demand for medical services and medications is almost limitless.

It would be unusual for a pensioner to pay extra for more than one or two prescriptions per year.

Q My wife has had a mastectomy for breast cancer. The doctor has prescribed Tamoxifen, which produces hot flushes and fevers. What are the risks if she stops taking the drug?

A Tamoxifen is a marvellous drug that has significantly improved the survival and cure rates for breast cancer in recent years. Cancers that were previously incurable have been cured with this drug, and it is now almost routine to use it for all cases of breast cancer.

Unfortunately, Tamoxifen does have side effects, some of which can be significantly more severe than those being suffered by your wife. The side effects must be weighed against the risks, but unless the side effects are very severe, I would strongly recommend that the Tamoxifen be continued as it will significantly improve the chances of totally curing the cancer.

The matter is one that is best discussed with the surgeon or oncologist who is caring for your wife, as individual circumstances and risks can vary very significantly.

Q My mother has been on Aldomet tablets for many years to control her blood pressure. Are there any adverse effects from taking this medication for such a long time? What would happen if she stopped them?

A Aldomet can best be described as 'an oldie but a goodie'.

Aldomet has been on the market in Australia for over 40 years. It was one of the first medications introduced that was really effective in controlling high blood pressure. Although not many people would be started on Aldomet today, there are thousands of patients who are still taking this medication after many years with no significant side effects.

There are no problems associated with taking Aldomet long term, but if your mother stopped them, her high blood pressure may return.

It is sometimes reasonable, with the cooperation of your general practitioner, to reduce the dosage of blood pressure medication slowly over several months to see if the blood pressure rises again. It may be that after all these years a lower dose is all that is necessary, or the medication may be ceased altogether. Do not do this without medical supervision, as sometimes the blood pressure can rise very rapidly and cause serious medical problems.

Q 35 years ago I was prescribed Stilboestrol to reduce the risk of miscarriage. I understand there may be side effects from this treatment that affect the daughters of those mothers who took the drug. What are these side effects?

A There is evidence that the daughters of women who were treated some decades ago with Stilboestrol are at a higher risk of developing cancer of the endometrium (lining of the uterus) than the average woman in the community.

Women in this situation should advise their general practitioner of the circumstances, so that additional screening tests can be performed, and the woman can be advised of additional risk factors.

Mothers should certainly inform their daughters if they have been given Stilboestrol in these circumstances. The use of this medication in women has ceased now, and has been minimal for the last 20 years.

The earliest symptoms of endometrial cancer are irregular and heavy menstrual bleeding.

Q After successfully taking Aldactone for nine months to treat oedema and period problems I noticed a loss of hair from my scalp which has caused the development of two small bald patches. I have stopped the Aldactone, but the hair loss has continued. Is this a recognised side effect of Aldactone? How can I treat the bald patches?

A Scalp hair loss and baldness are not listed in the detailed literature supplied to doctors as recognised side effects of Aldactone (spironolactone).

There are many causes of alopecia areata (the technical term for bald spots on the scalp) that vary from anxiety and stress to anaemia and thyroid disease.

I would suggest that you ask your GP for a referral to a specialist physician or dermatologist so that any cause for the hair loss can be determined and appropriate treatment given.

Treatments could include potent steroid creams, steroid injections into the scalp, minoxidil lotion (Regaine), hormone tablets or surgery to the scalp.

Q I have been prescribed Xanax for post-traumatic stress. At the moment I would barely be sleeping at all if I were not taking it. Can you tell me which group of drugs Xanax falls into, can it cause addiction, and what are its side effects?

A Xanax is a benzodiazepine, and is very useful for the short term relief of stress and anxiety. If the problem is long term it is better to change to a medication that is designed to be used for months on end, as regular use of Xanax over this period of time may cause dependence, and make it difficult to relax or sleep normally when it is ceased.

Xanax does not cause addiction, which is far more serious than dependence, but it may cause drowsiness, loss of interest, depression and poor coordination if taken inappropriately. If you find that you cannot do without the medication, talk to your general practitioner about using a more appropriate drug.

Q What are tranquillisers? The chemist told me that the pills my doctor prescribed for my problem were this type of drug. Are they dangerous?

A   Serepax, Valium, Ativan, Murelax, Frisium, Xanax, Ducene. These are just a few of the trade names for the tranquillisers marketed in Australia by several pharmaceutical companies.

Tranquillisers, or anxiolytics (anti-anxiety drugs) are excellent medications if used correctly. Unfortunately, they have received bad press in recent years because of their abuse by a small number of patients.

Tranquillisers are designed to control the stress associated with short term crises in a person's life. Loss of job, death in the family, marriage problems, trouble at work, disobedient teenage children, financial shortfalls—the list of stresses experienced in modern life goes on and on.

If these problems are causing a patient to have sleepless nights, lose concentration, become tearful, temperamental or just feel that they can't cope, a course of tranquillisers over a few weeks can enable them to see their problems in a more reasonable light and work to overcome them.

Doctors are very much aware of prescribing these products correctly to avoid their long term potential for dependence.

Q My doctor has started my sister on Lithium. How safe is it and what is it used for?

A   Lithium is a medication used in a number of psychiatric conditions. It is very successful in treating many patients, but normally must be taken long term. It is a safe drug, provided it is not used by patients who suffer from heart or kidney disease, and it should not be used in pregnancy or while breast feeding. It is sensible for patients on this treatment to ensure that they take plenty of fluids, particularly in hot weather.

Most doctors do blood tests regularly to ensure that the patient is receiving the correct dose of Lithium, and your sister will need to be reviewed by her doctor on a regular basis while taking the drug.

Q Can you tell me about a drug called Sinemet? My husband has been taking it for years, and I don't know why.

A   This medication is used for only one purpose—the treatment of Parkinson's disease.

The tablet actually contains two medications, which work together to control the stiffness, tremor and mental deterioration that can accompany this disease. It is important to remember that there is no cure for Parkinson's disease, only control, so the tablets must be taken for long periods. If they are stopped, the symptoms of the disease may return, and a person who is well controlled may deteriorate rapidly. Unfortunately, the disease tends to worsen with time, so often the dosage of medication must be slowly increased, or other drugs added to maintain control.

It is a very safe drug, and there are no problems in using it long term. Any side effects are usually experienced in the first few weeks of treatment, and then subside.

If your husband ever sees a doctor or dentist for any treatment, he must make the practitioner aware that he is taking Sinemet, as it can interact with other medications, and can cause problems with general anaesthesia and some diseases.

Q **I was exposed to malaria-carrying mosquitoes for 20 years, and had many severe attacks of malaria. Is there any evidence that the anti-malaria medications can affect the eyesight?**

A Certain anti-malarial medications based on quinine, such as chloroquine, if used at high doses for long periods of time, can cause damage to the eyes in some people. The low doses used by most travellers cause no problems.

More sophisticated drugs are now used for the prevention of malaria, but for many years, quinine and its derivatives were the mainstay of prevention and treatment.

Quinine is now used by patients with severe rheumatoid arthritis, as it can act to control this disease as well. These patients are required to see an ophthalmologist (eye doctor) on a regular basis to detect any early signs of eye damage.

It is likely that some if not most of your attacks of malaria were treated by a quinine drug at high doses for some weeks or months.

You would be well advised to ask your general practitioner for a referral to an eye specialist to ensure that your eyes have not been affected by quinine.

Q **I have just been prescribed Sinequan. Is it a safe drug? What is it used for?**

A Sinequan (also known as doxepin) is a very safe drug if taken strictly as directed. You should not use any more tablets than instructed by your doctor.

The main side effects are a dry mouth and drowsiness. It should not be mixed with alcohol, and you should be careful if driving or operating machinery.

Sinequan is used primarily for the treatment of depression, but may be useful in insomnia, anxiety and other conditions. It is designed for long term use, and it may take two weeks or more after the treatment is started for the medication to become completely effective. The side-effects are more noticeable when the medication is first started, and wear off as time passes.

Q **I have been prescribed Serepax to help me cope with my divorce. What are the main side effects of Serepax? Are they addictive?**

A The main problems associated with Serepax and the other anti-anxiety drugs are drowsiness and slowed reflexes. These are usually due to a dosage that is too high, but it may just require a few days on treatment for the side-effects to subside. Care should be taken with driving and operating machinery on the first few days of any tranquilliser course. Alcohol will exacerbate the side-effects, and must be avoided.

The major problem is dependence, when too many tablets are taken for too long. This is different to addiction, where severe withdrawal symptoms occur if the drug is removed. Dependence is easier to deal with, but still requires the cooperation of doctor and patient to slowly reduce the dosage of the medication over many months.

If your doctor prescribes a course of tranquillisers for you, please don't throw up your hands in horror and refuse to take them. He or she will be doing this for good reason, and will be aware of both the problems requiring their use, and the problems that must be avoided by their use.

Q I have a daughter who takes Tegretol for nocturnal fits. She has only had three in three years, and they follow overwork and stress. Do these tablets cause any liver or kidney trouble, and if she did not take them and had more fits, would she get brain damage?

A Pseudo epilepsy is a term that is sometimes used to describe the type of stress-related fits that affect your daughter.

If the fits are always related to overwork and stress, it may be possible for her to take a medication on only those days when she feels that she may have a fit because of these factors. This would probably be more effective, and less annoying, than taking medication long term.

On the other hand, Tegretol is a very safe and effective medication for controlling and preventing many different types of fits, and there are no serious long term effects from taking this medication.

Brain damage from fits only occurs in rare situations if the fits are very prolonged, very frequent, and cause serious side effects. This is not the case with your daughter.

Discuss using intermittent medication, rather than constant medication, with your daughter's doctor.

Q My husband and I have taken Mucaine and Quickeze for many years for a hiatus hernia and reflux. With the scare about aluminium and Alzheimer's disease, I don't know if we should keep taking them. We need them despite being on Losec. Can you let me know if there is any proof that they are harmful?

A There is evidence that people with Alzheimer's disease have an increased level of aluminium in their brains, but there is no evidence that the aluminium causes the Alzheimer's disease. In fact, the reverse may be true, in that the Alzheimer's disease causes the increased levels of aluminium.

There is no reason why you should not continue to use Mucaine and Quick-eze in moderation to relieve your symptoms, but better still, you should discuss with your general practitioner using a higher dose of Losec, or an additional medication, to prevent your discomfort.

Losec is an extremely effective medication, but sometimes it is necessary to use a second medication in combination with it (eg. Tazac, Zantac—all of which require prescriptions) to add to its benefit, or to change to a different medication in the same group (eg. Zoton) to obtain greater benefit.

As a last resort, surgery can be performed to prevent acid from running back up from the stomach and causing the pain. The surgery is relatively major, but this may be a better solution than taking pills and mixtures for decades to come.

Q I have suffered episodes of constipation, flatulence, burping and a dry cough since taking a course of iron tablets. What can I do to correct this problem?

A Iron tablets are well known to cause constipation as a side effect. Other side effects include other forms of stomach discomfort and rarely tiredness, but it is generally well tolerated. I therefore suspect that many of your symptoms may have some other cause other than the iron tablets if the symptoms are continuing after finishing the course.

As the symptoms could be caused by any one of a number of diseases of the gut, it would be sensible to have a check up by your general practitioner. A bowel infection, problems in absorbing food, or a more sinister problem could be responsible.

MENOPAUSE
See also FEMALE PROBLEMS

Q **I am 50 years old and still taking the contraceptive pill. How will I know when I have my change of life?**

A It is possible for the periods to continue long after the menopause if you continue to take the contraceptive pill. There are two ways to find out whether you still need contraceptive cover.

(1) You can stop the pill, use alternative forms of birth control (eg. condoms), and see if the periods return in the next six months. During that time your doctor can take blood tests to assess your hormone status.

(2) These tests can be done while you are still on the pill, but they are less reliable and harder to interpret. Women over 40 who continue to take the pill should ensure that they are on the lowest possible dose, and should not smoke, as this will greatly increase the risk factors.

Q **As I get older I am scared about the problems of menopause. My mother had a terrible time and I have no desire to follow in her footsteps. Can the menopause be controlled?**

A. I find the biggest problem with the menopause is the failure of my patients to tell me exactly what they are feeling and what effects the menopause is having on them.

The first step in treating someone with menopausal symptoms is explanation.

The sex hormones are controlled by the brain, and are released from the ovaries into the bloodstream on regular signals from the pituitary gland, which sits underneath the centre of the brain.

Once in the blood, these hormones have an effect on every part of the body, but more particularly the uterus, vagina, breasts and pubic areas. It is these hormones that make the breasts grow in teenage girls, give you regular periods as their levels change during the month, and cause hair to grow in your groin and armpits.

For an unknown reason, once a woman reaches somewhere between the early forties and early fifties, the brain breaks rhythm in sending the messages to the ovaries. The signals become irregular and sometimes too strong, at other times too weak. The ovaries respond by putting out the sex hormones in varying levels, and this causes side effects for the owner of those ovaries. The periods become irregular, vary in length and intensity, and may become painful.

Other symptoms can include bloating and associated headaches and irritability as excess fluid collects in the brain, breasts and pelvis; hot flushes, when hormone surges rush through the bloodstream after excess amounts are released by the ovaries; abdominal cramps caused by spasms of the uterine muscles; and depression which can be a reaction to the changes in the body, a fear of ageing or a direct effect of the hormones on the brain.

Menopause cannot be cured, because it is a natural occurrence, but doctors can relieve most of the symptoms. Hormone tablets or patches are the mainstay of treatment. One hormone is taken for three weeks per month, and a different one is added in for the last 7 to 14 days. Minor symptoms can be controlled individually. Fluid tablets can help bloating and headaches, ane other agents can help uterine cramps and heavy bleeding. Depression can be treated with specific medications.

Q Should all women use hormones after menopause to prevent osteo-porosis?

A   Women should consider their options at the time of the menopause and discuss them with their doctor. Generally, all women should be on hormone replacement therapy (HRT) after the menopause, not only to prevent osteoporosis, but to also prevent heart disease, strokes, premature ageing of the skin, Alzheimer's disease and generally protect the body from ageing too quickly.

It always necessary to exclude any contra-indications to HRT, such as liver disease or blood clots.

If a woman is small boned and has a family history of osteoporosis, she has an increased risk of osteoporosis, and HRT is even more important.

The main problem most women complain of with HRT is the continuation of their periods beyond the normal time for their cessation. These periods are usually very light though, and often cease with time. Other side effects are usually related to an incorrect hormone dosage. They include headaches, depression, flushes and pelvic discomfort. As all women are different, finding the correct dosage can sometimes be a matter of trial and error.

Q I have had breast cancer and a total hysterectomy at a relatively early age. I am concerned about premature ageing but my doctor says I cannot take hormones. What can I do?

A   This is an extraordinarily difficult problem to deal with. Most women who have a total hysterectomy take oestrogen to prevent the problems of menopause, but if you have had breast cancer, most doctors believe that you should not use this hormone because it may result in a recurrence of the cancer. More recently, some doctors are using oestrogen in this situation as they argue that oestrogen does not cause breast cancer. I would suggest that you avoid oestrogen unless it is absolutely necessary to use it.

To prevent osteoporosis you should eat plenty of dairy products and take calcium tablets. The premature growth of facial hair can be controlled by a medication called spironolactone. Exercise is important to keep your body toned up as much as possible. A well-fitted bra and possibly plastic surgery may help the sagging breasts and can replace a breast removed for cancer. Skin moisturisers and plastic surgery can be used to control premature skin ageing in all parts of the body.

By being careful with your body and taking the appropriate medical advice there is no reason why anyone should place you in an older age group than you are, and you should live a full and normal life well into your 80s.

Q **I am 58 years old and recently started on hormone replacement therapy with Premarin tablets prescribed by my GP. Another GP I consulted for a second opinion is most alarmed that taking this drug alone will increase my risk of cancer. I am confused! Which GP is right?**

A Hormone replacement therapy is of great benefit to the majority of women who are menopausal, and there is sometimes a period of trial and error in getting the doses and balances of hormones just right.

In the majority of women, both an oestrogen (such as Premarin) and a progestogen (eg. Provera, Primolut) should be taken, as these are the two hormones that are normally present during your reproductive life.

If oestrogen is taken without progestogen, there is over stimulation of the tissue in the uterus (womb) which can increase the risk of cancer of the uterus. When the two are taken together, either cyclically (progestogen for only part of the month) or constantly (both hormones all the time) there is no increased risk of uterine cancer.

In a hysterectomy your uterus is removed, and so women who have had a hysterectomy cannot have an increased risk of cancer of the uterus, and these women only need to take the oestrogen. Progestogens are usually unnecessary.

If you have had a hysterectomy, the first GP was right (oestrogen only is necessary). If you have not had a hysterectomy, you should follow the advice of the second GP (take both oestrogen—Premarin, and progestogen).

Q **I heard recently that women who could not produce hormones naturally, either due to the change of life or after a total hysterectomy should have hormone replacement therapy to prevent osteoporosis. What is your opinion?**

A Women who have a total hysterectomy (removal of the womb and both ovaries) will age prematurely, and have an increased risk of osteoporosis, particularly if the surgery is performed at an early age. Unfortunately, the most common reason for a total (as opposed to sub-total) hysterectomy, is cancer in the area of the ovaries or womb.

Any hormones given to these women in the future may rarely cause a recurrence of their cancer. These women are therefore caught in a cleft stick, and will need to discuss their individual problems carefully with their gynaecologist. The treatment will depend on what type of cancer they had, where it was, how advanced it was, and how severe the symptoms caused by the lack of hormones.

Fortunately, most women who have a hysterectomy have a sub-total one, where at least one ovary is left behind. These women can be treated the same way as those who have never had any surgery.

Women who are going through the menopause and who are suffering from significant effects of this natural change can be helped by regular hormone supplements. This usually involves taking oestrogen either constantly or for three weeks a month, and those who have not had a hysterectomy will need a course of progesterone for ten days or so every month.

If the symptoms of the menopause are not severe, the family history should be checked, and if the patient's mother or grandmothers suffered from osteoporosis, again hormone supplementation is advisable. If there is no history of osteoporosis, and no significant effects from the menopause, hormone

MENOPAUSE

supplementation can still be beneficial by reducing the incidence of strokes and heart attacks, and improving skin tone and appearance.

Q   If you have a hysterectomy, do you still go through menopause?

A   In a hysterectomy, it is normal to remove the cervix, uterus (womb), both Fallopian tubes and sometimes one of the two ovaries. The remaining ovary will produce sufficient hormone, in most cases, to maintain the woman's normal sexual functions and prevent the menopause.

In due course, this remaining ovary will cease its production of female hormone, and the woman will develop the hot flushes, depression, irritability and headaches characteristic of the menopause. Because her uterus has been removed, she will not suffer from the heavy and irregular bleeding or the uterine cramps that can also occur with menopause.

If during the hysterectomy it is necessary to remove both ovaries because of disease, the woman will lose her female hormones instantly and go through a premature menopause. It is important for these women to take hormone supplements until they are in their early sixties to prevent premature ageing, bone weakness, facial hair, sagging breasts and the other unpleasant effects of the menopause.

Women who have had cancer of the ovaries that has resulted in both ovaries being removed may not be able to use hormone replacement, but should carefully discuss this option with their gynaecologist.

Q   I am 62 and on treatment for blood pressure. I am concerned about osteoporosis and heart disease and I am considering using the oestrogen patch. I finished my menopause 9 years ago. Are hormones going to help me now? What effect will it have on blood pressure?

A   Hormone replacement therapy (HRT) using oestrogen and progestogen is very beneficial to women during and after the menopause. If you have had your uterus removed in a hysterectomy, only the oestrogen hormone is required.

These female sex hormones not only relieve the symptoms of the menopause such as hot flushes, irritability, irregular bleeding, breast tenderness etc., but protect women against osteoporosis (weakening of the bones), hardening of the arteries and heart disease.

It is a treatment that I highly commend to all women, and may be taken until you are well into your seventies. There is absolutely no evidence that it will cause any increase in the incidence of breast cancer.

Your blood pressure may actually improve using HRT, but there is no guarantee of this. It will certainly not get worse or interact with your medication.

Both oestrogen and progestogen can be taken as a tablet, a stick-on patch that is replaced twice a week, or as an implant every three months. Oestrogen is also available as a vaginal cream that is used once or twice a week.

I strongly suggest that after further discussion with your general practitioner you commence hormone replacement therapy.

Q   I am in my fifties and would like to know the pros and cons of hormone replacement therapy. How should I take them and how safe are they? What do you think of vaginal oestrogen creams?

A   I personally recommend HRT to all my patients, unless there are specific reasons that they should not take hormones. Generally speaking, HRT has been a major advance in the health of women, who now outlive men by an average of more than seven years.

The points for and against hormone replacement therapy (HRT) are outlined as simply as possible in the following points.

PROS: • Prevents osteoporosis (thinning of bones) and fractures.
   • Slows the development of wrinkles and keeps the skin moist and more elastic.
   • Lubricates the vagina and enhances sexual pleasure.
   • Slows the sagging of breasts by maintaining breast tissue.
   • Relieves the hot flushes, depression, bloating and other symptoms of menopause.
   • Regulates irregular periods to make them milder and less painful.

CONS: • Menstrual periods may restart, or continue, for a year after HRT commenced.
   • May cause breast tenderness if dosage too high.
   • Nausea and belly cramps may occur.
   • Migraines may be aggravated.

Except under special circumstances, HRT should not be used in women who have had:

   • Cancer of the breast, uterus or cervix.
   • Hormonal mastitis (breast pain).
   • Endometriosis.
   • Blood clots (thromboses), liver disease or strokes.

Q   Why can't all women who have troubles with the menopause have hormone replacement therapy with oestrogen? Why can't they stay on treatment until they are 60, 70 or indefinitely?

A   The vast majority of women can take hormone replacement therapy with both an oestrogen and progestogen to overcome their problems. It is necessary to take both hormones to prevent some of the long-term complications of constant oestrogen use. Women who have had a hysterectomy need only take oestrogen.

There are a small number of women who should not use hormone replacement therapy, including those who have had breast or gynaecological cancer, blood clots or liver disease.

Most GPs are sympathetic to these women, who may suffer flooding, cramps, depression, flushes, headaches, irritability etc. etc. etc.!!!

There are a number of different types of oestrogen, and varying dosage regimes, and it sometimes takes a little trial and error to get the dosage just right for an individual woman.

Oestrogens also protect against osteoporosis, heart disease, dementia, skin ageing and improve the libido (sex drive) of older women.

There is a great deal of controversy about how long this treatment should continue, but there is no reason why they should not be continued beyond 70 years of age. Oestrogens are not a long term 'youth pill', but can certainly help women through a difficult period in their lives and prevent a lot of the complications of ageing.

Q I began menopause six months ago. I've been on HRT (hormone replacement therapy) but have a period just before or just after the tablets finish. The doctor said I need a curette and told me not to take the tablets because of a higher risk of cancer. However, I wish to continue taking them because I can't bear the hot flushes. What should I do?

A Any form of abnormal bleeding while on HRT needs to be investigated, and that is why your doctor is quite rightly showing concern.

Bleeding should occur each month just after finishing the hormone tablets. Some women are on constant hormone regimes and will not have any bleeding. Bleeding that occurs before the tablets finish each month is what will be concerning your doctor.

The chance of cancer or any other serious disease is very slight, but if it is present, it is far better to detect it early when it has a good chance of cure, rather than leave it until too late.

A curette will quickly diagnose any cancer and possibly cure other causes of abnormal bleeding. It is a simple procedure, requires only one day in hospital, and has minimal after effects.

Because HRT can aggravate an existing cancer (but it does not cause cancer) it is sensible to stop it until after the curette. You will only need to be off the HRT for a few weeks until the after the operation, and if all is clear, you can restart the HRT and control the annoying hot flushes again.

MOUTH and THROAT

See also NECK; NOSE and SINUSES; SMELL and TASTE; TEETH

Q What are cold sores? I get one every few months, and I hate them, because they look so ugly.

A Cold sores are caused by a virus.

About a quarter of the population is susceptible to this condition, while the rest of us are immune.

Once the virus is contracted, it settles in the tissue around the lips, nostrils and other areas of sensitive skin. At times when the body's resistance is lowered, the virus will start rapidly reproducing and an itchy, painful, blistery and later weeping sore will develop. Eventually this dries out and heals, but while in the blistery stage, the virus can be spread to other people in the community.

There are ointments that can be used (eg. Zovirax) in the very early stages of a cold sore to prevent it from developing further. Once the sore is established, only soothing and drying preparations can assist in healing the sore.

Tablets are available to prevent cold sores, but these are very expensive, available only on prescription, and must be taken all the time.

Q What causes a venous lake to appear on the lip? Can it be removed without leaving a scar?

A An injury from a blow, bite or burn may damage the lip tissue and allow blood to accumulate under the fine skin on the lip, or any other part of the body. They are caused by the rupture of a very small vein near the surface of the skin, while the skin over it remains intact. Blood leaks out of the vein and accumulates as a dark blue blob under the skin.

They are easily removed by bursting the venous lake with the tip of a needle that has been sterilised by holding it in a flame or soaking in antiseptic. The blood will rapidly come out through the hole made, and healing will occur very quickly, with no scarring, particularly on the lip, which is probably the best healing part of the whole body.

Q I am 82 years old and dribble saliva from the corner of my mouth all the time. This causes soreness and is embarrassing. What is the cause, and do I need to see a specialist?

A Unfortunately, as we grow older, our muscles and other tissues do not remain as trim, taut and terrific as they were in earlier years. This is very obvious in the face, where the jowls droop and the skin wrinkles.

We all produce saliva in our mouths constantly, but the flow increases at times when we eat or smell food.

The saliva is contained within the mouth by the tone of the muscles that circle around the mouth, and by the elasticity of the skin and other tissues. Excess saliva is normally swallowed every minute or two, and this actively aids digestion.

Elderly people frequently find that their tissues are less elastic and their muscles less taut, so that the normally produced saliva can escape from the corner of their mouth. If teeth have been lost, and the gums are worn down, it is easier for the saliva to escape from under the tongue to the area just inside the lips.

Plastic surgery would be a very radical solution to this problem, and is rarely performed. Medications that reduce the amount of saliva can be tried, but often leave the mouth feeling dry and uncomfortable.

Unfortunately, using a barrier cream at the corner of the mouth to protect the skin, and a tissue to dab away the excess saliva, is the most practical, if least aesthetic, way of managing the problem.

Q I keep getting mouth ulcers. What can I do to treat them?

A Mouth ulcers are caused by an imbalance between the normal bacteria, viruses and fungi in the mouth; by injuries to the mouth from false teeth or biting on hard food; infections of the mouth; and numerous less common diseases.

It is worthwhile having a check up by your doctor to see if there is some significant disease causing your recurrent mouth ulcers, but if no cause is found, it will mean using one of the innumerable mouth ulcer preparations available from chemists. All of these work to some extent, but it will be a matter of trial and error to find the preparation that suits you best. A combination of mouth wash and paints or pastes to put on the ulcer is probably the best form of management. Doctors can prescribe stronger preparations for resistant cases.

Q When I go for long runs to keep fit I get gum ulcers. These infections only occur a few days after a hard run. Can you explain this phenomenon for me?

A Mouth ulcers are commonly caused at times when you are stressed or run down, and excessive exercise is obviously the trigger in your case.

In your mouth, billions of bacteria, viruses and fungi live in your saliva. Digestive enzymes are also present in saliva, which is secreted from glands under your tongue and at the angle of your jaw. These organisms are meant to be present, and actually assist in the process of digestion.

If you have a cold, other infection, more serious disease, or are under emotional or physical stress, your body's immune system may be affected, as may the types of bacteria, viruses and fungi in your saliva. When these imbalances occur, instead of starting to digest your food as you chew it in your mouth, the various organisms and enzymes in the saliva start to digest the lining of your mouth to cause mouth ulcers.

The mouth ulcers can remain for days or weeks to cause discomfort and pain.

Q I have a recurring ulcer and lump inside my bottom lip that sometimes fills with blood. Should I get it checked?

A Any recurrent ulcer or lump anywhere on (or in) the body should be checked by a doctor. Quite often they will be found to be of no consequence, and a simple remedy will be prescribed, but occasionally the answer will be cancer.

Any cancer can be cured more easily if found early in its course rather than later, so asking a doctor to check a worrying spot such as yours soon after it develops may be life-saving.

Q What causes a dry mouth? I am always having to take a sip of water, and it gets very embarrassing.

A When you next visit your GP, tell him or her that you have xerostomia and see what sort of reaction you get—he or she will probably curse me for using the technical term for the annoying condition of a persistent dry mouth.

The most common cause for the problem is the side effects of drugs. These can be antihistamines, those used for treating depression, some blood pressure medications and a score more. People with fevers also have dry mouths, and some infections—particularly with a fungus—give the sensation of a dry mouth when it is really quite moist. A number of other rarer diseases may also be responsible, along with radiation therapy for cancer, but most patients find that a modification of their medication cures the problem.

Q I have have suffered from a continuously watery mouth since becoming pregnant with my baby girl, who is being breast fed and is now three months old. The excessive saliva is hard to swallow, and I end up with a sore throat. Please help, as I am tired of it.

A This is probably a hormonal effect caused by the higher levels of oestrogen during pregnancy and breast feeding. I suspect that when you eventually stop breast feeding the problem will settle, but unfortunately, in the meantime, any medication that your doctor could prescribe to dry up your excess saliva would probably have an adverse effect on your breast milk.

Take hope from the fact that it will only last a few months more, and in the meantime, soothing lozenges or gargles can be used for your sore throat.

Q I have a problem with my tongue. It has been very uncomfortable for 4 years. My doctors says it is covered in veins. What do you suggest?

A   Tongue pain and discomfort can be associated with many diseases. Many older people develop obvious veins on the tongue, but these are not normally the cause of any problems, and are barely noticed by the patient.

Pernicious anaemia and iron deficiency anaemia can both be associated with a sore, red, uncomfortable tongue. A fungal growth called thrush causes a sore tongue with a white coating. Dental problems can cause irritation and soreness of the tongue, and patients who are run down and affected by other diseases can develop persistent painful ulcers on the tongue. A hard, stiff tongue can be caused by a cancer within the tongue tissue, but this is a very rare disease.

You will need to return to your doctor for further assessment, and if s/he is unable to help you further, you should ask for a referral to an ear, nose and throat specialist.

Q   **What causes a white coating on the tongue? I find that I can scrape the coating off, but it returns soon afterwards. What can be done to overcome my problem?**

A   A white coating on the tongue may be caused by poor mouth hygiene, a fungal infection of the mouth (thrush), excessively fast reproduction of the surface cells of the tongue (leukoplakia), cancer of the tongue, and a disease called lichen planus. There are also a number of rarer causes.

Oral hygiene can be improved by using a mouthwash twice daily. These are readily available from chemists. In the initial stages, a very potent mouth wash made from hydrogen peroxide may bring rapid relief.

Thrush (a fungal infection of the mouth) can be cured by anti-fungal lozenges that can be prescribed by a doctor.

A steroid mouthwash or tablets (both on prescription) may be necessary to control a severe case of leukoplakia or lichen planus.

Cancer of the tongue is a serious condition, that is more common in pipe smokers. As you can scrape the coating off temporarily, this is unlikely to be the cause of your problem.

The treatment obviously depends upon the cause, and the correct diagnosis can only be made by your doctor.

Q   **I have had a terrible sore throat that has come and gone for weeks. It wakes me at night, and it hurts to swallow. Even moving my neck hurts. I have gargled with Milton, and wrapped socks around my neck at night. I am well over 80 and would appreciate your advice.**

A   You must see a doctor. A persistent sore throat may merely be a recurrent infection, or it may be something far more significant, particularly if you are a smoker.

There are many causes for pain in the throat including tonsillitis, quinsy, abscesses, foreign bodies (eg. fish bones), leukaemia, arthritis in the neck, and cancer.

Gargling with Milton (I don't know how you could stand the taste!) has probably killed every bacteria on the surface of your throat lining, but they may still be causing trouble in deeper tissue layers. A fish or chicken bone may have lodged in your throat, and not have caused trouble until some hours after the responsible meal. More serious causes can be dealt with by appropriate surgery, medication or irradiation.

Abandon the socks and Milton, and seek professional advice tomorrow.

Q   I have what can only be described at putrid breath. It is so embarrassing. I seem to have a permanent mouth full of peppermints or chewing gum to try and disguise it. I have tried everything without success. My mother had the same problem. What can I do?

A   There is a wide range of diseases that can cause bad breath, and all these must be investigated and excluded. Dental disease is the most likely problem, so see your dentist before a doctor. Infections in the cracks between teeth, and the crevices where the teeth leave the gums can cause a constant foul breath.

Chronic nasal and sinus infections are another common cause, as is smoking and lung infections or diseases. Generalised infections of any sort can cause bad breath (halitosis) for a few weeks or months. Rarer causes run into the hundreds, but include pharyngeal pouches (an outpocketing of the lower part of the throat, which contains rotting food, and may be a characteristic passed from mother to son), gut infections or diseases, liver or kidney failure, diabetes (another inheritable cause), a nasal disease called ozaena, salivary gland diseases, dehydration and dozens more.

Some medications, including lithium and griseofulvin (used for fungal infections) may cause bad breath.

See your GP again and again, and if you still have no success, ask him/her to refer you to both an ENT specialist and a general physician.

Q   My ten year old son has recurrent tonsillitis. Should he have his tonsils removed?

A   Possibly. An initial attack of tonsillitis, and a subsequent one, are usually treated with a short course of antibiotics. A third attack within a couple of months would normally result in a prolonged course of antibiotics. If there are more attacks beyond this, the child can be put on long-term antibiotics for many months, or have the tonsils removed. If tonsillitis develops despite the preventative antibiotics, tonsillectomy will almost certainly be required.

As a rule of thumb, five attacks of tonsillitis a year in a child should result in removal of the tonsils. If you are unsure, or in doubt, ask your GP to refer you to a specialist ear, nose and throat surgeon for his opinion. The operation is simple, safe and effective if carried out by experienced doctors in a recognised hospital, and can make an enormous difference to a child's general health.

Q   I am 19 years old and keep getting one or two attacks of tonsillitis every winter. I find it very embarrassing to tell my friends I'm off work because of this children's disease. What can I do to stop it?

A   As a general rule, two attacks a year for two years in an adult is sufficient reason to surgically remove the tonsils. Antibiotics can certainly cure nearly all acute attacks of tonsillitis, but you will still experience several days of severe throat pain, fever and misery before they can work.

I would suggest that you discuss the possibility of referral to an ear, nose and throat specialist with your general practitioner. The operation is quite simple in an adult, and you will only be in hospital for one or two days, and off work for a week. Once the tonsils are out, you can still get throat infections, but these should not be as bad as tonsillitis.

Q My GP has referred me to a specialist to have my son's tonsils removed, but I am not sure that I want him to have this operation. When should tonsils be removed?

A. The tonsils are glands, similar to those in your neck, armpit or groin, which lie in the throat on either side of the back of the tongue. They are made of lymphoid tissue which is responsible for producing antibodies to fight off infection. The tonsils are only one percent of the total body lymphoid tissue, so are not essential from this point of view. Tonsillectomy was a much more common operation in the pre-antibiotic era before World War 2, as tonsillitis without antibiotics was a severe disabling disease that could be life-threatening. Today the operation is still necessary under certain circumstances. These include:

- Five attacks of tonsillitis in 12 months in a child, or three a year in an adult.
- An attack of quinsy (the formation of an abscess under the tonsil).
- Obstruction of the airway or food passage by grossly enlarged tonsils.
- Tonsillitis complicated by middle ear infections on two occasions.
- Other rarer complications of tonsillitis.

Age is no barrier to the operation, provided the reasons are present, but it is unusual under 12 months of age and in the elderly.

Q My husband had his tonsils out at seven years of age. Recently he became very sick, and was told a tonsil had regrown and he had quinsy. Is this possible, as I have never heard that tonsils can regrow?

A When tonsils are removed, it is impossible for the surgeon to remove 100% of the tissue, as it is embedded into the side wall of the throat. Usually, 95% at least is removed, but it is possible for the remaining tiny amount of tonsil tissue to become repeatedly infected and slowly grow over many years.

Quinsy is the formation of an abscess in the side of the throat underneath an infected tonsil. Surgery is usually needed to drain away the pus, and any remnant of tonsil tissue can be removed at this time.

Q I've heard of infected tonsils, but is there such a thing as infected glands?

A What most people think of as glands are actually lymph nodes, which are collections of white blood cells. Lymph nodes are scattered throughout your body, but are concentrated around the neck, in the armpit and groin, and along the back of your belly. Their purpose it to remove infecting viruses and bacteria from the blood stream, and destroy them.

In this task, lymph nodes are spectacularly successful, as we are invaded by millions of germs every day, but only infrequently do we suffer from infection.

If a germ overwhelms the defence mechanisms contained within the white cells of a node, it may become infected. The patient will then suffer from tender, swollen lymph nodes, and a fever. This infection, if caused by a bacteria, can be cured by antibiotics. If caused by a virus (eg. glandular fever, mumps), time and rest are the only cures.

The tonsils are merely lymph nodes that protrude into the back of the throat. Because of their position in the main pathway taken by germs entering the body, they are more susceptible to infection than most lymph nodes.

Q **I have foul phlegm in the back of my mouth that I find very difficult to remove. It started after a bad bout of the flu a year ago. Telfast tablets from my doctor do not help. What can I do?**

A Cattarh is a very common and most annoying problem, and one that is difficult to treat. It may be due to a bacterial or viral infection, allergies and sometimes strange things such as stress and temperature changes can cause the excess production of phlegm.

The mainstay in treatment are the drugs in the antihistamine class. These are divided into broad spectrum antihistamines that have a side effect of sedation, and specific anti-allergy antihistamines that do not usually cause sedation. The non-sedating antihistamines are very specific for allergy reactions, and will not dry phlegm produced because of viral infections or other non-allergy causes.

There is a lot of variation in the way an individual reacts to an antihistamine. The drug that helps one person may not help another. If one does not work, then others should be tried.

All antihistamines are available over the counter from chemists without a prescription. Broad spectrum (sedating) antihistamines include Polaramine, Periactin, Zyrtec and Zadine; while specific anti-allergy antihistamines include Telfast and Claratyne.

Pseudoephedrine tablets or capsules (eg. Sudafed, Drixora) and a medication called Bisolvon, are also very useful in liquefying phlegm so that it clears away more rapidly.

A course of antibiotics will remove any bacterial infection, and if your phlegm is particularly foul, this may be appropriate. Otherwise gargles, inhalations and various nasal sprays may also be tried.

To dry up your persistent phlegm problem I would suggest using a course of Zyrtec tablets, which are the least sedating and most effective of the broad spectrum antihistamines.

Q **Tell readers about salivary stones. I have just been through the worst imaginable agony, and all people do is laugh at me—and it's not funny!**

A Under your tongue and in the side of your jaw you have salivary glands—three on each side of your mouth. These produce the saliva to keep your mouth moist and start the digestion of food. A small tube leads from each gland to open into the mouth under the tongue or at the back corner of the mouth. If the gland becomes infected or injured, or the saliva becomes too concentrated, a stone may form in the gland. This stone then moves along the duct towards the mouth, causing excruciating pain with every movement.

When you see, smell or taste food you automatically salivate. In patients with a salivary stone this salivation causes pain because the pressure of saliva behind the stone moves it in the delicate duct.

These patients require urgent treatment to temporarily dry up their saliva and ease the pain. Surgery is often necessary to remove the stone and relieve the condition. It is certainly no laughing matter, but one that is fortunately fairly uncommon.

Q **At 84 years of age, I am having trouble swallowing and have a dry throat. What could cause this?**

A The first thing that springs to mind in an older person is that the dryness is causing the difficulty in swallowing, and that side effects from medicine you are taking is causing the dryness. You should ask your doctor to review your medication to determine whether it may be responsible for your problems.

There are, of course, dozens of medical reasons for both a dry throat and difficulty in swallowing, and only appropriate investigation and examination will determine if any of these are present.

Possible causes can include fungal or bacterial infections of the throat, ulcers, allergies, tumours, anaemia, liver failure, excess alcohol, several different syndromes and a number of rarer diseases. Stress and anxiety can also cause a dry mouth and difficulty in swallowing in a condition known as globus.

A dry mouth is far more common in older people than younger ones, merely because the salivary glands are not working as well as they used to. Frequent sips of water and having a sips of a drink with your meal is the simplest way to overcome this problem.

Q **I find that I am always hiccupping when I am nervous or anxious. What causes hiccups and how can they be cured?**

A The diaphragm is a sheet of muscle that stretches across the body to separate the chest from the abdomen. It has holes in it to allow the major blood vessels and the gullet (oesophagus) to pass through.

Hiccoughs are due to spasms of the diaphragm. When it contracts, a small amount of air is suddenly forced out of the lungs, causing the characteristic sound. The diaphragm goes into spasm because it, or the nerve that controls it, becomes irritated.

If you swallow large chunks of food, swallow quickly, or overfill the stomach (by overeating, or swallowing air when nervous), it causes pressure on the diaphragm, and therefore irritation. The cure for the condition is to cause a counter-irritation or relieve the pressure.

Drinking water may remove a piece of food lodged in the oesophagus. Holding a deep breath causes counter pressure on the diaphragm. A fright can cause a sudden generalised muscular spasm. Burping can relieve pressure too. Most of the well-known remedies work this way.

In the rare cases where the hiccoughs are prolonged, medications can be given to relax the diaphragm muscle.

MUSCLES, TENDONS, LIGAMENTS

Q **What is the best treatment for tendonitis?**

A Tendons are the ropes of the body. They connect a muscle to a bone, so that when a muscle contracts, the bone is pulled by the tendon. Whenever you see the suffix '—itis' after a word, it means inflammation. Thus appendicitis is an inflamed appendix, and tonsillitis is an inflamed tonsil. Tendonitis is inflammation of a tendon due to injury or overuse. If you start at a new job, sport or hobby, it is possible to use tendons (and muscles) that cannot stand the new type of repetitive strain. This will result in inflammation and pain in the tendon. It may also be caused by one sudden over-stretching injury of the tendon.

The primary treatment is rest. The affected part may be strapped, bandaged or even plastered to ensure adequate rest of the tendon. Anti-inflammatory medicines may also be used along with physiotherapy. Physio is particularly valuable on return to work to prevent a recurrence of the problem. In severe or chronic cases, injections of steroids may be given, but these cannot be repeated too frequently.

Q What is tenosynovitis, and how is it treated?

A Tendons run inside a fibrous sheath in many parts of the body, particularly the hands and feet. Between the sheath and the tendon is a very thin film of lubricating oil called synovial fluid.

Tenosynovitis is an inflammation of the sheath around a tendon, and usually occurs due to overuse or injury. Treatments include heat, anti-inflammatory tablets, physiotherapy, immobilisation in a splint, injection of steroids, and as a last resort, an operation to remove the sheath.

Q How long do torn ligaments take to heal?

A There is no easy answer to this because it depends on how badly torn the ligament is, and which ligament is involved. If a ligament is completely torn through, it will sometimes need to be surgically repaired but always immobilised in plaster.

A partly torn ligament will heal with rest, and immobilisation in a firm bandage or a plaster cast for a few weeks. A ligament that is strained (stretched but not torn) will settle in a few days to a couple of weeks with adequate rest.

The basic rule is to rest the injured joint until all pain has gone and for a week afterwards. Any exercise that causes pain should be avoided. The well intentioned advice of some sport coaches to work through the pain of a sprain or strain is not correct.

Q I have calcific tendonitis of my shoulder that was very painful initially, but has settled to pain when lifting my arm above my shoulder. I have been told there is no treatment. Will it ever go away?

A If the tendons that run across the top of your shoulder are repeatedly overused or strained, they are damaged and develop small areas of hard callus (calcification). These areas can prevent the tendons from sliding smoothly as the shoulder moves, and pain results.

The tendons usually affected are those that move the arm away from the side of the body and up to horizontal.

The problem often subsides slowly over several months or years, but may give some trouble almost permanently.

The treatments available are anti-inflammatory medicines, physiotherapy, steroid injections, and as a very last resort, an operation to remove the lump in the tendon. If your general practitioner is unable to help you, request a referral to an orthopaedic surgeon.

Q I have frequent painful cramping spasms in my right foot and right hand. Is this arthritis? I am 67.

A   Muscle cramps in the small muscles of the hand and foot are not due to arthritis, but may be caused by poor circulation of blood to the extremities, excessive exercise and overuse of the muscles, compression of nerves in the arm, leg or back, a lack of thyroid hormone, a lack of salt in the blood and as a side effect of some medications (eg. fluid tablets).

You should see your doctor to have tests done to see if there is any significant cause for the problem that can be corrected.

Q   **I am worried that a relative in her late 60s may have progressive muscular atrophy. What are its initial symptoms and how do you diagnose it? Is there any treatment available? How should she cope with the disease?**

A   There are several different types of muscle wasting that may occur in older people. These vary from the mild wasting that is associated with ageing to serious conditions such a dermatomyositis (where a rash accompanies the muscle wasting), polymyositis (multiple bundles of muscles that weaken), and inclusion body myositis (progressive weakness of the arms and legs). Very rarely does the weakness affect the chest, heart or abdomen.

These disorders can only be diagnosed by a combination of clinical examination, blood tests, measurement of muscle electrical activity (electromyelogram—EMG) and biopsy (surgical sampling) of an affected muscle.

Once the exact diagnosis is determined, specific treatment can be given in some cases, but unfortunately, in many cases, there is no treatment available, and the condition is slowly progressive over many years.

Physiotherapy to strengthen the remaining muscle function may be helpful in some cases, but encouraging your friend to remain as active as possible is probably the main treatment.

Q   **I have been told that my aches and pains are due to polymyalgia rheumatica. Can you tell me more about this disease?**

A   Polymyalgia rheumatica (PMR for short) is thought to be a post-viral syndrome in that it usually commences after a bad cold, flu or other viral infection.

The patient is weak and has muscular pains that vary from one limb to another over days or weeks. He or she is usually irritable, unable to concentrate and depressed. Good days and weeks will alternate with bad periods. The disease may last for many months, and then recur after it appears to be cured.

Its exact cause is unknown, but blood tests indicate a generalised inflammation of the body tissues. Other symptoms can include nausea, headache and loss of appetite. The only treatments available are pain killers, anti-inflammatory drugs and steroids. Steroids are very effective in relieving the symptoms.

Eventually recovery occurs, but the sufferer may have had many days off work and considerable discomfort in the meantime.

Q   **My doctor wants me to take cortisone for my polymyalgia rheumatica. Is this safe?**

A   Polymyalgia rheumatica is a most distressing condition, but not serious or fatal. It involves inflammation of the muscles and can attack any muscle group at random.

The treatment involves heat, painkillers and anti-inflammatory medications. If these are not successful, steroids can be used. These are potent drugs that reduce the swelling, pain and tenderness associated with many diseases. They may have serious side effects, but if taken strictly as directed they are unlikely to do any harm. It is probably better to have your condition settled by steroids rather than suffer for many weeks to come.

Q Can you tell me about the serious muscle meltdown condition that marathon runners sometimes get.

A Rhabdomyolysis is the disease you are talking about. It is a form of muscle destruction caused by massive overuse.

In conditions of extreme exertion, when a muscle is forced to work despite an inadequate blood supply of oxygen and energy, the muscle will briefly use its own material as an energy source and destroy itself.

The athlete suddenly collapses during extreme exertion and is unable to use the affected muscles, which become excruciatingly painful.

There is no treatment available as the muscle is permanently damaged and is replaced by scar tissue or fat.

Q What can cause muscle stiffness? I am elderly and it is not due to overuse.

A You do not give me any further clues about your symptoms, so I will run through all the possible causes of this problem.

Nerves run from the brain down the spinal cord to connect with a nerve to a muscle at the point where the nerves leave the spinal cord between each vertebra in the back. If the nerve from the brain is damaged by an injury, tumour, abscess or other disease (an upper motor neurone lesion), the brain will be unable to control the contraction and relaxation of the muscle, and it will go into a mild spasm to become stiffer and more rigid.

Damage by an injury, stroke, tumour, abscess or infection to the parts of the brain that control muscle movement will have the same effect as an upper motor neurone lesion.

Parkinson's disease is caused by degeneration of part of the brain that coordinates muscle movement. The usual symptoms are tremor, shuffling walk and increased muscle stiffness.

Steele-Richardson-Olszewski syndrome is a variation of Parkinson's disease that usually affects elderly women, and is characterised by muscle rigidity in the back, chest and belly; dementia; difficulty in swallowing; inability to look downwards; and frequent falls.

Multiple sclerosis is a nerve disease that can affect any nerve in the body in a random and intermittent way. The covering (myelin sheath) of the nerve degenerates and it ceases to function. The myelin sheath may then regenerate to allow nerve function to return, but then another nerve is affected. Abnormal signals reaching muscles through the damaged nerves may result in rigidity. Treatment is very difficult.

There are numerous rarer possibilities, including an underactive thyroid gland, the neuroleptic-malignant syndrome (usually a side effect of the excessive use of tranquillising medication in psychiatric conditions) and the Shy-Drager syndrome (a form of progressive brain degeneration).

The bottom line is that you should have your muscle stiffness assessed by a doctor to determine its correct cause.

NAILS

Q My life is a misery because of constantly ingrowing toenails. What can I do?

A It is often the small problems that can cause significant disability, discomfort, inconvenience and pain. An ingrown toenail may involve only a small corner of your big toe, but it can totally disable you. Almost invariably, it is the big toe that is involved, but the smaller toes can occasionally develop the problem.

Ingrown toe nails are caused by tight shoes (particularly those with high heels), tearing nails rather than cutting them, and poor foot care and hygiene. If the corner of the nail is not allowed to grow outside the flesh of the toe, tearing and damaging the nails may lead to the formation of a spicule of nail that will steadily grow into the tissue, causing severe pain and eventually an infection.

Obviously, prevention is better than cure, and correct foot care, with particular emphasis on careful nail cutting and properly fitted shoes should prevent most cases of ingrown nails. Treatment will depend on the severity of the condition, and the degree of infection present. Pulling back the proud flesh that overgrows the ingrown nail and inserting antiseptic, antibiotic or antifungal creams and lotions may be all that is necessary in early stages. Antibiotic tablets may be necessary in more severe cases, and carefully cutting a wedge from the centre of the nail seems to relieve the pressure at the sides.

Severe or recurrent cases will require a more long-lasting surgical procedure. Several of these are available, but the most common involves cutting away the edge of the nail and the proud flesh over the ingrown part of the nail, as well as removing part of the nail bed, in a procedure known as a wedge resection. This is normally done under local anaesthetic by your own general practitioner or a surgeon.

Q I have had an ongoing problem with an ingrown toenail for ten years. The nail has been removed twice, and despite having both sides of the nail bed removed by a podiatrist, the nail is still growing back and getting infected. I have heard that laser surgery will help this problem. Do you know where I can obtain this treatment?

A Lasers are a substitute for a scalpel, and are used to cut through flesh, while at the same time searing the flesh to prevent it from bleeding. In most cases they are of more assistance to the surgeon, by preventing bleeding, than they are to the patient.

Removing both sides of the nail bed (Zadek's procedure) should cure the problem if it is carried out correctly, but if even a small amount of nail bed is left behind, the problem would recur, often worse than before, because the nail will be deformed.

You need to have a radical Zadek's procedure performed so that the nail bed at both sides of the nail is totally, completely and utterly removed, thereby permanently narrowing the nail by about half its width. This procedure is very well performed with a scalpel rather than a laser, will prevent the nail from growing into the adjacent flesh, and can be done by some general practitioners and orthopaedic surgeons.

Q **What causes ridges in your nails? Mine look horrible, and even with nail polish on, the ridges show through. They make my hands look far older than the rest of me.**

A Lengthwise ridges of the nails are common in elderly people, but can also occur with poor circulation to the fingers.

A single lengthwise ridge may be due to a cyst or growth in the nail bed.

Crosswise ridges are due to eczema of the fingers, recurrent nail bed infections, chronically wet nails (eg. a dishwasher, laundry worker), and the habit of pulling back the quick at the base of the nails.

A single crosswise ridge is called a Beau's line, and occurs after an episode of severe physical or emotional illness.

Depending on the type of ridges you have, treatment may or may not be possible.

Q **I have a horrible looking black/green growth under one of my toenails. What is it?**

A Probably a fungus.

Fungi are microscopic algae (or mushrooms) and they like warm, damp places on the body. People who put their hands frequently in warm water (eg. dishwashing) can develop fungal infections under the nails. The growth slowly spreads back into the finger, lifting the nail off the nail bed. There is usually no pain, but the patient complains of the horrible appearance of the nail, which may be white, yellow, brown, black or green depending on the type of fungus causing the disease.

There are several methods of treatment. The nail over the infection normally can be cut away to allow antifungal creams or lotions to reach the infection. Tablets (Griseofulvin) have been available for many years to kill the fungus, but these may cause liver problems, and must be used for many months.

In 1993 a new tablet (Lamisil) was introduced. This cures the vast majority of fungal infections under nails in a few weeks with minimal side effects, but tests must be done to prove that the nail has a fungal infection before this expensive medication can be prescribed under the Pharmaceutical Benefits Scheme.

There is also a nail lacquer (Loceryl) that can be applied to the nail weekly, and penetrates through the nail to kill the fungus. This is expensive though, and slow to work.

Until the introduction of Lamisil and Loceryl, these infections were notoriously difficult to treat. Even today, the sooner treatment is started, the easier it is to cure, so see your doctor today.

Q **My toenails are thick, brown, scaly and ugly. I can't wear sandals or thongs, or go barefoot without people looking at me and feeling revolted. What can I do?**

A Onychogryphosis. Try saying it three times quickly! This is the medical term used to describe your condition. It may be caused by a chronic fungal infection, poor circulation, tight shoes, injury, old age, psoriasis and numerous less common conditions.

Treatment used to be extraordinarily difficult and involved prolonged and often ineffective medical treatment, or removal of nails, which often grew back just as badly deformed as before. Now we have some very effective medication that can cure the problem in three months, but only if it can be proved to be caused by a fungal infection.

Go to your general practitioner and s/he will take clippings and scrapings from your affected nails and have them tested to see if a particular fungus is present. If the test is positive, a tablet called Lamisil can be prescribed to be taken for three months. This has a 90%+ cure rate, but the tablets are extremely expensive, and the government will only subsidise the prescription under the Pharmaceutical Benefits Scheme if the presence of a fungal infection is proved.

Q I wish to inquire why my fingernails are so extremely soft, and keep breaking off, flaking and splitting. Will my bones be similarly affected? Could diet be the problem?

A Fortunately for you, there is no direct link between most cases of nail softening and bone softening (osteoporosis). If you had a severe lack of calcium in your diet, which is very unusual in Australia, it is possible that you could have a rare condition called osteomalacia in which osteoporosis and soft nails occur, but it is far more likely that your nail problems are due to your choice in parents, and hormones.

Soft nails are usually caused by a genetic tendency, changes in sex hormone levels at menopause, alcoholism and sometimes persistent infections of the nail bed by a fungus or bacteria.

A diet high in calcium is always a good idea, and may help your problem slightly, but nail-hardening lacquer is probably your best treatment. The fact that so many nail-hardening products are available in the chemist and beauty shops will give you some idea of how common this problem has become.

Q I have had a greyish blister just behind my fingernail for six months. When I nicked it, I got out a clear jelly substance. It is now sore, and X-rays and blood tests for gout are negative. What could it be?

A Without seeing your finger, it is obviously difficult to make a definitive diagnosis, but you may have a mucous cyst of the nail bed. These cysts cause a lengthwise ridge in the nail, and often contain a grey coloured jelly. They are quite harmless, but may be disfiguring.

If your general practitioner is unable to help you, you should ask him/her for a referral to an orthopaedic specialist so that the condition can be appropriately diagnosed and treated.

If your problem is a mucous cyst, it can be cured by an operation under local anaesthetic, in which the cyst is scraped out, and the skin and nail bed allowed to heal slowly across the defect.

Q I am told that black splinter-like longitudinal markings under my finger-nails signify dire and dreadful things. Is this so?

A There are a number of significant conditions that can cause these splinter-like black lines under your fingernails, but by far the most common cause is repetitive minor injuries to the nails.

Other causes include skin conditions such as eczema and psoriasis, fungal infections of the nail bed, rheumatoid arthritis, bleeding disorders and, most seriously, a rare type of heart infection.

If these marks are something that you cannot easily account for, it is worthwhile having a comprehensive check-up by your general practitioner.

NECK

See also ARTHRITIS; BACK; MOUTH and THROAT

Q My doctor keeps feeling my son's neck for glands every time I take him for a cold or sore throat. He prescribes antibiotics if the glands are tender. Why do your glands get sore when you have an infection?

A If you have an infected cut on a finger, the bacteria can enter the lymph ducts, and slowly move along them towards the vital organs of the body. The neck glands are not really glands at all (glands secrete hormones) but are correctly called lymph nodes.

The lymph nodes act as filters along the lymph ducts, removing unwanted bacteria and viruses from the lymphatic fluid, and preventing them from progressing further. This filtering process is occurring every second of every day, but in the process of collecting and destroying germs, the lymph nodes are occasionally overwhelmed by the vast numbers of bacteria or viruses, and themselves become hot, red, sore, enlarged and infected. Some germs can then get past the nodes, and cause the fevers and muscular pains associated with a generalised infection.

Without the vital lymph nodes and their vast numbers of white cells that can engulf and destroy bacteria and viruses, severe body infections would be a regular occurrence rather than an occasional nuisance.

Once lymph nodes become infected by a bacteria, antibiotics are required to assist the body in the fight against them. If treated promptly, the nodes will soon return to normal, but delay may result in an abscess forming in the node.

After a severe infection, some nodes may remain as hard lumps due to the scar tissue within them caused by the overwhelming infection. These painless lumps may take months or years to disappear.

Q I have a lump on the side of my neck that seems to go up and down, and every time it goes up it causes headaches and a general feeling of being unwell. My specialist wants to remove it, but says I will be left with a sizeable scar that cannot be avoided. Aren't there more advanced techniques such as plastic surgery that can minimise the scarring?

A A neck lump that increases in size when you are unwell and decreases when you feel better is almost certainly a lymph node. Removing it may well remove a source of chronic infection, and therefore cure the problem.

Whenever any operation is performed, a scar must remain behind. Some areas of the body heal poorly (eg. the back) and a bad scar is inevitable. Other areas heal very well (eg. the face), and scarring is usually minimal. The part of your body being cut is far more important than the surgeon in determining the type of scar you will develop.

Plastic surgeons are not able to perform miracles. They have techniques that will minimise scarring, but most general surgeons are aware of these techniques also. Making the initial cut along the natural skin folds of the body, using fine stitches, using stitches under the skin rather than through the skin, and removing the stitches at just the right time are some of the tricks of the trade.

There would be no benefit from having a plastic surgeon perform your operation, as I suspect your scar will be far less noticeable than you expect. The neck is an area of the body that heals quite well, but if the scar does worry you six months or more after the operation, a plastic surgeon can be consulted about having a scar revision operation.

Q **My wife has had a slowly enlarging lump below and in front of her ear for months. After numerous X-rays and an ultrasound scan, she has been told that she has a tumour of the parotid gland, and it will have to be removed. Is this a dangerous procedure? Are there any complications of the operation?**

A The parotid gland is one of three glands on each side of the face that produce saliva, which is discharged into the mouth through a duct that opens at the back corner of the tongue. The parotid glands are the ones that usually swell up with a mumps infection.

Rarely, a tumour can arise in the parotid gland. These tumours are usually relatively benign (not cancerous), and are called mixed parotid tumours. Their cause is unknown, but they slowly enlarge with minimal symptoms other than a vague discomfort. Eventually, they start to break down and ulcerate, at which stage they cause severe pain. If left for a long period, the tumour may press on the facial nerve to cause permanent paralysis, or become malignant.

The only treatment is removal of the affected parotid gland. This is not a serious operation, but a very technically difficult and tedious operation. The gland is not easy to reach as it is tucked underneath the angle of the jaw, and more importantly, the facial nerve runs through the gland.

As it leaves the brain, the facial nerve divides into nine smaller nerves that supply the muscles of the face, the tear gland in the outer corner of the eye, and some of the taste glands and sensation of the tongue. During the operation to remove the parotid gland, the surgeon must dissect out these tiny nerve fibres from the gland and tumour, because if any of the fibres are cut, the area of the face supplied by that nerve will be permanently paralysed.

Even if the operation is completely successful, the irritation to the nerve caused by the operation will cause temporary paralysis to the face for a few weeks. During this time, the patient will not be able to smile, close the eye, suck, whistle, frown, puff out the cheeks or produce tears on the affected side of the face.

After removal of the gland, a recurrence of the tumour is uncommon, provided it has not been left to develop into a cancer.

Q **I have seen a chiropractor for a painful neck, but it is not getting better. What other treatments are available?**

A The first step is to have an accurate diagnosis made as to the cause of the neck pain. This is best done by consulting a doctor who will examine you and probably order X-rays.

Once the diagnosis is known, the appropriate treatment can be given. This may involve anti-inflammatory medications, supporting collars, heat and physiotherapy. Physiotherapists are very competent in manipulation techniques, but can also apply many other modes of therapy to ease the pain associated with neck and back injuries.

Q **I have a neck that is always stiff and sore. I work as a typist and computer terminal operator, and I believe this is the cause, as my doctor cannot find any cause. He said I should exercise my neck to make it move more freely. Can you suggest some exercises for me?**

A Certainly! The following neck exercises and positions are useful for all forms of neck stiffness and arthritis.

A. POSTURE

This is very important! Don't slouch, shoulders back, chin in, think tall!

B. STRETCHES

1. Move neck SLOWLY in all directions every day (eg. in hot shower):
   —tilt to side
   —rotate
   —forwards & back
2. Rotate shoulders forwards and backwards.
3. Tuck chin in and hold for 2–3 seconds.
4. Push shoulders back and attempt to bring shoulder blades together.
5. Drop one shoulder, tilt head towards opposite shoulder thus:

C. STRENGTHEN

1. Lie on back with knees bent. Tuck chin in. Lift head JUST off the floor thus: Aim to hold for 30 seconds.

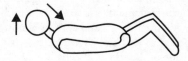

2. While sitting, tuck chin in, and push shoulders back and attempt to bring shoulder blades together. Use your hand to push against the side, front and back of your head in turn, but tense the neck muscles to prevent the head from moving. Hold for 6 seconds and repeat 6 times.

Q My husband has had problems with his neck for eleven years, which causes pain and stiffness down his right side. The doctor says his extra pair of ribs is a problem. Can this explain his shoulder pain?

A In a small percentage of people, a pair of accessory ribs grow out from the base of the neck. These are usually very short, and serve no useful purpose, but may sometimes interfere with the normal path of a nerve from the spinal cord in the neck to the shoulder and arm.

Most of these accessory ribs are only discovered when a patient complains of symptoms such as your husband's, and an X-ray is performed.

The extra rib may be responsible for pain in the neck, shoulder and arm, but not other parts of the body.

Treatments may include anti-inflammatory medications, physiotherapy, injections around the affected nerve, and surgical removal of the additional rib.

Q I have trouble with ingrown hairs on the neck below my jaw that cause redness and pimples. I have been told that this is caused by shaving with the grain and I should shave against the grain. Is it OK to shave against the grain on the neck?

A I am not aware of any specific problems in shaving with or against the grain (the way the hairs lie naturally on the skin), except for a slight discomfort. If you find that shaving against the grain on the neck prevents your ingrown hair problem, then this is naturally the way to proceed.

If you continue to have this problem, using one of the anti-pimple creams or lotions that teenagers often require can reduce the inflammation in the skin and reduce the problem. These are available without a prescription from chemists.

If the problem still persists, mild steroid lotions or creams can be prescribed by your general practitioner to further reduce the inflammation in the skin.

NERVES

Q I suffer severely from trigeminal neuralgia, which is not relieved by pain-killers. What causes this dreadful pain?

A The trigeminal nerve leaves the brain and passes through a hole in the skull just beside the ear. From there it fans out across the face to receive sensations from the skin of the face and to give instructions to the muscles in the face.

Neuralgia is nerve pain, and patients with trigeminal neuralgia (also known as 'tic douloureux') experience sudden, severe pain in the trigeminal nerve. The pain often arises beside the mouth, and spreads almost instantly up to the eye, down to the jaw, and across to the ear. The pain may last a few seconds or several minutes. Only one side of the face is affected.

Attacks of pain may be started by cold winds, eating, yawning or touching the face. The pains tend to come in episodes, with attacks coming every few minutes for a few days or weeks, and then disappearing for a time. Unfortunately, each successive attack tends to last longer than the preceding one, and the pain-free periods become shorter.

Occasionally, trigeminal neuralgia may be caused by a brain or nerve disease such as multiple sclerosis, but usually there is no specific cause, and there are no tests available to prove the diagnosis.

A number of drugs can be used to control the condition. Pain-killers are not particularly effective, but antiepileptic drugs are quite successful.

If these medications prove unsuccessful, surgical exploration of the nerve may find an area of compression or abnormality as a cause of the pain. Very rarely, as a last resort, the nerve may be destroyed to give relief from intractable pain, but this leaves the face numb and paralysed.

Q **I awoke last week with half my face paralysed. I am very scared, but my doctor says it will get better in a few weeks and she won't give me any treatment. She says it is a Bell paralysis. What should I do?**

A You should not worry. Your GP is doing just the right thing—nothing!

The muscles of the face are controlled by the facial nerve, which comes out of a hole in the skull just below and in front of the ear. From there it spreads like a fan across the face, with branches going to each of the many tiny muscles that control our facial expressions. Damage to this nerve causes all these facial muscles to stop working, because the nerve tells the muscles when to contract and when to relax. The patient can no longer smile or close the eye properly.

By far the most common cause of this type of paralysis is Bell's palsy. Bell's palsy is caused by an inflammation of the facial nerve as it leaves the skull. The exact reason for this inflammation, and subsequent paralysis, is unknown. When the condition starts, the patient develops a sudden paralysis of the face muscles on one side only. There may be some mild to moderate pain at the point where the nerve leaves the skull beside the ear, but this settles after a few days. There may also be a disturbance to taste sensation.

Two-thirds of patients recover completely within a few weeks with no treatment. Most of the others obtain partial recovery, but 10% are significantly affected long term by facial paralysis. No treatment is necessary for most patients, but if the victim is elderly, the paralysis is total, or if there is severe pain, treatment may be tried. High doses of prednisone, a steroid, to reduce the inflammation in the facial nerve, is the usual medication. It is important that the treatment start within five days of the onset of the condition. Unfortunately, there is varying evidence about the value of any treatment, but at least it rarely causes any harm.

Q **I get the shakes. Sometimes my hand is alright, but at other times it shakes terribly. Can you help me?**

A Tremors are very common in older people, and there are a variety of causes. One of the most common is Parkinson's disease, which is due to a deterioration of the coordination centre in your brain. Some drugs, alcohol and caffeine (from both tea and coffee) can precipitate or aggravate tremors.

There are dozens of other causes that vary from anxiety and psychiatric conditions to an overactive thyroid gland or a stroke.

The first step is to have an accurate diagnosis made. This may involve a visit to a neurologist—a specialist brain and nerve doctor. Many tests will be done and a thorough investigation undertaken, and once the diagnosis is made, treatment can commence. Some types of tremors can be completely cured, others controlled, and a few cannot be treated at all. You will not know what can be done to help you until that diagnosis is made, so arrange to see your GP as soon as possible.

Q   I have been told that my deafness is due to an acoustic neuroma, but my doctor is not treating it. Is this serious?

A   This is a benign (not cancerous) tumour of the nerve that transmits sound from the hearing mechanism in the ear to the brain. It can enlarge to put pressure on other nerves and blood vessels in the base of the brain, and can cause a wide variety of symptoms other than deafness and noises in the ear. Poor balance, ear pain and paralysis of part of the face can also occur.

It can be diagnosed by a special type of X-ray known as Computerised Axial Tomography (CAT scan for short) that can show its exact position and size. The only treatment is surgical removal of the tumour. If it is small, the nerve may be saved and hearing restored, but larger tumours will result in permanent hearing loss.

Q   I keep getting pins and needles in my arm. What could cause this problem?

A   Pins and needles (or paraesthesia as doctors call it) is almost invariably due to the pinching of a nerve. In your situation, one of the nerves running from your neck to the hand is being pinched. The most likely areas for this to occur are in the neck, the armpit or at the elbow.

The 'funny bone' in your elbow is actually a nerve that is close to the surface of the body. If this is hit lightly, you will experience a tingling (or pins and needles) sensation down your arm. If it is hit hard, or compressed for a long time, the tingling will become pain. In treating this condition, doctors will ask you to precisely outline the area of your arm affected, and from this, the point at which the nerve is being pinched can often be determined. X-rays of this area are then taken to detect any arthritis or other disease.

Treatment will depend on the cause, but may include anti-inflammatory medications, slings, splints and physiotherapy. Rarely, surgery is necessary. Other causes of pins and needles can include severe anaemia, diabetes and some psychiatric conditions.

Q   My mother has motor neurone disease. Can you explain this condition for me?

A   This is one of the nastier diseases that can attack humans. We do not know its cause, and there is no cure; but doctors do know what happens inside the body, and to the patient.

Nerves occur in two main types—sensory and motor. The sensory nerves detect heat, cold, pain and touch. The motor nerves send messages from the brain to make every muscle in the body move as we want it to. In motor neurone disease, these motor nerves slowly degenerate, often in a random pattern around the body, causing weakness in the arms and legs, poor posture, difficulty in speech, and eventually difficulty in breathing. It may get better spontaneously for a few weeks or months, but eventually the disease progresses to the point where the body cannot function adequately.

It is a tragedy to see these people deteriorate, particularly as they maintain their normal mental state and intelligence. Active physiotherapy, good nursing care, medications to relieve muscle spasm and infections, and lots of T.L.C. are the main forms of treatment.

Q My sister has just been diagnosed as having multiple sclerosis. How is this treated, and is there a cure?

A Once the diagnosis of multiple sclerosis is made, the patient is NOT condemned to life as an invalid. The disease goes through a series of attacks and remissions, and periods of good health can last for many months or years. Most patients can lead independent, active and satisfying lives and can take care of their own needs for many years after the diagnosis is made. The life span of victims is not significantly altered.

Unfortunately, no effective treatments are available to cure the disease, but doctors combine with physiotherapists, speech therapists and occupational therapists to help these young patients cope with a most unpredictable and distressing condition.

Q I was astonished to read in your column your advice that an orthopaedic surgeon would perform an operation to do a carpal tunnel repair. My operation was done by a neurosurgeon. You should know better. Does some layperson write your column?

A Some of the less polite and wildly scrawled letters bring up some of the most interesting subjects.

I can assure readers that the column is written by a doctor, in fact by a general practitioner in private practice.

There are no set rules about which doctors may perform which procedures, but by training, certain surgeons tend to perform operations on certain areas. Legally, there is no law restricting me as a GP from performing routine brain surgery, but it would be ethically wrong, and no reputable hospital would allow me to perform such surgery, as I have not been trained to perform this work.

Once a doctor has a surgical fellowship (and all surgeons have the same qualifications, but with emphasis in their training in a certain area), it is very difficult to delineate certain areas of the body to a particular type of surgeon. The simple operation on your wrist could have been equally well performed by an orthopaedic surgeon, neurosurgeon, general surgeon or a general practitioner with only moderate surgical skills (eg. in a rural area). Most are performed by orthopaedic surgeons.

Many other areas of overlap occur, particularly in the head and neck where otorhinolaryngologists (ear, nose and throat surgeons), plastic surgeons, general surgeons and even dental surgeons all may be involved.

Geographic location is another factor, and in major cities, more highly specialised surgeons are available. The emergency of a burst blood vessel in the brain would be dealt with by a neurosurgeon in the city, by a general surgeon in a major country town and by a general practitioner in a small country town.

Q For 6 weeks I have had a strange pins and needles like sensation in both feet associated with numbness. It seems to be slowly progressing from my soles and toes up my legs. Walking is becoming a problem as a result. I would appreciate your advice.

A   The technical term for the pins and needles sensation that you are experiencing is paraesthesia, and it is caused by irritation of the sensory nerves supplying the area affected. The big question is, what is irritating the nerve.

If you are having difficulty walking, it is probable that the nerves supplying the muscles, and telling them what to do, are also affected.

For both types of nerves to be damaged, the most likely explanation is that they are being compressed in the lower back, at the point where they pass through narrow gaps between the vertebrae on their way from the spinal cord (and therefore the brain) to the legs.

In some people, this can be a temporary problem from a back strain or injury, but if it is steadily progressing, you should see a doctor as soon as possible, as you may have a disc that is pressing on the nerve, or more seriously, the spinal canal may becoming narrowed due to injury to a disc or a vertebra.

You will need appropriate investigations, usually X-rays and CT scans of the spine, to see what damage there is to the back, and blood tests to exclude less common causes of this problem (eg. poorly controlled diabetes). In many cases, surgery is necessary to correct the problem.

Q   **I have had tingling like pins and needles in my left arm for three months. I would like to know what is causing it. Can you help me?**

A   When a nerve is squeezed, you initially feel a tingling sensation, then if the nerve is squeezed steadily harder the sensation becomes one like pins and needles, then pain, numbness and finally paralysis. The area affected is the place where the nerve ends.

If a nerve running from your fingers to the spinal cord is squeezed at your shoulder, the sensation will appear to come from the fingers, and there may be no abnormal sensation at the shoulder.

In your case, the pins and needles sensation is due to the nerve being squeezed at some point between where the sensation occurs, and where the nerve ends in the neck. The most likely areas for a nerve to be squeezed are at the elbow, shoulder and neck.

A strained shoulder, twisted elbow, whiplash injury to the neck and similar injuries are possible reasons for a nerve being squeezed. You should see your GP so that s/he can examine and X-ray you to determine the cause of the problem. Appropriate treatment can then be given to relieve the problem (eg. physiotherapy, anti-inflammatory medication).

Q   **I have a numb patch to one side of my spine. I often feel a twinge or burning sensation in this area. I have noticed the numbness for some time, and it seems to be getting worse. Your advice on this matter would be appreciated.**

A   Almost certainly the small nerve that supplies the area of the back that has become numb, has been pinched as it emerges from the spinal cord, and has now ceased to function. The pain or burning that you feel at times will be caused by pinching of the nerves immediately beside the damaged one.

The problem should not be ignored, as it may be an early sign of a more significant problem. If caught early, treatment is easier and more effective.

There are a number of possible causes for a nerve being pinched, most of which are not serious, but occasionally a tumour may be responsible, and this problem must therefore be fully investigated. The first step is to have an X-ray of the back at the level of the numb patch to see if there is some damage to the vertebrae, or arthritis in the joints of the back.

Whatever the diagnosis, I doubt that the numb patch will ever regain its normal sensation, but this will be an inconvenience and not serious.

Q My father has recently been diagnosed with peripheral neuropathy. Is there any cure?

A Peripheral neuropathy is damage to a nerve that supplies the arms, legs or trunk of the body, as distinct from the nerves that supply the head, internal organs or occur in the spinal cord or brain.

Unfortunately, peripheral neuropathy is not a true diagnosis, as there are many different causes for this condition, and the exact cause must be determined before any treatment can be given or any idea of the likely outcome can be known. Sometimes only one nerve is involved, other times many, and sometimes only one sensation (eg. fine touch) fails to function.

The simplest form of peripheral neuropathy is the temporary injury to a nerve from a bruise or swelling. The mildest form of this would be the tingling sensation experienced down your arm when you knock the 'funny bone' (which is really a nerve) in your elbow.

Other causes of peripheral neuropathy vary from the innocuous to the very serious and include uraemia (kidney failure), autoimmune diseases (the body inappropriately rejects its own tissue), inherited disorders, poor blood supply to the nerve, alcoholism, severe diabetes, leprosy, serious infections, AIDS, poisons (eg. insecticides, solvents) and dozens of other conditions.

Q There was a famous American baseballer who died with a very rare nerve disease many years ago. I cannot think of the name of the baseballer or the disease, but I am hoping you might be able to help me win a bet about this disease. Do you know of the disease and baseballer?

A Now this is a question right out of left field, but I actually do know what you are talking about. The disease is amyotrophic lateral sclerosis, which is often known in the United States as Lou Gehrig Disease after the 1930s baseballer who developed the condition.

It is a rare form of motor neurone disease that affects the nerves that supply the muscles of the body. The absolute cause is unknown, but it may run in families, and results in a steadily progressive degeneration of the motor nerves in the body.

The symptoms include a muscle weakness that usually starts in the hands or feet, muscle cramps and twitches, difficulty in swallowing and talking, drooling of saliva, inability to cough effectively, reduced tongue movement, and progressive weakness up the arms and legs. Eventually the muscles used for breathing are involved.

No cure is available, and treatment is aimed at relieving muscle spasm, assisting feeding, preventing infections, aiding breathing and making the patient as comfortable as possible. Physiotherapy on a very regular basis is essential.

Lung infections such as pneumonia develop, and often lead to death, usually within three to five years.

NOSE and SINUSES

See also MOUTH and THROAT; SMELL and TASTE

Q I keep getting nose bleeds at the most inconvenient times. Blood started dripping into my dinner at a restaurant last night from my stupid nose. What causes blood noses, and how can I stop them?

A The nose is lined with a moist membrane that has numerous arteries and veins running across it. These blood vessels are very close to the surface, and can therefore be easily damaged and bleed. In the nose lining just inside the nostrils, there is a large network of arteries and veins that start to warm the air as it enters the body, and keeps this exposed area as moist as possible. In very dry, windy weather, or in an air-conditioned restaurant, this area may dry out, and crack. These tiny cracks can involve a blood vessel, and bleeding results. This type of bleeding usually starts without warning, but settles quite quickly with the correct treatment.

The patient should sit upright in a chair, and the soft end part of the nose should be pinched firmly with a clean cloth held between the fingers. This pressure is applied for five minutes without letting go. When the pressure is released, the bleeding will probably have stopped. If the bleeding continues, the pressure should be applied for two more five-minute periods.

If the problem continues after this time, medical assistance must be sought. An ice pack applied to the nose during this time may also be beneficial.

Bleeding from the back of the nose, when the blood runs down the throat, rather than out through the nostrils, is much more serious. It may be due to a wide variety of diseases including high blood pressure, ulcers, cancers and blood abnormalities. This type of bleeding always requires urgent medical attention and investigation, as it may be difficult to stop.

Q What can be done for a 9 year old with recurrent nose bleeds? My son has one at least once a week, and often at the worst possible time.

A As a first step, try preventing the nose bleeds by moistening the lining inside the nostrils. This can be done by using an antiseptic cream applied by a cotton bud or little finger to the inside of the nose.

If the bleeding persists, medical attention should be sought. In the acute case, doctors can pack the nose with gauze, blow up a small balloon inside the nose, or use adrenalin swabs to stop the bleeding. To prevent recurrences, the bleeding spot needs to be identified and cauterised.

This is best done by a specialist ear, nose and throat surgeon who can examine the inside of the nose with a special instrument, identify the bleeding spot, determine the cause of the bleeding and destroy the offending blood vessel with an electric current (cautery), or remove a growth or polyp that may be bleeding.

Q I have a constantly runny nose and need to use antihistamine tablets all the time. All the ones that work make me drowsy, and I can't work as a driver. Is there anything else available to help me?

A Runny noses are caused by irritation to the moist membrane that lines the inside of your nose and sinuses. This irritation can be due to allergies, viral infections, temperature changes, changes in your emotional state, changes in position and hormonal fluctuations.

The normal way to deal with this problem is to use antihistamine preparations, but until a few years ago, all of these caused some degree of drowsiness. This side effect varies from one drug to another and from one person to another, so trialling several different types may be necessary to find the best one for you.

New antihistamines are now available (eg. Telfast, Claratyne, Hismanal). The effectiveness in drying up runny noses varies between patients, but they have the great advantage of not causing drowsiness and can be safely used by drivers and others in similar positions.

Unfortunately, these non-sedating antihistamines only work if your runny nose is caused by an allergy. If the cause is a viral infection, due to temperature changes or other problems, you are better off staying with the traditional antihistamines. Even with these, newer versions such as Zyrtec are less likely to cause sedation than older preparations.

There is also an antihistamine nasal spray (Avil spray) available, which works very well in some people, and a nasal spray (Rynacrom—prescription required) which reduces the sensitivity of the nasal lining to pollens and dust.

The other way to deal with the problem is to reduce the inflammation of the nose membranes by coating them with a fine layer of steroid spray. A number of medications, including Beconase, Rhinocort and Aldecin, are available in a pressure pack or pump spray that is squirted up the nose to prevent it from running. These sprays have minimal side effects.

Many of these medications require a doctor's prescription, so discuss the matter further with your GP.

Q My husband sneezes for an hour or more every morning when he wakes. How can he stop this?

A He is probably suffering from vasomotor rhinitis or hay fever. Vasomotor rhinitis is an excessive secretion of phlegm in the nose and sinuses due to changes in temperature, emotion and posture. Hay fever is caused by allergies to pollens, dust etc.

If your husband takes a long-acting antihistamine tablet each night, it should prevent the reaction in the nose, and therefore prevent his sneezing fits. New, non-sedating antihistamines are now available. Special nasal sprays containing a steroid (available only on prescription) may also help the problem if used regularly.

Q My doctor describes the constant rubbish I swallow as cattarh. What causes catarrh?

A Catarrh is the post-nasal drip that drives some poor patients crazy with the constant cough and irritated throat, and may be associated with bad breath and nausea as the creek of foul phlegm winds its way down the back of the throat and into the stomach.

It can be caused by many different factors, and normally two or three are responsible, making it almost impossible to cure, and difficult to control.

The causes include both bacterial and viral infections, allergies, emotional changes, hormonal changes, temperature changes, climatic changes and changes in position.

Bacteria can be treated by antibiotics, but the other causes will all require combinations of antihistamine tablets, nasal decongestants, steroid nose sprays, liquefying agents and anti-allergy sprays.

After some trial and error with numerous medications, and sometimes surgery to aid in the drainage of the sinuses, most people can achieve some degree of relief from this most annoying condition.

Q Every morning I vomit because of all the mucus that has been running down my throat from the back of my nose during the night. This is only an irritation in summer, but in winter it can become a problem because I get sinusitis.

A Prevention is possible in this situation, but a permanent cure is unlikely, although you may find that moving to another city or suburb may change the situation.

I suspect that you are producing the excess mucus throughout much of the day, but because it is swallowed during the night while you are asleep, it irritates the stomach, and causes you to vomit on waking. The mucus may be caused by an allergy reaction, reaction to temperature change, emotional change, change in position, a viral infection or any one of a dozen other reasons.

Taking a simple antihistamine in the evening may be all that is necessary. These can be purchased without a prescription from a chemist. There are many different brands, but a long-acting one like Zyrtec is the one I usually recommend.

If this measure is ineffective, using a steroid-based nasal spray once or twice a day may reduce the sensitivity of the nose and sinuses so that they do not react as readily to irritants. These are only available on prescription from your general practitioner.

As a last resort, ear, nose and throat surgeons can perform an operation to reduce the amount of tissue in your nose and sinuses that is available to produce mucus.

Q What are the sinuses that everyone complains about when they get a runny nose?

A Below, above, between and even behind your eyes, your skull bone is riddled with cave-like spaces called sinuses. All these sinuses are connected together by small holes and tubes, making a complex interconnecting system. Lining this network is a moist membrane, the same as that inside your nostrils. The whole system is thus kept constantly moist, and this moisture slowly flows out of the drain holes in the sinuses, into the back of your nose and throat. This system is designed to keep the sinuses clean, as any dust or other small particles that may enter them is washed out.

Some people secrete excess amounts of fluid in the sinuses, while others may have drainage holes and tubes that are too small to cope with the secretions produced. If bacteria or viruses enter the sinuses, sinusitis may result. The phlegm produced is no longer watery, but thick and pus-like, and it is very easy in this situation for the drain holes to become blocked, and the sinuses become very painful and tender.

Q **My sinuses are always blocked. I can't breathe through my nose, which runs constantly, and my face aches. Nothing seems to help me. What can I do?**

A Those of you with the constant irritation and annoyance of a blocked nose and sinuses should work steadily through a 'therapeutic crescendo'. This means that you start with the simple remedies available over the counter from chemists, and gradually use the stronger medicines and procedures available from doctors.

The starting point is to use nasal decongestant sprays. To these can be added pseudoephedrine tablets (to be used with caution by people with high blood pressure) and then antihistamines (which may make you drowsy). If there is still no success, doctors can recommend stronger antihistamines, and some that will not cause drowsiness. More effective nasal sprays, that can be used long term to prevent the problem, are also available on prescription.

If you continue to be blocked up, the last step in medication is to use mucus-liquefying drugs, and if these combinations fail, a minor procedure to wash all the 'gunk' out of your sinuses may be performed.

Physiotherapists can use ultrasound on the sinuses to break up the mucus and allow it to drain.

The last resort is surgery, to cut and burn away the mucus-secreting lining of the nose, remove some of the bones inside the nose, and to drill larger drain holes into the sinuses. At some stage of this treatment crescendo, nearly everyone should receive some relief, but it is important to persevere with a doctor until you reach that point.

Q **My sinuses are always full of gunk, that is absolutely foul. None of the medicines I have been prescribed work. I am absolutely fed up with having a thick head. What type of surgery could be done for my sinuses?**

A An antrostomy and turbinectomy is the technical name for an operation that involves drilling additional drain holes from the nose into the sinuses, and removing the curly bones (turbinates—look like a turban) that are inside your nose.

People who have recurrent attacks of sinusitis often have small or poorly placed drainage holes from the sinuses, allowing them to fill up with foul phlegm.

The turbinates are covered with a moist skin that is designed to warm and moisten the air as it enters the body, but these can swell up excessively to block the nose and the sinus drain holes. There are three turbinate bones in the top of each nostril, and normally only one or two are removed.

The operation is done under general anaesthetic, has no serious complications and is often very successful in giving relief to sinus sufferers.

Ask your GP to refer you to an ear, nose and throat specialist, who will consider your problem, and its possible surgical solution.

Q **I suffer from chronic sinusitis. My face is one big ache. I can't breathe, and feel absolutely lousy. I need help before I go mad!**

A Chronic sinus infections are best prevented rather than treated. This can be done by the regular use of chemist medications to dry up excess nasal and sinus secretions. If these are not sufficient, more potent medications can be prescribed by your doctor. There are also prescription nasal sprays that will keep your nose clear and aid sinus drainage. Some people may require low-dose antibiotics on a regular basis if they are particularly bad.

Operations to improve the drainage of the sinuses and remove the phlegm-secreting lining of the nose are the best option in those who have suffered repeatedly over several years. Once a sinus infection is present, antibiotics are essential. The congestion in the sinuses may also be relieved by physiotherapists using short-wave treatment to liquefy solid phlegm, or by doctors washing out the sinuses.

OBESITY

See also DIET

Q   Is there a simple and cheap way to lose weight?

A   There are no easy ways to lose weight, only hard ones, but losing weight can be simple and cheap. There is no need to buy costly diet foods or attend expensive courses. Following these five points, while using a lot of willpower, and I guarantee you will lose weight.

1.   EAT ONLY THREE TIMES A DAY.
     Never eat between meals, and drink only water or black tea/coffee if thirsty. Set aside three half-hour periods a day for eating, and do not eat at any other time.

2.   EAT ONLY THE CORRECT FOODS.
     There are scores of diet charts available that will tell you which foods are low in calories. Do not stick to only one food group, but eat a balanced diet.

3.   EXERCISE REGULARLY.
     Get up a good sweat and make your heart race at least once a day.

4.   EAT LESS.
     If you are not losing weight at the rate of four kilograms (nine pounds) a month, you are still eating too much. Do not weigh yourself more than once a week, and remember that weight loss does not occur steadily, but with sudden weight loss, and then a period of no loss. That is why the loss must be averaged over a month.

5.   KEEP GOING.
     It is pointless spending months losing weight, only to put it on again. Your diet should be one for life, not just a few weeks or months.

Q   What causes obesity? I am very careful with my diet, but still over-weight.

A   Your choice of parents is the most important factor in your weight, particularly if you do stick to a good diet. Obesity is hereditary, and children of fat parents should be carefully watched to make sure they do not put on too much weight in childhood.

The other big factor (pardon the pun!) is of course your diet. Many fat people claim they eat nothing, but when monitored they are seen to nibble little bits of food all the time between meals. Their meals may be small, but their calorie intake is enormous.

Exercise is the third factor, and obviously people who exercise regularly are going to burn off more calories and fat than those who lead a sedentary lifestyle.

There are some diseases, such as an under active thyroid gland, which may be responsible for obesity, but less than 1 in 100 fat people have these diseases, and they can be easily tested for by your GP.

Q   I have been told to exercise to lose weight. Is jogging the best form of exercise?

A No. The most effective forms of exercise, that work all the major muscle groups with minimal risk of stress injury, are swimming, gymnastics and cycling.

Swimming is without doubt the ideal exercise, as there is no stress on the support structures of the body, while every muscle is being worked. Group activities such as gymnastics (or variations of this such as aerobics) tend to give more encouragement to exercise, and are less boring than endlessly pacing around a grass oval by yourself. Cycling does not cause foot and leg stress, and the scenery changes rather more rapidly than in jogging.

Any form of exercise is better than none in an attempt to lose weight, but jogging has several disadvantages. It tends to cause leg and foot injuries, particularly if running on a hard surface; there are dangers in jogging on roads; and only the lower half of the body receives adequate work. Those who do like jogging should ensure that it is done on a grass surface in good quality shoes, and where there are no traffic hazards.

Q **I am seventeen years old and over the last six months I've gained ten kilos in weight. I can't control my eating. I grasp chocolates, ice-cream, candy etc. even after a full meal. My stomach is always upset and I'm vomiting because of overeating. I'm desperately out of control with a constant desire to eat. Please help, as my body is becoming horribly distorted.**

A Rapid weight gain is usually due to a compulsion to eat. This in turn is usually attributable to a psychological problem, and recent stress or emotional shock may have triggered your problem.

Weight gain is caused by a greater intake of food than output of energy and wastes.

There are some rare diseases such as an underactive thyroid gland, Cushing's syndrome and pituitary gland disorders that can cause obesity, but the vast majority are caused by overeating and inadequate exercise.

You need to see your GP to have any of the rarer causes of obesity excluded by investigation. If these tests are normal, referral to a psychiatrist is appropriate. This is not because you are mad or insane, but because your body is reacting inappropriately to some form of stress in your life.

Q **I am a thirteen year old girl, 164 cm tall and weigh 55 kg. I feel fat because I have fat legs. Am I overweight? What is the average weight for a girl my age?**

A The average weight for someone of your age and height is 47 to 51 kg, so you are a little overweight statistically. It would be equally important for me to know your degree of maturity.

Girls at thirteen can still be flat chested and have no sign of changing into a woman, or they may be well developed and appear to be a grown woman. Those with a woman's figure will weigh more than those who are still girls.

Almost certainly you will grow taller in the next year, so the sensible thing to do is to watch your diet, get some exercise and make sure that you do not put on any more weight, and let your height slowly increase. You will grow up into your present weight, and thin out as a result. Losing weight is NOT a good idea at your age unless you are grossly obese.

Q I am fat! Not just a bit overweight but superfat, obese and gross! I have tried every diet in existence, and with great difficulty, I can lose a few kilos. The moment I relax my vigil, I put on five kilos again. My parents and grandparents were also fatties, but all are still alive and well. Do I really have to lose weight to live longer as my doctor tells me?

A Doctors have now differentiated two types of obesity— 'android' and 'gynoid'. Android obesity occurs more often in men, and the fat is distributed mainly around the abdomen, chest and neck. Gynoid obesity is more common in women, and the fat is found on the hips, buttocks and thighs.

The android form of obesity is believed to cause an increased risk of strokes, heart attacks and diabetes, but only if the person's weight is 20% above the average for their height and age.

There appear to be no fatal complications associated with gynoid obesity, but there is still an increased incidence of arthritis from the additional wear and tear to the joints, and skin problems from sweat and friction.

Interestingly enough, very thin people actually live shorter lives than the very fat, as they have a greater tendency to develop lung diseases and some forms of cancer.

Obesity is certainly an inherited characteristic, and you seem to have little chance of avoiding it. If one parent is obese, 40% of the children have the problem. If both parents are obese, the risk rises to 80%. It has also been found that the way in which the individual cells in fat people use energy is different to those from thin people, explaining the reason why so many fat people find it almost impossible to lose weight.

Fat is very much a fashion, and at the beginning of the twenty-first century, thin is 'in' and beautiful. If you moved to Turkey or Egypt you would find yourself to be a fashion hit, as voluptuous women are in demand in these countries. The Europe of Rembrandt was also a time when rolls of fat were appreciated, as his huge canvases covered with well endowed nudes will attest.

My advice is to assess your own position in the light of the information above, eat sensibly, exercise regularly, and unless there is good medical evidence to the contrary (for example a raised cholesterol level or diabetes), do not ruin your life by trying to match those who parade in their size 8 creations on the shopping centre catwalk.

Q I have a son who is nearly 14. His height is 144 cm and his weight 53 kg. People comment that he is too big in the stomach, and he will have to lose some of it. What can he do about it?

A Your son is certainly a bit overweight for his height, but he is still quite short. He is also quite short for his age, with 97% of boys his age being taller than he is, but only 40% are heavier.

He should eat only healthy and nutritious foods, and avoid the junk and sweet foods. The easiest way to do this is to prohibit all between-meal snacks, and allow him to eat only the three normal meals a day.

Avoiding sugary soft drinks is also important—refreshment can be given by water or natural fruit juice.

Exercise plays a part in burning off the excess fat and strengthening the muscles of the stomach. He should be encouraged to play sport, or undertake an exercise programme. Swimming and cycling are excellent forms of exercise.

I do not believe that he should actually lose weight, as he is likely to grow in height significantly in the next couple of years. He should avoid gaining any weight, and allow his body to become leaner as he grows taller.

Q I have heard that when tablets containing cider vinegar, kelp, vitamin B6 and lecithin are taken along with a sensible diet and no extra exercise, you lose weight fast—12 lb in two weeks. Is this true?

A There is no easy way to lose weight, and anyone who believes in the above formula will also believe in the tooth fairy and Easter bunny!

There is a simple (but not easy) way to lose weight—eat less and exercise more. This method has the great advantage of being not only effective, but cheap! Millions of dollars are spent by Australians every year on special diets, magic formulas, 'guaranteed' tablets, patent mixtures, acupuncture, hypnotherapy and quack remedies in order to lose weight. None of these are more effective than the simple formula of eat less and exercise more; all are more expensive, some may be harmful, and none work long term.

Being overweight is not a crime, although women's magazines make it seem to be, as all have diets of some type or other. You do not have to look like Princess Diana to be acceptable in society.

There are no medical risks in being up to 20% greater than average weight for your height, age and sex. Only over 40% greater than average weight do medical risks become significant.

The most important factor in your weight is your choice in parents, followed by your diet and exercise levels.

Many fat people should accept their weight, avoid gaining any more, and not damage their health by yo-yoing up and down by ten kilos every few months as they go on and off diets. This is more damaging to health than staying overweight.

If you plan to lose weight, start on a sensible diet that you can maintain for years to come, exercise regularly, and certainly do not try to lose 12 lb in two weeks!

Q I have been obese all my life, since childhood in fact, and now I have diabetes. Some doctors think I may have Prader-Willi syndrome. I have had my stomach stapled, been on innumerable diets, medications, padlocked the fridge—you name it. Nothing works. I have even been locked up in a girl's detention centre, not because I broke the law or anything like that, only to lose weight. What would you suggest?

A One can only take treatment so far, and then one must call it quits. I do not think any suggestion that I make to you will make the slightest difference, considering the extraordinary lengths that you have gone to in the past.

You may have Prader-Willi syndrome, but that is almost impossible to prove. This syndrome is a disorder of the hunger centre in the brain that leads to compulsive eating, regardless of consequences. It is often associated with diabetes, is present from birth, and may be due to a low birth weight and overstimulation of the hunger centre at that time. There is no cure for this syndrome that I can discover in my texts, but you should be assessed by an endocrinologist and a neurologist if this has not already been done.

I can only suggest that after consultation with your doctor it may be appropriate to use high doses of appetite suppressants to control your hunger and maintain your present weight. Your chances of losing weight are almost nil.

I have sympathy for your plight, but can offer nothing more.

Q **I am 25 kg overweight, but after dieting, I always revert to my old bad habits, and regain any weight lost. I would appreciate it if you could provide information on having a balloon inserted in my stomach to assist with weight loss.**

A A technique is being used by a small number of specialist doctors, in which a tube with a deflated balloon at its end is swallowed. Once in the stomach, the balloon is inflated, to fill up approximately three-quarters of the stomach volume. The tube is removed, and the balloon can remain in place for weeks or months.

While present, the balloon fools the stomach into believing that it is already full, thus reducing the appetite and desire to eat. The obvious aim is to reduce the calorie (kilojoule) intake of the patient to the point where they lose weight.

There are complications with the procedure. It is possible for the stomach to become inflamed, ulcers to develop, the outlet from the stomach may become blocked, uncontrollable vomiting may occur, and in very rare instances the stomach may rupture.

Obesity and overeating in some people is a habit that is extremely hard to control, and they continue to eat, and further expand the stomach, despite the presence of the balloon.

The balloon cannot remain in place permanently, and once it is removed, those who may have lost a great deal of weight often start gorging again and regain all the lost weight.

There is no easy answer to obesity—only lots of different difficult and/or expensive ones. The cheapest and most effective is self-discipline, diet and exercise—but that is certainly not an easy option.

Q **I am 18 years old, female, slightly underweight, very attractive and have a perfect figure. I can eat anything I like and still maintain my figure. How long will it be before I start to put on weight every time I eat something fattening? Will I be like this forever?**

A I am delighted that you have such self-confidence in your appearance, but I would suggest that you act cautiously around any friends who are even slightly overweight or who have a figure a little less spectacular than your own, or you may not live long enough to find out if you will ever become fat and flabby!

The best way to find out if you will have a weight problem in the future is to look at your parents, grandparents, uncles and aunts. If they are overweight, then you have a high risk of following in their footsteps.

Your weight is determined by several factors including inherited tendencies, the metabolic rate of your body (rate at which cells burn energy) and obviously your diet and exercise level.

You should decide on an ideal weight, and merely eat a nutritious diet, low in fatty and processed foods until you reach that weight, be that in a few months or a few years. Once at that weight, modify your food intake and exercise level to maintain that weight.

Remember, that as you age, your ideal weight will increase, at about 2 kg per decade of life.

OTHER PROBLEMS

Q Why are some people left-handed? I am 12 years old and the only left-hander in my family. Will it be a problem for me?

A The lefties in our society should not feel apologetic for their 'preferred laterality', to use the correct medical term for left-handedness. There is an impressive list of left-handed leaders, artists and sports people including Queen Victoria, Harry Truman, Gerald Ford, Michelangelo, Paul McCartney, Judy Garland, Picasso, Jimmy Connors and John McEnroe.

Hand preference does not appear to be a characteristic of animals, but is exclusive to humans. There are many theories to explain this. Some experts claim it is due to emotional contrariness in childhood, others that it is inherited, still others that it is an acquired learning process. It may well be a combination of these factors.

Because most sporting equipment, tools and appliances are designed for right-handed people, this has created preference in the community for the right hand. Parents tend to give children toys and the like in their right hand, thereby adding to the learning process of the child. Hand preference usually begins around 9 months of age, and is established around 18 months to two years.

There is increasing research interest in the proficiency with which left-handers are able to use their right hand. Some left-handers are quite hopeless using their right hand, while others are much better.

Q I was a soldier in Japan after the war, and visited Hiroshima. I also worked with yellowcake at a uranium treatment plant in South Australia in the 1950s. Is there any way of telling if I have been damaged by radiation?

A Unfortunately there is no way of finding out if you have had any long-term damage to radiation from many years ago. At the time of radiation, blood tests may be abnormal, and if cancer or other disease does develop, once again pathology tests will be able to detect the damage, but in between these two stages, there are no tests that will give any meaningful result.

In order to give you some reassurance, I would point out that yellowcake has a very low level of radiation, and even today is transported in 44 gallon drums with no more protection than a thin layer of steel. It is extremely unlikely that working with yellowcake (which is a uranium ore concentrate) will cause any long-term problems.

I have checked with the Department of Veterans Affairs, and they claim that no Australian servicemen were adversely affected by radiation while serving in Japan.

Q What are spastics? My friends at school are sometimes rude and call me names, and say I am a spastic. I see them in the streets sometimes, and they scare me. I don't want to get like that. How do you become spastic?

A Your so called 'friends' need a lesson in manners, because those who are spastics are the innocent victims of a family tragedy.

Cerebral palsy is the correct medical term for most forms of spasticity. It is due to brain damage which usually occurs during development while a foetus before birth, or because the brain is deprived of oxygen by a placenta that is functioning poorly.

Children and adults who suffer from cerebral palsy are trapped inside a deformed and crippled body for the rest of their lives. They are subjected to cruel jests, rude stares, and an acute lack of understanding.

Try to imagine yourself, a normal, intelligent human being, having a body which refuses to respond to your commands and needs—a body that twists itself into grotesque shapes because of the inexorable spasms of your muscles. The frustration of such a situation is hard to comprehend.

Many spastics have normal intelligence, and some are university graduates. A few have competed successfully in the international Paralympics, but do not receive the acclaim that our normal Olympic champions achieve.

Q My sister has just found out that her son has cerebral palsy. He is only four months old, and I would like to know how do doctors treat children with this problem?

A Cerebral palsy can vary dramatically from one person to another. Some have slight difficulty in controlling one limb, others may be unable to talk clearly, yet others may be totally unable to care for themselves in any way.

Understandably there may be emotional and social problems associated with this incurable disease. Doctors do their best to control the muscle spasms, give emotional and psychiatric support and treat the skin, chest and orthopaedic problems that beset these people; but the most effective help comes from teams of nurses, physiotherapists, occupational therapists, social workers and volunteers who devote their lives to the management of these patients in a lifestyle which is as near to normal as possible.

Early recognition that an infant has cerebral palsy can be very beneficial, because the sooner treatment is started, the less severe the long-term problems are likely to be.

Operations to correct deformities and release spasm in limbs can complement medications which also reduce the uncontrollable twitching that may occur. Paramedical staff can instruct the child in the control of an unwilling body.

There is no likelihood in the future of any cure being found for spastics, because once part of the brain is damaged, it is unable to repair itself.

Q My daughter recently had the most terrifying experience of an oculogyric crisis after taking medication for vomiting. Can you please warn people about this problem?

A An oculogyric crisis may be caused in several different ways. It may be a very rare complication of using the medication prochlorperazine (Stemetil), or due to encephalitis (a brain inflammation) and some types of Parkinson's disease. In 30 years of general practice I have never seen a case.

Stemetil is a widely used, very safe, and effective medication for the treatment of nausea, vomiting and dizziness. It has been on the market for nearly 40 years.

The effect can occur after just one tablet of Stemetil, or may be associated with an overdose.

An oculogyric crisis can vary in severity from a mild abnormal twitching of the eyes, to a constant upward gaze, inability to move the eyes in their sockets, and extension of the neck to the point where the back of the head almost touches the back of the chest due to spasm of the muscles in the neck.

In extreme cases, where medical attention is not available, it can cause difficulty in breathing due to the extreme neck extension.

The crisis is easily and rapidly treated by giving an injection of a drug (benztropine) into a vein to reverse the muscle spasm.

Your daughter was extraordinarily unlucky to suffer from such a reaction, and she should make all doctors she comes in contact with in the future aware that she should never use Stemetil again. As this medication is so widely used, wearing a charm or bracelet with this information may be appropriate.

Q **In the past two months I have experienced bouts of queasiness, loss of appetite, general tiredness, a weight loss of 4 kilograms and an itchy rash around my neck. Should I seek medical attention for these vague symptoms?**

A The one word answer to your query is yes.

All your symptoms are vague, but combined they give a clinical picture that may indicate anything from a minor condition to a serious disease. The possibilities include a chronic viral infection, pernicious anaemia, prolonged stress, and cancer.

The only way to differentiate between these possibilities is to be appropriately investigated by a doctor. See your GP as soon as possible.

Q **My cousin is very ill with lead poisoning. How can you get lead poisoning?**

A Older people who suffer from lead poisoning have probably picked up the lead from old flaking paint that may have stuck to their fingers and is then swallowed. Modern paints do not contain lead, but many old houses still have lead coats of paint buried under more modern finishes, and this can be a trap for restorers. Petrol sold in Australia used to contain lead, and low-grade lead poisoning could occur in people who breathed in large quantities of petrol fumes in their work. Toll collectors and car park attendants are classic cases. Unleaded and lead replacement petrol has overcome this problem.

Some types of alternative fad treatments taken in large quantities can be dangerous, as they may contain lead. Workers in the lead industry (eg. with batteries) are obviously at risk, and some old toys (eg. toy soldiers) were made with lead and can cause trouble to modern youngsters if found in grandfather's trunk. Only very small amounts of lead can cause problems.

Lead poisoning can be very serious and can lead to a wide range of symptoms and severe organ damage. Treatment is difficult as the lead is hard to shift once ingested. It is becoming an unusual disease due to greater care with this metal.

Q **A relative has repetitive strain injury (RSI), fibromyalgia and irritable bowel syndrome. Is there any connection between these conditions?**

A Repetitive strain injury is caused by performing the same action thousands of times until eventually the tendon, muscle or ligament that is being stressed finally gives way and tears. It is rather like taking a thin piece of metal and bending it back and forwards along the same line a few dozen times until finally it breaks.

Fibromyalgia occurs when normal muscle tissue is replaced with fibrous scar tissue after an injury or tear. This can cause persistent pain and weakness in the muscle because it cannot contract properly around the scar tissue.

Fibromyalgia can therefore be the result of RSI.

The irritable bowel syndrome is caused by excessive contractions of the large bowel which can cause belly pains that come and go, and may result in diarrhoea. Stress is a common cause of irritable bowel syndrome.

Stress and anxiety caused by the constant discomfort of RSI and fibromyalgia may lead to the development of irritable bowel syndrome.

Its amazing how various problems in medicine can be connected together, even though the connections can be fairly tenuous at times!

Q **What organ in the body controls one's personal body heat? My husband feels the cold far more than I do.**

A The body's temperature is controlled by balancing the heat produced by the body with the heat lost. Heat is produced by the exertion of muscles, the breakdown of food in the liver and the basic functioning of the body's organs (the metabolic rate). Heat is lost by the evaporation of sweat, radiation from the skin (a person feels hot or cold to the touch), loss of heat in breathing out warm air, and in the warmth of the urine and faeces.

The balance of these inputs and losses is maintained by an area at the base of brain known as the hypothalamus. If the hypothalamus perceives that you are too hot, it will increase heat loss by making you sweat. If it perceives that you are too cold, muscle activity will be increased by shivering. In between these ranges, the individual will also sense heat or cold, and adjust their clothing or environment accordingly.

An individual who feels the cold (or heat) more than another is reflecting that person's variation in basic metabolic rate (the rate at which the bowel, kidneys, heart, liver and all the other organs work) from another's, or their learned experience of temperature change (eg. a Tasmanian can swim in winter in Queensland, while a local finds it far too cold to do so).

Q **My father suffers from amyloidosis. Can you explain this disease to me in simple terms? All I get from his doctors is jargon.**

A Amyloidosis is one of the most complex, rare and poorly understood diseases in the text books. This is why you hear so much jargon, because there is no simple way in which to describe it. There are also several different forms of amyloidosis that vary in severity, age of onset and outcome.

The disease occurs when amyloid, a proteinaceous material that can be best described as a dense red jelly, is deposited in different parts of the body. It may replace the normal tissue of the skin, heart, kidneys, lung, liver, muscles etc. When sufficient amounts of the normal tissue has been replaced by the amyloid, the involved organ will fail to function properly, leading to the symptoms of the disease. These symptoms can be very varied, depending on which organ is involved. There is no treatment available other than rather crude surgery to cut out the larger deposits of amyloid. The cause of the disease is also unknown.

Q **I sweat a lot, to the point where it is very embarrassing. Can doctors do anything to help?**

A Obviously, you should first try the proprietary antiperspirant preparations available from chemists.

A tablet called probanthine is available on script to reduce sweating, but it should not be used all the time as it dries up saliva and other secretions too.

Iontophoresis is a method of reducing the number of sweat glands in an area by passing an electrical current through them.

If you are a very severe sufferer, and the problem is significantly affecting your lifestyle, you may wish to consider a surgical cure. The most successful of these is removal of the sweat glands in your armpit by a plastic surgeon. You will not want to raise your arms for a few weeks after the operation, but the long-term results are excellent.

In another technique, the nerves supplying an area of excess sweating can be cut to prevent the sweat glands from functioning. There is help available from doctors, the type depends on the severity of your problem.

Q **My 17 year old son lacks energy and seems almost lethargic most of the time, although he eats well and plays sport. What could be the reason for his lack of energy?**

A 17 year old boys are usually growing and developing rapidly, eat huge amounts of food, and most seem to remain extraordinarily thin. They may be undertaking normal activities, as your son is with school, sport and other activities, but it is also quite common for them to tire easily and sleep ten or more hours a day while they grow several centimetres in height during the year.

Girls seem to go through this developmental stage earlier and more gradually, and stop growing by about 16 or 17, while boys may grow until 19.

It would be sensible to ask your general practitioner to give your son a physical check up, but the vast majority of boys are found to be perfectly normal, and just passing through an interesting developmental phase.

Q **We have an hereditary disease in our family, and I am concerned about my children developing it. Where can I get further information?**

A Start with your general practitioner. Some inherited diseases have regular and easily predicted patterns of inheritance that he or she will be able to work out for you. If the problem is complex, the GP will refer you to a specialist physician, or to one of the genetic clinics that are established in some major teaching hospitals.

It is always wise for prospective parents who have relatives suffering from a disease that may be inherited to have adequate genetic counselling. Doing this before pregnancy may prevent heartbreak later, as some diseases can be detected before birth, and treated accordingly.

Q **My daughter in North Queensland has Ross River fever. Please tell me about this disease.**

A   Ross River fever is an infection carried from one person to another by mosquitoes. It is found throughout northern Australia, and as far South as Brisbane. It is caused by an organism that is a primitive form of bacteria.

Antibiotics do not ease the disease, and often the person suffers muscular aches and pains, swollen glands, poor appetite, nausea and flu-like symptoms for many weeks or months. There is no way to prevent the spread of the disease except for control of mosquitoes, and treatment generally involves prolonged rest and aspirin. It has no serious consequences, but may be debilitating for a long time, and may recur after recovery seems complete.

Q   **I am always tired. I just have no energy. Even writing this letter is an effort. Please help me.**

A   This is a very common reason for attending a doctor, and it is one of the most difficult to diagnose and treat. You should see your GP who will ask you a lot of questions about your lifestyle and habits. He or she will give you a thorough examination, and then probably order some blood tests. Hopefully this will reveal a cause for your lethargy, but often there is no apparent reason.

Chronic tiredness may be due to your lifestyle, with excess stress and anxiety, too much or too little exercise, sleep disrupted by infants or neighbours, obesity and alcohol excesses being common factors. Diseases as diverse as anaemia and cancer or chronic infections and thyroid gland disorders may be responsible.

Medications you are taking such as antihistamines (for runny noses), pain-killers or some blood pressure tablets may also be the cause. A poor diet lacking in essential elements can cause fatigue, but this normally only occurs in people taking unbalanced fad diets in Australia. Depression is a hidden disease that is often responsible for chronic tiredness, and there are no specific blood tests that can diagnose this.

It is a test of the doctor's clinical acumen to find the correct cause, and then initiate the appropriate treatment, but this may take several visits and a number of investigations. In the long run, persistence usually pays, with the problem disappearing spontaneously or treatment giving relief.

Q   **When I go shopping, and stand for a while waiting to be served, or stand anywhere for a time, I black out. I don't know when these attacks are coming. Please let me know why this happens.**

A   Blood is pumped out of your heart, and through the arteries, to every part of your body. To return to the heart, the blood relies upon the action of muscles squeezing on veins as the person moves about during their normal daily activities.

In the veins are one-way valves, that allow blood to travel only towards the heart. When the soft, thin-walled vein is squeezed by the movement of muscles in the arms or legs, the blood moves along the vein, back towards the heart.

If you stand still for any period of time, there is no muscle activity to pump the blood back from the feet and legs. The heart continues to pump out blood, but without the return supply, begins to run out of blood to pump. The brain then becomes starved of blood and switches off, causing you to faint.

When you fall to the ground, blood can easily flow from the legs to the heart because gravity is no longer holding the blood in the legs. The heart pumps properly again, the brain obtains an adequate blood supply, and you recover.

Soldiers who must remain at attention for long periods of time are taught to tense the muscles in their legs, and to rise slightly on the balls of their feet in order to keep their leg muscles working and thus the blood moving back to the heart.

Try not to stand still for long periods, or adopt the soldier's trick, and keep those muscles working.

Q **I am a 19 year old male and I want to find out if there is a cure for shortness. I am only 5 ft 4 in and I really get depressed about being so small. It's just so horrible being short, and I really don't enjoy life at all the way I am. Nobody takes me seriously, and I find great difficulty in finding work of any kind.**

A The simple answer to your question is no. At your age, there is no cure available for shortness, and even if detected at an earlier age, it is most unlikely that you would have been given growth hormone to increase your height, as 5 ft 4 in (163 cm) is not particularly short.

Growth hormone is a substance that can be given to children in their early teens, who have not yet finished growing, to promote their growth, if it is found that they will be extremely short.

I feel that there is a lot more behind your question than just being short—a lot of very successful people have been your height or less—Napoleon was only 5 ft 3in tall. You are obviously lacking in self-confidence, and you are blaming your social and employment problems on your height. I do not believe that there is any significant discrimination against shorter people unless that shortness is very marked—and you do not fit into that category. You need help in coping with a situation that is going to be with you lifelong, and I suggest that you discuss with your general practitioner the possibility of obtaining counselling from a psychiatrist or psychologist. You do not have to be mad or crazy to see a psychiatrist, just someone in need of help to cope with problems.

Q **My 12 year old daughter is a head taller than everyone else in her class. Is there any way of stopping her from becoming too tall?**

A The first thing to determine is her final height. Because children mature at different rates (eg. some girls start their periods years before others), statistical tables and comparison with peers is not a very accurate method of estimating final height.

Radiologists have developed a sneaky way of giving a quite accurate estimate of final height (plus or minus 2 centimetres) by x-raying the child's wrist. There are many different tiny bones in the wrist that harden at different stages of a child's physiological (not chronological) age. By seeing what these bones look like on the X-ray, and comparing the results and their present height with a previously devised table of results, the estimate of final height can be made.

If it turns out that your daughter will be 190cm (6ft 4in) or more in height, your GP can refer her to an endocrinologist (gland specialist), who, after further blood tests and other investigations, may give special hormones to slow or stop further growth if that is desired. It is very important to do this at an early stage, because it is better to slow growth than to try and stop it suddenly when the rapidly maturing woman may already be far taller than she wishes. See your GP to arrange the initial X-ray.

Q **I have been stuttering since early childhood, and am now 25. Could you please tell me the cause, and recommend a medicine which will be of some benefit.**

A Stuttering is the involuntary repetition of a sound during speech. The speaker is unable to proceed past this point in speech for some seconds, but eventually s/he overcomes the barrier, and the remaining part of the sentence or phrase comes out in a rush.

The cause of stuttering is unknown, but it tends to start with the commencement of speech between two and four years of age. It is more common in boys than girls, and more likely if one parent is, or was, a stutterer.

Some experts believe that emotional insecurity, anxiety and disturbances in childhood can be a trigger for stuttering, but this theory is not accepted by all. It may be that the insecurity and anxiety is caused by the stammer, rather than the converse.

An association between left–right confusion and stuttering has also been noted.

If the person is tense, hurried or confused, the stammer will be worse. Helping a stammerer to finish a sentence only agitates him/her more, and worsens the problem with the next sentence.

The consonants are the usual block in stammerers, and the letters 'p' and 'b' are the most commonly involved.

Interestingly, stammerers can usually sing without stammering, even if it is a sentence they had been totally unable to complete previously. Some stammerers use a sing-song cadence to their speech pattern to overcome their problem, and speech therapists may use singing as a starting point in their treatment of stuttering. A metronome may also be used during treatment to correctly pace the speech pattern.

Treatment involves assessment by a paediatrician to exclude any of the rare underlying brain conditions that may contribute to stuttering, followed by long-term treatment by a speech therapist. Psychologists and/or psychiatrists may also be involved in counselling at intervals through this treatment.

Other than brief use of minor anti-anxiety drugs, no medication can help stuttering, but given persistence over many months or years, most patients can learn to cope with their disorder with the dedicated assistance of a speech therapist.

P

PATHOLOGY

Q My doctor wants me to have a blood test, but I am scared stiff. What actually happens during a blood test? Does it hurt?

A The doctor may take the blood in the surgery or you may be asked to go to a nearby pathology clinic. Either way, the sample will be sent to a laboratory for analysis, unless a relatively simple test is required, in which case the doctor may have the necessary equipment in the surgery to perform the analysis (eg. for blood sugar).

Blood is extracted by inserting a hollow needle into a vein and allowing an amount of blood to flow into an attached tube. The blood will usually be taken from a vein at the bend in your elbow, but if that is not sufficiently prominent, the nurse may try your forearm or the back of your hand. It takes only a minute or so. Once the nurse has sufficient blood for the tests that have been ordered, the needle will be withdrawn and a dressing or cotton wool pressed on to the point of entry to stop the flow. You will need to leave it in place for half an hour or so until the blood clots naturally.

Sometimes the blood can be taken at any time of the day, but if the test is to measure your metabolism (how your body converts food into energy), the test must be performed in the early morning after a 12 hour fast, or at particular times after you have eaten a certain measured amount of food.

Blood tests to measure the amount of certain drugs in the system are also taken at specific times after the tablets are swallowed.

Blood tests hurt far less than a normal injection such as a flu shot because nothing is injected. If you do not watch the nurse, you will barely notice the discomfort, which will be no worse than having someone pinch your skin.

Q I had a blood test at a local shopping centre that showed my urea to be 10.9 instead of between 2.5 and 7.9. What does this mean?

A Random blood tests at shopping centres are notoriously unreliable, particularly for substances such as cholesterol. I assume that in your case, the high urea reading was an isolated finding on a machine that scans for many different substances.

A urea reading of 10.9 is certainly high, and the first thing you should do is to arrange for your GP to repeat the test using a recognised laboratory. This reading can then be compared to other results, the results of a physical examination, and your medical history, to make an appropriate diagnosis.

Elevated urea levels are usually found in kidney disease, but other tests are usually abnormal as well.

Don't start worrying until you confirm that there really is a problem.

Q I am a 50 year old male. My total cholesterol is 4.2, my HDL is 0.7 and my LDL is 3.0. I have encountered a difference of opinion between doctors as to whether this is a good level or a bad level, and one doctor has said that I cannot get Medicare benefits for a blood test at these levels. What do you think?

A   There is considerable debate between doctors over just what the ideal level of cholesterol should be, and this debate is now even more controversial because the government has delineated a set of criteria that must be met before Medicare payments for cholesterol blood tests will be funded. There is also a very complex formula for deciding who is allowed subsidised treatment for high cholesterol levels under the Pharmaceutical Benefits Scheme.

The following criteria are mine personally, and do not necessarily reflect any official line.

A total cholesterol of under 5.5 is of no concern. A cholesterol between 5.5 and 7.0 is a grey area, and treatment would depend on the ratio of the two main types of cholesterol (high—HDL, and low—LDL), family history of heart disease and stroke, smoking, blood pressure and obesity. Over a level of 7.0, most patients should be treated.

The HDL (high density lipoproteins) are generally good for you, while the LDL (low density lipoproteins) are bad. HDL should be above 0.9 and LDL below 3.0.

On the total cholesterol criteria you do not require treatment, but your ratios are slightly unfavourable. Your doctors are right in saying that under present government criteria you cannot have a blood test for the ratios under Medicare, and the government will not subsidise any treatment.

I do not know your family history etc., but unless other factors are extremely bad, I do not believe that you require treatment at this time.

Q   **On a routine blood test, my ESR was high, and now my GP keeps ordering new tests to find out why. What could this mean?**

A   The erythrocyte sedimentation rate (ESR) is a frequently performed blood test that gives an indication of inflammation, infection or cancer in the body, but gives no indication of where the disease is located, or the nature of the disease. It is a measure of the rate at which erythrocytes (red blood cells) settle in a thin tube. The higher the rate, the more significant the result.

It is a warning sign to doctors to watch out for some significant disease, but may be raised in anything from a simple viral infection or pregnancy to a heart attack or most types of cancer.

It is sensible to find out whether the cause for your raised ESR is serious or inconsequential. If the level rapidly returns to normal, there is usually nothing to be concerned about, but if it continues to rise test after test, the cause must be found.

Q   **My doctor says I have to stop my wine drinking because my GGT is high. What on earth is GGT and why is it affected by wine?**

A   Liver function tests are performed on a sample of blood and measure the presence of certain enzymes in the blood that are produced by the liver. If these enzymes are present in excessive quantities, the liver is under stress or damaged. Conditions such as hepatitis, liver abscess, gall bladder disease, cancer, drug reactions (eg. to epilepsy medications) and alcoholism may cause abnormal liver enzyme levels.

One particular enzyme, gamma glutamyl transferase (GGT), is usually raised in association with alcohol abuse. The fact that your level of this enzyme is raised indicates that too much alcohol has been entering your body, thus your doctor's warning to slow down before more serious liver damage occurs.

Q   What do the results of the prostate cancer blood test mean?

A   A test for the prostate specific antigen (PSA) can be used to follow the success of treatment for prostate cancer and infection. If the levels drop, treatment is successful, if they rise it is not.

There has been a lot of controversy about the use of this test as a screening test for prostate cancer. A level of PSA below 4 micrograms per litre is nearly always normal, but unfortunately, many conditions other than cancer can cause the results to be high, and so it is not an absolute test for prostate cancer. A combination of tests for different types of PSA (free and combined PSA) may be a better form of screening, but is quite expensive.

At present the best way to determine if a person has prostate problems is to question them about their toilet habits (can they start their stream of urine easily, and does the urine come out freely and hit the porcelain, or does it dribble on their boots), and to examine the prostate gland directly by placing a finger through the anus to feel the gland.

Q   How can blood tests determine if you had a particular infection years ago? I am pregnant and my doctor said after doing tests that I had German measles in the past, but I cannot remember this.

A   If you get an infection, or a vaccination against an infection, your blood produces antibodies to fight it. These antibodies remain even after the infection has cleared, and usually prevent most viral infections from developing again, in other words you are immune to it. Rubella (German measles) and chickenpox are examples of infections which, once suffered, will not usually recur.

A doctor may order a blood test to find out if a patient is at risk from a particular disease. For example, the doctor will want to know if a woman has had rubella (which can harm the foetus if the mother develops it during early pregnancy) or whether she should be immunised against it—although immunisation during pregnancy is not advisable.

Sometimes tests are carried out to detect the presence of antigens themselves (antigens are substances that the body regards as foreign and to which it will develop antibodies). The presence of particular antigens in the blood indicates that the organism is still active and that, even though the symptoms have subsided, the person may be a carrier of a disease such as hepatitis B.

The progress of certain diseases can be assessed by testing the blood for specific immunoglobulins (antibodies) which differ according to whether the disease is current or past. Many infectious diseases such as glandular fever, AIDS, various forms of hepatitis, Ross River fever and measles can be diagnosed and followed by this type of test.

Q   My doctor has ordered an FBC on the pathology form, and the receptionist said this was a full blood count, but couldn't tell me why it was being done or what it involves. Can you help me?

A   A full blood count (FBC) is the most frequently performed of all blood tests. It gives an enormous amount of information about your blood and the state of your overall health. A blood sample is taken from the vein on the inside of your elbow and smeared onto a glass slide.

The smear of blood is examined under a microscope and the number of different types of cells present are counted. Computers have now been programmed to do these counts very rapidly and automatically.

Blood cells consist of three different types—red cells (erythrocytes), white cells (leucocytes) and platelets (thrombocytes). Red cells carry the red pigment haemoglobin which is used to transport oxygen. There are several different types of white cells that fight infection, and platelets are one of the main factors that enable blood to clot.

A blood count determines the number of all these cells, their size, and the proportions in which they exist, as well as the amount of haemoglobin present. If you consult a doctor because you are unduly tired and lacking in energy, it may mean that you are anaemic, that you have an infection or some other disease, or simply that you are working too hard. By ordering a blood count, the doctor can often find out which it is.

If you are anaemic, you will have insufficient haemoglobin or too few red blood cells. If you have a bacterial infection it is likely that your white blood cells will have increased (leucocytosis) to fight it, while a viral infection often decreases white blood cell levels (leucopenia) as the virus destroys them. A lack of platelets (thrombocytopenia) will cause excessive bruising and bleeding as the blood is unable to clot normally.

If the full blood count is normal, further tests may be necessary to determine the cause of your tiredness, or reassurance may be all that is required.

Q What are electrolytes? I have been told by my GP that mine are a bit low, and he wants to do another blood test.

A The levels of the ions (electrically charged particles) of sodium, potassium, chloride and bicarbonate in the blood must be in perfect balance in the body in order to maintain the acidity of the blood within very narrow boundaries. These are collectively known as electrolytes, and all can be very accurately measured.

If the levels of these ions varies significantly from normal, the electrical activity of the brain and nerves, and the function of the heart and other organs may be adversely affected. Conditions such as severe diarrhoea, prolonged vomiting, dehydration, kidney failure, massive infection, diabetes and starvation can affect electrolyte levels.

Your doctor has probably found a minor irregularity and is doing further tests to see if it persists and warrants further investigation.

Q My mother and sister have had breast cancer, and my doctor wants me to have expensive blood tests every year to see if I will get it. How do these work and are they reliable?

A The development of blood tests for specific antigens that are produced against particular types of cancer is one of the most exciting recent developments in pathology. Unfortunately the technology is still far from perfect, but antigens against a number of cancers including those that occur in the breast, pancreas, liver, colon, ovary, uterus and prostate have so far been detected.

Unfortunately they are unreliable as a way of detecting cancer as there is no absolute value in any one person above which a cancer can be said to be present, but a series of tests over a period of months or years may show increasing levels of the antigen which may indicate the presence of a particular cancer.

The tests are particularly useful in following the progress of treatment in a patient (if successful, antigen levels should decrease steadily), or in watching a patient who has a bad family history of a particular type of cancer.

The cost is not covered by Medicare, and so these tests are expensive, but may be useful in your situation. You must, of course, continue to regularly examine your breasts yourself, and have mammograms every year or two.

Q **I have been told to take warfarin tablets life long as my heart beats irregularly, but I have to have blood tests every couple of weeks. What are these tests for?**

A A clotting or coagulation test measures how long it takes the blood to clot. This test may be ordered for someone who bruises or bleeds excessively to find out if they are a sufferer from an hereditary disease such as haemophilia (in which the blood does not clot and so even a minor accident can cause excessive bleeding), or one of the many other diseases that can reduce clotting.

Patients with a high risk of blood clots forming in the heart, an artery or vein, which may result in a heart attack, lung damage or stroke, may be placed on anticoagulant drugs such as warfarin. Clotting tests are carried out regularly to monitor the effect of these drugs and to ensure that a balance is maintained between preventing a clot forming and stopping the blood clotting at all.

These tests are often reported as a ratio (international normalised ratio—INR) which measures how much longer the patient takes to stop bleeding than normal. A person with an INR of 3 takes three times as long to stop bleeding as a normal person. The doctor will determine the INR which is desirable for the patient (usually between 2 and 3.5), depending upon their diagnosis.

Warfarin may be life-saving in the correct dose, but if too much or too little is taken, there may be excessive internal bleeding, or the drug may not act to prevent dangerous blood clots in arteries. This is why regular blood tests are essential.

Q **I have a funny looking patch on my leg and my GP wants to biopsy this to make a diagnosis. Why is this necessary and what does it involve?**

A A biopsy is the removal of a small piece of tissue from a part of the body so that it can be examined under a microscope to detect the presence of abnormal or diseased cells. It is one of the surest ways to determine what disease is present.

Biopsies are particularly important in the diagnosis of cancer and will often be performed when there is a skin abnormality for which there is no apparent cause and when the doctor feels that the only way to reach an accurate diagnosis is by taking a piece of that skin and looking at the cells directly.

The procedure is quite simple—a piece of skin is merely cut away, using a local anaesthetic. Once the tissue has been extracted, it is usually placed in preservative and sent to the laboratory, where it is set in wax and finely sliced. The slices are then mounted on a glass slide and stained with various dyes which highlight different characteristics. Abnormal cells can be identified and treatment can be decided upon according to the results.

Once the correct diagnosis has been made, appropriate treatment can be given.

Q   What can doctors find out about you with a test on your faeces?

A   Because faeces have passed through much of the body, an analysis of their composition can be an indication of abnormalities and disorders existing in the body.

A faeces sample is collected by using a disposable plastic spoon to place a small amount of faeces into a sterile plastic container.

One of the most common reasons for testing the faeces is the suspected presence of parasites or worms in the intestines. In such a case, the eggs, body parts or entire bodies can often be seen quite easily in the faeces using a microscope.

The colour of the faeces can indicate something abnormal. Black or red faeces may indicate bleeding in the stomach or intestines, while tan or white faeces may be a sign of liver or gall bladder problems.

Even if nothing abnormal can be seen in the faeces, chemical tests may show that blood is in fact present.

An analysis of the fat and salt content of the faeces tells if food is being properly digested and absorbed, or if there is some digestive disorder present.

A culture test performed on the faeces may be carried out to determine a possible infectious cause of diarrhoea.

Q.   What tests can be done to see if you are allergic to different foods?

A   This is not as easy as it seems. You must have a fair idea of what you might be allergic to before the tests can be done, because they are very specific for every possible food, animal, dust, pollen or other substance that you can react to.

There is a screening blood test that measures the number of eosinophils (a type of white blood cell) in your blood, and if this is normal, you almost certainly have no allergies. If it is raised, you may have an allergy or viral infection.

Skin tests for allergies consist of the injection of various substances under the skin. These substances, called allergens, are found in cat fur, house dust, pollen from various plants etc. Allergies to certain foods and drugs can also be tested. If you react to a particular injection, then the source of the allergy has been identified. The process is one of elimination, and consequently may be very slow.

There are also blood tests (RAST test) that can be performed to detect reactions in the blood to specific substances. These are expensive though, and only half a dozen at a time are usually covered by Medicare.

Allergy testing is especially important for people who react violently to things such as bee stings, since they may need desensitising treatment or to carry a supply of adrenaline in case of emergency.

PREGNANCY

See also BABIES

Q   I plan to fall pregnant soon. Should I see a doctor for a check-up first?

A   Before a woman embarks on her first pregnancy, a physical examination may reveal unknown factors in her health that may have a significant effect on her ability to fall pregnant or successfully carry a child. High blood pressure, diabetes, back disease and gynaecological problems are examples of these. A woman should be taught how to examine and care for her breasts, and one of her regular Pap smear tests should be performed.

A A blood test for a past history of Rubella (German Measles) infection will be arranged and a vaccination given if necessary. Advice on correct diet and eating patterns, weight control and bowel habits can all have a bearing on fertility. Even details on how to get pregnant (no, I don't mean what position or sexual technique, but at what time of the month to try) can be useful.

A pre-pregnancy check-up is of great benefit to all women. It is a custom that should be encouraged.

Q **My first child was a boy, and I want to have a girl next time. Is there any way in which I can improve my chances of having a girl?**

A There is no way in which the sex of a child can be guaranteed, but the following system (known as Shettles' system) may increase the odds in your favour. At best, this system increases the chances of a child of a particular sex from 50% to 75%. It is definitely NOT a guarantee of success, and it may make it more difficult to fall pregnant at all!

Ovulation (release of the egg from the ovary) occurs 14 days before a period starts. If you usually have 28 days from the beginning of one period to the beginning of the next, you will ovulate 14 days after the first day of your last period. If your cycle is usually 30 days, you will ovulate 16 days after the first day of your last period. For the following system to work, you must know when you usually ovulate.

TO INCREASE THE CHANCE OF HAVING A GIRL:
1. Ten minutes before sex, use a vaginal douche consisting of 20 mL of white vinegar in 500 mL of cooled boiled water.
2. Have sex frequently in the seven to ten days before you ovulate.
3. No sex from one day before ovulation until ten days after ovulation.
4. Your partner should ejaculate just inside the vagina, and not deeply inside as usual.
5. Your partner should withdraw immediately after ejaculation.
6. It is better for the woman not to have an orgasm.

TO INCREASE THE CHANCE OF HAVING A BOY:
1. Ten minutes before sex, use a vaginal douche consisting of 5 g of baking powder in 500 mL of cooled boiled water.
2. No sex from the end of your period until the day ovulation occurs.
3. Twice daily sex from the day of ovulation for four days.
4. Your partner should ejaculate deep inside the vagina.
5. Your partner should withdraw immediately after ejaculation.
6. It is better for the woman to have an orgasm, ideally just before ejaculation.
Good luck!

Q **My period is a week late and I've never been late before. Is this serious?**

A 'All females between fifteen and fifty should be considered to be pregnant until proved otherwise'. This saying was pounded into me as a medical student so that

I would not commit the sin of prescribing damaging medications to a pregnant woman. In your case, the first thing to do is exclude (or confirm) pregnancy.

There are other causes for a missed period though. These include stress and anxiety, other illnesses (even a bad cold can delay a period), the onset of menopause, an underactive thyroid gland, ovarian diseases, rapid weight loss, strenuous exercise (highly competitive athletes often stop menstruating), drugs (including the contraceptive pill, which may harmlessly stop your periods with time) and a host of rarer diseases.

See your doctor to get a pregnancy test, and take the matter further from there if necessary.

Q I know a woman's periods stop when you get pregnant, but are there any other signs in a woman that she is pregnant? My girlfriend says she is pregnant, but she is acting very peculiarly, and I am not sure if she is being truthful.

A When a woman becomes pregnant, her body undergoes many changes, but I'm afraid that none of these are really specific enough for you to tell by looking at her if your girlfriend is really pregnant.

Very early, the breasts will enlarge and become tender, and a tingling sensation will be felt in the nipples. With a first pregnancy, the skin around the nipple (the areola) will darken, and the small lubricating glands may become more prominent to create small bumps, but this darkening may also occur with the oral contraceptive pill.

Hormonal changes in early pregnancy cause the woman to want to urinate more frequently. This settles down after the twelfth week, but later in pregnancy the size of the womb puts pressure on the bladder, and frequent urination is again necessary.

Some women find that they develop dark patches on the forehead and cheeks. Called chloasma, these patches are caused by hormonal changes affecting the pigment cells in the skin. Such changes can also be a side effect of the contraceptive pill. The navel and a line down the centre of the woman's belly may also darken. These pigment changes fade somewhat after the pregnancy but will always remain darker than before.

It is obviously time for you and your girlfriend to have a serious discussion, and you may offer to accompany her to her first antenatal doctor's visit, as I am sure you wish to be fully involved with the new baby. See what her reaction is, and take things from there.

Q How soon can pregnancy be diagnosed by blood and urine tests?

A Modern urine pregnancy tests used by doctors are now nearly as accurate as blood tests. These new urine tests have been developed through genetic engineering techniques to enable the unique hormone of pregnancy (known as human chorionic gonadotrophin) to be detected as early as two days BEFORE a period is expected, or twelve days after the sexual intercourse that is responsible for a pregnancy.

Any woman who is at all late in having her period, and feels she may be pregnant, should visit her general practitioner. Most doctors will not accept the results of a home testing kit as proof of pregnancy.

Blood tests are only marginally more accurate, and usually only ordered in women who have kidneys that fail to excrete the pregnancy hormone.

Q Is there an easy way to calculate when a pregnant woman is due to deliver?

A Add 7 days to the day the woman's last period started, and 9 months to the month of her last period. eg: If the last period started on 5th January 2002 (5.1.02), she will be due on 12th October 2002 (12.10.02). The calculation is shown again in the example below:

$$
\begin{array}{r}
5 \ . \ \ 1. \ 02 \\
+ \ \ 7 \ . \ \ 9 \quad\quad \\
\hline
= 12 \ . \ 10. \ 02
\end{array}
$$

A pregnancy lasts 40 weeks from the beginning of the last period, but only 38 weeks from conception, because a woman ovulates two weeks after her period starts.

Q I have just learnt that I am pregnant for the first time, and I am very anxious that nothing should go wrong. I keep hearing about women who have done something during their pregnancy that has caused a deformity. What drugs and medicines should I avoid in pregnancy?

A Many things should be avoided in pregnancy, and not just the medicinal types of drugs that you are considering.

Smoking causes you to inhale many drugs that can cause small and immature babies and has been associated with birth deformities. The embryo is bathed in hundreds of foreign chemicals that are inhaled with every puff. If you smoke and plan to get pregnant, ask your doctor how to stop now!

Alcohol should be avoided during the first three months of pregnancy when the vital organs of the foetus are developing. Even in later pregnancy, only one drink every few days with a meal is allowed, and never get drunk.

All medications should be avoided during that vital first three months unless prescribed by a doctor who knows you are in early pregnancy. Later in pregnancy, check with your pharmacist or doctor before using even the simple grocery type pharmaceuticals.

All illegal drugs, including marijuana, will cause damage to the developing infant. If you are addicted, discuss the problem confidentially with your doctor well before you fall pregnant, so that expert help can be obtained. Avoid the temptation to have the spontaneous smoke of pot or sniff of cocaine during the pregnancy—the consequences could haunt you for life every time you look at your child.

Q I had some bleeding early in my pregnancy, and had to rest in bed for two weeks. Will this increase the risk of an abnormal baby?

A No! Exhaustive studies have not shown any increase in infant abnormalities after bleeding in early pregnancy. The bleeding may have been due to a slight separation of the placenta from the wall of the womb as it was growing, and almost certainly did not involve your baby directly.

About 30% of all pregnant women suffer from some degree of bleeding during pregnancy, and some have quite severe bleeds without losing the baby.

A bleed may indicate the early stages of a miscarriage, but not necessarily so. There is no treatment available for a threatened miscarriage except bed rest. Women who have repeated miscarriages may be given additional hormonal or surgical treatment by a gynaecologist.

Q **What can I take for a headache in pregnancy? Is aspirin safe?**

A Both aspirin and paracetamol are safe to take in pregnancy for headaches or other minor pains, but aspirin should be avoided in the last few weeks of pregnancy as it may cause minor problems with bleeding during the delivery and jaundice in the baby if taken at this late stage.

As a general rule, no woman should take any medication during pregnancy unless she checks with her doctor first. The most dangerous period is the first twelve weeks after conception, when all the vital organs are forming and joining. After 12 weeks, there is no new development, and the perfectly formed miniature human spends the next six months growing to a size suitable for delivery.

Many medications are safe in pregnancy, and should be used to treat the symptoms and diseases that develop, but only after being carefully checked by your doctor.

Q **I am only three months pregnant, but very keen to breast feed my baby when he/she is born. How soon should you start breast feeding after having a baby?**

A Breast feeding may be started immediately after birth in the labour ward. Babies have an instinct that enables them to turn towards the nipple when it is brushed against their cheek, and the suckling at this early stage gives comfort to both mother and child.

In the next few days, relatively frequent feeds should be the rule to give stimulation to the breast and build up the milk supply. The breast milk is initially called colostrum and is thin and yellow. It slowly becomes thicker and whiter over the next week, and contains vital ingredients for the baby's growth and health.

After the first week, the frequency of feeding should be determined by the mother's and child's needs, not laid down by any arbitrary authority. Each will work out what is best for them, with the number of feeds varying between five and ten a day.

Unfortunately, for a variety of reasons, not all mothers are comfortable with breast feeding (despite what the ardent supporters of lactation may say). These women should not feel guilty or failures, but should accept that this is a problem that can occur through no fault of theirs, and be grateful that there are excellent feeding formulas available for their child.

Q **Can you give me information on a blighted ovum? My pregnancy ended earlier this year in grief, although I am now pregnant again and due in seven weeks. I was told that 9 out of 10 miscarriages are caused by a blighted ovum.**

A The term 'blighted ovum' is one used by doctors to describe a pregnancy that is not producing a baby and will inevitably end in a miscarriage.

At least 15% of pregnancies end as a miscarriage before the end of the third month, and most of these because of a blighted ovum, so what has happened to you is not at all abnormal.

In a pregnancy, two things are produced—a baby, and the placenta. The placenta acts to take nutrition and oxygen from the mother to the baby in the womb, and remove wastes from the baby to be taken away by the mother.

If in the first few weeks of pregnancy, a baby does not develop, but the placenta does, then the woman has a blighted ovum. Women who do have a miscarriage for this reason should not think that they have lost a baby, but have never had a baby, and just a placenta-like growth that is of no use to the mother, and is discarded by the body in the same way that a normal placenta ('afterbirth') would be discarded after the birth of a baby.

I am delighted that you have now achieved a successful pregnancy, and this is the normal pattern, because a blighted ovum in no way prevents you from having a normal pregnancy at a later time.

Q **Recently my first pregnancy ended in its 7th week because I have a bi-horn uterus. What chances do I have of a normal and successful pregnancy in the future?**

A A bihorn uterus is one that is split down the middle into two separate, but smaller uteruses. They usually open into the vagina through the one cervix, but rarely two cervixes are present. It is a developmental defect, and has been present since you were born. It is an uncommon condition, but does not prevent a normal pregnancy from developing. There is a slightly higher rate of pregnancy complications, but there should be no reason that you cannot in due course have your own child.

Q **What can I do for morning sickness? I'm nine weeks pregnant, can't keep anything down and I'm losing weight. I'm worried it might affect the baby.**

A Debendox was the medication used for over 20 years to very effectively control morning sickness in women around the world until 1985. Some very flimsy evidence led to some suits in the United States that cost the manufacturer a great deal of money. Not for any medical reason, but because they could not afford to defend the suits bought by women who had abnormal babies, the manufacturer stopped making Debendox.

There is now NO medication available specifically for morning sickness. For women afflicted by the problem, a diet of dry food, small amounts taken frequently rather than three meals a day, is probably the best solution. Some women get relief from vitamin B6 capsules 200 mg per day (but NO more!). Antihistamine such as Phenergan can also be used in severe cases, but they cause significant drowsiness and other annoying side effects. A mixture called 'Emetrol' helps women with mild to moderate morning sickness. Merbentyl is another drug that has been used successfully in some women.

If the problem cannot be controlled, and the vomiting persists to the point where the woman is losing weight and becoming dehydrated, hospitalisation is necessary to give intravenous feeding and bed rest. You should keep in regular contact with your doctor so that the condition of yourself and the baby can be closely monitored.

Q I have fallen pregnant to a boy I don't really like and I'm considering an abortion. I would like to know what happens in this operation.

A I will not enter into the moral, ethical or legal side of this debate, but will merely give the bare clinical facts.

Provided you are less than twelve weeks pregnant, an abortion is a technically simple procedure. More advanced pregnancies are more difficult to terminate.

On attending the clinic where the procedure is to be performed, you should be questioned about your overall health and the details of the pregnancy. You will be examined generally and internally, a pregnancy test may be performed, and an ultrasound scan should normally be done to determine the exact stage of pregnancy.

Once these details are completed, and you are determined to proceed, you will be taken to an operating theatre and a general anaesthetic will be given. While you are anaesthetised, a thin tube is introduced up your vagina and through the cervix into the uterus (womb). Suction apparatus is attached to the other end of the tube, and the tube is moved around inside the uterus, sucking out the contents which includes the developing foetus and placenta.

There are several other techniques, but this is now the most common.

The operation lasts only ten to fifteen minutes, and you will wake up from the anaesthetic in a recovery room. After a couple of hours you will be allowed to go home, but should have an internal check by a doctor (often your own general practitioner) in the next day or two to ensure that there are no complications.

If you have any abnormal bleeding, discharge or develop a fever in the week or two after the abortion, you should see a doctor immediately.

Q How dangerous is smoking during pregnancy? Does it cause miscarriages?

A There is no doubt that the babies of mothers who smoke are smaller (by 250 g on average) than those of non-smoking mothers. There is also an increased rate of both premature labour (delivering the baby too early) and miscarriage in these women.

After birth these babies continue to suffer both directly and indirectly from their mothers' smoking. The smoking by the mother appears to reduce their resistance to disease, and infections in particular, so that babies born to smoking mothers die in infancy more often than average. By inhaling the smoke from either of their parents, these infants have more colds, bronchitis and other respiratory problems than babies in non-smoking homes.

Any woman who smokes should ideally cease before she falls pregnant, but certainly no later than when the pregnancy is diagnosed. This is far easier said than done, but if the husband stops at the same time, support and encouragement is given by family and friends, and assistance is obtained from the family doctor, women who are motivated to give their baby the best possible chance in life will succeed in kicking this very addictive habit.

Q My last pregnancy ended as a miscarriage, and I am now ten weeks pregnant again, but I am 38 years old, and my doctor wants me to have an amniocentesis in a few weeks. What do you think about these tests?

The obstetrician says there are some risks with it.

A   There is no simple answer to this question, so you must understand as much as possible about the test to enable you to make up your own mind.

While a foetus is in the womb, it is surrounded by the amniotic sac which contains fluid that protects it from harm. Amniocentesis is a procedure in which a small amount of the amniotic fluid is drawn off, and the cells it contains are cultured and analysed under a microscope to give information about the health of the baby. It will also disclose the baby's sex. The cells contain the baby's chromosomes, which it has inherited from its parents. These chromosomes can be analysed to give information about nearly 100 different genetic disorders, such as Down's syndrome.

There is a slightly increased possibility of miscarriage as a result of amniocentesis, and it will not usually be carried out unless there is some risk of abnormality.

Risk factors include:

— A woman who is over 37 years of age, especially if it is her first child. Older mothers are significantly more at risk of giving birth to a Down's syndrome child and will usually be offered this test as a matter of routine at between 16 and 18 weeks of pregnancy.

— One or other parent with a known chromosomal abnormality. For example, a woman may be a carrier of a genetic disorder such as haemophilia, which does not affect her, but which her sons have a 50% chance of inheriting.

— Certain diseases that run in either parent's family (eg. muscular dystrophy).

— The fact that the mother has had three or more miscarriages.

— An earlier abnormal child, or a close family member with an abnormal child.

Before the procedure, an ultrasound scan will be performed so that the position of the foetus and placenta can be pinpointed. The woman will then be given a local anaesthetic in the abdomen, following which a hollow needle will be inserted through the abdominal wall into the uterus. About 14 mL (roughly two dessertspoons) of fluid will be removed by a syringe attached to the needle.

Amniocentesis is performed not less than 14 weeks (and usually 16–18 weeks) after the last period, because until then there is not enough amniotic fluid or cells to analyse.

Amniocentesis results are 99% reliable. The risk of injury to the baby is practically nil. The risk of a miscarriage occurring is very slight—about one in 200. Complications such as infection and bleeding are also rare.

It is not, however, a procedure that should be undertaken lightly. There is a risk, albeit a slight one. You will need to think about what your reaction will be if the results should prove to be abnormal. If you would not consider having the pregnancy terminated under any circumstances, the test is probably pointless. There is a long wait for the results and this can be stressful. Terminating a pregnancy at the stage the results become known is distressing and may need to be the same as an induced labour.

Q   **I am eight months pregnant, but I am worried that my beautiful breasts will be ruined if I feed my baby. Why is breast feeding better than bottle?**

A   'BREAST FEEDING IS BEST'. This admonition features prominently on cans of infant formula and on advertising for breast milk substitutes in many third world countries, and there is little doubt that it is true. The advantages of breast feeding include the obvious convenience of avoiding the need to sterilise bottles and prepare formulas, but more significant is the advantages it gives the child in protecting it from some childhood infections, and stimulating the mother's uterus to contract to its pre-pregnant size more rapidly. Being a cost-free food, it can also help the strained budget of a young couple.

Breast feeding does not necessarily mean that your breasts will become saggy or alter adversely. You will have to decide upon the relative benefits to your baby and yourself.

Q **I am well into my pregnancy, and keep hearing all these horror stories about childbirth. What really happens? Is it really terrible for the woman? Can you just be knocked out with an anaesthetic?**

A No, things are not that bad. Although I am a male doctor, I have delivered over 300 babies, and so have reasonable experience of observing women in the last stages of pregnancy and labour. I will do my best to describe what happens.

In the last few weeks you waddle around uncomfortably. Every few hours you have Branxton-Hicks contractions that can be quite uncomfortable and sometimes wake you at night, but they always fade away. Your back aches, and you are going to the toilet every hour because your bladder has nowhere to expand.

One day you notice that you have lost some blood-stained fluid through the vagina, and the contractions are worse than usual. You have passed the mucus plug that seals the cervix during pregnancy, and if a lot of fluid is lost, you may have ruptured the membranes around the baby as well. Labour should start very soon after this 'show'.

Shortly afterwards you can feel the first contraction. It passes quickly, but every ten to fifteen minutes more contractions occur. Most are mild, but some make you stop in your tracks for a few seconds. They are rather like the cramping pains you may have with a heavy period. When you find that two contractions have occurred only five to seven minutes apart, it is time to be taken to hospital or the birthing centre.

You are now in the first of the three stages of labour. This stage will last for about 12 hours with a first pregnancy, but will be much shorter (4 to 8 hours) with subsequent pregnancies. These times can vary significantly from one woman to another.

Once you arrive at hospital, you change into a nightie and answer questions. Soon afterwards, you may be given an enema. By the time the obstetrician calls in to see how you are progressing, the contractions may be occurring every three or four minutes. The obstetrician examines you internally to check how far the cervix (the opening into the womb) has opened. This check will be performed several times during labour, and leads may be attached through the vagina to the baby's head to monitor its heart and general condition. The cervix steadily opens until it merges with the walls of the uterus. A fully dilated cervix is about 10 cm in diameter, and you may hear the doctors and nurses discussing the cervix dilation and measurement.

As the labour progresses, you are moved into the delivery room. In a typical hospital delivery room, white drapes hide bulky pieces of equipment, there are large lights on the ceiling, shiny sinks on one wall, and often a cheerful baby poster above them. The contractions become steadily more intense. If the pain in your abdomen doesn't attack you, the backache does, and your partner (who has hopefully attended one or two of your antenatal classes) should massage your back between pains. The breathing exercises you were taught at the antenatal classes should prove remarkably effective in helping you with the more severe contractions. Even so, the combined backache and sharp stabs of pain may need to be relieved by an injection offered by the nurse. Breathing nitrous oxide gas on a mask when the contractions start can also make them more bearable.

Eventually you develop an irresistible desire to start pushing with all your might. Your cervix will be fully dilated by this stage, and you are now entering the second stage of labour, which will last from only a few minutes to 60 minutes or more.

Then you are being urged to push, and even though it hurts, it doesn't seem to matter any more, and you labour with all your might to force the head of the baby out of your body. The contractions are much more intense than before, but you should push only at the time of a contraction, as pushing at other times is wasted effort. Another push, and another, and another, and then a sudden sweeping, elating relief, followed by a healthy cry from your new baby.

Immediately after the delivery, you are given an injection to help contract the uterus. A minute or so after the baby is born, the umbilical cord which has been the lifeline between you and the baby for the last nine months is clamped and cut. A small sample of cord blood is often taken from the cord to check for any problems in the baby.

About five minutes after the baby is born, the doctor will urge you to push again and help to expel the placenta (afterbirth). This is the third stage of labour.

If you have had an episiotomy (cut) to help open your passage for the baby's head, or if there has been a tear, the doctor will now repair this with a few sutures.

You should be allowed to nurse the baby for a while (on the breast if you wish) after the birth. Then both you and the baby will be washed and cleaned, and taken back to the ward for a good rest.

Your pregnancy is over, and you have a new baby to prove it.

Q I have been told that I will have to deliver my baby by Caesarean section. Can you tell me about this operation?

The operation is extremely safe to both mother and child. A light anaesthetic is given to the mother, and the baby is usually delivered within five minutes. The anaesthetic is then deepened while the longer and more complex task of repairing the womb and abdominal muscles is undertaken. In many cases, the scar of a Caesarean can be low and horizontal, below the bikini line, to avoid any disfigurement. The latest innovation is epidural anaesthesia, where a needle is placed in the middle of the mother's back, and through this an anaesthetic is introduced. The woman is feels nothing below the waist, and although sedated, is quite awake and able to participate in the birth of her baby, seeing it only seconds after it is delivered by the surgeon. Some doctors and hospitals allow husbands to be present during these deliveries.

Recovery from a Caesarean is slower than for normal childbirth, but most women leave hospital within ten days. It does not affect breast feeding, the chances of future pregnancies or increase the risk of miscarriage. If your doctor has recommended, or performed a Caesarean section for you, it will have been to ensure the safety of both you and your baby.

Q I will be having my baby by Caesarean section, and the obstetrician said he would arrange for a spinal anaesthetic. What is a spinal anaesthetic? Why do doctors use them?

A The spinal cord inside the vertebrae of your back carries all the nerve impulses to and from the lower part of your body.

If a needle is inserted between two vertebrae in the back and an anaesthetic agent injected, the nerves below that level will cease to transmit the pain sensations from the legs, pelvis and abdomen to the brain. The nerves that control your muscles and their movement are not affected. This is a spinal anaesthetic.

Doctors use this type of anaesthesia in a difficult childbirth and Caesarean section because it has no effect on the baby. They are also used in elderly and debilitated people who may be at risk with a general anaesthetic.

A tube is left in your back during the operation, so that the anaesthetic can be topped up as required, and you have to lie flat in bed for a day or two afterwards. A severe headache is the most common complication.

Q I saw the placenta after I had my baby and it looked really yukky. It hurt almost as much to push this out as having the baby. Can you explain how this works and why is it necessary?

A The placenta is a special outgrowth of the foetus that is firmly attached to the inside of the mother's womb. It has blood vessels that penetrate into the wall of the womb and interact with the mother's arteries and veins to enable the foetus to draw oxygen and food from the mother's system and send waste products to the mother for removal.

The foetus is connected to the placenta by the umbilical cord, which contains three intertwined blood vessels (an artery and two veins) which convey nourishment from the mother to the foetus and waste products the other way. At birth, this is between 15 and 120 cm long and runs from the navel to the placenta, where the artery and veins it contains fan out to interact with the mother's circulatory system. The mother's and baby's bloodstreams remain separate and do not mingle. Doctors will check the cord after birth, and if only one vein is present instead of two, it is probable that the baby will have some hidden birth defect.

The placenta is a flat, circular organ consisting of a spongy network of blood vessels. It acts as a combined lung, liver, kidney and digestive tract for the developing foetus. Oxygen, nutrients, waste products and other substances (eg. alcohol and some drugs) can pass freely through the placenta from the bloodstream of the mother to the bloodstream of the foetus. Infections (particularly viruses such as German measles) may also pass to the foetus through the placenta.

Several minutes after the birth, the placenta (the afterbirth) is expelled by further contractions of the uterus, assisted by gentle traction on the cord by the doctor or midwife. This may be an uncomfortable experience, but is not normally painful.

Q I was told my baby had an 'Apga' of 8 when he was born. Is this good or bad? What does it mean?

A The Apgar score is a number that is given by doctors or midwives to a baby immediately after birth, and again five minutes later. The score gives a rough assessment of the baby's general health. The name is taken from Dr Virginia Apgar, an American anaesthetist, who devised the system in 1953. The score is derived by giving a value of 0, 1 or 2 to each of five variables—heart rate, breathing, muscle tone, reflexes and colour. The maximum score is 10.

APGAR SCORE

SIGN	0	1	2
Heart Rate	Absent	Below 100	Above 100
Breathing	Absent	Weak	Good
Muscle tone	Limp	Poor	Good
Reflexes	Nil	Poor	Good
Colour	Blue/pale	Blue hands and feet	Pink

When estimated at birth, a baby is considered to be seriously distressed if the Apgar score is 5, and critical if the score is 3, when urgent resuscitation is necessary. The situation becomes critical if the score remains below 5 at five minutes after birth. A score of 7 or above is considered normal.

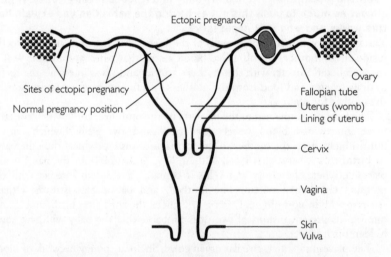

Female reproductive organs showing possible sites of ectopic pregnancy

Q I've had two ectopic pregnancies leaving me with two 'stumps' for Fallopian tubes. What is the danger of having another one?

A 'Ectopic' means 'in the wrong position', so an ectopic pregnancy is one in which the baby is developing in the wrong position.

The Fallopian tubes run from each ovary to the womb (uterus) and transport the egg from the ovary to the womb, where it can be fertilised by a sperm and grow into a baby. If the baby starts growing in the Fallopian tube instead of the uterus, then you have an ectopic pregnancy.

As the baby grows, the tube eventually bursts, causing an internal haemorrhage in the mother, and the almost inevitable death of the baby. An operation is then performed to remove the damaged Fallopian tube and the remains of the pregnancy. This operation leaves you with a 'stump' of Fallopian tube.

To have two ectopic pregnancies is extraordinarily unlucky. Your chance of having a pregnancy of any sort is not good, probably 1:1000, but if you do beat these very long odds and become pregnant, it is possible for you to have a normal pregnancy, although an ectopic pregnancy in some other abnormal position cannot be ruled out.

PROSTATE GLAND
See also MALE PROBLEMS

Q **I am 72 and I can't pee very well any more. I have to stand for ages, and then go back again after half an hour. What can I do to speed things up?**

A The tube from the bladder to the outside in men runs through a golf ball sized gland called the prostate before passing along the penis. The prostate gland is responsible for secreting part of the semen a man ejaculates during sex. There is no female equivalent.

As a man ages, the prostate slowly enlarges, putting pressure on the urethra (the urine carrying tube) so that it is narrowed, and the urine has difficulty in passing. When you go to the toilet, the bladder is usually not emptied completely because of inadequate pressure to keep the narrowed tube open. Therefore the urge to pass urine comes on again after only a short period of time.

The enlargement of the prostate gland is normally benign in older men, but it can be due to a cancer. For this reason it is essential for any man with a poor urinary stream to be checked by a doctor. If a benign enlargement is the cause, a simple operation will set the problem right, and you will rejoin the jet set!

Q **My prostate has been giving trouble, and my surgeon says he is going to remove it—through my penis! How on earth can he do that?**

A Impossible as it may seem, most (but not all) of the prostate can be removed through the penis.

The prostate secretes a fluid that lubricates the urethra (the tube that carries urine from the bladder to the outside) and nurtures sperm. It sits at the base of the penis behind the pubic bone. The gland is the size and shape of a small egg, but in older men it can enlarge to be two or three times this size. There is no cancer or other disease necessarily present when this enlargement occurs, but because of its position around the opening of the urethra from the bladder, it can constrict the outflow of urine from the bladder when it is enlarged (see diagram).

If the flaccid penis is held straight, it is quite easy (under an anaesthetic) for an instrument to be passed down the urethra to the prostate. This instrument has a sharp edged cup at the end, which is used to scrape away layer after layer of the prostate to remove any blockage that is present. The scrapings are then washed out of the bladder and urethra. In this way, a quite large internal gland can be removed through a very small tube.

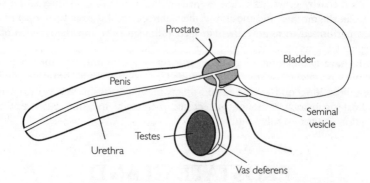

Q **I had my prostate gland removed by an open operation that left a scar across my belly. Now, six months later, I have an egg-sized lump at one end of the scar for which I am wearing a corset. What should I do with this lump?**

A It is possible that you have a cyst in the scar caused by a stitch that has been left behind, but the far more likely explanation is that you have an incisional hernia.

In older people, the frail tissue may break down after an operation, allowing part of the bowel to escape through the deeper layers of the wound to the area just under the skin. If the lump goes away when you lie down, but recurs when you stand or exercise, the problem is almost certainly a hernia.

The development of such a hernia can be caused by a wound infection, but is often just bad luck, as the deeper tissue gives way under the strain of supporting your belly after an operation.

The lump certainly needs to be checked by a doctor, but if it is causing only minimal discomfort, a corset may be all that is required to control it. In other circumstances, further surgery, often with insertion of some surgical mesh to strengthen the area, will be required.

Q **I'm an old codger, stuck in a nursing home—but I've still got my wits! Ever since I had my prostate out, I have to have a horrible tube up my private bit to get rid of my piss. My doctor says it has to stay in, and keeps pushing them in and out every month. It's damned embarrassing! How can I get rid of this tube for good?**

A There are a number possibilities here, but the most likely is that you cannot pass urine normally because of a bladder that will not contract properly after the operation. The prostate is certainly responsible for a lot of problems in older men, and if it is enlarged, you sometimes cannot pass urine at all because of its size, and after the operation the bladder may be so slack that it cannot force the urine out.

It is often unfortunate that the body gives out before the brain, leaving you having to deal with the embarrassment and inconvenience of urinary catheters. They have to be changed every month because if they are left for too long infections can develop, and the rubber of the catheter deteriorates.

I fear that you will not be able to get rid of the tube for good, because if there was any way in which this could be done, your doctor would have tried it. Ask your doctor why the catheter is required, and ask if you can try for a couple of days without it—you may soon wish to have it back in again.

Q   I had a prostate operation ten years ago, and no problems since until recently. Now I pass a few drops of blood before the urine with my first trip to the toilet in the morning. I am very embarrassed about this, and as I don't have a regular doctor, would appreciate your opinion.

A   The best thing you could do would be find a GP whom you like and trust. Ask friends and neighbours who they go to, then visit that GP for a routine matter. If satisfied, return to discuss your intimate problem, and let the doctor know that you intend to be a regular patient.

If you are not satisfied, keep trying until you find a doctor with whom you are compatible.

As far as your current problem is concerned, you do need to be thoroughly assessed, and in particular, your prostate requires further checking, both by blood and urine tests, and probably by a specialist urologist. It is likely that your prostate is causing the bloody discharge, but the bladder, sperm storage sac or even the testicles could be responsible.

Investigation and treatment as soon as possible would be appropriate.

Q   My doctor has told me that I have cancer of the prostate, but doesn't seem too worried about it, but I am! How serious is this? Can it be cured?

A   The prostate gland sits inside the body at the base of the penis, and secretes a fluid that lubricates the urine tube from the bladder through the penis, and supplies part of the man's ejaculate during sex. Cancer can develop in this organ, but it occurs normally in old men and early signs include difficulty in passing urine, pain and bloody urine.

The seriousness of this (and most other cancers) depends on how far advanced it is when the diagnosis is made and treatment started. Doctors consider a five year survival after diagnosis to be equivalent to cure, and with cancer of the prostate, 70% of all patients survive for five years. If the diagnosis is made early, the survival rate exceeds 90%.

Treatments will involve one or more of several different medications, surgery to remove all or part of the prostate, radiotherapy (high intensity x-rays), removal of the testes (to stop the male hormone being produced that encourages the cancer to grow) and female hormone tablets.

It is possible that your cancer was diagnosed during an operation to clear a blocked urethra (urine tube). This operation, carried out by passing an instrument up from the end of the urethra, is the most common way in which this type of cancer is found, and if only a small number of cancer cells were detected, the operation you have already had may have cured the cancer.

Q   My old friends are too embarrassed to see a doctor about their prostate problems, and several of them have poor flow when they urinate. Others are very worried about the side effects of prostate surgery such as

impotence. I have recently had prostate surgery with no problems. Please tell others about this problem.

A   You have put the problems of men's health in a nutshell. The golden rule is 'If in doubt, check it out.' Prostate cancer is certainly a significant problem in older men, but may occur in men as young as 40. The main symptoms are difficulty in starting the flow of urine, and then instead of a jet of urine, a dribble that splashes on your shoes instead of the porcelain.

There are other causes for these symptoms other than cancer, particularly an enlarged prostate gland which is not cancerous, but the only way to find out for sure is to be examined by a doctor.

The examination will consist of an examination by the doctor placing a gloved and lubricated finger through the anus (back passage) to feel the gland, and a blood test. If there is any suspicion of a problem, further tests such as an ultrasound scan, will be performed.

If a prostate cancer is found early, it can be removed. There may be side effects of surgery such as impotence and difficulty in controlling the urine flow, but these are more common if a bigger operation is necessary for an advanced cancer.

If impotence occurs, there are tablets and injections available that will enable the man to have a normal erection and sex life.

Remember, if delay in making the diagnosis because you do not go to a doctor leads to complications, or even premature death, the only person to blame is yourself.

PSORIASIS
See also SKIN

Q   **What is psoriasis? I have been told this is the cause of my skin problem, but know nothing about it.**

A   The most complex organ in the body after the brain is probably the skin. It must be waterproof, and yet let out water in the form of sweat. It must be strong to resist damage, yet flexible and sensitive to touch. Skin must repair itself rapidly when damaged, or vital body fluids may escape in a quantity sufficient to threaten life. It is easy to see, but difficult to treat, because few medications can penetrate through it. Because of the complexity of skin, many diseases can arise in our outer covering, and dermatologists are the doctors who specialise in diagnosing and treating its ailments.

One of the most annoying and distressing skin diseases, because it tends to be chronic and difficult to treat, is psoriasis. Psoriasis (the P is silent, and it is pronounced almost as 'sore-eye-asis') affects up to 2% of the population. It is unusual in children but becomes more common as age increases. One of the most frustrating aspects of this disfiguring dermatitis is the way in which it can come and go without any treatment. It almost invariably returns, and often in a worse form than previously.

Psoriasis is an autoimmune disease (like rheumatoid arthritis or systemic lupus erythematosus) in which the body's immune system is inappropriately triggered to reject tissue as though it was a foreign material. In psoriasis, varying parts of the skin are rejected.

It first appears as a small patch of red skin covered with fine scales. The elbows, shins, knees and scalp are the most common sites affected, but the rash may cover any part of the body. The small spot gradually enlarges, roughens and the skin thickens. Then other spots start in other areas of the body over a period of months, until a large part of the body is affected. In the scalp, it may appear to be a bad case of dandruff until the doctor makes the diagnosis. The nails may also be affected, and they become rough and pitted.

Psoriasis has many sub-types, and it is not always easy to make the diagnosis. It may be necessary to cut out a small piece of skin for a pathologist to examine under a microscope before the diagnosis is finally confirmed.

Q How can I cure my psoriasis? I have seen dozens of doctors, naturopaths, homeopaths and faith healers, but none can help me.

A The sad truth is that there is no cure for psoriasis, but doctors do have a number of quite successful forms of control that help most patients. It can also come and go without any treatment.

Because of this tendency to improve spontaneously, many forms of alternate medical treatments have claimed success in its management.

Treatment involves one or more of a number of creams or ointments that are used regularly on the skin. Coal tar in various forms is the mainstay of treatment, but steroid creams can supplement it. Many other less common creams (eg. Daivonex) can be used on the skin, along with ultraviolet irradiation, and some newer very potent tablets that are giving great relief to the more severe victims.

Although chronic and sometimes severe, psoriasis can be successfully controlled if a doctor's advice is carefully followed.

Q Are there any new treatments for psoriasis?

A This plaintive cry for help is constantly heard by general practitioners and dermatologists. Psoriasis is one of the most annoying, but rarely serious, skin diseases to afflict mankind. It can come and go for no apparent reason, may flare in varying parts of the body, and can even cause arthritis. Traditional treatments involve a combination of various messy creams from coal tar to steroids. Most help to some extent, but none cure. Ultraviolet light, steroid injections and anti-cancer drugs have all been tried in severe cases. One of the most successful skin preparations is dithranol.

The latest advance is a drug called Neotigason. This has been available for only a few years, and is very successful in controlling (not curing) severe (not mild) cases of psoriasis. This drug cannot be used during pregnancy, and has other side effects that will have to be considered by your doctor and yourself.

Anyone with psoriasis should be under the regular care of a doctor, because keeping the rash under control is the long-term way to prevent its spread and the more serious complications of the disease.

Q My brother's children have psoriasis in their hair. Has there been any recent development that will cure psoriasis?

A There is no cure for psoriasis, but there are many drugs that will control most cases of the disease.

The mainstays of treatment for scalp psoriasis are coal tar shampoos and steroid lotions. There are several different brands of these, and they should be used just frequently enough to control the psoriasis, and no more. The reason for this is that coal tar and its derivatives may cause scalp dryness and irritation if overused, and the steroid lotions are quite expensive and may cause skin damage if used excessively.

The condition will come and go, have good periods and bad periods, no matter what treatment is used, but the bad periods should be reasonably controlled if the patient is prepared to use the correct medication consistently.

Q How can a doctor diagnose psoriasis? I have been told that I have it, but it just looks like a patch of eczema to me.

A This distressing, and sometimes disfiguring skin disease, affects up to two out of every one hundred people in the population.

Psoriasis first appears as a small patch of red skin covered with fine scales. The elbows, knees and scalp are the most common sites affected, but the rash may cover any part of the body. The small spot gradually enlarges, roughens, and the skin thickens. Then other spots start in other areas, and over a period of months, a large part of the body may be affected.

In the scalp, it may appear to be a bad case of dandruff until a doctor makes the diagnosis. The nails may also be affected, and they become rough and pitted. In severe cases, it can even cause a form of arthritis.

Skin diseases often appear similar, even to doctors, and if there is doubt about the diagnosis, a small piece of skin may be cut out and sent to a pathologist to examine under a microscope. Once the diagnosis is confirmed, appropriate treatment to control the disease can be commenced.

Q I have had psoriasis for years, and now I'm getting bad arthritis. I'm told there is a connection—is this so?

A Arthritis means 'a painful joint' and nothing more. It is important in any patient with arthritis to determine the type of arthritis present.

One fairly uncommon type of arthritis is psoriatic arthritis, in which the lining of the joint is affected in the same way as the skin in patients with psoriasis.

Psoriasis is a distressing skin disease which causes red, scaling, unsightly patches to occur in many parts of the body. The disease will wax and wane over the years, but usually slowly worsens in most patients, but some find it suddenly disappears.

The arthritis that may accompany the skin disease is treated in the same way as osteoarthritis, with the addition of medication to control the psoriasis. A relatively new drug called Etretinate appears to be effective in both the skin and arthritis forms of the disease.

In your case, it may or may not be psoriatic arthritis. If your skin disease is not active, it is unlikely that the arthritis is due to psoriasis. The only way to find out for sure is to have an orthopaedic specialist remove some fluid from the joint for examination by a pathologist—this can give a definite diagnosis.

PSYCHIATRY

See also DEPRESSION

Q   When should someone see a doctor about anxiety?

A   Doctors become concerned when you become anxious about routine matters that the majority of people take for granted. Anxiety about catching a bus, meeting new people, going shopping or using household appliances is not normal, and if allowed to continue, may cause you to become steadily more anxious about more and more things.

Doctors call this an anxiety neurosis, and it can become so severe that the patient is unable to lead a normal life.

Unfortunately, some of these people are also anxious about seeing doctors, and may not seek help until the situation has reached a crisis.

It is important for close friends and relatives to intervene in this situation, to ensure that medical assistance is obtained at an early stage.

Treatment may only involve regular counselling sessions with your general practitioner or a psychiatrist, but sometimes medication is required to give the patient an initial boost back to the normal world. The earlier treatment is started, the shorter the course required, and the more successful the eventual outcome.

Q   My wife is in her thirties and suffers from extreme swings of mood which last for about a week. One day she can be extremely happy, then the next she is throwing pots at me and screaming. I try talking to her about it, but this only makes things worse. She seems unable to control these mood swings. Please help!

A   You are describing a quite classic case of manic-depressive psychosis.

Normally we all have our good days and our bad days. Days when the world seems to be with us, and days when the opposite appears to be true. Everyone accepts these minor mood swings and copes with them, but in some people these changes are dramatically exaggerated into the scenario that you have described. These swings are caused by alterations in the balance between the different chemicals in your brain that control mood.

The problem is not a psychological one, but a biochemical imbalance, in the same way that diabetes is an imbalance of sugar, manic-depressive psychosis is an imbalance of these mood chemicals, and is beyond the control of the individual.

There are successful forms of treatment available. The first step is to discuss the problem with your general practitioner, who can often prescribe medication that will assist your wife, but as with diabetes, there is no cure, only control, so the medication must be taken long term. Spontaneous recovery can sometimes occur.

If the condition is difficult to control, your general practitioner will refer your wife to a specialist psychiatrist who has the knowledge and training to better analyse and treat the problem.

Q   My wife's general practitioner and psychiatrist believe that she is manic depressive, but her sister has talked her out of taking any medications

as she does not believe in doctors or medication. She now refuses to see her doctors and I am having great difficulty in coping with her wild mood swings and neglect of our children. I would appreciate your assistance.

A   Manic depression, or a bipolar personality, can affect anyone in the community. It causes patients to have episodes of severe depression when they may feel suicidal, and at another time they may be excessively happy and do things they may later regret.

These swings in mood may occur every hour or two, or may be weeks apart. In a depressed mood the patient will be withdrawn, sleep poorly, loose interest in work and friends, and appear generally gloomy. When manic they may spend excessive amounts of money, take outrageous risks, become sexually promiscuous or party till dawn.

Women are far more likely to be affected than men.

Medication can be used to reduce the highs and lows so that the patient has normal mood swings, without stopping them from being the person that you know and love.

A bipolar personality is no different to any other chronic disease that requires long-term medication. In the same way that people with high blood pressure, diabetes or asthma must take medication on a regular basis to control their condition, so must people with a bipolar personality.

These people cannot pull themselves together without medical help, and unless they do take medication, in one of their extreme mood swings, they may harm themselves permanently.

Doctors cannot force patients to take medication, so it is a matter of convincing your wife (and her sister) that she may be better off receiving appropriate medication than taking risks with her life and damaging the lives of her family.

Q   **A friend of mine has an overwhelming fear of contamination and spends hours a day washing his hands and taking showers to the point where he cannot work. What can be done to help him?**

A   I am very concerned that your friend suffers from an obsessional neurosis. This is a psychiatric condition that requires treatment by a supportive specialist psychiatrist as soon as possible. The longer it is left before appropriate treatment is commenced, the harder successful treatment will become.

The first step is to take your friend to his family doctor, using a pretext if necessary to get him to attend. It is often worthwhile warning the doctor beforehand about your concerns. Hopefully the GP will be able to convince him to accept referral on to the psychiatrist. Further treatment will involve the use of medications, psychotherapy (analysis to find out why he has these fears) and behavioural therapy (training him to avoid the compulsive behaviour) to rid him of his unreasonable fears and his compulsion to wash himself.

It will take several months, and possibly years, to control the problem adequately. Some patients require continuing management by doctors for the rest of their lives.

Q   **In my late teenage years, I was a victim of anorexia nervosa and bulimia. I am now happily married, and worried about the long-term consequences of my earlier irresponsible behaviour. Could my fertility be affected?**

A   Anorexia nervosa is a psychiatric disorder in which the girl (almost invariably a teenager) refuses to eat, and loses weight dramatically. Bulimia is a related condition, in which large amounts of food are eaten, and then regurgitated.

These are both very serious conditions that may persist for several years, and a significant proportion of the victims may die during that time.

Once the woman (very rarely are men affected) has recovered, regained her normal weight, and started menstruating regularly, there should be no long-term effects.

If you are having some irregularity or abnormality in your periods, it would be wise to consult a gynaecologist. Otherwise, it is unlikely that the anorexia nervosa or bulimia will have any effects on your future health.

Q   **My 18 year old daughter is quite short and thin, weighing only 37 kilos. The doctor said she is just skinny but I'm worried about her. Is there something I should do?**

A   37 kilos (5 stone 9 lb) would be the correct average weight for an 18 year old who is 145 cm (4ft 9 in) tall. This is obviously very short (99% of girls would be taller than this), but by 18 years of age, growth has virtually ceased, and there is nothing that can be done to increase her height.

If your daughter is significantly taller than this, then her weight is of considerable concern.

The most common possibility is that she is suffering from anorexia nervosa or bulimia. Girls are often very good at hiding this problem from their families, and may appear to eat normally, but later vomit all the food they have just eaten. These people have a distorted body image and believe they are fat even though they are actually very thin. Treatment is possible, but usually spreads over many years.

Other possible causes of being very underweight include an overactive thyroid gland, liver and bowel disease, blood disorders, depression, infections, heart failure and cancer.

Because this list is so widespread, and because many of the conditions are serious, it is essential that if your daughter is taller than expected from her weight, she must be further investigated to find out just which problem is affecting her.

Q   **For the past twelve years, my husband has been diagnosed and treated for schizophrenia. He is now seeing a psychiatrist who says he isn't schizophrenic, but has a bipolar affective disorder. Could you please explain what this is, and why now a difference in the diagnosis?**

A   If a patient has high blood pressure, diabetes or even epilepsy, there are specific tests that a doctor can perform to confirm the diagnosis. With the vast majority of psychiatric disorders there are no specific tests available, and it is the clinical judgment of the doctor that makes the diagnosis.

There are no definite boundaries between one type of psychiatric disorder and another, and so a group of patients with one type of disorder gradually merge into a group that are classified with another disorder. It is rather like the varying colours in a rainbow, with one colour gradually merging into the next, without any definite border, but the individual colours can still be seen.

The same applies with schizophrenia and bipolar affective disorders—one tends to merge into the other.

Patients with bipolar affective disorders tend to have moods that swing rapidly from being over-happy (euphoric) to very sad (depressed). They tend to be rather eccentric in their behaviour (like schizophrenics), but their mood swings tend to be faster than those who have another psychiatric condition called cyclothymia.

The treatment of these conditions also follows a spectrum of activity, and the diagnosis is merely a guide to the types of treatments that may be tried. The change in your husband's diagnosis may well reflect the fact that he is responding better to medications that help bipolar affective disorders than those that help schizophrenia.

Q Could you please write an item on schizophrenia and its consequences? One of the members of my family is marrying someone who has it.

A Schizophrenia is a condition that can have widely varying effects. Many people may have only minimal symptoms and no effect upon their daily life, while at the other extreme, a minority may be permanently hospitalised with severe problems.

The symptoms of schizophrenia may be very subtle at the beginning, with minor changes in personality, and friends commenting that the patient is just not the same person they used to know. This is followed by a deterioration in work, conflicts in relationships and a deterioration in self-care and hygiene.

Patients become perplexed about the way they are feeling, tend to isolate themselves from others and, as the condition worsens, become very anxious and frightened. This may progress to the final stage with the patient being in constant terror caused by a world that is perceived to be out of control.

Other symptoms may include hallucinations, delusions, incoherence in speech, inappropriate emotional reactions, bizarre behaviour, the inability to control bodily functions, hearing imaginary voices, odd beliefs and a lack of energy.

There are no specific blood or other tests that will diagnose schizophrenia. Only the clinical skill of the treating doctor can make the final diagnosis.

There is an hereditary tendency, but it is certainly not the case that people with parents who have schizophrenia will inevitably develop the condition.

The majority of victims can be adequately treated and lead a normal life provided that they use regular medication in the form of daily tablets or injections that are given every few weeks.

Schizophrenia is a disease in the same way that asthma or diabetes are diseases. All can be controlled by medication, but none can be cured. It is unfortunate that because schizophrenia affects the mind rather than the lungs or blood sugar it is put in a different category by many members of the public.

RADIOLOGY
(X-Rays, MRI, Ultrasound etc.)

Q Can you explain what happens in mammography? My doctor has suggested I have this done, but it scares me.

A Mammography is merely an X-ray of the breasts, and there is no reason for concern. During the procedure, the breasts will be X-rayed from top to bottom and side to side. There may be some discomfort as your breasts are squeezed between the X-ray plates, but it only takes a few seconds, and the results can be life-saving.

There are now many doctors who believe that all women of 40 years should have a routine mammogram, and this should be repeated every five years. Combined with monthly breast self-examination, mammography is an extremely effective way of detecting breast cancer at an early stage. Women are now having tiny breast cancers removed, without disfiguring scarring, before they or their doctor can feel any lump or discomfort.

Early detection is the key to successful cancer treatment, and if you are concerned about your breasts, or if there is a family history of breast cancer, do not hesitate to have a mammogram arranged by your general practitioner.

Q My son has been having stomach pains that are quite severe, and his doctor wants him to have a CAT scan of the abdomen, but because he has diabetes and allergies, I fear he may be at risk from such a scan. Could you please explain the complications and risks involved?

A A CAT (computerised axial tomography) scan is merely a form of X-ray, a very sophisticated X-ray, in which dozens of low dose X-rays are taken at different angles of the area of the body being examined, to produce a detailed cross-sectional view. There are no more complications from a CAT scan than from a normal chest X-ray.

The exception to this rule is when contrast dyes are used. These dyes show up areas that are not normally visible on a normal CAT scan or X-ray. An example would be the Barium meal, where a mixture of Barium is swallowed so that the stomach and intestine can be seen. In some CAT scans, dyes may be injected into the bloodstream and travel to areas of particular interest.

Some people can be allergic to these dyes, and because your son has many allergies, it is possible that he may react adversely to a dye being used for an X-ray or CAT scan. It is probable that no dye will be used in a CAT scan of the abdomen, but they are commonly used in brain CAT scans. You should discuss this with the radiologist performing the scan, and if a dye is essential for the examination, a very small test dose of the dye may be given to see if your son reacts.

There are no risks associated with diabetes and CAT scans.

Your doctor would not advise your son to have this test without good reason, and I therefore suggest that you proceed as outlined above.

Q   My husband recently underwent a CAT scan, but suffered severely with diarrhoea for two weeks afterwards, and was at one stage considered at risk of dying. A doctor told him that he had an allergic reaction to the dye injected for the CAT scan. Can you warn people of these risks?

A   The contrast dyes that are injected into some patients before an X-ray or CAT scan to get a better picture can cause rare fatal reactions but are 20 times less risky than travelling by car.

There is no evidence that new contrast dyes recently introduced are safer, even though they cost up to six times as much.

In one recent study, only eight deaths occurred after more than 600,000 dye injections—an extraordinarily low risk, considering that many of those injected were critically ill.

In those under 65 years of age, the risk was far less than in those over 65, and there was a close relationship to the health of the patient. Survival after a severe reaction depended upon the availability of resuscitation equipment.

There has been much public anxiety over this issue, but when the benefits are weighed against the risks, proceeding with a potentially disease-identifying and therefore life-saving procedure is far safer than waiting until the disease becomes more obvious.

Q   My husband had a myelogram three weeks ago and has suffered from severe headaches and nausea ever since. Is this a normal side-effect of a myelogram? Can these side effects be prevented or treated?

A   Myelograms have largely been superseded by CAT and MRI scans, which give much the same information with fewer side effects, but sometimes a myelogram is still necessary to diagnose particular problems.

When a myelogram is performed, a needle is pushed through the skin low down on the back, and between two vertebrae so that the tip of the needle is in the spinal canal. This canal contains the spinal cord (which carries all the nerves from the brain to the body) and a fluid called cerebrospinal fluid.

A small amount of fluid is removed, and an equal amount of a dye is injected into the spinal canal. The patient is then tilted so that the dye runs up the canal. This dye is visible on X-rays, and as the patient is tilted backwards and forwards, numerous X-rays are taken of the back to see where the dye moves to. If there is a blockage in the spinal canal caused by a slipped disc, or any abnormality of the spinal cord, it should show up on the X-rays.

At the end of the procedure, the dye is run back down to the area where the needle has been inserted, and as much dye as possible is removed, and an equal amount of saline solution is injected to keep the volume and pressure of the cerebrospinal fluid constant.

If the pressure changes significantly, a headache will occur. A headache (sometimes quite severe) is normal for a few days after the procedure, and these headaches are notoriously resistant to any treatment, but three weeks is excessive. It may be that too much or too little fluid was injected into, or removed from, the spinal canal, and this change in fluid pressure is causing the headache.

The other possibility is that the disease leading to the myelogram being performed may be responsible for the headache. In either case, you should return to see the specialist who ordered the myelogram as soon as possible for further assessment.

Q **My obstetrician wants me to have a scan to check on the size of my baby. I am only 4 months pregnant. Are these scans safe in pregnancy?**

A YES! There is absolutely no doubt that an ultrasound scan is safe in pregnancy. Thousands of experiments into its safety have been carried out, and millions of women have had the procedure during pregnancy with no evidence of problems.

Ultrasound is not an X-ray, but actual waves of sound, rather like the dog whistle that animals can hear but which humans cannot.

A greasy substance is rubbed onto your abdomen, and an instrument that contains a miniature high-frequency sound-producing element is then rubbed across your tummy. The sound waves pass through your body, but are reflected and distorted in different ways by different types of tissue, fluid and bone. These distortions can be picked up and measured to give a detailed picture of the growing baby.

The size, shape, position, development and sometimes the sex of the child can all be determined, so it is a very useful tool for measuring the progress of a pregnancy, and making pregnancy safer for both mother and child.

Q **I am 66 years old and the report on a recent X-ray of my chest says that 'the aorta is unfolded'. Could you please explain in a good old-fashioned way what takes place with this complaint, and are there any exercises that could help?**

A There is absolutely no reason for you to be concerned about this problem, and there is no need to undertake any specific exercises, as I will explain.

The aorta is the main artery of the body and is about 2 cm across. It starts from the top of the heart, bends (or folds) over, and then runs down the back of the chest and belly along the inside of the backbone. It looks like an upside down 'J'. Just below your umbilicus (tummy button) it splits into two slightly smaller arteries that continue through the pelvis and down each leg.

In an X-ray of the chest, the heart and aorta can be seen quite clearly. As you age, the bend in the aorta as it curls around from the top of the heart to run down the back of the chest becomes a less sharp bend. The aorta does not fold over on itself as much as it did before, and so in medical jargon, the aorta is said to be 'unfolded'.

In your case it is a sign that you are no longer 21, and nothing more. In some people the aorta is unfolded and dilated by an aneurysm, which is quite a serious condition, but this can usually be seen on the X-ray and there is no sign that this was the case with you.

Q **I have an X-ray request slip from my doctor to have an air-contrast barium enema done. What will happen to me?**

A This is an X-ray that shows the lower part of the gut from the anus up to the appendix, and sometimes the last part of the small intestine. This part of the gut is about one and a half metres long in an adult.

The day before the X-ray, you will have to use special medicines to clean out all the faeces from the gut. When you go to the radiologist's rooms, you will be undressed and lie on your side on a rather narrow table. A small tube will be placed in your back passage, and through this a mixture of barium will be run into the large gut. You may be given injections in the arm to relax you and the gut during the procedure.

You will be rolled around from side to side while X-rays are taken, and air will be introduced into the gut to display any abnormalities more readily. The procedure may be a little uncomfortable when your gut is inflated with air, but this settles rapidly.

After half to one hour, all the pictures necessary will have been taken, and you will be asked to go to the toilet to pass the barium mixture that was previously introduced. Your bowel function will return to normal after a couple of days.

The procedure can diagnose most diseases of the lower gut, and will only be requested if your doctor considers there are good reasons for doing it.

Q   I keep having funny turns, and my doctor has ordered a 'dopple' test on the arteries in my neck. What will this involve? Are they safe?

A   What your doctor has ordered is a doppler ultrasound.

When listening to a fast-moving vehicle approaching you, its engine noise changes pitch as the vehicle passes you and moves away. This change in the pitch of a sound due to movement is known as the doppler effect. This same effect can be used to measure the movement of fluids (such as blood) within the body.

Using a blunt probe that is placed against the skin, a high pitched sound wave (ultrasound) is passed into the body, and the reflection of the sound wave from stationary tissue and moving blood is measured and compared. In this way, the rate at which the blood is flowing can be determined.

The carotid artery in the neck is commonly one to be examined to see if there is any blockage or narrowing that may be responsible for your funny turns, but other arteries near the surface of the body (eg. in the groin) may also be checked to see if there is any blockage of the blood flow caused by a clot or build-up of a cholesterol plaque.

There is absolutely no discomfort to the patient during the procedure, it is completely safe, and you only have to lie still for a few minutes.

Q   What is the test done to see if you have thin bones in old age?

A   Quite often osteoporosis (thin bones) can be seen on a plain X-ray of major bones, but there is also a specific test known as dual photon densitometry scan.

The density of bone can be ascertained from the amount of mineral contained in it. This type of scan is able to measure the mineral content of bone and is a way of diagnosing the onset of osteoporosis, or thinning of the bones. The machine is called an osteodensitometer. The whole body, or just the forearm of a patient can be tested.

In a whole body scan, the patient lies on a bed with a flat plate underneath as a (very mild) source of radiation, and a long-armed scanner then moves slowly down the body emitting photon beams which can determine the density of the tissue they are passing through. The procedure takes about half an hour and is completely painless.

A bone scan cannot necessarily predict osteoporosis in normal people, but is very useful for high-risk subjects or people who already have signs of osteoporosis, so that remedial treatment such as medications to replace the lost calcium, hormone replacement therapy and calcium supplements can be administered.

Dual photon densitometry costs are not rebateable under Medicare except in very specific circumstances.

Q **What is involved in an MRI scan? I have seen numerous doctors about my headaches and fainting, and now a neurologist wants me to have one of these tests.**

A Magnetic resonance imaging (MRI), or nuclear magnetic resonance (NMR) as it is sometimes called, is a new technique of scanning the body. It is based on the fact that living tissues give off their own special electromagnetic signals, depending largely on their water content, and if the tissues are exposed to a magnetic field the signals can be picked up and read. Hence, a very strong magnetic field is created by special magnets, and different areas of the body absorb different amounts of magnetism according to their water content. A magnetic absorption photograph is then built up, and can be seen and analysed, slice by slice, on a computer screen in much the same way as a CT scan. MRI is particularly useful as it ignores bones (which contain little water) and shows up soft tissue, which is the opposite of X-rays.

MRI is especially helpful in diagnosing diseases in the brain and spinal cord. The picture obtained by MRI of the brain clearly shows the difference between the white matter (nerve fibres) and the grey matter (nerve cells). Tumours that are not apparent on a CT scan are sometimes revealed by MRI, not only in the brain but in organs deep within the abdomen such as the liver.

MRI is completely safe. Its main disadvantage is that the equipment is enormously expensive (approximately twice as expensive as a CT scanner) and must be housed in a special magnetically sealed room. As a result, high fees must be charged for its use, and not all of these are covered by Medicare or private health insurance.

S

SEX

See also BREASTS, FEMALE; FEMALE PROBLEMS; MALE
PROBLEMS; PROSTATE

Q I have a very embarrassing sexual problem, which I cannot bring myself
to discuss with my GP. I have not been able to have intercourse for many
years because of it. Can you please tell me of a doctor who looks after
these problems?

A General practitioners hear about all sorts of very strange and personal problems,
and keep the details of these completely to themselves. Your GP is not going to
laugh at you, or think any less of you if you tell him/her of your problems.

If you still can't bring yourself to speak to your GP, you are probably seeing
the wrong doctor, and need to change to one with whom you can establish a
better relationship.

Your GP may well be able to help you with your problem, as an amazingly
large number of people do present to their GP with sexual problems, and many
GPs have considerable expertise in successfully treating them.

If the problem is more complex, your GP can refer you on to the appropriate
specialist. This may be a urologist, gynaecologist, sexologist or psychiatrist.

Pluck up courage, and see your GP. Taking along a note, with the details of
your problem written down, may help break the ice.

Q Six months ago I gave birth to my first child, and stopped breast feeding
after five months, and started on the contraceptive pill. Ever since the
birth I have had no sexual appetite whatsoever, and this is putting a
strain on my marriage. Will I ever be normal again?

A A low libido (sex drive) is quite common during breast feeding, due to the
hormonal changes at this time, as nature's way of preventing pregnancies too
close together. The mother also tends to be preoccupied by the baby's welfare,
and is under a constant low-grade stress from the demands the baby puts on her.
Sleep, calm rest, and privacy also tend to be rare commodities in the first six
months (or more) after a birth.

Any form of stress will reduce the libido of both males and females, and many
couples are slow to restart sex after the birth of a child, particularly the first one.

Sometimes the hormones in the contraceptive pill may also reduce libido, but
most women finds that the pill enhances their sex drive rather than reduces it.
The modern, low-dose pills are particularly unlikely to reduce libido.

The best way to kick-start your sex life would be to pass the care of the baby
over to a grandparent or friend, while you and your frustrated husband head off
alone for a relaxing long weekend away from home.

Q Almost every time I have sexual intercourse I suffer a strong burning
feeling around my vagina and urethra. Doctors' tests show no germs
present, and their treatments do not help. Every day there is a discharge
on my panties. I hope you can help me.

A   There are a number of possibilities that could explain your problem, including inflammation caused by inadequate lubrication during sex, or the rare condition of an allergy reaction to sperm or the rubber in a condom, but the explanation that readily comes to mind is that you have a chlamydial infection.

Infections of this type are very difficult to detect with normal methods, and even a perfect technique by the doctor and laboratory may fail to prove the diagnosis; but the correct treatment subsequently clears the symptoms.

Discuss the possibility of this being the cause with your GP. S/he may order the specific tests to prove the diagnosis, but often it is easier to treat than to confirm.

It is essential that both you and your partner be treated at the same time with a course of antibiotics that will destroy a chlamydial infection.

If the problem persists after this, you should ask for a referral to a gynae-cologist so that some of the rarer causes of your problem may be excluded.

Q   **I gave birth vaginally five months ago. Since then I have found sex very painful, and have only attempted intercourse four times, each time being very uncomfortable. I had an episiotomy which still does not feel completely healed. What can I do to help this problem?**

A   Your problem needs to be properly assessed by a gynaecologist, because you have been suffering for far too long.

The probability is that the scar tissue from the episiotomy (the cut at the opening of the vagina to allow the baby's head to escape more easily) has become excessively inflamed, and the episiotomy scar may need to be cut out and restitched.

It is also possible that you may have had some damage to the cervix during the birth, and this may the source of your pain.

Q   **I am female, 18 years old, and have always had trouble using tampons. I've had sex only once, and although I had no pain, my partner did. I now realise I have an extremely short vagina, as I can feel my cervix only 10 cm away from my vaginal opening. I am very embarrassed and don't want to get involved with anyone until it is fixed, or am I doomed to live my life alone?**

A   Do not despair, almost certainly you are normal!

It is very common for young women to have difficulty inserting tampons, as they find them uncomfortable, embarrassing, scratchy, dry and ineffective. The last is often because they are not inserted far enough into the vagina. Smaller sizes are available for younger women, and these should be used first.

Sex for the first time may also be uncomfortable and unsatisfactory, due to lack of experience, nervousness, lack of natural lubrication (the probable cause of your partner's pain) and the tearing of any remnant of the hymen. When you first learn to ride a bike, you tend to wobble and fall a few times, but after a short time, you can ride smoothly along a straight line. Sex can be considered in the same way—practice makes perfect.

The vagina is a very elastic and expandable pouch of tissue. It tends to be the mirror image of the penis. When sexually aroused, the male penis enlarges, and so does the female vagina.

Feeling the cervix 10 cm from the outside is completely normal. During sex.

the cervix will be pushed forward and out of the way, so that the vagina can expand naturally to accommodate the penis. It is not appropriate to judge the capacity of the vagina when you are not sexually aroused.

You are not doomed to live your life alone, and when you are comfortable with your partner, you will find sex the enjoyable and bonding experience nature intended.

Q Every time I have sex with my husband, I am in agony for two or three days afterwards because of burning when I pass urine. How can I prevent this?

A This is a very common problem, and one that is relatively simple to overcome. When you have sex, the urethra (tube from the bladder to the outside) becomes bruised and inflamed. It is also easy for bacteria to be massaged up the tube into the bladder. In these circumstances an infection can occur, which leads to your discomfort.

The problem is more common with those who are not used to having sex (thus honeymoon cystitis), in those having very frequent and gymnastic types of sex, and in those who have infrequent sex. The way to prevent it is to have something to drink before sex, and then pass urine immediately after sex to remove any germs that have entered. Douching should not be done. If this is not sufficient, you can use a urinary alkalinising agent either all the time, or on days when you expect to have sex. There are numerous brands of these (eg. Ural, Citravescent) available from chemists, and they come as a powder which adds to water to make a flavoured drink. They make the urine unpalatable to the bacteria that like to breed in your bladder.

As a last resort, your doctor can give you special antibiotics to use long term to overcome the problem. A small number of women may need surgery to correct a defect in the area.

Q I am now nearly seventeen and about two years ago I started to masturbate regularly because it makes me feel good. Will this have a bad effect on other parts of my body? Will it weaken my eyes or heart? Will it make my penis grow bigger or smaller?

A Masturbation has no detrimental effects on any part of the body in either sex, other than the possibility of friction burns on the part of the anatomy being stimulated.

It is an extremely common form of self-stimulation, and if anyone tries to tell you it is dirty and dangerous, or that they have never masturbated, do not believe them. It is far more common in teenagers than older people who are in a position to have sex on a regular basis. Experimentation by teenagers with their developing bodies and sexuality is a normal part of growing up.

Masturbation may become a habit that interferes with other activities, and then it may become a minor problem.

You may be disappointed to learn that it will not make your penis grow any larger.

Q I am 58 years old, and am married with a loving wife and 6 children. Would you please advise me as to where I could go to seek assistance to cure a habit of masturbation.

A Masturbation itself is not a disease or problem that will cause any damage to you, and virtually all men, and many women, masturbate at some time.

As with all things, it may become excessive, and cause you to become preoccupied with the habit. Some people are obsessive about collecting, others become dependent on cigarettes, others are obsessed about doing things in a particular way every time. In your case you are performing excessively the normal activity of masturbation.

Assistance is available from psychiatrists and psychologists who can teach you methods to reduce this (or any other) excessive activity.

Your first step is to confide in your general practitioner, who will be able to refer you to the most appropriate specialist in your area.

Do not be embarrassed, see your GP as soon as possible, and arrange the necessary referral.

Q **I have noticed over recent months that I enjoy almost no pleasure when I ejaculate after masturbating. Orgasms are almost non-events. Could this be a sign of something serious?**

A Ejaculation is only the climax of an activity that normally takes two people some time to reach, and sex should not be merely a physical act but a mutual sharing of emotions, sensations and pleasure. Masturbation can be used to give relief of sexual tension, but in the same way that you can tire of eating liqueur chocolates if given them every day, regular masturbation without any emotional involvement can soon become boring.

This is not a sign of anything serious, other than a need for some more emotional and interpersonal involvement in your life.

Q **Some twelve months ago I suffered from a bout of impotence due to mental stress. I purchased a vacuum penis pump to help things along, and this helped me to get back to 'working order'. The makers of the penis pump claimed that with regular use, the penis will enlarge by up to two inches, but this hasn't happened. Is it possible to extend the length of the penis? If body-builders can exercise and build their muscles, why can't the same be done for the penis?**

A Both mental and physical stress, as well as disease and a number of unexplained factors, can all lead to impotence, and a vacuum pump (used carefully) may help overcome the problem by both boosting your confidence, and increasing the blood supply to the penis.

The penis becomes erect because blood is pumped into the penis, and valves close around the veins leading from the penis so that the blood cannot escape. The penis is blown up with blood, rather like a sausage-shaped balloon.

There are virtually no muscles in the penis, and so unlike the body builder, there is nothing to develop and increase in size with exercise.

A vacuum pump will not increase the size of your penis. There is no simple way to achieve this, but plastic surgeons can perform quite major surgery to increase its size, but usually only in men who have an abnormally small penis.

The size of the penis does not greatly affect a woman's pleasure in sex. How the penis is used, and who it belongs to, are far more important factors.

Q **Practically every morning I wake with an enormous erection, which at my age of 45, I feel is a precious thing, not to be wasted. My wife does not share my point of view, and detests sex in the mornings. This causes a lot of friction between us. Why do these erections occur, and what is #*!#*! wrong with sex in the morning?**

A Normally, blood circulates into your penis through the arteries, and out again through the veins. When you are sexually stimulated, tiny muscle rings around the veins contract, which prevents the blood being pumped in by the arteries from leaving the penis. The penis is therefore pumped up to an erect position by the blood entering through the arteries.

An early morning erection is a very common phenomenon, and is caused by mildly erotic dreams, and stimulation of the nervous system controlling the blood valves in the penis, while asleep. There is nothing abnormal about these erections at all, and they normally subside rapidly on awaking.

There is nothing wrong with sex in the morning, the afternoon, or at any time—provided it is desired by both partners. When it is desired by only one partner (male or female) and forced upon the other, sex becomes rape.

If there is a problem between you and your wife over sex in the morning, and you have difficulty in obtaining an erection at other times, a calm rational discussion of the problem, at some other time of day, is essential. If you cannot resolve this conflict, marriage guidance by your doctor or a counsellor becomes imperative.

Q **My wife and I enjoy frequent bouts of sex. I would like to know if protein increases male sperm and sexual performance. Also, are there any vitamins that will increase sexual performance in an already sexually active male?**

A The rhinoceros population of Africa has been almost wiped out because some Asians believe that rhinoceros horn powder is an aphrodisiac. This belief is unfounded. There is also no truth in the rumours that oysters, avocados or certain vitamins and proteins can increase sexual prowess.

Medical practitioners have drugs that can help men who are impotent due to inadequate levels of male hormone, but there is no medication available that will increase the sexual potency or arousal of a normal sexually active man.

Those who have an inadequate diet, vitamin deficiencies, or a lack of protein may find that they are unable to perform sexually as well as they would wish, but that does not mean that greater than normal amounts of these substances will increase sexuality.

The first person to invent an aphrodisiac will make a fortune and be blessed by the protectors of rhinoceros populations, but may well be cursed by women!

Q **My GP gave me Andriol tablets to help my sex life, and now I can get an erection, but I can't ejaculate with sex, only with masturbation. I would rather ejaculate while having sex. Can you help me?**

A Andriol is the trade name of capsules filled with form of testosterone, the male hormone. It is normally used if there is a measurable lack of testosterone on blood tests which is causing problems in obtaining an erection.

An erection and ejaculation are triggered by totally different nerve pathways.

It is possible (but uncommon) to ejaculate without an erection, and many men find it difficult to ejaculate with sex.

Because of these different nerve pathways, different types of stimulation to the penis and brain are necessary for these two activities. You may be able to modify the stimulation during masturbation to allow ejaculation, but sex may not give the same type or intensity of stimulation.

I would suggest that you try different positions for sex, which may increase the stimulation to the skin just behind the head of the penis, which is the most sensitive area. You may also be able to ask your partner to position herself or tighten her vaginal muscles in a way that increases your stimulation. Additional medications are not going to help the problem.

Q **I am 57 and lately cannot get an erection. Are there any pills or devices that can help my problem?**

A There are many reasons for failure of penile erection, and it is necessary for a doctor to examine you, and test you carefully, to determine which cause is affecting you.

Psychological factors are by far the most common reason. Once a man fails to have an erection (as all do at some time), he is anxious about the next time, which makes failure more likely, and a vicious circle develops.

Depression, anxiety, stress and over tiredness are also common problems that can result in impotence. Work problems, arguments, money worries, and a host of other matters may be the initial cause.

Alcohol can enhance the desire, but reduce ability. When you are intoxicated, erectile failure is common, and long term alcohol abuse may result in permanent impotence.

Diabetes is a common problem in late middle age, and can cause the arteries to become clogged. The only reason a man can get an erection is because he has a good blood supply to the penis, which becomes engorged with blood during an erection. If the arteries are not up to the task, nor is he!

Many different medications, including those that may be used to treat high blood pressure, depression, kidney failure, some types of cholesterol excess, and ulcers may have a side effect of impotence. The illegal drugs (eg. marijuana, heroin) are also responsible for the problem.

Other less common causes include injury to the spine or pelvis, hardening of the arteries, and various gland problems.

Your first step is to find out which problem is responsible for your impotence. Once that has been determined, it may be possible to correct the problem.

If no specific problem is found, there are tablets (Viagra) which will assist in giving an erection when you are sexually stimulated, and injections into the penis that can give an erection within half an hour. Both are only available on prescription, and your doctor will need to explain how to use them.

There are also mechanical devices available that can pump out the air from a tube that is placed around the penis and result in an erection. These are available from 'marital aid shops' and by mail order, but should be used with caution. Discuss the use of these devices with your doctor.

Q **I am 68 years young, very healthy, cut wood, mow the lawn, and walk for miles but I have an erection problem. I can get an erection, but I can't**

sustain it. As soon as I try to have sex, it droops. I believe an implant in the penis that I read about in an American magazine will solve the problem. Are they available here? My wife is 20 years younger than I am, and I don't want to lose her.

A   The implants to make a penis erect are available in Australia, and have been implanted by plastic surgeons into appropriate patients for many years. You are not an appropriate patient.

These devices are used only in men who cannot obtain any form of erection. A squeeze bulb is placed in the scrotum (so that you have three balls instead of two), and two long balloons are placed on either side of the penis. The bulb is squeezed to pump up the penis, and a valve at the base of the penis is pressed to deflate it.

In your case, a very simple device can be used. When the penis is erect, place a piece of rubber around the base of the penis and clamp the rubber so that it acts as a tourniquet, to prevent the blood that keeps the penis erect from escaping. This should not be applied too frequently, or for more than fifteen minutes, or the penis may be damaged.

Injections are also available to give you an erection. These can be prescribed by your general practitioner after appropriate investigations to exclude any disease that may be causing impotence. Viagra tablets for impotence can also be used.

Q   **I am having trouble maintaining an erection during sex. Approximately 12 months ago I failed miserably twice with this problem. Since then I have separated, and have now met a woman with whom I have become friendly, but I fear I will not be able to fulfil my love. I am 68 years old, a war veteran, had a prostate operation, high blood pressure and two heart attacks.**

A   Sir, it obviously takes a great deal to keep an old soldier down!

There is no reason why elderly people should not maintain an active sex life until well into their seventies, but you have a number of factors which will make the task more difficult. The main reason for a failed erection at any age is psychological pressure to perform. If you are anxious about the event because of a new partner, conditions that are not ideal, or stress and worries, there is a good chance that these nervous signals will override the stimulating signals, and the penis will not become erect. If you have failed previously, then there is even more anxiety, and every successive failure makes you more anxious to perform, and therefore less likely to perform.

The way to overcome this is not to plan sex, but to relax and wait until the time when something occurs spontaneously.

The other factors that can be affecting you are the male menopause, and there is no doubt that this does occur. From the mid-fifties onwards, the amount of male hormone in the system slowly decreases. Unlike the female menopause, where there is a relatively sudden drop in hormone levels, the drop in men is so gradual that it may not be noticed until the early seventies, when sexual responsiveness and libido (desire for sex) starts to decrease. This will obviously vary from one man to another.

Some types of treatment for high blood pressure can also affect your ability to have an erection, and you should discuss your medication with your doctor. Unfortunately, a prostate operation may have an adverse effect upon sexuality in some patients.

If you continue to have problems obtaining an erection, Caverject injections or Viagra tablets may be worthwhile discussing with your general practitioner.

Q   I am a 52 year old man, and have noticed blood in my urine after intercourse. It occurs at no other time, and all sorts of urine, blood and X-ray tests by my doctor are normal. I am otherwise fit and well. What could cause this problem?

A   This is an uncommon problem, but almost invariably it is not serious. Tests should be performed on the urine to detect any possible infection, blood tests can be performed to exclude prostate disease and clotting disorders, and sometimes X-rays of the kidneys and bladder may be done. If the problem persists, referral to a urologist for cystoscopy is appropriate, but in nearly all cases, all these tests are negative. All the patient requires is a large dose of reassurance, even if the problem persists.

The bleeding is caused by microscopic injuries to the penis and sperm sacs during sex, and does not interfere with the man's performance or fertility.

It is a problem that is more common after middle age, and in men who have sex infrequently.

Q   Is circumcision necessary to be able to have children?

A   Circumcision was a fad in Australia from after the First World War until the 1970s, but is now fading away, and less than 20% of Australian boys are now circumcised. It is certainly not necessary to father children, and is not necessary for the sexual or general health of a man.

Some cultures and religions use male circumcision as a right of passage or symbol, but there is no more medical reason for circumcising men than women, and female circumcision is considered to be genital mutilation and banned by law in this country.

There are a very small number of men who do need to be circumcised for good medical reasons, but there is no need for this to be carried out routinely.

Please be reassured that if you are having trouble fathering a child, it will not be because you are uncircumcised.

Q.   I am 62 years of age, and somewhat concerned that I no longer ejaculate. I am not unduly concerned about this but would like to know if this is a normal or expected condition for a man of my age?

A.   Ejaculation is the result of a complex series of occurrences. The sac that stores the sperm must contract, and at the same time, sphincters (muscular valves) must open or close to prevent the ejaculate fluid from going the wrong way.

In older men, particularly those who have had a prostate operation, the valves may not operate appropriately, and instead of the ejaculate fluid going to the outside, it goes up and into the bladder. Doctors call this phenomenon retrograde ejaculation. Some men notice this the next time they pass urine as a stringy mucus. There are no serious consequences from this failure to ejaculate, but it is obviously not possible to father a child. It should not reduce your sexual pleasure, as you still climax and feel you have ejaculated, even though nothing happens.

Unfortunately, there is usually nothing that can be done to correct the problem, but if for some reason you are keen to become a father, you should ask your GP for a referral to a specialist urologist.

Q After a prostatectomy at age 59, I am suffering from retrograde ejaculation. Will this stop me from fathering further children as I am contemplating marriage to a younger woman? Is there any treatment available?

A During the operation to remove the prostate, which is a gland at the base of the penis, the flow of sperm from the sac (seminal vesicle) where it is stored to the outside may be disrupted. Normally a valve prevents the sperm from entering the bladder during ejaculation, but in the operation of prostatectomy, this valve is usually damaged or destroyed. Sperm can the take the shorter route from the seminal vesicle into the bladder, rather than the long route down the shaft of the penis to the outside.

This problem is called retrograde (backwards) ejaculation, and is a very common complication of the operation.

As the vast majority of men requiring operations on the prostate are elderly, fathering further children is not usually a problem, but you have had the operation at a particularly young age.

Do not despair, because there are techniques that will still enable you to father a child despite the problem of retrograde ejaculation. All these methods involve the cooperation of specialist doctors and your wife.

The most successful technique involves taking medication to alkalinise your urine, emptying your bladder, then ejaculating by masturbation. Immediately after ejaculation, the bladder is emptied again, when you will pass almost equal amounts of urine and sperm. The sperm are then separated from the urine, washed in a nutrient solution, and introduced artificially into your wife.

The other method involves inserting a needle into the tubes around your testes that carry sperm to the penis, and extracting sperm. These are then artificially introduced into your wife; but this method is not quite as successful as the other.

Both these procedures must obviously be carried out at the fertile time of the month for your wife.

You should discuss the problem further with your general practitioner who will refer you to the appropriate specialists.

Q I am a 33 year old man and suffer from premature ejaculation. This situation is threatening my relationship with my girlfriend. We have tried to solve the problem ourselves, but to no avail. Can anything be done medically?

A Premature ejaculation is a common problem, but many men do not complain for fear of being ridiculed by their doctor. This should not be the case, as GPs see a large number of sexual problems, and are used to dealing with them.

There is no medicine, drug or device that can help this problem, but there are techniques available that are very effective in teaching the partners in a relationship how to cope.

Premature ejaculation certainly requires the cooperation of the female partner, and without this cooperation, treatment is doomed to failure.

One technique is called 'the squeeze method'. At any time after an erection is present, before or during intercourse, if the man feels he is about to ejaculate, he gives a signal to his partner, by word or touch, and she then immediately uses her forefinger and thumb to squeeze the penis firmly just below the glans (head) until the erection starts to subside slightly. Intercourse or sexual stimulation can then start again until the urge to ejaculate is felt, when the technique is once more applied immediately.

There are other similar techniques advocated by different sex therapists, and you should discuss referral to a specialist in this area if your problem persists.

Q **I am a 42 year old male and my problem is I am not very well endowed when it comes to genitals. My penis is so small that one woman friend commented 'How do you have anything to hang on to when you pee?' This is very embarrassing when in the intimate company of a woman, and some have openly laughed at me and walked out. Is there a cure for my problem?**

A Some people have big noses, others have small. Some people are short, others are tall. Some men have a large penis, others have a small one.

A small penis can function just as well as a large one, and your partners may have been surprised if they had given you the chance to use it appropriately. The most sexually sensitive areas of a woman are her clitoris (just outside the vagina at the front), and the front wall of the vagina about one centimetre from the outside (the so called 'G' spot). The other sexually stimulating areas are the nipples, lips, ear lobes and cervix.

You can become a good lover by stimulating all the sexually sensitive areas on your partner's body with the possible exception of the cervix (at the top of the vagina), but even this can be stimulated by a finger. In other words, you can make up for a lack of size by improving your technique.

As an absolute last resort, plastic surgeons can perform a series of operations to increase the size of your penis to some extent. These are uncomfortable, prolonged and expensive, but if you are particularly interested in having such surgery performed, discuss the choice of a suitable plastic surgeon with your general practitioner.

Q **I am a 52 year old man who has recently remarried. My new wife is also a divorcee. We now find sex to be very painful to the point where I have a very sore penis, and she bleeds afterwards. We have tried gel but it was still painful. We need your advice.**

A. There are numerous reasons for this problem, which is a relatively common one. The main reason is a lack of lubrication of the vagina, so the reason for the lack of lubrication is what must be determined.

In younger couples, nervousness, lack of experience, and worries about privacy may be factors.

When the male partner is rather over-enthusiastic, he may not 'warm up' his partner sufficiently. Sexual foreplay is necessary to stimulate the glands in the vagina to produce adequate mucus for lubrication.

In older women, menopause may be a factor, and assuming that your new wife is close to your age, this may be the problem here. If there is insufficient oestrogen produced by the ovaries, then the vaginal glands shrink and cease to function effectively. This can be fixed by appropriate hormone replacement therapy.

There are also a number of generalised diseases that may affect vaginal lubrication, including an underactive thyroid gland (again a problem of middle-aged women). These need to be sought and diagnosed by appropriate blood tests.

Please discuss your personal problems in more detail with your GP, who will be able to assess and investigate the problem further.

SKIN

See also ACNE; FUNGAL INFECTIONS; HAIR; NAILS; PSORIASIS; SKIN CANCER; SKIN INFECTIONS

Q   Why do some children get warts and not others?

A   About 25% of the population are susceptible to the virus that causes warts. The rest of us are immune. Once the virus enters the skin, it develops extremely slowly until the low-grade infection induces the growth of a wart at that site. This can then spread the virus to other parts of the body.

The virus causing warts is widespread in the community and cannot be avoided.

Eventually the body develops antibodies to the wart virus that cause the wart to drop off and give protection against further warts developing.

Q   I have multiple warts, but do not want to resort to surgery to remove them. How can I remove warts at home?

A   If you apply the following treatment diligently for two or three months, the warts MAY disappear.
- Soak the warts in warm water for five minutes. Dry with a special towel to prevent spreading the virus to other parts of the body.
- Pare the warts with an old emery board or pumice stone. Do not pare too deeply, because the wart will become tender and bleed, but ensure that any crust is removed.
- Apply one of the commercially available acidic wart paints to the wart, avoiding the surrounding normal skin. Apply several coats, and allow to dry between each coat.
- Cover the wart with a waterproof sticking plaster and keep dry for 24 hours.
- Repeat above procedure every day.
- If the wart becomes tender, stop applying acid, and leave covered for a couple of days before starting again.

Once you are completely clear of warts, wait for at least two months before relaxing, as they may recur in this time. Treat any recurrence as above.

Q   What are the best treatments for warts?

A   The best treatment depends on the size, position and age of the wart.

The simplest treatment for small warts is one of the various acid preparations that can be purchased from chemists. These must be used regularly for several weeks, and both persistence and patience are necessary for success.

The next treatment is some form of minor surgery. This may be freezing the wart with liquid nitrogen or carbon dioxide snow, burning off the wart with cautery, or cutting it out. These are fairly definite procedures, but even so, a small percentage can recur.

Another method for recurrent or resistant warts is to inject a drug called Bleomycin under the wart. This destroys the rapidly multiplying cells at the base of the wart, and it falls off after a few days.

If warts still keep coming, despite these treatments, it may be necessary to investigate the victim's immune status to find out why they are not becoming immune to the wart virus.

Q **I find the application of castor oil regularly to warts makes them disappear in a couple of months. Please pass this advice on to your readers.**

A Warts that occur on fingers, knees, elbows and other areas away from the sex organs, will all disappear eventually. Those on the genitals have more sinister implications.

Warts are caused by a virus, to which about a quarter of the population are susceptible. The virus has a very slow growth and development cycle, and when it irritates an area of skin, a wart develops, usually over or near a joint. After six to 24 months or more, the body slowly develops antibodies to fight off the wart virus, and when the antibody levels reach an adequate level, the virus dies, and all the warts on the body disappear.

Obviously, any medication given for long enough will therefore cure warts, and dozens of remedies have been recommended over the years. There is no harm in trying castor oil, but I know of no references that indicate that this is any more effective than any other substance.

Medically, acid ointments or paints, freezing, diathermy, excision (cutting out), and injecting irritants under them, are the main forms of treatment for warts that are particularly annoying.

Q **My skin specialist said he would be using cryotherapy on my next visit to him, but he didn't explain anything more about it. What is cryotherapy?**

A 'Cryo' means 'cold' in Greek, so cryotherapy is any treatment involving low temperatures or freezing.

Cryotherapy is most commonly involved in the freezing of small skin cancers and warts by general practitioners, dermatologists and plastic surgeons. Liquid nitrogen or carbon dioxide snow is applied to the lump, and freezes it instantly. This destroys the mole, and it shrivels up into a small black lump, which after a few days falls off leaving a small sore that then heals.

It is a very safe and effective procedure, and is associated with only minimal discomfort. The only complication is that if not all of the wart or skin cancer is frozen, after a time it may regrow.

Q   I always feel too hot and sweat too much. Other people around me sweat far less and feel the heat far less than I do. Could you please help?

A   Sweating is an individual characteristic, and some people normally sweat more than others, but it is first necessary to determine if there is some medical condition that is causing your excessive sweating. Conditions that can do this include an overactive thyroid gland (diagnosed by a blood test), diabetes (excess sugar in the blood), infections such as malaria and tuberculosis, and a number of rarer diseases that can affect the function of the glands in your body. You will need to see a doctor to be investigated for these conditions.

If no specific cause can be found, there are antiperspirant sprays and lotions that can relieve the problem, and tablets (Probanthine) that can be taken to reduce sweating. It is important to exclude any serious disease before such tablets are taken.

Q   I sweat excessively. My armpits are disgusting. On a hot day my shirt can be soaked from armpit to waist. Help!

A   By the time they get to a doctor, most people with this problem have tried every antiperspirant on the chemist's shelves. Some people are born with more sweat glands in their armpits than others, and some people have overactive sweat glands.

Doctors can prescribe tablets that dry up sweat, but these also dry up all your other secretions, and many patients find the side effects unacceptable. Potent drying agents such as aluminium chloride alcoholic solution, can be used in the axilla too.

The best solution is surgical. Plastic surgeons can remove most of the sweat glands from your armpit in a relatively simple operation that is very effective, and lasts lifelong.

Q   My six year old daughter has very sweaty hands, feet and armpits. At times her feet actually drip! What can be done?

A   Some people are born with overactive sweat glands or a greater number of these glands. This is an inherited characteristic, and is no different to some people having big noses and others small noses. There is nothing seriously wrong with your daughter, but it is obviously a nuisance.

At her age, only the antiperspirants available from chemists can be used to control the problem. Those containing aluminium hexahydrate solution are the most successful.

The most successful procedure for the sweaty armpit is an operation to remove most of the sweat glands in this area, and your daughter may wish to consider this later.

Operations to cut the nerves causing the hands and feet to sweat are also available, but are considered a last resort rather than a first choice.

Q   After I shave every morning, my neck becomes red raw and itchy. I am seriously contemplating growing a beard. How can I prevent this annoying razor rash?

A   Razor rash is due to irritation of the skin by the scraping of the razor, and an ugly, red itchy rash results. Many men avoid the problem by shaving lightly with an electric razor, and not applying pressure as the razor is used.

Astringents and alcohol rubs may harden the skin to prevent the problem, but unfortunately it may persist. A mild steroid cream can be applied to settle down the rash when it flares up. More frequent, gentler shaves are better than infrequent, harder ones.

Q I have severe pain after I had shingles on my chest 6 months ago. Can you help me?

A Shingles is a viral infection of one particular nerve. Anywhere on the body can be affected.

Post-herpetic neuralgia is a severe pain that persists in the affected area long after the skin rash and blisters of shingles have gone. The pain can be quite excruciating, and the slightest touch of clothing can trigger off spasms of agony. It is a most unpleasant condition!

Shingles can now be cured by a course of specific antiviral tablets, that are available on prescription, but unfortunately they will not help you as they must be started within three days of the rash appearing.

Once post-herpetic pain is present, treatments are not particularly successful. Pain killers are certainly used, but often prove ineffective. Anti-inflammatory drugs, anti-depressants and sedatives can all be tried. In the end, some patients have injections or surgery to destroy the affected nerve, leaving a permanent numb patch at the site of the infection.

If you are not receiving adequate relief you should arrange for your GP to refer you to a physician or a pain clinic for further assessment.

Q I have a big problem—my skin on my face and scalp has itched awfully for a long time non-stop. What causes such itching? Could it be playing football in the sun years ago? How can I get rid of this nuisance?

A Itching of the skin in any part of the body can have a very large number of causes, some of which I shall list below:

- overcleaning of the skin with soaps and shampoos that remove too much of the natural oil from the skin.
- drying of the skin from long exposure to the sun, which may be helped by oily creams (eg. sorbolene).
- dermatitis of many different causes may result in a minimal rash but a maximal itch. Mild steroid creams may assist.
- psoriasis, a skin disease that is more common in older people, and causes red, scaly, itchy patches, particularly on the scalp, elbows and knees.
- scabies, caused by a tiny insect burrowing under the skin. Small red dots or lines may be seen, but the whole area may be very itchy.
- liver failure can cause a generalised itch of the skin in many parts of the body.
- allergies may occur in any part of the body in response to a wide range of substances in the environment, and result in intensely itchy skin.
- a nerve rash may flare at times of stress and anxiety to cause an itch.

If I continued the list, I would probably fill several pages, but the above suggestions may be helpful. Obviously the best solution is to take your itchy skin to a doctor so that s/he can examine it carefully, make a diagnosis and prescribe appropriate treatment.

Q   I am 20 years old and have extremely sensitive skin. If I scratch or bump myself, even lightly, my skin comes up in welts. Several different doctors have been unable to help. I can't play sport or socialise. Help!

A   You are describing a classic case of dermographia. This extremely annoying condition is effectively an excessive reaction to pressure on the skin, resulting in a localised attack of hives (urticaria) at the point where you are scratched or bumped.

It is a condition that can develop at any age, but is far more common in women than men.

Any part of the body can be affected, and although the welts develop in a few minutes, they may take many hours or days to fade away.

The cause of the condition is unknown and there is no permanent cure, but patients who have serious problems with the condition can take antihistamine tablets on a regular basis to reduce the severity of attacks. Most victims find that the condition is severe at some times, and less severe at others. There is a tendency for the severity of the reaction to slowly subside over many years.

Q   I am in my seventies, and generally well, but I have noticed a number of raised moles coming up on my back and shoulders. They can be surgically removed, but more keep coming. What are they and what causes them?

A   The spots you are describing are benign pigmented naevi or seborrhoeic moles. They are a common problem in older people, and it is an inherited characteristic. The most important thing you ever do in life is choose your parents!

There is nothing you can do to prevent more from coming, and the only treatment is cutting them out as they occur.

They are totally harmless, and not a sign of disease elsewhere in the body, but sometimes more sinister growths (eg. melanoma) can be confused with them, so it is wise to have them checked every year or so by your doctor.

Q   My skin is terribly dry and cracked. When I play with my grandchildren they complain that my hands are like sandpaper, and this upsets me. What is the best treatment for dry skin?

A   Many different types of moisturising creams and oils are available for the treatment of dry skin. As a first step, baby oil is cheap and often effective. If this does not control the problem, or proves too messy, your chemist will be able to recommend a suitable cream. Many of these contain urea as an active ingredient. Any cream used should be non-perfumed to avoid any sensitivity or allergy problems.

The excessive use of soap is often a cause of dry skin, and the use of soap substitutes (again your chemist can advise you) is one way of preventing dry skin. If none of the simple remedies help, see your general practitioner, as there are many skin diseases that may be responsible for skin dryness.

Q   I am developing little red spidery things on the skin of my face. What causes them and how can they be removed?

A   Spider naevi are relatively common. They appear when a number of tiny blood vessels (capillaries) can be seen diverging from a central point. In Australia, they are most commonly caused by sun damage to the skin, and this is one of the reasons for doctors to be constantly urging the public to slip (on a shirt), slop (on sunscreen) and slap (on a hat) to protect themselves from skin damage and cancer later in life.

A number of diseases can also cause spider naevi. These include liver failure, an overactive thyroid gland, alcoholism and rheumatoid arthritis. Some unfortunate women also find that the hormonal changes of pregnancy can cause the blood vessels to dilate and mark their skin.

When a patient presents with this problem, it is important to determine the cause before any treatment is undertaken. Each individual spot can be treated by placing a fine needle in the central blood vessel of the spider, and passing an electric current through it for a moment. This diathermy process destroys the central vessel, and therefore the radiating vessels collapse, and the disfigurement disappears. A small white spot will remain at the site. Lasers are now being used by some doctors for this procedure.

Q What is a sebaceous cyst? My daughter has one behind her ear, and her GP wants to cut it out.

A Sebum is the oil-like substance that keeps our skin moist and supple. It is produced in glands beneath the skin, and is discharged through small ducts. These glands are present all over the body, but in areas that may become sweaty, dirty or injured it is possible to block the duct leading from the gland. The sebum continues to be produced, and a cyst (known as a sebaceous cyst) slowly fills up under the skin.

Sometimes the pressure is sufficient in the cyst for its contents to be discharged through the previously blocked duct. Unfortunately, the cyst usually regrows again.

The worst thing that can happen is for these cysts to become infected, and if antibiotics are not given soon enough, an abscess may form.

Any cyst that is unsightly or becomes infected should be cut out. This is a simple procedure that can be performed under local anaesthetic by most general practitioners.

Q Why would I get eczema on my chest from ironed shirts but not drip-dry shirts?

A The most likely explanation is contact dermatitis. When ironed, your shirts may be sprayed with a product that makes ironing easier and more effective. Your skin may be reacting to one of the components of this spray.

As a first step, I would check ensure that no sprays are used when your shirts are ironed. If the dermatitis settles, you have your answer. Different products contain different chemicals, and it may be that your shirts can be ironed in future with a different type of spray. The other possible cause is a synthetic material that may be in some shirts but not others. As a last resort, see a doctor when the rash is bad, to have it identified.

Q I am 71 years old and have had an ulcer on my ankle for 2 years, in spite of visiting the doctor all the time. Could you please let me know how to get it better as I am so depressed by it.

SKIN

A   Ulcers on the ankles of elderly people are notoriously difficult to treat, and success usually involves many months of careful treatment and the careful following of a doctor's instructions.

Often a small graze or cut develops into an ulcer because the lower leg has a very poor blood supply in many older people, and the correct nutrients cannot be supplied through the blood to allow healing.

There are as many treatments for chronic leg ulcers as there are doctors, but the one that I have found most successful is the following three-point plan:
1. Apply a piece of Duo Derm over the ulcer. This is a sheet of a jelly like material, which should be cut to a size slightly larger than the ulcer, and left in place for three or four days at a time. The ulcer should be gently rinsed with a dilute antiseptic (eg. Dettol, Savlon) between dressings. Duo Derm is available from chemists without a prescription.
2. Firmly (but not too tightly) bandage the lower leg from toes to just below the knee with a wide, good quality elastic bandage.
3. Keep the leg elevated as much as possible—on a foot stool when sitting, or on a pillow in bed.

With time, and a lot of patience, the ulcer should very slowly heal.

Before undertaking this treatment, all patients with ulcers should have them checked by a doctor to ensure that there is no serious underlying disease.

Q   **My daughter suffers terribly from pilonidal sinuses in the groin. She has had several removed, but they keep returning. Will waxing help the problem? How can she prevent these terrible sores? Could they be caused by her hairy husband? Thank you for your assistance with this matter.**

A   A pilonidal sinus is the infection of a hair follicle, which then becomes a small abscess. Some people are unlucky enough to be prone to this problem, but they are normally hairy men rather than women.

All women have hair on their bodies, and if those fine hairs are supplied with oil glands that secrete a thick, viscous oil, the hair follicle may become clogged with oil, and develop an infection. Once an infection is present, it rapidly develops into an abscess that must be drained surgically, and treated with antibiotics.

In your daughter's case, prevention is essential. There is unlikely to be any permanent cure available, but medication to prevent the problem should be used long term.

I am sure her husband cannot be blamed for the problem.

Waxing will possibly aggravate the situation by damaging the hair follicles.

I would suggest that you make a long appointment with your GP to discuss two possibilities. Long-term antibiotics, similar to those used by people with severe acne, may prevent any infection developing in the hair follicles. The use of a mild steroid/antibiotic combination lotion (eg. Neo Medrol—prescription required) may thin out the oil in the skin, and again prevent infection.

Q   **For at least ten years I have had a body itch from my head to my knees. Different ointments have helped for a time, but it keeps coming back. Can you help me?**

A   There are hundreds of causes of itchy skin, with and without a rash. You do not mention a rash, and I will therefore assume that you do not have one.

The common causes of this problem include stress reactions, excessively dry skin from using soap, allergies, liver failure, leukaemia, thyroid gland abnormalities, anaemia, kidney failure, fibreglass exposure, several types of cancer, diabetes, drugs and poisoning.

As you can see from this far from complete list, the causes vary from the mild to the very severe. After ten years, it is unlikely that one of the severe causes is responsible, as other symptoms should have developed.

Nevertheless, you should be thoroughly investigated by the appropriate blood and urine tests to exclude any possible cause for your constant itching. If no cause is found, it is possible to use anti-itch creams when appropriate, but when large areas are involved, this is impractical. Anti-itch tablets such as Dilosyn can then be used to control the problem, but these can cause drowsiness in some people.

Discuss the matter further with your GP, and if necessary request a referral to a dermatologist for a more detailed examination.

Q **My husband has a skin problem which a dermatologist has diagnosed as erythema multiform. Could you explain what this condition is?**

A Erythema multiform is an acute inflammation (redness) of the skin, that may be triggered by drugs, bacterial or viral infections, cold sores and other herpes infections; or it may appear for no apparent reason. 75% of cases occur after a herpes or cold sore infection, and half the remainder are caused by drugs—particularly sulpha antibiotics.

The attacks that are caused by cold sores and other infections tend to be mild, but those that occur as a result of drug sensitivity can be very severe.

Patients with erythema multiform suddenly develop several types of rash simultaneously. This gives the disease its name, which can be loosely translated as 'red spots of many shapes'. Almost any imaginable skin problem can occur.

The inside of the mouth and vagina, and the eyes may also be involved.

The rash may occur anywhere on the body, but is most common on the front of the leg, over the shoulders, and above and below the elbow on the outside of the arm. The soles and palms are other areas that are commonly attacked. In most cases, the rash is evenly distributed on both sides of the body.

Most patients have only a mild fever, but severely affected victims may be acutely ill with a very high fever and generalised weakness.

There is no cure for this condition, but the vast majority of cases are mild, and settle in two to four weeks. Severe cases may persist for up to six weeks, and rarely, with lung involvement in the elderly or chronically ill, it may be very severe.

Treatment is aimed at minimising the symptoms and discomfort with painkillers such as paracetamol and aspirin; and creams, lotions and dressings to ease the irritation of the rash. Steroids may be prescribed in severe cases. Recurrent attacks of erythema multiform are quite common.

Q **I have been diagnosed with lichen planus, which mainly affects my mouth. I would like to know more about this condition, what causes it, method of treatment and prognosis.**

A   Lichen planus is an uncommon skin condition which normally starts in the twenties or thirties. It causes small, shiny, flat-topped growths that may grow and join together to form a plaque. It is more common in skin creases such as the inside of the wrists and elbows, but can occur anywhere on the body surface, including the insides of the mouth, nose, ears, vagina and anus. It may start at a point where the skin has been injured, or may be triggered by some drugs, but the actual cause is unknown. One theory is that it may be a chronic viral infection of the skin, but this is as yet unproven.

The only way to be certain of the diagnosis is to cut out a part of the skin affected by the rash (a biopsy) and have a pathologist examine this under a microscope.

Mild cases are usually not treated, but more serious cases are treated with steroid creams and then covering the area with a plastic dressing. Further treatments include steroid pastes in the mouth, taking steroid tablets, injecting steroids into the affected skin, exposing the rash to ultraviolet light, and using potent prescription medications such as Tigason, Retin A and Dapsone in serious cases.

The long-term course of the condition is very variable, with some patients recovering in a few months, while others may suffer for years. Virtually all patients recover from the condition completely eventually, but there may be some pigmentation of the skin left behind after the rash has cleared.

Q   **I have been diagnosed as suffering from 'acne rose asia'. Is there a cure? What will happen to my skin?**

A   Acne rosacea is a skin condition that is far more prevalent in females and those of middle age than any other group. It presents as pimples, flushing and redness of the face that is usually symmetrical. The cause is unknown, and there is no evidence that foods or vitamins can play any part in its cause or treatment.

Tetracycline type antibiotics usually clear the condition, and there is a skin preparation also available (Rozex). A complete recovery may take many weeks and the rash may recur after the treatment is ceased, but if this occurs the drug is merely taken for a longer period to control the disease. The medication is not a cure, but will control the majority of attacks.

Q   **I have a very itchy rash on my arms after putting insulating batts in my ceiling, and it's driving me batty (ha, ha)! What can I do about it?**

A   Insulating batts are usually made of fibre-glass that is loosely spun. Tiny slivers of glass fibre can easily break off and penetrate the skin to cause pain, irritation and inflammation. While the glass remains, the rash will persist. With time, the body will reject the tiny pieces of glass, but until then, irritation may be intense.

Secondary infections may develop in some areas, and these will require antibiotic treatment.

Various anti-itch and anti-inflammatory creams can be prescribed by your doctor, but unfortunately time is the usual cure. Anyone dealing with uncoated fibre-glass should wear protective clothing, and eye protection, to prevent this problem. Coated and sealed fibre-glass as used in boats and car bodies is quite safe unless it is cut or sawed, when the dust produced may cause irritation.

Q   **Is there any treatment for stretch marks? I am covered with them from my legs to my upper arms, which greatly limits what I can wear. I am willing to do anything!**

A   The simple answer to your question is unfortunately no. There is no effective treatment for stretch marks, particularly when they are severe.

On the other hand, some unconfirmed research by a limited number of doctors in the United States indicates that a cream called Retin A may reduce the severity of stretch marks, but not remove them entirely. Regular use for six months is required, and extreme care is necessary when first using the cream as some people react adversely to it. Retin A is available from chemists without prescription.

Unfortunately, there is nothing that can be done to prevent stretch marks either, and the expensive creams promoted by some cosmetic companies are next to useless.

The tendency is one that you will inherit from your parents, and if your mother, aunts or grandmothers had bad stretch marks with pregnancy, your chance of developing the same problem is considerably increased.

Possibly you should consider living in a cold climate where revealing sun dresses and bikinis give way to the all-covering wool suit and heavy coat.

Q   **I have a lot of blackheads on my nose. How can I get rid of them? Squeezing them doesn't work.**

A   Please do not squeeze your blackheads! The most likely consequence is further infection and damage to the tissue around the blackhead, which can lead to more pimples. The worst result would be infection spreading into the surrounding tissue from the squeezed blackhead to cause a serious condition called cellulitis.

The first step in treatment is keeping the skin clean by washing twice a day with a good soap. Then one of the numerous proprietary creams and lotions available from chemists can be used. These must be used regularly for some weeks to give them a fair trial, but if they are unsuccessful in clearing the skin, the next step is to see your general practitioner.

Your general practitioner can prescribe stronger lotions and creams, as well as special antibiotics to prevent the skin infections that cause blackheads.

Q   **Are there any dangers in having several birth marks? I have about 25, and my 2 year old son has about 13. A paediatrician commented that future children could have problems. I also have a couple of soft lumps under my skin. A second opinion would be appreciated.**

A   Generally speaking, provided your birth marks are not moles that may become skin cancers, there is no cause for concern about them.

What your paediatrician is probably concerned about is a condition called Von Recklinghausen's disease of multiple neurofibromatosis. Besides having one of the longest names in any medical textbook, this disease has the characteristics of multiple light brown marks on the skin, soft fatty lumps under the skin and in a small number of cases, nerves may be damaged.

The disease passes from one generation to the next, but has a very variable result. Some patients merely have a couple of brown spots that never concern them, while others may be severely disfigured and disabled by the lumps under the skin, nerve weakness and large brown patches.

There is no treatment other than plastic surgery for any particularly bad lumps and patches. There is also no way in which you can determine whether a future child will have the condition, or how badly affected that child will be. Your son should not marry someone who also has this condition in her background. Further advice can be sought from your paediatrician or a geneticist.

Q My son has a red rash around his mouth. No creams seem to help. What is it?

A Peri-oral dermatitis is very common in children, and often requires no treatment. If severe, it may be due to an allergy, fungal infection, bacteria or just irritation from excess salivation—particularly in children who suck their thumbs!

If the simple barrier creams obtainable from chemists are not helping, take your son to a doctor to ensure that there is no treatable cause. Fungal and bacterial infections can be serious and require appropriate treatment. If it is a severe rash due to an allergy or excess salivation, a mild steroid cream may help.

Q I have a very itchy scalp, but there is nothing to see except occasionally a tiny red spot. I have used Diprosone without success. Any advice would be appreciated.

A The first condition that comes to mind is head lice, but there are many more possibilities including fungal infections of the scalp, psoriasis, dermatitis, allergies and nerve rashes.

Head lice are almost impossible to see with the naked eye, but can cause considerable irritation from their bites. They are easily spread from one person to another by close contact or sharing combs, brushes, caps etc.

A number of preparations are available from chemists to treat this condition, but if after using one of them a couple of times the problem persists, you should consult your doctor.

Diprosone will ease inflammation of the scalp, but it will not cure infections or infestations of any sort.

Q Does the skin naturally get thinner with age? I am just over 60 and recently noticed the skin on my fingers getting very wrinkled.

A The reason that young people, and children in particular, have smooth, firm skin is that there is a layer of fat immediately under under the skin, and the skin cells are large and full of fluid. As you age, the amount of fat in the skin (as distinct from the amount of fat that may be present elsewhere in the body), and the amount of fluid in the skin cells, gradually diminishes. This causes the skin to become thinner and wrinkled.

The elastic fibres that are present in young skin, also stretch and become replaced by fibrous tissue with age, so that the skin does not react to changes in shape (eg. over joints such as the elbow) as readily. Ageing is a process that involves every cell in the body, and unfortunately wrinkles, thin skin, age spots, poor healing and sagging tissue are all part of this inevitable process.

Q I have a medical condition called angiokeratosis, which appears as little blood blisters on my scrotum. These are unsightly, and I have to convince my partner they are not some form of STD. Is there any way of removing them?

A Angiokeratosis consists of dilated blood vessels which form red lumps that are then covered by a fine scale. There may be one or two present or several dozen. Their cause is unknown, they cause no specific problems other than bleeding excessively if damaged, and they are certainly not contagious. They usually persist long term, but sometimes resolve spontaneously.

They can be quite easily removed by diathermy (burning under a local anaesthetic), cryotherapy (freezing) or laser coagulation. This type of procedure is done by some general practitioners and most dermatologists and plastic surgeons.

It will depend on how much they worry you as to how much you worry them.

SKIN CANCER
See also CANCER; SKIN

Q I was a sun bunny in my youth, and now I am petrified that I will develop a disfiguring skin cancer. If one is going to come, I would like it removed before it causes any serious damage. What are the danger signs to look for with skin cancer?

A Australia is blessed with far more sunshine than most nations with a predominantly white-skinned population. As a result, it is also blessed with a far greater percentage of sun-induced skin cancers.

Nasty skin spots fall into several different categories.

Cancers of the outermost layer of skin are called squamous cell carcinomas (SCC). They occur most commonly on the exposed parts of the body such as the face, scalp, arms and hands. An SCC looks like a red spot covered in fine white scales. They may be itchy or sore, but often attract attention because they are unsightly.

Another type of tumour develops if the next layer down in the skin is involved. These growths are called basal cell carcinomas (BCC) and are generally not as serious as the more superficial cancers. They appear as shiny, rounded lumps that often change in size and colour.

Malignant melanomas are the most serious and deadly of them all. Even with the best medical care, a significant proportion of these patients will die, often because they have been seen too late by a doctor. Melanomas can be flat or raised as lumps, and can be any colour from mid-pink to jet black. They are due to overgrowth of the layer of skin that causes pigment to be laid down in the skin. Because they are deeper in the skin, they can move more easily to other parts of the body.

The signs to watch for in a spot or sore are:
* any change in colour, shape or size
* soreness or itchiness
* bleeding or weeping.

If any of these signs occur, see your doctor immediately!

It is far better to find out the truth now, be it good or bad, than to worry for months unnecessarily, or have a far worse outcome because of the delay.

Q It is many years since I have holidayed at the beach, but I plan one soon. Should I go to a solarium to get a tan before I go so that I don't get burnt when I go to the beach. Is a solarium tan dangerous, or are chemical tans better?

A Ultraviolet (UV) rays cause tanning of the skin, and it does not matter whether these rays come from the sun or an artificial source, the results are the same.

If excessive amounts of UV rays hit the skin you will burn, and the more you are exposed, the higher your risk of skin cancer. A tan will not protect you from further burning or skin cancer.

Chemical tans can give you the brown colour you desire without any risk (except allergy to the preparation), but will not protect your skin in any way.

Be sensible, and avoid both the solarium and the sun's rays. Go on your beach holiday but follow the Anti-Cancer Council's advice, and 'slip, slop, slap' to avoid burning, excessive tanning and skin cancer.

Q I want to get a good tan, but not get skin cancer. What are the best sunscreens to use?

A The answer to this depends on what you want your skin to do. All reputable sunscreens are numbered from 1 to 30+. The higher the number, the greater the protection. If you want to avoid burning and tanning, use a 30+ sunscreen. If you want a light tan, use a 10 to 12. If you are already tanned, and merely wish to keep it perfect, use a 6 or 8 rated preparation.

Sun tans may look attractive, but remember that it can take 10 or 20 years for skin cancer to develop. Have a look at the skin on some of the older beach-side residents. Most of us do not want leathery skin covered in red, scaling, lumpy cancers when we are in our middle or later years. It is therefore better to limit tanning as much as possible, particularly if you are fair-skinned and red-haired. Your beach bumming now may cause you to spend many hours under a doctor's scalpel later.

Q I have been told that I must have a suspicious mole cut out, but I am frightened of any surgery. Can you please explain what will happen?

A An area is excised (cut out) to remove a skin cancer, a mole that is annoying or cosmetically unacceptable, to improve the appearance of a scar, or part of a growth may be removed to see if it is malignant.

After you lie down on a couch in the doctor's surgery in a position that makes the area to be excised easily accessible, the area will be cleaned with a solution that destroys most of the germs on the skin.

The doctor will then inject an anaesthetic around the area to be excised, or sometimes into the base of a finger or toe, to anaesthetise the area. The injection stings for about 15 seconds, and with larger areas, two or more injections may be necessary. The area injected will become numb within a few seconds, and no further pain or discomfort should be experienced. If any discomfort is felt, tell the doctor immediately, and further anaesthetic can be injected.

A tray with instruments, solutions, drapes, swabs, sutures etc. will have been placed near you, and the doctor will wear sterile gloves, and possibly a mask and gown. The doctor will thoroughly clean the skin again, and then take a drape from the tray, and arrange it near or around the area to be excised.

Using a scalpel, which has an edge sharper than a razor, the doctor will cut around the lesion being excised. You may feel pressure, but no pain. It is not possible to cut out closely around the lesion, as a round hole cannot be closed without using plastic surgery techniques to extend the size of the wound, so in most cases, a diamond shaped excision is made, and the scar is usually about three times longer than the lesion is wide. Over the next few minutes, the doctor will cut out the area of concern, and in most cases put the tissue removed into a bottle of preservative for further analysis by a pathologist.

The repair of the wound then commences with stitches (or sometimes staples) being inserted to close the wound. This often takes longer than the excision of the lesion, and once again, you should feel no pain.

Once the wound is closed, a dressing will be applied (unless the wound is on a sensitive area where it is inappropriate) and you can go home. The anaesthetic will last for one to three hours (depending on which type has been used), but after it has worn off there should be nothing more than a slight ache and paracetamol is normally the only medication necessary.

There may be some slight ooze of blood onto the dressing in the first hour or two, but for no longer, and the dressing may need to be changed at this time. The wound should be kept clean, dry and, if possible, covered until the stitches are removed. You can normally have a shower, but not a bath or a swim. After a shower, remove the damp dressing, pat the wound dry and apply a clean dry dressing. Antiseptics, powders and other medications are not normally necessary

If the wound becomes red, painful, discharges pus or you develop a fever, return to see the doctor immediately. Otherwise the stitches will be removed in a few days or weeks, depending on the area affected and the size of the wound. Sometimes only some of the stitches are removed, and a further visit is necessary for removal of the remainder.

The scar will continue to heal after the stitches are removed. It will form a red line initially, but this usually fades to a white line after a few months. The scar will not reach its final form until a year after the excision.

Some parts of the body heal better than others. The face and hands heal very well, while the back, chest and lower leg heal poorly and will scar more. Scars on areas of tension often spread, and will not appear as neat as scars that are not under tension.

Your procedure may not exactly follow the outline above for multiple reasons. Please ask your doctor if you have any other queries. An example of how an excision is performed is shown below.

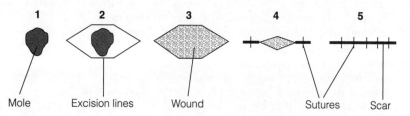

| 1 | 2 | 3 | 4 | 5 |
| Mole | Excision lines | Wound | Sutures | Scar |

Q   I have a black, hairy mole on my cheek. It has been there as long as I can remember and I'm now 45. Could it be dangerous?

A   There is only one way to find out, and that is to have it checked by a doctor, because any black mole could be serious.

As a general rule, hairy moles and those that have not changed in appearance for many years are unlikely to be a cancer—but you never really know unless a professional has a look. It is far better to be reassured now that all is well, than to leave it too late to get the bad news, by which stage effective treatment may be impossible.

Even the nastiest malignant melanomas (the worst form of skin cancer) start as a small mole that can be easily removed, but once the cancer has spread to the internal organs, cure is impossible. And remember, nearly all skin cancers are due to sun exposure.

Q   I keep hearing about people who have skin cancers that can kill them if they are left for too long. I have worked out in the sun most of my life, and would like to know what a skin cancer looks like?

A   Cancers of the outermost layer of skin are called skin cancers or squamous cell carcinomas. They occur most commonly on the exposed parts of the body such as the face, scalp, arms and hands. Men with receding hairlines are at greatest risk, because they lack nature's own sunshade.

A skin cancer looks like a red spot covered in fine white scales. They may be itchy or sore, and often attract attention because they are unsightly. Most of them can be very easily removed, and if the doctor is sure of the diagnosis he or she may burn the cancer off with a diathermy machine, or freeze it off with liquid nitrogen.

If the skin cancer is large, it is necessary to cut out the spot and the surrounding tissue to prevent it from spreading further.

The signs to watch for in a spot or sore are any change in colour, shape or size; soreness or itchiness; or bleeding or weeping. If any of these signs occur, see your doctor immediately!

Q   My 61 year old mother is rapidly developing a large number of squamous skin cancers on her legs, despite the fact that she has always kept them well covered. As soon as one is cut out, another appears. Is there anything that can be done about this.

A   Skin cancers are caused by exposure to excessive amounts of sun in childhood, but it can be decades later that they develop.

All of us are producing cancer cells in our bodies every day, but these abnormal cells are normally rapidly destroyed by the body's defence mechanisms. In old age, these defences do not work as well, and this allows skin cancers (and other forms of cancer) to develop more easily.

Many older people develop multiple skin cancers, particularly if they spent their childhood in sunny climates, despite protecting themselves from the sun later in life.

These skin cancers can be removed by cutting them out, freezing them off, burning them away or by using special chemicals on the skin.

Larger spots must be cut out, but multiple small skin cancers may be frozen with liquid nitrogen spray as soon as they appear. This is probably the best option for your mother, as there is no way to prevent them from developing.

A cream called Efudix, which can only be obtained on prescription, can also be used to control multiple small skin cancers. It destroys the cancer cells directly, and the skin heals with minimal scarring.

Moisturising creams applied freely to sun-damaged skin will keep that area supple and less likely to develop skin cancer.

Q **My GP checked over my skin yesterday when I went to see him about my blood pressure, and said that I had a lot of skin cancers that would need to be treated, and he wants me to make a long appointment so that he can have time to treat them. I am very worried. How are skin cancers treated? Can they be cured?**

A There are many sun-induced skin sores which are not the nasty cancerous type, but there are also some which can spread rapidly enough to eventually kill the unfortunate owner of the spot!

Most of them can be very easily removed, and if the doctor is sure of the diagnosis he may burn the cancer off with a diathermy machine, or freeze it off with liquid nitrogen. Both methods are very effective in early stages of the disease.

If the skin cancer has spread, it is necessary to cut out the spot and the surrounding tissue to prevent it from spreading further. Some people are unlucky enough to have areas such as the nose or ears involved, and in severe cases these can be completely eaten away by the cancer cells.

It is often difficult for doctors to be absolutely certain about a spot when examined on the patient, and so if there is any doubt at all, the spot is cut out. This can be done very easily in a general practitioner's surgery. The lesion is then sent to a pathologist, who will examine it further under a microscope to make the exact diagnosis.

The vast majority of skin cancers can be cured, but early treatment is vital.

SKIN INFECTIONS
See also FUNGAL INFECTIONS; SKIN

Q **Why are school sores different from other sores?**

A School sores (also known as impetigo) are bacterial infections of the skin. They get their name because they are easily spread from one child to another in the school environment. They are not necessarily a sign of poor hygiene. They respond quickly to the correct treatment of antibiotic ointment and/or antibiotic tablets.

Other members of the family should protect themselves from infection by avoiding close contact, not sharing towels etc. and using antiseptic soap.

Q **I have recently had a horrible abscess on my buttock. Can you please tell me all about these messy things?**

A An abscess is a collection of pus in a tissue-lined cavity. They occur due to the destruction of normal tissue by a bacterial infection. Rarely, fungal infections may cause an abscess.

When a bacteria infects an area, it destroys the normal cells. The wastes produced can normally be removed through the blood circulation in the area, but if the destruction is too great, the waste products accumulate as pus, and an abscess forms. There are two main types of abscess: those that occur in or under the skin, and those that occur in internal body organs.

An abscess in or under the skin appears as a red, painful swelling. It is initially hard to touch, but as the pus formation increases, it becomes soft and obviously fluid filled. In due course, it will 'point' and form a head that will eventually burst and allow the pus to escape. Treatment in the early stages will involve antibiotics by mouth or injection, and hot compresses on the area. Once there is obvious fluid present, the abscess should (under local or general anaesthetic) be drained, scraped out, and the drain hole kept open by a small piece of cloth (a wick) to allow any further pus to escape quickly. The wick is changed regularly, and the abscess cavity will slowly reduce in size until it heals.

Particularly nasty abscesses may develop around the anus and require quite major surgery to allow for the adequate drainage of pus.

Q **My daughter has just been started on treatment for a ringworm. How do you catch ringworm?**

A Ringworm is not a worm, but a fungal infection of the skin. The disease is caught from another animal (human, cat, dog etc.) that already has the disease.

The fungal spore that causes the disease penetrates into the skin, and then starts growing. It first appears as a red spot that gradually enlarges and then develops a pale centre. As the fungus grows, the edge of the spreading infection becomes red and inflamed, while the area that has recovered returns to a normal skin colour. Thus a slowly enlarging ring appears.

The same phenomenon can be seen in the toadstool rings that form in damp grass.

Q **I have patches of white scales on my body. In my armpit they look red. I've had it for years and it comes and goes. What is it?**

A It is almost certainly pityriasis versicolor. This is a fungal infection of the skin that is very common in the tropics and becomes less common as you move south. It is unusual south of Queensland and unheard of in Tasmania.

This fungus can flare and settle, depending on the season, and produces the type of rash you describe. It tends to be chronic, and although treated in an apparently successful fashion, tends to recur in the next summer. The infection prevents the ultra-violet rays of the sun from reaching the pigment layer of the skin, and so in exposed areas you develop a tan that is covered in white spots where the infection is present, giving a polka-dot effect.

Curing the infection does not remove the white spots, because they are due to lack of a sun tan. In areas not exposed to the sun the infection produces red scale-covered patches.

Treatment involves lotions, foams and/or tablets from your doctor. The infection can usually be cured, but don't be surprised if it comes back again next year.

Q **I have been troubled with fungal skin infections since coming to Australia 5 years ago. It is always worse with the higher temperatures**

of summer. I have used numerous creams which settle it down, but it always recurs. Is there any cure for it?

A   I suspect that you are describing a fungal condition called pityriasis versicolor, which causes patches on the skin that spread steadily across the body, often worsening in warm humid conditions, and settling in winter. The patches are red coloured on white skin, but white coloured on suntanned skin, as the fungus prevents suntanning of the area of skin it covers.

There are numerous antifungal creams and lotions that can be bought from chemists without a prescription that control most of these infections, but if these are failing to control your problem, you should see your general practitioner.

Your doctor can confirm the diagnosis, and then prescribe stronger lotions, or tablets that can control the condition. Total cure is difficult unless you live in a cold climate, and many sufferers require a course of treatment at the beginning of each summer.

Q   **I developed a very itchy rash in my crotch area while recovering from a knee fracture. None of the anti-itch creams helped. The rash disappeared when the fracture healed. Can you explain this?**

A   When you had a fracture, you would have been less active than normal, and certainly moving the fractured leg less than normal. You would also have been unable to bathe or shower yourself properly because of the plaster.

In these circumstances it is possible for the sweat to build up in the crease between your leg and groin, and with the heat of summer, the friction between your leg and groin skin and sitting down more than standing, the irritated skin in the area would become a prime site for a fungal infection. Technically, this problem is called tinea cruris.

Fungal infections will not recover with the normal anti-itch creams, but require specific fungus-killing creams for a cure. These are available from chemists and on prescription from doctors. Keeping the affected area cool, dry and clean is also important.

Once your fracture healed, you became more active, did not spend as much time sitting, and could bathe more easily—thus curing the rash.

Q   **I am 70 years of age and have developed a skin rash between my legs in the groin area. The rash is itchy after a shower, and all sorts of creams and ointments from the chemist have failed to fix it. They just seem to control it for a while, then it comes back. I hope you can help me.**

A   The most likely cause of your rash is a fungal infection of the warm, moist skin in the groin area. Fungi are microscopic plants, rather like the green slime on stagnant ponds, that can infect the skin and gut. They like areas that are warm (under clothing), moist (from sweat) and irritated (by scratching or folds of skin).

There are a number of antifungal creams and lotions available from chemists and on prescription from doctors that can kill the fungal infection of the skin, but the condition often recurs if the source of the infection is not removed. The fungus can remain deep in the skin for some time after the rash has settled, so it is important to continue with the treatment for several days after the rash has cleared.

The other source of infection is the gut. Fungi live quite normally inside your intestine, but if excess numbers are present, they can come out the back passage, and infect the warm, moist skin around the anus. From there the infection can easily migrate to the groin. It is therefore sensible for a doctor to prescribe an antifungal tablet that will clear the gut of infection when a skin infection recurs repeatedly. Some types of tablets can also assist the creams or lotions in clearing the infection from the skin itself. You should see your doctor for further advice and treatment.

Q **I am a 19 year old girl, and for five years I have been trying to overcome my terrible under-arm scent. I am light in colour, but my armpit is black and stinks. I can't wear anything like a tank-top because it is easily noticed. How do I get rid of the blackness and smell?**

A First, see a doctor. S/he will probably take swabs from your armpit to send to a laboratory. Hopefully, they will be able to determine what is causing the infection in your arm pit.

The most likely explanation is a fungal infection. These can certainly cause a smelly, black coating on warm, moist areas of skin. If this is found to be the cause, antifungal lotions or creams, and possibly tablets, will be prescribed to cure your problem.

Q **I went to my doctor with an itchy rash and she says I have an insect in my skin called scabies! What is this disease?**

A Scabies occurs when tiny insects, which are barely visible to the naked eye, start burrowing under the skin. It is rather like a microscopic mole, digging burrows that can be one centimetre or more long in the outer layers of your skin. These burrows, and the tissue around them, then become red, itchy and inflamed.

The only way to catch scabies is by close contact with someone who already has the disease. In its early stages, a person may not realise that the couple of itchy spots they have on their hands are scabies, and so shaking hands with that person could spread the disease.

Treatment involves painting the entire body below the neck with a lotion or cream. All other members of the family, and anyone else closely connected to the sufferer, should be treated at the same time. The bed linen needs to be changed on that day too. The treatment is repeated after a week, so that any mites that hatch from the eggs remaining after the initial treatment will be killed.

Scabies need not be a disease of unhygienic families, and can occur in the children of the most scrupulously clean mother. It does tend to come in epidemics every couple of years, and obviously the sooner it is treated, the less it will spread.

Q **What diseases could cause me to get sores around my neck and armpit all the time?**

A Weeping infections of the skin can take on many different forms, but they all look and feel most unpleasant. They will include diseases such as school sores, boils and carbuncles.

School sores are caused by one or more of several different bacteria. The bacteria spread easily from one person to another, and are known as school sores because of their rapid spread from one child to another in a crowded classroom.

A boil or furuncle, is a localised infection of the skin, often caused by the 'Golden Staph' bacteria. It usually starts in a hair root, and appears as a rounded, red, sore lump with a central core of pus. They are most common on the back and neck.

A carbuncle is an area of infected skin through which there are many openings for pus to escape. Unlike a boil, it is only slightly raised, but still quite red and sore.

Once a sore is present, a doctor should be seen as soon as possible for an appropriate antibiotic to be prescribed.

SLEEP

Q Why do old people have trouble sleeping?

A You require less sleep as you grow older. Babies may need 14 hours a day, children 10 hours and adults 7 to 8 hours. The elderly can often feel quite comfortable with 5 or 6 hours of sleep. They are also less active than younger adults, and tend to take naps during the day, both of which reduce their need for night-time sleep. Sleeping tablets merely force artificial sleep upon people who do not require it.

Q My wife and I are in our seventies, and sleep seven or eight hours a night, and often have an afternoon nap as well. Many other people our age have a lot of trouble sleeping, or sleep for far less time. Is there something wrong with us?

A Sleep patterns are an extremely individual characteristic, and vary markedly from one person to another.

Generally, the amount of sleep required slowly decreases from infancy, through childhood to adult life and old age, but there are exceptions to every rule.

Some adults cope quite well on five hours sleep a night, while others (particularly teenagers) seem to require nine or even ten hours a night to function well. Others have frequent brief naps and cope well with life.

The ease of sleeping also varies—those who cannot easily get to sleep and wake frequently, are annoyed by those who can fall asleep in a minute and remain in that state, oblivious to their partner's restlessness, for the entire night.

The amount of sleep that you need is the amount that suits you—and only you.

Inadequate sleep makes you tired (obviously), but also irritable and decision making can be affected. On the other hand, too much sleep can also be detrimental, causing headaches and light-headedness.

There is nothing wrong with you or your sleep pattern, and you are probably the envy of your peers.

Q I am always sleeping. I fall asleep at work, in the train (and miss my station), in front of TV etc. What could be wrong with me?

A Doctors will immediately consider the diagnosis of narcolepsy, which is a rare form of epilepsy that causes people to suddenly fall asleep, sometimes in the middle of a sentence, or when half-way across a pedestrian crossing. This condition has obvious dangers, and requires urgent treatment.

It is far more likely that you are merely over tired from work, play and activities. Many medical conditions from anaemia and chronic infections to an underactive thyroid gland and the side effects of medications can cause you to be tired and fall asleep. Your quality of sleep may also be poor, leading to chronic tiredness. You will need to be examined and investigated by a doctor to get to the bottom of the problem.

Q **In my job I have to work shifts. I work two days from noon till 8 pm then have a day off, then two days from 8 pm till 4 am, then a day off, then two days from 4 am to noon, followed by another day off. This has gone on for four years, and for most of that time I have not been able to sleep properly. I can't sleep during the day on night shift, or at night when on day shift. I'm getting irritable, lose my temper easily, can't relax and have headaches. What should I do?**

A You have an atrocious job, with an employer who has no conception of the effects such irregular hours can have on an employee.

There are many jobs which require workers to be on site 24 hours a day, but rapidly rotating shifts do not give the body's natural clock and biorhythm any chance to catch up. You are suffering from perpetual jetlag, and I am surprised that you do not have more symptoms than you have mentioned.

I suggest that you join with other employees in approaching your employer with a request for a more reasonable roster. This does not mean that you avoid night work, but you change shifts less often.

For reasons of health and employee productivity (you won't work well if you are tired and irritable) you should spend four to six weeks on each shift, and then change to another shift. With a prolonged period on one shift, you can adjust your sleep patterns to a regular one, be it night or day.

On days off, you should try to keep roughly the same sleep times. This can interfere with your family and social life, so if there is some special function you need to alter your sleep time for, ask your doctor to prescribe a mild sleeping tablet (eg. Stillnox, Normison, Halcion) to help you get off to sleep.

Far too many shift workers are being forced to work unreasonable rosters, with rapid changes in shifts. I believe this is something that unions should be investigating, and acting to protect their workers.

Q **I get eight hours sleep a night, but always have dark circles under my eyes, and my eyes get bloodshot in the evening. I am also very fatigued. I would appreciate your professional opinion.**

A Dark circles under the eye have no specific diagnostic meaning, and many people are just unlucky enough to develop them far more easily than others. If you are ill, suffering from an allergy, or under stress, they occur more readily, but it is impossible to make any diagnosis or form a reasonable opinion about a person from that symptom alone.

In your case, it may be possible to link the widely varied symptoms together. Your bloodshot eyes may also be the result of an allergy, as dust, pollutants and pollen can enter the eye during the day, and cause a reaction in the eye to make them red, itchy and watery. They can recover overnight, as the closed eyes prevent any more irritants from entering. Chronic fatigue may also be the result of allergy problems, so all your symptoms may be due to the one cause.

Discuss this possibility further with your general practitioner.

Q I am a female aged 30, and I sleep 3 hours, or at most 4 hours, every night. I would like to take some tablets to make me sleep, but my friend said if I start with tablets now, I'll have to take them every day.

A The amount of sleep needed varies dramatically from one person to another. Some require only three or four hours a day; most require seven or eight hours; others may need ten hours.

There are, of course, those who genuinely cannot get to sleep for a variety of reasons, and 15% of the population fall into this category. There are many things other than medication that can be done to ease the problem.

The simple steps that anyone can use to aid sleep include:
- Avoid exercise immediately before bed. Take time to wind down before going to bed.
- Avoid drinks containing caffeine such as tea, coffee or cola. Caffeine is a stimulant.
- Lose weight if you are obese. A slight weight loss can significantly improve sleep.
- Avoid eating a full meal immediately before bed time. Give your food a couple of hours to settle.
- If you cannot sleep once in bed, get up and read a book or watch television for half an hour before returning to bed. Never lie there tossing and turning.
- Learn to relax by attending specific relaxation classes which your doctor may recommend. Follow up by listening to relaxation tapes.
- Instead of counting sheep or worrying about your problems, focus your mind on a pleasant incident in your past (such as a holiday, journey or party) and remember the whole event slowly in great detail from beginning to end.

If all else fails, and you still find you are unable to sleep, consult your general practitioner. He or she can prescribe medications that can be taken ideally for a short time only, to relieve the problem.

Q My husband snores a lot, and at times during his sleep he seems to stop breathing for ages. Is this dangerous?

A Sleep apnoea is a condition that affects one or two in every hundred people, and males are more commonly affected than females. 'Apnoea' means 'no breathing', and patients with sleep apnoea stop breathing for periods from 10 to 60 seconds on many occasions during the night. There are two reasons for sleep apnoea developing.

The most common cause is due to the small muscles at the back of the throat and in the roof of the mouth relaxing completely, and allowing this tissue to become very soft and flabby. The airway tends to collapse as the patient breathes in, closing it off, and preventing breathing. Snoring is also caused in the same way. Most patients with this form of sleep apnoea are overweight, middle-aged men.

The other far less common cause is an effect in the brain, whereby the urge to breathe is suppressed during very deep sleep. Elderly men with high blood pressure most commonly fit into this category.

Patients complain of tiredness during the day, morning headaches, personality changes, poor concentration, failing memory, bed wetting and impotence. These may become bad enough to cause car accidents and job loss. The sleeping partner complains about the other person's loud snoring, and thrashing restless sleep.

Treatment involves weight loss, and avoiding alcohol, sedatives and smoking. These steps alone may be sufficient to cure the problem. In persistent cases, surgery to clear the nasal passages and/or shorten the soft palate at the top of the mouth may be performed. This surgery performed by ear, nose and throat surgeons, is very successful in selected patients as the slack tissue that falls back to block the airway is removed.

Other treatments include, a rather cumbersome but effective face mask and machine that supplies air at higher than normal pressure to force open the airway. A number of other devices that can be inserted into the mouth to keep the airway open have also been devised.

Q **After several hours of sleep I wake with a very dry mouth and have to take a drink of water. This happens several times a night. Any suggestions for a cure?**

A The most likely cause is that you are breathing through your mouth rather than your nose. The nose is designed to warm and moisturise air as it enters your body, but if the nose is blocked by a cold, hay fever, narrowed nostrils from a polyp or other cause, air has to enter through the mouth.

During the day you may clear the nose or it may drain better while you are upright, only blocking when you lie down at night.

You will need to have your nose checked by your doctor to find if there is a cause for it blocking. If hay fever or a cold is responsible, medications can be given regularly to clear out the nose and prevent it from reblocking.

People who snore may also develop a dry mouth. Snoring can lead to disturbed sleep for both the victim and others nearby, and in severe cases can cause breathing to stop during the night. Snoring can be dealt with in a variety of ways including medications to clear a blocked nose, devices in the nose, surgery and machines that increase the air pressure you breathe through a mask.

There are a number of rare conditions and many medications that can cause a dry mouth, so these should also be excluded by your general practitioner.

Q **After a whiplash injury to my neck, and blows to my head in an accident last year, I have had nothing but sleepless nights. I also injured my arm and leg. I am a male aged 29 and would like some advice on how to stop my sleepless nights.**

A You will need to be investigated to find if there is any permanent damage to your neck, head, arm or leg from the accident. If damage is discovered, this will need to be treated.

If no damage is found, the cause of your sleeplessness may be pain, anxiety, discomfort, depression or a combination of these factors.

Obviously, if you are in pain, or you can't get comfortable at night because of your neck injury, taking a mild to moderate pain-killer (eg. paracetamol with codeine) will settle you down.

If you are anxious, upset, depressed or under stress from the memory of the accident or other events in your life, you may need further help.

You should avoid exercise, tea, coffee or cola drinks before going to bed. Once in bed, do not toss and turn for hours on end. If you are not asleep in 20 minutes, get up and entertain yourself for half an hour before going back to bed again.

Having a radio playing quietly in the bedroom may put you to sleep. Concentrating in great detail on a pleasant event in the past, and trying to relive every moment of that day in you memory is another trick you can use.

If all else fails, see your doctor to obtain a mild sleeping pill. These should be used intermittently rather than regularly, as it is quite easy to become dependent on them.

Q **All my life I have found that waking up in the morning is the hardest thing I do each day. I can easily drop back to sleep at any time in the first half hour I am up in the morning. I am often late for work as a result. Can I be helped?**

A Some people seem to be morning people, while others are evening people. You are unable to function well on waking, while others can bounce out of bed and be fully alert and active within seconds. On the other hand, you may be able to outlast others in the evening.

The Spanish and other southern Europeans seem to be able to function well at both ends of the day, but then they enjoy a siesta in the early afternoon.

Why this phenomenon of preferring mornings or evenings for activity exists is not really understood, but it is certainly well recognised.

The agent probably responsible is melatonin, which is produced by the pineal gland. This tiny gland lies at the front of the brain, just behind the point where your eyebrows would meet. It acts as the time-keeper of the body, and regulates all sorts of natural daily rhythms. When it goes out of rhythm with jet lag, the inappropriate production of melatonin by the pineal is responsible.

It seems some people have their pineal glands set at different times to others, but whether this can be reset is another matter, although some people have commented that after a trip from Europe they can cope better at different times of day than they could previously.

Maybe you can cure your problem with a long-distance holiday? It is certainly a more attractive option than any medication or procedure!

SMELL and TASTE
See also NOSE and SINUSES; MOUTH and THROAT

Q **I have lost my sense of smell. My doctor just says there is nothing that can be done. What should I do?**

A It is important that the reason for the loss of smell is found. The most common causes are nasal infections, colds and hay fever. These only cause a temporary loss of smell, as you regain your sense of smell when the problem settles.

Some older women lose their sense of smell because of an underactive thyroid gland, and this problem can be proved by blood tests. If confirmed, the appropriate tablets can be prescribed to correct the lack of thyroid hormone.

The most sinister cause is a brain tumour, as this can put pressure on the smell nerves at the top of your nose. Anyone with a permanent loss of smell must have tests to exclude this possibility.

Q **With my usual winter cold this year, I lost both my sense of taste and smell. I worry that this may be due to my age (70) and would appreciate your advice.**

A It is possible to taste only four flavours—sweet, sour, salty and bitter. Our ability to smell is far more important, and the smell of the food in our mouth is most of what we perceive as taste.

The cells which sense smell are covered in fine, microscopic hairs and are situated at the top of the nasal cavity at a level that is just below our eyebrows. These nerves send appropriate signals into the brain.

When you have a cold, thick mucus may cover the fine hairs and prevent them from reacting to the odours in both the environment and the mouth. As a result, you perceive that you have lost your sense of taste, when in fact it is smell.

In most cases, the problem disappears as the cold resolves, but if there has been a severe bacterial infection of the nose, the smell cells may be damaged, and the sense of smell will not return until these cells are able to repair themselves.

To prove what I am telling you, next time you feel that you have lost your sense of taste, with your eyes closed have someone put a crystal of sugar and then salt on your tongue—you'll immediately be able to tell which is which!

Q **I have suffered for many months with a failure of the sense of taste and cannot distinguish one type of food from another. I am 88 years old and am wondering if this problem is due to old age or illness.**

A A wide range of conditions can cause a loss of taste. These include lead poisoning, a lack of saliva causing a dry mouth, an underactive thyroid gland, some forms of stroke, a condition called Sjögren's syndrome and numerous rarer conditions.

In older people a dry mouth is a common cause of poor taste sensation.

You should get your general practitioner to give you a thorough going over to exclude any illness as a cause of your problem. If nothing specific is found, old age may have to be blamed.

Q **For two years I have had a strong metallic taste in my mouth that makes me feel sick. Have you any ideas as to a cause?**

A By far the most common cause of abnormal taste sensations is the side effects of any one of a number of medications. Different drugs used for arthritis, bacterial and fungal infections, psychiatric disturbances, high blood pressure and heart failure may all cause strange tastes.

Other causes include thyroid gland disease, strokes that affect the taste-sensing area of the brain, radiation treatments to the face, viral infections and degeneration of the brain with age.

Differentiating between these various causes may be quite difficult, but if you are on medication of any sort (including vitamins, minerals and over-the-counter medicines) it would be worthwhile discussing with your doctor if these can be safely ceased to see if they are responsible.

Q **From time to time I have a very bitter taste in my mouth. What could cause this?**

A Almost certainly you are suffering from waterbrash.

Waterbrash is a bitter taste in the mouth caused by the reflux of a small amount of acid from the stomach up into the mouth where it stimulates the taste buds at the back of your tongue. If the amount of acid is significant, you may get further symptoms such as heartburn and burping.

The treatment is to eat slowly, have sips of water (or other non-alcoholic fluid) between mouthfuls, have small meals and if necessary use an antacid lozenge or mixture. If the symptom persists, see your general practitioner, as more significant problems may need to be excluded.

Q **I am 68, and over the past 3 years have gradually lost my sense of smell, but can still taste sweet and sour. A specialist has told me that nothing can be done. Is that true?**

A The senses of smell and taste are totally independent of each other, and so it is certainly possible to lose one sense and not the other.

The sense of smell comes from tiny nerve endings that project through the thin bone at the top of the nose. These nerve endings respond to different aromas in different ways, the subtlety of which is poorly understood by physiologists. The appropriate nerve impulses are then carried to a part of the brain that interprets these as the smells we know.

Man has a relatively small part of the brain devoted to smell (it is much larger in dogs), and if the blood supply to this part of the brain, or the olfactory (smell) nerve is reduced, the sense of smell may be lost. This can occur in old age from a mild stroke or hardening of the arteries, and is relatively common in smokers. There is no treatment available.

Taste results from four different types of receptors on the tongue, which can detect sweet, salty, bitter and sour (and combinations of these). Taste is a far coarser sensation, and it is only the combination of smell and taste that makes us appreciate different foods.

I regret, that with taste alone, your garlic prawns and fresh strawberries are not going to be the pleasure of years past.

Q **After having a heart attack, my brother has been left with no sense of smell for hot foods. Doctors have come up with all sorts of suggestions to explain this, but no help. He is getting despondent and I hope you can help.**

A Your sense of smell comes from a nerve that sends tiny sensitive hairs into the top of your nose. These detect certain different odours, and convey the sensation back down the nerve to the part of the brain that can recognise them as particular smells.

During a heart attack, the heart stops working as an effective pump, and some parts of the body may be deprived of an adequate blood supply. When this happens, the more sensitive parts of the body (eg. the brain) may be permanently damaged.

It is also possible for a small stroke to accompany a heart attack.

In either case, it is probable that the part of your brother's brain that is responsible for the sense of smell has been partly damaged, so that he can no longer smell as well as he could previously.

Unfortunately, brain damage is usually permanent, and although some recovery may occur by new nerves taking on old tasks, once a few months has passed, no further improvement can be expected. There is no effective treatment available.

Q Everything I eat and drink tastes of salt. Chocolate is the worst. The only thing that is not bad is milk. Have you ever heard of a case like this?

A I must admit that I haven't heard of a case like this, so I have been scouring my medical texts and cross examining my colleagues to find some answers for you. A wide range of conditions have come to my attention, some very rare, some probably too simple to account for your symptoms, but I will list them all for you.

The most likely cause is the side effects from a medication, and this includes many herbal and 'natural' preparations. These medications, or their breakdown products, can be secreted as a salt in your saliva, and the more you salivate (eg. with something tasty like chocolate) the saltier the taste.

Tongue infections such as thrush can alter your taste sensations.

A chronic postnasal drip can affect taste as the phlegm slides down the throat past the back of the tongue.

Poisoning from heavy metals such as lead and mercury can cause abnormal tastes. If you have ever worked with these metals (eg. in a battery factory) you should have the levels of these metals in your blood checked.

There are a number of rare diseases that can affect taste including liver failure and the syndrome of inappropriate antidiuretic hormone secretion (SIADH), which causes a build up of the salt levels in your body.

You will need to discuss these options with your own general practitioner to have them investigated, excluded or treated.

SMOKING

Q I can't stop smoking! I can't stand the withdrawal symptoms! Help!

A Before anyone can stop smoking, they must really want to stop. No-one who is half-hearted about wanting to stop will ever succeed.

Once you have decided to stop, set a time and date for the event. Tell everyone you know of your intentions, and take side-bets if you can to reinforce your incentive. Make lists of reasons why you must stop, and leave them everywhere at home and work.

Make sure that from the moment you stop you have no cigarettes available to you, and resist the temptation to buy more—carry no more than your bus fare on you.

Start a savings account with the money you save by not smoking (this will add up to several thousand dollars a year), and if you don't succeed, pay the balance to the Cancer Fund!

If these incentives are not sufficient, see your pharmacist or doctor. Pharmacists can recommend nicotine-containing gum, inhalers or patches that will ease the craving for cigarettes. Doctors can also teach you how to stop, and may prescribe a tablet (Zyban) that acts on the brain to break the addiction to nicotine.

Group therapy sessions, hypnosis, rewards at the end of each successful week and reinforcement visits to your GP can all help you win the fight.

Q Can you tell me about the new anti-smoking drug that doctors are prescribing. Is it safe and effective?

A The drug you are referring to is bupropion which has the trade name Zyban. It aids cessation of smoking and counteracts nicotine addiction, and was introduced late in 2000. It is very effective in easing the craving for nicotine, but does nothing to help ease the habit of doing something with your fingers and lips.

The dosage is one tablet a day for three to seven days, then increasing to one tablet twice a day when smoking is stopped.

It must not to be used in pregnancy, breast feeding and children, and must be used with caution in patients with any liver or kidney disease, head injury, brain tumour, alcoholism and diabetes. Patients using the drug should have their blood pressure checked regularly.

You must not take Zyban if you suffer from epilepsy or other condition causing seizures, a bipolar psychiatric disorder, eating disorder, or severe liver disease (eg. cirrhosis).

Common side effects include sleeplessness, headache, fever, dry mouth and nausea. Unusual side effects include diarrhoea or constipation, brain irritation, skin reaction and taste disorders. Rarely it may cause a convulsion.

Zyban may interact with other drugs including antipsychotics, antidepressants, theophylline, steroid tablets, benzodiazepines (eg. Valium), medications used to treat epilepsy and convulsions, and levodopa. It may also interact with alcohol and stimulants.

A prescription is required, and it is subsidised by the Pharmaceutical Benefits Scheme, but once only, as it is very expensive normally.

Overdosage may be serious. Drowsiness, hallucinations, seizures, coma and rarely death may occur.

Q Have you heard of cigarette smoking as a cause of pain in the calf when walking. I heard it was called 'smoker's foot'?

A Smoker's foot, or Buerger's disease, is a cause of peripheral vascular disease (narrowed arteries in the extremities). Other causes include hardening of the arteries, high blood pressure, excess cholesterol and diabetes.

The other technical name for Buerger's disease is thromboangiitis obliterans, which when translated into English means 'clotting, inflammation and obliteration of arteries'. Dr. Buerger, who first described the disease, was an American urologist (urinary tract specialist) who worked in New York and Los Angeles in the first half of the twentieth century.

Smoker's foot is a dreadful disease which causes the loss of fingers, toes, then arms and legs; and it occurs only in smokers (thus the common name), nearly always in men, and often young men.

Due to the influences of toxins within tobacco smoke, segments of the small arteries in the hands and feet become inflamed. This inflammation causes a clot to form in the artery, which becomes completely blocked. The tissue beyond this blockage is then starved of blood, becomes painful, white and eventually gangrenous.

The process starts in the fingers and toes, and slowly moves along the arteries, further and further up the arms and legs. A limb may eventually be totally amputated, but often over several operations, as each successive area becomes deprived of blood.

The first symptoms are a pain in the foot when walking which settles with rest, red tender cords caused by involved blood vessels may be felt under the skin, and a finger or toe may be white and have reduced sensation.

The next stage is characterised by pain at rest, loss of pulses in the hands and feet, and ulcers around the nails. Cold weather may aggravate the symptoms. If the disease progresses further, gangrene results.

Treatment involves trying to stop these patients from smoking, but because they are even more addicted to their habit than the average smoker, this is extremely difficult. If smoking is stopped, the disease usually does not spread any further.

If the disease progresses, surgery to the nerves supplying the arteries to make them totally relax and open up as much as possible may be tried, but progressive amputation of the limbs is often necessary. If the patient cannot stop smoking, clots may form in vital organs and cause death.

Q **My husband complains of aching legs and sore feet especially after walking. His feet are sometimes very white. He is a heavy smoker, and often quite short of breath. What does the future hold for him? He is 42 years old.**

A His future is not good! He is showing the early signs of two very serious, and potentially fatal diseases, associated with heavy smoking.

Buerger's disease is a condition in which the arteries in the arms and legs go into prolonged spasm in response to nicotine. The fingers, toes, hands and feet are initially cold and white, then the circulation problem becomes so severe that gangrene sets in, and first the fingers and toes, and then parts of the arm and leg have to be amputated. If you think I'm kidding you about the seriousness of this condition, talk to any doctor, or look up Buerger's disease in the library. There is no cure for this condition other than stopping smoking.

The other condition your husband may be developing is chronic bronchitis. This is a constant inflammation of the lungs caused by the irritation of smoke. It becomes steadily harder to breathe as more and more lung tissue is damaged, and the victim becomes far more susceptible to pneumonia and other lung infections, as well as lung cancer. Your husband MUST stop smoking NOW, and see a doctor to determine just how much damage has been caused already.

Q **How does smoking cause poor circulation? Does it damage the blood vessels, or does it cause the blood to thicken?**

A With the first inhalation of cigarette smoke, the nicotine and other chemicals in the smoke enter the lungs and the blood stream. Within seconds, there is an effect on the arteries and veins throughout the body.

Smoking primarily acts upon arteries and veins by causing them to go into spasm. The tiny muscles in their walls contract, and the blood vessel shrinks in size, narrowing the tube through which the blood passes, and therefore depriving of oxygen the tissue supplied by that artery.

In elderly people or those who have high blood pressure, excess cholesterol or heart disease, this narrowing of the arteries can have very severe consequences, as a vital organ may have its already limited blood supply reduced to a point where it is unable to function properly.

The heart muscle itself is supplied with blood that comes through small arteries. If these go into spasm, angina or a heart attack may result. For this reason, it is imperative for those with other risks of heart disease to stop smoking.

In advanced cases, a condition known as Buerger's disease (or thrombo-angiitis obliterans) can result from smoking.

Smoking can have serious affects upon every body organ, not just the lungs.

Q **How dangerous is passive smoking? I share an office with a girl who has a cigarette in her mouth all day long, while I choke and splutter. She says I complain about nothing, but I am concerned that it may affect my health.**

A Almost everyone is forced to inhale fumes containing toxins such as form-aldehyde, acetone, arsenic, carbon monoxide, hydrogen cyanide and nicotine at some time. You have no choice in the matter, and you have to suffer the consequences, because these chemicals are just a few of the scores of irritants found in cigarette smoke.

Fortunately for most of us, the result of passive involuntary smoking is only a minor itch of the nose, a cough or a sneeze, but some people can develop life-threatening asthma attacks, or have their heart condition aggravated by someone exhaling tobacco smoke in their direction.

In some situations, the non-smoker may be more affected than the smoker, as the smoke coming directly from the cigarette contains more toxins, nicotine and carbon monoxide than that inhaled by the smoker, as the inhaled smoke has been more completely burnt, and passed through a filter.

In the workplace, employers are required to provide a safe and healthy work environment, and this can include an area where non-smokers can work. Unfortunately, some bosses still smoke, and have little sympathy for the enforced passive smoking of their employees. This situation may change in the future, as more and more workers are successfully claiming workers compensation payments for the complications of passive smoking in their work place.

Smokers should now be aware of the health risks that they are taking every day (90% of lung cancer occurs in smokers), but they can no longer claim personal freedom to smoke where and when they like, as their habit is adversely affecting the health of those around them. In some cases passive smoking can be life threatening, and legal suits against smokers for causing bodily harm have been successful in the United States.

POSTSCRIPT:

It is 8.30 pm on a Tuesday night, and I have just seen my last patient for the day. Rather than heading home to my family and dinner, I have turned to my keyboard to tell you about a patient I saw earlier today.

He was 68 years old, once a solidly built man, and a bomber gunner during

World War Two. He first presented with shortness of breath and a chronic cough some five years ago. He had smoked 20 cigarettes a day since his teenage years.

After listening to his chest on that examination some years ago, I sent him for an X-ray. He returned, and after examining the films, I told him the diagnosis—emphysema.

Since then he has been slowly dying, fighting a battle with repeated attacks of bronchitis and pneumonia, taking more and more medication, but getting weaker every month.

Often he was desperate and scared. Was there some new miracle cure? How long would he take to die? Would it be quick or slow? He already knew the cause—his decades of smoking.

No—there was no new miracle cure, only medications to try and control the damage already done. If he stopped smoking, and if he was lucky enough not to catch too many attacks of bronchitis, he had a chance of living a bit longer and more comfortably. I kept giving him scripts for the bronchodilator drugs he would need for the rest of his life.

This morning he died.

Death from emphysema is not a quick, clean death at an advanced age, but a slow, lingering, coughing, gasping, blue death that takes many months.

Please do not risk it—stop smoking now!

SPORT

Q **I am very worried about my son who has started boxing at a local club. I don't think this is a suitable sport for him, and I am concerned that he may be injured. How safe is boxing?**

A The aim of boxing is to render your opponent unconscious, or to injure him sufficiently that he is unable to continue. It is not surprising that a significant number of the participants in this activity suffer from permanent brain, eye and other bodily injuries that destroy the quality of their life, and shorten their life span.

Even in the amateur arena, with short bouts and headgear being worn, the acceleration forces applied to the head by a punch cause the brain to rattle around in the skull like a dried pea in a pod. During the 1980s, 7% of amateur boxing matches in the United Kingdom were won by a knock out, and that amounts to a lot of brain-damaged people.

Every episode of unconsciousness associated with a head injury leaves some permanent damage, but it is not necessary to be knocked out to become 'punch drunk'. The famous Cassius Clay (Mohammed Ali) was knocked out only once in his career, but he now suffers from advanced cerebral degeneration, and is barely able to care for himself.

If a boxer is found to be brain-damaged, it is too late to stop him from further fights; the damage is already permanent. The outstanding feature found at autopsy in the brains of dead boxers, is the massive number of altered nerve cells spread throughout the brain, which must have significantly altered the thought patterns and activity of the boxer in life.

Injuries occur in most sports, from fractures in rugby to injuries from a hard ball in cricket, and even golfers strain backs and joints, but no other sport comes close to the trail of wrecked bodies and premature death created by boxing. No other sport has the stated aim of damaging the opponent, and in the other martial arts such as judo and karate, deliberately injuring your opponent can count against the competitor. I would urge your son to consider one of these other martial arts.

Q **My son has just started football, and I am very worried about him. Why do so many footballers need knee operations?**

A The knee joint is the same as a finger joint, it is designed to move in only two directions, backwards and forwards.

Inside the knee, there are cartilages that form a deep cup on the top of the tibia (the bone in the calf) for the rounded end of the femur (the bone in the thigh) to move in.

When playing body contact sports such as football, the knee may be forced in abnormal positions or twisted. When this happens, the cartilages inside the knee tear. Because these tissues have a very poor blood supply, they heal poorly if at all.

If left torn they cause pain and limitation of knee movement, so an operation is performed to remove all or part of the cartilage, and the knee can move freely again, but is not as stable long term.

Q **I am a seventeen year old male and work out a lot at the gym. My dream is to have a body like Arnold Schwarzenegger. What are your views on steroids, and where can I obtain them?**

A The main reason that Arnold Schwarzenegger looks the way he does because of his genes (most important), then his exercise program and diet. You may improve your muscle definition, strength and fitness by exercise and a good diet, but still not look the same as your idol.

Anabolic steroids may artificially increase your muscle bulk and strength, but as a side effect you may suffer impotence, shrunken testes, infertility, development of breasts, vomiting, headaches, jaundice (liver damage) and heart damage. Their use for this purpose is also illegal, and anyone supplying you with them may be prosecuted.

Be sensible, rationalise your ideals, and enjoy life!

Q **My son is determined to learn scuba diving, but I am very scared about the dangers to him. I remember hearing about divers dying from the bends. Is this still a problem? Can this be treated?**

A When we breathe, the oxygen and nitrogen in the air are taken into the lungs, and fill up millions of tiny bubbles (called alveoli) that are covered by a fine network of capillaries (very small blood vessels). The gases pass across a fine membrane and are dissolved into the bloodstream. If the air pressure is high, more gases (oxygen and nitrogen) will be dissolved into the blood than if the air pressure is low.

Underwater divers must breathe air at a pressure equivalent to the depth of water in which they are diving. As a result, more oxygen and nitrogen than normal is dissolved into their bloodstream. When they surface, they must do so slowly (following rates of ascent that have been worked out from tables that allow for depth and time), or the lower pressure around their bodies and in their lungs will allow the previously dissolved gases to come out of solution, and form actual tiny bubbles within the blood.

Exactly the same phenomenon can be seen when the top is removed from a bottle of carbonated soft drink or beer, and it starts to fizz. Divers who develop the bends have blood that fizzes. The symptoms depend greatly on the fitness, age, and weight of the diver, as well as the amount of physical exertion s/he has undertaken. Joint pain may be excruciatingly severe, and permanent joint damage can result. If the bends remains untreated, it may progress to coma and death. The only effective treatment is to recompress the patient as rapidly as possible.

Compression chambers are maintained by the Navy, government and private institutions at a number of points around the Australian coastline. They are a reinforced cylinder that can have air pumped into it at the required pressure. The patient, and often a medical attendant, are placed in the chamber, the air pressure inside is increased to the necessary level, and then over several hours or days, slowly reduced back to normal again. This has the effect of redissolving the nitrogen bubbles into the bloodstream, and then allowing the gas to escape slowly and naturally through the lungs.

Prevention is better than treatment, and all divers should be aware of the correct procedures for the dive they undertake, and should avoid diving to greater depths, or for longer periods than planned. There is no reason for your son not to learn scuba diving provided he is careful and responsible. It will certainly give him a great deal of pleasure.

Q **My daughter and I have difficulty in breathing after exercising regularly for 12 months. In our beginners aerobic classes we have to stop after a few minutes because of difficulty in breathing. Is there something wrong with us?**

A You probably have exercise-induced asthma. This may only present in certain circumstances, and may be worse if the exercise is in a dusty hall rather than out of doors. This type of asthma may be hereditary, so it is quite conceivable that both you and your daughter could have the same condition.

Asthma can be treated by mouth sprays and other medications, and it may be possible for you to use a spray before exercise that will prevent the shortness of breath. You should see your general practitioner and discuss the matter further.

Q **I am a keen golfer and have developed a painful elbow. My GP says the diagnosis is golfer's elbow, but this sounds like an excuse for a diagnosis. Is there such a condition, and do I have to stop playing golf?**

A Golfer's elbow is a medical condition that is also known as medial epicondylitis. It is due to an inflammation of the tendon on the inside of the bony lump on the back of the elbow (olecranon).

The cause is over-straining of the extensor tendon at the inner back of the elbow due to excessive bending and twisting movements of the arm. In golfers it is not normally one stroke that strains the tendon, but repeated episodes of overstretching caused by hitting the ground with the club during a stroke. This leads to tears of the minute fibres in the tendon and scar tissue forms, which is then broken down again by further strains. It also occur in tradesmen who undertake repetitive tasks, housewives, musicians and many others who may put excessive strain on their elbows.

Painful inflammation occurs, which can be constant or may only occur when the elbow is moved or stressed. The whole forearm can ache in some patients, especially when trying to grip or twist with the hand.

Unfortunately for you, prolonged rest is the most important form of treatment. Exercises to strengthen the elbow and anti-inflammatory drugs may also be used. Cortisone injections may be given in resistant cases. The strengthening exercises are done under the supervision of a physiotherapist and involve using your wrist to raise and lower a weight with the palm facing up. Some patients find pressure pads over the tendon or elbow guards (elastic tubes around the elbow) help relieve the symptoms and prevent recurrences by adding extra support.

It is a condition that is not easy to treat and can easily become chronic. No matter what form of treatment is used, most cases seem to last for about 18 months and then settle spontaneously.

Q What is the best way to prevent injury when playing vigorous sport?

A Preventative medicine is important for all diseases, but especially so in 'sports medicine'.

Many hold the narrow view that prevention of sporting injuries relates simply to protective equipment used in the various sports, but the subject is much broader and has many implications and ramifications.

The physical fitness of the competitor is the most neglected area relating to the prevention of sporting injuries. If you are going to play sport, you must follow the axiom 'get fit to play' and not 'play to get fit'.

Children are playing more and more organised sport. It is recommended that all parents have their children examined by a doctor before they participate in sport so possible medical problems can be checked. If problems are found, children can often be directed into equally enjoyable sports which will not affect their health.

It is interesting to note how the range of protective equipment available to sportspeople grows every year, but not all is of proven value. Some protective equipment can itself inflict injury—abdominal injuries following blows to the abdomen with rigid American football helmets for example.

Three proven items of protective equipment have not received the acceptance they warrant, however.

There is no doubt that a mouth guard properly prescribed and fitted by a dentist will provide excellent protection for the teeth and jaws of those who play any type of contact sport. The average $50 cost becomes insignificant when compared with the cost of repairing a broken tooth, replacing a lost tooth or the permanent disfigurement which may accompany both.

Sight is one of our most precious possessions, yet thousands of squash and racquetball players all over the world sustain serious eye injuries every year, some producing total blindness of one eye.

Even if you don't require spectacles for normal daily use, wearing correct eye protection with non-shatter polycarbonate lenses available from optometrists and eye specialists can totally avoid the tragedy which occurs when a squash ball hits the eye socket at high velocity. The reason most players don't wear eye protection may be that the top international players have ignored this advance in protective equipment, and so it is not as yet 'fashionable'.

Taping of ankles has been shown to be almost 100 percent effective in protecting this joint from sprain. Taping does not offer the same protection to the more mobile knee and shoulder joints.

Non-stretch zinc-oxide tape is required for successful joint taping. It is a recommended procedure for all those involved in sports where running, jumping or twisting is required. You must learn the correct taping technique and it is best to have a partner tape your ankles and vice versa.

These three simple measures and checking for any potential problems before competing, may make your sporting future far more secure.

STOMACH

Q **I have not been well for three months, having a choking feeling in my throat and soreness of the oesophagus. Oesophagoscopy showed I have a moderate hiatus hernia. Is there any treatment, and what should one do and not do with this illness?**

A A hernia occurs when a part of the body slides through an opening into a position that is not its normal position. The stomach sits in the abdomen immediately below the diaphragm, which is a sheet of muscle that separates the chest from the abdomen. The oesophagus (gullet) runs from the back of the throat, down the back of the chest, through the diaphragm and joins the stomach. There is a hole in the diaphragm through which the oesophagus passes just before it enters the stomach. If part of the stomach moves up through this hole into the chest cavity, the patient has a hiatus hernia.

Pressure in the abdominal cavity from heavy lifting, obesity, and tension (muscle spasm occurs), or slack ligaments in the diaphragm in the elderly, may all lead to the formation of a hiatus hernia. Patients usually describe difficulty in swallowing, and sometimes pain from ulceration inside the hernia or pinching of the hernia. Further symptoms can include heartburn (which may be very severe), burping excessively, a bitter taste on the back of the tongue ('water-brash'), difficulty in swallowing, a feeling of fullness, bleeding from the damaged part of the stomach, and palpitations if a large hernia pushes onto the heart. Most of these hernias are small, but sometimes a large proportion of the stomach may push up into the chest.

The heartburn is usually worse at night when lying down, or after a meal. It is usually eased by drinking milk or an antacid, but this relief may only be temporary. Long standing reflux of acid into the oesophagus can cause peptic ulcers which may bleed and cause serious complications.

Most cases of hiatus hernia can be treated with medication, posture and diet. Antacids that neutralise the acid, liquids and gels that coat the lower oesophagus, anaesthetic mixtures, foaming granules that float on top of the stomach acid, and tablets that reduce the amount of acid secreted by the stomach (eg. Pepcidine, Zantac etc.) can all be used alone or in combination. Tablets that increase the emptying rate of the stomach, and strengthen the valve at the lower end of the oesophagus (eg. Motilium, Prepulsid) are also useful. Frequent small meals, rather than three large meals a day, and a diet low in fat and high in protein is beneficial.

Obese patients must lose weight. Gravity is the most important factor in keeping the stomach in the abdomen rather than the chest, and the acid in the stomach rather than the oesophagus. Bending over to garden or lift, and any heavy lifting are banned. The head of the bed should be elevated, and three or more pillows used to raise the chest higher than the abdomen. Lying on the right side rather than the left, to enhance the drainage of the stomach, can also be tried.

In only a small percentage of patients, who do not respond adequately to the above regime, should surgery be contemplated.

Q **For two months I have had bad stomach aches on and off. The pain seems to run up into my chest sometimes. I am getting worried. Please help.**

A There are several dozen possible causes for your stomach pains, but the most likely are a peptic ulcer, regurgitation of acid from the stomach into the gullet, and a hiatus hernia.

Peptic ulcers cause severe pains at the top of the belly, that are often worse at night, and eased for a short time by food.

The stomach is full of acid, but the cells lining the stomach are covered with an acid-resistant mucus. If the mucus breaks down, a peptic ulcer results. If excess acid is produced, it may be regurgitated from the stomach, and run up into the gullet, which has no acid-protecting mucus. This results in a severe burning pain just below and behind the breast bone.

A hiatus hernia occurs when a small piece of the stomach slips up out of the belly and into the chest. The hernia itself causes little discomfort, but the stomach acid is allowed to flow freely up into the gullet to cause pain.

You will need to see a doctor to have your problem more thoroughly investigated, possibly by gastroscopy. This procedure involves swallowing a thin tube while under sedation. Through this, a doctor can examine the inside of your stomach and gullet to detect any abnormalities.

Q **What sort of acid causes stomach ulcers? Why do we have acid in our stomachs?**

A Hydrochloric acid is known to most high-school students as a potent acid that can eat through many substances and cause nasty burns on your skin. This acid is also naturally produced in the body, and in its correct place in the stomach does no harm to the body but aids food digestion.

Specialised cells lining the stomach make the acid and release it in response to the sight or smell of food. We also start to produce more saliva when food is nearby, and if the food is not forthcoming, we are left drooling and with an ache in the gut, because no food has been eaten to soak up the saliva and acid. We normally end up eating the food we expect, and the acid works in the stomach to break it down to its basic components. Further digestive enzymes are added to the food when it passes out of the stomach into the small intestine.

The cells lining the stomach protect themselves from attack by the acid with a thin layer of mucus. If there is excess acid or insufficient mucus present, the acid may be able to attack the stomach wall. Many factors can produce either or both of these stomach problems. The most common triggers are smoking, stress,

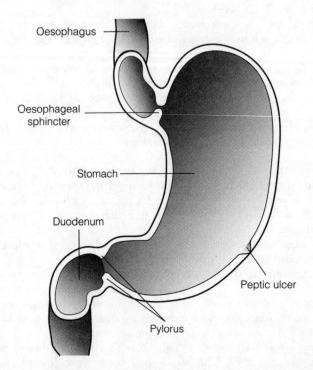

Oesophagus

Oesophageal
sphincter

Stomach

Duodenum

Peptic ulcer

Pylorus

alcohol, and aspirin-type medications that are used in treating arthritis (eg. non-steroidal anti-inflammatory drugs—NSAID). Anxiety can cause excess acid to be produced, which can then eat into the stomach. Smoking can reduce the mucus secretions that protect the stomach, while aspirin and some anti-arthritis drugs can directly damage the mucus layer. In recent years, a bacteria (*Helicobacter pylori*) has been identified in association with many ulcers, and it is believed that this bacteria may damage the mucus lining of the stomach.

Q **Could you please explain, just what is a peptic ulcer? One doctor told me I had a stomach ulcer, then another said it was a peptic ulcer. What is the difference?**

A Peptic ulcer is a term that is used to include any one of several different types of ulcers that occur in the stomach, pylorus (connection between the stomach and duodenum) and the duodenum (first part of the small intestine). If the hydrochloric acid in the stomach that is used for digestion attacks the stomach wall, it causes a gastric ulcer (stomach ulcer), the same as an acid burn on the skin. The duodenum may also develop an ulcer (duodenal ulcer), as excess acid overflows from the stomach. Pyloric ulcers develop at the point where a muscle ring acts as a valve between the stomach and duodenum.

Q **What are the early symptoms of a gastric ulcer? I am concerned that my constant burping may be due to one. How will doctors find out if I have an ulcer?**

A   Unlike the skin, the stomach has few nerve cells, and the acid may eat through to a blood vessel and cause bleeding, anaemia and weakness before any pain is felt. Most ulcers cause pain, which may be severe because the acid is attacking a nerve. The pain is often at its worst just before a meal when the acid levels are highest, and food (particularly milk) may relieve the pain. Once a person has the severe pain high up in the abdomen that is characteristic of an ulcer, it is important to have the diagnosis proved and treatment started quickly in order to avoid complications. Other symptoms can include a feeling of fullness, burping excessively, and indigestion, so your constant burping may well be caused by an ulcer, but it is also a hiatus hernia may be responsible.

Doctors will prove the presence of an ulcer or hiatus hernia by an X-ray or gastroscopy. The X-ray is known as a barium meal, and to perform this you swallow a liquid that can be seen on X-rays, and its course through the stomach can be followed.

Gastroscopy involves swallowing a fine tube, through which a doctor can see the inside of your stomach and small intestine. This procedure is performed under a light anaesthetic and patients experience no discomfort.

A very small percentage of ulcers can be cancerous, so it is vital that the disease is correctly diagnosed and treated.

Q   **Would you please tell me about the 'helicopter' virus that is causing my stomach ulcer? I have just been given a huge concoction of tablets to kill it.**

A   A significant proportion of stomach ulcers are caused by a bacteria (not virus) called *Helicobacter pylori*, which breaks down the protective mucus layer that lines the stomach.

An ulcer is often diagnosed by a gastroscopy, and during this procedure a biopsy of an ulcer can be taken if there is any risk of cancer, and a special test can be performed to identify the presence of the *Helicobacter pylori* bacteria.

Helicobacter pylori can also be detected by a test on the breath. A sample of your breath is collected in an airtight container and analysed for the presence of waste products from the bacteria. A blood test is also available, but less accurate.

If by any means the presence of this bacteria is detected, a specific course of antibiotics and anti-ulcer medication (triple therapy) can be given to eradicate the infection, heal the ulcer, and in many cases, prevent a recurrence.

In patients who have a negative test, or whose early mild symptoms do not warrant performing the test, numerous medications are available to control and sometimes cure peptic ulcers.

Q   **I am always burping, and it's sometimes very embarrassing. I don't seem to be able to stop it. Why do some people burp more than others?**

A   Burping is bringing up air or gas from the stomach into the mouth. That air has to get in to the stomach in the first place to be burped, and in the vast majority of cases, it gets in by being swallowed.

People who eat quickly tend to swallow air with their food. If you are nervous, before an exam or interview etc., you may swallow air as a sign of anxiety. If you drink fizzy liquids such as lemonade or beer, you will take gas in to the stomach. If small amounts of gas are swallowed, it will move on into the gut to be absorbed or passed through the anus as flatus. Otherwise, excess gas tries to escape by going up and out through the mouth.

This is not as easy as it seems because there is a muscular valve at the top of the stomach that stops the food and acid in the stomach from running back up the gullet into the mouth when you bend or lie down. Only when sufficient pressure builds up, or you are able to relax the muscular valve yourself, can the air escape, causing the often unexpected and embarrassing explosion. When the gas escapes, it may take small amounts of acid and food with it, causing heart-burn or nausea at the same time.

Eating slowly, sipping water between mouthfuls and using antacids are the main methods of treatment.

Q   What can you tell me about polyps in the stomach (which the doctor states I have) and what can be done about them?

A.   Polyps are growths on the inside of the gut that can be anything from micro-scopic in size to an inch (2.5 cm) across, and may be attached to the gut by quite long stalks. They are more common in the last metre of the bowel (the colon) than they are further up. In most people, they cause no symptoms, but they may become irritated, ulcerated and bleed; they can become twisted around a narrow stalk to become painful; or they may even be picked up by the actions of the intestine, which attempts to push it further along like a piece of food. In rare cases, they may become cancerous.

There are certain types of hereditary polyps which are large in number, and in which cancer is a particularly high risk. The polyps are usually discovered during endoscopy (a flexible telescope that is passed into the gut from either end) or on an X-ray of the gut. If your doctor was worried about them, s/he would have arranged for them to be removed.

If they are causing no symptoms, and are not likely to become cancerous, they can be left alone, but you should report any change in your bowel habits, or any bleeding or pain immediately to your doctor.

STRESS
See also DEPRESSION; EMOTIONS

Q   How do doctors define stress and its causes?

A   Doctors have no special definition of stress other than that used in everyday speech. Dictionaries define stress as a disturbing physiological or psychological influence which produces a state of severe tension in an individual.

The causes of stress are innumerable, and include everything from excessive mortgage repayments and marriage strife to coping with young children and your relatives, job security, separation and divorce, leaving home, exams, unemployment, poor health, work responsibility, and a death in the family. You name it, and it can probably cause stress in someone.

Stress is not something new to modern man. Stress has always been with us, but the form has changed over the years. Most of the above problems were experienced thousands of years ago, but in Australia we do not have to worry about starvation and a life expectancy, problems that still occur in many poorer countries.

Q **My marriage has broken up and I am losing a lot of weight. I have no appetite and look like a bag of bones. What can I do?**

A Stress and anxiety of any sort can lead to loss of both appetite and weight. Discussing the problems with a friend, counsellor or family doctor can often relieve a lot of the burden of anxiety. Making sure that you do eat at regular times and eat good nutritious food is an obvious way to help the problem.

Food supplements, such as Ensure, can be added to milk to help build you up. Appetite stimulants are the next step, and these can be prescribed by your doctor. Some medications that ease anxiety have a side effect of increasing appetite, and so may help combat both problems. Time is a great healer, and although divorce is a traumatic experience, most women survive to lead happy lives, free from a husband who may have caused them long-term distress had the marriage continued. Look for the light at the end of the tunnel.

Q **Every time I get anxious about anything, I break out in a very itchy, red rash on my ankles and wrists. Why?**

A I can sympathise with you, as I suffered from a neurodermatitis (nerve rash) before exams for many years when I was a medical student. It is a problem experienced by many people, and there is no adequate explanation as to why it attacks some people and only in some areas. The inside of the elbow and backs of the knees are other commonly affected areas, but a nerve rash may occur anywhere.

Avoiding stressful situations is the perfect way to avoid the rash, but that is usually not a practical solution. Relief can be obtained from anti-irritation creams from the chemist, but usually a prescription for a steroid cream will be needed. These creams come in many different strengths and forms, and some experimentation may be needed to find the weakest one to work for you. Steroids reduce inflammation in the skin, and are therefore useful in a wide range of skin rashes. They will aggravate any rash caused by a bacterial or fungal infection, so should not be used without directions from a doctor. If the cream is applied as soon as the rash appears, it should settle immediately.

Nerve rashes do not mean that you are neurotic or in need of psychiatric care. They are merely an outward manifestation of a sometimes minor stress in an otherwise normal human.

Q **What symptoms does a person with stress develop? How can you tell if those symptoms are due to stress or something else?**

A Everyone experiences stress in their lives, but some people cope with it far better than others, and some experience far more due to their individual circumstances.

Stress can cause a very wide range of physical illnesses. Chronic headaches and peptic ulcers are probably the best known diseases due to stress, but depression, heart disease, migraines, diarrhoea, shortness of breath, sweating, passing excess urine, rashes, vomiting and a host of other symptoms may be an outward manifestation of inward emotional turmoil.

There is often no easy way to tell if the symptoms are due to stress or some other underlying disease, and doctors may perform numerous blood and other tests to exclude any other possible diagnosis.

Q How can stress, as a diagnosis made by my GP, be treated?

A There are four ways to treat stress:

- The obvious, most successful, but hardest to achieve, is removing the cause of the stress. If your mortgage repayments are in arrears, winning the Pools will solve your problems and remove the stress, but this is a solution for the minority, not the majority. Marriage stress is probably one of the most difficult forms of stress to remove, as bitterness and wrangling over children and property may last for many years after a divorce.

- The next, and most practical way to deal with stress is to rationalise it. This can involve a combination of several different techniques. Talking is an excellent way of relieving anxiety. Discuss the problem with your spouse, relatives, friends, doctor, work mates or anyone else who will listen. Problems often do not appear as insurmountable once bought into the open. Writing down the details of the problem is another excellent way of relieving anxiety. An insurmountable problem in your mind often appears more manageable on paper, particularly when all your possible options are diagrammatically attached, to enable a rational view of the situation to be obtained.

- Professional assistance in discussing your problems is also very helpful. This may be given by your own general practitioner (who can often be a friend as well as counsellor), a psychiatrist (not because you may be insane, but because they have specialist skills in this area), a psychologist, marriage guidance counsellor, child guidance officer or social worker. Many people are reluctant to seek this type of assistance, but it is far preferable to the fourth type of treatment for stress.

- Drugs that alter your mood, sedate or relieve anxiety are very successful in dealing with stress, but should only be used in a crisis, intermittently or for short periods of time. Some antidepressant drugs and treatments for psychiatric conditions are designed for long term use, but most of the anxiety relieving drugs can cause dependency if used regularly. When prescribed and taken correctly they act as a very useful crutch to help patients through a few weeks of extreme stress, and allow them to cope until such time that the cause of the stress is removed or counselling can be started.

Q I am a very timid person, and do not like any change in my life. I have been prescribed antidepressant medications by my doctor, and they seem to help, but I don't think I am depressed. Could there be some other cause?

A I think you may be suffering from social anxiety disorder. This is a common form of neurosis in which the patient realises that they have an irrational level of anxiety or fear. It may be due to an unfortunate experience earlier in life, depression, trauma or stress, but often no cause can be identified.

Patients have a prolonged (greater than six months) marked and persistent abnormal fear about one or more social activities such that fear of embarrassment causes avoidance of others, avoidance of activities that draw attention, and a fear of looking stupid in the eyes of others. The patient does everything possible to avoid these situations, or they are endowed with intense anxiety. If exposed to feared situation, the patient may develop a tremor, stuttering, sweating, rapid heart rate and collapse.

Treatment involves counselling, abreaction (gradual exposure under supervision to situations that provoke fear), and some types of antidepressant medications. Some patients may become totally housebound and unable to function in society.

Fortunately, there is usually a good response to appropriate treatment.

Q. After being involved in a car accident in which the driver of the car I was in was killed, I have been diagnosed with post-traumatic stress. Please tell me more about this problem as I keep seeing my dead friend as he was after the accident, in constant nightmares.

A Post-traumatic stress disorder (PTSD) occurs after experiencing a situation that causes extreme stress and a feeling of helplessness (eg. armed holdup, serious accident, war violence, being assaulted or raped, observing atrocities etc.). Most symptoms start between two weeks and three months of the triggering catastrophe, but may start as late as six months.

To make the diagnosis, doctors must observe in patients at least one symptom from each of the following four categories:

General category

—Symptom duration more than one month, with significant distress or inability to function normally in society.

Re-experiencing phenomena

—Experience intrusive recollections, nightmares, flashbacks as if the event was recurring, psychological distress on exposure to cues that may trigger memories, or physiological effects (eg. rapid pulse, rapid breathing) on exposure to cues.

Avoidance behaviour

—Avoiding thoughts, feelings or conversations about the incident; avoiding places, people or activities connected with the incident; selective amnesia about the traumatic event; reduced interest in everyday activities or detachment from others; unable to look forward to future events with pleasure; or abnormal personality compared to before the incident.

Excessive arousal

—Insomnia, irritability, anger, poor concentration, increased vigilance or increased startle response to frights.

Treatment involves psychological counselling and debriefing immediately after the event, and a trained counsellor should follow up the victim for at least six months. Normal work and activities should be resumed as soon as possible. Referral to a psychiatrist is necessary if the patient does not appear to recover within six months, or deteriorates sooner, when medication may be necessary. PTSD may also lead to recurrent minor illnesses, poor physical health, and in extreme cases, suicide.

In most patients, the problem usually settles within 3 to 6 months, but in some it may become chronic.

SYNDROMES

Q I keep reading about new medical syndromes that are being found, and treated. They always have unpronounceable names, and only a few people seem to have them. Just what is a syndrome?

A Syndromes seem to be multiplying exponentially in modern medicine. Some are just a passing fad, or have only local significance; others though, become diagnostic classics, and are handed down with the combinations of the original describers' surnames (the etymology of which can be quite fascinating at times) or Greek/Latin hybrids that are designed to paralyse even the most articulate tongue.

A syndrome occurs when several patients all present with the same combination of apparently unconnected complaints. They all follow the same course with their disease, and they all respond the same way to treatment.

Syndromes can vary from the now infamous AIDS (acquired immune deficiency syndrome) and Zollinger-Ellison syndrome (severe recurrent peptic ulcers) to Hand-Schuller-Christian syndrome (a children's disease characterised by a thin skull, protruding eyes and a type of diabetes) and irritable bowel syndrome (a relatively common condition accompanied by varied bowel habits and belly pain).

To be told you have a syndrome means nothing. It is which syndrome that counts, and some are quite mild and innocuous.

Q I have been diagnosed as having myalgic encephalomyelitis. Can you explain this disease for me?

A Myalgic encephalomyelitis (ME or chronic fatigue syndrome) is one of a number of diseases categorised as post-viral syndromes. No-one can fully explain the condition, because these syndromes have only recently been recognised and remarkably little is known about them.

It appears that in some people, a viral infection such as influenza is followed by a chronic inflammation of many organs of the body. It is rather like a prolonged dose of the flu, but without the runny nose and fever—just aches and pains and tiredness.

The symptoms of ME vary dramatically from one patient to another, and there are no specific blood or other tests to make the diagnosis. This makes the task for doctors very difficult, and explains why some of these people have at times been described as malingerers.

Symptoms can include arthritis, muscle pains, headaches, nausea, vomiting, diarrhoea, skin rashes, abdominal cramps, depression, mood changes and severe tiredness. A wide range of treatments have been tried to help these people, but all are experimental and there are none that I could justifiably mention here.

Most people have the disease for many months or a few years, and it then slowly fades away, but in the meantime the victim has lost job, career, pride, money and possibly family. The only other point of note is that women are affected five times more than men.

Q My son aged 30 years has been diagnosed as having chronic fatigue syndrome. What causes this, and is there anything that can be done to help him, as he is very depressed and always tired?

A Chronic fatigue syndrome is a chronic condition may affect anyone, as it is thought to be caused by a virus. It may start as a flu-like illness, that recurs several times until it becomes constant. The patient is tired all the time, every muscle in the body aches constantly, a severe headache occurs, skin rashes can develop, and there may be weakness of the arms and legs. It is like having the worst possible case of influenza, but without the runny nose and cough, and without improving for many years. It is far more common in women than in men.

Unfortunately there are no miracle cures available, but antidepressants, anti-inflammatories and other drugs may be helpful. There are also a few new medications being used on an experimental basis by some specialist physicians.

Q **You were inept in your description of the genetic disease chronic fatigue syndrome in a recent column. The disease is self-explanatory and is called Abnormal Cell Mediated Immunity in the Australian Medical Journal (sic). You did not mention the recovery techniques available, and 86% of patients recover using these.**

A The discussion of this problem always raises the ire of those who suffer from, or who have contact with victims with, the disease.

The review of Chronic Fatigue Syndrome (CFS) in the *Medical Journal of Australia* (MJA) that you referred to in your letter dates from 1990 and studied the increased prevalence of the disease in different areas of NSW. In this study, the disease was referred to as CFS, and not one of the other dozen or more names that it has been given in different parts of the world and by different groups (eg. myalgic encephalomyelitis, Tapanui flu, Royal free disease, post-viral syndrome).

The report in the MJA concludes that 43% of those with the condition were unable to work, and that the incidence in NSW was 37 cases in every 100,000 people (ie. about 6300 cases in Australia).

The study defined those as having the disease as:
— having long-lasting fatigue that was aggravated by minor exercise or alterations to daily routine.
— impaired concentration.
— no alternative diagnosis after extensive investigation.

No blood tests or other reproducible criteria could be found to make the diagnosis. Females were found to be 30% more likely than males to develop the disease, and 75% believed that their condition followed a viral illness (eg. influenza).

The medical literature list numerous treatment regimes, but with the possible exception of antidepressant and anti-inflammatory medications and immune globulin infusions, none of these stand up to rigorous assessment, as the majority of patients recover in a year or two regardless of any treatment. There is no evidence that the disease is genetic in origin.

Q **I have chronic fatigue syndrome, and wonder what treatment you would prescribe, as many doctors maintain there is nothing that can be done for it.**

A Medical science is constantly advancing, discovering more about the body and its interactions with the environment and diseases. Unfortunately, we are a long way from knowing all the answers about what is an extraordinarily complex biochemical machine that can have its equilibrium disturbed by everything from cancer and infection to stress and allergies.

There are no tests that can confirm a diagnosis of chronic fatigue syndrome. Everything in the sufferer appears completely normal except for the fact that they are so tired that they cannot perform their normal daily activities. It is therefore a diagnosis of exclusion, and some doctors claim it is purely psychiatric, but after seeing some of my own patients suffer, I am sure that there is something more to it—the question is what?

Because we don't know what causes chronic fatigue syndrome, we don't know how to treat it. There are as many theories and treatments as there are doctors, and every alternative therapist from osteopaths to naturopaths seems to claim that they can cure the problem.

I know of nothing that works. The medical press is constantly full of trial results, letters, case reports and anecdotes from doctors, but nothing conclusive has yet come to light. What we do know is that most victims do fully recover, but this may take many years.

Some patients are affected more than others by the condition, not only because they are more tired, but because in desperation they have spent large amounts of money from their already depleted reserves in trying exotic and expensive cures that are promised by charlatans. If there was anything that could be proved to work, the medical profession would be delighted to use it, but because the condition eventually cures itself, any treatment that is being used at that time will be credited with the benefits. Antidepressant and anti-inflammatory medications seem to be the best options currently available.

Q My mother has just been diagnosed as having Cushing's syndrome. What causes Cushing's syndrome? Is it serious?

A. Cushing's syndrome occurs when an excess amount of steroids (such as cortisone) are given to a patient, or a gland becomes overactive to produce steroids within the body. The glands involved are the pituitary, which is in the middle of your brain, and the adrenals which sit on top of your kidneys.

The syndrome may cause obesity, skin markings, headaches, weakness, bone pain and other diverse symptoms.

Steroids are very useful in controlling a wide range of diseases from asthma to arthritis and skin disorders, but they must be used judiciously to avoid complications.

Q I have been told that Sjøgren's syndrome is the cause of my arthritis. I have never heard of this disease before, and I am naturally very worried about it. Is it serious? What does this strange name mean?

A There are certainly a very large number of diseases and syndromes known to medical science. Many receive names that are derived from the Greek or Latin words to describe the disease (eg. polymyalgia rheumatica means 'many muscles aching and inflamed') while others are named after the first doctor to describe or write about the disease.

Sjøgren's syndrome fits into this latter category, as it is a disease consisting of arthritis, dry eyes, dry mouth, dry skin and dry throat first described by a Swedish ophthalmologist.

It is closely related to rheumatoid arthritis, and is treated in much the same way with the addition of artificial tears and skin moisturisers for the dryness problems. There is no permanent cure, but reasonable long-term control is normally possible.

Q **I have a continuing interest in Prader-Willi syndrome, and would appreciate it if you could bring this condition to the attention of your readers.**

A The Prader-Willi syndrome is a rare congenital (present since birth) condition that affects mainly boys. It is characterised by babies who are small at birth, but soon become obese children due to compulsive overeating as a result of an abnormality in the part of the brain that controls hunger. They are usually short, have under developed genitals, and are some are mentally retarded. The muscles are weak, and have very poor tone, which combined with the excess fat, results in a very flabby belly. There is a significant tendency to develop diabetes later in life.

The cause of the syndrome is a lack of a specific chromosome, and there is no effective treatment.

Q **My mother is paralysed from the waist down with Guillain-Barré syndrome. She has diarrhoea, pins and needles and feels cold. Will her condition ever improve?**

A The Guillain-Barré syndrome is fortunately rare, and often follows a stress to the body such as an infection, surgery, vaccination or injury. Its exact cause is unknown.

The symptoms vary significantly from one patient to another, but include weakness of the legs and/or arms, paralysis of some facial muscles to cause grimacing, pain in various nerves, pins and needles sensation, poor control of bladder and bowel and abnormalities in heart rhythm and breathing.

The disease is difficult to diagnose, as there are no specific tests that will confirm its presence.

It is uncommon for patients to die from the condition, and most make a good recovery over many months, but as many as 20% are left with some long-term disability.

Numerous treatments have been tried, but none are generally successful in all patients. The main form of care is good nursing in hospital during the worst stages, then at home for the months that recovery will take. Physiotherapy is often beneficial in maintaining limb movement.

Unfortunately, it is impossible to predict the outcome in any individual, but patience may be rewarded with recovery, often after nearly all hope has gone.

Q **Would you please write something about carpal tunnel syndrome? My doctor tells me that this is the cause of my hand problems.**

A. Carpal tunnel syndrome is a form of repetitive strain injury to the wrist. It is caused by the excessive compression of the arteries, veins and nerves that supply the hand as they pass through the carpal tunnel in the wrist. This tunnel is shaped like a letter 'D' lying on its side and consists of an arch of small bones which is held in place by a band of fibrous tissue. If the ligaments become slack, the arch will flatten, and the nerves, arteries and tendons within the tunnel will become compressed. It is far more common in women and in those undertaking repetitive tasks or using vibrating tools and in pregnancy.

The symptoms include numbness, tingling, pain and weakness in the hand. The diagnosis is made by x-rays of the wrist, and studies to measure the rate of nerve conduction in the area confirm the diagnosis.

Treatment involves splinting the wrist, fluid tablets to reduce swelling, non-steroidal anti-inflammatory medications, and occasionally injections of steroids into the wrist. Most patients will eventually require minor surgery to release the pressure.

The main complication is permanent damage to the structures in the wrist and hand if the syndrome is not treated.

The operation normally gives a life-long cure.

Q A very good friend of mine in England has told me in her last letter that her new baby has Down's syndrome. Can you please tell me about this condition, and how serious is it?

A   Down's syndrome and 'mongolism' are one and the same thing.

It is a chromosomal defect that occurs at the moment of conception as the sperm and egg join. Chromosomes are the incredibly small strings of protein inside the nucleus of a cell that carry the genes. Genes determine every function and appearance of your body.

When the woman's egg is fertilised by a sperm, the chromosomes from the mother and father come together. Rarely, the chromosomes break and rejoin inappropriately, or extra chromosomes may form.

Many different conditions can result from this occurrence, and Down's syndrome (also known as Trisomy 21 because chromosome number 21 is triplicated) is one of the more common syndromes caused in this way.

The characteristics of the syndrome include mental retardation, flattened facial features, small stature, protruding tongue and several other internal problems.

It occurs more commonly in mothers over 40 years of age, and special tests can be performed before birth to detect the condition if there is a significant degree of suspicion.

There is no treatment available other than special education, physiotherapy and other paramedical services.

Q 30 years ago my son was born mildly mentally retarded. No-one then could explain what was wrong, but I have recently heard of the fragile X syndrome. Could my son be suffering from this? Can you tell me more about this syndrome?

A   The X and Y chromosomes determine an individual's sex. Males have an X and a Y chromosome (XY), while women have two X chromosomes (XX). In women, if one X chromosome is faulty, the other one can take over. In men, if the one X chromosome is faulty (fragile), there is no back up, and so the abnormalities become apparent.

The fragile X syndrome occurs almost entirely in males, but females can carry this inheritable complaint from one generation to the next. It is responsible for about a quarter of all cases of mental subnormality in men, and can be diagnosed by pathological examination of the genes in a cell sample that may be taken from the blood after birth, or by a biopsy of the placenta before birth.

Men with this syndrome suffer from mental retardation, excess activity, epilepsy and autism. They are often large babies, with large ears, forehead and jaw. Other problems may include short sightedness, enlarged testes, cleft palate and slack joints.

There is no cure, and treatment involves the use of appropriate support services and medication to reduce excitement and excess activity. You could have genetic tests performed to see if this is the reason for your son's problems. Genetic counselling of families in which this condition occurs is essential.

Q **I have had an operation on the salivary gland under my ear for a tumour, and I have been left with Frey syndrome. If I had known this would happen, I would not have had the operation.**

A Mixed tumours of the parotid gland, the main gland behind the jaw and under the ear that produces saliva for the mouth, are very sinister growths. Although usually not cancerous initially, they may grow to a very large size to cause disfigurement and pain, and may in time turn malignant.

Once one of these tumours is discovered, removal at the earliest opportunity is sensible. Unfortunately, the facial nerve, which controls the muscles of the face and other nerve fibres (sympathetic and parasympathetic nerves) that control blood vessels and sweat glands, runs through the centre of the gland, and an enlarging tumour may engulf more branches of the nerves, making it very difficult for a surgeon to avoid all the tiny filaments when the tumour is removed.

If the nerve or some of its branches are cut, you will lose the ability to move the facial muscles on one side supplied by those nerves, including those that control the lips.

Frey syndrome occurs when the facial and other nerves to the face are damaged by an infection of, or surgery to, the parotid gland. It results in sweating and flushing of the face, and drooling when eating.

It is very unfortunate that you have developed this syndrome as a complication of the surgery, but without the surgery, your life could be even more miserable with a tennis ball sized mass on the side of your face, and an early death from malignant change.

Q **What can be done to help my wife's Raynaud's phenomenon?**

A Raynaud's phenomenon is often associated with cold weather, and sufferers should choose the warmest climate possible for their home.

The symptoms occur in the hands and feet and are due to spasm of the small arteries in the extremities. Patients have fingers and/or toes that go red, then white and finally blue, while swelling up and causing considerable pain.

Treatment involves wearing gloves, bathing in warm water, and medication to dilate the arteries. There are a number of drugs that can be used. Nicotinic acid is the one most commonly prescribed, but a drug called Adalat also shows considerable promise. These must be used regularly to prevent the problem, and are only available on prescription. An ointment that is used to dilate heart arteries can also be used in very small amounts on the hands to dilate the arteries in the acute situation.

Q   I have been told that a cousin has Klinefelter syndrome. Is this an hereditary problem that I should be worried about in my family?

A   One in every 500 males is afflicted with Klinefelter's syndrome. It is named after Harry Fitch Klinefelter, who practised as a physician in Baltimore, USA, until the 1990s. He described a condition in which males have very small testes and penis, develop small breasts, have scanty body hair and are impotent. These men are always sterile.

The syndrome is caused by an abnormality in the chromosomes that govern the activity of every cell. At the moment of conception when the sperm fuses with the egg, the chromosomes from the mother and father of these men combine incorrectly with two X chromosomes and one Y being present (XXY) instead of one of each (XY). Because every cell in the body is affected by the abnormal chromosomes, no cure is possible.

Testosterone (male hormone) tablets or injections can be given to improve the general body shape and impotence of the man, but the infertility cannot be corrected. Plastic surgery to remove the breasts is sometimes necessary.

Please be assured there is absolutely no chance of the condition being present in your family, as it is an error of fertilisation, not an inherited condition.

Q   I have had pins and needles in my arms for years on and off. Sometimes my arms really ache. It can't be the arthritis my doctor says it is because I am only 28 years old. Do you have any ideas?

A   Naffziger syndrome, which has numerous other names including cervical rib syndrome, scalenus anticus syndrome and thoracic outlet obstruction, is the diagnosis that springs to mind.

Patients with this problem have an additional rib present in lower neck above normal first rib. Nerves and arteries can be compressed between the extra cervical rib and the scalenus anticus muscle in the neck. This is a congenital (present since conception) problem.

The syndrome causes abnormal pressure on ulnar nerve then pain and pins and needles sensation in the arm and hand, muscular weakness of small hand muscles, and altered sensation in the forearm and hands. In severe cases patients have cold blue hands, and reduced pulsation and blood flow in the radial and ulnar arteries in the arm.

The diagnosis can be confirmed by an X-ray of the neck, which shows the extra rib.

Treatment involves rest, neck traction, and sometimes surgical excision of extra rib. Without treatment, symptoms are slowly progressive, but there is a good result from surgery

Q   Please tell me about Turner syndrome. I have met this girl who when I asked her out told me that she has this problem, and explained it by saying she is not a complete woman. I am confused, and she is embarrassed, so I'd like to know more, but can't really ask her.

A   Turner syndrome (also known as XO syndrome) is a rare defect in sex chromosomes.

The person is born with only one X chromosome (XO), and no matching X or Y sex chromosome. The sex chromosomes are named X and Y. Normally two X chromosomes (XX) occur in a female, and one of each (XY) in a male.

Patients look female, but are really asexual, as they do not develop testes or ovaries and are infertile. At puberty, the breasts and pubic hair fail to develop, the genitals remain child-like in appearance, and menstrual periods do not start. Other signs are short stature and a web of skin that runs from the base of the skull down the neck and onto the top of the shoulder. The diagnosis can be confirmed by blood and cell tests that show the chromosome structure.

Giving female hormones (oestrogens) in a cyclical manner from the time of expected puberty will encourage the development of female characteristics such as breasts. Growth hormone can be used to improve height, and surgery can correct the heart defects and neck webbing.

The main complications of the syndrome are eye disorders, heart valve defects, narrowing of the aorta (main body artery), a stocky chest, the early development of diabetes and thin frail bones (osteoporosis).

Patients can function as females in every way except fertility, and can otherwise lead a normal life.

Your friend may feel that once you know all the facts you may reject her, and she may have been hurt before. Provided you do understand the long-term implications, if you still feel attracted to her, by all means ask her out again.

Q **Would you please explain Noonan syndrome to me? We have a lovely little woman who has just started at the office as a cleaner who has this problem.**

A Noonan Syndrome is an uncommon developmental abnormality with wide-spread effects.

It is a congenital (present from birth) condition that occurs in both sexes and without any chromosomal defects.

Patients are short in stature, have a wide neck, broad chest, abnormal heart valves, slanted eyes, low-set ears, depressed bridge of the nose, broad tip of the nose and some mental retardation.

There is no cure, but surgical correction of the heart problems is possible and plastic surgery corrects cosmetic deformities. Life expectancy is normal.

TEETH

See also MOUTH and THROAT

Q **Should children be taking fluoride supplements if they use fluoride toothpaste?**

A The fluoride in toothpaste acts directly on the tooth enamel from the outside, hardening it and helping it resist decay, but it can only act upon the very outermost layer of the tooth enamel.

Fluoride in tablet form does the same thing, but enters the tooth from the inside via the bloodstream, and permeates the entire tooth. Fluoride tablets can therefore protect the entire tooth far more effectively than fluoride toothpaste alone.

Many areas of Australia have adequate supplies of fluoride added to the drinking water, giving everyone protection. If you live in an area that has fluoride added to the water supply, or if the natural level of fluoride in the water is high, you do not need to give your children fluoride tablets. This information will be available by phoning your local council. If there is no fluoride in the water, it is advisable to give fluoride supplements to protect your children's teeth.

Q **My two year old is still bottle fed but has white spots on his teeth and bleeding gums. He often cries when feeding. Should he see a dentist at this early age?**

A. This case describes the typical presentation and outcome of 'nursing bottle decay' or 'bottle caries', which is seen in young children who are not yet weaned from the bottle.

Bottle caries is caused by frequent feeding of sweetened liquids from a bottle, especially before the child goes to sleep. Sugar in the liquid mixes with bacteria in the dental plaque to form acids that attack tooth enamel. Each time a sweet liquid is taken, acids attack the teeth for at least 20 minutes.

When children are awake, the saliva is able to remove some of the liquid. However, during sleep, the saliva flow decreases and the sweet liquids collect around the teeth for prolonged periods, bathing the teeth in acids.

The earliest appearance of decay is the enamel turning a chalky white colour, usually around the gum line. Then as more calcium is lost from the tooth, a hole finally appears. In severe cases of bottle caries, the cavities can ringbark the teeth and cause them to break off.

At the early stages, the cavities do not cause pain, but as they enlarge, increasing discomfort may be experienced, and dental abscesses may result.

Bottle caries may be treated by fillings or extractions, but because most children are not cooperative at such a young age, they usually need to be sedated. Very often, general anaesthetics have to be given.

The best form of treatment for nursing bottle decay is prevention. Children should not be allowed to sleep with a bottle of sweet liquid. If a child needs a bottle for comfort before falling asleep, fill the bottle with plain water, milk or formula, and remove the bottle as soon as the child is asleep. Dummies should never be dipped in honey.

Q My son obtains his water for drinking from an underground well. Do his children need to take fluoride tablets?

A Some water supplies, be they from the local dam or an underground well, contain adequate amounts of fluoride to protect children's teeth. The fact that children in some communities were noticed to have far healthier teeth than others, led to the discovery of fluoride in the water supply of the healthier children, and the subsequent development of fluoridation of many water supplies around the world to protect the teeth of children.

Your local council can tell you if your water supply contains adequate amounts of fluoride. If it does not, your children should take fluoride tablets or drops to protect their teeth from premature decay.

When using water from a well, it will be necessary to have a sample of the water analysed to determine its fluoride content. Industrial chemists undertake this work, and it is important to obtain these results, as giving fluoride supplements to children who already have adequate fluoride in their diets can lead to teeth discolouration (but not damage). The minerals in the ground around the well will determine the amount of fluoride in the water.

Water obtained from rooftops and tanks will never contain any fluoride, as this is very close to distilled water, which contains no minerals of any sort.

Q I am one of those people who listen to television commercials about bad breath and try everything they suggest, but my problem persists. Help!

A Bad breath, with its social implications, is one of the major problems facing Australians today, if the health content of television commercials is to be believed!

Halitosis (the technical name for bad breath) may be due to smoking—the most common cause—poor dental hygiene, periodontal (gum) disease, sinusitis, bronchitis and other infections. Fad diets that contain excess protein and not enough carbohydrates are another possibility because the breakdown products of proteins are highly volatile acids that are expelled in the breath.

Alcoholics have halitosis because the alcohol alters the balance of micro-organisms in the gut, causing an increase in the number of odour-producing bacteria.

Other serious diseases that can cause halitosis include diabetes, hepatitis and cancer. Drugs such as those used to treat angina, fluid tablets and certain tranquillisers may also be responsible.

Those of you with bad breath should stop smoking, clean your teeth regularly, use dental floss, and gargle with antiseptic mouthwashes. If these measures fail, then see your doctor to have some of the more serious potential causes excluded. A dental appointment may also be necessary.

Q Is it necessary to spend a lot of money getting wisdom teeth out because of infection or gum growing over them? Can't they be left to rot without affecting the body?

A Wisdom teeth are removed because they cause constant pain, crowd other teeth, or become infected. Most people do not have their wisdom teeth removed, because (like the appendix) they are meant to be there.

On the other hand, if these teeth are causing discomfort or damage to other teeth, it is in your long-term interest to have them removed.

Leaving an infected tooth to rot is certainly not an option. The toxins and infection can spread throughout your body, to make you extremely ill, and possibly even cause death. Even if you recovered after several months from the infection, the tooth would still be present.

Fear of dentists is a common phenomenon, but you can arrange to have a general anaesthetic, and although your jaw will be sore for a few days afterwards, the long-term relief will be worthwhile.

Q **Would you know any reason why my 8 year old daughter grinds her teeth while sleeping? She has a large overbite. Would this be the cause?**

A The grinding of teeth is called bruxism by doctors, and is most commonly a sign of stress or tension, or it may be a nervous habit. I am sure the over bite has nothing to do with it.

Bruxism during sleep could occur during nightmares, and if your daughter ever wakes with night terrors this is the probable explanation.

Prolonged bruxism may cause damage to the teeth, so have them checked by your dentist.

If the problem continues, a mild medication (on script from your GP) to alter the depth of sleep, and thus reduce the number of dreams, may be appropriate.

TRAVEL

Q **I am travelling overseas soon, but I have to take with me a lot of different tablets and sprays for my heart and chest condition. Do I need a letter from my doctor so that I can take these tablets through customs in foreign countries?**

A Doctors have been unnecessarily inundated with requests such as these since a woman tourist was arrested in Greece for carrying headache tablets containing codeine. The Greek government has been trying to live down this embarrassing mistake ever since.

There is no need for people taking medication to take with them a letter from their doctor for customs purposes. The chemist's label on the medication, with your name and the directions for taking the medication, are sufficient proof that the medication is genuinely required.

The one exception to this rule could be the traveller carrying narcotic pain-killers, but I would doubt that anyone requiring such medication would be in any fit state to travel anyway.

If you have significant medical problems, it is a good idea to carry with you a letter from your doctor outlining your medical condition, so that you can show this letter to any doctor you may need to consult during your journey.

Q **How can I work out how long it will take me to recover from jetlag after a trip to America? I don't want to waste time, but I want to enjoy myself and not feel terrible at Yosemite or Disneyland.**

A The table below looks complicated, but once you get started it works out quite easily, and will give you a good guide to the length of time it will take to recover from an intercontinental flight. If possible, you should adjust your departure

$$\text{REST TIME in hours} = \left(\frac{\text{Travel Time in hours}}{2} + \text{Time zones in excess of 4} + \text{Departure time coefficient} + \text{Arrival time coefficient} \right) \times 2$$

1 Time Zone = 1 Hour difference in time

TIME PERIOD	0800–1200	1200–1800	1800–2200	2200–0100	0100–0800
Departure time coefficient	0	1	3	4	3
Arrival time coefficient	4	2	0	1	3

$$\text{REST TIME in hours} \left(\frac{16}{2} + 3 + 1 + 2 \right) \times 2 = 28 \text{ hours}$$

and arrival times to give the lowest possible time coefficient. All times are local times.

An example for a trip to the west coast of America, departing at 2 pm and arriving at 1 pm (local time) on a 16 hour flight, and covering 7 time zones, has been worked out above to give a rest time of 28 hours.

Q What vaccinations do I need for a trip to South East Asia?

A No vaccinations are needed for Hong Kong and Singapore. For travel in other countries in the area you should have a typhoid vaccination (which is now available in tablet form) and hepatitis A vaccination 4 weeks before your departure. If you are planning to travel away from the major cities in Asia, a cholera vaccine is also advisable, and it is essential to take tablets to prevent malaria (start 2 weeks before departure). Also make sure your tetanus shots and polio vaccination are up to date.

Hepatitis B protection is advisable, but not essential. If desired, it can be combined with the vaccine against hepatitis A in the one injection.

It is a good idea to ask your doctor for some diarrhoea and vomiting tablets to take with you—just in case.

Q How do I avoid getting sick on a trip through Vietnam? I'm very scared I will catch some horrible tropical disease, but my husband is keen to visit there.

A Getting sick on a holiday is always a major disappointment, and in a strange environment can be very difficult to cope with. A few simple preparations can reduce the likelihood of disaster.

You should ask your doctor about any local diseases against which you should be immunised, and the availability and cost of medical treatment. In Vietnam, the main problem is malaria, and you should take regular medication against this, and use insect repellent to avoid being bitten. Vaccinations against typhoid, and both hepatitis A and B, would also be advisable.

It is critical to be very careful about everything that passes your lips. Do not eat or drink anything unless it is straight from a bottle or can, hot on your plate, or a thick skinned fruit (such as a banana) that you can peel. This includes cleaning your teeth with bottled water, and not gargling under the shower. Remember, even bottled drinks can be interfered with, the original contents being replaced, so check the seal on the bottle, and fizzy drinks are unlikely to have a substitute in them.

Remember, the only ways you can catch an exotic disease is to:
— eat it
— drink it
— be bitten by it
— have sex with it!

Q   I don't think Australians are told enough about the risks of overseas travel. I caught a disease called dengue fever in Fiji that I have never heard of before. The doctors back here took ages to work out what was wrong with me, and don't seem to know how to treat it. Is there any cure?

A   I agree that Australians are sometimes naive when travelling abroad, particularly to places like Bali and South-East Asia, where there are many quite nasty diseases present. Fiji is generally disease free, and you were particularly unlucky to catch it there. It is more common in Vanuatu and New Caledonia, which may explain why your doctor did not suspect it at first. Dengue fever may be caught from a mosquito bite in most tropical countries, including northern Australia.

Because it is caused by a virus, there is no effective treatment available. Medical science cannot cure any viral infection, be it the common cold, measles or AIDS. The most important therapy is prolonged rest and the regular use of aspirin for the pain and inflammation. Although the fevers, muscle pains, headaches, sore throat and depression caused by the disease are distressing, fatalities are rare. Total recovery may take several months.

Q   What vaccinations are available to protect you against diseases when travelling in poorer countries?

A   There are a wide range of vaccinations available, but not all are necessary for all destinations. You will need to check with your GP to see which ones you need for your itinerary.

A vaccination programme for overseas travel should commence five weeks before departure but may be completed in two weeks if absolutely necessary. Vaccinations that may be required include:

Cholera. A new oral vaccine now gives good protection for six months.

Hepatitis A. One vaccination of the latest vaccine (Havrix 1440) will give six to twelve months protection. A booster at this time will give long-term protection. Hepatitis A occurs everywhere in the world, but is more common in areas of poor hygiene.

Hepatitis B. Two vaccinations four to six weeks apart will give six months protection. Boosters at six months and five years will usually give long term protection. A combined hepatitis A and hepatitis B vaccine (Twinrix) is also available.

Malaria. Prevention involves taking the appropriate tablets for the areas being visited. Numerous combinations of tablets may be used. Some drug regimes must be taken for up to two weeks before entering a malarious area, and for up to a month after leaving. Dosages vary between a tablet every day to two tablets a week.

Meningococcal meningitis. One injection, five weeks before departure.

Typhoid. Three capsules, two days apart, give 12 months protection, OR one injection gives three to five years protection.

Yellow fever. One injection, five weeks before departure, gives ten years protection.

Immunoglobulin. In situations where there has been exposure to hepatitis A or other serious illnesses, or there is insufficient time for a normal course of vaccinations, one immunoglobulin injection gives protection for 6 to 12 weeks against numerous viral infections, depending on dose.

Japanese encephalitis. Two vaccinations, two weeks apart. It is required only for residence in rural areas of India, Nepal, China and South-East Asia.

All travellers should also ensure that their tetanus and polio (Sabin) vaccinations are up to date.

Q Do I need any vaccinations or special medicines to travel in England, France, Germany and the Czech Republic? I am taking a bus trip from London to Prague, then flying back to London.

A. No vaccinations or special medications are necessary for your planned trip, but make sure you have appropriate medical insurance.

No vaccinations are normally necessary for visits to any of the following countries:

Austria, Bahamas, Belgium, Bermuda, Canada, Croatia, Czech Republic, Denmark, Estonia, Finland, France, Germany, Greece, Greenland, Grenada, Hong Kong, Hungary, Iceland, Ireland, Italy, Japan, Latvia, Lithuania, Luxembourg, Malta, Moldova, Nauru, Netherlands, New Zealand, Norway, Poland, Portugal, Slovakia, Slovenia, Spain, St. Vincent, Singapore, Swaziland, Sweden, Switzerland, Trinidad, United Kingdom and the United States.

If you are visiting any other countries, discuss your vaccination requirements with your GP.

Q My daughter married a Rhodesian man some years ago, and has moved to Zimbabwe to live. She wrote saying that she had caught a disease called 'Bilharsia', but not to worry. Naturally I am worried, but my own GP says he has never heard of it. Do you know anything about it? How serious it can be?

A This disease cannot be caught in Australia, as it is transmitted by a species of snail that is not found in this country.

Bilharzia can be caught by bathing in fresh-water streams, rivers and lakes in Egypt, tropical Africa as far south as Zimbabwe, the Caribbean and eastern South America. It is caused by a microscopic animal called a fluke (trematode) that enters into the body by burrowing through the skin, often of the foot.

Once into the bloodstream, the fluke travels to the veins around the large bowel. Here, eggs are laid, and pass out with the faeces or urine to infect water supplies. Once in the water, the eggs hatch, and the larvae seek out and burrow into the flesh of certain species of fresh water snail. Here they mature, and emerge from the snail ready to enter and infect another human host.

The first symptom is an itchy patch at the site of skin penetration. Varying symptoms then follow, depending on the areas affected. Patients are infectious for a week or more before the symptoms become apparent, and so it is difficult to stop the spread of this disease by the fluke as it moves through the body, and the individual's reaction to those changes. Long-term symptoms include diarrhoea, abdominal pain and bloody urine.

A number of drugs can be used to kill the fluke inside the body. The outcome of treatment is good if commenced early in the course of the disease but advanced disease may be difficult to cure. You should hold no great fears for your daughter, because doctors in Zimbabwe are very experienced in the treatment of this condition, and she should recover after a few weeks of medication.

VACCINATIONS, ADULT
See also VACCINATIONS, CHILDREN

Q I've had a terrible flu this year and I don't want to get it again. When should I get my annual flu shot?

A The best time is between March and May. The Influenza vaccine does not become available until the end of February each year, as the new types of influenza virus in the environment have to be identified and the appropriate vaccine must be developed and produced. Unfortunately, the influenza virus has the ability to change its form regularly, so a flu shot one year will not necessarily protect you the next year.

Q I am 42 years old, and often work in the garden and get small nicks on my hands. Is it still necessary to have a tetanus injection? I have never heard of anyone catching this disease. If so, how often should I have a tetanus injection?

A Imagine a disease, the seeds of which are in the soil around us. A disease not restricted to the third world nations of Asia and Africa, but present in Australia. A disease that causes the death of nearly half the people who catch it, and which causes excruciating pain from muscle spasms triggered by the slightest noise. A disease that can be caught by having a relatively small cut anywhere on the body. A disease called tetanus.

We are fortunate in Australia to have access to vaccinations which prevent this terrible disease and the number of people who catch it is not therefore high. In less fortunate countries, the population is not as well educated and medical services are not as readily available. Thousands of people die a terrifying and tortured death because of the unavailability of a simple vaccine. Tetanus vaccination is still necessary, and if you have not had one for ten years, you could catch tetanus!

All children should have a series of vaccinations known as triple antigens at two, four, six and eighteen months of age. This contains vaccines against whooping cough and diphtheria as well as tetanus. A further booster is given prior to school entry at five years of age.

Adults are also at risk. The tetanus vaccine does not give life-long protection, and revaccination is necessary every ten years. If you have a wound likely to be contaminated by tetanus, the vaccination should be given again after only five years. Deep wounds, such as treading on a nail, are particularly likely to cause tetanus.

The tetanus vaccine is one of the smallest and least painful injections of all, and it has no side-effects. There are no excuses for you and your children not being adequately protected. See your general practitioner soon. Tomorrow may be too late!

Q What causes tetanus? Is it a serious disease? Why do doctors insist on jabbing everyone who has a cut with a tetanus shot?

A A bacteria called *Clostridium tetani* can live quite harmlessly in the gut of many animals, particularly horses. When it passes out of their bodies in faeces it forms a hard microscopic cyst which then contaminates the soil and waits for a chance to return to active life. The bacteria can remain inactive for many years until it enters a cut or wound in the dirt or dust that may be around when the tissues are exposed.

Once it has infected a cut, it starts multiplying and produces a chemical which is absorbed into the bloodstream and spreads throughout the body. This chemical (a toxin) attacks the small muscles used for chewing our food, making it difficult to open the mouth. Thus the common name for tetanus is lockjaw. The toxin gradually attacks larger and larger muscles, irritating them and causing them to go into severe spasm.

These spasms are similar to the cramps you may experience in your leg at night, except they are more severe and can attack every muscle in your body. The patient remains conscious throughout the disease, but eventually the muscles which control breathing and the heart are affected, and the patient dies.

There are very few effective treatments for tetanus, because although the bacteria may be killed, the toxin remains in the body. Tetanus can be prevented by vaccination, but it cannot be cured.

Q **I am about to get married. How can I find out if I need a German measles needle?**

A Your general practitioner can order a simple blood test to measure your immunity against German measles (rubella). If it is low, an injection will be given to give you long-term immunity. It is important for all young women to ensure that they are immune to this disease, because if it is contracted in the first few months of pregnancy, it may cause severe birth defects in the child.

All children should be routinely vaccinated against rubella at 12 months of age, and at 5 years of age by a council clinic or their general practitioner.

Q **Should an adult man have a mumps vaccine if he has never had the disease?**

A. Yes. Children should have a mumps vaccine at one and five years of age, so it is now an uncommon condition, but if an adult catches the disease, it is usually more severe than in a child.

If an adult (man or woman) has not had mumps, a vaccine that has minimal side effects is available to give life-long protection. Most general practitioners would carry a supply of this vaccine, and so it is a very simple matter to obtain protection.

Mumps seems to have the unfortunate ability to strike just before your annual holidays or at some other vital time, so for this reason alone it is worthwhile being protected. In addition, the testes of men and ovaries of women may be affected by a severe case of mumps. This complication is not common, but may lead to sterility in both men and women.

Q **I have heard there is now a vaccine against pneumonia. My GP wants me to have it, but I'm not sure about these things. I'm only 66, but have bronchitis sometimes.**

A   The vaccine you are referring to is called Pneumovax 23. It has been around for a few years now, and is given as a single injection. It will prevent lung infections caused by the Pneumococcal bacteria, which is a common cause of pneumonia, but gives no protection against other bacteria that may cause this infection.

The vaccine lasts at least five years, when a second injection can be given to give long-term protection. It can be used in almost everyone, but is not designed for use in pregnancy, and those very few receiving chemotherapy for Hodgkin's disease. It should be used with caution in people with reduced immunity, a fever, or currently on antibiotic treatment.

The side effects are minimal, mainly local soreness and redness at site of injection. Unusual reactions include a rash, joint pain and fever. Significant adverse reactions and allergy reactions may occur if a second vaccination is given to an adult within the five years, but children may require a second vaccination.

It is a vaccination that is not used routinely but is advisable for those who have any long term lung disease, the elderly, patients who have their spleen removed, who are chronically ill, or who are in an institution where the disease has occurred.

VACCINATIONS, CHILDREN
See also VACCINATIONS, ADULT

Q   **Do children still need a vaccine at 10 years of age? My old clinic book says my son does need a ten year old shot, but my doctor says it is not necessary.**

A   No. Provided your child has had all the necessary vaccinations as an infant, at 18 months and 5 years, no further routine tetanus or diphtheria vaccine is required until 15 years of age. It has been found that the effects of the vaccine last far longer than originally thought.

Everyone should still have their hepatitis B vaccine at 13 years of age.

Vaccination schedules change almost annually, and may have changed again by the time this book is published, so always check with your GP as to what vaccinations are necessary.

Q   **Should I give my baby the diphtheria, whooping cough and tetanus vaccinations, or are the side effects dangerous?**

A   All children should receive the full course of vaccines to protect them against these serious diseases unless there are very good medical grounds not to use them.

Unfortunately, some parents through ignorance or ill-informed advice are not vaccinating their children, and the diseases of whooping cough and diphtheria are increasing in the community.

Tetanus is always with us, and is potentially able to infect any wound. All three diseases may be fatal, may cause brain damage and may cause chronic ill health.

The risk of vaccination is infinitesimal, and when compared to the potential side effects of any one of these diseases, it is a far preferable course of action. Another person (adult or child) only has to breathe the infecting germs in the direction of your child and he or she may catch one of these dread diseases. Please vaccinate your child now!

Q I have never heard of any child catching whooping cough, but my doctor is insisting that my baby has this vaccine. Is whooping cough vaccination still necessary?

A. There is no treatment available to cure this distressing disease, but it may be completely prevented. Even so, increasingly large numbers of children are being left unprotected because their parents forget to obtain the necessary course of injections, or are poorly informed.

Whooping cough is not a disease of the past. Hundreds of Australian children contract the disease every year, and many of them die or are left as invalids. The bacteria that causes the infection is widespread in the community, and adults may have the disease and consider it merely a cold. Only in young children is the disease severe, and it is therefore important to start vaccinations as early as possible.

The vaccination against whooping cough is invariably combined with those for tetanus and diphtheria, and is given at two, four, six and 18 months of age. This triple vaccine has minimal side effects, and the most common ones are a slight fever for 6 to 24 hours after the needle, and sometimes prolonged crying. Any other risks are minimal, and certainly far rarer than the serious complications of any of these three diseases.

If the child has a fever or other illness, the vaccination may be delayed for a few days until he or she has recovered. The only children who should not be vaccinated are those with febrile convulsions, a history of epilepsy and allergies to certain elements of the vaccine.

Q I have read recently that there are dangers associated with the vaccination of children, and that homeopathic alternatives are just as effective. I would appreciate your opinion on this matter.

A Many parents believe that polio, diphtheria and whooping cough are diseases of the past, and that measles, mumps and rubella are only minor childhood illnesses, and don't warrant a vaccination. Nothing could be further from the truth.

It is still possible to catch all these diseases in Australia, and children are diagnosed with them on a regular basis. Another epidemic could easily occur if the vaccination rate among all children drops too low. In some research, vaccination rates as low as 60% for some of these diseases have been reported, and this is cause for grave concern.

Epidemics in past years, and in other western countries more recently, have resulted in the death, disablement, and permanent damage of hundreds of children. We should not allow this to happen in Australia.

Measles and mumps are often mild diseases, but in a significant proportion of children it can cause severe illness, and in a few, permanent brain damage or even death may occur.

Homeopathic remedies have no proven record of success, and have been discounted by every reputable scientist. The risks of vaccination are infinitesimal, and far less than the risk associated with catching any of these diseases.

Do not take chances with your child's life. Have him/her fully and properly vaccinated to avoid possible tragedy.

Vaccinations against tetanus, whooping cough, hepatitis B and diphtheria are given at 2, 4, and 6 months of age, and without the hepatitis B component at 18 months and five years of age; the oral Sabin vaccine against polio is given at the same time. Mumps, measles and rubella (German measles) can be prevented by a vaccination at one and five years. Some types of meningitis are prevented by the HiB vaccine at 2, 4 and 18 months.

Q How safe and necessary is the measles vaccine?

A It is very safe and very necessary.

Measles is usually a relatively mild disease, but it may cause severe problems in a small number of children. These problems can include brain inflammation, ear infections, pneumonia, eye infections, fitting and (rarely in Australia) death.

The complications of the vaccine are extremely rare, and relatively mild. The most common (3%) is a very mild attack of the measles.

It is a vaccine that is normally combined with that against mumps and rubella, and so is very beneficial. It is normally given at 12 months of age, and again at five years of age.

If for no other reason than to avoid the inconvenience of a child developing the disease the day before you depart for your annual holiday, you should ensure that your child receives this vaccine.

Doctors hope that with intensive vaccination campaigns, measles may be totally eradicated in Australia.

Q What vaccinations does a child require in their first five years?

A Far too many parents are neglecting their children's vaccinations. The diseases that affected and killed our parents' and grandparents' friends are still with us, and children still die or become brain damaged by diphtheria, measles, mumps and whooping cough. It is essential for all children to be adequately vaccinated.

The vaccinations required before starting school are:
— five vaccinations against tetanus, diphtheria and whooping cough at 2, 4, 6 and 18 months, and 5 years of age.
— two against measles, mumps and rubella (German measles) at one and five years of age.
— three against Haemophilus influenzae B (HiB), an infection that may cause meningitis or severe throat infections at 2, 4 and 12 months of age.
— three against Hepatitis B at 2, 4 and 6 months of age—usually combined in same injection as tetanus, diphtheria and whooping cough.
— four Sabin vaccines against polio, which is given by mouth at 2, 4 and 6 months, and 5 years of age.

Q What vaccinations does my son need before starting school at five years of age?

A Two injections and one oral vaccination are required.

The injections cover tetanus, diphtheria and whooping cough in one; and measles, mumps and rubella in the other. The polio (Sabin) vaccine is given by mouth as two drops on a spoon.

Many schools will not accept a child for enrolment unless they have evidence of being fully immunised.

Q **Can you tell me about the new chickenpox vaccine that I have heard is now available. Is it a good idea?**

A The chickenpox (*Varicella zoster*) vaccine was first introduced to Australia in 2000 and is obviously a good idea if you want your child to avoid this infection, but it is not yet a routine vaccination, is not subsidised by the government, and is quite expensive (but not as expensive as missing a few days of work to eventually look after your sick child).

It is recommended for children from 9 months to 12 years of age, and only one injection is necessary. Older children and adults require two injections six weeks apart.

It is not for use in pregnancy, and must be used with caution in breast feeding. You should not not have the vaccination if you are sensitive to neomycin, have received a blood transfusion recently or are suffering from a high fever.

The only common side effect is local soreness at injection site. Unusual side effects include a rash and a vaccinated person may rarely pass the virus on to an unvaccinated person to cause chickenpox.

VENEREAL DISEASES
(Sexually Transmitted Diseases)
See also AIDS

Q **Why do some very respectable people, who have never played around sexually, develop genital herpes?**

A Only in exceptional circumstances (hot spa baths being one possibility) can genital herpes be caught by anything other than sexual contact. It may be many years from the time it is caught until symptoms develop, and it may be transmitted by a person with no symptoms of the disease. It may be that a husband/wife had premarital sex, and caught genital herpes without developing the disease, but later passed the virus that causes it on to their partner.

Medication is now available on prescription that will cure an attack of genital herpes, but it is essential to start treatment as soon as symptoms are experienced.

Q **My (very) ex-boyfriend has donated his curse to me, and I am distinctly unimpressed! Is there a cure for genital herpes?**

A Genital herpes is caused by a virus that reactivates regularly for many months or years to cause painful blisters and sores on the genitals of both men and women. Usually, the attacks become less frequent and less severe as time passes, but some patients continue to have acute attacks for long periods of time.

The best treatment is to use soothing and drying lotions and creams on the sores.

In recent years, new antiviral medications have been developed which will settle a particular attack of Herpes, and if taken regularly will prevent recurrences, but do not give a permanent cure. If you are suffering severely, it is worthwhile discussing their use with your doctor.

Q I have heard that genital herpes can be caused by the same herpes virus that causes cold sores. If my partner has a cold sore on his lips, but no genital herpes, can I get genital herpes by kissing him? Is oral sex safe in this situation?

A Herpes simplex type two is the virus that causes genital herpes. It is closely related to Herpes simplex one that can cause the distressingly painful blisters of cold sores on the lips and nostrils. It is possible by direct contact with a sore to catch genital herpes from Herpes simplex one, and sores on the lips from Herpes simplex type two. The blisters they form appear similar. Oral sex can therefore transmit both forms of virus from lips to genitals and vice versa.

The majority of cases of genital herpes are caught by sexual contact with someone, male or female, who already has the disease. It is possible, but unlikely, for the virus to be caught in hot spa baths and from a shared wet towel, but these and similar incidents are not common.

Once a person is infected with the virus, it settles in the nerve endings around the vulva, penis, lips etc. and remains there for the rest of that person's life.

If sores are present, there is a very good chance of passing the disease on to your sexual partner. A victim is also infectious for a few days before a new crop of sores develop, as the virus is rapidly reproducing at this stage. An absence of sores does not guarantee that the infection will not be transmitted, but condoms will give some protection against spreading the disease.

At times of stress, illness or reduced resistance, the virus starts reproducing, and causes the painful blisters and ulcers that characterise the disease. The first attack may occur weeks or years after the initial infection. The attack will last for a few weeks and then subside. After weeks, months or years, a further attack may occur, but the usual pattern is for the attacks to become less severe and to occur further apart.

Antiviral tablets can be prescribed by a doctor to control an attack of genital herpes, and if taken for several months, will prevent further attacks. They are quite expensive, but are subsidised by the Pharmaceutical Benefits Scheme under certain circumstances.

The most serious side of genital herpes, is the effect it may have on the babies of women who develop an attack of the disease at the end of their pregnancy. If a baby catches the infection during delivery, it can cause severe brain damage in the child. For this reason, if a woman has a history of repeated herpes infections, she may be delivered by Caesarean section so that the baby does not come into contact with the virus particles that may be present in the birth canal.

There is some evidence that the incidence of gynaecological cancer is increased in women with genital herpes. All women should have regular Pap smear tests, but particularly so if they have this annoying, but rarely serious disease.

Q A friend of mine contracted genital warts and had intercourse with another female. Please tell me all about these horrible things. How serious are they?

A The human papilloma virus (HPV) is responsible for genital wart infections, and it is transmitted from one person to another only by sexual intercourse, or other intimate contact.

The obvious result of infection with this virus, is the growth of warts, sometimes of quite a large size, on the penis in men and in the genital area of women. They may appear as flat, pale areas on the skin, or the dark coloured, irregularly shaped lumps more commonly associated with warts. Both men and women can be carriers of the virus from one sexual partner to another, without being aware that they are infected. Only when the warts become large and obvious does the victim seek attention.

If a woman is infected by HPV, she may develop genital warts not only around the outside of her genitals, but internally where they are difficult to detect. There may in fact, be no warts present at all, but once the virus enters the vagina, it can attack the cervix, which is the opening into the womb (uterus).

HPV infections of the cervix may cause cancer of the cervix. It does not happen immediately, and may take some years to develop, but a significant proportion of women with this infection will develop cancer. Cancer of the cervix has few early signs, and is often not detected until it is well advanced and difficult to treat.

Every woman should have regular Pap smear tests every year or two while she is sexually active. These tests can detect this type of cancer, genital wart infections and other gynaecological problems at an early stage. When detected early, the cancer can be treated effectively, and completely cured.

The genital warts themselves, in both men and women, can be treated by destroying the warts with acid paints or ointments, freezing the warts with liquid nitrogen, by burning them away with an electric needle or lasers, or by using a special cream (Aldara).

Q   I have a most embarrassing problem that I am afraid to discuss with my doctor. I have some warty like growths around the head of my penis. Are they dangerous?

A   Genital warts are the probable cause of your problem. They are not particularly serious in men, but can cause significant problems, including a high risk of cancer of the cervix, to your female sexual partners.

Genital warts are caused by a virus. They occur in both men and women, but for obvious reasons are more easily seen in the male. They are passed from one person to another during sex, but it may be many months before the warts start growing after the infection is caught. The body eventually manages to defeat the disease, but his may take years, and in the meantime you can pass the infection on.

The infection can cause warty growths as large as a golf ball if they are neglected. For this reason, treatment should be sought as soon as the warts are seen. This will involve removing the warts and a small amount of surrounding tissue by regularly applying a special cream, freezing, acid application or burning. Regrowth after treatment is common, and should receive further immediate medical attention.

You will remain infectious until every last virus has been destroyed, and you will not know this until you have been free of wart growth for at least 6 months.

Q   I have large white lumps on my penis. Are these genital warts? Is there any cream or lotion I can buy from the chemist?

A   What you are describing could be genital warts, or they could be cysts, dermatitis or any one of a number of other skin diseases. The skin diseases that occur on other parts of the body can occur just as readily on the skin of the penis. The only way to find out just what these spots are is to have them checked by a doctor.

Far too many patients, both male and female, are embarrassed about showing certain parts of their anatomy to a doctor. As a result, they worry for weeks or months on end about something that may be easily cured, or they may be delaying treatment for a condition that could be quite serious.

Doctors are very used to seeing all parts of the body, and they will not be offended by what you show or tell them.

If these spots are genital warts, the best treatment is to have them properly removed by your doctor, because if they are left, they will enlarge and spread. Do not try to treat them with chemist preparations without obtaining a correct diagnosis.

Q   **What would cause my penis to burn every time I start to urinate, then desist? My urine is crystal clear.**

A   You have an inflammation of the urethra, the tube leading from the bladder and through the penis to the outside.

There are a number of causes for this condition, including bladder infections and gonorrhoea, but by far the most common cause in men is a venereal disease called non-specific urethritis (NSU). This may be associated with a slight white discharge from the penis, but many men have no other symptoms than burning when passing urine. Unfortunately, women may not develop symptoms until the disease has been present for months or years, by which time they may have develop a widespread infection in their pelvis that can lead to infertility, abnormal pregnancies, and damage to the cervix and womb.

Diagnosis is sometimes difficult, because a negative test does not mean that the disease is not present, only that the test has failed to detect it. All men with this problem, and all their sexual partners, will need to be treated with a special course of antibiotics. Fortunately this is successful in curing the vast majority of these cases.

Q   **After a business trip to Bangkok I have developed a yellow discharge from my penis and it hurts to urinate. My business partner dared me to go with a bar girl while I was there. What is it likely to be, and could my wife catch it?**

A   Sir, you are in big trouble! You almost certainly have a venereal disease, and if you have had sex with your wife since returning from Bangkok, she has probably caught it too.

The most likely infection is gonorrhoea, which is treated with a course of antibiotics. You may have caught other more serious infections at the same time though. It is essential for you AND your wife to see a doctor. Swabs will be taken from your penis and her vagina, and you will have blood tests taken for other types of infection. Once the correct diagnosis is made, effective treatment can follow. If you do not get treated, the infection can spread causing severe complications including sterility. If your wife is not treated, you can catch the disease back from her in the future. This is why both partners must receive adequate treatment.

Hopefully she will forgive you this one indiscretion—others be warned!

Q **My GP has diagnosed my vaginal irritation as a 'chlamidya' infection after taking some tests. She has given me some tablets to take, but I would like to know more about this problem.**

A Chlamydial vaginal infections are one of the most common forms of sexually transmitted disease in both sexes.

Chlamydiae are a group of organisms that are not bacteria, but closely resemble bacteria. They act as parasites inside human cells, cause the destruction of the cell where they multiply, and then move on to infect more cells.

They cause irritation of the vagina in women, and urethra (urine tube from bladder to outside) in both men and women, so that passing urine may be uncomfortable. In rare severe cases it can spread to the nearby lymph nodes in the groin to cause lymphogranuloma venereum.

The infection is difficult to diagnose, but swabs from affected area are sometimes positive. Blood tests can also be used to make the diagnosis with internal infections.

Once suspected, it can be successfully treated with appropriate antibiotics.

VIRUSES

Q **I have had 'glandular fever' for two years now. I take a lot of vitamins with a good diet. Could you tell me the story of this virus?**

A Although romantically named, the 'kissing disease', infectious mononucleosis or glandular fever, is a most unpleasant disease to catch, and doctors are completely powerless to prevent it or treat it.

Glandular fever is caused by a virus called the Epstein-Barr virus. The virus is passed from one person to another through all the bodily fluids, but most commonly in the tiny droplets of water that you exhale when breathing. If you are unlucky enough to inhale some of these virus carrying droplets from a person with glandular fever, you may catch the disease yourself.

Patients with glandular fever usually have a sore throat, raised temperature, large glands in the neck and other parts of the body, and generally feel absolutely lousy.

Doctors can perform a blood test to prove the diagnosis, and they can give advice on how to cope with the disease, but unfortunately, this advice will not cure the disease. The patient must rest as much as possible, take aspirin or paracetamol for the fever and aches, use gargles for the sore throat, and then wait until the illness passes. There is no evidence that vitamins or other herbal remedies have any effect upon the course of the disease.

The disease lasts about four weeks, but some patients are unlucky enough to have it persist for several months. The patient is considered infectious while s/he has the large tender glands, and during this time should avoid close contact with others.

After the symptoms have settled, the patient is often left very tired and weak, and it may be another week or two before s/he is fit to resume school or work.

The complications of the disease are rare. Some people develop secondary bacterial infections while their resistance is lowered by the glandular fever.

Others may have their spleen infected by the virus, or in even rarer cases, the liver, heart and brain may be involved. Recurrences of the infection for many months or years after the initial infection are not uncommon.

Q One of my pregnant daughter's blood tests shows that she has been exposed to cytomegalovirus. What does this mean? Could it cause a miscarriage?

A Cytomegalovirus (CMV) infections are very common, and almost everyone has these infections at some time, but they are usually so mild that they are not noticed. Only in patients who have reduced immunity from other diseases can CMV infections be a significant problem.

In pregnancy, it is possible, but rare, for a CMV infection to cause a wide variety of complications, but only if the infection spreads to the developing baby.

Your daughter will probably have two or more blood tests to determine whether the CMV infection is active or not. If it is active, it is possible for it to be the cause of a miscarriage, or other problems.

She will need to be further advised by her obstetrician.

Q How serious is hepatitis? My doctor tells me I have the A form and not the B. What is the difference?

A Hepatitis is a viral infection of the liver. There are several different forms, and the B form is one of the worst, as it can lead to a slow degeneration of the liver over many years.

The A form is also a nasty disease, but most patients totally recover within a few weeks or months. The different forms of hepatitis are produced by different viruses. They can only be separated by special blood tests done by pathologists.

In the A form, you probably ate food prepared by, or came into close contact with, someone who already had hepatitis A. That person may have had the early stages of the disease, a very mild form of the disease, or was a long-term carrier of the virus. Once the virus entered your gut, it migrated to the liver, and started multiplying rapidly. The damaged liver cells could no longer work effectively, and you became ill, feverish and yellow.

There is no specific treatment available other than rest, time and a high-carbohydrate diet. Alcohol must be avoided for a long time after the disease is cured. Any close contacts with a person suffering from hepatitis A can receive an immunoglobulin injection to give them immediate short-term protection from the disease. For long term protection it is necessary to have a specific hepatitis A vaccination, which is given in two doses, 6 to 12 months apart.

There is a series of three injections available to protect you long-term against hepatitis B. The B form can only be caught by having sex with someone who has hepatitis B, or by contaminating your blood with the saliva (eg. on an open wound) or blood (eg. shared needle in drug users) of a victim.

Q Could you please explain the symptoms, causes and treatment of an illness described as 'hand, foot and mouth disease'?

A Hand, foot and mouth disease has nothing to do with the foot and mouth disease that occurs in some animals.

It is a viral infection, caused by the Coxsackie virus, that affects virtually every child before the age of five years, but in most children the disease is so mild that its symptoms are overlooked.

In severe cases the virus causes a moderate fever and a day or two of being unwell, followed by the appearance of red patches and ulcers in the mouth, and tiny blisters on the soles of the feet and palms of the hand.

All these problems settle within a week, and the only treatment necessary is paracetamol for the fever and some soothing gel for the mouth ulcers.

The infection often occurs in epidemics, spreading rapidly through a family or kindergarten. The incubation period (time from contacting a child with the disease until the disease becomes apparent in another child) is three to seven days.

Q **What is the best cure for a cold? I get several a year, and I end up in bed for a week every time. Medical science must be able to do something to help me!**

A If you catch a cold, there is nothing a doctor can do to cure it. He or she can certainly prescribe medications to ease the symptoms and make you feel more comfortable, but please do not pester him or her for antibiotics, because they do not help the problem at all.

The more you rest, the faster the problem will go away. Those who insist on working while feverish and miserable prevent the body from building up its defences rapidly, and pass the infection on to their work mates.

Aspirin or paracetamol, rest at home and medications for the cough, sore throat, runny nose and blocked sinuses are the best remedy. The usual cold will last for a week, but some people are luckier and have a brief course, while others are particularly unlucky, and the first cold may so lower their defences that they can catch another one, and then another, causing cold symptoms to last for many weeks.

Many vitamin and herbal remedies are touted as cures or preventatives for colds, but when subjected to detailed trials, none of them can be proven. If any medication, vitamin or herb could be found to help this condition, the entire medical profession would be delighted to recommend it.

Q **I keep getting one cold after another. Why does it always have to be me?**

A You are just very unlucky. Several hundred viruses can cause a cold. Once one virus infects you, you should develop life-long resistance, but because there are so many possible causes, you will still catch colds. Gradually your resistance to infection will improve though, and colds will occur less frequently.

Because they have not been exposed to many viruses, children develop more colds than adults. Unfortunately, once you do catch a cold, it becomes easier to develop a second one. This second cold knocks you about even further, weakening you so that a third one can be caught. This unpleasant chain of events can sometimes continue for months.

Some people also have genetic factors that either protect them or make them more susceptible to viral infections. Stress, both physical and mental, can also reduce the body's resistance to infection. Extremes of temperature are a cause of stress, and an indirect cause of recurrent colds.

Q **I am just recovering from shingles, and my doctor says its connected with chickenpox. Can you explain this?**

A Shingles is caused by a virus called *Herpes zoster*, which is the same virus that causes chickenpox.

When you were a child, you had chickenpox at some stage. Since then, the virus has not left your body, but has migrated to the roots of the nerves along your spinal cord, where it can remain in an inactive stage for the rest of your life.

At times of stress, either emotional or physical, or when you have another illness that lowers your resistance, the virus may become active again and start to multiply and move along the nerve. This causes the skin and other tissues around the area the nerve supplies to become very painful, and this is the first symptom of shingles.

Usually only one or two nerves are affected, and almost invariably on only one side of the body. Any nerve may be affected, and it can occur on the belly or chest (which are the most common sites), or on the face or legs. The worst variety occurs around the eye and ear, where dizziness, ear noises and rarely blindness may occur.

When the rapidly multiplying virus particles reach the end of the nerve, an acutely tender blistering rash occurs. This often forms an acutely tender belt-like line around one half of the body. The rash dries out slowly and disappears over several weeks, usually healing completely, but occasionally leaving some scarring on sensitive areas such as the neck and face.

Tablets are now available to cure shingles, but you must start taking them within three days of the rash first appearing, so never hesitate to see your doctor if you develop a painful rash—you could save yourself weeks or months of pain and discomfort.

Q **I need help with my cold sores. They just keep coming and nothing seems to help them. What can I do?**

A Cold sores are best treated when they first develop. The first symptoms are pain and tingling at the site of the sore on the lips, nose or elsewhere. If antiviral ointment (eg. Zovirax) is applied every hour to the area at this stage, it may be possible to prevent the sore from developing. Once the sore is present, the ointment is not as effective.

The best treatment for developed cold sores are the many lotions and creams available from chemists that contain a drying agent to heal, an antiseptic to prevent further infection, and an anaesthetic to ease the pain. About a quarter of the population are susceptible to these sores, and develop them at irregular intervals for many years.

Unfortunately there is no permanent cure yet available.

Q **My grandson suffers severely from a recurrent blistering rash across his face that I believe are cold sores. I have read that there is a drug to cure herpes infections. Will this drug work on cold sores as well as genital herpes?**

A Zovirax (aciclovir) was the first effective antiviral drug ever developed. It is expensive, but also very effective in controlling infection by all forms of the herpes virus. There are several newer drugs that also act in this way.

The herpes virus causes cold sores, genital sores, shingles and chickenpox.

The drug has been used for some years to control genital herpes and shingles, but cases of severe cold sores can also be prevented and controlled by the drug. Because chickenpox is a self-limiting disease, it is only used to treat this disease in patients who have an inadequate immune system.

Zovirax can be used in a low dose long term to prevent infection, or at a high dose for a short time to settle an acute infection.

The government subsidises the cost of the drug under very strict guidelines. If your grandson falls outside these guidelines, be prepared for a very large bill from the pharmacist.

Q My daughter's best friend has Ross River fever. I am worried that she could catch it too. What is this fever, and how do you catch it?

A Ross River fever is caused by a virus-like germ that attacks the connective tissue of the body. It is transmitted from one person to the next by mosquitoes. When the mosquito bites an infected person, the germ enters the mosquito with the blood, and is injected back into the next person the mosquito bites, infecting them also.

The patient suffers from fevers, muscle aches, arthritis and headaches, and is very tired. It may last for a couple of weeks or a couple of months. There is no cure available. The only form of prevention is the liberal use of insect repellents, screening houses and long sleeves.

The disease is more common in north Queensland and the Northern Territory, but may occur anywhere in Australia that mosquitoes occur.

Q How can I cure my Ross River fever? It has lasted for weeks!

A Unfortunately there in no cure for this condition. Ross River fever (also known as epidemic polyarthralgia) is not limited to the Ross River in Townsville, but is a world-wide disease of tropical areas that is spread by mosquitoes. Once the condition is established, only medications to relieve the joint and muscular pains, fever and tiredness can be given.

The only treatment is symptomatic—medications to ease the aches and pains and remove the fever. Aspirin is the mainstay of treatment, but if this is insufficient, more potent anti-inflammatory medication or even steroids may be prescribed by your doctor to keep you comfortable for the 6 to 12 weeks the disease will last

Q It has taken several weeks, but finally my doctor has diagnosed my aches and pains as Barmah Forest infection. He says it is like Ross River fever, but different. Can you explain further?

A Barmah Forest virus is a blood infection that is more common in males than females and in the elderly, and is limited to the eastern states of mainland Australia. It is named after a forest in northern Victoria on the Murray River. The infection spreads from one person to another by mosquito bites. Carriers, who have no symptoms, can donate the virus to a mosquito that bites them.

The symptoms include arthritis that moves from joint to joint, muscle aches and pains, fevers that come and go, headaches and sometimes a rash. The diagnosis can be confirmed by a specific blood test, but the doctor must think of this specific disease as a cause of the symptoms.

Medications (eg. pain-killers, anti-inflammatories) can be given to relieve symptoms, but there is no specific cure. Fortunately, there are no significant complications.

The symptoms settle with time and rest, but regular recurrences are common.

INDEX

NOTE: Section headings are in listed in CAPITALS

Tenosynovitis 271
Tension headache 183
Terminally ill 77
Testicle 239
Testicle contracting 245
Testicle large 240
Testicle pain 241
Testicle small 242,243
Testicles not descended 239
Testicles uneven 241
Testicular torsion 244
Tetanus 397
Tetracyclines 24
Thalassaemia 53
Thoracic outlet obstruction 389
THROAT 263
Throat sore 266
Thromboses 31
Thrombosus from drip 32
Thrush 146
Thrush treatment 159
Thrush, oral 158
Thrush, vaginal 158
Thymus gland 79
Thyroid gland 160
Thyroiditis 161
Thyroxine 161
Tic removal 154
Tietze syndrome 79
Timid 382
Tinea 156
Tinea cruris 157,359
Tinea unguium 157
Tingling 283
Tinnitus 122,123
Tinnitus masker 122
Tired 299
Tiredness 296
Toe nail ingrown 274
Toilet fear 171
Toilet training 81
Tongue 266
Tongue pain 266
Tongue white coated 266
Tonsillectomy 267
Tonsillitis 267
Tonsils and adenoids 117
Tooth 391

Torsion of the testes 244
Total hysterectomy 203,206
Toxic shock syndrome 150
Tramal 33
Tranquillisers 247,255
Transfusion reaction 52
TRAVEL 393
Travel illness 394
Travel risks 395
Travel tablets 393
Travel vaccinations 393,395
Treatment for asthma 39
Treatment for psoriasis 322
Tremor 281
Trichologist 177
Trigeminal neuralgia 185,280
Trisomy 21 44
Tropical disease 394
Tubal ligation 86,91,92
Turbinectomy 288
Turner syndrome 389
Typhoid 395
Ubiquinone 14
Ulcer, ankle 347
Ulcer, peptic 376,377
Ulcers, mouth 264
Ultrasound 328
Ultrasound scan in pregnancy 329
Umbilical hernia 44,198
Underweight 294
Uranium 295
Urea 302
Uric acid 253
Urinary catheter 319
Urinary frequency 215,217
Urinary incontinence 142,218
Urinary tract infection 213,214
Urinate frequently 244
Urination at night 217
Urination difficult 318
Urine bloody 339
Urine burns 335
Urine protein 218
Urologists 216
Vaccination alternatives 400
Vaccination dangers 399
Vaccinations before school 401
VACCINATIONS, ADULT 397